T0296307

INTELLIGENT ENVIRONMENTS

INTELLIGENT ENVIRONMENTS

Advanced Systems for a Healthy Planet

Second Edition

Edited by

PETER DROEGE
Liechtenstein Institute for Strategic Development

Elsevier
Radarweg 29, PO Box 211, 1000 AE Amsterdam, Netherlands
The Boulevard, Langford Lane, Kidlington, Oxford OX5 1GB, United Kingdom

ISBN: 978-0-12-820247-0

For information on all North Holland publications visit our website at https://www.elsevier.com/books-and-journals

Publisher: Candice Janco
Acquisition Editor: Jessica Mack
Editorial Project Manager: Zsereena Rose Mampusti
Production Project Manager: Erragounta Saibabu Rao
Cover Designer: Vicky Pearson Esser
Cover Credit: Anis Radzi

Typeset by TNQ Technologies

Contents

Contributor biographies

Abdelrahman Ammar graduated with a bachelor's degree in building engineering from An-Najah National University in 2016. Afterward, he moved to Germany and graduated in May 2021 with a master's degree from the Department of Energetic-Ecological Urban Redevelopment at Nordhausen University of Applied Sciences. He is currently working with DSK GmbH as an urban planner in Climate, Energy and Mobility.

Jesús López Baeza holds a Ph.D. in architecture and works as a science lead in the Digital City Science group at HafenCity University Hamburg. He has led and participated in several national and international projects in Europe and Asia. Part of his work encompasses social cohesion, the livability of urban spaces, urban identity production, spatial perception, and agent-based modeling, among other dynamics in the field of advanced sociospatial analysis.

Jan Barski is a spatial planner and translator by training. In his career, he has dealt with a variety of topics from, in his Ph.D. dissertation, the geography of the industry via the city as a political idea, to migration, participation, employment, mobility, economy, and simulation, in proposals he coauthored. His main fields of activity are research funding applications and project management.

Nimish Biloria is an associate professor at the University of Technology Sydney, Australia, holding a Ph.D. degree in real-time interactive environments from TU Delft, the Netherlands. His research is centered around Empathic Environments: the study of human–environment interaction. He conducts multiscalar transdisciplinary research spanning architecture, smart cities, urban informatics, sustainable mobility, social robotics, and tangible and embedded interaction.

Janis Birkeland, a professorial fellow, University of Melbourne, taught architectural, planning, and legal dimensions of sustainability at several Australian universities. Before entering academia, she worked in these fields to understand the impediments to socioecological sustainability. Her Ph.D. topic was *Planning for Sustainability* (1993); books include *Design for Sustainability* (2002), *Positive Development* (2008), and *Net-Positive Design* (2020).

Guillermo Borragán, Ph.D., is a cognitive environmental scientist with experience integrating technology and data into the development of more sustainable territories. His work focus on the investigation of urban resilience and how the built environment impacts health. He has participated in numerous international conferences, and he is the author of several peer-reviewed publications.

Katharina M. Borgmann is a trained architect and city planner. She practiced in Israel, China, and India, before starting an academic career in Germany. Her Ph.D. focused on the cultural and contextual layer of the Chinese urban texture, and she has ever since focused on the transfer of holistic sustainable urban development strategies across the European and Asian cultural realms.

Michele Campagna is a professor of spatial planning at the Department of Civil and Environmental Engineering and Architecture of the University of Cagliari, where he teaches geodesign. Author of over 130 publications, his research deals with the use of information and communication technology in spatial planning, planning support systems, metaplanning, volunteered and social media geographic information, and geodesign.

Matthew Cook is a professor of innovation at the Open University where he founded and now leads the Future Urban Environments research team. Working on the intersection of urban studies and innovation studies, his research interests are in the development of more sustainable urban and regional environments, with particular reference to mobility and energy infrastructures.

Catalina Díaz works as a research associate and project manager in the research unit "Urban Economy Innovation" at the University of Stuttgart IAT. She has a background in architecture and a master's degree in sustainable urban development from the University of Stuttgart. With international experience, her expertise lies in content management, methodological processes, and the conceptualization of sustainable urban development strategies.

Peter Droege specializes in regenerative urban design and planning, and sustainable development in practice and research. He directs the Liechtenstein Institute for Strategic Development and has current and past positions with universities in Asia, Australia, Europe, and the United States. He published numerous books and papers on sustainable spatial development and has received several awards for his work. See also eurisd.org.

Bruna Felici graduated in sociology, studying content analysis techniques through the use of software for automatic text analysis and mining. She is a researcher at the National Agency for New Technologies, Energy and Sustainable Economic Development (ENEA), working on the analysis of the social aspects of the energy transition and on new forms of work organization (models of smart working, teleworking, co-working) along with the effects of changes in behavior on urban mobility.

Trinidad Fernandez is a senior scientist at the Fraunhofer Institute, Germany, holding a master's degree in integrated urbanism and sustainable design from Stuttgart University and an architectural degree from the Universidad de Chile. Her research focuses on urban systems engineering for sustainable, smart, and climate-sensitive urban transformation, participating in several international projects, including the coordination of the EU-SCC1 lighthouse project "Triangulum."

Thomas Fisher is a professor in the School of Architecture, Director of the Minnesota Design Center, and former Dean of the College of Design at the University of Minnesota. He is a former editorial director of *Progressive Architecture* magazine; he has written or edited 11 books, 70 book chapters or introductions, and over 450 articles in professional journals and major publications.

Dieter D. Genske, Ph.D., worked as Humboldt Research Fellow in Kyoto, then for DMT Essen. Later, he taught at TU Delft, EPF Lausanne, ETH-Zurich and Nordhausen University. His project work includes the IBA Emscher Park, the 2000-Watt-Society for Basel, and the IBA Hamburg. In 2012, he received the European Solar Prize.

Sophia German is a Ph.D. candidate in the School of Biological Earth and Environmental Sciences at the University of New South Wales. Her academic background is in environmental geography and GIS, and her current research uses geospatial technologies and spatial analysis to understand and report on gendered perceptions of safety in public urban spaces.

Jemma Green is chair and cofounder of Power Ledger, a leading energy blockchain company, and a research fellow at Curtin University in Western Australia, where she completed her Ph.D. in disruptive innovation in electricity markets. She holds a masters's degree and two postgraduate diplomas from Cambridge University in sustainability.

Keith Guzik, Ph.D., is an associate professor of sociology at the University of Colorado Denver. His research examines the role of technology in state institutions and its impact on people's legal experiences. He is the author of *Making Things Stick* (2016) and *Arresting Abuse* (2009).

Scott Hawken is the director of the Planning and Urban Design program at the University of Adelaide and holds a Ph.D. from Sydney University and a bachelor's degree and university medal from the University of New South Wales. He is a leading scholar in smart cities and critical urban studies having published a highly cited special issue, an edited volume, and numerous papers on the topic.

John Herr BFA is a data engineer with the Office of Information Technology, Duke University. His work supports researchers, physicians, and students on teams building novel and data-intensive software applications. He has particular interests in early-stage prototypes and experimental proofs-of-concept.

Ahmed Khoja is a lecturer and senior researcher at Munich University of Applied Sciences Institute for Construction and Building Climatology, holding a master's degree in energy-efficient and sustainable building from the Technical University of Munich, and a bachelor's degree from King Abdulaziz University. His research includes zero energy retrofits, urban renewal, smart and sustainable city development, and building performance evaluation.

Irena Kondratenko is a project manager with VITO/Energy-Ville, with a Ph.D. in building energy from Glasgow University, and an MSc in environmental science and policy from Central European University. His research focuses on climate change mitigation in urban areas through sustainable construction, low carbon energy efficient buildings and renewable technologies, and removing barriers toward Nearly Zero Energy Building (NZEB) renovations.

Hojung (Ashley) Kwon is an undergraduate student majoring in computer science and art history at Duke University. She discovers and conducts research on unexpected connections between her two majors. She is particularly interested in visualizing data using game engines and characterizing digital images of artworks using algorithms in computer vision and image processing.

Shawn Laffan, Ph.D., is a professor in the School of Biological, Earth and Environmental Sciences. His research interests are in GIS, geospatial analysis, and geocomputation, with applications across biophysical and sociocultural domains.

Ardeshir Mahdavi, is University Professor of Building Physics at TU Graz, Austria. He conducts research in the fields of building physics, building performance simulation, building ecology, and human ecology. Professor Mahdavi has published over 700 scientific papers and has supervised over 65 doctoral students. He is the recipient of the IBPSA Distinguished Achievements Awards.

Gary T. Marx, Ph.D., is a professor emeritus at MIT. His most recent book is *Windows into the Soul: Surveillance and Society in an Age of High Technology*. He is rooted in the sociology of knowledge and in the centrality of reflexivity, but with the firm conviction that there are transcendent truths to pursue and fight for. Figuring them out is what it is all about. For additional information, see www.garymarx.net.

Graciela Metternicht, Ph.D., is a professor of environmental geography at the Earth and Sustainability Science Research Centre of the University of New South Wales, Sydney. Her research is primarily in the field of geography, with a focus on geospatial technologies and their application in environmental management and policy, and in sustainability science and the UN Sustainable Development Goals.

Peter Newman, Ph.D., AO is a professor of sustainability at Curtin University in Perth, Australia. He has written 21 books and over 360 papers on sustainable cities. He has worked to deliver his ideas at all levels of government and is the co-ordinating lead author for the UN's IPCC on Transport.

Jörg Rainer Noennig is a professor of digital city science at HafenCity University Hamburg and director of the WISSEN-SARCHITEKTUR Laboratory of Knowledge Architecture at TU Dresden. He is a trained architect and holds a Ph.D. from Bauhaus University Weimar.

Brian Orland, Ph.D., held distinguished professorships at Pennsylvania State University, the University of Illinois at Urbana-Champaign, and the University of Georgia. He pioneered computer uses in visualizing community perceptions and citizen engagement, GIS-based virtual and augmented environments, serious games, and mobile apps. His recent work has been in unconventional fossil fuel development, climate-related coastal migration, and cultural influences on regional planning.

Marina Penna is a senior researcher at the National Agency for New Technologies, Energy and Sustainable Economic Development (ENEA). She has gained significant experience in the environmental sector, working at the Ministry for the Environment (1995–2011) in the fields of air pollution, sustainable mobility, energy, environmental impact assessment of projects, and strategic environmental assessment of plans and programs.

Stephen Potter is an emeritus professor of transport at the Open University. His research has explored the human and institutional aspects of transport innovation, the diffusion of cleaner vehicle technologies, low-carbon transport systems, and sustainable travel behaviors. He has participated in several research projects on transport innovations including the Milton Keynes *Plugged in Places* program, *MK:Smart* and on DRT system developments.

Anis Radzi is a city planner and urban policy analyst. She attained her PhD at Technical University Darmstadt, a master of urban design and a bachelor of architecture summa cum laude from Sydney University. She focuses on governance and design tools for renewable energy autonomous settlements. She has published in urban renewable energy areas, and both researched and taught in spatioterritorial assessment, decision-making, and planning settings.

Marco Rao works at the National Agency for New Technologies, Energy and Sustainable Economic Development (ENEA) in the Particle Accelerator and Medical Applications Development Laboratory; he also lectures in economics of markets and energy resources at the University of Siena. His research includes developing machine learning techniques, applying machine learning to energy systems analysis, and other topics such as the energy effects of smart work, environmental justice, and queuing theory in healthcare.

Roberta Roberto holds a Ph.D. in Energy Engineering. She works as a researcher and project manager at the National Agency for New Technologies, Energy and Sustainable Economic Development (ENEA) in the Energy Technologies and Renewable Sources Department. Her current research activities include smart energy systems, low-carbon energy transition strategies in EU and South-Mediterranean Countries, energy planning and implementation strategies, and energy and environmental impacts of smart working.

William O. Ruddick is a development economist and an associate scholar at the University of Cumbria. After graduate research in high energy physics and behavioral economics at Stanford and UCT, he founded Grassroots Economics Foundation and Community Inclusion Currencies as a humanitarian modality that connects communities to their own abundance.

Bill Seaman, Ph.D., explores computational media research in his work—recombinant poetics and recombinant informatics, through intelligent dynamic interactive and generative combinatoric systems, working in conjunction with specific databases. He has been interested in meaning production and has also explored ideas around computational meta-meaning systems. He co-directs the Emergence Lab, Duke University.

Dev Seth studies computer science and philosophy at Duke University. He works on next-generation human–computer interfaces and is especially interested in using transdisciplinary methods to facilitate collaborative systems leveraging both human and machine intelligence. He also researches adversarial methods to develop machine learning systems that behave reliably in complex real-world settings. His aim is to understand and develop artificial general intelligence (AGI).

Carl Steinitz is a professor of landscape architecture and planning emeritus at Harvard Graduate School of Design and an honorary professor at the Centre for Advanced Spatial Analysis, University College London. He is the author of "A Framework for Geodesign," Esri Press, 2012. He has lectured and given workshops at more than 170 universities and is cofounder of the International Geodesign Collaboration

Sonja Stöffler is a senior researcher and project manager at the University of Stuttgart, Germany, holding a master's degree in business engineering from the Karlsruhe Institute of Technology. Within national and international projects, she contributes to the digital mobility transformation of cities, regions, and companies. Her research focuses on future mobility ecosystems, evaluating the right measures and suitable cooperation formats for a sustainable transformation.

Alan-Miguel Valdez, Ph.D., is a lecturer in technology management and innovation at the Open University and a member of the Future Urban Environments research team. His research explores how various public as well as civic, industrial, and governmental bodies use urban experiments to make sense of innovative technologies and collectively negotiate the future of their city.

Han Vandevyvere is a project manager at the Belgian research institute VITO/EnergyVille and an associate professor at the Faculty of Architecture and Design of the Norwegian University of Science and Technology (NTNU). His work focuses on climate and energy action planning for cities, both as a consultant for local authorities and through EU projects regarding smart cities and communities.

Jan Verheyen, Ph.D., is a researcher at VITO/EnergyVille in the unit Sustainable Built Environment working on energy performance and indoor environmental quality aspects of the built environment. He is a construction engineer, holding a Ph.D. in energy sciences from VUB. He has 2 decades of experience in engineering sciences on sustainability-related themes both in an academic context and in practice.

James Warren, Ph.D., is a senior lecturer at the Open University whose specialisms include engineering, design, development, environment, and systems thinking, particularly with reference to transport studies. He currently works with University College London on a project based on public transport systems and urban design in conjunction with our partner in Ciudad Universitaria José Antonio Echeverría in Havana, Cuba.

Dawid Wolosiuk received his Ph.D. at TU Wien, Austria. The main foci of his scientific work are data processing and visualization, building simulation, visual performance, and renewable energy applications.

Preface

This second edition of *Intelligent Environments* presents sustainability-focused hard- and software applications, theories, and practices in a system representative, selected, and case-specific manner. Topics explored in this edition include intelligent and IT augmented region, smart cities, urban transactive energy, inclusionary monetary systems, advanced modes of governance, software facilitated geospatial design collaborations, IT supported gendered space, new transport paradigms, autonomous mobility, intelligent building retrofitting, smart neighborhoods, ontologically streamlined building design supports, new city design approaches, support tools for net positive design, geographic information system–based regional scenario planning tools, interactive energy case study, and conceptual explorations in the art of biomimetic systems as personal intelligent environments digitalization.

Digitalization is *de rigeur* in conversations about society's future. This has been a cultural feature since the 1980s when the *informatization* of the economy emerged as a major urban development theme. The promises and realities of digital innovation permeate everything from government to finance, art to medicine, astronomy to cities, politics to warfare, and from genetics to our sense of reality, and ourselves. This astonishing advance has made our world at once more fluid and more brittle. It presents enormous opportunities and risks, and with it great responsibilities: most of these have not been lived up to yet.

While digitalization has taken on the illusion of an existential escape hatch, the evolution of this planet's human habitability remains curiously elusive as an equally pervasive focus of attention. At stake is no less than Earth's very viability as a livable planet: and yet this challenge has so far overtaxed humankind's capacity for intelligent problem-solving. Rather than providing solutions at the needed massive scale, the sheer weight of IT's environmental footprint alone represents a heavy load on Gaia's jugular, constricting humanity's prospective. While E-tech gave rise to a cultural belief in systems superiority and technological mastery, it is far from a virtualizing phenomenon, in the popular sense of being without a physical footprint, and hence environmentally beneficial.

The gargantuan energy consumption of digitalization—the IT industry, its infrastructure, investment commitments, and flow-on impacts—grows larger each year. From crypto mining to the spread of data centers and the boost to productivity power consumption has surged, even when considering efficiency increases and sectoral change (Lange et al., 2020). Although cloud computing and associated efficiency gains have helped slow the increase of electricity use relative to data processing output dramatically (Masanet et al., 2020), power consumption has not been reversed either. On the resource side, the shift to electricity in transport has given rise to massive costs in human rights and environmental damage, from artisanal cobalt mines in the Democratic Republic of Congo to the water and environmental costs of lithium production in Bolivia. Add to this a combination of IT-enabled process acceleration, the rebound effect in the new-found efficiency gains, and the increasingly automated expansion of a globalized economic superstructure driven by short-term reward maximization, and it becomes clear that the search for solutions in this systemic struggle is only beginning.

This technospatial cyberculture has come to dominate humankind's construction of reality to the extent that it—despite all scientific evidence and knowledge—fails to fully appreciate that the determining factor of its very existence is not economic power or political will, but the state of its biosphere, as also measured in the chemical composition of the air we breathe. This is astonishing given the historical findings about the atmospheric heating dynamics by Joseph Fourier, Claude Pouillet, Eunice Foote, John Tyndall, and Svante Arrhenius throughout the 19th century, and the mountain of data, analysis, and insight that has accumulated since—all the way to both empirical and theoretical scientific evidence mounting since 1958, when Scripps Institution of Oceanography scientist Charles David Keeling began CO_2 measurements at NOAA's Mauna Loa weather station. By searching for life-sustaining features of environmentally geared IT and software tools, the true but hidden celebration of this book is owed to the planetary atmosphere as until recently stable result of a sentient, living, natural ecosysytem—until our species began to unravel it. The functional focus of this volume is trained on the existential commons of this planet—not the feeble figments and fleeting flashes of civilization's seemingly smart systems and advanced contraptions. This is the meaning of the cover image we have selected for this book.

This book explores in its introduction and key chapters both promises and pitfalls of spatial digitalization. The hope is that it contributes to a sense of responsibility in the application of digital tools and software-driven spatial innovations and interventions, leaving the judgment of whether these meet the standard set by this book to our readers. The great new goal for all technical systems must be to help stabilize a planet thrown into biospheric disarray by evolutionary misjudgments and wrong turns made by: *homo*—so far not so—*sapiens*.

The contributions by leading researchers and reflective practitioners seek to cope with these, and range from attempts at undoing historical choices of dead-end, non-renewable energy systems to banking on ways of correcting a fundamentally flawed global economy that is motivated primarily by immediate financial gains. This book is dedicated to this very environmental meaning and mission, and to those in its pursuit.

References

Lange, S., Pohl, J., Santarius, T., 2020. Digitalization and energy consumption. Does ICT reduce energy demand? Ecological Economics 176, 106760. https://doi.org/10.1016/j.ecolecon.2020.106760. October 2020.

Masanet, E., Shebahi, A., Lei, N., Smith, S., Koomey, J., 2020. Recalibrating global datae center energy-use estimates. Science 367 (6481), 984–986. https://doi.org/10.1126/science.aba3758, 28 Feb 2020.

1

Intelligent environments 2—Advanced systems for a healthy planet

Peter Droege
Liechtenstein Institute for Strategic Development AG, Vaduz, Liechtenstein

1. Intelligent environments in transition

Digital systems augmenting physical space, buildings, and cities occupy a special place in the wider discourse about advanced technology. The two *Intelligent Environments* books assembled by this editor focus on this dimension in an as broad and non-technical way as possible, spanning a quarter of a century across this genre. This second volume goes one step further than the first and asks: how does civilization approach thinking systems, and more specifically intelligent spatial models, design methods and support structures that are designed or applied for spatial sustainability, even counteract challenges to terrestrial habitability?

The result of this quest is at once useful, practical, and informative: it opens a door to what still only begins to emerge as a major focus. This book presents a range of explorative and innovative but also practical and typical, even humble and everyday attempts to be relevant in the pursuit of a more sustainable world, against the maelstrom of unfettered economic value extraction. These are visible in endeavors as diverse as the planned guidance of industrial change across regions, currency innovation, infrastructure architecture, network protocols of energy transaction, geodesign, net-positive design—and notions of artificial intelligence in understanding the most immediate spatial setting: the body.

Intelligent regions

Dr.-Ing. Anis Radzi's **The Ruhr Innovation Ecosystem—From industrial brownfields to regenerative smart environments**

Intelligent Environments. https://doi.org/10.1016/B978-0-12-820247-0.00017-5

paints an epic picture of one of the great success stories in post-industrial economic, technological and social change—one yet to be concluded. The Australian and German educated renewable energy and spatial planning expert documents a system of collectively conceived transformations that have powerful lessons to teach: about coordination, planning, improvisation, collaboration and the selective, careful deployment of information technology, knowledge economy geared planting of seeds for regenerative change, and their manifest depictions.

Intelligent cities

In **A tale of three intelligent cities: Triangulum** three smart-city researchers, Trinidad Fernandez, Sonja Stöffler, and Catalina Diaz, associates of Germany's Fraunhofer Institute, describe their quests and successes in one of the EU's first and largest Smart City research and development projects. It is focused on developing smart city frameworks across three European city regions, while endowing them with social benefit and environmental purpose. This chapter offers insight into the workings of large European grant programs, the social cohesion policy behind them, and the architecture of a research and development construct that reaches from basic, even everyday supports to higher-level regional transformations.

Intelligent energy

The **Transactive electricity** chapter explores how software enabled markets in renewable energy generation, distribution, storage and use may enhance security, resiliency, and decarbonization benefits. Australian authors, digital electricity trading pioneer Jemma Green, and sustainability academic Peter Newman elaborate with this editor an emerging power paradigm as a way of achieving low-cost, ubiquitous, and democratic access for everyone producing and using renewable electricity, particularly rooftop solar energy.

Intelligent money

In **Community inclusion currencies,** the Africa-based community currency innovator Will Ruddick conveys the making, management, and messages that come from running Africa's most successful alternative currencies. The chapter illuminates the logic of community money supporting the fostering, strengthening, and management of sustainable local economies based on blockchain and other software enabled tools, side-stepping the risks and local-value siphoning dangers of what many experience as an environmental black hole: the "real economy."

Intelligent governance

In **Managing uncertainty/making miracles**, social scientists Keith Guzik, University of Boulder, and Gary T. Marx, MIT, describe the unexpected consequences, uncertainty and even unpredictability of digitalization, evident here in linking intelligent environments to intelligent governance. But, as Marx and Guzik assure us, failure is not assured. Two successful cases of digital government—digital democracy—open government in Estonia and US motor vehicle department in the United States—draw out lessons for aspiring to and supporting intelligent environments more broadly.

Intelligent design collaboration

In **Geodesign to address global change** Carl Steinitz, Harvard University, multi-university affiliated Brian Orland, the University of Minnesota's Thomas Fisher and Michele Campagna, University of Cagliari, deploy a series of case examples to describe geodesign as a discipline to methodically and purposefully transform geography by design. Their International Geodesign Collaboration uses online and geographic information system based cooperation protocols that allow many multidisciplinary teams to cooperate across international boundaries in coping with accelerating environmental, economic, and social change.

Intelligent work

In **Massive smart-work deployment,** Italy's ENEA sustainability and energy experts Roberta Roberto, Marina Penna, Bruna Felici, and Marco Rao elaborate on their explorations of smart work with a view to broad applications. The setting is the global SARS-2 coronavirus pandemic that was triggered in 2019 and exploded across 2020, 2021, and 2022, leading to a world-wide humanitarian and economic crisis with long-term repercussions and a boost to remote, distant and, indeed, "smart" work.

Intelligently gendered space

Intelligent technologies for gender-inclusive urban environments are the focus of Australian authors and academics Sophia German, Graciela Metternicht, Shawn Laffan, and Scott Hawken, of the University of New South Wales and Adelaide, respectively. Encompassing various spatial design backgrounds the author team highlights the many ways in which urban environments and public space are often gender biased and segregated but also can facilitate abuse and harassment. The paper examines technologies available to help overcome this.

Intelligent transport

Toward an intelligent mobility paradigm is the focus of British Open University author team Stephen Potter, James Warren, Matthew Cook, and Miguel Valdez. It advances an important perspective on the lag between policy and both technology and societal needs, across the socio-technological regime. The authors anticipate the future of transport and transportation in an intelligent mobility sphere—a paradigm capable of transforming urban transport.

Intelligent automobiles

Autonomous vehicles and the built environment is the focus of Sydney based automobility expert Nimish Biloria at the University of Technology Sydney. He grounds his characterization of important technological and regulatory developments on a brief history of vehicular autonomy, assesses recent advances and establishes rules derived from an analysis of both failures and successes, risks and rewards of automobile autonomy.

Intelligent retrofits

Smart building and district retrofitting for intelligent urban environments is the result of a European Union supported project, recognizing that the existing building stock is the most important focus in transforming the built environment. The authoring consortium consists of Han Vandevyvere, Jan Verheyen, Pedraz Guillermo Borragán, Francisco Rodriguez, Koldo Urrutia Azcone, and Irena Kondratenko: it describes an important EU project and its findings resulting from deploying software tools for urban retrofit projects.

Intelligent neighborhoods

In **Intelligent integration software for energy neighborhoods** Munich Applied Sciences University research academic Ahmed Khoja focuses on software driven ways of integrating, optimizing and sharing the benefits that come from pursuing so-called near-zero energy buildings in neighborhoods, developing, deploying, and testing software tools to optimize the interaction and performance of renewable energy and efficiency measures in cities.

Intelligent building design

In **Ontologically streamlined data for building design and operation support** leading building physics and ecology expert Ardeshi Mahdavi and his doctorate candidate Dawid Wolosiuk, both University of Vienna based, describe the need for increasingly larger building performance data sets, in order to take full advantage of information and communication technology in the design and management of sustainably intelligent built environments. The authors introduce a building performance data ontology to streamline and manage this burgeoning flow.

Intelligent city models

In **Digital City Science—a platform for sustainable urban development** Hamburg HafenCity University experts Jörg Rainer Noennig, Jan Barski, Katharina Borgmann and Jesús López Baeza describe how the merger of computer science and urban sustainability planning can be organized and focused into an inclusive research and innovation framework in pursuit of a new kind of city making science capable of helping stabilize the climate, lower resource use, and empower communities.

Intelligent design tool

In **Open access software for net positive design**, the design sustainability augmentation expert Janis Birkeland presents a tested open-access software tool capable of guiding planning decisions toward net positive outcomes. These result in buildings and urban environments that improve environmental conditions in fundamental and measurable ways, from small spaces to regional plans.

Intelligent scenario planning tool

In **Strategies to improve energy efficiency in residential buildings on Ambon Island, Indonesia,** Abdelrahman Moufeed Hassan Ammar and Dieter D. Genske describe the application of the geographically referenced STAR Energy Model as a spatially relevant energy efficiency scenario building tool. The model is based on an expert system integrating empirically reliable knowledge about the behavior of space types in energetic and carbon management terms.

Intelligent energy case project

A second contibution by Jemma Green and Peter Newman, **Transactive electricity markets: RENeW Nexus,** assembled with the research and development expert Nick Forse, describes in a working urban application in the Western Australian city of Fremantle the role of software driven platforms in intervening in the conventional energy marketplace and accelerating the penetration of variable renewable energy. In applying software protocols to optimizing low-cost solar energy production across local communities they arrive at findings of significance to a wider scientific, policy, and application-minded audience.

Intelligent environment par excellence: the body

In **Existential ethics of bio-algorithms** media academic and artist Bill Seaman and his group of young collaborators and apprentices at Duke University explore the dynamics and logic of the human body as an intelligent environment within the greater environments of nature and the artificial world. They describe a linked set of cognitive processes as extended intelligence technologies. These frame interactions between humans and their experience as a new expression of human sentience that is both socially and linguistically framed. By abstracting this kind of sentience they define a model branch of AI, exploring synthetic sentience through biomimetics, raising the question of purpose in intelligent sentience.

2. The rise of intelligent environments: early inklings

The first edition of *Intelligent Environments* (IE1) was subtitled "Spatial Aspects of the Information Revolution"(Droege, 1997a). It had been developed over a decade, from the late 1980s to its release in the final years of the second millennium AD. It focused on the intersection of physical, cultural, institutional, and technological aspects of new information-system enabled virtual space, the suffusing of that ancient collective information machine "City" with distributed, ubiquitous computing, modern telecommunications and hybrid media—embedded mass media, narrow-casting, and early web-based network channels. The background tenor of the first edition was the quest to find societally ethical direction and even environmental purpose in the accelerating maelstrom of digital innovation as it impacted and undermined the traditional conceptual frames of what cities were and how their economies and spaces functioned: in semantics, symbolism, and infrastructure.

IE1 was composed in a late 20th century frame of mind, imbued with the delight of anticipation in facing what many saw as a new information-technology enabled era of citizen empowerment and democratic liberation, political freedom and potentially even environmental redemption in the purposeful application of information and telecommunication technologies. This aspiration was already then—and is even more so today—overshadowed by an automated quest for advanced—in the sense of more efficiently performing and hence putatively more competitive—buildings, cities, and regions—yielding improved opportunities for civil society in the expanding market space of "smart everything"—but all in the service of short-term profit maximization. At this more skeptical end of the attitudinal spectrum the first volume was also trepidation tinged because many saw Big Brother taking command, and a globalized form of Taylorism rising.

Social media, big data, and commercial grade autonomous vehicles had not yet broadly arrived as commonplace notions even if they all have deep roots in the technological history of the 20th century. Today's most prominent household names in this wider genre, Apple, Amazon, Facebook, Google and Tesla had either not been born or not yet billowed into the supernova state these spatially relevant tech giants expanded into by the third decade in the third millennium AD.

While their early stages—as in the case of the Baby Boomers Apple and Microsoft—and other predecessors were already very much present in the 1980s, if not earlier, the first edition's main focus was trained onto some of the more practical foci of digital cities: urban globalization, Teleports, Smart Regions, software tools for regional design and planning, monitoring and controlling systems for everything from city traffic to smart homes, and the rise of marketing digitally enhanced cities and development projects.

Japan and the information city

The first volume was shaped in the wake of a seminal city design competition that had been organized in Japan more than 35 years prior to the publication of the present book. The 1986 *International Concept Design Competition for an Advanced*

Information City focused on creating a city-wide open-learning world without reliance on traditional educational institutions, but using the city as a whole as virtual campus (Droege, 1997b). It had been co-organized by the Japan Association of Planning Administration, Tokyo Institute of Technology and Kawasaki City with corporate and conceptual support by the likes of NEC, Dentsu, Obayashi, Mainichi Newspapers, Mori Building, Toshiba, and many others.

The initiative was carried by the late social-engineering visionary Professor Yoshinobu Kumata, and the model municipal host of the project ideas, the City of Kawasaki in Kanagawa Prefecture, set hard against and along the Tokyo border to the northeast, across the Tama river. The city had been among the leading steel manufacturing centers worldwide—and here the former post-war giant Kawasaki Heavy Industries—parent of Kawasaki Steel Corporation—had been born from the historical breakup of the city's dockyards. Kawasaki City in the 1980s hence epitomized the profound structural transformations and shifts of manufacturing under technological and trade paradigmatic advances, affecting of nation and world throughout the fourth quarter of the 20th century. In this early *Campus City Competition*, all current aspirations coalesced. The results carried some influence, accompanying a massive wave of finding educational and community development benefits in IT suffused building and urban and development initiatives. The drive was to usher Japan from an era of heavy industrialization into the postindustrial information society age, in a glorious, but also frantic, and even desperate quest to overcome an age of heavy pollution.

The cancerous toxicity of the post-war industrialization era now became retrospectively rationalized as a sacrifice that had to be made to achieve the level of prosperity and advancement required for the late 20th century leap into the hallowed Information Age, driven by the so-called quaternary sector of the knowledge economy: in the early 21st century, it came to be referred to as the *fourth industrial revolution* of 'advanced advances', in an almost amnesiac, permanent anticipation of the new across a time span of half a century, a collective phenomenon of *jamais vu*. This inability to technologically learn from or even remember experiences led to the remarkable persistence of nuclear power—the most toxic energy system ever devised — being still marketed as clean, even after the melt-down accidents at Three Mile Island in 1979 and Chernobyl in 1986—leading a generation later to the massive and long-lasting global contamination legacy of Fukushima. This, too, is a feature of the "fourth industrial age"—extreme absorption in a manufactured reality while enormous risks are piling up—from dozens of mostly unreported nuclear (near-)accidents annually to the explosion of a rising global carbon cocktail into the affecting environment: from atmosphere to oceans, and still largely unabated for generations to come.

While Japan's heavy industries moved off-shore to other global hubs of yet lower pay and without the concerns about pollution that began to mount in the industrial world ever since the 1960s, Tokyo's rise as a global financial command and control center (Sassen, 1991) came to epitomize the postindustrial mirage of the knowledge economy and digital life: Japan and several other quaternary industrial leadership aspirants embraced the new era of advanced IT, telecommunications, and consumer service industries with a vengeance.

These early days of spatial digitalization were a true cultural phenomenon, touching all aspects of mid-1980s life, from advanced building controls to electronic music, founded on earlier scientific and cultural developments from the late 1960s on—over half a century before this book's publication. Fashion design's Grand Dame Competiton, won by the author of this chapter, Hanae Mori chaired the jury of the Advanced Information City—and Keio University's ingenious Professor Kei Mori, inventor of the *himawari* sunlight transmission system for internal or underground spaces, ranked among the creative judges. Kei Mori was the father of multimedia artist Mariko Mori and first son of ultra-wealthy Taikichiro Mori, the professorial founder of the developer empire Mori Building. He initiated ARK Toshijuku in 1988—the city school renamed Academic Hills in 1996 (Academy Hills, 2021) perched atop Mori Building's ARK Hills, the pioneering mixed-use, smart-building branded high rise complex in Tokyo's Roppongi district. This modeled a new urban vision: information technology suffused professional learning and general enlightenment—of limited impact perhaps in its exclusive rarefication, but positively and purposefully aimed at seizing the new digital environment for a "smarter" technology augmented reality (AR).

Despite the rising enthusiasm for the intelligent city though the 1980s and 1990s, the informational dimension of constructed environments was not a new feature in the sense of their conveying social meaning and political as well as cultural information. The human environment—the terrestrial systems as perceived, used, and shaped by humans throughout time—has always been fundamentally designed for information conveyance and exchange. The very spatial structure of cities and buildings is organized and shaped to facilitate motion for communication (Hillier, 1996). Information is central to the cultural systems connecting us to one another and binding us to a common past and emerging future—troubling, disruptive, hostile—or empowering, supportive, or enchantingly paradisal. Flora, fauna, and microbial life exchange information: transmission of information is elementary to the very genetic code and structure.

But can the kind of technology that is associated with the "smart" in the built environment also help solve today's most vexing challenges? Are there technological answers to a problem that at the same time is exacerbated, amplified, even proliferated through the deployment of advanced technology? Can humanity extinguish the fires it has lit? This compelling question quickly reveals an implicit assumption framing this seeming paradox. Technology cannot be divorced from the human economy and its financial system, rewarding ever shorter payback horizons, and the very inventions and innovations that serve that goal. It hence must be endowed with an active and powerful societal purpose and the appurtenant mechanisms and tools to overcome the trap of this seeming inevitability—and this was both spirit and mission of the initial inquiry in IE1.

Liberation and empowerment

The first edition was shaped by the sincere belief in social empowerment, information democracy, the leveling of class distinction and an end to poverty through digital access. Nicholas Negroponte's 2005 OLPC project—'One Laptop Per Child', manifested in the robust, hand cranked (and in later editions pedal powered) XO-1 computer set a late landmark in that very 1980s quest, a combination of gizmotic optimism and the kind of messianic dedication to techno-enlightenment that also had energized a young Steve Jobs. The XO initiative was bound to fail – in part due to inexorable technological change in a rising competition – but illustrated the dreamy dedication to a new techno-democratizing and empowering info-marketplace perfectly. In the urban design arena, too, new information technology made deep inroads as early as the mid-1980s, with the aspiration of what I in the first edition of this book called "making the city intelligible": information system augmented urbanism and community development ideas in what later reincarnated as the "smart city" drive—in an homage to Richard Saul Wurman (1971) eye opener "Making the City Observable." Wurman initiated TED in 1984, in an event of features demonstrating the convergence of Technology, Entertainment and Design. The mood was positively one of pure elation about the new possibilities.

The resulting book's title was coined by the editor of this book to frame a new era in understanding urban space in the dusk of the Anthropocene. The neo-moniker "Intelligent Environments" became adopted by IBM and IEEE, and a faithful band of exceptional researchers organizing annual conferences and publications around software and IT applications in various sectors, something the first edition of this present book had called for, in presenting itself as the pilot for such journal. IBM's interest spans from Intelligent Environments to Environmental Intelligence, most recently providing predictions and forecasts on risk and opportunities in aspects such as weather patterns and carbon performance, ranging to generative agriculture and renewable energy (IBM, 2021).

Unrelated to the present edition a computer science oriented, IEEE affiliated conference series commenced in 2005, organized by 'Intelligent Environments' of enthusiasts continuing each year, its proceedings published since 2009 by the German based Digital Bibliography & Library Project (dbpl, 2021)—the computer science bibliography at the Schloss Dagstuhl Leibniz Center for Informatics (Intelligent Environments, 2021a). A colorful group of educational programs persists. One example is the Integrative Design, Arts, and Technology (Intelligent Environments, 2021b) program at Carnegie-Mellon University that offers a rich curriculum of selections for an undergraduate Minor requirement in Intelligent Environments since the fall semester of 2018. The Center for Intelligent Environments at the University of Southern California (CENTIENTS, 2021) is a conglomerate of cross-disciplinary fields and interests. Others can be found under the references provided by Wrede et al. (2013).

The digital construction of social reality

The efforts took a special focus on spatial IT applications and issues—manifest in communities and the built environment: urban, regional, rural, global, and local. Today the systems have become even more pervasive and ubiquitous: the intelligent environment is omnipresent, shaping reality, informing society of risks and opportunities—but also deluding civilization in a technologically augmented illusion of the possible, while accelerating environmental and ultimately economic destruction in near-autonomous automation and AI enhanced efficiency. Perhaps this is why Warner Brothers' 1999 cyber spatial drama *Matrix* struck such a cord, in a faint flicker of popular realization that something was terribly amiss. And perhaps this is partially the existential flight motivation for NASA, ESA and a bevy of other space travel enterprises from the Emirates to China—not to speak of billionaires Musk and Bezos' spacecapades, or Branson's orbital outings—began to sell missions to 'space', the moon or Mars as to 'other worlds'—as if these barren rocks were somehow worthy to be called 'other' and 'worlds'—that is, comparable alternatives to this, humanity's only 'world' Earth, except perhaps to the mind of a mining magnate or a tour operator.

Is this kind of language designed to help us anticipate Earth's demise semantically? Is this the frame AI chatter and robotic ravings cocoon the popular imagination in, in evolutionary algorithmic flourish, to carry artificial life into a post-Anthropocene future? Is Elon Musk's 'relax, this must be a simulation' probability calculation really enough to assuage our existential anxieties? It must be simulation of a simulation, to be sure—unless carrying the stamp of an NFT—a nonfungible token encapsulating your very persona, proving to the digitally adept that you indeed are the proverbial real McCoy. The unauthentic—say, digital imagery—has become authentic, but not distinguishable—through the brute algorithmic force of non-fungibility via blockchain contracts. Is reality really nonfungible, deserving of the paradox label 'NFR', or has information system suffusion and CRISPR capacity made the very idea of the authentic meaningless? Can an NF code carrying token really remake, synthesize so to speak, the lost aura of authenticity Walter Benjamin had ascribed 95 years earlier to the means of mechanical—let alone digital—reproduction (Benjamin, 1935)?

Digitalization takes command: control and surveillance

Since then digital disillusion has been only thinly and temporarily swamped by a wave of industry led euphoria over *smart everything*, IoT and bigger and faster data streams yet, with the invasion of privacy, surveillance, abuse of personal data by government and media, internet, consumer products, general and specialized services, and even energy companies largely submerged in the popular discourse, but still visible. The capture and exploitation of user behavioral data streams are profoundly important across most major digital business leaders—including in the distributed energy industry where entire companies have begun to train their very business focus onto data harvesting and commercialization.

The concerns about the perils and promises of digitalization fall into the general, more popularized genre of "Surveillance Capitalism," as aptly framed by Shoshanna Zuboff (2019), endemic to the entire landscape of digital life having fallen prey to itself. Is society's digital tail being swallowed by itself, now a proverbial snake-inparadise, metaphorically representing human civilization's internalized urge to acquire short-term profit and reward, endlessly reproducing and exploiting itself? Does "the digital" complete the Fordist nightmare of mass production, exposed by Gideon in his 1948 master piece "Mechanization takes Command," into an automated and accelerating production-consumption automaton in which humans have become hapless agents moved and manipulated into a self-fulfilling but ultimately meaningless process of coagulation into an intelligent, sentient but uncontrollably voracious mass, a software and technology infused primal life form devouring its own existential nutrient base, the miraculously balanced, and supremely intelligent biosphere?

The message of almost every environmental campaigner and cyber-cultural critic is: we can overcome our technological fate, however inexorable it seems, through criticism and emancipation. Indeed, the extreme banality of a hyper-monitored data harvesting community does not always exude great confidence or attraction. Toronto has turned its back to the Smart City, and looks at good old people-oriented place design and old-fashioned energy efficiency and renewable energy solutions, to begin and build a more resilient city (Cecco, 2021). Sidewalk Labs, the design and infrastructure company owned by Google parent Alphabet, wanted to drive urban development and community life "from the internet up," as Google Chief Executive Eric Schmift had put it. Google inaugurated the commercial use of personal data harvesting from a myriad of users in 2001, and it became only natural to expand that drive into the replicant world of Smart Cities.

Almost halfway through the first half of the 21st century digital urbanists find themselves contemplating smart cities as "living labs" of a more sinister kind: wholly owned front ends of surveillance capitalist data mining, commercialization, consciousness shaping behavior management machines. What Berger and Luckmann **had framed in their Social Construction of Reality (1967)** as 'social construction of reality' had through the integrated "Doomsday Machine" Facebook (LaFrance, 2020) and the other pervasive digital empires Google and Amazon become a hyperreality creation machine. Along with a gargantuan armada of commercial operators virtually all avail themselves of microlocation and other tracking applets embedded in a myriad of standard apps, capable of more and less subtly nudging the "user" into defined behavioral, emotionalized and preconceptionalized consumer and voting responses in real time and real, as well as virtual space.

Toronto may have been able to reject the prying googly eyes of Google City—but the growing private surveillance networks of

Amazon Ring cameras perpetually gaze outside, combined with all-sensing street lights, surveillance cameras for store security and traffic safety, including police operated *Milestone* cameras—these began to turn United States cities and suburbs into online panopticons, comparable to the long-ubiquitous video cameras monitoring the streets of London, Great Britain. Amazon not only charged for the privilege of processing user surveillance data on its cloud servers but also marketed that individually harvested and paid-for information to law enforcement agencies across the United States (Bridges, 2021). It even promoted it as tool in combating domestic violence through police partnerships and the *Neighbors by Ring* application—but the scant evidence of actual benefits revealed this as sales messaging rather than a public and private security and safety program (Guo, 2021). At the other end of the surveillance response network operators were shackled to this very system in squalid conditions, subjecting Ring response call center workers to stress and even squalid conditions, for example, in the Philippines (Lee, 2020; Solon and Glaser, 2020)—a practice that Amazon even rewarded with incentives (Suppa, 2020).

The surveillance business took on even darker forms in Project Nimbus, a 1.2 billion cloud service contract between the Israeli public sector and both Amazon and Google, primarily serving the military's operations. This was revealed and protested against in an anonymous letter by Google and Amazon workers, following fears that the data technology was to be used to ever more effectively and systematically segregate, persecute and kill Palestinian children, women and men (Anonymous, 2021). Project Nimbus extended deep and highly lucrative surveillance, defense and cooperation contracts for Amazon Web Services, here for example with Israeli aerospace contractor IAI, who also was reported as experimenting with automating Gaza border control through sniper robots and drones (Chua et al., 2021). Drone manufacturers, weapons businesses, surveillance contractors and putatively AI enhanced lie detector equipment makers have found the growing European and U.S. migration protection fortification system ecology to be a lucrative yet deeply troubling playground (Ahmed and Tondo, 2021).

Surveillance through personal assistance devices, recording of personal data and communications, ubiquitous home information monitoring and systematic biasing of customer and vendor preferencing are some of the practices that Amazon's epic campaign against user privacy and disclosure protection legislation is reported as safeguarding successfully (Dastin et al., 2021).

Renewable energy risk and redemption

The electronic energy sector demonstrated the fundamental hope for survival in the transition from fossil to renewable resources. Digitalization is part of the electricity revolution—and this in turn opens, at least theoretically, the path to a fossil resource und uranium free future. Solar photovoltaic derived energy is the fastest growing form of renewable energy—and here pivots one promise: that of decarbonizing industrial and household energy. The twin needs to urgently cope with the twin challenge of related resource depletion and to reduce the carbon concentrations already in atmosphere and oceans are another matter.

Taking this one special feature, the digitalization of distributed energy resources, as a case in point: a pervasive perversion of early notions of "energy democracy" has ensued. In the context of distributed energy it has become salient to the discussion and the questions informed readers will have. Once networked into low-cost solar energy production and consumption microgrids and beyond, virtual trading communities and their distributed collectable "smart" data points and meters can be more dangerous in the cybersecurity, privacy and commercial data exploitation sense than centralized "dumb" systems were. The need for solutions to this quandary goes to the very heart of the resistance against Open P2P.

Two measures would seem required, one in terms of policy, and one of principle in a system architectural sense. A universal e-web (Droege, 2006) *Data Ownership Protocol* is originally suggested here, and long overdue to bar the central public or commercial collection and control of distributed user data. Equally critical is a structurally framed focus on decentralization, through consistently regulated bottom-up approaches to growing a loosely linked network architecture that is always fit for local purpose—not masterminded, projected or woven from above or afar. This would also inhibit the ease with which scam- and attack-bots are disseminated and propagated through the system. Both sets of measures together could assuage the legitimate fear increasingly felt by distributed renewable energy producers and users toward putatively enabling digitalization tools.

Digital salvation

This second IE edition revisits the genre by scanning its horizons a generation later for a congenial but far more urgent quest: finding purpose and redemption of sustainability in so-called advanced technology driven cities and regions. It is as if there is another purpose awakening, deep within the digital slumber of the “smart” or “digital” city. Or is there?

Be it as it may: Terra, Great Analog Mother Gaia shows herself unimpressed by the extremely marginal efforts of environmental risk management or greening, its carefully balanced biosphere unraveling under the polluting onslaught of a human economy driving her exploitation for short-term gain in accumulation of wealth expressed, at its pinnacle, in the conspicuous acquisition, consumption and exhibition of luxury goods. It is not until ‘advanced’ industrial civilization’s *Short-term Economic Return Syndrome* is overcome by an *Earth Rescue Finance System* urged here, an advanced monetary framework capable of representing community over individual prosperity, natural capital over corporate accumulation, long-term survival over short-term value extraction.

There is no question that digital technology has become a powerful element in the resilience—but not in the sustainability of, say, the retail and hotel services sectors. Among the earliest decliners—and yet, quickest to recover but also strongest performers during the Covid-19 pandemic of the early 2020s was the luxury goods industry. The high end was particularly adept in latching onto the lavish life style opportunities posed by digital technology. Whether the private sale of diamonds, art or private fashion shows over a catered five-star champagne lunch—the luxury goods, services and hospitality sector in the exclusive brand range did comparably well, thanks to online marketing and delivery (Aloisi and Cristoferi, 2021), although not as stunningly as the mass online retail market, epitomized by the stratospheric rise of Amazon, purveyor of all and everything, from masks to governance services.

The slow and reluctant rise of “smart” responsibility

There is a veritable universe of environmentally and climate mitigation and adaptation geared systems and applications, from investment fund rating tools to remote sensing and other geodata sampling, sounding and modeling devices and program—all the way to the sizable and growing online fund raising industry, environmental activism, and mobilization domain. Disappointingly and tellingly it has yet to create a noticeable upward push in the downward trajectory of terrestrial habitability systems.

The overwhelming, pervasive cultural focus on digital technologies has been peculiarly elsewhere, and largely distracting from any sense of existential purpose. Instead of being squarely and ubiquitously focused on Earth's atmospheric and terrestrial systems in their rapid decline, so-called advanced human civilization has become obsessed with finding entertainment, entrepreneurial energy and salvation in digital technologies. Since the second half of the 20th century, the Digital or Information Age has not only become accepted but even promoted, welcomed, and celebrated as a kind of pinnacle of human evolution. While its rise has also long evoked fear, criticism, condemnation, ridicule and dissent with infotech rule as end in itself, seekers of social or environmental purpose or structural solutions in applications have remained in the clear minority.

Even when this quest is articulated it seldom rises above greenwashing. As a typical example of "corporate responsibility," 2021 Facebook released four 'Responsible Innovation Principles' in the context of rebranding itself as the aspiring ruler of the metaverse while relabeling the company "Meta" (Meta, 2021a), a move similar to its USD 50 million pledge to "build the metaverse responsibly" (Meta, 2021b). Neither represented anything as grand or fundamental as what these defensive gestures sounded like, but merely referred to rules governing the development and administration of AR, virtual reality (VR), and other metaversal modes and protocols of user interaction (Carter and Egliston, 2021).

Sociotechnical and political frames involved in the digitalization of processes and procedures range from robotics in manufacture and construction, building sensors and controls, vehicle automation, big data mining, the notion of an internet of things—and one of energy, sensorial, and sentient urbanism—all the way to software augmented warfare, and increasingly rampant extrajudicial killings by remote controlled and sometimes autonomous, AI enabled drones—as if the virtualizing connotation of digitalization in itself served to sanitize mayhem and absolves the perpetrator of personal accountability in such incursions.

AI-enhanced *everything* is accepted as feature of an almost natural, "evolutionary move from atom to bit," from an analog to an information technology augmented, even simulated world—a transformation seemingly as natural as the demise of dinosaurs and the rise of sharks, penguins, otters, sloths, and dragonflies were 66 million years ago. The extinction analogy is apt: is an AI empowered meta-world supplanting a reality grounded one, in an illusionist act of existential transcendence? The degree of distraction in this invasion is uncanny: one late-Anthropocenic

AI ethicist even likened one feature of the digital revolution—domestic robots—to cuddly pets and perfect personal partners (Darling, 2021).

From the failure of modeling science: a call for action

New information realms form their own environments, with their own dynamics: data spheres, cyber space, social networks, corporate business process, marketing and accounting online and conventional video worlds, the suffusion, infusion, and extrapolation of 'reality' with ubiquitous media and omnispatial publication. A recent example was the anointment of a TV creation, the 45th U.S. President, into the political sphere, or better, the shaping of the political sphere around the aim to anoint. Media management has long been a central feature of elections but this was perhaps the first and so far only example of a voting populus being electronically and emotionally structured for a specific outcome—bar perhaps the choice of the UK to leave the European Union in 2020.

The technology is powerful. But how powerful? Powerful enough to save humankind from the flaming fossil-fuelled fireball its planetary habitat threatens to become? The 45th U.S. President's power rested more in appealing to and appeasing the destructive forces already in place instead of assembling capital and finance to stem the tide of fossil (doom). That effort was left to be attempted (by his successor) in seeking to pitch a countervailing wave of regeneration. At the end of the second decade in the second millennium AD the world witnessed the awesome power of a technologically powered globalized social media putsch machine, not broadcasting, not narrowcasting but micromanaging minds and memories into alternate realities (LaFrance, 2020).

Meanwhile, the world watches itself—in horror, apathy, or oblivion—burn in accelerating atmospheric and oceanic heat waves, consuming forests and glaciers, harvests and fresh water bodies—a slow motion nightmare of tens of millions—and possibly up to 2.5 billion—years of stabilization efforts by a Gaian planetary biosphere coming apart under the massive and rapid heat trapping gas injection of carbon dioxide, methane, nitrous oxide, and half a dozen other elements in the waste plume emanating from burning geologically sequestered carbon strata throughout the 20th century, accelerating exponentially in its second half.

Climate science through its models has been remarkably inaccurate in predicting the course of climate destruction—and ineffective in impressing on society and its lead agents the need to abandon fossil fuels and industrial agriculture. Much of climate science's public presence has been reduced to a group of individuals and institutions expressing their amazement and shock to see the world melt and combust by generations faster than predicted—70, 80 years sooner. Ultimately, the economic institutions bent on pursuing the established path have led to ignoring precaution and prioritizing short-term profit perpetuation—and casting into the wind any scientific caution in mistaking models for reality.

A similar failure is brought about by the incumbent machinery of entrenched institutions perverting the quest for climate stability by appending costly demands to the call for climate neutrality. While climate neutral or net zero action is in itself an inadequate goal, since it (a) is founded on the continued emission of greenhouse gases while notionally compensating these—without there being sufficient scope for doing so on a finite planet; and (b) it aims to hold carbon concentrations at far too high level. The call for climate neutrality serves the actual agenda of at once simulating and postponing action while creating a profitable market for carbon offseteering. A good example of this is the demand by Tenessee Valley Authority's CEO Jeff Lyash in the April of 2021 for a shopping list of 'technological advances in storage, carbon capture and small modular nuclear reactors' (Loller, 2021). The TVA is a federal authority, established by an act of congress in 1933, to, inter alia, provide low-cost electricity and environmental stewardship—in 2020 42% of TVA's electricity was derived from nuclear, 28% from gas 15% from coal and 12% from water power. Wind and solar provided only 3% of TVA's power.

The Biden administration offered in 2021 another example of the extent to which climate action had become virtualized and supplanted in symbolic rituals such as the United Nations Framework Convention's Conferences of the Parties (UNFCCC COP). Immediately after declaring that "America was back in the climate negotiations" during the 26th COP held in Scotland—where his predecessor Barack Obama—the greatest public policy developer of domestic oil and gas resources in U.S. history—gave a rousing speech, his administration allowed itself to be compelled into releasing more than 80 million acres of oil and gas prospecting leases for sale (Nilsen, 2021). A virtual, media created world characterizes the primacy of aspirations over reality. Seeming climate action characterizes a pervasive psycho-social reality, and manifest in cognitive detachment from reality of the planetary kind.

At this point the book picks up with its central message as a wake-up call from the paradoxical and pervasive digital slumber: that spatial and other information technologies and software systems are not just a genre within a genre but must be revealed as the very existential purpose of IT, AI, digital twins, networking tools and modeling power. The disconcertingly all-encompassing reliance, even utter dependence of civilization on digital hardware and software is revealed in periodic events such as malware attacks, or supply chain disruptions such as the great microchip shortage of 2021 and 2022—plain old black-outs, or the ever-present threat of EMP, electromagnetic pulse.

Untact or intact?

The pandemic commencing in early 2020 charged environmental virtualization with a new meaning: the US primaries of 2020 were abruptly transformed into remote events—without hitch and to great theatrical advantage and reach. This was stunning since the technical capacity to do so had been available for 2 decades, while laboring under the sheer inertia of physical events. In 2020 also a new consumer service strategy emerged in South Korea: remote shopping without human contact: *Untact* (Lee and Lee, 2020). This effective but empty concept provides a boost to pandemic weary shoppers, but only a faint hint at what may be possible when technology is applied broadly and systematically.

Can IE technology keep humanity intact, while it is becoming increasingly untact? Since human civilization is brittle and bound to suffer technology breakdowns the only way to cope with this technology is to not merely accept risks and failures but place entirely into the service of an Earth rescue mission of unheard of proportions. A myriad of isolated examples for positive action already exist. The time has come to reinforce this shift to positive action and place both hardware and software capabilities into the service of a planetary rescue mission, here referred to as the Regenerative Earth Decade (see also Droege, 2022).

3. The regenerative earth decade: intelligent environments for a habitable planet

What IE technologies are needed for the rapid transformation to a climate positive, carbon negative world? This depends on the specific purposes for which they are to be deployed. The Regenerative Earth Decade (RED) plan has been devised by the author, here for the Regenerative Earth Decade 10-point (RED10) action framework (Droege, 2022), for a war-like mobilization in a first- and last-ditch Earth rescue effort. These 10 policy and action points require concrete implementation. They can be supported by special, essential and nonessential but helpful intelligent-environment tools to achieve a stable climate, in a bold and comprehensive planetary emergency program.

3.1 Redefinition of emission targets: ubiquitous climate emergency gauges

Climate neutrality, a favorite rallying cry of mainstream climate policy advocates, is not enough to avoid a colossal climate calamity. So-called zero emission targets alone are no longer sufficient. The long-term stable atmospheric CO_2 level peaked at 280 ppm, current levels have reached 420 ppm at the time of writing this chapter: that is 150% of long-term stable concentrations. While long-term stable methane levels peaked at 600 ppb over the last 800,000 years, current levels will soon exceed 2000 ppb—at Arctic hotspots this value is already significantly higher. Conventional emissions targets are not only set too high—they should aim at well below zero. The global economy needs strategies that are suitable for reducing greenhouse gas (GHG) concentrations in the atmosphere by reversing the flow of emissions. This is also needed in an emergency effort to slow the disintegration of subsurface Arctic methane hydrates, and of the seafloor permafrost that has long begun to thaw, accelerates in disintegration and has begun to release potentially massive streams of thermogenic methane from ancient deep pools (Steinbach et al., 2021).

If there were a major policy lead and effectively related implementation push to concerted climate stabilization measures, then ubiquitous and precise, action sensitive and responsive atmospheric sensorial systems and a potentially AI reinforced global alert system could assist in actions to help maneuver humanity from the dire state of emergency it currently is in to a lower level of concentrations. In itself, without policy and action commitments, it cannot yield success. Atomized distributed action does not work unless it is guided by systemic financial and policy incentives. To arrive at these, the news and media outlets have to regularly inform the global communities of this internal threat: new means of daily and effective information sharing on climate indicators are essential.

3.2 Climate defense budgets

A central vision of the Regenerative Earth Decade involves the introduction of national climate defense budgets for the rapid phase-out of fossil fuels and a switch to renewable energies—this may account for five to 10 percent of gross national product, equivalent to four to eight times that of average military budgets, in need of redirection and repurposing to climate defense action. This is only a conservative estimate: the United States economy during mobilization for and conduct of World War Two rapidly exceeded these levels. The global economy must be prepared for this level of readiness, in effort and immediate engagement.

Whole-of-economy requisitioning of material, machines, renewable energy generators, carbon sequestration measures—and, above all, the financial flows required: their facilitation and understanding will benefit from tools and systems that are optimized to enable the coordinated and monitored flow of resources to construct the entire remaining economic capacity of nations and international networks to the termination of fossil fuel emissions, resource depletion and the preservation, regeneration and ramping up of atmospheric CO_2 and CH_4 removal—see here the bio- and industrial sequestration points under Sections 3.7 and 3.8 below.

3.3 Climate peace diplomacy

Presented here is the emergency response concept of Climate Peace Diplomacy. It speaks to the ending of wars and military aggression in the common interest in the fight for survival - against the *common enemy* of global warming (LISD, 2021). Climate peace diplomacy includes an unwavering focus on climate migration management plans: billions of human beings will be forced to migrate very soon: the business-as-usual Representative Concentration Path RCP8.5 / three degree Kelvin mean average temperature rise scenario implies that up to one third of the world's population may have to migrate over the next 50 years (Xu et al., 2020).

Planet-wide Climate Peace accords must be achieved to deal with this most threatening common enemy: the scourge of anthropogenic climate change. Supreme communication lines are crucial to muster diplomatic channels at all levels, for peaceful cooperation, to increasingly share resources. To avert the ultimate calamity in the short history of humanity the peaceful unification and a rallying around the cause of bold and comprehensive climate stable action is a basic, essential condition.

Comprehensive climate positive action diplomacy of this kind requires new and open means of direct communication, and the negotiation of an unprecedented integration of renewable energy transformation, agricultural soil regeneration, the "healing abandonment" that is, renaturalization and renurturing of deforested areas and wetlands, biodiversity rescue, and support—to name only a very few of the most essential areas. This will also require a new monetary framework rewarding planetary support agendas over short-term individual gain.

3.4 Fossil fuel industry restructuring

The most urgent and challenging of all emergencies in the battle for geo-climate stabilization is fossil industry restructuring, because its entrenched interests and spheres of influence permeate so much of the command and control apparatus of industrialized and so-called developing Planet Earth. The influence and inertia of incumbent industries, and after-tax subsidies of 5.9 trillion U.S. dollars in 2020 (IMF, 2021) have meant a very slow transition—frequently going in reverse, as demonstrated in the great slowing and structural reversal of the German energy transition from 2012 through 2021, when hundreds and thousands of jobs in renewable energy sectors were lost.

A systematic and targeted restructuring of fossil industries is needed: through technical substitution programs, the elimination of the widespread subsidies and structural measures such as transformation assistance. This complex includes also the immediate dismantling of the massive regulatory blocking of renewable energy grids, storage, and distribution systems—supported by new energy market frameworks. The new industries offer entrepreneurial and employment opportunities for diehard fossil-fuel industrialists and their employees alike. This "pull" effect will not be enough: the system has to be pushed into another state.

Here we need software solutions for retraining, and investment intelligence in renewable industries and resources. An intelligent market space of innovation is required to boost, coordinate and guide investment flows to the highest transformative value and effect. Of equal importance is the modeling and recognition of revenue compensation needs in states reliant on fossil income.

3.5 Regenerative employment programs

Transforming and healing the vast fossilized parts of the economy is key: changing the careers and business models of those reaping rewards from the subsidized extraction, processing, distribution and application of fossil energy resources. At the same time the replacement of jobs in the fossil industries by prioritized structural reforms toward renewable industries is essential: conventional employment markets alone would respond too slowly. By structuring opportunities in renewable energy and other regeneration-oriented retraining, research, development, manufacturing, maintenance, investment, and policy development we can not only ease the transition of workers, job opportunities but also dramatically boost the sheer number of available jobs, as well as of those competent to fill them.

Creating jobs is easy in any dramatic mobilization of the economy, for conventional war preparations and fighting—and as here for climate stabilization wars. Distributing them and making them accessible in systematic, open, and equitable ways is much harder. Here social integration programs are needed. Ubiquitous online education, and community nurturing support are critical—an entirely new global migration framework with a view on targeted employment programs is needed. The cultural shifts required are enormous, and intelligent online media require recruitment and targeted deployment to prepare humanity for it.

3.6 Source taxation of fossil fuels and their regulatory phasing-out

The classification of fossil resources as toxic is an essential measure of sustainably evolving forward: their extraction and for combustion should become highly taxed in a short transition period to prohibition. Paths and means to this aim are based on precedents and routes to success in other area of emission and waste regulation—although none, from carcinogenic tobacco to industrial air pollutants have proven so utterly and universally threatening, and lethal to all.

Global lethal resource tracking systems are needed to map, expose, and disincentivize fossil fuel prospecting, extraction, and production in a focused and targeted manner. The fossil fuel content in global and local value chains can be traced to its variegated sources: it makes more sense to tax the toxin at the source than after it has been produced, processed, refined and distributed. This requires substantial measures to guide the transformation away from state and corporate reliance on fossil fuel revenue—a feature of the Intelligent Environment Society that is already on its way.

3.7 Biosequestration: the rapid development and regeneration of healthy, climate-active agricultural soils, wetlands, and forests

Carbon concentration reduction in the atmosphere requires as one of the most available mechanisms the activation of the natural capacity of healthy soils and natural land cover in drawing down and absorbing and retaining atmospheric carbon. A few tools are available to gauge, map and measure biosequestration and potential—too few and far between. Also, their use is at best sporadic. The CO_2 removal and sequestration opportunities are relatively well modeled, tracked and understood, for CH_4 only a beginning has been achieved, if anything. Jackson et al. (2021) discuss the logic and potential, and propose a globally and locally relevant Methane Removal Model Intercomparison Project, an indication of how dauntingly early these steps still were at the time of writing this chapter.

This makes atmospheric concentrations tracking tools even more powerful: expanding the understanding of land use and planning as a key to preserving, protecting, and nurturing carbon removal and sequestration potentials.

3.8 Industrial sequestration: transformation for carbon removal and uptake

The transformation of the construction industry and all industries and manufactories into carbon-sequestration processes demands the large-scale conversion of atmospheric CO_2 into wood, carbon fibers and other solid carbon products. Atmospheric carbon: the concentrations of CO_2, CH_4, NOx, and other climate heating gases have to be lowered. This is a revolution in the very concept of a circular economy. It has already begun, with hundreds of business initiatives and some University ventures such as Michigan University's Global CO_2 Initiative focusing on the atmospheric GHG removal opportunities (University of Michigan, 2021).

Tracking these developments will require the massive deployment of whole-of-economy performance. True atmospherically cyclical economies will benefit from reliable mapping and accounting systems of resource flow, and the transparent crediting of reliable, sustainable, and proven permanent atmospheric GHG removal.

3.9 Planning and utilizing regenerative economic boosts from migrant streams

There are two aspects to this enormous shift in human civilizational evolution. To transform the economy into an NCS, a negative carbon society for existential reasons also will take full advantage of the resulting unprecedented productivity and innovation in the new regenerative industrial reality and massively expand high-quality employment opportunities for all citizens – and especially for existing and new migrants. It is of paramount importance to plan for something utterly unprecedented in human history: the global migration of billions assuming a by now optimistic future of the business-as-usual Representative Concentration Pathway RCP of 8.5 and population growth/socioeconomic pathway SSP 3, that is, a global Mean Average Temperature rise of 3°C, translating into a 7.5°C rise over continents, or some 29°C (Xu et al., 2020).

To model, analyze, track and plan for this extraordinary move requires computing power akin to that to run advanced climate and global weather models, since climate as well as economic and political shifts are essential to consider. The model or models also have to consider where employment opportunities will arise, and consider the policy and support frameworks available in the respective countries: for example agricultural jobs in Siberia, or mining in Greenland.

3.10 A regenerative finance mechanism

New mechanisms are needed to reward long-term investments at a large, systemic scale: in defossilization, agricultural reform and afforestation - with higher returns than short-term ones. This calls, for example, for "Future Banks" that create special currencies with demurrage charges or negative interest rates, thus incentivizing spending tied to sustainable products and services.

An entire universe of intelligent environment tools is needed to construct as well as support the financial transactional space needed to reverse-engineer the reward structure of investments from short to long term. The current monetary system requires augmentation with a rich ecosystem of demurrage payment and investment tools trained on ecosystem services from atmospheric carbon removal to biodiversity regeneration.

In order to construct and maintain a new monetary framework rewarding planetary support agendas over short-term individual gain fintech innovations will be useful, capable to constructing a new market space for regenerative goods and services that can be tracked and registered, whether through blockchain or other reliable, simple, and ubiquitously affordable means.

4. The case for an intelligent planetary support environment

At the time of this writing, no real effort was underway to construct an Earth-listening, action and communication network, informing the planet's human population with daily updates on emergency actions taken. The popular discourse about artificial intelligence and its inexorable taking over of human affairs: none of it has been programmed or even guided to preserve this planet as habitable for human purposes. This only gives rise to the utterly dystopian notion of a posthuman world living in a self-replicating robotic world permanently adjusting to ever higher temperatures. Here is an obvious lacuna in the application of advanced intelligent environment technology, ranging from plotting likely policy paths to modeling financial reward systems to guiding global migration policy and climate peace initiatives.

The only faintly, very remotely related effort at assembling an earth rescue network of sorts was a promotional project by the Clemenger Group, a Melbourne based marketing and communications agency working with the University of Tasmania and others, to propose "Earth Box," a "black box for Earth" to be built in 2022, in order to "record every step we take toward the catastrophe" (Clemenger, 2021; Kilvert, 2021). It was unclear whether this was a serious proposal or a marketing flash in the pan to mark the University on the global map. For about 24 h in the initial global news rotation, the device worked.

But much more than such short-term marketing ploys are needed, feeding off fear and fostering despondence. Instead, the time of a concerted drive toward climate stabilization has arrived: the mobilization of Intelligent Environments for the Regenerative Earth Decade, an attempt at short-, medium-, and long-term climate stabilization efforts that cannot wait another single hour.

5. Conclusion

A definite success has been the democratization of media access and the rise of citizen justice and science—see the ability by citizens and bystanders to support racial justice and human rights worldwide. In the Unites States, this was long epitomized by the video graphed police power abuse, from the widely broadcast Sony Handycam capture by George Holliday and the resulting public exposure of Rodney King's beatings in Los Angeles of 1991 to 17-year old bystander Darnella Frazier's capturing of George Floyd's street side suffocation on her iPhone 11 (Canon, 2021) for Facebook upload—leading to the subsequent trial and murder conviction of the police perpetrator, in Minneapolis of 2021 (Sandoval, 2017; Stern, 2020). This capacity had already been in the focus of Ithiel de Sola Pool's pamphlet "Technologies of Freedom" (Sola and Ithiel de, 1983), in this case placed into the service of a political argument about presumed media-liberated democracies versus dictatorships.

The capacity of information technology to monitor, map, model, and analyze the state of the natural environment has been utterly explosive. This capability helps comprehend both depth and breadth of 'nature's' complexity—but also the staggering scale of loss being incurred as result of the modern human economy having being unleashed on this small planet, on its growth-hormonal diet of cheap hydrocarbons for easy combustion. While the electronic microscope and mirror onto our own demise has boosted the potential for easy comprehension no overall effective action has yet resulted from it.

The application of Jay Wright Forrester's 'World' model as deployed by his MIT students Donnella and Dennis Meadows presented to a global audience its inexorable futures in simple line drawings: in the exponential rise, leveling off or collapse of industrialization, population, food, use of resources, and pollution. The Volkswagen-Foundation funded and Club of Rome commissioned project is still unsurpassed in its compelling accuracy today (Meadows et al., 1972, 2004a, 2004b).

An extraordinary success has also been the explosion of analysis and visualization tools, or the myriad of efficiency and environmental monitoring systems and their hand-held apps and devices. From 20 years of NASA's Aqua satellite mounted atmospheric infrared sounder (AIRS) renditions of a planet in distress—allowing say the animation of massive plumes of carbon monoxide emanating from South American, African, and Siberian forest fires in 2019, visualized at 5500 m (NASA, 2019)—across the other exceptional work by ESA, NASA, the

Geographic Survey, NOAA, and a number of international agencies and organizations and their modeling efforts yielded an exemplary and vast array of hypothetical and empirical mappings, modelings, visualizations, and informed albeit limited predictions. The work of either the IPCC or the UNFCCC, too, is steeped in a vicarious, surrogate world of scientific modeling—alas, much of it bearing little resemblance to the real world to date.

References

Academy Hills, 2021. https://www.academyhills.com/english/index.html. https://www.academyhills.com/english/mission_history.html.

Ahmed, K., Tondo, L., 2021. Fortress Europe: the millions spent on military-grade tech to deter refugees. The Guardian, 6 December 2021. https://www.theguardian.com/global-development/2021/dec/06/fortress-europe-the-millions-spent-on-military-grade-tech-to-deter-refugees.

Aloisi, S., Cristoferi, C., 2021. Buying Diamonds in Lockdown? WhatsApp Can Be Your Best Friend. Reuters Technology. https://www.reuters.com/technology/buying-diamonds-lockdown-whatsapp-can-be-your-best-friend-2021-04-14/.

Anonymous Google, Amazon Workers, 2021. We Are Google and Amazon Workers. We Condemn Project Nimbus, 12 October 2021. https://www.theguardian.com/commentisfree/2021/oct/12/google-amazon-workers-condemn-project-nimbus-israeli-military-contract. (Accessed 15 October 2021).

Benjamin, W., 1935. Das Kunstwerk im Zeitalter seiner technischen Reproduzierbarkeit. (2008. The Work of Art in the Age of Mechanical Reproduction. Penguin).

Berger, P.L., Luckman, T., 1967. The social construction of reality: a treatise in the sociology of knowledge. Anchor.

Bridges, L., 2021. Amazon's Ring Is the Largest Civilian Surveillance Network the US Has Ever Seen. The Guardian Opinion, 18 May 2021. https://www.theguardian.com/commentisfree/2021/may/18/amazon-ring-largest-civilian-surveillance-network-us.

Canon, G., 2021. I cried so hard': the teen who filmed Floyd's killing and changed America. The Guardian. https://www.theguardian.com/us-news/2021/apr/20/darnella-frazier-george-floyd-derek-chauvin-trial-guilty-verdict.

Carter, M., Egliston, B., 2021. Facebook relaunches itself as 'Meta' in a clear bid to dominate the metaverse. The Conversation, 28 October 2021. https://theconversation.com/facebook-relaunches-itself-as-meta-in-a-clear-bid-to-dominate-the-metaverse-170543.

Cecco, L., 2021. Toronto Swaps Google-Backed, Not-So-Smart City Plans for People-Centred Vision. https://www.theguardian.com/world/2021/mar/12/toronto-canada-quayside-urban-centre.

CENTIENTS, 2021. Center for Intelligent Environments – A Human-Centered Initiative to Improve Built Enviroments. USC Viterbi School of Engineering. https://www.intelligentenvironments.usc.edu.

Chua, C., Alimahomed-Wilson, J., Potiker, S., 2021. Amazon's investments in Israel reveal complicity in settlements and military operations. The Nation. June 22, 2021. https://www.thenation.com/article/economy/amazon-prime-day-israel/. (Accessed 15 October 2021).

Clemenger, B., 2021. Earth's Black Box. https://www.earthsblackbox.com/.

Darling, K., 2021. AI ethicist Kate Darling: Robots can be our partners. Interview statements to Zoë Corbyn. The Observer Interview Sat 17 Apr 2021 16.00 BST. https://www.theguardian.com/technology/2021/apr/17/ai-ethicist-kate-darling-robots-can-be-.

Dastin, J., Kirkham, C., Kalra, A., 2021. Amazon Wages Secret War on Americans' Privacy, Documents Show. Reuters Special Report filed November 19 2021. https://www.reuters.com/investigates/special-report/amazon-privacy-lobbying/. (Accessed 22 November 2021).

dbpl Digital Bibliography & Library Project - computer science bibliography, 2021. Schloss Dagstuhl Leibniz Center for Informatics. Retrieved on 2021-04-17 07:24 CEST: https://dblp.org/db/conf/intenv/index.html.

Droege, P., 1997a. Intelligent Environments – Spatial Aspects of the Information Revolution. North Holland.

Droege, P., 1997b. Tomorrow's metropolis – virtualization takes command. In: Intelligent Environments – Spatial Aspects of the Information Revolution. North Holland. https://doi.org/10.1016/B978-044482332-8/50003-2.

Droege, P., 2006. Renewable City – Comprehensive Guide to an Urban Revolution. Wiley.

Droege, P., 2022. Regenerative Earth Decade. EUROSOLAR - European Associat ion for Renewable Energy e.V. http://www.earthdecade.org. https://www.youtube.com/watch?v=JFYqfeM8Pq0.

Gideon, S., 1948. Mechanization Takes Command – A Contribution to Anonym ous History. University of Minnesota Press.

Guo, E., 2021. How Amazon Ring Uses Domestic Violence to Market Doorbell Cameras. Technology Review. https://www.technologyreview.com/2021/09/20/1035945/amazon-ring-domestic-violence/.

Hillier, B., 1996. Space Is the Machine. Cambridge University Press.

IBM, 2021. Environmental Intelligence Suite. https://www.ibm.com/products/environmental-intelligence-suite.

IMF International Monetary Fund, 2021. Still Not Getting Energy Prices Right: A Global and Country Update of Fossil Fuel Subsidies. September 21, 2021. https://www.imf.org/en/Publications/WP/Issues/2021/09/23/Still-Not-Getting-Energy-Prices-Right-A-Global-and-Country-Update-of-Fossil-Fuel-Subsidies-466004. https://www.imf.org/en/Topics/climate-change/energy-subsidies. See also the earlier report.

Intelligent Environments, 2021. dblp. https://dblp.org/db/conf/intenv/index.html.

Intelligent Environments, 2021. IDeATe. https://ideate.cmu.edu/undergraduate-programs/intelligent-environments/index.html.

Jackson, R.B., et al., 2021. Atmospheric Methane Removal: A Research Agenda. The Royal Society Publishing. https://doi.org/10.1098/rsta.2020.0454.

Kilvert, N., 2021. Earth Is Getting a Black Box to Record Our Climate Change Actions, and It's Already Started Listening. 5 December 2021. ABC Science. https://www.abc.net.au/news/science/2021-12-06/climate-change-earth-black-box-recorder/100621778.

LaFrance, A., 2020. Facebook is a doomsday machine. The Atlantic, 15 Dec. 2020. https://www.theatlantic.com/technology/archive/2020/12/facebook-doomsday-machine/617384/.

Lee, D., 2020. Amazon Contractors Enduring, subhuman' Conditions in the Philippines. Financial Times. https://www.ft.com/content/8b7bc787-4f33-4909-85f0-8df36d165b69.

Lee, S.M., Lee, D., 2020. Untact – a New Customer Service Strategy in the Digital Age. Springer, pp. 1–22. https://doi.org/10.1007/s11628-019-00408-2. Published in Service Business 14 (2020).

LISD, 2021. Climate for Peace. Liechtenstein Institute for Strategic Development AG. http://www.climateforpeace.org.

Loller, T., 2021. TVA CEO: US Needs Tech Advances to Reach Carbon Goals. AP News. https://apnews.com/article/technology-environment-and-nature-business-359b81ae94b8411fe550f0c43f17e714.

Meadows, D.H., Meadows, D.L., Randers, J., Behrens III, W.W., 1972. The Limits to Growth. A Report for the Club of Rome's Project on the Predicament of Mankind. Universe Books. http://www.donellameadows.org/wp-content/userfiles/Limits-to-Growth-digital-scan-version.pdf.

Meadows, D.H., Randers, J., Meadows, D.L., 2004a. Limits to Growth: The 30-year Update .White River Junction: Chelsea Green.

Meadows, D.H., Randers, J., Meadows, D.L., 2004b. Limits to Growth: The 30-year Update. Chelsea Green Publishing.

Meta, 2021a. Responsible Innovation Principles. https://about.facebook.com/realitylabs/responsible-innovation-principles/. (Accessed 30 October 2021).

Meta, 2021b. Building the Metaverse Responsibly. https://about.fb.com/news/2021/09/building-the-metaverse-responsibly/. (Accessed 30 October 2021).

NASA, 2019. NASA's AIRS Maps Carbon Monoxide from Brazil Fires. Jet Propulsion Laboratory. https://www.jpl.nasa.gov/images/nasas-airs-maps-carbon-monoxide-from-brazil-fires.

Nilsen, E., 2021. Why the Biden Administration Is Reopening Oil and Gas Leases in the Guld of Mexico. CNN. https://edition.cnn.com/2021/11/17/politics/biden-oil-gas-leasing-gulf-of-mexico-climate/index.html.

Sandoval, P.X.de, 2017. Meet the Man Who Recorded the World's First Viral Video. El Pais. https://english.elpais.com/elpais/2017/05/25/inenglish/1495709209_218886.html.

Sassen, G., 1991. The Gobal City - Tokyo. Princeton University Press, London, New York.

Sola, P., Ithiel de, 1983. Technologies of Freedom. Harvard University Press.

Solon, O., Glaser, A., 2020. Amazon Ring Call Center Workers, scared to Go to Wrk during Pandemic. NBC News. https://www.nbcnews.com/tech/security/we-don-t-have-choice-amazon-ring-call-center-workers-n1243439.

Steinbach, J., et al., March 9, 2021. Source apportionment of methane escaping the subsea permafrost system in the outher Eurasian Arctic Shelf. Proccedings of the National Academy of Sciences United States of America 118 (10). https://doi.org/10.1073/pnas.2019672118 e2019672118.

Stern, J., 2020. They used smartphone cameras to record police brutality – and change history. The Wall Street Journal. https://www.wsj.com/articles/they-used-smartphone-cameras-to-record-police-brutalityand-change-history-11592020827.

Suppa, A., 2020. Can Multinational Corporations be responsible for human rights violation of its outsourcee company? Response of national or international law? International and Comparative Law Review 20 (1), 153–179. https://doi.org/10.2478/iclr-2020-0007. https://www.researchgate.net/publication/346763258_Can_Multinational_Corporations_be_responsible_for_human_rights_violation_of_its_outsourcee_company_Response_of_national_or_international_law.

University of Michigan, 2021. Global CO_2 Initiative. https://www.globalco2initiative.org/.

Wrede, J.C.A., Callaghan, V., Cook, D., Kameas, A., Satoh, I., 2013. Intelligent environments: a manifesto. Human-centric Computing and Information Sciences 3 (1), 12. https://www.researchgate.net/publication/270793368_Intelligent_Environments_a_manifesto.
Wurman, R.S., 1971. Making the City Observable. MIT Press.
Xu, C., Kohler, T.A., Lenton, T.M., Svenning, J.-C., Scheffer, M., 2020. Future of the human climate niche. May 26, 2020 PNAS 117 (21), 11350–11355. https://doi.org/10.1073/pnas.1910114117. first published May 4, 2020.
Zuboff, S., 2019. Surveillance Capitalism: The Fight for a Human Future at the New Frontier of Power. PublicAffairs.

2

The Ruhr innovation ecosystem—From industrial brownfields to regenerative smart environments

Anis Radzi
Liechtenstein Institute for Strategic Development, Berlin, Germany

1. Climate change and urban infrastructure transformations

The urgency of climate change presents an existential challenge to metropolitan regions around the world. The scale and complexity of the problem demand systemic solutions as well as structural changes that disrupt existing ways of governing economies in order to protect the environment, work toward mitigating climate change, and prepare for their impacts.

The Ruhr Metropolis in the state of North-Rhine Westphalia, Germany is one region that has undergone such changes. A product of robust structural change policies implemented over many decades, the Ruhr has effectively replaced a once highly industrialized mono-structural coal, iron, and steel economy with one based on advanced information and communication technologies (ICT), environmental and energy innovation, and sustainable urban development. The shift not only completely transformed and reinvigorated the region but over time has successfully addressed local environmental challenges and enhanced socioeconomic efforts to tackle climate change through local energy transition projects.

Changes in the Ruhr began in the 1960s with the need for environmental repair and rehabilitation from heavy industrial pollution. State legislation demanded cleaner industry processes and improved waste management. Integrated policies in economic rationalization and diversification soon included set

Intelligent Environments. https://doi.org/10.1016/B978-0-12-820247-0.00005-9

targets for climate protection and carbon emissions reduction. These policies set the basis for the first major infrastructural interventions in the region.

Beyond mere environmental remediation and protection, the German energy transition strategy of 2010 became the catalyst for more ambitious urban energy trajectories to reduce emissions and to invest in renewable energy. Progressive changes in the world economy and the growing impacts of climate change also pushed cities in the Ruhr to rethink municipal practices in environmental and energy planning as well as urban redevelopment. Through collaborative networks involving universities, research institutes, companies, and associations, future-oriented solutions for a postfossil fuel society were conceived and implemented. The construction of new universities and start-up incubators initiated the reprogramming of Ruhr's economy based on science and research. A portfolio of projects in low carbon development and sustainable urban transport soon affected wider economic and societal transformations.

When the European Commission set the long-term objective of a climate-neutral Europe by 2050 (EC, 2018) in 2018, accompanied by the EU Green Deal in 2019 and a Climate Law in 2020 (EC, 2020a and b), these set forth another round of structural demands for the Ruhr.

Energy transition in the Ruhr Metropolis is currently in progress. New networked approaches based on advanced ICT developed within the region are being deployed to formulate smart-city and sustainable development plans; modernize urban energy infrastructures for the intelligent generation and management of renewable energy sources; establish new renewable energy markets; develop advanced environmental technologies; and conserve cultural and environmental landscapes through digitized monitoring. Innovations in the new green technology and infrastructure systems are duly expected to bring successive economic and employment opportunities to the region.

This chapter traces the development history of the Ruhr Metropolis, and the critical phases of structural change, and presents three cities in the region that have pursued advanced science and technology to transform local economies and achieve their energy transition goals. The chapter presents the concept of "innovation ecosystems" as the critical "spaces" which have enabled these transformative processes to take place. These are spaces where the harmonization of policy conditions and stakeholder milieu afford the ideal means to develop and implement new concepts, products, and services. Exemplified in the various policies, platforms, and environments created by the different levels of government in the Ruhr, such spaces have engendered high economic creativity, productivity, diversity, and growth. The chapter concludes with a brief discussion of the key moments, lessons, and socio-economic aspects of these ecosystems.

2. The Ruhr Metropolis innovation ecosystem

The Ruhr Metropolis (*Metropole Ruhr* - MR) is one of Europe's largest and densest metropolitan regions. Located in the state of North Rhine-Westphalia (NRW), it is the largest conurbation in Germany with an area of 4435 km^2. The region comprises 53 cities and four counties with around 5.1 million inhabitants. It lies in a prominent central position within the national and European context (see Fig. 2.1).

The Ruhr is a polycentric urban region characterized by robust, economically strong cores with surrounding hinterlands (see Fig. 2.2). The main cities of Dortmund, Bochum, Essen, and Duisburg represent the largest local economies with specializations in logistics and environmental technology. Its dense academic and scientific infrastructure comprises 1700 schools, 20 universities, 71 research institutions, nine technology transfer

Figure 2.1 Location of Ruhr Metropolis (RM) within Germany and the German state of North-Rhine Westphalia.

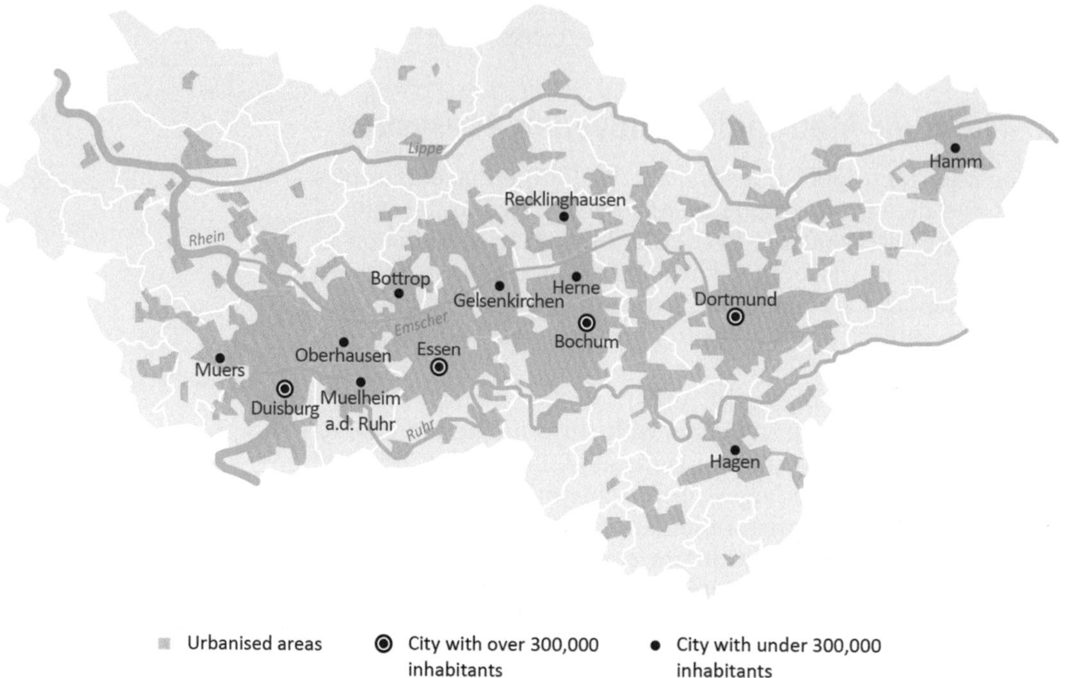

Figure 2.2 The major cities of the Ruhr Metropolis.

agencies, and 30 start-up and technology centers (Keil and Wetterau, 2013). The region's highly developed transportation network (international rapid transit, commercial airport, dense road network) makes it a leading gateway for business in northwestern Europe and a vital logistics hub. It has the world's largest inland port and Europe's most dense canal system. Many corporate headquarters are based in the region, and important political and economic decision-making takes place here. Its rehabilitated industrial structures have become internationally recognized historical monuments and cultural centers, serving to celebrate the Ruhr's history in coal and steel.

In 2018, around 1.75 million people were employed in the Ruhr. There were over 42,000 companies, with the greatest number active in the lead market of urban construction and living (business.metropoleruhr.de, 2021). The region has experienced good employment growth in the leading markets of digital communication (+6.5%), mobility (+4.6%), and education (3.4%). As an influential and aspiring region in the digital economy, local companies are taking advantage of innovations in digitization to develop new business models and value chains. In

2018, there were 6580 small and medium-sized IT companies mostly specializing in data processing and software development. The highest sales in the region were achieved by the industrial core and entrepreneurial services with a turnover of EUR 82 billion (business.metropoleruhr.de, 2021). Overall, the region accounts for almost 24% of the GDP of NRW's state economy (rvr.ruhr, 2020a).

2.1 The structural phases of the Ruhr Metropolis innovation ecosystem

Historically, the Ruhr developed into an economic powerhouse based on coal mining, coal power generation, and coal-reliant steel production. In the 1810s, the population was around 200,000 but rose to four million before the First World War, and to six million in the 1950s when the accelerated output of coal and steel caused a huge rise in the labor force through large-scale migration. Europe's largest industrial agglomeration consisted of only a few very large firms. During the two world wars, the region became the center of military industry. It was a key exporter of plants, equipment, chemicals, and vehicles. Following the Second World War, the coal and steel industries provided resources for Germany's economic recovery (*Wirtschaftswunder*). The region formed the center of the European Coal and Steel Community, which later evolved into the European Union.

By the late 1950s, the core heavy industries of the Ruhr were in a decline. The cost of extracting German hard coal was rising. World market prices for coal and steel were falling below the production costs of the Ruhr industry. New mines in the U.S. and Eastern Europe were supplying the markets with cheaper coal mined near the surface. The demand for coal was also being replaced with oil and gas. The traditional customers—the shipping, railways, steel, and chemical industries—were reducing their coal consumption.

Within 30 years, the mines and factories in the Ruhr had shut down, with more than half a million jobs lost. The German economic growth of the 1960s partially offset the job losses but it could not stop the 15% unemployment rate reached in the 1980s, which resulted in large-scale emigration (Reicher et al., 2011).

The large-scale losses triggered major structural change policies over 5 decades and several notable phases resulting in the replacement of the region's mono-structure economy with tertiarisation based on science and research.

2.1.1 Integrated reindustrialization (1966–74)

A long-running series of interconnected progressive responses to the historic collapse of economic activity and employment in coal and steel in the region ensued from the late 1950s.

At the start, subsidy policies for hard coal mining were instituted to safeguard national energy security. Given that the complete closure of Germany's high-cost hard coal mines could not be averted, the subsidies also served to structure the slow decline in coal production, prevent large-scale unemployment caused by mine production cuts and closures, and manage the labor market transitions of dismissed coal workers.

When the NRW state government launched the "Ruhr Development Program" (EPR) in 1968, the aim was to approach economic repositioning in a more integrated manner in order to draw new business sectors into the region. With a volume of 17 billion Deutsche Mark (DM) (EUR 8.7 billion) financed by the state and the German national government, the 5-year program focused on radical improvements to the three major public infrastructures of transportation, education, and recreation (Goch, 2009) (see Fig. 2.3).

Figure 2.3 Education, transport, and green infrastructure priorities in the Ruhr between 1966 and 1974.

Increased and improved mobility for all was essential for stimulating economic growth. In the late 1960s, the cities in the Ruhr were poorly connected due to weak public transport systems and incomplete road and highway networks. With the construction of new motorways and arterial roads, the region was finally opened up to more people, businesses, and investment. It triggered growth in the service sector and prompted the establishment of new industries related to modern transport logistics planning, design, monitoring, and control, all built upon a long regional history in industrial freight by road, rail and water. Extensions to the public transport network also substantially eased and improved access to wider areas in the region for work, living and leisure.

New learning and training environments prompted new business impulses and became critical to economic diversification. Before 1965, there was no university in the Ruhr. Up to then, an "educational blockade" was implicitly enforced by the region's core industries and political lobbyists who did not consider educational institutions necessary in a region running on the manual labor of coal, and steel. But the realization that new academic and vocational training capacities were essential to prepare new graduates and reskill retrenched workers for a new economy, huge investments by the NRW state government set forth the development of a number of universities, starting with the Ruhr University Bochum (1965), the Technical University of Dortmund (1968), and the universities of Duisburg (1968) and Essen (1972)—which merged to become the University of Duisburg-Essen in 2003.

Healthy and clean environments enabled economic activities to flourish and helped sustain new industry presence. Poor environmental conditions caused by the polluting coal, steel, and energy industries created a region that was long unpleasant to live and unattractive to set up a business in. By remediating several industrial estates and integrating them into the region's existing green belts, attention returned to improving the quality of life of the region's residents. The extension of the parkland system, initially created in the 1920s to provide ecological compensation from the heavy industries and prevent the uncontrolled expansion of cities, enhanced the greening of the Ruhr. It also increased recreational opportunities and raised awareness of environmental conservation.

The EPR achieved significant improvements in transport, education, and environmental infrastructures. The major core industries in the Ruhr collaborated to improve their productivity and competitiveness, eventually leading to mergers between former competitors, such as the case of steel companies Thyssen and Krupp. The alliance ensured company viability and maintained close ties with customers and suppliers. Meanwhile, a few local city governments attracted some investment in the new sectors of microelectronics, chemicals, and cars. The trade unions worked with the governments to minimize hardship on retrenched workers from the mining and steel industries with compensation, retraining, or pensions. Many new positions were offered in postmining activities such as pit water management, surface water management, and groundwater purification, critical expertise in the construction of new roads, schools, and parkland infrastructures.

The immediate economic impacts of the EPR were modest and highly sectoral. The decline of traditional industries persisted due to the continual changes in international markets. The focus on building roads over public transport led to urban sprawl. The creation of new educational institutions and technical schools did very well in retraining workers and producing highly skilled graduates, but there were very few jobs in the region to fill the demand. Very few new businesses were drawn to the region and unemployment remained high. Environmental pollution levels were still elevated despite the expansion of the regional park system, largely because the large industries continued to operate as usual. Meanwhile, there remained a widespread reticence, at all levels, to accept that the Ruhr's heavy industries had entered a phase of historic, structural decline, even with the onset of the global oil crisis in 1973 and the steel crisis in 1974. Rationalization policies were in place to address the steel crisis but even these could not tackle rapid deindustrialization, as unproductive parts of steel works were closed, and sites were completely shut, due to altered market conditions.

The state government invested huge sums into diversifying the economy and lessening the impact of job losses on workers but there was still significant investment in propping up the failing hard coal industry. From 1958 to 2002, the total cost of subsidies amounted to EUR 158 billion (Storchmann, 2005).

During this period, the state government predetermined investments and projects with minimal input from local and regional stakeholders. Structural change remained top-down. There was an attempt to exert more control over projects when in 1975, the NRW state government secured the regional planning tasks from the Ruhr Area Settlement Association (*Siedlungsverband Ruhrgebiet*) to promote its "Four Technology Program". Driven by the hope of a coal resurgence due to the oil crisis, and a recovery in the steel industry, the reindustrialization program invested DM2 billion (EUR 1 billion) into the modernization of the mining, energy, economy, and steel sectors. It was expected that the optimization of the four core industries would boost competitiveness, limit pollution, improve technology transfer, and create new jobs. The program succeeded in maintaining a certain level of productivity in the region. However, it was unable to tackle on-going industrial decline, rising unemployment, low development of new businesses, and limitations to sectoral specialization.

2.1.2 Centralized neoindustrialization (1975–86)

The introduction of the "Ruhr Action Program" (APR) by the state government in 1979 marked the onset of economic neoindustrialization in the Ruhr. This strategy focused on improving technology transfer between universities and companies; growing the service sector by supporting research and development (R&D) and innovation, reorienting the economy by removing development barriers through the purchase of abandoned industrial lands, and remediating and releasing said brownfields for redevelopment.

Technology transfer took place by establishing the first technology centers in the Ruhr. The centers would provide collaborative environments for academic institutions, research groups, and private industry to develop new products and services. One particular goal was to attract new industries in the fields of ICT and bio-medical science. The Technology Center established at the Technical University of Dortmund is a notable example (See Section 2.2.1).

By allocating EUR 2 billion for the purchase, demolition, decontamination, and development of sites via the "Ruhr Property Funds", the state government was able to support the reuse of derelict industrial lands and buildings by cities, and guarantee the responsible and cost-oriented treatment of industrial pollution. The Fund vitally abolished the "ground-lock" situation created by the coal and steel industries. For years, the core industries resisted selling or redeveloping their abandoned mining and manufacturing sites due to persistent land-banking practices, and for fear of competition from new industry sectors entering the region.

The purchase and restoration of 150 former industrial sites by the state immediately made available opportunities for new commercial and industrial developments as well as for new high-quality urban environments combining living, working, leisure and culture. It provided the chance to transform the physical image of the region for the better. The technology centers kicked-off science and research activities, attracting a range of technological fields, and creating new employment opportunities albeit mainly in the scientific arena. The modernization of neighborhoods accompanied the construction of new affordable housing, and the upgrade of old industrial mono-structures incorporated new historical monuments and cultural functions.

The APR ran for 4 years with a budget of DM 6.9 billion (EUR 3.5 billion). The NRW state government provided DM 5.1 billion (EUR 2.6 billion) while the national government funded the remainder (Dahlbeck et al., 2019). Unlike the earlier program, which failed to integrate local actors and thus made spatial planning and practical implementation difficult, the APR involved the participation of local and regional stakeholders from the outset.

When the APR ended in 1984, the NRW state government decided to directly support the development of small and medium-sized enterprises (SMEs) in the fields of renewable energy and environmental systems by forming the Center for Innovation and Technology (ZENIT). The center comprised several innovation and technology transfer centers and supported new energy and ecology start-ups via a range of services. ZENIT provided financial and funding advice, helped mediate between the firms and technology transfer centers, supported joint R&D projects, and offered marketing and management support. Activities especially supported focused on the themes of energy efficiency, renewable resources, recycling, and waste combustion, chosen as explicit responses to the enormous fossil fuels consumed and a huge amount of waste produced by the coal and steel plants in the region. The start-ups also benefited from assistance provided by city governments through improved local infrastructures.

2.1.3 Regionalized economic diversification (1987—99)

In 1985, the “Coal and Steel Regions Future Initiative” was introduced by the NRW state government to reverse the high unemployment trends in the Ruhr. Joblessness by this time had tripled within 6 years to 14.2%, compared to 8.7% in the rest of the country. Urgent investments were thus needed to achieve economic and social renewal.

The strategy invited local institutions to propose projects that specifically promoted innovation and technology, enabled future-oriented skills acquisition and job creation, expanded local and regional infrastructures, and improved local ecology and energy systems. Financial support for projects was predicated on proposals being developed and implemented through local networks comprising local enterprises, trade unions, chambers of industry, communities, and city administrations. Pooled funds from the EU, national, state, municipal, and governments to a volume of two billion DM (EUR 1.0 billion) ensured the implementation of projects (Herpich et al., 2018).

Almost 95% of the 1200 proposals submitted were carried out (Bross and Walter, 2000). Several technical schools, art colleges, technology centers, and research institutions were established (see Fig. 2.4). New start-up businesses entered the local markets, boosting new technology research and development activities. The capacities of larger companies already existing in the region were strengthened and diversified, enhancing the growth of smaller companies all along their value chains. New jobs were created in the new environmental and energy technology-related industries, but more substantially so in the auxiliary services sector. Projects also involved a much larger network of local and regional players, which helped form a social consensus on structural changes.

The initiative also succeeded in preventing mass outward migration and long-term economic decline. Annual economic

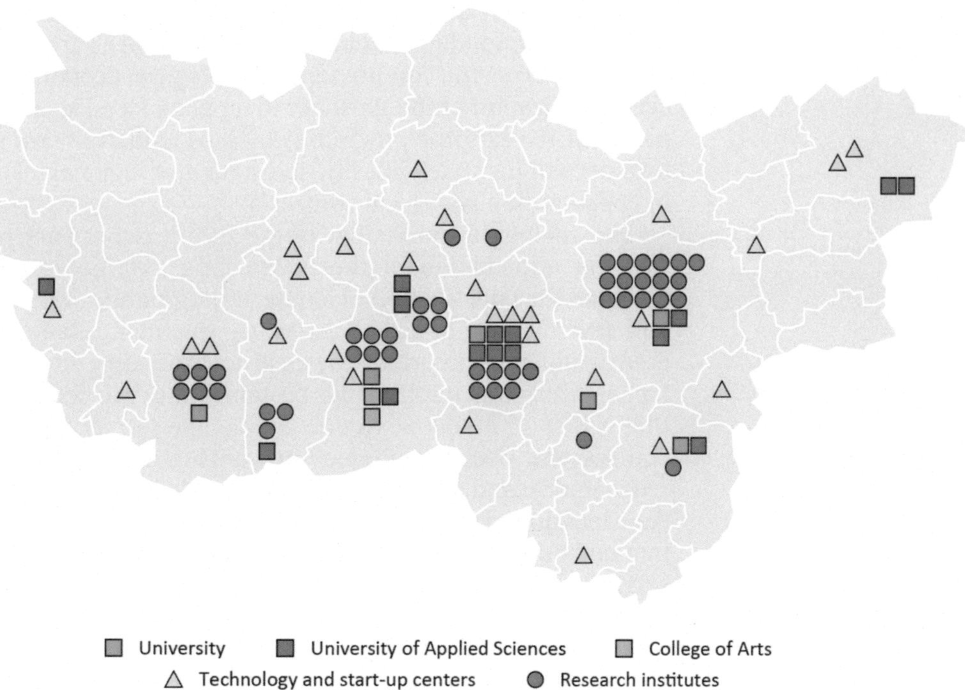

Figure 2.4 Academic, start-up, and research institutions in the Ruhr Metropolis.

growth of around 1.3% was reached, a good achievement considering the magnitude of the structural decline alongside the frequent cyclical crises experienced by the coal and steel industries (Taylor, 2015:6). The initiative also marked the first time that control by the national government was lessened. The state broadly guided the long-term planning of projects but design and implementation moved largely to local actors.

2.1.4 Environmental remediation, urban regeneration, and cultural development (since 1989)

2.1.4.1 Environmental remediation

The Ruhr was a severely polluted region by the late 1980s. Toxic waste from heavy industry, untreated sewage, a high water table, and subsiding ground, made water and land remediation very difficult. Basic measures to control pollution introduced in the 1960 and 1970s were no longer sufficient. The Emscher River, which formed the backbone of the Ruhr, flowing east to west across a catchment area of 865 km^2, was considered biologically dead. With deteriorating environmental conditions, immediate attention was required, as well as enormous public investments.

In partnership with municipalities, universities, and private actors, the NRW state government launched the "Emscher Park International Building Exhibition" (IBA Emscher Park) in 1989 in order to oversee the comprehensive ecological, economic and social revitalization of the Emscher River zone (see Fig. 2.5). Over a period of 10 years, the program witnessed a flurry of new sustainable development activities by the state and regional institutions in collaboration with local consortia.

The ecological foundation of the IBA Emscher Park program was the remediation of the 80 km long riverine zone. It also included the construction of a new underground sewage network and several decentralized wastewater treatment plants. Considered a public health priority by local governments, environmental regeneration was the basis for sustainable urban redevelopment that was soon to follow. In due course, the re-naturalized watercourses and decontaminated brownfields attracted new urban regeneration and conservation projects all along the river system. New technology parks were built, often alongside new and rehabilitated housing, with new leisure facilities, and a range of public services. Former workers' settlements and historical garden suburbs were regenerated. Vacant factories were converted into cultural monuments. Former industrial harbors were redeveloped to house new business and entertainment facilities. Abandoned mining rail tracks were converted into bicycle routes, and

Figure 2.5 Location of IBA Emscher park in the Ruhr Metropolis.

incorporated into new linear river parks. New green spaces formed an ecological web linking the major towns and cities in the region (see Fig. 2.6). Today, the 450 km^2 Emscher Parkland system is the central landscape reconstruction project of the IBA Emscher program, and plays a vital role in the region's climate change mitigation and adaptation strategy.

Figure 2.6 North Duisburg Landscape Park (left) and Anger Park Duisburg (right).

The expertise required for the implementation of the IBA Emscher Park program, from waste management to pollution monitoring, benefited from experience long gathered since the 1960s when strict environmental requirements first sought to minimize industrial pollution. Then, the energy, chemical, steel, and coal industries were challenged to develop new solutions and technical innovations that prevented toxic waste, and that used cleaner technology and production processes. Environmental compliance demanded new methods in environmental rehabilitation project design, development and implementation. These fields later became the bases for a new eco industry in the region.

With investments of EUR 4.5 billion, the Emscher River transformation was one of the largest infrastructure projects in Europe (Reutter et al., 2017). The IBA process itself was a positive economic direction for the region not only in terms of establishing an environmental rebrand but also in turning environmental problems into market opportunities.

2.1.4.2 Urban regeneration

The polycentric nature of the Ruhr meant that a good distribution of local-area development was key. The area-by-area strategy was to renovate neighborhoods, create good public spaces, establish cultural centers, and ensure high-quality public services. Business and technology parks were established where needed. Municipal land-use and building guidelines steered these processes.

Urban planning practices shifted considerably since the postwar years in the region when the primary task was to quickly rebuild the severely damaged cities, with the utmost urgency given to housing. The 1950s witnessed urban sprawl with large plot sizes, increased private motorization, and much new multi-story housing. In the 1960s, urban renewal prioritized large-scale redevelopment through the demolition of old housing quarters in inner city areas. Small businesses and inhabitants moved to the outskirts in order to make way for larger retail and financial companies coming into the city.

By the 1970s, the energy and steel crises transferred the focus to urban renewal through careful rebuilding. Work began on regenerating the large modern housing estates built in the 50 and 60s, which were by then empty and in poor condition. Local inhabitants were involved in the renewal process to help preserve social structures. The city centers were transformed to improve their socio-economic functionalities and competitiveness. Public spaces were prioritized with the redesign of main streets into new shopping streets, the redirection of traffic by ring roads, and the replacement of old tramlines with new underground networks.

By the early 1980s, ecological and sustainable urban development was the basis for urban planning in the Ruhr. In the course of the IBA Emscher Park program, for example, some 30 residential quarters were created based on historical preservation (garden cities), sustainable housing (ecological development), gender equality (oriented toward women's needs), and affordability (self-built houses). Much support was given to projects that dealt with the refurbishment of existing settlements and the creation of new residential areas with very high energy efficiency standards.

In order to improve the quality of life in deprived neighborhoods, it was recognized that urban projects in the Ruhr had to strategically consider all of the built, social, economic, and cultural aspects of a project. In 1993, the NRW state government launched the integrated action program "Urban districts with special needs of renewal – NRW Social City" (*Soziale Stadt NRW*) in order to facilitate processes that addressed a range of local problems related to job availability, housing affordability, traffic congestion, pollution, and social disorder.

Since 2009, new concepts for the utilization of land in the region have been taken over by the Ruhr Regional Association (RVR), which works to develop 10–15-year regional master plans for the Ruhr. The masterplans help coordinate local projects according to a common regional vision and are devised through open, multi-leveled dialogues between state institutions, local governments, and regional communities. They serve to complement municipal land-use and development plans autonomously created by cities, which incorporate more specific local priorities according to the sectors of housing, economy, mobility, environment, and energy. The masterplans have since coordinated the development of hundreds of projects across the region based on climate protection and energy transition principles.

2.1.4.3 Cultural development

The purchase and remediation of derelict industrial lands and structures through the state's Ruhr Property Fund, followed by robust redevelopment activities, resulted in several important cultural landmarks.

Through the IBA Emscher Park program, for example, over 200 projects comprising parks, museums, monuments, and historic settlements were implemented, making it one of the most developed cultural parks in Europe. In 2010, the Ruhr was named the "Cultural Capital of Europe." The various locations of industrial culture, adapted with state-of-the-art entertainment and convention facilities have attracted local, regional, and international events in music, performing arts, and film, as well as scientific and industry conferences. The restored mining sites and structures serve as striking reminders of the cities' industrial past as well as important symbols of a new start.

The Zollverein World Heritage Site in Essen in particular is a major drawcard to the region (see Fig. 2.7). Today it is representative of the Ruhr Metropolis' new identity as a hub for arts, culture, innovation, and technology. Created through the redevelopment of the former Zollverein coal-mining complex, the architectural monument today houses two museums, shops, restaurants, an ice rink, a public pool, and a start-up incubator. It educates the public about the geology, archaeology, and industrial and social history of the region, and anchors the European Route of Industrial Culture, a 400 km round course combining 25 industrial culture sites of the Ruhr (see Fig. 2.8). In 2001, the Zollverein Complex became a UNESCO World Heritage Site and has since attracted more than two million visitors a year.

Cultural development in the Ruhr has enhanced the region's locational advantage by attracting creative SMEs engaged in the creation, production, and media distribution of cultural goods and services. Fields that have most particularly flourished have been in the areas of design, music, games, architecture, press, and advertising. In 2011, the creative industries sector comprised

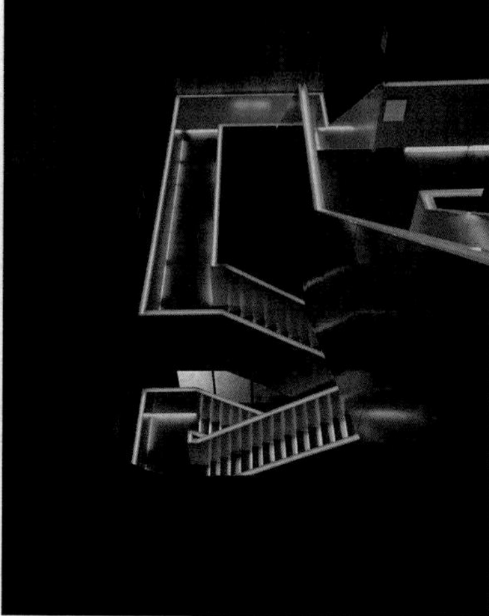

Figure 2.7 European route of industrial culture in the Ruhr Metropolis.

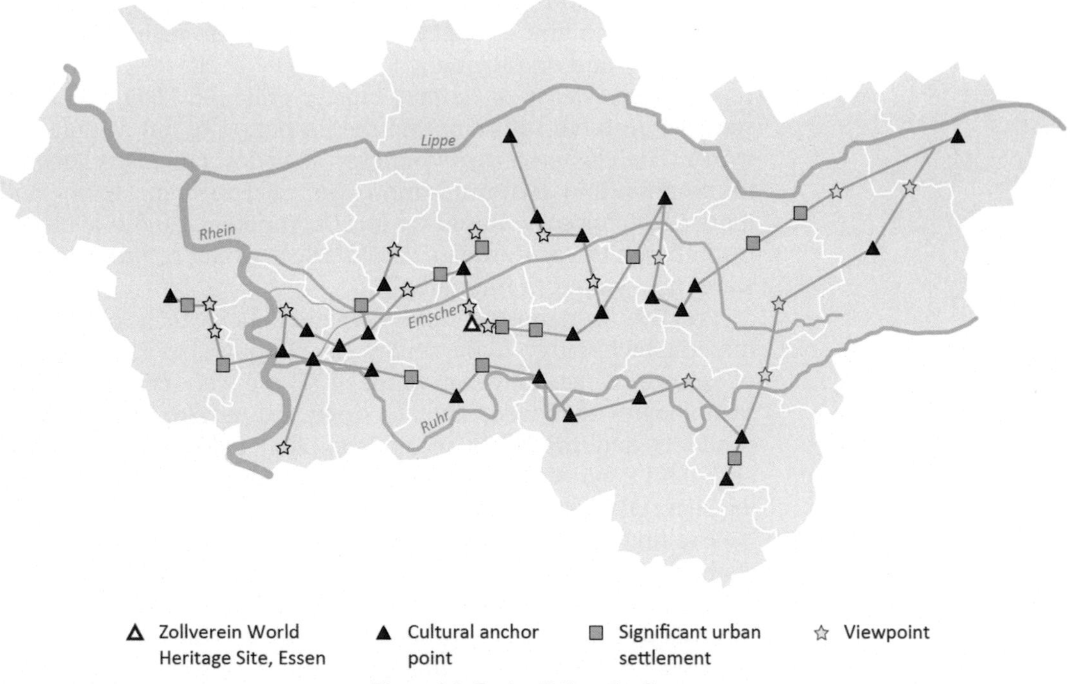

Figure 2.8 Zeche Zollverein, Essen.

11,100 companies and generated around EUR 6 million in sales (wmr, 2011). Their presence has elevated the profile of the region, and stimulated local city growth through the development of "Creative.Quarters" (Lauderbach, 2012).

2.1.5 Fields of competence (since 1990)

Global discussions about fields of competence or expertise-oriented clusters began to influence structural policy actors in the Ruhr from the mid-1990s. Policy attention was shifting away from large-scale industrial projects and toward improving competencies in networks of promising sectors or clusters. The new emphasis was on increasing the competitiveness of the region, developing and distributing technologies and products, and creating and preserving jobs. Support was received from the European Regional Development Fund (ERDF) to pursue these goals.

Clusters are networks in which loosely connected companies, research facilities, and political and nonprofit institutions of a specific economic field cooperate all along a value chain to advance the development, testing, and marketing of new technologies and applications. A successful cluster exhibits particular economic strengths that contribute to regional growth, innovation, and employment.

With the release of its first Cluster Policy in 2000, the NRW state government set in motion the formation of innovation networks. The clusters targeted energy, logistics, chemistry, health, information and communication, and microsystem-, nano- and material technology. Based on local competencies and available resources, city governments would select which of these sectors were most suited to their area.

Progress in nano-technology, microsystems technology, and material technology, in particular, gave impulses to a wider range of fields in which they were applied. These were cross-sectional technologies that were able to drive the development of new products and processes in such applied fields as mechanical and plant engineering, communication technology, automobiles, logistics, chemistry, and health.

The first clusters program was financed and managed by the state, through a cluster agency that distributed support based on a cluster's capacity for self-supporting growth in the medium term, as well as its ability to rely on a considerable number of enterprises and expertise in the region. Each cluster was individually managed by staff seconded through the cluster's group of companies, and logistically supported by city governments through a range of local services.

The clusters concept in the Ruhr was later subsumed by the lead markets concept, which worked to ensure that new products, applications, and services created in the region were given access to wider regional and global export markets. The new system comprised eight lead markets structured based on an industrial core flanked by corporate services. These included health, urban construction and housing, mobility, sustainable consumption, resource efficiency, leisure and events, education and research, and digital communication. Each lead market was divided into a core area of production or services, and into sections that provided the materials, processes, engineering, and supporting services (Keil and Wetterau, 2013).

The self-organized cluster policy was well received in the Ruhr because projects and activities in the selected competence fields were broadly spread across the region. No districts were excluded (see Fig. 2.9).

The energy clusters in particular have provided an expansive landscape for energy research, development, and manufacturing in the Ruhr. The "EnergyRegion.NRW", "Energy Research.NRW", and "Environmental Technologies.NRW" industry clusters

Figure 2.9 Location of competence fields in the Ruhr Metropolis.

formed by the state government kicked off new projects in energy technology and brought them to market. The state's energy agency networked those involved in the energy economy throughout the value chain, and facilitated information exchange between them.

New renewable energy industries greatly benefited from these networks, many formed as start-up offshoots from established environmental technology industries already operating in the region. Former coal and steel companies also took advantage of incoming expertise and markets to develop new energy products and services. Companies that were once manufacturers of coal-mining machinery in the Ruhr became prominent fabricators of wind turbine parts. Original producers of coal-fired power plants turned to the production of biomass generators. Former mining technology suppliers have switched from drilling machinery for coal to geothermal energy equipment (Galgóczi, 2014).

By 2011, the "EnergyRegion.NRW" cluster alone comprised 3300 companies, 64 universities, 107 institutes, and 94 associations. These included the subclusters of solar photovoltaics, power plant engineering, fuel cells and hydrogen, biomass, solar building construction, geothermal energy, and wind power (Galarraga et al., 2011). It is estimated that the energy clusters generate a combined turnover of around EUR 47 billion a year (wmr, 2011).

2.1.6 Energy transition (since 2010)

Efforts to transition to highly efficient renewable energy infrastructures have generally been slow in the Ruhr. In the 70 and 80s, the high cost of renewable energy technologies and the availability of cheaper imports of oil, natural gas, or coal hindered the widespread uptake of renewables and building energy refurbishments. Similarly the modernization of, or extensions to, district heating systems was cost preventative for most city governments. There were some small-scale solar energy installations on individual homes and wind power turbines installed by farmers but these had minimal impact on the overall energy system. Energy consumption remained dependent on fossil fuels.

Large-scale systematic efforts in renewable energy in the Ruhr began in earnest with the introduction of national legislation in renewable energy and energy transition.

The national Renewable Energy Sources Act (EEG) of 2000 really drove the expansion of renewable energies in Germany by encouraging the generation of renewable electricity via a feed-in tariff scheme. Its successive editions set the foundation for the German energy transition (*Energiewende*) strategy, which was introduced a decade later. In 2010, the "Integrated Energy and Climate Program" (IEKP) was launched by the national government to transition the country to a low-carbon, nuclear-free economy based on environmentally sound, reliable, and affordable energy supplies (BMWi and BMU, 2010). The primary goal was to reduce CO_2 emissions by 40% by 2020 relative to 1990. This was to be achieved by promoting the construction of energy-efficient buildings and power plants, increasing the uptake of cogeneration technology, conducting energy monitoring of urban infrastructures, funding building modernization, and expanding the regional electricity networks. Several pieces of legislation were key to driving implementation. Revisions to the Renewable Energy Sources Act (EEG) enhanced the adoption of wind power and solar PV technologies. The Renewable Energies Heat Act increased biogas and geothermal production. The Motor

Vehicle Tax Act promoted incentives for biofuels and electromobility, as well as provided tax relief for fuel-saving vehicles.

In the Ruhr, municipalities began working together with local groups and the Ruhr Regional Association to develop local climate protection concepts, energy transition plans, and implementation strategies that complemented the national energy transition policies. Most focused on sustainable procurement, energy retrofits of municipal buildings, small-scale renewable energy systems integration, low carbon development guidelines, and sustainable mobility.

The InnovationCity competition was launched by a consortium of 70 companies from the region to push for more ambitious implementation. Influenced by the IEKP, the contest challenged local governments to nominate pilot districts that could undergo low-carbon redevelopment and achieve carbon emissions reductions of 50% within only 10 years. The participatory urban regeneration proposal by the city of Bottrop was the winning plan and its rapid success set the benchmark for other cities across the Ruhr. Fig. 2.10 illustrates the combined energy transition efforts in the region to date.

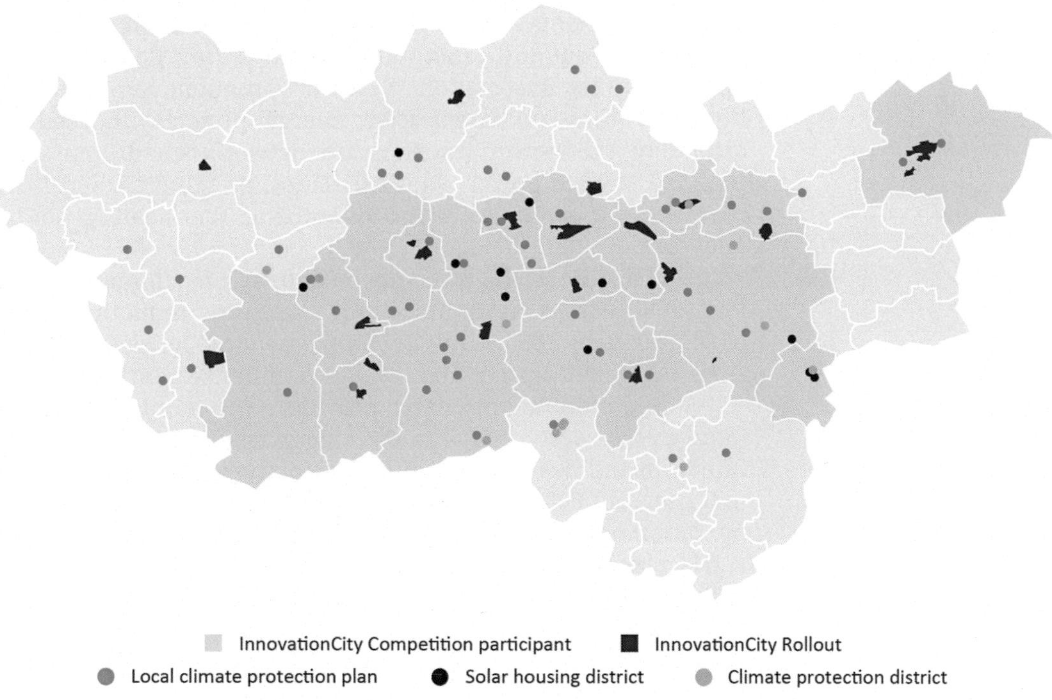

Figure 2.10 Energy transition activities in the Ruhr Metropolis.

Several cities in the Ruhr collaborated with municipal energy utilities to implement local energy infrastructure improvements. Tasks included modernizing local combined heat and power (CHP) plants to be fueled by renewable energy sources, expanding the local heating networks, and developing intelligent power grids with the help of research partners. Efforts were qualified by the IEKP which specified further rights for cities to secure repowering, develop spatial planning plans for renewable energy, and set up energy efficiency funds for project implementation. A few cities began the energetic modernization of large residential complexes and the construction of new energy-efficient settlements or solar housing. Some municipal utilities began investing in or procuring energy from, onshore and offshore wind farms when renewable energy generation within city boundaries was limited.

In 2013, the NRW state Climate Protection Law applied the national emissions and energy reduction targets to state policy. It also outlined a comprehensive plan of measures according to the various economic sectors of energy, building, transport, agriculture, services, industry, land use, and forestry. Loans and grants were allocated to support low carbon investments by businesses in building renovation, cogeneration, and resource efficiency. Cities could receive guidance on municipal energy planning and promotions via the state's Energy Agency and Consumer Association. Research programs supported by the state took on larger-scale energy projects, focused on extending the power transmission network, quadrupling the pumped storage power plant capacities, merging the local district heating systems, and modernizing the heating supply networks.

In 2016, the IEKP was superseded by the Climate Action Plan 2050 with a more ambitious emissions reduction target of 80%–95% by 2050. A raft of complementary policies and measures by the NRW state and local governments soon followed.

As the predominant energy providers, the municipal utilities (*Stadtwerke*) were central to the energy transition efforts in the Ruhr. The utilities supply around 70% of the population with natural gas, and 60% with electricity. They are responsible for the operation of most local decentralized combined heat and power (CHP) plants in the region and are considered the most flexible and secure way to supply heat and electricity. The plants range from small CHP for the supply of individual buildings, to large gas and steam CHP with a capacity of several hundred megawatts to supply entire districts. Collectively, the systems contribute to a 4300 km long district heating network, which makes it one of the largest in Europe (Wuppertal Institute, 2017). Heat and power plants are conventionally fueled by coal, oil, or natural gas, but in recent years, several cities have switched to alternative energy fuels such as industrial waste heat, heat from waste incineration plants, and heat derived from biomass and biogas. The new sources of fuel have required modifications to existing energy plants.

In the Ruhr, municipal utilities actively engaged with cities and their residents in renewable energy systems implementation through the sale and supply of renewable energy services. The Stadtwerke Bochum municipal energy company, for example, began offering products related to building energy management, as well as the planning, construction, and operation of micro-CHPs, while the Stadtwerke Unna started leasing solar energy systems, and took on all tasks in their planning, installation, and maintenance.

Cities without municipal utilities have pursued pursue carbon emissions and renewable energy targets by collaborating with independent energy companies to develop energy supply contracts and new business models for building modernization and renewable energy installations. Through the energy advisory centers established by cities, information and expertise provided by the utilities effectively guided the development of energy projects by companies and residents.

Indeed cities with ownership of their local energy utilities had better control of the decarbonization of local energy systems. They were able to make critical decisions with regard to plant and system efficiencies, network operations and storage, and renewable energy production and distribution. There were able to turn to more innovative approaches in ICT. A few explored the integration of intelligent management systems to allow for the modulation of electricity demand with the supply of renewables into the grid. Others examined ways that retrofitted energy systems could link the different branches of public services to new digitized infrastructures such as integrating electro-mobility systems into the public transport network.

Ultimately, the collective goal of the Ruhr is to connect the decentralized local energy systems into a single regional virtual grid over the long-term. The networking of energy systems and public services will be critical to mitigate and adapt to climatic changes as severe winter storms and summer heat periods are becoming more prevalent in the region.

2.2 City energy transition and smart specialization strategies

There are three cities in the Ruhr which have exemplified the success of innovation-led structural policies to foster a high degree of innovation and enterprise in project development and implementation to achieve ambitious climate and energy targets. The cities of Dortmund, Bottrop, and Gelsenkirchen have established highly networked environments that have enabled administrations, businesses, and communities to not only collectively tackle socio-economic challenges but also address the urgent demands of climate change.

2.2.1 Smart city Dortmund

The city of Dortmund is the largest city in the Ruhr Metropolis, covering an area of 280 km^2 with a population of around 588,000 inhabitants (2019) (rvr.ruhr, 2020b). The city began its structural transition following the demise of the coal and steel industries in the city. The first transformative initiatives in the 1980s spurred growth in the tertiary sectors, especially in new technologies, research and development (R&D), insurance, and financial services.

Much of the growth in the new technology sectors came from the development of scientific institutions in the city. The Technical University of Dortmund was established in 1968, followed by the University of Applied Sciences and Art in 1971. The Dortmund Technology Center was founded at the university in 1985 to serve as an incubator for young enterprises, and as an R&D department for established companies. The rise in the number of start-ups led to the creation of the Dortmund Technology Park in 1988. After a 5–7 year incubation period, the start-ups at the Technology Center were relocated to the Technology Park. The three scientific institutions combined their academic, testing, and production expertise to advance the development, marketing, and manufacture of new products and services.

In Dortmund, the institutions steered the upsurge of technology-based activities. Early emphasis on industrial production technology and environmental management technology was quickly augmented by the fields of information technology (IT), biomedicine, logistics, robotics, and micro and nano-systems. Today the Dortmund Technology Park (see Fig. 2.11) is the largest of its kind in Germany with more than 100,000 m^2 of incubation space. Since 1985, it has supported 350 companies and 10,000 employees and has generated a turnover of around €1.1 billion (UA Ruhr, 2018). It has also led to the establishment of a further 30 technology centers across the Ruhr.

Figure 2.11 Dortmund Technology Campus. Image from Google Earth.

Economic restructuring based on technology clusters was boosted with the launch of the "Dortmund Project" in 1997. Devised by the city administrations of Dortmund and Duisburg in cooperation with the NRW state government, the steel companies Krupp-Hoesch and Thyssen, and trade unions, the project's aim was to create new employment opportunities and strengthen the local economies by fostering new jobs in the new SME clusters of software engineering, IT, e-commerce, microsystems technology, biotechnology, and logistics. The project was a response to major job losses incurred due to the merger of ThyssenKrupp. Along with the coal mining industry, around 80,000 jobs had been lost. With support of around EUR 200 million in European, national, and local subsidies, the project succeeded in achieving its goals. By 2010, there were 800 IT enterprises, 831 logistics companies, 100 e-commerce enterprises, and 45 micro and nano-technology businesses in Dortmund (Keil and Wetterau, 2013).

With the release of the German energy transition strategy, the cities in the Ruhr were faced with an immediate challenge. For Dortmund, it meant the need to reduce energy consumption and restructure local energy supplies so that they were safe, sustainable, and economically viable—a complex task given that the former industrial city had long relied on coal-based centralized energy infrastructures. New expertise, large investments, and the cooperation of many stakeholders were required to create new or adapted energy systems based on renewable resources.

Under the banner of the "Dortmund Climate Action Program 2020", the city began working with scientific and business partners to compile carbon emissions and energy accounting for the city in order to derive appropriate projects and measures. An energy advisory center was set up to provide information to the general public on the topics of energy efficiency, renewable energy, and mobility.

In 2014, the "Dortmund Energy Transition Master Plan" was introduced to steer energy transition by all urban sectors. The masterplan extended the scope and budget of the Climate Action Program in order to achieve better energy savings and implement more energy projects. It also provided the framework for collaboration between citizens, scientists, the energy industry, trade unions, businesses, and the government. It ensured that energy transition concepts were embedded into Dortmund's technology and innovation clusters and that measures were compatible with other action programs carried out by the city, such as Dortmund's Smart City Strategy, and Mobility Strategy.

The masterplan focused on five fields of action: municipal building and urban development, energy modernization of existing buildings, renewable energies integration, cross-structural improvements, and enhanced mobility. Its implementation was managed by the Dortmund Energy Transition Control Center (LED) established by the city. Headed by the Institute for Energy Systems, Energy Efficiency, and Energy Management at the Technical University of Dortmund, the center developed projects and coordinated the masterplan's content with the work of relevant city departments. The center made sure that projects were innovative and included relevant partners from business, science, and civil communities.

The first projects by the city dealt with climate-stabilizing procurement policies for municipal facilities and operations and the renovation and energy management of municipal buildings. Schools for example were modernized using a raft of climate-friendly technologies such as new systems in solar energy, high-efficiency lighting, heat pumps, ventilation, and water management. The energy consumption of municipal properties and services was monitored and evaluated, with new intelligent energy control solutions applied.

The city promoted renewable energy by purchasing green electricity based on hydropower for its public buildings, street lighting, and light rail. Its municipal utility DEW21 created a "Solar Fund" to finance the implementation of solar technologies. The electricity product enabled energy customers to make a donation of several cents per kWh in their energy bills, amounts that were matched by DEW21 and transferred to the fund. The result was an uptick in solar installations on government buildings, industrial wastelands, landfills, warehouses, commercial structures, and community facilities.

Spatial planning in the city was geared toward the optimization of renewable energy systems. A solar roof cadastre mapped out the solar energy generation potentials of all roof surfaces. The municipal land use plan was amended to allocate sites for large wind turbines, and an output study examined the potential for small wind turbines on buildings. These efforts led to an increase in solar systems installations and the construction of seven wind turbines with capacities of between 500 kW and 2,000 kW.

The city also encouraged innovations in green buildings. The "100 Energy Plus Houses" initiative promoted the construction of 100 residential buildings that were not only energy autonomous in terms of heat and power but also produced surplus electricity of 1,000 kWh per year. The buildings featured advanced energy-efficient construction techniques, and the integration of photovoltaic systems or microcombined heat and power (CHP). In order to attract property owners to the scheme, the city reserved 80 building plots distributed across the city with optimal solar energy conditions and guaranteed free advice and quality assurance by local architects and energy consultants.

The transformation of the city's energy infrastructure required the simultaneous coordination of a range of measures. The modernization of the district heating network for example necessitated the adaptation and repowering of existing technologies, the maximization of the waste heat recovery system, the conversion of steam networks to hot water, the consolidation of the existing supply areas of the inner city, as well as the integration of new renewable sources of energy. Coal and oil-fired steam plants along with decentralized natural gas-fired CHP plants were replaced or retrofitted to run on renewable sources of industrial waste heat, mine gas, landfill gas, sewage gas, or biomass.

With the help of the municipal energy utility DEW21, the city analyzed the potential of renewable energy sources in the local heating market. The utility created an online "Heat Map" which plotted the location and use of existing plant technologies, heating consumption patterns, network connections, and thermal energy sources. Through the visualization of the heating market's spatial distribution, the extent of the various district heating areas in the city area was better understood.

Similarly, a thermographic analysis of city areas helped derive an energy savings program for the entire urban building stock. The visualization of heat losses of homes motivated many building owners to invest in building modernizations. Joint renovation contracts encouraged property owners of semidetached houses or adjoining multi-family apartment buildings to consolidate energy refurbishment projects. This enabled legal, financial, and technical aspects to be addressed in a more efficient and cost-effective manner.

Accompanying the modernisation of municipal and energy infrastructures were various urban design and regeneration strategies implemented since the 1980s. Urban regeneration began with the extensive reconfiguration of its city center and the revitalization of distressed neighborhood districts. Through the "Old Buildings Regenerated" (ALTBAUNEU) program, an initiative supported by the NRW State Ministry of Economics, Medium-Sized Enterprises, and Energy, the energy modernization of residential buildings were effectively boosted. Integrated city planning concepts, which carefully considered all relevant aspects of housing, ecology, economy, social affairs, and culture, helped improve urban quality as well as maintain social cohesion.

The most significant large-scale urban development project in Dormund was the "Phoenix Lake" project. The 6-year project was led by the city government and managed by a development agency through the municipal utility Stadtwerke Dortmund AG. Formally the site of a large steel mill complex, the 200-hectare redevelopment incorporated a mix of new luxury and affordable housing, new community buildings, and a Technology Park, all surrounded by a large artificial lake with green spaces and leisure facilities. The lake formed part of the wider Emscher River System remediation project, a key component in Dortmund's climate adaptation and protection plan (see Fig. 2.12).

The focus on state-of-the-art working environments impacted other urban regeneration projects in the city. The Stadtkrone East Technology Park was a former army barracks site acquired by the city in 1997. Benefiting from close proximity to the city center and access to major motorways and regional airports, the 50-hectare

Figure 2.12 Phoenix Lake urban regeneration, Dortmund.

site was transformed into a gateway for electronic and mobile phone businesses. The park soon triggered the redevelopment of other coal and steel sites in Dortmund into new logistics and distribution centers and set the foundation for the city to function as a service center for the surrounding regional manufacturing economy.

Dortmund's energy transition extended to its mobility strategy, achieving success in reducing fuel consumption and promoting alternative transportation fuels. It developed a comprehensive public transport network, added state-of-the-art hybrid buses and trams, and created an infrastructure for electric vehicles. Cycling is promoted through an expanded cycle network with many bicycle parking and storage facilities, and rental bike stations. Pedestrian activity increased following upgrades to public spaces and the creation of speed reduction zones in residential areas. The city set itself as a role model for local businesses by instituting a local carbon vehicle fleet management system.

Participation in EU research projects aided the city's efforts in pursuing its energy transition goals. The projects provided an environment where concepts were actualized through immediate communication with experts and business partners.

The city's energy efficiency campaigns in the area of retail and logistics real estate, for example, were aided by a project, which helped companies to jointly analyze energy issues in the supply chain and to find more efficient ways of producing, transporting, storing, and selling goods. Companies in business parks were challenged to reduce their carbon emissions and energy costs by reducing energy consumption in operations and applying solar installations on roofs, a precedent that could be copied across other industrial parks across the region.

With the municipal utility and several industry and scientific partners, the city worked on a number of renewable energy-related research projects. The "DesignNet" research project explored strategies for an intelligent electricity grid fed with wind power, solar, and biogas energy. At TU Dortmund, the "Smart Grid Technology Lab" project tested smart grid components in real-time by simulating electricity systems and examining their communication and control technologies. The "SyncFueL" digital infrastructure project examined the utilization of photovoltaic electricity for the home charging of electric cars. Also, the "IQN –Innovative district heating solutions" project worked on the gradual conversion of Dortmund's heating supply to decentralized heating networks based on renewable energy.

Raising awareness of the energy transition strategy, and developing an urban climate brand were other key strategies of the city. Pursued through community workshops and mobilization groups, voluntary work by citizens in projects was widely encouraged. A "Citizens' Fund for Climate Protection" for example, enabled citizens to invest in various city projects in energy for a return on investment of some 3% a year. Via the "Energy Transition Education Initiative", the city worked with schools to adapt curricula and create instruction apps that taught children and adolescents on the topics of climate change, resource efficiency, and energy.

And beyond community outreach, the emphasis on research and innovation also drove the development of scientific platforms in the city that combined scientific, entrepreneurial, and political knowledge. The Technical University of Dortmund joined the universities of Bochum and Duisburg-Essen to form the University Alliance Ruhr Metropolis (UAMR). The Alliance develops common fields of teaching and research and works with research institutes, companies, municipalities, business development agencies, and associations to solve complex regional problems in mobility, energy, and IT. The Alliance oversees some 90,000 students, 1250 professors with a budget of EUR 840 million (Keil and Wetterau, 2013).

The "Allianz Smart City Dortmund" is another participatory network, which implements smart city and digitization strategies in the city. With more than 150 partners, the platform gathers interdisciplinary teams of experts in the fields of energy, mobility, logistics, demographics, IT, security, and urban infrastructure to jointly develop projects that reduce costs, save resources, and give more effective control of the city. Projects to date range from intelligent traffic and parking solutions, fast charging infrastructure for e-vehicles, digitization of cultural landscapes, open data systems, smart systems for assisted living, and digital district development. A "Smart Citizen App" for example allows the local population to better and faster record deficiencies in the urban infrastructure, serving to inform the city's spatial planning. Such projects aim to increase the quality of life in the city and strengthen Dortmund as an attractive business location.

2.2.2 InnovationCity Bottrop

The city of Bottrop is the forerunner of the Ruhr Metropolis' energy transition efforts and has successfully embraced green energy and sustainable development strategies to transform its local economy. The city covers an area of 101 km^2 with a population of around 117,000 inhabitants (2019) (rvr.ruhr, 2020b). Like most cities in the Ruhr, the former coal mining city suffered a severe socio-economic decline in the 1960s following the collapse of the mining economy. The population stabilized with the emergence of new industries in packaging, logistics, and mobility equipment in the 1980s. The adoption of the "small steps, small companies" approach saw the entry of SMEs into the city in the 1990s. However wider diversification of the economy did not really take off until policies in sustainable development, energy, education, and tourism were formally enacted. In 2018, Germany's last black hard coal mine Prosper-Haniel colliery in Bottrop was closed (Fig. 2.13).

Strict environmental standards set by the state government in the 90s initiated the development of Bottrop's first environmental policies. The city created a new department for environmental protection within the administration and implemented simple municipal energy conservation measures.

In 2010, the city was named "Innovation City" after winning the urban development competition to create "The Climate City of the Future." The contest was devised by the Ruhr Initiative Group, a group of 70 companies based in the region, which challenged municipalities to nominate urban districts capable of reducing carbon emissions by 50% in just 10 years.

Figure 2.13 Prosper-Haniel Colliery in Bottrop.

Bottrop's plan was to revitalize seven districts in the city according to low carbon principles. Covering an area of 25 km^2 with 70,000 inhabitants and 14,500 buildings, the strategy was to reshape the existing municipal, housing, transport, economy, and energy sectors in the city, and to transform the local economy by building upon existing knowledge of energy systems. Instead of new building development, the focus was on regenerating and modernizing existing buildings and neighborhoods, as well as retrofitting existing energy infrastructures in order to gradually replace fossil fuel sources of coal and natural gas with renewable energy.

The regenerated districts would serve as living laboratories for climate-friendly urban development and sustainable economic growth. Projects would benefit from knowledge transfer with the local technical college and research institutions and include the participation of local services and trades. The emphasis on urban regeneration meant that the plan was replicable in the region because the city's building stock, energy system, and social structures were typical for a Ruhr city.

A "Climate Friendly Urban Regeneration Masterplan" with 350 measures tailored to specific city sectors drove concept implementation in Bottrop. The master plan prioritized the creation of quality jobs, the promotion of private sector development, and fighting climate change. There were five fields of action: "Housing" (systematic retrofitting of residential buildings); "Work" (energy modernization of working environments through company collaboration); "Energy" (smart, decentralized, efficient, and renewable energy supply); "Mobility" (sustainable transport/ logistics); and "City" (facilities energy management and urban development). It was important that projects implemented served as models for other cities in the Ruhr.

The masterplan was made consistent with the city's "Integrated Energy and Climate Protection Concept" (IEKK), which focused more specifically on energy efficiency, renewable energy, climate adaptation, awareness raising, and education. Projects in these fields had to demonstrate an ability to achieve direct savings in energy and CO_2 emissions, initiate offshoot projects, and expand networks and capacities. Priority was given to those that were self-supportive in terms of budget and expertise.

The InnovationCity Management GmbH (ICM) was established by the city to steer the implementation of the master plan and to serve as an interface between stakeholders. It consisted of five public and private shareholders: the Ruhr Initiative Group, the city of Bottrop, the local energy company, one public sector consultancy, and one real estate company. The group combined urban planning experience, city governance knowhow, and project management capabilities.

A scientific advisory board representing 10 universities and nine research institutes guided the input of scientific research into projects, a critical aspect for the city as a real-life laboratory and testing ground for environmental technologies and low carbon urban development. Quarterly meetings with ICM and NRW State Ministry for Innovation, Science, and Research were able to scientifically assess projects, identify procedural errors, and determine areas that demanded more research.

A network for technology partners comprising local tradespeople, architects, and energy consultants was established to realize the various sector-specific projects, and to ensure the quality and sustainability of projects completed. Its members, for example, had to show high technical abilities in such tasks as preparing expert assessments and thermographic studies, installing heating and photovoltaic systems, and planning and completing renovations according to the best energy standards.

Initial projects by the city were carried out close to home and were centered on energy savings and energy management in public buildings and municipal operations. This was then followed by energy renovations of the urban building stock. The city established the Center of Energy Information and Advice

(ZIB) to guide households and businesses on building refurbishments. It provided technical services including energy consumption analyses and thermal imaging of properties, which aided the development of retrofitting plans. Depending on the type of building and potential for CO_2 reductions, the city granted up to 25% of the modernization costs to property owners. Tenants could also receive a subsidy for the purchase of new energy-efficient electrical appliances.

The city promoted the construction of energy-self-sufficient buildings in the municipality by working with industry partners and homeowners to implement the "Future Homes Plus" initiative. These were buildings that produced more energy than they used and were achieved by combining renewable energy systems with passive solar building design. In this project, three types of buildings—a single family, multifamily, and commercial building—were retrofitted to demonstrate how buildings with plus energy standards could achieve very low energy costs. The design, planning, and implementation of the project were recorded for replication.

The city supported the integration of a range of renewable energy systems in the municipality. It installed solar and battery storage systems in government buildings, and photovoltaic panels on the municipal waste landfill as well as on noise barriers along its highways. It was the first town in the Ruhr to create a planned zone for wind energy. It worked with developers to provide homes with geothermal systems in all new residential settlements. By 2017, Bottrop sourced 40% of its energy from renewables—10 percentage points above the national average (Urry, 2017).

Systematic energy refurbishment in Bottrop encompassed 2000 buildings housing industry, trade, commerce, services, and public facilities. The city collaborated with businesses to find energy savings potentials, instill energy-efficient practices, and promote renewable energy integration. The "Zero Emissions Park" project, for example, challenged companies and their research partners to create replicable energy concepts for the sustainable redevelopment of industrial and commercial areas. Small firms were urged to reduce energy consumption and install solar energy systems on office roofs, while larger manufacturers were encouraged to supply the city with energy surpluses for the local district heating network.

The city also worked with local housing associations and housing industry partners to guide refurbishments of large affordable housing complexes. The impact of modernization on the cost of rent was minimized by focusing on simple installations of energy-efficient heating systems, new windows, and basic insulation. Historical qualities of districts and social structures of communities were conserved by ensuring that community facilities and public space development always accompanied any redevelopment. Between 2012 and 2020, an estimated EUR 23 million was granted to the city for urban renewal measures, resulting in a residential modernization rate of 3% per year, higher than the national rate of 1% (Reutter et al., 2017).

Low-carbon development would not have been possible without a district management committee in each of the pilot districts to help coordinate projects. The committees comprised members of the community and made certain that local interests were considered, that building owners, tenants, and businesses were given good advice, and that projects were realized. By carrying out projects district by district, district-specific problems were solved systematically.

Contributions to the urban development process in Bottrop by several large well-known companies, such as E.ON, RWE, Bayer, Viessmann, and many others, were invaluable. They provided project cofinancing, free or discounted materials, technical know-how, and/or staff support. While most applied existing products and services in projects, some made use of the city's modernization program to test and promote new technologies, or to develop new sales and business models.

Energetic modernization also extended to public utilities. The retrofit of existing heating plants and district heating networks helped increase energy efficiencies and eased the use of renewable energy sources to fuel local CHPs. Hydrogen derived from sewage gas was fed into a fuel cell cogeneration plant to produce heating and fuel for municipal buildings and public buses. Biomass and biogas sourced from sewage sludge fueled several micro-CHP plants. There were plans to turn Bottrop's former underground coal mine into a 200 MW pumped-storage hydroelectric power station and heat storage. The mine was the last in the region to be shuttered when coal subsidies finally ended in 2018.

Despite lacking a municipal energy utility, which it could have used to directly decarbonize the local energy infrastructure, Bottrop pursued its energy goals by working directly with local energy companies and participating in several state and EU-funded energy research projects.

In the "Dual Demand Site Management" project (2011–14), the city worked with the RWTH University of Aachen to explore how buildings and neighborhoods could be used as energy storage systems for drawing energy from both a central energy generation source and decentralized energy supply sources. The research examined ways that intelligent energy management systems at the building and district scales could be linked in a virtual grid, thus helping to compensate for increasing generation and fluctuations of renewable energies into the grid. By analyzing the electricity and thermal dynamics of buildings, shiftings, and reductions of energy loads in the power network could also be determined.

In the "100 Cogeneration Systems" project (2013–16), the city examined ways to multiply the use of micro-CHP systems in homes and businesses within the city area. Through systems implementation, project partners conducted a daily test of systems, which were adjusted to achieve high-energy efficiency in their operations according to building type. The systems served as models of experience enabling wider replication.

In the NachbarschaftsWerk (neighborhood plant) research project (2015–19), the city was involved in the development of an online communication system tool that enabled building owners and tenants to participate in the energy planning of their building or neighborhood. If an owner plans to install a PV solar system, or if a tenant may like to suggest certain efficiency improvements, such proposals can be rapidly posted. Through the clustering of plans and ideas, potential synergies can then be visualized and joint activities actively initiated.

Another important aspect of Bottrop's energy transition strategy was education. In order to build awareness, provide practical information, and mobilize the community in projects, the city conducted sustainability campaigns and hosted community workshops and events such as "InnovationCity Day". It worked with schools and universities to develop activities and projects geared toward climate protection and energy transition.

The active participation of local citizens was without a doubt critical in the implementation of local renewable energy technologies. Individual households tended to opt for small-scale solar PV or solar thermal panel installations, while farmers preferred to invest in bigger systems such as biogas CHP plants or wind turbines. Residents that did not own a roof directly participated in community solar initiatives. The local citizen solar cooperative Sonnenkraft eG for example enabled citizens to invest in PV solar systems installed on roofs of public buildings such as the town hall and schools. They receive a fixed return through the sale of electricity generated and fed into the grid.

Apart from urban development, electro-mobility was another vital strategy to reduce CO_2 emissions. The city established a car-charging infrastructure, promoted the sharing of electric cars, and introduced fuel cell-powered buses. It developed and expanded cycle paths and extended its public transport network. It took part in the "Sustainable Urban Truck Routing" project, which created an application that optimized the transportation of freight cargo. Through the electronic tracking of traffic and road conditions, the quickest, safest, cleanest, and most energy-efficient routes in the city could be rapidly ascertained.

In order to adapt to the growing effects of climate change, projects in urban greening, open space development, and water management were also undertaken by the city. It commissioned a heavy rainfall study, a vulnerability analysis, and a green infrastructure integrated development concept as part of its climate plan. Rainwater management was addressed by prioritizing green open spaces in all developments. These helped retain and filter water in order to reduce the amount of stormwater to be processed and thus save energy.

The city also heavily invested in the construction of new entertainment and recreational facilities, turning former industrial brownfields into cultural monuments with public art, cycleways, hiking trails, and amusement parks. It turned one coal heap into Europe's largest indoor skiing arena. The projects demonstrated the city's emphasis on public urban and cultural space development as a long-term development approach (see Fig. 2.14).

Since 2010, around 370 individual projects were implemented in Bottrop. By 2015, the measures and projects resulted in a reduction of CO_2 emissions of around 100,000 tons, equivalent to a 38% reduction compared to 2010 emissions levels (Schepelmann, 2018). The city's low-carbon energy transition received EUR 473 million in support via European structural funds (ERDF), state, municipal, and corporate investments, as well as national research and development grants (Schepelmann, 2018). Local businesses benefited from investments totaling EUR 110 million in contracts (Reutter et al., 2017).

Figure 2.14 Tetrahedron (left) and Theater Arena in Bottrop (right).

Following the end of InnovationCity Bottrop in 2020, the program was rolled out to other municipalities across Ruhr. The climate-friendly masterplan was used as a blueprint by cities but adapted to local conditions.

2.2.3 Solar City Gelsenkirchen

The city of Gelsenkirchen lies at the heart of the Ruhr, and covers an area of 104 km^2, with a population of around 259,000 (2019) (rvr.ruhr, 2020b). The city was once the leading coal mining town in Europe and was known as the "City of a Thousand Flames" due to the flaring of gases from its many coal mines. Its strategic importance meant that Gelsenkirchen was a target of heavy bombing during the Second World War. Postreconstruction witnessed a certain level of prosperity but the decline of the coal and steel sectors in the 1960s marked the beginning of a slow decline. By the late 1980s, the city's unemployment rate was one of the highest in Germany. Air quality was extremely poor and contaminated industrial brownfields dominated the city.

Following the transfer of ownership of industrial sites to the NRW state development corporation, Gelsenkirchen was presented with ideal redevelopment opportunities to establish a new positive future vision for the city. It set itself the goal of achieving economic diversification and job creation by using the redeveloped sites to attract new environmental technology and renewable energy industries to the city. Climate protection policies with ambitious emissions and energy targets were introduced. Urban regeneration projects and education strategies were implemented. Energy and eco clusters were supported, setting the basis for strong local economic growth based on green local entrepreneurship. Today the city calls itself "Solar City Gelsenkirchen" and according to its 2030–50 climate strategy, aims for carbon neutrality by 2050. The city works to protect the climate and improve the share of renewable energy through structural changes in urban planning and green industry development.

The first step in the city's structural and energy transition was marked by the conversion of a former coal-powered steel factory into the Gelsenkirchen Science Park (*Wissenschaftspark*) in 1995 (see Fig. 2.15). In partnership with the State Development Company of North Rhine-Westphalia (LEG NRW), the city built the Science Park to serve as a technology and start-up center for research institutions and new businesses, as well as act as an information hub on all energy-related matters. By facilitating exchanges between universities, research and development institutions, and commercial enterprises, knowledge was translated into practice.

Figure 2.15 Aerial view of Gelsenkirchen Science Park and interior. Aerial image from Google Earth.

The Science Park represented one of the flagship projects of the IBA Emscher Park, the EUR 10 billion program responsible for the redevelopment of the Emscher River region in the Ruhr. Extending across 45ha, the Science Park featured the latest in solar architecture including a 300-meter long technology center consisting of 12,500 m^2 space for offices and laboratories, and a 210 kW photovoltaic power plant installed on its roof, the largest in the world of its kind at the time. Around EUR 50 million pooled from European Regional Development Funds and state and federal level funding was invested into its development (Jung et al., 2010). Initially, activities at the Science Park focused on research, development, and marketing of renewable energy technologies. Today a small fraction of the companies and institutions work in the area of sustainable energy, with the rest engaged in environmental engineering, media, social sciences, and health-related fields.

The Gelsenkirchen Science Park, and the large-scale installation of solar technology manufactured in the city, set the foundation for implementing the city's overall Solar City strategy. They set off joint efforts by the local and state governments to cultivate a clean energy industry cluster. A series of demonstration projects were initiated to qualify the energy concept, and business and community support were gathered to establish trade networks and create a local identity (Jung et al., 2010).

The national "Renewable Energy Sources Act" (EEG) of 2000 also triggered the solar boom in Gelsenkirchen. New support schemes for PV from the state and federal levels accelerated the growth of solar technology companies, with businesses engaged in various activities from the planning and installation to the maintenance and marketing of solar. The Science Park drew in Europe's biggest solar cell factory (Shell Solar International). The city's first solar-module plant was built by Flachglas AG, one of the first automated solar production facilities in Germany. A photovoltaic laboratory and service center was opened by the world-renowned Fraunhofer Institute for Solar Energy Systems (ISE) to support innovation in solar cell technologies.

Several new local companies were established with expertise in different aspects of the new green economy. Manufacturing and engineering of renewable energy technologies thrived in the city. Abakus Solar, a wholesaler, and trade supplier of building-integrated photovoltaics realized over 1000 solar projects. Scheuten Solar Group Solar, a mass-producer of solar modules and solar cells, was involved in several major architectural projects around Germany, such as the Akademie Mont-Cenis in Herne, the exhibition center in the Messe Essen, the Berlin central train station, and the roof of the Reichstag parliament building also in Berlin. Wind power company BBB Umwelttechnik GmbH oversaw more than 16,000 MW of planned or already completed wind farms around the world, generating an output equivalent to the capacity of five coal-fired power plants. August Friedberg GmbH, a former manufacturer of bolts for the mining industry, became the world leader in wind power station components. Other businesses acquired expertise in alternative fuel technologies. This included the operation of solar and natural gas filling stations (Emscher Lippe Energie GmbH), the development of hydrogen fuel cell powered bicycles (Masterflex AG), the construction of biogas installations for heat generation (Hese Biogas GmbH), and the distribution of biogas in the natural gas network for domestic fuel (Gelsenwasser AG) (City of Gelsenkirchen, 2011).

In Gelsenkirchen, the skills of individual sector players were critical. There were regular training programs conducted at the Science Park. Advanced energy technology became the central focus of research and teaching at the Gelsenkirchen University of Applied Sciences. Interdisciplinary work at the Energy Institute was conducted in the areas of energy-supply systems modernization, fuel cell technology, solar technology, low-pollution combustion, cogeneration, and modern gas- and steam turbines. In collaboration with industry partners, real-time research of technologies applied in industrial practice was carried out at the Fraunhofer ISE Laboratory and Service Center. The Center is equipped with state-of-the-art technology and has access to the expertise of Europe's largest solar research institute, the Fraunhofer ISE, in Freiburg Germany.

In 2016, the city began collaborating with global telecommunications company Huawei, and regional IT and telecommunications provider GELSEN-NET to create a city-wide security system based on ICT infrastructure. The smart city system works to maximize safety and minimize crimes, optimize the efficiency of existing public services, and establishes effective frameworks for future services. By linking local companies, city departments, and law enforcement through the cloud, network, and platform technologies, the system helps to improve decision-making processes, and strengthen the provision of services, via three distinct avenues. The secure cloud data center facilitates the rapid open exchange of data. The linked data network allows city departments to more intelligently respond to an array of government, community, and business needs. The Big Data support platform accommodates data services for new industrial applications, and permits the sharing of historical and real-time city data between government agencies. Through a 13,000-kilometer, fiber-optic cable network connecting all industrial parks and major municipal institutions, the project is Germany's first "Safe City" solution (e.huawei.com).

Innovations in energy research and technology as well as ICT complemented the concerted efforts by the city of Gelsenkirchen to apply solar urban planning as a means to advance urban development. The planning principle was in concert with the "Solar City Gelsenkirchen" study commissioned by the State Ministry for Urban Planning and formed part of the state's "Solar City" program and energy clusters policy.

Studies were ordered by the city to determine the best course of action, including a CO_2 inventory of the city, and a potential study for the application of solar technologies on buildings and development areas. Sectoral climate action plans were compiled with the help of local energy utilities, incorporating community feedback from public hearings and workshops.

The development of solar power plants in the city was the first major effort in solar urban development. The city began leasing the roofs of municipal buildings to investors for the installation of photovoltaic systems. It facilitated the installation of a solar plant on an ore- and coal bunker of the former steel works, which later became an important cultural landmark.

The city then worked with local companies and research institutions to carry out major improvements in the city's housing infrastructure. Given the city's pursuit of solar city principles to guide urban regeneration, advanced energy performance criteria were set for new and existing buildings characterized by energy efficiency retrofits, integrated renewable energy systems, and solar passive design. These were demonstrated through the development of solar housing estates across the city.

The Gelsenkirchen-Bismarck solar housing estate was the first to display the use of renewable energy technologies (see Fig. 2.16). The estate was developed at the edge of the former coal mine Graf Bismarck over an area of 4 hectares and was the first of its kind in the Ruhr. Part of the "50 Solar Housing Estates NRW" state program launched in 1997, the estate featured innovative energy concepts for a school and self-built houses. For example, building space heating requirements were 40%–60% lower than the German standard at the time. Solar thermal and photovoltaic systems were installed on roofs, and passive solar energy techniques were deployed impacting building design,

Figure 2.16 Aerial view of Gelsenkirchen-Bismarck solar housing estate. Aerial image from Google Earth.

orientation, and internal layout. A life-cycle assessment calculated the total energy required to construct the entire estate. Information meetings were held, and brochures were designed touting the benefits of the solar estate via the Association for Solar Energy and Quality of Life, a local environmental advocacy group founded by locals to attract new residents to the area.

The solar estate soon led to the development of the larger Graf Bismarck City Quarter on the power plant located adjacent to the former coal mine. The 80-hectare quarter included 5000 new working places and 700 new dwellings, with office buildings, and facilities for trade, commerce, and recreation, all meeting high-energy efficiency, electricity, and heating standards. The city also imposed solar requirements in the contracts of land purchases such as the minimum output of PV installations on residential buildings, and the inclusion of PV on nonresidential buildings.

The city also engaged in the regeneration of older buildings in the establishment of solar housing estates. The Gelsenkirchen-Lindenhof solar housing estate, for example, involved the modernization of a former miners' settlement. In order to raise environmental standards while keeping rental costs down, measures focused on improving insulation and integrating new systems in heat recovery, space heating, and warm water. The measures resulted in reductions in CO_2 emissions of more than 85%, and energy costs per square meter by almost 60%. Completed in 2003, the project attracted new residents to the estate and set the stage for the systematic integration of clean energy solutions in other housing projects in the city. It also stabilized the social mix and lifted the image of the city district (Jung et al., 2010).

The city launched a program to assist smaller housing companies and cooperatives to evaluate their building stock and investment potentials in order to boost the replication of solar housing. One major achievement was the Gelsenkirchen-Schaffrath solar housing estate, which featured an 800 kWp solar system on a former miners' estate. It became the largest PV community in Germany and the second-largest in the world.

Projects in Gelsenkirchen owed their implementation to the commitment of the city's economic promotion, environmental protection, and urban planning departments. Processes and budgets were optimized to raise awareness, offer consultancy for private investors, and commission studies to support the development of additional policies and instruments. Given that energy issues were relevant to all city sectors, and required the systematic involvement of many stakeholders to tackle the inherent complexity of sectoral implementation, an energy team with members from various departments of the city administration was formed and led by a climate protection and solar officer. By participating in the European Energy Award scheme, the Climate Alliance program, and ICLEI's Cities for Climate Protection (CCP) Campaign energy and climate activities were effectively qualified.

The networking of local economic stakeholders was improved by the foundation of the Solar City Gelsenkirchen Association formed by the local utility, university, district crafts and trades guild, a local housing company, and the local solar industry. Members included all major actors along the chain from research and development, to production, installation, and maintenance of renewable energy technologies.

Public participation in the implementation of the solar city strategy was also encouraged through activities devised and coordinated by the Local Agenda 21 network. The group was formed in the late 90s for the implementation of sustainable development projects with local communities. Monies raised through charity events were spent on photovoltaic installations on public buildings, and for solar energy projects in developing countries. Larger solar projects in Gelsenkirchen received support from the local trade and commerce chambers, the representative bodies of many industries, and local banks via the Gelsenkirchen Solar Development Association.

Climate change campaigns were launched by the city to raise awareness about energy use, renewable energy, and sustainable mobility. Environmental education was promoted via the "EnvironmentDiploma", a program that supported carbon literacy in schools. Solar clubs and public events enabled citizens to obtain information on all things energy-related. The Energy Lab at the Gelsenkirchen Science Park offered hands-on educational activities for high school students to inspire future careers in environmental and renewable energy technologies. In recognition of its efforts, the city of Gelsenkirchen was the recipient of the UNESCO Learning City Award for sustainable development in 2017. The transition to a "learning city" has provided it with the necessary tools to develop and transform the city.

3. Innovation ecosystems for regional structural change

Policies and programs in industry diversification, urban regeneration, and environmental improvement have improved the economic resilience, growth potential, and liveability of the

Ruhr Metropolis. The most effective structural actions were the promotion of research and innovation, the creation of new industry clusters, and sustainable urban development based on low-carbon principles. The transdisciplinary networks ensured a range of expertise to pursue energy transition and address the challenge of climate change.

The cities of Dortmund, Bottrop, and Gelsenkirchen have demonstrated the ability of urban areas to harness their innate capabilities and experiences to create new diversified and green economies through the development of collaborative smart environments, ecosystems that have stimulated innovation through scientific research and systematic project implementation.

3.1 Industry clusters and sectoral diversification

New business development was most successful when it was linked to local and regional strengths. The cities drew upon existing local economic knowledge, competencies, interests, and experiences. In all three cases, energy transition was the commonality, with differences in logistical approach based on infrastructural capacities, industry and political support, and institutional presence.

In the Ruhr, regional waste disposal and water management expertise initiated the development of new environmental services industries in the areas of site remediation, recycling, and waste disposal, which later grew to include environmental technology research and development. By combining the mining, engineering, and energy technologies experience, new renewable energy industries were established as advanced offshoots in the fields of scientific research, manufacturing, retailing, installation and servicing, and maintenance of systems or components for solar, wind, geothermal, district heating, and power grid technologies. In making use of strong manufacturing, IT, and logistics base, new ICT industries grew to create jobs in the interface of these sectors such as e-logistics, e-commerce, and robotics. Consequently, the services sector boomed in support of the new industries, with employment growth in retail, health, tourism, sports, and media services. The sectoral variations translated into variegated work-based landscapes with large industrial conversions, business and technology parks, and university complexes.

Industries with thematic synergies thrived in Ruhr's new green economy. The energy, environmental technology, and IC sectors, in particular, achieved good growth because of their high compatibility. By developing alongside each other, the sectors were able to establish major competitive advantages in comparison to other industries. These relationships were outcomes-based, driven and highly cooperative. As they suited the development trends of the particular city where they resided, innovations in each sector were able to take place, making them sustainable and self-supportive. Their entry into the local markets strategically considered the gradual phase-out of the coal and steel industries, and took into account the structural and private support available. Their growth and continuing presence in the cities were assured by good local infrastructures provided by the local administrations, combined with dynamic project implementation through active stakeholder and community engagement.

In the Ruhr, the competence fields concept was able to bundle various projects under specific thematic umbrellas such as energy, environmental technology, and mobility. It enabled the appropriate support and funding of the required activities needed for the clusters' development. The clusters not only generate economic growth and employment but established sustainable institutional structures for future sectors to develop.

Logistically, the clusters were able to connect industry and academia, and offer vital assistance from economic and political circles. They provided the critical mass of businesses and suppliers necessary for the development of new products and services or the implementation of large-scale city projects in urban redevelopment and landscape rehabilitation. New start-ups and SMEs were able to take advantage of the sharing of knowledge, expertise, experience, and resources within each network. With input from industry partners, research facilities, and political and nonprofit institutions cooperating all along the value chain, the acts of decision-making, strategic positioning, and risk sharing were facilitated. By creating formalized but loosely structured intelligent environments, a collaboration between science, business, politics, and civil society was more effective.

Economic diversification through local and regional innovation, production, and manufacturing benefited from robust efforts in local and regional rehabilitation, modernization and redevelopment of the built and natural environment. The clusters approach in particular succeeded in making available the expertise and resources needed for these processes to take shape.

3.2 Advanced education and transdisciplinary networks

Substantial public investment into the establishment of universities, technical colleges, professional education institutes, and technology centers and parks resulted in highly positive socio-economic outcomes. They helped retrain workers retrenched from the coal, steel, and energy industries and brought immediate employment through their construction. Training and reskilling assisted the continuing employment of large numbers of people of different ages across many and very different job classifications. Institutions with links to growth industries were able to educate, attract, and keep personnel qualified for the new growth sectors in the region. Incoming working populations contributed to the local economies by augmenting local consumption and spending patterns, as well as increasing the demand for local goods and services.

The educational institutions created learning milieus that enhanced connectivity and boosted activity between stakeholders. Academic bodies aided product development, testing, and manufacture, as well as identified relevant markets for distribution. Independent research institutes facilitated the diversification in research areas, activating new cross-sectional technological innovations and business concepts, as shown in the evolution from pure IT and environmental technology, to e-mobility and virtual grids. Established industries assisted new startups in gaining entry to wider commercial markets, clients, consumers, and expertise for their products and services once matched as project partners. New companies in turn injected fresh creativity, new methods of working, and advanced skills with new technologies into existing industry practices. Regional associations, business development agencies, and city chambers of industry and commerce assisted in project development, funding, location marketing, and site and investor services. These interdependencies provided the resources and relationships necessary for activities to advance.

Knowledge and technology transfer were intensified through project collaboration. Networks that connected the universities and technical colleges with nonuniversity research facilities and industry partners resulted in the development of new technological products, applications, and services. By widening the networks to include city administrations, businesses, and local communities, outcomes became focused on much larger infrastructural and urban development projects. With the help of industry partners in such projects, new energy concepts and products were widely applied and usefully tested in real-world conditions.

In Ruhr, the learning environments or ecosystems are physically manifested in three ways. First, through in-house research projects largely conducted within the educational institutions;

two, through the development of real-time built projects within the city as demonstrated in neighborhood rehabilitation or energy pilot projects; or three, through promotional activities and events and local advisory services taking place in city energy centers, workshops, and clubs. Whether taking place in the laboratory, city district, or community center, the dynamic and flexible environments enabled innovation cultures to come together to generate ideas and navigate project implementation. Through strategically arranged and harmonized project groupings, knowledge and working practices were able to interact to produce innovations in systems-oriented technical solutions, products, and services.

Energy transition challenges in particular were better addressed through systematic approaches developed by way of transdisciplinary cooperation, in which the knowledge ecosystems provided. Energy transition was not a task to be solved in isolation. The three cities revealed that energy transition was a complex and multivariate process, involving many stakeholders, many methods of implementation, and concurrent project timelines. Measures were of different scales, importance, size, cost, and jurisdiction, ranging from municipal procurement, and energy studies, to large-scale housing modernization and power plant retrofits. These required varying expertise and careful coordination. However, by unifying projects on the basis of common emissions and energy targets through the application of low-carbon or energy transition masterplans, cities were able to structure these processes most effectively.

3.3 Intelligent climate-resilient infrastructures

Creating good conditions for ongoing learning and innovation set the basis for the pursuit of energy transition goals in Smart City Dortmund, InnovationCity Bottrop, and Solar City Gelsenkirchen. New and inspiring living and working environments were constructed to accommodate the rapidly growing workforce and new enterprises engaging in the new energy and environmental sectors. Urban regeneration integrated the latest in low-carbon building and renewable energy technologies, and incorporated climate adaptive blue and green landscape design. Around the universities and technology parks, a new urban quality emerged with high-quality services and cultural centers. These were served by new stormwater and sewage systems, retrofitted cogeneration technologies, and expanded and intelligently managed power and heating distribution networks.

Programs and projects achieved practical emissions and energy targets as part of ambitious climate protection and energy transition plans. As the foundation of activities in the region, they represented the cities' commitment toward achieving economic growth that also protected the environment and enhanced the quality of life of its residents. The region benefited greatly from the climate and environmental rebrand. Large-scale infrastructural investments into public institutions, transport, and open space over several decades resulted in cities that were well connected, economically dynamic, and environmentally healthier.

Climate protection and energy transition master plans ensured that developments were strategically and efficiently pursued, often beginning with the city administrations acting as a model, shifting from small-scale municipally targeted energy projects to multidisciplinary research projects that explored large-scale energy infrastructure transformations. Improved living, working and leisure environments were the practical outcomes, but the many projects also served as testing environments for new energy concepts and technologies in construction, production, and facilities management. The public and private works proved the capacity for new energy technologies to improve the urban building stock in a cost-effective and socially acceptable manner.

The three cities successfully turned abandoned brownfields and environmental blight into fields of opportunity for urban regeneration and economic redevelopment. Employment for local trades and businesses was identified along the entire process of site clean-up and remediation, to construction and management. Over time, innovation in environmental technologies branched out into more advanced eco industries and renewable energy systems.

The dynamism and infrastructural demand of the new industries and start-ups were highly influential on the urban development trends within cities. Cities were able to improve public infrastructures to create supportive working environments for start-ups to develop, create, and maintain their presence. The new industries influenced the design of solar architectures, with low-carbon buildings and photovoltaic systems featured in numerous technology parks. Ambitious goals were extended to energy-self-sufficient housing and solar housing estates. The expansion of new energy technologies was aided by solar, wind, and geothermal mapping, which when made accessible to the general public through online platforms, greatly improved the uptake of renewable systems and raised the resilience of local energy infrastructures.

Smart city projects encouraged more optimized and resilient city growth. By creating intelligent links between numerous research and real-time projects in different subject areas, energy transition was able to take place both top-down and bottom-up. It influenced the chain of activities in managing the demand, generation, storage, and distribution of energy through the transformation of local energy infrastructures. It impacted ongoing environmental protection and conservation responses through the intelligent monitoring of carbon emissions, air, water, and soil quality.

3.4 Socio-cultural considerations for cohesive smart environments

The expanding local economies of the Ruhr are becoming more globally oriented and competitive, influenced by continual innovations in science and research. In order for the region to progress, economic diversification must work to also maintain social cohesion, stability, and equality.

Significant demographic changes are taking place in the Ruhr. More tech workers and their families are moving into the region while younger educated people are leaving to seek better jobs and living conditions. Immigration from EU member states and refugee resettlement have also added to the social mix. Although the regeneration of old residential areas and derelict industrial lands have helped to preserve social structures and conserve cultural identities, such methods may not be sufficient to address the needs and concerns of a rapidly changing region facing new socio-economic challenges. Social segregation and tension between the different social groups are growing, and concerns regarding gentrification and housing affordability persist. Inclusive and transparent planning and support measures will be called for.

The disruption will apply to energy governance and urban infrastructures in the region. The Ruhr remains reliant on fossil energy sources, and thus great effort will be required by all actors to break the dependence. In economic and even psychological terms, it will entail changes to established social alliances of companies, politicians, trade unions, and suppliers, and the disruption of common interests in maintaining existing economic arrangements. Transformations in urban and regional energy systems running on renewable energy will demand varying expertise and feedback loops involving scientific, industrial, political, and civil networks.

Future policies focusing on SMEs, infrastructure, and the like, must prevent burdening the poor and marginalized groups—whether based on gender, age, ethnicity, or disability—with the increased costs due to structural changes. Large investments into new energy systems and extensions to networks will impact the price of heat and power. Systematic energy renovation of urban housing will place pressure on rents. The promotion of high-performance or self-sufficient buildings will raise capital outlays by building owners. Structural transition measures must therefore seek to reverse patterns of social and economic inequality by ensuring that such aspects are carefully considered and addressed.

Social acceptance will rely on equal access to information, employment opportunities, and services in the Ruhr. The success of "innovation cities" and "smart cities" in particular will require a high level of engagement and a certain level of technological literacy among resident and working populations in order for those cities to come to be. While this is achievable among the younger population, older and disadvantaged groups may face difficulty in navigating the workings of a new high-tech city, notwithstanding the privacy and accessibility issues inherent in integrated and intelligent city environments, where ways of living and working in the future will increasingly rely on virtual and digital application-based tools. Furthermore, with the high priority given to technological specializations in the Ruhr, some societal imbalance may ensue, creating a "lock-out" of certain sectors of society who are less technologically proficient. Cities must therefore consider the manner in which different sectors of society are able to engage with the city, and what choices are available to them to sustain their engagement.

And as societies begin to increasingly inhabit virtual environments, the importance of good urban quality cities will also rise. The pursuit of smart city programs will promise low carbon, well-connected, highly competitive cities. But the increasing prioritization of urban systems that are managed through virtual environments may overtake the focus on the physical, tangible qualities of cities, and the design of urban spaces that people actually inhabit. Instead, there are opportunities to make use of the savings and efficiencies achieved in the remote management of urban infrastructures - whether it be energy, transport, housing, or workspaces—to improve the physical design of cities, enhance urban environmental qualities, and thus lift the socio-economic conditions for all.

4. References

Research and writing supporting this chapter were funded by the Gesellschaft für Internationale Zusammenarbeit (GIZ).

References

BMWi - Federal Ministry of Economics and Technology, BMU - Federal Ministry for the Environment, Nature Conservation and Nuclear Safety, September 28, 2010. Energy Concept for an Environmentally Sound, Reliable and Affordable Energy Supply. Federal Ministry of Economics and Technology, Berlin, Germany.

Bross, U., Walter, G.H., 2000. Socio-economic Analysis of North Rhine-Westphalia. Working Papers Firms and Region No. R2/2000. Accessed from. https://core.ac.uk/download/pdf/6625278.pdf.

business.metropoleruhr.de, 2021. WIRTSCHAFTSBERICHT RUHR 2020. Accessed from. https://www.business.ruhr/fileadmin/user_upload/Bilder/Presse/Verschiedenes/bmr_wirtschaftsbericht20_210319.pdf.

City of Gelsenkirchen, 2011. SOLARSTADT GELSENKIRCHEN: Stadt der Zukunftsenergien. Accessed from. http://www.solarstadt-gelsenkirchen.de/fileadmin/solarstadt/Download/Flyer/Broschuere_GE_Solarstadt__3_.pdf.

Dahlbeck, E., Gärtner, S., 2019. Just Transition for Regions and Generations—Experiences from Structural Change in the Ruhr Area. WWF, Germany. Accessed from. https://www.iat.eu/aktuell/veroeff/2019/wwf-studie-englisch.pdf.

e.huawei.com. 'Gelsenkirchen: A Small, Smart City with Big Plans'. Accessed from https://e.huawei.com/en/case-studies/global/2017/201709071445.

EC - European Commission, 2018. A Clean Planet for All - A European Strategic Long-Term Vision for a Prosperous, Modern, Competitive and Climate Neutral Economy. Accessed from. https://ec.europa.eu/clima/sites/clima/files/docs/pages/com2018733en.pdf.

EC - European Commission, 2020a. Green Deal. Accessed from. https://ec.europa.eu/info/strategy/priorities-2019-2024/european-green-deal_en.

EC - European Commission, 2020b. Committing to Climate Neutrality by 2050. Accessed from. https://ec.europa.eu/commission/presscorner/detail/en/IP_20_335.

Galarraga, I., González-Eguino, M., Markandya, A., 2011. Handbook of Sustainable Energy. Edward Elgar, Cheltenham, Northampton.

Galgóczi, B., 2014. The long and winding road from black to green: decades of structural change at the Ruhr region. International Journal of Labour Research 6 (2), 217—241.

Goch, S., 2009. 'Politik für Ruhrkohle und Ruhrrevier - Von der Ruhrkohle AG zum neuen Ruhrgebiet'. Kumpel und Kohle. Der Landtag NRW und die Ruhrkohle 1946 bis 2008", Schriften des Landtags NRW. Düsseldorf.

Herpich, P., Brauers, H., Oei, P.-Y., 2018. An Historical Case Study on Previous Coal Transitions in Germany. DIW Berlin, German Institute for Economic Research; Berlin University of Technology.

Jung, W., Hardes, A., Schroeder, W., 2010. From Industrial Area to Solar Area—The Redevelopment of Brownfields and Old Building Stock with Clean Energy Solutions. City of Gelsenkirchen, Germany.

Keil, A., Wetterau, B., 2013. Metropolis ruhr. A regional study of the new ruhr. In: Ruhr, R. (Ed.), Translated by Hans-Werner Wehling. Essen: Regionalverband Ruhr. Accessed from. https://www.geographie.uni-wuppertal.de/uploads/media/Metropolis_Ruhr-1_02.pdf.

Lauderbach, M., 2012. Effective governance to develop creative quarters: three case studies from Germany. Quaestiones Geographicae, Sciendo 31 (4), 77—86.

Reicher, C., Kunzmann, K.R., Polívka, J., Roost, F., Utku, Y., Wegener, M. (Eds.), 2011. Schichten einer Region – Kartenstücke zur räumlichen Struktur des Ruhrgebietes (Berlin: Jovis).

Reutter, O., Müller, M., Esken, A., Fekkak, M., Gröne, M.-C., Treude, M., 2017. Report on the state of the environment in the ruhr metropolitan area 2017. Regionalverband Ruhr (RVR). Essen. Accessed from. https://www.rvr.ruhr/fileadmin/user_upload/01_RVR_Home/02_Themen/Umwelt_Oekologie/Umweltbericht/Report_on_the_State_of_the_Environment_in_the_Ruhr_Metropolitan_Area_2017__Webdatei__1_.pdf.

rvr.ruhr, 2020a. Wirtschaft und Innovation. Accessed from. https://www.rvr.ruhr/daten-digitales/regionalstatistik/wirtschaft-und-innovation/.

rvr.ruhr, 2020b. Bevoelkerung. Accessed from. https://www.rvr.ruhr/fileadmin/user_upload/01_RVR_Home/03_Daten_Digitales/Regionalstatistik/Bevoelkerung/Bevoelkstand_und_entw._2000_bis_2019.xlsx.

Schepelmann, P., 2018. Governance of Low-Carbon Energy System Transitions - A Case Study from North-Rhine Westphalia, Germany. Asian Development Bank. Issue 32. https://www.adb.org/publications/low-carbon-energy-system-transitions.

Storchmann, K., 2005. The rise and fall of German hard coal subsidies. Energy Policy 33, 1469–1492.

Taylor, R., 2015. A Review of Industrial Restructuring in the Ruhr Valley and Relevant Points for China. Institute for Industrial Productivity. Accessed from. http://www.iipnetwork.org/Industrial%20Restructuring%20in%20the%20Ruhr%20Valley.pdf.

UA Ruhr, 2018. University Alliance Ruhr: The Academic Hub for Research, Teaching, Studying and Networking in Germany's Vibrant Ruhr Area. Accessed from. https://www.uaruhr.de/mam/content/120718_uar_imagebroschure_2018_lowres.pdf.

Urry, A., 2017. 'Life after Coal'. The Grist. 29 Nov 2017. Accessed from. https://grist.org/article/inside-the-last-coal-mine-germany-appalachia/.

wmr – wirtschaftsfoerdering metropoleruhr, 2011. The Metropole Ruhr. A Good Place to Live, a Good Place to Invest. Accessed from. https://slideplayer.com/slide/5891760/.

Wuppertal Institute, 2017. Die Energiewende Regional Gestalten. Accessed from. https://www.stiftung-mercator.de/content/uploads/2020/12/Energiewende_Regional_Gestalten_Auf_dem_Weg_zu_einer_Energiewende-Roadmap_im_Ruhrgebiet_Publikation_2017.pdf.

3

Triangulum: the three point project—findings from one of the first EU smart city projects

Trinidad Fernandez[1], Sonja Stöffler[2] and Catalina Diaz[2]

[1]*Fraunhofer Institute for Industrial Engineering IAO, Stuttgart, Germany;* [2]*University of Stuttgart, Institute of Human Factors and Technology Management IAT, Stuttgart, Germany*

The digital era offers new opportunities for planning and developing cities, infrastructures, and communities: the Triangulum Project provides insights into this quest. Concluded on January 2020, this 29,5 Million Euro project was one of the first European *Smart Cities and Communities Lighthouse* projects that received funding within the European Union's Horizon (2020) Research and Innovation Program. The project worked with three forerunner cities and three follower cities during its 5-year lifetime. From these two triads, the inspiration for the name of the project was taken; Triangulum is the Latin word for triangle (see Fig. 3.1). The focus on the Dutch forerunner city of Eindhoven addresses urban transformation as an outcome of city vision and strategy setting, the bold pursuit of technological innovation, and broad participation by the public and industry.

1. European social cohesion, climate, urban innovation, and industrial development aims/H2020 and the green deal

Urbanization in Europe is on the rise and is expected to increase to 84% by 2050 (UNDESA, 2018). Cities consume more than 70% of final energy—and emit an equivalent share of greenhouse gas—in the European Union (EU) (European Commission, 2020). To address these challenges, the EU's executive branch, the European Commission (EC) works through its policy departments, known as Directorates-General (DGs), to develop,

Intelligent Environments. https://doi.org/10.1016/B978-0-12-820247-0.00010-2

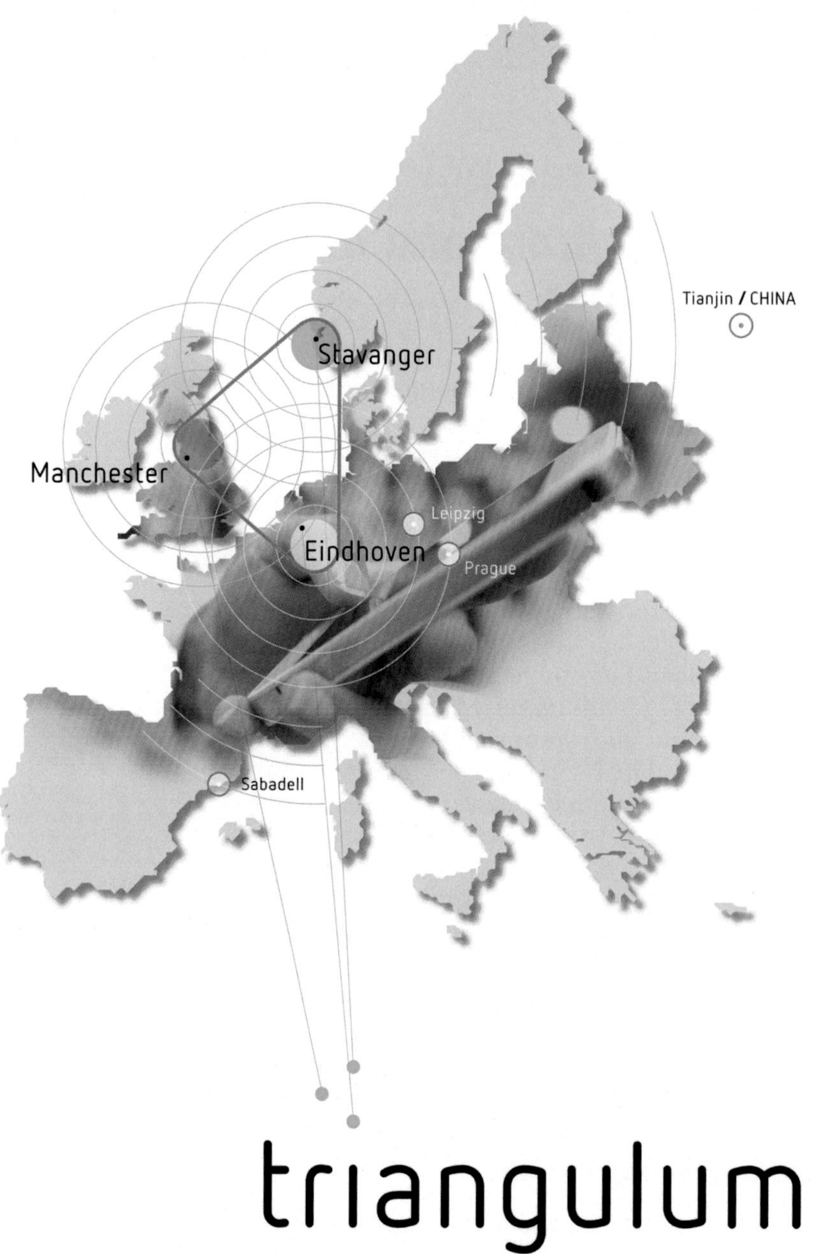

Figure 3.1 Triangulum logo (2015–20). Source: Triangulum.

implement and manage EU policy, law, and funding programs. In the year 2010 the DGs launched a strategy to reach climate change and energy targets, defining and allocating funding for smart city solutions that contribute to sustainable and inclusive growth in the region. Its investment focused on research and innovation programs and policy development on smart cities to achieve a triple aim for Europe: better quality of life for citizens, more competitive industry and SMEs, and more sustainable, efficient, and user-friendly energy, transport and information technologies, services, systems, and infrastructures (European Commission, 2010).

2. The European Union (EU) initiatives on smart cities: innovation, resilience, climate change mitigation

The EU has developed an extensive implementation process in various initiatives and programs to support the cities' transition to smart cities. According to the EC, a smart city offers services and provides networks more efficiently with the support of digital and telecommunications technologies for its citizens and businesses (European Commission, 2018). In this sense, the most relevant transformational instruments are the European 2020 Strategy: the European Union's 10-year plan for growth and jobs, the Innovation Union flagship initiative: together with the Digital Agenda it highlights the formation of European Innovation Partnerships, and the European Innovation Partnership for Smart Cities and Communities (EIP-SCC), which brings together cities, industry and citizens to improve urban life through sustainably integrated solutions. From the EIP-SCC the *Smart Cities and Communities Lighthouse* (SCC1) program emerged.

The SCC1 program was conceived to promote large-scale "urban laboratories" where existing or near-ready smart city technologies and solutions are demonstrated and innovatively integrated into the urban systems in the following action areas: low energy districts, integrated infrastructures, and sustainable urban mobility. The initiative brought together cities, industry, academia, and citizens, fostering innovation to demonstrate solutions and business models that could be scaled up and replicated in other European cities.

In order to find, foster and maximize the impact of solutions, the EU built on this type of projects based on best practice reflection, benchmarking, transfer, and replication of solutions to reduce risks for both public decision-makers and businesses. The implementation of smart city solutions brings multiple and measurable benefits in energy and resource efficiency, economics, social aspects, environment, and new markets (Harrison and Donnelly, 2011). Furthermore, smart city ideals of high technology, efficiency, and connectivity are aligned with the open, interactive exchange culture. Here, mobilizing, transferring, and replicating cities' policies and ideas are increasingly part of policymaking and urban planning.

The SCC1 lighthouse projects were funded primarily as part of the EU's innovation action program (IA). This program required financial contributions from local, regional or national sources as well as private investments. In the case of Triangulum, the volume of the project was 29,5 million euros, of which a large amount of it (25,4 million) were part of the funding provided by the European Union under the Horizon 2020 IA program for its development.

These projects were meant to develop the research and innovation strategies for smart specialization proposed by the Commission as an integrated approach to exploit the potential for smart growth in all regions and cities in Europe. The Commission conceived lighthouse project consortia to have the four main characteristics (European Commission, 2012). First, the project should rely on robust and performance-oriented partnerships, including cities, research partners and key industry, service, and technology innovators. Second, the participation of cities from at least two EU Member States or Associated States to try the solutions and transfer knowledge within the EU was a requirement. Cities and local stakeholders needed to prove their ability and plans for engaging citizens and end-users at a large scale and enabling systemic change (e.g., a district of a city, or a corridor). Additionally, the EC was seeking for a strong commitment to support the generation of new open standards that facilitate interoperability between systems, avoiding supplier dependency and fostering competition for the technological solutions deployed. To conlcude, commitment toward scaling up, innovation adoption, and replication within the city, to and in other cities and communities was listed and highlighted as a requisite to be encouraged. This includes getting involved in measuring, collecting, and disseminating data to foster further replication and development in other contexts, in particular information on costs and impact (energy savings, CO_2 reductions, financial savings, jobs created, environmental impacts, etc.). Also, preparation and customization of comprehensive roll-out business cases related to the deployed solutions to secure leverage of significant public and/or private co-funding to ensure further implementation outside the project scope and maximize the impact of EU funds.

3. The role of Triangulum

The Triangulum project began in 2015 and concluded in 2020. As one of the first projects in the SSC1 program, it relied on replicating solutions to minimize technical and financial implementation risks for both decision-makers and companies. Under the format of lighthouse and follower cities, the Triangulum cities served as testbeds for innovative projects focusing on sustainable mobility, sustainable and efficient energy supply, information technology, and business opportunities. The lighthouse concept refers to a city ready to deploy large-scale demonstrations that are first of a kind.

The project consortium combined the interdisciplinary expertise of 22 partners from industry, research and municipalities. All of them shared the same objective and commitment to develop and implement smart solutions in the lighthouse cities Manchester (UK), Eindhoven (NL) and Stavanger (NO) and replicate them in the three follower cities Leipzig (D), Prague (CZ) and Sabadell (ES). Triangulum project was coordinated by the Fraunhofer Institute for Industrial Engineering (IAO) in Stuttgart (EC Research Results CORDIS, 2015) and exhibits 29 solution modules and 69 use cases addressing the individual challenges and requirements of its lighthouse cities and involved stakeholders.

This powerful combination and partnership in six different countries and cities reflects an urban population of between 100,000 and 1.2 million inhabitants, demonstrating successful replication in a wide range of typical European urban areas. Triangulum served as an accelerator and built on each of the participant cities strengths toward smart sustainable urban development.

The project name Triangulum refers to a constellation where the three brightest stars form a long and narrow triangle, referring to the structure of the project developed in triads ("the three-point project"). Three lighthouse cities and three follower cities, as brighter stars within the smart city European constellation, aiming to demonstrate, disseminate, and replicate smart city solutions.

4. Aims and scope

The Triangulum project aimed to stimulate proactive smart city development, by implementing smart city pilots in its lighthouse cities featuring the main European city typologies and scaling them up in follower cities. A set of projects was developed around zero/low energy districts, integrated infrastructures and sustainable urban mobility, designed to deliver cross-sector and multi-stakeholder outcomes. Triangulum served as a “trial” for the European Commission’s Strategic Implementation Plan (SIP) and made recommendations to the Commission on how it could be improved to facilitate wider replication. The project’s objectives pointed to a number of direct impacts in terms of reducing the energy consumption of buildings, increasing the use of renewable energy, increasing the use of electric vehicles, deploying smart energy management technologies and deploying an adaptive and dynamic ICT data center. One of the crucial cross-cutting elements identified and developed for anchoring technologies in real urban environments and facilitating their replication were innovative business models and the activation of citizens as co-creators. The project included the generation of a Smart City Framework among other activities to gather to support these crucial elements and the need for cooperation.

The project performance concentrates on the implementation of an integrated set of technologies and interventions that consider the overall complex urban landscape, including policy, planning, citizens, and local governance structures in one or more districts of each one of the lighthouse cities. This phase runs for the first three years of the project and represents the heart of the project.

After completion of implementation in years four and five of the project, efforts are primarily focused on monitoring and tracking the impact of the pilots to upscale and transfer the knowledge to the follower cities.

Throughout the project, activities around the implementation are established to provide a framework for catalyzing the vertical integration of the lighthouse cities projects through joint impact assessment and monitoring aiming to capture the impact of the pilots, delivery of a joint ICT reference architecture, design of a smart cities framework, management, transfer and replication of knowledge between the cities and the development of a joint corporate project design and dissemination of project results within the participating cities as well as across Europe.

It is intended that the partner cities will use the project to develop several demonstration activities and strategies aimed at sustainable economic growth and sustainable places to live, while reducing their environmental impact. Moreover, an evaluation and scaling-up strategy is developed to capitalize and maximize the project outcomes, showcasing as a reference the pathway of the participating cities for the implementation of smart cities in Europe.

5. Participating cities and their expectations

As mentioned before, the participating cities represented different typologies of European cities that share features but present different socio-economic and political systems and individual local conditions. The expectation at the beginning of the project was to test their Strategic Implementation Plans (SIP) first in the three lighthouse cities of Manchester, Eindhoven, and Stavanger, and to continue before the end of the project with the follower cities of Prague, Leipzig, and Sabadell. Each SIP document defines a deployment plan outlining the resources, assumptions, and predictions, short- and long-term outcomes, roles and responsibilities, and the budget. The combination of these six cities, allowed the project to demonstrate successful replication across a wide range of typical urban areas in Europe. By the time of the selection, each city had already made significant progress toward the transition of becoming a smart city, developing their own individual approach reflecting specific local circumstances. These inherent advantages served as a base to accelerate the smart city development across proposed demonstration sites within the project.

The interaction between the cities was very diverse over the course of the 3 years. At the beginning the main focus was on the lighthouse cities and their local constellations of partners and stakeholders to identify their needs and areas of work within the project scope. The implementation, monitoring, and evaluation of the pilot demonstrations covered a good second portion of the project. The follower cities had the chance to travel to the lighthouse cities and take insights and references from their existing demonstrations. During the course of the 5 years, and to support the follower cities a Training Mission was designed, which helped them to define their visions and own smart city strategies. Toward the end of the project, the implementations shifted to the follower cities, to replicate use cases deployed during the first part of the project in Manchester, Eindhoven, and Stavanger. Fig. 3.2 illustrates the different steps throughout the project timeframe, the main implementations, and key milestones.

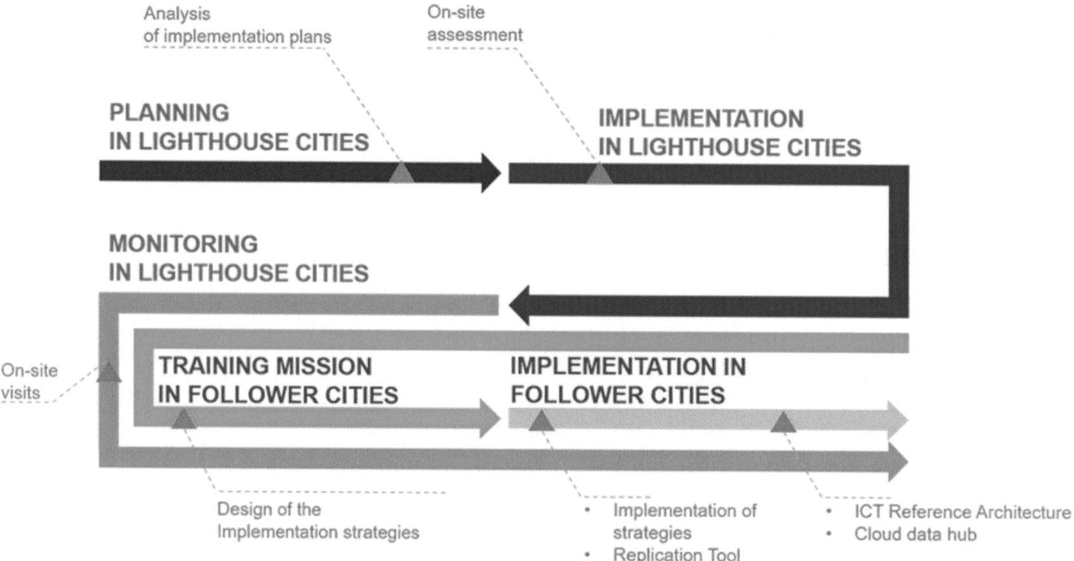

Figure 3.2 Triangulum project timeline (2015–20). Source: Triangulum Management Team by Fraunhofer. Copyright © 2021 Fraunhofer.

6. Leading technologies and their purpose

To secure an efficient smart city development, different cutting-edge technologies from the sectors of mobility, energy and information and communication were selected to be implemented during the project. The purpose was to demonstrate to cities across Europe how to integrate smart city technologies with a high technology readiness level TRL into existing socio-technical urban systems and how to adapt existing socio-political frameworks for an improved and accelerated smart city development. Therefore, the project considered technologies ranging from TRL 7 to TRL 9, meaning from system prototype demonstration, to an actual system proven in operational environment.

The implemented technologies were either complete and qualified systems, for example, TRL 8—Smart lighting in Eindhoven; or functioning actual systems that had already been tested, for example, TRL 9—electric buses in Stavanger. Only some systems were TRL 7, for example, shared on demand mobility solution with e-bikes in Manchester. Here, it was built upon the demonstration of system prototypes in operational environments.

The clear advantage was the high transferability of the implemented solutions as stand-alone and as integrated district solutions. Rather than providing technology development, the focus lay on the demonstration of the great synergy potential of market-ready and feasible technologies when applied and combined in a defined area like the lighthouse districts.

7. Expected outcomes and success measures

In order to embed the previously mentioned technologies in wider socio-technical urban systems, all three cities involved the citizens and local stakeholders into the transition process of the districts. The lighthouse cities Manchester, Eindhoven, and Stavanger thus acted as a source of the smart city development, focusing on the replication of the solutions in the follower cities and beyond. The project achieved several impacts, for example, energy savings, increase in sustainable mobility, rise of citizen engagement, and socio-economic benefits. Different specific indicators were defined in each of these domains to measure and monitor the impacts in the lighthouse cities. In the energy domain those indicators included, for example, the amount of buildings retrofitted, the carbon emissions per building, share of renewable energy in the grid or smart meters installed and used. Regarding mobility, indicators such as the modal split, carbon emissions, use of smart mobility apps or the number of electric/fuel cell vehicles charging stations were monitored. The number of smart apps developed using open data platform, E-participation and E-governance are examples for the citizen engagement indicators. For the evaluation of the socio-economic domain, indicators like the number of patents, small- and medium-sized enterprises created, skills and training delivered or the number of technologies from the lighthouse cities adopted elsewhere came into use.

In Manchester the electric vehicles provided within the project saved 35 tCO_2e from 2016 until project completion in January 2020. These came along with four eCargo bikes, each one of them making three journey per day across the city (see Fig. 3.3). In Eindhoven, the Sanergy-biomass system generated over 15% of all energy produced in the district of Strijp-S. This 100% renewable energy was used for heating. Furthermore, 14 electric vehicle charging stations were implemented and the fiber-optic network was expanded to 350 home and over 7000 office connections. Stavanger brought out Blink, an innovative video solution that communicates between smartphones, tablets and the TV. It was one of

Figure 3.3 Green-delivery vans and cargo bikes in Manchester (2019). Source: Manchester City Council.

the solutions replicated and demonstrated in the area of care services in the follower cities Prague and Sabadell.

A core part of Triangulum was to improve the capacity and integration of knowledge and its commercial exploitation through a robust assessment and upscaling strategy. Therefore, not only quantitative indicators were used to measure the impact, but also qualitative factors, such as capacity building, financing strategies, regulatory barriers, or the collaboration between urban local actors were monitored.

The project had wider impact than originally thought. It had an influence on the strategic and governance processes in the lighthouse and follower cities and helped to create new stakeholder constellations and shape strategic developments. Triangulum has also been the means of access for new projects with a total budget of more than 50 million euro. One example is City Verve in Manchester, a program that demonstrates the application of IoT technologies to the city. Also, Leipzig successfully turned from a follower city to a lighthouse city as part of the SCC1 project SPARCs. This project will create a network of Sustainable energy Positive & zero cARbon CommunitieS in two lighthouse and five fellow cities.

8. Case study: Eindhoven

In the case of Eindhoven, one of the main drivers of urban development over time has been the long history of entrepreneurship epitomized by companies such as the electronics conglomerate Philips and the commercial vehicle manufacturer Van Doorne's Aanhangwagen Fabriek DAF. The founding in 1891 and the gradual, international evolution of Philips turned this city from a rural farm into a major industrial center that triggered rapid urban growth during the 20th century. In addition to creating jobs, the company played an active and significant role in the city's urban development, for example, by building neighborhoods for workers, running schools, providing health services, building a library, supporting the local football team and the Technical University of Eindhoven.

During the 1980 recession, Philips was forced to relocate its factories outside Eindhoven, leaving 14,000 locals unemployed in 1993. In the same year, DAF's financial situation deteriorated rapidly, and the company was forced to stop production and cut more than 2,500 jobs (Padilla and Stöffler, 2017).

In response to these events, the regional government created the Greater Eindhoven Regional Authority in 2014 as a public-sector initiative to improve the economic situation through cooperation at the regional level. In order to mobilizse European funds, the economic development office NV REDE was founded in 1983 and started by then a strong collaboration between local actors, for example, the Chamber of Commerce, the Eindhoven University of Technology (TU/e) and the municipalities from the metropolitan region of Eindhoven. This collaboration resulted in the Regional Opportunities Commission, which eventually led to the foundation of the Brainport Development. The latter is a regionally active public–private partnership that has shaped itself into an innovation hub.

Eindhoven began to become known for applying a so-called quadruple-helix concept. Built upon a triple-helix model that comprises academia, industries and governments, the new model incorporates citizens and civil society as the fourth helix. The system is based on the idea that innovation is the result of an interactive process involving different "spheres" of actors ("helixes"), each contributing according to their "established" or "institutional" role in society (see Fig. 3.4) (Cavallini et al., 2016; Borkowska and Osborne, 2018). In Eindhoven, the helix consists of the city itself, research institutions (e.g., TU/e), industry representatives (e.g., the construction company Volker Wessels, the social housing corporation Woonbedrijf or the telecommunications company KPN) and citizens. All these actors were involved within the Triangulum project and are the ones who implemented smart city solutions in Eindhoven. The solutions used contain robust technological approaches mostly related to the ICT, energy and mobility sectors. These included a system that generates energy and clean the soil (Sanergy), 3D ICT citizen participation tools for housing renovations (Woonbedrijf refurbishment) and an illuminated jogging path completed in a co-creation process. This constellation of actors in the project enabled face-to-face cooperation and collaborative development facilitated by flat hierarchies and only a minimum of bureaucracy.

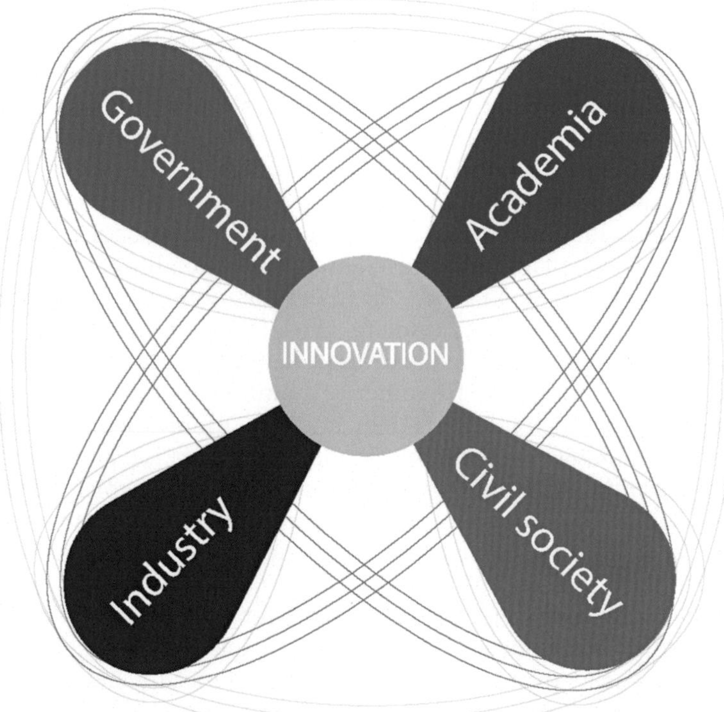

Figure 3.4 The quadruple helix model. Adapted by Fraunhofer (2021), originally developed by Carayannis and Campbell (2009). Copyright © 2021 Fraunhofer.

The Brainport Eindhoven concept was developed on the basis of programs and projects around the understanding that it was urgent to adapt to changing circumstances within the wider high-tech economy. Together with the help of the (European Commissions' funding programs) projects around this vision could become a reality. The funding programs started with the FP1 funding program in 1984 with an estimated funding budget of some 3.8 billion Euros over a 5-year period. The programs continued for six periods (FP1-FP6) but quadrupled their funding for research and innovation Actions over time. From the *Seventh Framework Program* (FP7) onwards, including the recent Horizon 2020 and the upcoming *Horizon Europe* program, these funding cycles have a duration of 7 years with a budget of 50, 77, and 95 billion Euros, respectively. Supported by these programs, the cooperation between industry, research, and academic institutions and the regional government came to light and had the opportunity to work together on the development of a strategic plan called *Brainport Navigator* in 2003 going beyond the Lisbon Agenda (the action and development plan devised in 2000 from the European Union between 2000 and 2010) and paving the way to the new Brainport 2020 strategic plan in 2011 (EIPO, 2015).

Concerning the smart development of the city, factors such as political commitment and local championship are highly relevant. During the past years, Eindhoven was involved in various sustainable smart city projects, Triangulum being one of them. This reflects the interest of the city in deploying smart solutions. However, isolated solutions are less powerful when they are not part of an overarching, deliberate strategy. A shared vision was therefore vital in Eindhoven to align plans and unite efforts toward a common goal, namely, the Brainport Strategy as the economic and innovation engine of the Netherlands (Padilla and Stöffler, 2017).

Besides the vision and strategy definition, it was important for the city to reinforce and synthesize these ideas directly and compellingly. Developed by the marketing organisation Eindhoven 365, the Eindhoven Innovation System consists of three elements. $E = U \times C$, where E stands for Energy, U for unconventional, and C for collaboration. Thus, Eindhoven's smart city drivers are based on start-up incubators, living labs, coworking spaces, research and inhabitants, among others. Together, they highlight the importance of cooperation among actors and frame the city's Brainport structure (Padilla and Stöffler, 2017).

9. Cooperation process and interaction

In applying the quadruple-helix model of innovation Eindhoven included citizens and communities in the overall decision-making processes and the shared development of products and services—the city considered their participation is considered as a key to building successful smart strategies (Calzada and Cowie, 2017). The social and human dimension of smart cities promulgates the conviction that interacting communities will provide more elegant solutions than individual experts, delivering inclusive, open and user-responsive innovations. In Eindhoven, the development of Brainport Eindhoven is considered as one of the most important economic pillars nationally as it concentrates knowledge-intensive manufacturing as a driver of high-tech innovation for the Netherlands. The Brainport Foundation counts with a strong political support from the government, with the mayors of the region as members of the foundation and the mayor of Eindhoven as chairman, as well as members of the committees of the most important companies and universities in the area.

Although the quadruple helix concept continues to be promoted in the smart city discourse, examples of cases that positively influence citizens' services are scarce (Cavallini et al., 2016). One of these examples is the successful transformation of the Eckart Vaartbroek neighborhood in Eindhoven from a 1960s social housing into a smart social housing district. Using a 3D digital software tool called WoonConnect, this district aims at becoming Eindhoven's leading innovative low-energy district. The software enables an interactive renovation process by providing tenants or owners with the opportunity to manage their energy consumption through renovation measures and behavioral insights (Gemeente et al., 2018). WoonConnect is an online platform developed by the company De Twee Snoeken WoonConnect that enables creating a digital 3D model of a house, including all relevant construction, architecture and artifacts details, so that residents can easily choose for themselves which adjustments and improvements they would like to make to their homes. Various scenarios can be compared, for example, to make living more sustainable, safer, more comfortable, more lifecycle-resistant, or cheaper. The platform calculates what the wished invervention and scenarios would cost, but also what it yields in investment return by, for example, a lower energy bill. This information can be not only relevant in a single home, but also for planning purposes in a neighborhood and eventually even at a regional or national level. The social housing organization Woonbedrijf has organized the use of this software for the renovation of the houses within Triangulum.

The creative approach was based on an active participation model, which allowed tenants to make personal choices for the renovation of their home, especially compared to a standard social housing renovation process. The participation model started with direct interviews at the kitchen table in 200 households and continued with renovation plans based on the outcome. All renovation measures and improvements were designed and developed from these participatory sessions with the tenants. Every plan of the houses was prepared and drawn into the WoonConnect tool for each tenant, and a guided process accompanied this phase to familiarize them with the platform. This platform allowed tenants to make informed decisions about renovation options. Initially, the project expected a fast process and engagement of the tenants to use the tool. However, it was not until the third year of the project that renovations could start as much of the effort had to go into engaging the tenants and working with the community to renovate their houses. While the development and work around the 3D tool took between two and 3 years, while the execution time of the renovation was less than half a year (Fernandez et al., 2020; Lämmel and Stöffler, 2020). Fig. 3.5 shows one of the houses already renovated with solar panels installed on its roof.

Figure 3.5 Renovation of social housing in the Eckart Vaartbroek neighborhood in Eindhoven (2018). Source: Trinidad Fernandez for Fraunhofer IAO.

While turning citizens into collaborators in the design of services and policies improves the innovativeness and effectiveness of those services, new forms of interaction between government and citizens must be pursued. It is challenging for governments to implement and create participatory spaces and activities in a sustained manner. Governments often struggle with the complexity of processes and issues, the time needed to invest in such methods, the diverging interests at stake in the complex value networks, or the interactions' unclear objectives (Linders, 2012; Cavallini et al., 2016; Walravens, 2016). Reaching the right target group is one of the most important challenges. In the Triangulum project's scope, 70 houses were renovated with EC funding; however, by the end of 2020, Woonbedrijf had continued the renovation of more than twice as many houses by other means. The combination of top-down and bottom-up approaches in the quadruple helix model highlights socially inclusive innovation and meets the aim of leaving no one behind.

Another example of Triangulum inspired co-creation is the Lighting Route in the same neighborhood. The intervention focuses on the smart use of lighting to reduce energy consumption. It provides a testing ground for the development of smart lighting applications in public spaces. The cocreation part of the project was quite exhaustive and involved users and residents' participation, something that is already common in this type of operation. Input was provided by representatives from the community center, health center and the Municipal Sports Department. The whole neighborhood was invited to a design workshop to codesign. The government focused on the ultimate goals of the lighting design: safety for the neighborhood and incentive to exercise, where smart lighting contributes to them. This new park lighting system is sensor activated to maximize and ease the use of the space in the hours of darkness as well as to avoid light pollution and energy waste. The "moving light route" adds extra functionality for runners in the Eindhoven Eckart neighborhood who can guide their run by the lights illuminating in front of them at a set pace. A steady pace, slightly faster, or in intervals can be chosen the lighting sets the running pace. Users can activate the system by stepping on the lighting tiles located at different around the park in a circular route every 20 m. The lights work as pace setters also during the day and are powered with solar energy. The design involved the public, the government, the private sector for possible solutions and the Technical University of Eindhoven. The latter recorded experience and behavior for research purposes: who uses it, what are the user's needs and results, but also to further improve the system as a whole.

10. Outcomes and legacies of the project

To achieve the ambitious implementations, all cities, including the Triangulum consortium members, must comply with national and European legislation. They have also been confronted with the possibilities and barriers of implementing local, national and European objectives. Political willingness, commitment, and support are needed if cities want to achieve smart and sustainable communities.

Cities have shown a strong political commitment that has established long-term strategies beyond the temporality of governments. One example is Eindhoven and its "Brainport" vision aiming to become one of the smartest regions in the world based on strengthening the regional economy based on innovation, creativity, and design. Another example is Manchester, where the results from the monitoring and impact assessment are informing actions to reach the city target and become a zero-carbon city by 2038, 12 years earlier than the UK national 2050 target. These policy decisions have affected each of the intervention elements: low-energy districts, sustainable mobility and ICT. Following engines are driving Stavanger's smart city development ambitions: technology, cross-sectoral cooperation and citizen participation. One landmark of the cooperation between local actors is the Nordic Edge Expo, which takes place every year in Stavanger and is considered the largest smart city event in the Nordic countries. The conference puts Stavanger on the world map as a vibrant and vital region where innovative solutions for a smarter, safer, greener and better world are promoted while accelerating the cooperation and exchange toward smart city development. All three cities have identified the need to address a combination of requirements and incentives to optimize urban development and sustainability (Garcia-Fuentes et al., 2019).

For city development to be successful, it is essential to understand how cities and their citizens behave. Leaders must make decisions regarding for whom, when, and how to manage the city's resources, ideas and potentials. A clear vision, implemented by inspiring and robust leadership, contributes to promoting and implementing innovative plans. The city will emerge as the ideal place for specific sectors and lifestyles, strengthening the administration's core objectives and growth directions. City leaders set the goals and objectives for actions and plans to determine the future of their cities, including the type of people they would like to see living and working in their cities and the type of businesses they would like to see investing in their cities. Decisive, coherent, and coordinated actions are to be taken to attract them and pursue the city goals. Following this vision will help maintain and enhance a city's character and differentiate it from others (KPMG, 2016).

Like living organisms, cities constantly change, so a stagnating or even declining city needs a clear purpose and vision of its future identity, with people as the focus, to reach its destiny and grow. For a city, it is crucial to set geographic, demographic, and thematic priorities; understand the financial sources required for viable projects and actions; and institute a process that leads to a strategic vision, involving key decision-makers and influential stakeholders on its pursuit. It is also essential to incorporate broad and repeated consultation on the plan to ensure everyone's commitment. Once the strategy is launched, it needs to be maintained for several years and progress should be monitored and reviewed periodically and adapted as necessary.

City leaders in Eindhoven focused on the type of businesses or industries they wanted to attract. Triangulum's experience with the development of smart city solutions in this city reveals the city's success as an innovation hub for the Netherlands, creating prosperity, jobs, and building communities.

The experience in Eindhoven reveals that once city leaders have identified whom they want to attract—entrepreneurs, young families, or creative people—the planning begins, where representatives of the target groups must contribute to the planning process. In general, the most successful projects have arisen when city representatives' hand over planning to the end-users to design their own space and allow citizens to identify with their city and its surroundings.

The iCity tender is one of the projects carried out in the Triangulum project to adopt smart city solutions in Eindhoven. The iCity competition aims to challenge enthusiastic entrepreneurs to develop innovative smart city solutions. The top 20 submissions received €5000 each in October 2020, which they used to build a prototype. The competition has yielded remarkable results and opportunities, with 63 companies bidding: 20 further developed their prototype, and 8 obtained additional funding to move closer to the market.

11. Learning from Triangulum

The Triangulum project has demonstrated the importance of establishing strong partnerships to connect and facilitate rapid and joint innovation in smart cities. Smart city processes are driven by strong political and citizens' will, creating new products and services from the private sector and research and innovation from the academic sector. The active participation of all four sectors with a strong focus on citizens and new forms of communication become crucial for the realization and implementation of such projects. Governance approaches such as the quadruple helix model have successfully addressed local and regional urbanization, industrialization, and economic challenges. Strategic partnerships have not only been the key to better interconnectedness but have also formed the basis of the innovation landscape and are one of the main drivers of economic success at all levels.

In Eindhoven, the involvement and commitment in ambitious projects and programs, such as Triangulum, evolved to build an international profile and reputation. While there is no instant or "one-size-fits-all" solution to becoming a lighthouse city, strong partnerships, active involvement of citizens in city planning and an environment of innovation can—based on Triangulum's experience—be considered important preconditions for starting a successful journey toward sustainable and smart urbanism.

Promoting new design tools such as the 3D tool for renovation or codesigning a running route requires training and awareness-raising and a willingness to try something new. The first interventions will always be a challenge, but they will grow and spread to the rest of the neighbors like a snowball effect when successful.

It is worth considering staff training and mentoring, as well as citizen's guidance and participation in the development of technologies within the city. For example, renovations have shown that residents not only choose these improvements because of the energy efficiency and clean energy solutions, but rather because of the services, advantages—also economic—and comfort they bring.

Legal policies are indeed essential supporting factors for the success of this kind of development. In Eindhoven, public policy has been one of the main drivers for smart city solutions. Privileges on the part of the public administration for the realization of such projects have boosted this technology. Other factors, such as incubators for the generation of new projects and the inclusion of entrepreneurs searching for new and innovative technology-based solutions, have contributed to this development.

Citizens' involvement from the very early stages and throughout the process has been crucial to the successful implementation of smart city projects. Considering citizens' needs and preferences from the outset and involving them in the creative design process increases the likelihood of subsequent acceptance. These processes require providing and communicating information in a way that is easy to digest, interpret and work. The more people can visualize and understand a specific solution or application, the easier it is for them to contribute and provide feedback.

References

Borkowska, K., Osborne, M., 2018. Locating the fourth helix: rethinking the role of civil society in developing smart learning cities. International Review of Education 64 (3), 355–372. https://doi.org/10.1007/s11159-018-9723-0.

Calzada, I., Cowie, P., 2017. Beyond data-driven smart city-regions? Rethinking stakeholder-helixes strategies. Regions Magazine 308 (4), 25–28.

Cavallini, S., et al., 2016. Using the quadruple helix approach to accelerate the transfer of research and innovation results to regional growth. Consortium Progress Consulting Srl & Fondazione FoRmit. https://doi.org/10.2863/408040.

EIPO Eindhoven International Project Office, 2015. Background of Brainport Eindhoven. https://eipo.nl/background-eindhoven/#:~:text=The%20company%20started%20building%20houses,on%20the%20Strijp%2DS%20complex.

European Commission, 2010. A European Strategy for Smart, Sustainable and Inclusive Growth. https://ec.europa.eu/eu2020/pdf/COMPLET%20EN%20BARROSO%20%20%20007%20-%20Europe%202020%20-%20EN%20version.pdf.

European Commission CORDIS Research Results, 2015. Triangulum: The Three Point Project (Demonstrate, Disseminate, Replicate). Factsheet. https://cordis.europa.eu/project/id/646578.

European Commission CORDIS Research Results, 2020. Triangulum: The Three Point Project (Demonstrate, Disseminate, Replicate) Periodic Reporting for Period 4. https://cordis.europa.eu/project/id/646578/reporting.

European Commission, 2012. Smart cities and communities. European innovation partnership https://ec.europa.eu/transparency/documents-register/api/files/C(2012)4701_0/de00000000627953?rendition=false. Communication from the Commission.

European Commission, 2018. What are Smart Cities? https://ec.europa.eu/info/eu-regional-and-urban-development/topics/cities-and-urban-development/city-initiatives/smart-cities_en.

European Commission, 2020. State of the Union: Questions & Answers on the 2030 Climate Target Plan. https://ec.europa.eu/commission/presscorner/detail/en/qanda_20_1598.

Fernandez, T., Díaz, C., Stöffler, S., 2020. Smart cities for smarter citizens. Participatory planning in housing renovation using 3D BIM tools: the case of Eckart Vaartbroek. REAL CORP 2020. Shaping Urban Change, ISBN 978-3-9504173-9-5, pp. 761–766. https://doi.org/10.48494/REALCORP2020.9077.

Garcia-Fuentes, M.A., et al., 2019. Policy paper: from dream to reality: sharing experiences from leading European Smart Cities. European Commission Research and Innovation. The Smart Cities and Communities Lighthouse Projects. https://publica.fraunhofer.de/handle/publica/299925.

Gemeente, E., et al., 2018. Living Lab Eckart-Vaartbroek. https://triangulum-project.eu/wp-content/uploads/2018/10/LivingLab-Eckart-Vaartbroek.pdf.

Harrison, C., Donnelly, I.A., 2011. A theory of smart cities. In: Proceedings of the 55th Annual Meeting of the ISSS – 2011. Hull, United Kingdom, vol 55, 1. https://journals.isss.org/index.php/proceedings55th/article/view/1703.
KPMG, 2016. The Future of Cities: Creating a Vision. https://assets.kpmg/content/dam/kpmg/pdf/2016/04/the-future-of-cities-creating-a-vision.pdf.
Lämmel, P., Stöffler, S., 2020. Triangulum - Demonstrate, Disseminate, Replicate: D6.10 Smart City Framework - Update. WP6, Task 6.6. January 2020. https://publica.fraunhofer.de/handle/publica/300466. Fraunhofer Publica.
Linders, D., 2012. From E-government to we-government: defining a typology for citizen coproduction in the age of social media. Government Information Quarterly 29, 446–454. https://doi.org/10.1016/j.giq.2012.06.003.
Padilla, M., Stöffler, S., 2017. On the path towards smart mobility. The journey of three forerunner cities Eindhoven, Manchester and Stavanger. PANTA RHEI—a world in constant motion: 22. In: International Conference on Urban Planning. Regional Development and Information Society; Tagungsband; proceedings REAL CORP, ISBN 978-3-9504173-3-3, pp. 383–390, 2017.
UNDESA, 2018. United Nations, Department of Economic and Social Affairs, Population Division. World Urbanization Prospects: The 2018 Revision, Online Edition. https://population.un.org/wup/Download/.
Walravens, H., 2016. Rückblick auf ein Leben für die Wissenschaft. Orientalistische Literaturzeitung 111 (1), 88–89. https://doi.org/10.1515/olzg-2016-0040, 2016.

Further reading

C40, 2015. Case Study Cities100: Stockholm - Becoming Fossil Fuel-free by 2040. https://www.c40.org/case_studies/cities100-stockholm-becoming-fossil-fuel-free-by-2040.
Lopes, A., Stöffler, F., 2020. Following the Smartness: Leipzig as a Follower City in a Horizon 2020 Smart Cities and Communities Lighthouse Project. REAL CORP 2020. Shaping Urban Change, ISBN 978-3-9504173-9-5, pp. 335–343. https://doi.org/10.48494/REALCORP2020.3106.

4

Transactive electricity: how decentralized renewable power can support security, resilience and decarbonization

Jemma Green, Peter Newman and Peter Droege
CUSP, Curtin University, Perth, Australia

1. Introduction

In the autumn of 2015 a significant tipping point in a particular electricity index emerged: for the first time, electricity from renewables became cheaper than from fossil fuels. The levelized cost of electricity (LCOE) from solar became lower than electricity from coal and natural gas (Fig. 4.1). Wind had already been cheaper than coal and gas for some time, and solar was already cheaper than coal. The cost of solar finally dipping below that of natural gas is a final and highly notable milestone in energy history.

With the cost of solar dropping below that of natural gas, numerous new possibilities and situations were expected to arise that would make renewable energy irresistible.

In Fig. 4.2, solar electricity costs fell by 89%, and those of wind power by 70%, in the 10 years 2009–2019. It is important to see that this is the cost of power as sourced at the generator, not the price to the consumer. These costs include network and grid stabilization costs, but also the many and varied costs added due to line losses, taxes, external cost charges, incumbent system phase-out burdens, and energy use disincentivizing levies.

This chapter will set out the implications of this dramatic shift in the power systems of the world now that solar and renewable are the big winners in the next economy. It will follow through how this revolution in energy is like a Kuhnian revolution (Kuhn, 1996) and already shifts the whole system built around the previous fossil-fuel-based power system. The threats to the system are

Intelligent Environments. https://doi.org/10.1016/B978-0-12-820247-0.00006-0

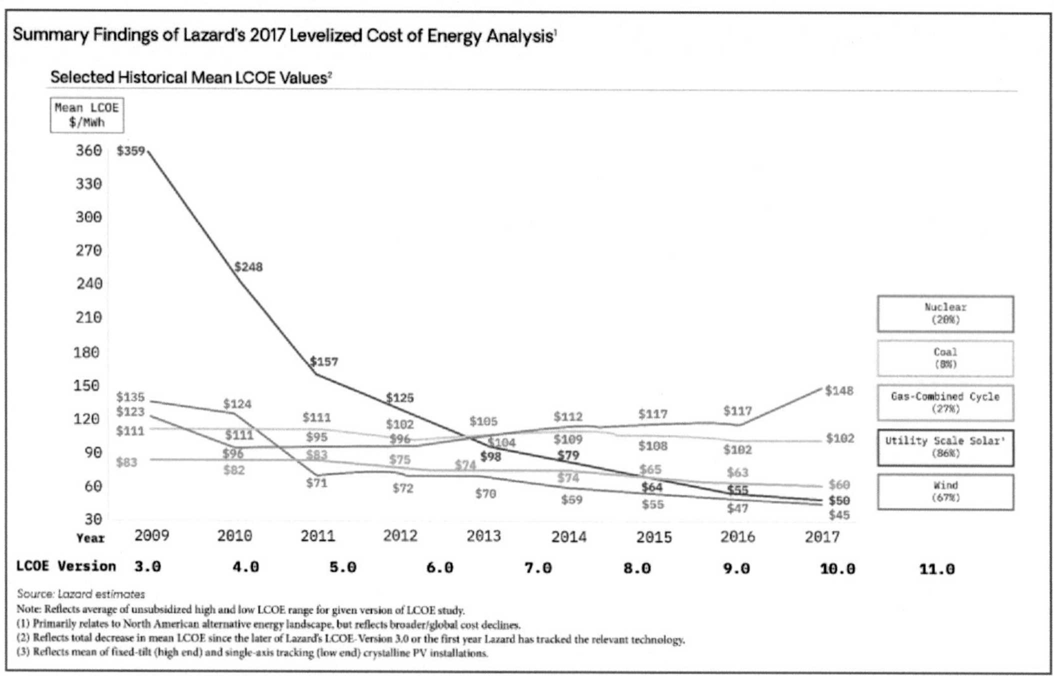

Figure 4.1 Transition in levelized cost of power production. Source: Modified from Lazard (2017).

such that we need a whole new approach that we have called Transactive Electricity, following similar ideas around the tools seen to assist in making a Distributed Energy System or DER, first set out by the Grid-Wise Architecture Council in the US Department of Energy in 2011 (GWAC, 2019; Lezama et al., 2019).

With such trends in costs for renewables at the point of power production, it seemed inevitable to some that coal power and gas for power - their main markets - would become economically unattractive to extract, resulting in the reclassification of many coal and gas fields as stranded assets. Due to the very nature of electricity as a commodity the cost of variable renewable energy (VRE) production, and the price to the consumer, are generally unrelated. As shown in Fig. 4.3 the reduction in the cost of renewables is not necessarily leading to reductions in the price of power. And as outlined in Box 4.1, Germany has high electricity prices, in part due to centralized planning, administrative restrictions, and stifling price signals for renewables - besides the rise in network and network stabilization costs.

This paradox of low-cost wind and solar, and high-cost electricity also came as no surprise to some energy system and energy market experts. J.P. Morgan CIO, Michael Cembalest, and Vaclav

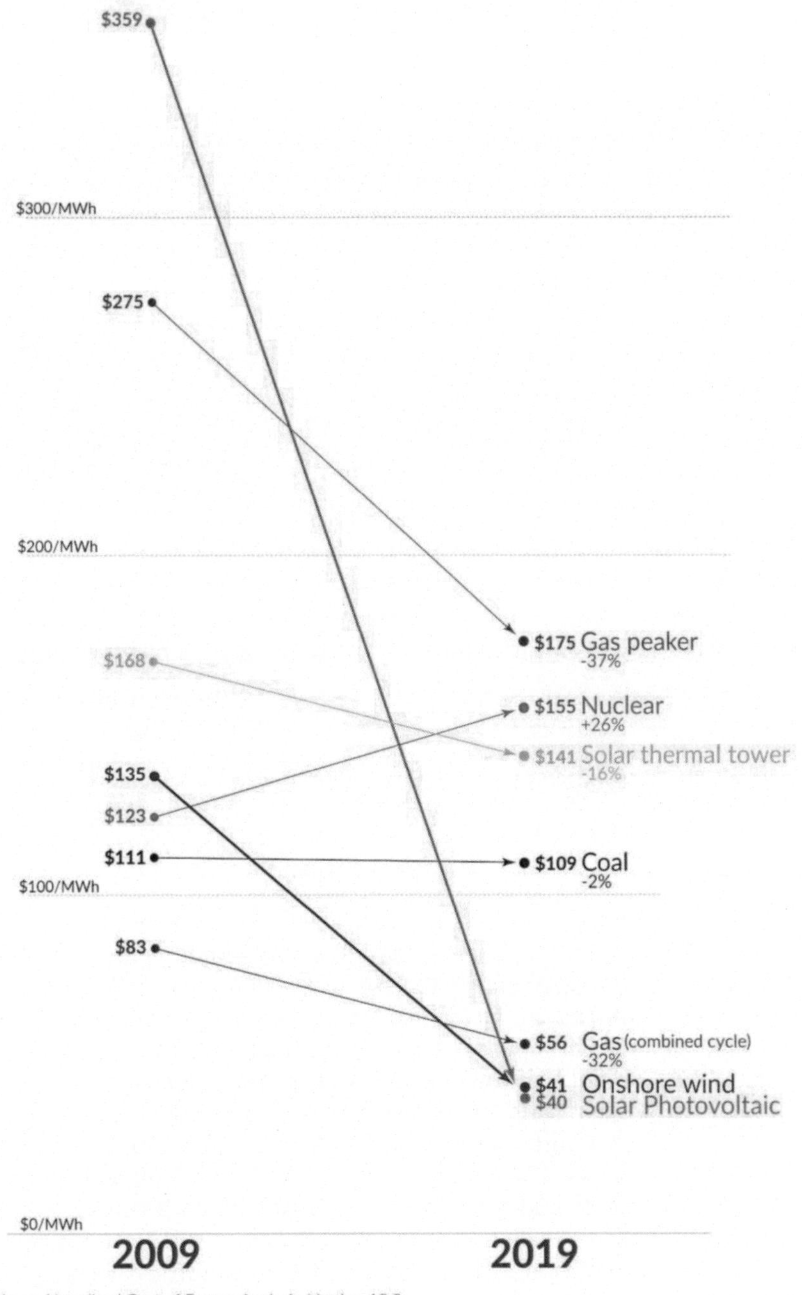

Figure 4.2 Levelized cost of electricity production from new power plants, 2009 to 2019. The cost of onshore wind production declined by 70% in this time period, and the cost of electricity from solar by 89%. The levelized cost of energy (LCOE) contains the new power plant construction costs, lifelong plant operation expenditures and ongoing fuel resource costs. Source: Modified from Roser (2021).

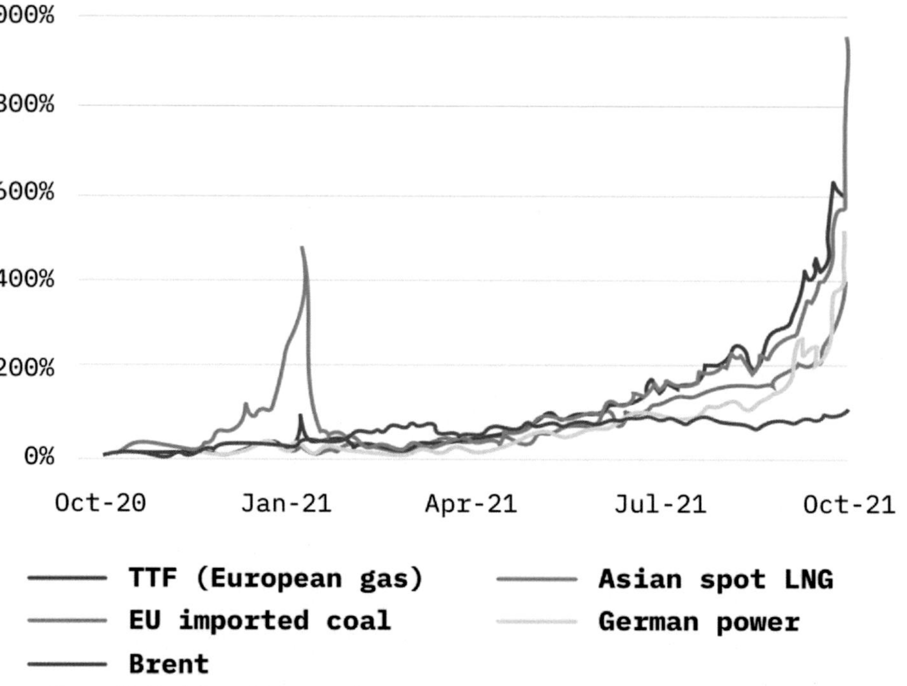

Figure 4.3 Evolution of energy prices. Redrawn by Jemma Green from Brownings (2021).

Smil, a Czech-Canadian scientist, policy analyst, and well-known thinker on energy and its history, noted somewhat archly in their Stargazing piece (2020): "*Thou shalt not conflate the speed of wind and solar cost declines with the speed of de-carbonization.*"

This chapter seeks to illuminate why the reduction in the cost of solar and wind power generation does not necessarily lead to the reduction of fossil fuels if these continue to be supported by traditional approaches to managing energy markets and networks. The chapter suggests that while political change is crucial, time- and place-based price signals in a transactive process are also needed to grow renewables, and the corollary local prosumption, distribution, and storage infrastructure.

The shift from dirty fossil fuels to clean renewables is more than a simple technological transition: a more fundamental, techno-political challenge is to be overcome. It is better understood as the before and after of a paradigm shift, one that needs an extended

Box 4.1 Germany's three-way problem highlights the renewables transition challenge

Germany has been a leader in pushing the renewable power agenda for many decades, inaugurating and using a highly effective feed-in tariff-based renewable energy producer compensation system since 2000. This system was designed to be phased out as renewable energy costs declined and markets expanded. But just at the moment when wind power became cheaper than coal and gas Germany did not cut its ties with lignite coal within its borders but extended the phase-out to 2038, due to the firm grip by incumbent interests on local, state, and national policies. Germany did not distance itself from natural gas either, Russian or otherwise—and began to double down on the limiting of distributed renewable energy especially, under heavy incumbent industry pressure. It had, however, already committed to exiting its nuclear program in 2000, and then again in 2011—after the year of the catastrophic Fukushima reactor melt-downs (Anzai et al., 2011).

Germany's actions had several consequences. According to McKinsey's report, *Germany energy transition: A country at a crossroads* (Pflugmann et al., 2019), the nation became home to some of the highest-priced electricity and missed carbon dioxide reduction targets. Wind power may have been the cheapest to produce in Germany, but that did not mitigate the fact that German residential customers experienced some of the highest electricity tariffs in Europe.

The McKinsey report is not the only one to highlight Germany's plight; auditor reports emerged highlighting high prices with potential undersupply risks (Wacket, 2021). New restrictive government auctioning systems with high transaction and bidding costs, and fixed ceilings placed on the permissible wind or solar energy maxima led to a dramatic drop in investment and new installations in solar and wind, and a collapse in the previously thriving renewable energy employment market.

The situation in Germany highlights the pitfalls of stifling the rapid renewable energy transition by insisting on a centralized, conventional power system for too long.

period of time to take place and bears the classic hallmarks of a Kuhnian revolution or paradigm shift (Kuhn, 1996). In Kuhnian terms, distributed electricity as a paradigm is incompatible with centralized electricity and the two sides simply do not integrate well. This is also the approach of the socio-technical transitions movement that recognizes the need to address issues concerning regulations and professional practice in any technological transformation (Geels, 2017). This chapter recognizes that there are many barriers to the shift, but they are not beyond the scope of small towns, cities, regions, and nations. In fact, much of this shift will occur in buildings within cities, as they become new sources of grid energy and grid stability and in the coming additional component of transactivity, which is how the electric vehicle will fit into the grid from a multitude of sites throughout the grid (Newman, 2020).

Solar and wind cannot just be simple substitutes for nuclear, coal, or gas for a range of reasons that form the basis for the rest of this chapter. Solar and wind, located in close proximity to consumption, and supported by storage - mostly from batteries in homes, businesses, communities, and electric vehicles - are variable sources capable of supplying users virtually on demand at the lowest volume of energy required at a particular time in a particular location. Nuclear and coal reactors have been generally relegated outside of major cities and hence the traditional, highly centralized grids with substantial transmission and distribution systems have grown throughout the 20th century, becoming more and more interlinked across continents—but leaving communities and industries as hapless consumers, as vulnerable to cyber-attacks, ransomware extortion, climate change, terrorism and natural disasters as the incumbent infrastructural behemoths of yesterday. The same can be said about transcontinental gas and oil pipelines.

To function efficiently, distributed energy systems require local storage together with mechanisms of sharing and managing these cheap and clean resources locally. The structures for this change are likely to be distributed "citizen utilities" that are managed still within a broader grid framework (Green and Newman, 2017a). This means a completely new business model and a new architecture for energy systems and markets that we have called the Transactive Electricity system. Only by taking these major system-wide changes seriously will the world be able to absorb a tripling in the renewable power system within this decade as outlined by the IPCC (2021). Below we discuss some of the issues and the key features that are needed in a 21st-century decarbonized Transactive Electricity grid.

2. The security and resilience challenge

Cyber-attacks have been increasing on all 21st century infrastructure. Conventional energy systems have long become run by digital systems so nuclear power plants, coal reactors, and continental oil pipelines have all long become targets for terrorist cyber-attacks, assaults by ransomware extortionists, and ordinary hacks as well as accidental crashes that can bring down large grids. There are new considerations in cybersecurity that are necessary if a more localized, transactive grid becomes the new normal in citizen utilities (Green and Newman, 2017b).

Surveillance capitalism (Zuboff, 2019), has increasingly manifested itself in the siphoning off and exploitation of massive data streams from web operations, search engines, and social media platforms—but also from smart grids, smart meters, and multilateral energy trading regimes. Governments and corporations use their surveillance capabilities to encroach into realms of privacy and personal liberty. These matters are the focus of researchers and utilities increasingly seeking ways to manage such data flows to avoid them being altered, corrupted, sabotaged, or stolen (Dasgupta et al., 2021).

Distributed renewables have long been seen as being in a country's potential national security interest and both climate change and cyber security challenges drive performance demands from the protocols and redundant yet secure, encrypted, and island-based tangles of distributed energy supply and demand ecosystems. Much more work on the cybersecurity aspects of any future power system is going to be needed but it is possible to see that a distributed, decentralized power grid, like the internet, can indeed be at once more secure and resilient and yet potentially viral-attack prone than a highly centralized grid with a few very obvious large power generators. The details of this security issue are outlined below.

Resilience is also a growing issue as the world warms and more energy enters the climate system each year. Climate change heating and drying up of rivers used for cooling reactors have already led to shutdowns of power plants. High-tension transmission lines have failed under high temperatures. Sudden freezing events brought about by a destabilized Arctic polar vortex have driven extreme disturbances by stratospheric heat waves and damaged grids across the northern hemisphere. One of these frost events collapsed the Texan gas supply system in early 2021; the entire conventional, brittle centralized energy system and its reliance on nuclear and gas failed, abruptly exposing communities to subzero temperatures.

Fluctuations in power prices are inevitable in such a warming world but are also caused by the changing of fuels and associated systems. In the 2020s it occurred in the power, oil, and gas sectors as shown in Fig. 4.3.

Such fluctuations and rising resilience issues are likely to be seen as the key character of the post-Covid economy of the 2020s. In response, the world is under pressure to remove fossil fuels and reduce the potential impacts of a warming climate. But few see that the necessary rush to renewables will need a much deeper commitment to a more appropriate localized, transactive grid.

3. The dispatchability deficit and transactive energy

The common argument against solar panels and wind turbines is that they are not like-for-like replacements for coal, nuclear, and gas, i.e., that they are not dispatchable: they cannot be summoned, nor delivered at will or short notice - unless provided with batteries, hydro and other forms of storage.

Implicit in the architecture of a traditional grid with its large power stations, transmission lines, and distribution system is the seemingly high reliability and dependability required from the central source of energy—until they fail. Coal and nuclear are capable of generating electricity consistently and generally without unplanned interruption, regardless of the weather and time of the year within narrow temperature margins. It is described as providing baseload power because the old grid was designed for a more predictable generation and demand of electricity.

3.1 Variable energy

The locations of nuclear and fossil generation sites were decided many years ago by striking a compromise between distance to load centers and balancing this with the environmental threat to the population. This placed them at a medium to the long distance from the center of the populations. Variable renewable energy sources do not present these environmental threats and hence can be brought close to where the power is going to be used, even sitting on the roof of the consumer's home or work.

Transmission can represent the most expensive part of electricity and often accounts for up to 45% of total costs (Fant et al., 2020). So, if solar fields and wind arrays simply replace an aging coal-fired power station, for example, it will lower emissions but not save much cost even though existing wiring could be used to achieve bringing the power back to the center. It also forces upgrades or flexibility management of the electrical congestion created when the variability overshoots the capacity of the lines. There are many similar potential additional costs of renewable energy sources unless the model is changed to a different market system that addresses the new needs and the very systems architecture of the new energy paradigm.

Variability can create a problem for the grid with the need for extra power resources to be ready when weather conditions or time of day require it. This is where high-capacity-battery or pumped-hydro storage is needed to allow the centralized system to be maintained. But this can consume a lot of land area for the extra renewable power. There is no shortage of solar and wind but there is a shortage of land, especially near cities, to produce the power from these sources although in some places the use of off-shore wind has been able to reduce this conflict —but here, too, new direct current transmission lines may be needed. However, the generation and transmission costs are still high and hence this centralized-renewables approach to power will remain costly. Importantly, it concentrates control and economic benefits on corporations rather than communities, which could also readily become contributors and beneficiaries of a renewable energy paradigm, and even its owners and operators.

Large-scale, stand-alone renewable power sources are the fastest growing among renewables today though recent trends are favoring small-scale roof-top photovoltaics (REN21, 2021). Large-scale systems require land and space at great distances from the center of population. Clearly some of this is needed, but to drive system efficiencies, price signals should encourage distributed agglomerations of energy generation and consumption. When electricity is needed to process minerals or create manufactured products then this may work well being located where such industries are likely to be. If a settlement just needs to be focused and low-power intensity needs then they may work better being situated inside the settlement—such as distributed on its rooftops.

Electricity system planning that only looks at network planning will be flawed if it only considers wholesale upgrades of transmission infrastructure without also first analyzing how much of that could be reduced by maximizing the consumption of renewable energy in the distribution part of the grid. A cellular approach to energy significantly reducing distribution transmission costs and interrupting the correlation seen in expenditures on renewables and on networks is needed—a trend that is beginning to be shown in Fig. 4.4.

3.2 Local energy markets

The way to drive efficiencies in the transmission is to address the duck curve as shown in Fig. 4.5. Solar panels produce electricity at a peak during the middle of the day, but the peak demand for residential electricity is usually during the evening. This creates a curve of deficit that resembles a duck's head and bill. The same issue exists for excess wind, albeit at different times

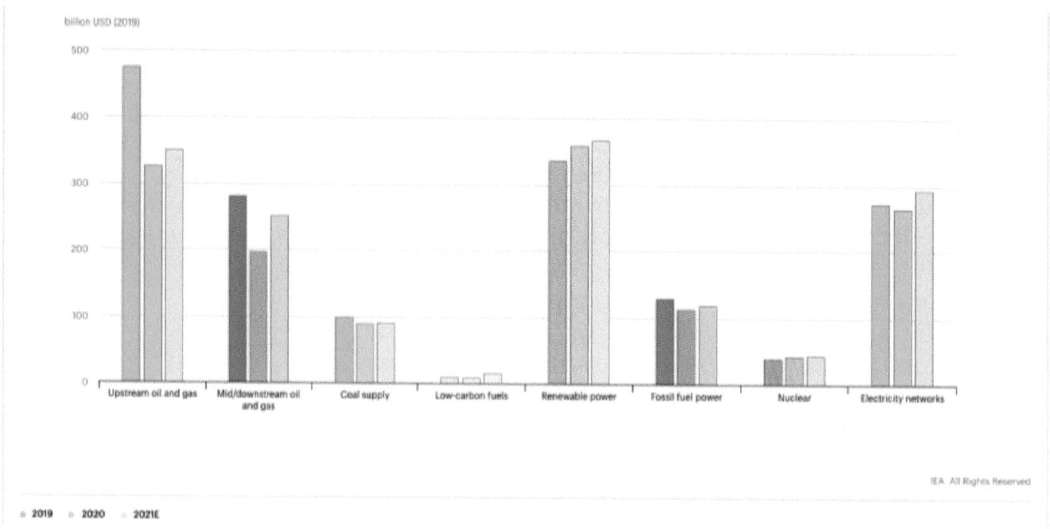

Figure 4.4 Global energy supply investment by sector, 2019–21. Source: Modified from IEA (2021).

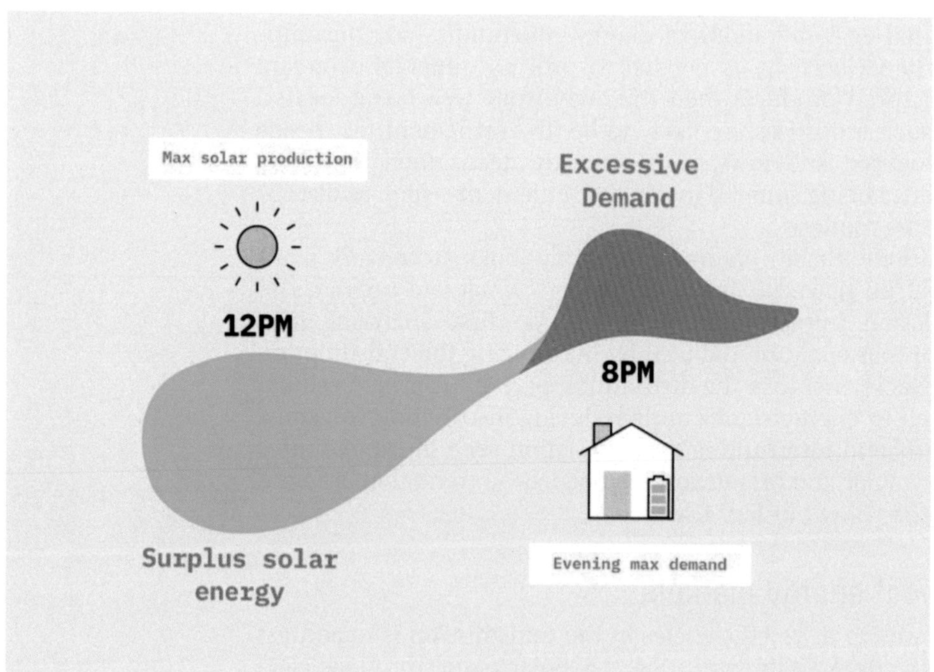

Figure 4.5 The "duck curve" shows that time of variability in renewables does not coincide with demand in the residential sector. Courtesy of Jemma Green.

of the day. In total, these are grid limit violations where supply exceeds demand at a particular time and place.

The solution to the duck curve and efficient expansion of network infrastructure is time and place-based transactive electricity. This is the basis of managing distributed energy to fit the demand for instantaneous, daily, and seasonal power requirements. To do so efficiently requires a comprehensive reconfiguration of electricity systems and markets, allowing trading of power to occur between prosumers and consumers in a discrete part of a grid such as a substation or a feeder. And in doing so, this increase in the number of electricity transactions between producers and consumers reduces grid export during the day and import at night as shown in Fig. 4.6 and outlined further below.

Schema A: NEM + ToU + PV (standard supply system).

Schema B: NEM + ToU + PV + R_BESS (Self-Consumption).

Schema C: NEM + ToU + PV + R_BESS (P2P Trade).

Fig. 4.6 shows how local energy markets including net energy metering, and time of use tariffs with solar and batteries can reduce the duck curve by 37% in the day and 25% in the evening with existing network pricing. Under this arrangement, network

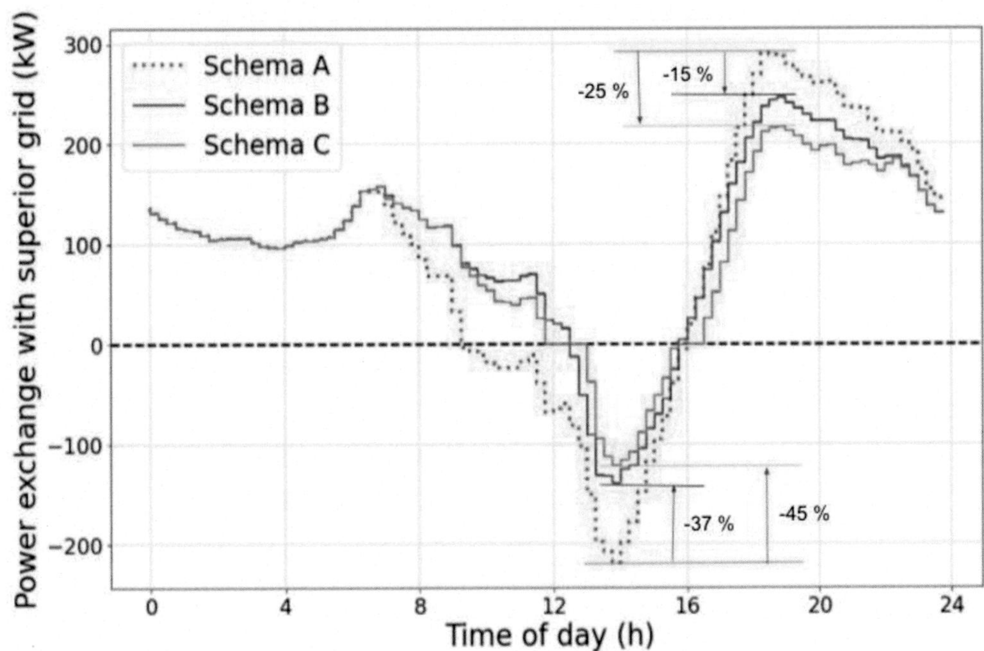

Figure 4.6 Reducing the duck curve with transactive power systems. Source: Modified from Powerledger, AusGrid, Australia.

income and electricity retailer margins would remain stable and consumers would be better off. The research showed that grid export can be reduced by a further 12% during the day and import by 10% in the evening with changes in pricing.

Time and place-based transactive electricity is an enabler of this distributed reconfiguration; it involves energy shared and traded in relatively small amounts by large numbers of participants. This concept of transactive energy is sometimes referred to as interoperability - it is about how the sources for control in a grid become in the millions rather than the few major power plants that managers use to control a traditional centralized grid. These millions of transactions are created by prosumers interacting with each other, managed by smart technology systems programmed to allow the distributed grid to be optimized for the outcomes sought. It is a rapid and multi-directional process like the internet and indeed it is best understood as an Internet of Energy (Strielkowski et al., 2019).

As distributed, transactive or peer-to-peer exchanges become commonplace, they start to replace the central feed of power. The distribution network becomes a major source of consistent electricity and grid services, a storage system in itself. This makes for a more cellular structure as explained further below, involving connected microgrids and virtual powerplants as well as a series of market mechanisms. The transactive grid embraces not just the energy production and consumption "prosumers" that are distributed, but everything else too: the storage systems, the fault protection systems, the regulatory systems, and the economic signal and pricing systems. The entire management system and business model of the grid have to adapt to being distributed and transactive if the scaling of renewables is to occur efficiently.

The chapter will therefore consider how all the features of the distributed, Transactive Electricity grid are integrated into a new socio-technical system and there is evidence of how it is emerging in many global experiments.

4. Decentralization of price—from FIT to transactive electricity storage

The main policy approach to help create more renewables in the grid has been to compensate solar panel owners through a subsidized feed-in tariff or FIT. This was still part of the centralized fixed grid system, but by necessity depended on a distributed producer reward system at preset prices or blunt price signals. Continents, countries, and states keen to meet renewable energy targets set high subsidized feed-in tariffs to make it possible for people to invest in solar and wind resources—and to compensate for the massive fossil fuel subsidies that totaled 5.9 trillion USD after tax in 2020 (IEA, 2021). Naturally, this resulted in a building and employment boom for renewable resources, helping to establish the culture of believing in solar as a credible solution to energy problems in the 21st Century.

Subsidized FiTs were designed to be lowered gradually to allow for renewable generation prices to come down enough for growth to continue without subsidy. Since around 2021, many of the feed-in tariffs around the world have been retired, but fixed price feed-in tariff structures persist, under electricity tariff offerings. The tariff rates are supposed to be reflective of an average of the yearly price of energy during the day. This blunt price signal still results in the duck curve albeit with less of an economic impact on the taxpayer, still creating economic impacts on the grid.

Fixed tariffs and FiTs, as instruments of balancing supply and demand in different geographical locations within an electricity grid, are very limited. In the absence of appropriate, fossil-fuel subsidy-free market mechanisms, and the elimination of political interference the curtailment of renewables is prevalent and growing. Transparent or otherwise: it discourages the uptake of VRE, ironically against overt policies to promote renewables. Curtailment is also politically bad, particularly if penalizing solar over high carbon energy.

Another intervention being pursued to address the deficiencies of centralized planning of renewables, with FiTs is charging renewables to export. This punitive system applied often ex-posttax, is generally seen as a bad taxation principle. Furthermore, this approach will encourage battery sizing for self-sufficiency only which will reduce grid utilization and net income. Consumers without financial ability to procure storage will be forced to buy electricity from the grid at high grid tariff rates. Prosumers with adequate financial capability would also be constrained to procure higher-sized batteries besides the fact that it is difficult to optimize battery sizing to fit exactly to self-sufficiency requirements.

A far better approach, without perverse outcomes, is to match supply and demand and address phenomena like the duck curve or other forms of grid violations, time and place-based price signals, i.e., dynamic rather than flat FiT price signals are needed. This will provide an additional economic opportunity for these energy generation and storage assets beyond self-consumption and participating in wholesale energy and ancillary services markets, thereby enhancing the return on investment in them. This would maintain grid utilization and network income.

But how can this be realized? If a distributed grid is to price the millions of transactions across its system there is a need to generate a price based on the market-grid interaction. This pricing can maintain a quality power system and reduce overall costs. The typical household scenario is that a distributed, transactive grid should pay households to charge their battery and discharge it when it is needed. The grid avoids having to curtail the output, as well as the evening peak production of electricity. It can defer or eliminate the need to augment the network to accommodate DERs. It can be a source of network services such as voltage and reactive power. The distributed price signal has done its job when this happens. The bigger the differential in price over the shortest time and distance in space, and the more often this happens, the larger the incentive. This is the missing link of a price signal that explains why renewables are so problematic if pursued in a centralized grid environment.

Once this is seen and the grid is built around the architecture not just of variable renewable energy production but also storage, then the cost of the system can be reduced even further. The key factor is not the technology of storage so much as how the transactive process links variable renewable power production and storage into the demands of the economic system.

5. Decentralizing and distributing the grid: optimizing digital technology with a purpose

In a distributed, transactive model among households, houses, or energy communities of the real or virtual kind, prices can be determined in a very different way. This can occur using customer choices, and a supply and demand model in an extensive microeconomy of prosumers transacting in peer-to-peer trading. Digital technology to help manage distributed, transactive power, is primarily artificial intelligence, machine learning, and blockchain for record-keeping, automated complex trading at scale, and settlement.

The following describes how such a model operates to create an Internet of Energy (Kaffle et al., 2016), in an automated electricity infrastructure yielding locally optimized outcomes in a flexible and agile distributed grid.

A digital energy system can be optimized to maximize the flow of local solar energy from the consumer's roof and to retrieve solar-based energy from a shared storage system so that by virtue of peer-to-peer trading the system effectively is 100% percent solar. This can be managed across the grid and within a microgrid, residing physically distinct in a larger grid.

Once close proximity energy sharing or trading of electricity is established in a market, the amount of transactions becomes significantly larger compared to that of a classical network operator charging consumers for a month's electrical usage. This is the nature of peer-to-peer trading. And while the number of transactions is large, the actual amounts of energy transacted in any one trade can be quite small. This opens up the possibility that a large and corrupt player or group of players could subvert the many transactions by a small amount, much the way the LIBOR rate was manipulated by rogue Barclay traders (Elliot, 2012).

This is where blockchain can become significant as it is a block of data produced in a way that is completely impossible to manipulate, hack or copy. By basing the entire edifice on a completely trustable decentralized blockchain rather than a vulnerable centralized system, this risk of corruption is removed.

We don't advocate entrusting the entire energy supply to a single digital system—a hyperweb of energy. This would be risky and may not even be impossible. Rather in the future state, we suggest the assembly of smart, largely energy autonomous buildings, user hubs, and communities. In this upgraded grid, they only require a modicum of data exchange to connect via a shared grid—without universal access to all points everywhere. The notional IoT equivalent—a ubiquitous IoE—would not be a desirable or even workable model.

The solution to this potential vulnerability then is another layer of decentralization. Under a decentralized model, the central bank or electrical retailer would be replaced by a blockchain-enabled transaction and settlement system. In this regime, many small transactions can be undertaken while keeping the system incorruptible. The management of a blockchain system of peer-to-peer trading can be distributed into a series of local areas or groups that are able to respond to their needs directly but are also part of the broader grid.

In the decentralized transactive and settlement scheme, a network of verification agents confirms a series of transactions that are written into a blockchain. They do this by setting original mathematical problems for the rest of the network to solve, which demand a certain amount of computing power and work. These mathematical problems are ways of validating the transactions without a central trusted agency. A decentralized scheme is responsible for making it impossible to write false entries into a spreadsheet containing all the transactions between peer groups exchanging electricity and money in the form of a digital currency. This approach also allows instantaneous settlement at each time period interval within the energy market, in itself improving market behavior.

6. How does the distributed, transactive electricity grid work?

The starting point for this is net electricity metering from the consumer's solar PV system, then offsetting or reducing electricity bills by a corresponding amount. This way the system provides a time-based credit for any excess of solar energy generated. This option reduces energy imports from the grid and promotes efficient production and consumption.

Some places have introduced an evolution of this, known as virtual net metering, which allows for the credit accumulated to be shared against another meter's bills, so if a prosumer has several houses or buildings the excess can be shared amongst them. This is not peer-to-peer energy trading, which is much more transactive and forms the basis for how the Internet of Energy works. For this to happen, consumers need to set their own "buy and sell" prices for energy. The market created on the energy trading platform is a dynamic one, acting like an auction pool. Each individual can be a market actor, setting a price that influences market behavior. A prosumer sets both a minimum sell price and a maximum buy price. A consumer sets a maximum buy price only. The available energy to trade is settled among these participants, matching their bids and offers in a way that rewards the prosumers that set the lowest price they are willing to accept, and rewards the buyers that set the highest price they are willing to pay. The whole process is automated based on local needs and with local energy managers and regulations set by governments through utilities.

The software that can enable this local energy market operates in concert with a number of virtual and physical elements (Fig. 4.7).

The Physical Layer includes the grid connection, metering hardware, and communication infrastructure.

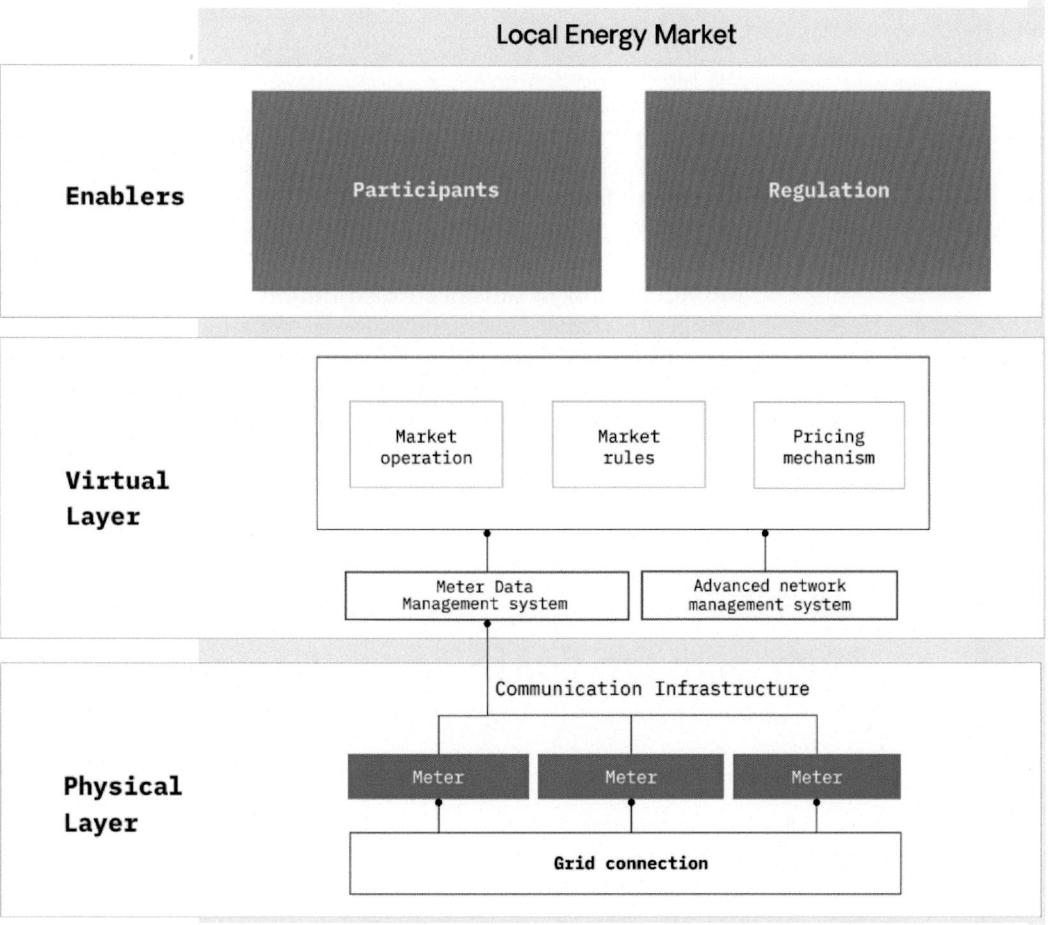

Figure 4.7 Elements of the distributed, transactive electricity grid for a local market. By the authors.

The Virtual Layer includes the marketplace information system incorporating an accessible user interface where the market participants interact through their bids and offers. This system is also required to provide market participants with their energy and trading data in real-time, to ensure efficient market outcomes, depending on the time-horizon for market activities. Additionally, this marketplace information system will be responsible for the market operation - matching buyers and sellers and providing settlement of trading activity, required at the granularity of market intervals and multiplied by the number of market participants.

Also in the Virtual Layer is the meter data management system, which stores the generation and consumption data from the metering infrastructure in the Physical Layer.

The Enablers Layer consists of the participants and the regulations that enable the system to have an operational framework. The market rules and operations are required to be designed into the marketplace information system. These are not necessarily simple design transpositions from other energy markets as they depend on the dynamic requirements of the network. Therefore, the integration of advanced distribution management systems, within the Virtual Layer, allows for the location and state of connected network resources to be known, along with power quality, in order to inform market events for market participant response.

Peer-to-peer energy trading suggests that the engagement of users is typically driven by the control they have of their benefit,

Box 4.2 Distributed, transactive electricity case study one: the der in perth, Western Australia

Australia is a global leader in distributed solar uptake rates with Western Australia being among the highest Australian jurisdictions. Unlike other locations where solar has primarily been associated with utility or large commercial installations, uptake in Australia has been largely driven by small household installations. Almost one in three homes in the South West Integrated System (SWIS) has solar PVs, with more than 3000 households adding a solar PV system each month. AEMO estimates that 50% of households will have solar PVs in the next 10 years.

The popularity of rooftop solar PVs in Western Australia is driven by a favorable climate and solar resources, high levels of homeownership and suitable housing, installer competition, and financial incentives, including beneficial tariff structures and government subsidy programs. Rooftop solar PVs are ideally suited to the Western Australian climate. SWIS experiences an annualized average of 8.8 h of sunlight a day, and Perth has the highest number of cloud-free days of all Australian capital cities.

Over 75% of all dwellings in Western Australia are free-standing houses, with medium- and high-density dwellings accounting for 21% of the housing in 2016. Residential lot sizes are also larger than the Australian average, leading to larger roof areas ideal for rooftop solar PVs.

Unlike other grids, SWIS is unable to rely on interconnections for system support services to maintain voltage and frequency when there is a large contribution from nonsynchronous intermittent generation. The Western Australian government responded to this rapidly approaching challenge by launching an Energy Transformation Strategy. This also addressed the opportunities presented by the energy upgrade to renewable and distributed energy technologies. The strategy contains three interlinked pieces of work:

- ✓ *a new market design*, to respond to the need to integrate high levels of renewables
- ✓ *the Whole of System Plan*, to identify through scenario modeling the least-cost investment required in a large-scale generation, transmission, and energy storage and to identify emerging challenges for SWIS over a 20-year horizon
- ✓ *the DER Roadmap*, to safely and reliably integrate customer DERs in SWIS.

Distributed, transactive electricity case study one: the der in perth, Western Australia—Cont'd

Storage is viewed as an essential component to ensure power system stability and security in a high-DER environment. Uptake of behind-the-meter storage is currently low in SWIS as high technology costs and a flat tariff structure have prevented storage systems from providing an attractive economic proposition for households. However, the use of front-of-the-meter battery storage in the distribution grid provides an opportunity to unlock the full capability of storage across the electricity service value chain. They offer economies of scale for technology and installation costs while presenting a chance for more efficient coordination of storage capacity to provide broader benefits.

A distribution-connected battery can be located in areas to provide localized network benefits. For example, batteries can be operated to store energy generated by local solar PVs and exported later during the evening peak. This can help distribution feeders that are under thermal stress and defer the need for costly network augmentation by reducing energy flows across low-and medium-voltage distribution transformers at these times. At sufficient numbers and capacity, several distribution-connected batteries can be coordinated to respond to broader system requirements and deliver market services.

This Box is a quote from the paper by Hadingham et al. (2021) Distributed Energy Resources Roadmap, IEEE Power and Energy, 19(5) pages 76–88.

Case study two: Quartier Storm, Switzerland

For 1 year, 37 households in Walenstadt traded locally produced solar power within their own neighborhood. Participants could directly buy and sell solar power within their neighborhood via a portal on which the participants could set their own purchase and sales price limits for solar power. The resulting transactions were processed automatically via a blockchain. The local electricity supplier, Water and Electricity Works Walenstadt (WEW) provided access to its distribution grid but also purchased surplus solar power and supplied the community with 'normal' power when the supply of solar power was insufficient. The aim as with Renew Nexus was to verify technical feasibility and also to study user behavior.

"The basic idea of the Quartierstrom project is for locally produced solar power to be consumed locally. In this local electricity market, local residents buy and sell solar power among themselves."

"One new feature of the system was that participants could use a portal to set a minimum sales price for their solar power and a maximum purchase price to buy solar power from their neighbors. The participants frequently adjusted the price limits, especially at the beginning. But the price limit they set for buying local solar power was rarely higher than for normal power from the grid," says Tiefenbeck. On average, the participants were willing to pay just under 19 centimes per kilowatt hour—less than the cost of mains power, which stands at 20.75 centimes. Fewer than 10% of offers were above this rate, despite the fact that many people had declared their willingness to pay more for local solar electricity in the surveys conducted beforehand.

"This gap between attitude and action is seen in behavioral research time and time again," says Tiefenbeck. The researchers also attribute this to the fact that the participating households knew that local solar power was subject to lower grid fees and that, accordingly, the power suppliers were getting more for their power, even at lower prices. For their part, the households with solar power systems also sought to make a proFiT, asking for around 7 centimes per kilowatt hour. When selling to the power plant they made only 4 centimes.

not necessarily in the act of trading itself, which becomes automated - see also the following case studies below.

Emerging examples of how the system set out in Fig. 4.5 can work are now appearing as illustrated in Box 4.2.

Such trials strongly suggest that agile, flexible pricing could become commonplace when prosumers are presented with the opportunity to transact electricity on their own terms and have the technology of storage available to them. This emergent behavior is an important cornerstone of distributed electricity. However, the use of smart technology systems is also necessary to make millions of transactions be rapidly optimized in a transparent and trustworthy way.

The electrical grid is one of the great systems created in the 20th century for growth in productivity and equity. It is changing now to accommodate variable renewables but must continue to provide both productivity and equity. This requires new regulations that are enabling the new distributed market, not regulations from the traditional centralized grid. The distributed, transactive grid also needs various new market mechanisms to enable it to flourish.

7. Market mechanisms for a distributed, transactive electricity grid

Centralized electricity systems across the world with growing amounts of variable renewables are beginning the journey toward energy market services for a distributed transactive grid. There are three ways this is happening: Tendering Mechanisms, Renewable Energy Certificates, and Flexibility Services.

7.1 Feed in tariffs

Tendering mechanisms for power purchase agreements (PPAs) have grown in popularity in the past decade with many multinationals, corporates, and governments buying renewable energy directly from the generator via a PPA. If the electricity demand profile of the PPA buyer is matched by the PPA, i.e., supply and demand are matched, then the grid system can remain stable. However often this is not the case and the energy is dispatched into the grid, the associated renewable energy certificates (RECs) are retained and energy is purchased at other times to match against the load profile. Virtual PPAs exacerbate this kind of financial arbitrage activity that may happen in two different electricity grids. For example, a company may purchase a PPA in Texas to cover load demand in California. Like the FiT, when only a small number of consumers were doing these things, it didn't have much of an impact on the grid, but as this has grown in popularity, grid impacts are becoming significant.

In Fig. 4.8 we can see that the number of countries with FiTs plateaued in about 2013 and the growth is now in tendering for procurement of renewable energy from PPAs and VPPAs.

At their peak, there were 115 FiT schemes globally, but of these only 69 remain active, with at least four announced to end in 2021—as they were intended to.

Of those FiT schemes remaining, as the price of solar has come down and penetration has gone up, many jurisdictions have reduced the FiT to be a closer reflection of average wholesale electricity rates—see Table 4.1.

Whilst at first glance it may seem that fixing the FiT price to the average wholesale energy rate is a fair and sensible approach,

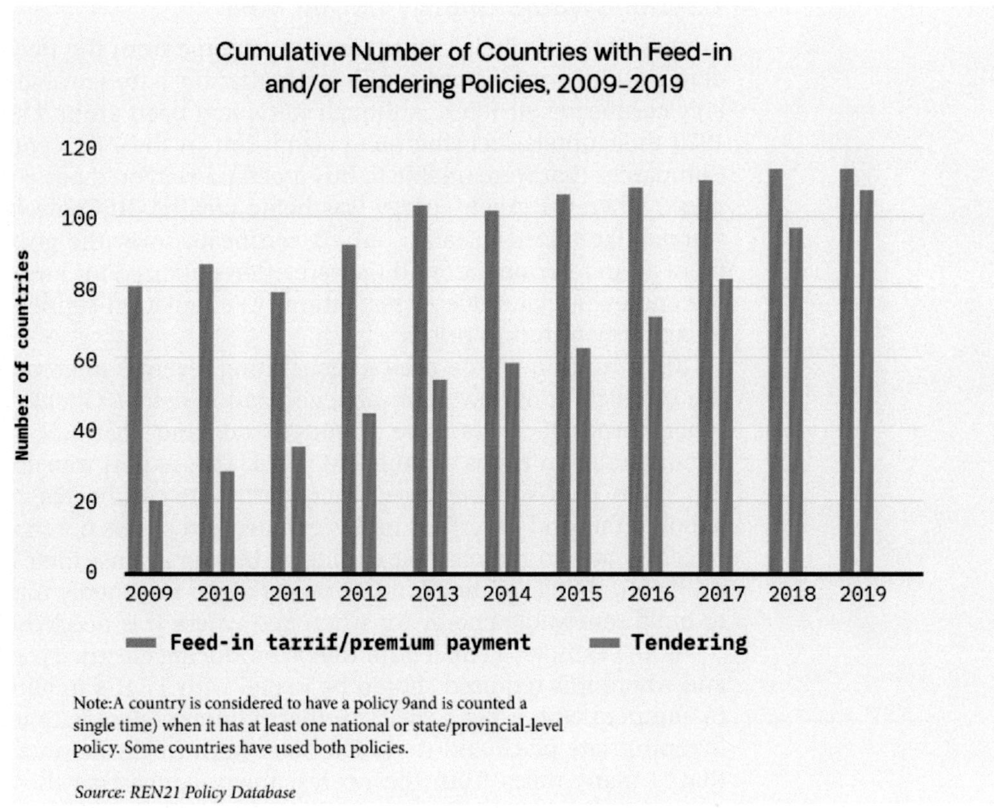

Figure 4.8 Comparison of feed-in tariff policies to tendering policies. Source: Modified from REN21.

Table 4.1 Comparison of FiT and wholesale/retail power rates in selected countries.

Country/State	Average wholesale rate range	Average retail energy rate	Feed-in-tariff
France	4–8 €c/kWh	11 €c/kWh	18.73 €c/kWh
Austria	4.1–9.1 €c/kWh	16–24 €c/kWh	7.91 € cent/kWh for PV at buildings
Western Australia	5 c/kWh	28.8229 c/kWh	3 c/kWh all other times 9 c/kWh 3–9p.m.

Source: Modified from REN21.

an average wholesale price signal does not produce supply and demand equilibrium in the electricity grid.

7.2 Renewable energy certificates

One of the financial instruments to emerge from the need to demonstrate commitment to decarbonization is renewable energy certificates or RECs. Although RECs had been around since 1970 their uptake became quite significant in the 21st century. Companies that were unable to buy green power could pay a premium wherever green energy was being created. RECs de facto worked like a feed-in tariff, but via certificates over the government as an intermediator. RECs were often criticized for lowering the energy upgrade due to restrictions in circulation supply and uncertainty in future prices.

RECs continue to be used in generating revenue to stimulate the installation of new renewable generation assets. Google and other corporate users have begun to demand that RECs are denominated in terms of time and place. This in part transforms RECs into TEACs - time-based energy attribute certificates - into a tool of the kind described in this chapter and allows purchasers of certificates to match their certificate buying against their load profile. In doing so, they send price signals to the energy market to build renewable energy for when and where it is needed.

As an example, a small farm that is producing electricity when and where it is required should be issued with TEACs to allow it to compete with a big solar farm that produces electricity in an inappropriate place and time. The solar farm might be on a site that is many miles from the nearest town, congesting the grid and requiring a hydro storage plant to manage the time differential. In this example, the small farm has much more value in terms of decarbonization for the grid than the big one as it is being used most of the time, whereas the solar farm's power may have to be shed when it is congesting the grid. Time-denominated RECs create more sophisticated incentives for the supply of renewable energy, and until blanket incentives are eliminated, this efficiency cost problem may bedevil the electricity industry.

7.3 Flexibility services

As renewable energy generation has grown to be a significant contributor to the grid, it has placed ever-increasing stress on grid managers. A system designed for largely centralized power is being asked to accommodate sources of energy in new and multitudinous places. A solar PV farm in the outback is a perfect spot for producing solar electricity. A wind farm on a collection of hills or offshore locations can produce megawatts of electricity. But there is no provision for the network to carry this much

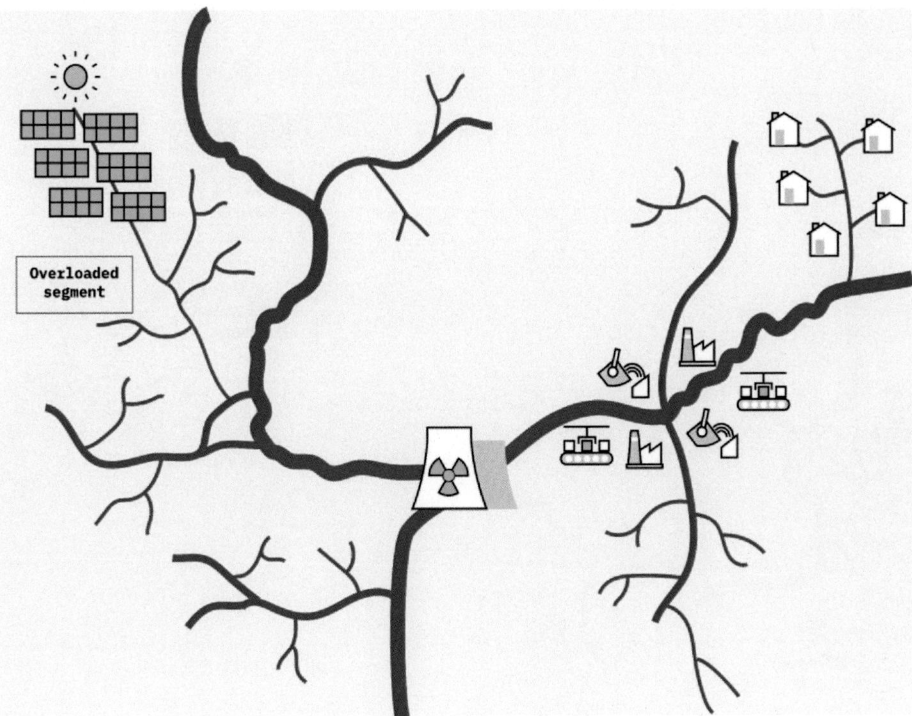

Figure 4.9 Overloaded segment illustration due to large solar farms away from consumers. Courtesy of Jemma Green.

power from these rural locations. A network operator has a choice, therefore, to either pay a significant sum of money to refurbish the transmission and distribution capacity or to decentralize and start to create a flexible services contract. In Fig. 4.9, we see an overloaded segment caused by a solar farm being installed in a "thin" part of the grid.

However, if a highly energy-intensive smelting work or similar is put on a flexible contract near the site of the solar farm, the amount of network reinforcement or refurbishment is reduced to a fraction (Fig. 4.10). To really derive maximum benefit from this, this kind of approach would need to be policy-driven, to encourage industrial facilities to be built, close to electricity generation, which could be derived from the reduced cost of electricity in the vicinity. The geopolitics of the location of industry in a world of distributed, transactive energy is still to emerge.

By creating flexible, distributed, transactive arrangements between local producers and consumers of power, to balance supply and demand and stabilize grids in discrete areas, significant savings in network costs and grid stabilization costs can be

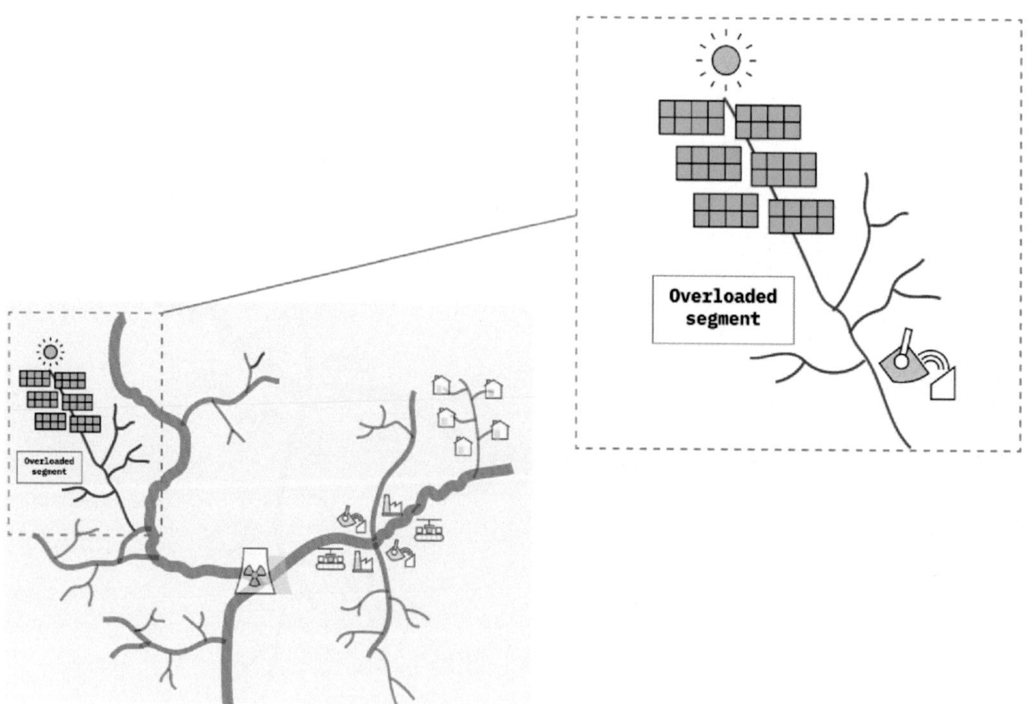

Figure 4.10 Overloaded segment reduced due to industry location policy. Courtesy of Jemma Green.

achieved. This is the essence of flexibility services and of interest to many network operators seeking to defer investment or invest more wisely.

Network or flexibility services procurement has been largely driven by tenders to date. Some networks may publish on their website maps of upcoming network grid constraints, for which they would be willing to agree to some kind of flexibility service in exchange for payment. Flexibility services can be in one or a combination of three forms: load shifting, storage, or curtailment. Tenders have proved to be an ineffective way to procure these kinds of services for several reasons. For the seller of flexibility services, there is no visibility on price, there is difficulty in ascertaining long-range income streams, and they are slow, time-consuming and tedious. For the buyer of flexibility services, they often net a poor result in terms of supply, they are time-consuming and costly to administer and often contracted on a standby basis that can be more expensive than participation on a forward-facing voluntary basis. As a result, network augmentation is often favored, citing a lack of firmness or expense with flexibility services.

To ensure enough supply and efficient procurement, the way flexibility services are procured needs to be more seamless and automated. Fundamental to this concept of the grid is enabling a group of prosumers to produce energy in the service of the grid, using a highly automated version of a frictionless stock market. The prosumers could be home owners aggregated together or scaled up to the level of shopping mall owners or industrial/warehouse areas with already large existing rooftop capability. Although there are many issues to resolve in such a system, the logic of having locally produced power right next to where it is produced is very powerful. The waste in the distribution network is a huge gain in the whole system, as long as the system can be managed to enable stability and resilience in the grid at the same time. The chapter begins to show how that is emerging in the distributed grids of the future using transactive technology systems.

There would be a very attractive business proposition if excess renewables capacity created locally is integrated with battery storage and the ability to solve hot spots on the grid. Such opportunities are preventing either a shut-down of the grid or reinvestment in traditional grid balancing mechanisms. This can be very expensive.

Electric vehicles can also provide vehicle-to-grid (V2G) services from their substantial batteries. How they fit into the distributed, transactive grid is beginning to emerge with

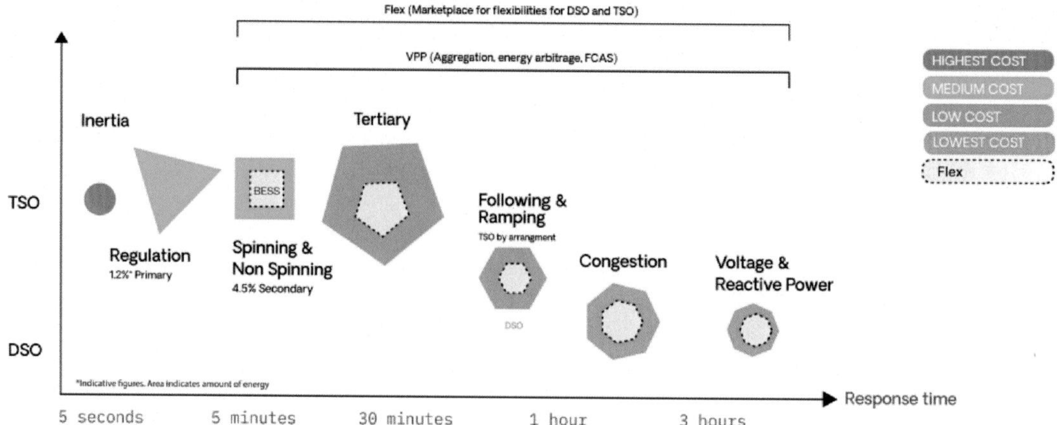

Figure 4.11 Various flexibility or balancing services for the grid in terms of response and agency. Courtesy of Jemma Green.

substantial opportunities for depots with electric buses, fleets of cars, or transit-based corridors with recharge hubs for all electromobility in station precincts (Newman, 2020).

The grid is in continual need of balancing itself, and there are various response systems with different times and costs associated with them. All of them protect against overloading or under-delivering on frequency or associated power. Fig. 4.11 sets out flexibility services in terms of response time and the agency that they concern; the DSO is a distribution service organization, and the TSO is a Transmission service organization for wholesale markets.

Flexibility services can deliver balance in almost all cases. By creating an agile, frictionless energy stock market to deliver the power exactly where and when it is needed, network operators can save many millions on investment in the traditional provision of back-up power like gas turbines, pumped hydro, and expensive large-scale substations.

Fig. 4.12 sets out how to create an automated Local Energy Market for flexibility services.

The distributed energy supply, integrated with a trading platform, combining standby contracts and voluntary forward-facing markets has the ability to produce a stable electricity service. The response zone of 3 h–7 days can be managed with an automatic market system. Sellers of flexibility services would receive a bracket price from the system operator and use this as the basis for an offer to owners of DERs, typically entrepreneurs who have invested in solar and wind and are exploring the new

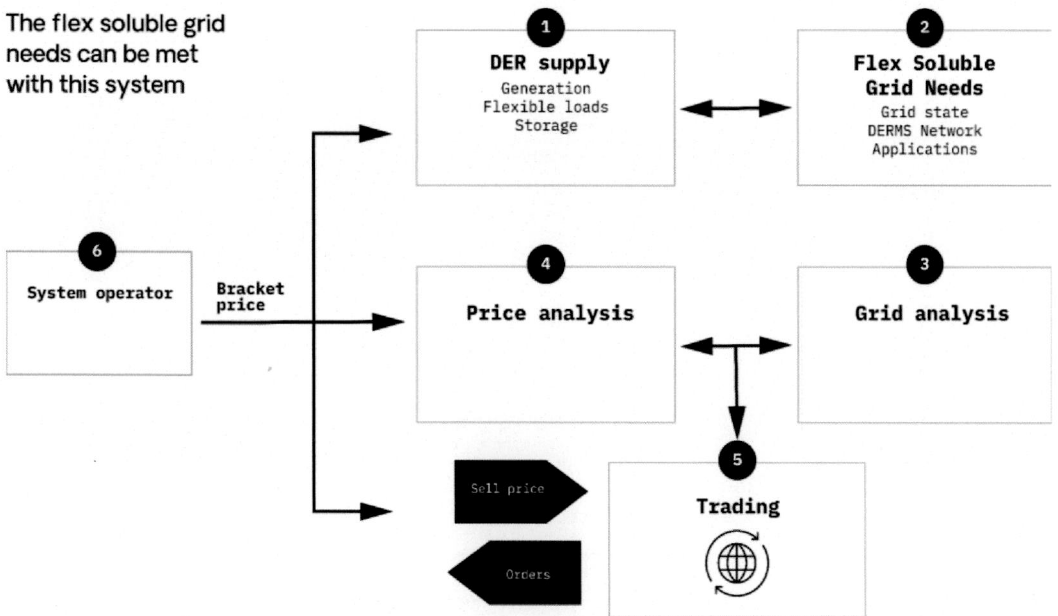

Figure 4.12 How flexibility services are integrated into grid operations. By the authors.

electrical landscape as pioneers. If using blockchain technology, offers can be settled by means of smart contracts and the electricity would then be delivered to the grid with the time, place, and energy contributions that have been agreed upon. A trading engine that is fully automated, using machine learning, and linked to a blockchain settlement system can manage to price. This is the model of how distributed, transactive power can become the solution to the problem of variable renewables.

The revolution to a distributed, transactive grid dominated by renewables will emerge and develop a regional configuration; this will require new elements ensuring that renewables are the dominant factor in how the grid is operating. Fig. 4.13 shows how the emerging Distributed, Transactive Grid will combine a Regional Flexibilities Market system; this will work with elements similar to the earlier P2P market system set out in Fig. 4.5 but with additional elements.

Fig. 4.13 shows how various functions are added to each layer - except for the Enablers Layer, which remains the participants and regulation - but the new dimensions build on the fundamentals of the demonstration scale exercise set out earlier.

Microgrids are physical connections linking variable renewables - mostly solar - to a group of nearby prosumers who want

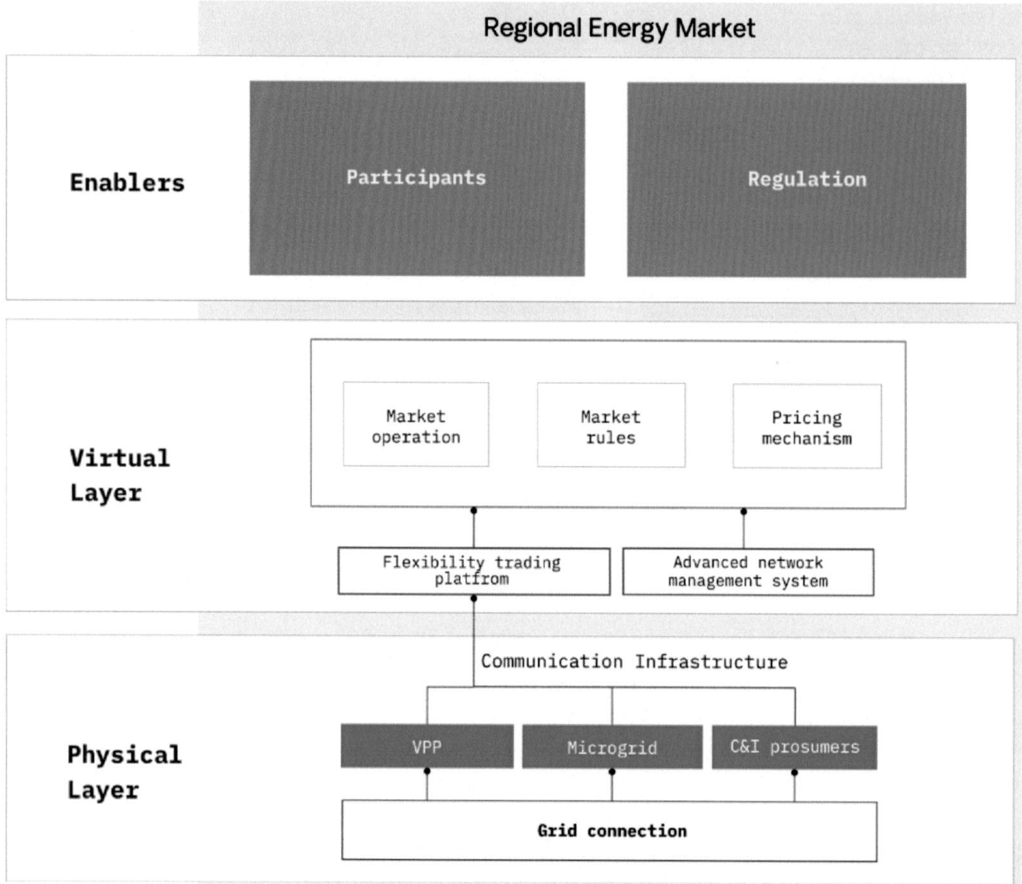

Figure 4.13 The emerging distributed, transactive grid with a regional flexibilities market system. By the authors.

to be part of a decarbonized future. Such microgrids are emerging as part of large traditional grids and provide resilient services when the grid is threatened by storms as well as operating to meet the daily needs of its customers.

A virtual power plant (VPP) is a region of distributed solar or wind and storage producers, an embodiment of the mathematical ideal we discussed earlier. It delivers the same amount of power as its equivalent power station, but the virtuality is that it is spread over a region of space. VPPs can bid to provide flexibility services. In a local energy market, batteries are orchestrated in a disaggregated way, managing local demand in a discrete part of the grid. For electricity retailers, this can offer a way to maintain retailer margin, and reduce their customer's electricity bills.

Box 4.3 The privacy, security, and resilience issues implied by digitalization in a transactive electricity grid

A distributed, transactive electricity grid has a built-in de facto centralized decentralization. So every address in the grid will be a transactive participant and so every participant or node will be equipped with a digital identifier, not unlike an IP address. The identifier is the way the grid will connect at an information level with the inhabitants of the dwelling or the owner of the electric vehicle using the grid for recharge.

Associated with that digital identifier (DI) will be a wealth of user data that might convey a plethora of private information. The very nature of having the mass data of electrical usage shareable to a wider community for the purposes of maintaining a stable grid thus opens up various privacy issues.

In the old centralized model of electricity there wasn't so much of a problem. The data resolution was very poor, in other words, it was just a customer's meter count at the end of a quarter, and maybe the customer's credit card details. But now there is a range of important data that is open to hacking as it is a shared, transactive microgrid.

Recognition of this issue is the first step in managing the issue. Second is the need for cybersecurity software to be designed for the issues that could be raised by the microgrid. Businesses have been struggling with cybersecurity issues for many years including ransom demands that are made through hacking their businesses' emails. Cybersecurity will need to be a big part of the distributed grid. Indeed the sheer number of distributed microgrids and their multiply functions should make a system based on this distribution of risk, much less of a target for hacking than a big centralized grid. These matters will need to be carefully pursued as grids decentralize.

The various elements outlined in Fig. 4.13 are emerging in traditional grids around the world. Box 4.3 sets out some case studies of places where these socio-technical changes are being trialed. Decentralized, transactive, regional grid systems are needed for the cities and regions of the world if they are to reach anything like the "net zero by 2050" goal being adopted across the world.

Apart from these market mechanisms, there are some human dimensions to the decentralized, transactive energy transition.

8. Emerging roles for entrepreneurs in the decentralized, transactive electricity grid

Implicit in the notion of having participants who are willing to invest in helping the grid meet its obligations is a new kind of investor. Sometimes called Flexipreneurs, this is a new profession who are producing power for flexibility services. They are simply a scaled-up version of prosumers who are delivering energy and grid services to the network operator. The new distributed transactive grid relies on people willing to get involved like this. The deeper social changes beneath this reflect a new preoccupation with energy, where it comes from, and how to create and use it correctly and ethically.

The rise of the Climate Emergency movement, the increase in climate anxiety in a generation of children and adults (Newby, 2021), and the rise of *flygskam*, or flight shame, are all manifestations of our new social landscape around energy. The backlash against this is due to the fear of renewable energy driving up energy costs and causing grid instability, as a result of centralized planning of renewable energy. But from this anxiety-based manifestation of the energy crisis is emerging a set of new more positive possibilities, which is creating new opportunities for new energy related products. Such hope is based on the perception that the most sustainable outcomes are win-win (Newman, 2020). Two examples illustrate the kind of emerging roles for energy entrepreneurs: ekWateur and loyalty energy sharing.

8.1 ekWateur

ekWateur is a new type of electricity provider for the energy-discerning consumer. The ekWateur business model is based on a customer archetype identified by the CEO, Julien Tchernia, whereby the company offers its customers a choice of where their power comes from. They are able to select biogas, solar, and wind as part of their mix, which still involves some fossil and nuclear.

Founded in 2015 the company now boasts more than 350,000 customers. The significance of the ekWateur offering is that the provenance of energy had become as important as price alone. This approach accords with the 24/7 carbon-free energy movement that was started by Google and Microsoft. Under their Choose Your Mix tariff, each kilowatt hour of energy consumed will be matched against renewable energy produced.

Fig. 4.14 shows the distribution of ekWateur's customers, mostly in France, and though a small and dispersed group is nevertheless enabling the transition. The vision of the company as an agent in a distributive energy world is stated as:

"These are the members of the ekWateur community, suppliers of renewable gas, and green electricity, who by harvesting energy from the sun or the wind are also our small producers. These small points may seem trivial, but put end to end it is a universe of possibilities that emerges: it is the possibility of exploiting the multiple sources of energy present locally, to achieve an energy mix respectful of the environment" (eKwateur, 2021).

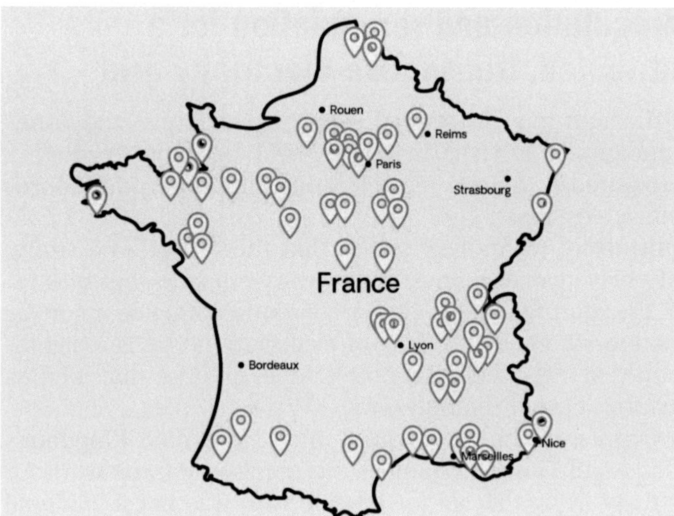

Figure 4.14 Distribution of eKwateur customers. Source: Modified from Ekwateur (2021).

8.2 Swapping solar for products: loyalty peer to peer electricity trading

Owned by Asahi, Victoria Bitter, or VB is one of Australia's best-known beer brands, and their new energy policy also tells us much about the social context of the distributed, transactive energy transition. Starting in 2021, Carlton United Brewery is sourcing some of its electricity directly from its own consumers, in exchange for beer. The exchange rate is set at 1 MWh for 3.5 'slabs' of beer - 84 bottles. The customer gets a carton of beer when it has supplied $32 worth of electricity to the brewery, whereas beer delivered to their home would normally cost nearly $60. But the value goes beyond the financial transaction. There is also significant brand value being developed, as customers get to see the company "living the renewable energy brand", to use marketing parlance, and not just talking about it. Customers also engage with the brand on a daily basis and have a new pathway to purchase.

The swapping solar for products and services offering demonstrates as much as anything else that energy sharing is becoming a reality through a receptive social base. The trends in deregulating and regulating the grid to achieve dominance of renewable energy over the next few decades is set out with some case studies that illustrate the emerging political agenda.

9. Deregulation and reregulation for a distributed, transactive electricity grid

With the shift to a distributed electricity supply as the dominant paradigm, it is clear that there will be some regulatory change required if there is to be a rapid shift toward an affordable, renewables-based grid.

The history of technology shows that there is often a strong regulatory bias against innovation in every era, and that bias resides in the statute books and professional practice manuals across nation-states. In the case of electricity, there is a significant amount of legislation and professional practice that inhibits the transformation of the networks.

For example, in the early 1980s, until the United Kingdom's chancellor Nigel Lawson changed the regulatory framework for UK electricity, it was illegal for anyone who was not a National Electricity Board employee, i.e., employed by the state, to enter premises and read an electrical meter.

Another example comes from Tortola, one of the British Virgin Islands. The legislation set up in 1978 conferred a monopoly on the state generation system and effectively outlawed self-generation. For an island that is prone to hurricanes that wipe out the transmission of electricity, the prospect of self-generation with abundant sunlight was a good one. It was, in fact, a necessity, but would have been a criminal act until the law was changed in 2015 (British Virgin Islands Electricity Corporation (Amendment) Act, 2015).

Law and professional practice based on a century of nondigital fossil fuel-based power inevitably enshrined centralization. As renewable energy emerges with its conflicting requirements, the pressure to change many laws that restrict the new paradigm is building. Evidence of this can be seen in many parts of the world.

Power regulators who are trying to free up the capacity of rapidly emerging distributed, transactive renewables generally find that their system must move from large centralized players to allow the aggregated small player access. Terms like the democratization of energy have particular resonance when it comes to understanding this. However, there is one issue that needs to be assessed with some caution as the changes to centralized systems emerge (Box 4.3).

9.1 Deregulation in the United States

In the United States, consumers can sell energy in limited ways, but there are restrictions on access that prosumers can have to the higher rate services and opportunities. FERC2222 (Office of Energy Policy and Innovation, 2020) will change that (Roberts, 2020). This will allow many different distributed, transactive sources and load shifting concerns to be legally aggregated as a single entity. That is significant because it allows distributed entities to participate in the market with far fewer entry barriers.

As the excerpt below states, this helps the system because it removes scenarios leading to the dispatch of more expensive resources than is necessary to meet the system's needs.

"For example, the Commission noted in the NOPR that, as a general matter, distributed energy resources tend to be too small to meet the minimum size requirements to participate in the RTO/ISO markets on a stand-alone basis, and may be unable to meet certain qualification and performance requirements because of the operational constraints they may have as small resources .... These restrictions on competition can reduce the efficiency of the RTO/ISO markets, potentially leading an RTO/ISO to dispatch more expensive resources to meet its system needs. By removing barriers to the participation of distributed energy resource aggregations in the RTO/ISO markets, this final rule will enhance competition and, in turn, help to ensure that the RTO/ISO markets produce just and reasonable rates." US Federal Energy Regulatory Commission FERC222 (page 5).

9.2 EU deregulation

In the EU two sets of legislation are changing, which together recognize the legal issues that need to be addressed. There is the Clean Energy For All Act (The European Parliament and the Council of the European Union, 2018), which covers energy communities and peer-to-peer trading.

The intention of the Clean Energy Package, and specifically the introduction of Renewable Energy Communities, has aims that are stated in loftier terms than in the US:

> *"to provide individuals the opportunity to realise their own environmental, economic and social benefits, from participating in a local energy market."*

Just how effective the regulation will be in delivering this intention remains the subject of debate. Schuman (2021) provides an overview of the EU approach to changing the regulatory environment:

> *"From a historical point of view, the right to sell self-generated energy is not at all naturally given. Prosumers were not entitled to the same level of market access as traditional parties, such as large energy producers, suppliers and traders. Researchers find that this historical background has led to a regulatory disconnect" (de Almeida et al., 2021).*

The Clean Energy Package in Europe has provisions around the creation of Energy Communities and Collective Self-Consumption, which encourages close proximity trading of energy in exchange for reduced network costs.

In other words, much like the US sentiment about the incumbent regulation, it recognizes that the playing field as it now stands is slanted against the individual with their solar panel on their rooftop because that individual has not been constituted as a corporation or an entity bigger than themselves. As such, they aren't granted any kind of privilege or access they need to help the process of decentralization.

The EUI paper also details the many other issues that need to be addressed. From data protection restrictions that could conflict with successful peer-to-peer trading to prohibitions on the use of smart contracts with Blockchain:

> *"If P2P trading is organised without intermediates, for example, based on blockchain technology, further legal questions arise. The use of a blockchain per se might already violate the European legal framework. There is quite some legal uncertainty as to the legality of blockchain-based smart contracts. (139) EU data protection law appears to pose major obstacles to blockchain applications, especially where they are public-facing. If personal data (140) within the regional scope of the GDPR is processed using a blockchain, the legal framework seems to be generally incompatible with the specific technology. This is because data subjects have the right to access their personal data and information relating to the data processing (141), the right to the rectification of inaccurate personal data (142), and the right to the erasure of personal data, the so-called 'right to be forgotten".*

The EUI paper concludes:

> *"The European legislator demonstrated a legislative will to implement new concepts in the system. However, many legal questions remain unresolved, which leads to legal uncertainty that may deter investment in the sector".*

Perhaps electrical transformation will be a phenomenon like Uber; the urge to transform will overtake the legal restrictions inhibiting change, and a court battle will ensue only after the new paradigm is already established.

There is also a deregulatory activity being pursued in the UK in the form of Elexon P415 (Macsween, 2021).

9.3 Indian deregulation

In India, there are changes too that have to be addressed before widespread peer to peer becomes something the state makes a significant reality.

9.3.1 Uttar Pradesh: a case study

In 2020, the Indian province of Uttar Pradesh drew up a plan that integrated many of the ideas in this chapter. Critical to this process even beginning was a shift in regulations. The India Smart Grid Forum and local utilities worked with the state regulator Uttar Pradesh Electricity Regulatory Commission (UPERC) to deregulate and legislate a space that would enable a distributed, transactive grid.

The project involves a P2P trading trial of about 15 sites that allows residents in Uttar Pradesh to sell their excess energy to other residential customers in a dynamic pricing environment. The software platform maintains a blockchain audit trail of energy transactions providing near the real-time settlement and complete transparency throughout the entire process. The first results are not yet available.

As a result of this project, UPERC issued a tariff order and has directed the distribution utilities (DISCOMs) in the state of UP to take the P2P pilot project to the next phase including billing and financial settlements so P2P rooftop solar can become operational throughout the state (UPERC, 2021).

9.3.2 Tata power, Delhi: a case study

In 2015 the Modi Government set out its aims to have India fulfill its UN climate obligations while also making energy cleaner and cheaper for all its citizens. The target was to reach 175 GW of renewable power by 2022 for India as a whole. As India's largest utility power company at $300 billion, Tata Power was also keen to help its government achieve this with its own ambitious targets on carbon. Tata set itself the goal of reaching 60% renewable energy by 2025 with its 9.5 million energy customers.

Through its subsidiary, Tata realized this would pose a challenge to them in retaining customers in what was to be a newly deregulated world. But the transformation would also bring opportunities that expanded their sphere of influence and could bring in new revenue streams (Bloomberg, 2018).

Hearing about the work in Uttar Pradesh, Tata Power realized they needed to do something similar, i.e., they needed to run a cross-grid peer-to-peer project that brought together 150 consumers and prosumers. They also discovered that there would have to be some regulatory adjustment first to enable all of this to happen.

The following provision has now been incorporated into regulation:

> *"1. Peer-to-peer energy (P2P) trading is the buying and selling of rooftop solar PV energy between two or more grid-connected parties in a secured and reliable way with proper accounting and billing mechanisms implemented with the help of blockchain technology. Any excess energy from rooftop solar PV can be transferred and sold to other consumers via a secure platform."*

> *"To provide flexibility to rooftop solar power prosumer, taking a progressive view, the Commission is proposing provision of mutual sale and purchase of electricity through peer-to-peer transaction in a secured and reliable way with proper accounting and billing mechanism implemented with the help of Blockchain technology. Provided that for such arrangement prior approval of the Commission shall be required. To further take up development of peer-to-peer transaction of electricity generated through renewable sources, the Commission directs that UPPCL and UPNEDA shall put up a proposal jointly." (RSPV Regulations, 2019).*

Much of the switch to distributed, transactive networks will have the characteristics of some of this case. A major authority tasked with a huge complex transformational challenge may be seen to be best able to specify what they want often only when they see it happening somewhere else first. But to go down this path would carry the risk of reintroducing a major centralizing factor: a new major authority tasked with a huge and new challenge. In order not to require such, in many ways utopian and risky new major authority lower-tech solutions with simplified regulatory environments, and stripped-down cost structures will have to be made available to users.

Perhaps there is a message that India is emerging as a good case study for change in its socio-technical grid system as it has a history of distributed planning (Ghandian philosophy) and because it is more agile in recognizing the need to leapfrog over such barriers. Leapfrogging in technology (Ndlovu and Newman, 2020) is rapidly happening in solar and wind systems in the emerging world and the next move to renewably-charged electric transport will drive the need for preparing the way with new regulations for a distributed, transactive grid.

10. Conclusion

The world faces the need to transition rapidly to achieve electrical grids and supply systems free of emissions. The first step in achieving this transition has been reached: solar and wind power production is the cheapest sources to produce power. This does not guarantee that stable, affordable clean power will follow as the traditional grid is built around highly centralized and concentrated power sources since the 20th century. These must shift to carbon-free electricity.

Because these resources are variable in an instant and on a daily and seasonal basis, there is a need for the grid to shift to having a distributed, Transactive Electricity grid system and in time a decentralized system. The paper argues that this will require new market mechanisms that will create a focus on storage plus software systems supporting internet of energy and a series of controls and professional practice procedures including issues such as cybersecurity. It is an entire infrastructural socio-technical paradigm shift of a Kuhnian revolution, one that does not need to be taken at once, but rather in a cellular or modular fashion. But it will be essential once the grid approaches a substantial proportion of renewables.

In the near term, renewable-electricity-supplied buildings and communities can also provide their own power, manage their uses with a storage system, and interact with the grid without a large number of data exchanges. Here the pricing policies will have to ensure that the savings made possible by low-cost renewables accrue to the user, and that self-consumption is not penalized via artificial surcharges and taxes. A Transactive Electricity grid will need to be fair.

This chapter has described how far-reaching that Transactive Electricity transformation has to be, from the pricing and banking systems to the electrical and legal spheres. All are now feasible and if implemented can help complete the transition so fundamentally required in the global economy.

This model can first leapfrog into places where regulatory push-back from traditional grid and supply interests is least intense and then expand across energy markets in a Kuhnian way, creating the new energy paradigm.

In countries where there is ambivalence or resistance to change with simple enabling regulation and a failure to grasp the need for ubiquitously distributed renewable energy markets, the result is likely to be higher cost and system instability.

11. Short glossary of terms

Peer to Peer: Where two or more prosumers transact electricity directly.

Loyalty Peer to Peer: Where customers of a brand produce electricity for those brands in return for the product itself.

Power Purchase agreement: Where a big organization such as a multinational or a university purchases its electricity in bulk from a source.

Sleeving agreement: Where an organization buys renewables under a PPA but also contracts with a fossil energy company to make up the difference when wind and solar are in short supply.

RECs. Renewable energy certificates. Proof that an MWh has been produced according to appropriately renewable standards. The certificate can be detached from the green MWh and sold separately.

Flexibility services: The maintenance of voltage and avoidance of congestion at various points in time and places along the grid. Such services are becoming increasingly popular as renewables increase their penetration.

Flexipreneurs: A contraction of Flexibilities and Entrepreneurs to denote a person who invests in battery and solar to provide flexibility services for the grid.

Prosumer: A contraction of producer-consumer of electricity. A more domestic equivalent of flexipreuner, the prosumer is the smallest unit of production and consumption of electricity in the distributed grid.

Transactive Electricity: A combination of economic and control techniques to improve grid reliability and efficiency. These techniques may also be used to optimize operations within a customer's facility. They are tools that enable consumers and prosumers to interact in a way that makes grids perform better.

Acknowledgments

The authors would like to thank Anand Menon, Gideon Todes, Jan Peters, Dr. Liaqat Ali and Holly Hyder for their assistance.

References

Anzai, K., Ban, N., Ozawa, T., Tokonami, S., 2011. Fukushima Daiichi Nuclear Power Plantaccident: facts, environmental contamination, possible biological effects, and countermeasures. Journal of Clinical Biochemistry and Nutrition 50 (1), 2–8.

Bloomberg, 2018. Tata Power Plans $5 Billion Push to Boost Renewable Energy Capacity - ET EnergyWorld [online]. ETEnergyworld.com. Available at: https://energy.economictimes.indiatimes.com/news/renewable/tata-power-plans-5- billion-push-to-boost-renewable-energy-capacity/64157447. (Accessed 28 April 2021).

Browning, N., 2021. Energy crisis could threaten global economic recovery, says IEA. Reuters. October 21, 2021. https://www.reuters.com/article/iea-oil-idCAKBN2H40OZ.

Dasgupta, R., Sakzad, A., Rudolph, C., 2021. Cyber attacks in transactive energy market-based microgrid systems. Energies 14, 1137. https://doi.org/10.3390/en14041137.

de Almeida, L., Klausmann, N., van Soest, H., Cappelli, V., 2021. Peer-to-Peer trading and energy community in the electricity market - analysing the literature on law and regulation and looking ahead to future challenges. SSRN Electronic Journal.

Ekwateur, 2021. Ce sont les membres de la communauté ekWateur, fournisseur de gaz renouvelable, d'électricité verte (et plus encore) qui en récoltant l'énergie du soleil ou du vent, sont aussi nos petits producteurs. Ces petits points, ça peut sembler anodin, mais mis bout à bout c'est un univers des possibles qui se dessine : c'est la possibilité d'exploiter les multiples sources d'énergies présentes localement, pour aboutir à un mix énergétique respectueux de l'environnement. https://ekwateur.fr. (Accessed 15 October 2021).

Elliot, L., 2012. Barclays Libor case could have severe consequences for banks [online] The Guardian. Available at: https://www.theguardian.com/business/2012/oct/28/barclays-libor-guardian-care-homes.

Fant, C., Boehlert, B., Strzepeck, K., Larsen, P., White, A., Gulati, S., Yue, L., Martinich, J., 2020. Climate Change Impacts and Costs to U.S. Electricity Transmission and Distribution Infrastructure, Energy (Oxf), p. 116899. https://doi.org/10.1016/j.energy.2020.116899. Mar 15.

Geels, F.S., Schwanen, T.B., Sorrell, S., 2017. Sociotechnical transitions for deep decarbonization. Science 357, 1242–1244.

Green, J., Newman, P., 2017a. Planning and governance for decentralised energy assets in medium-density housing: the WGV Gen Y case study. Urban Policy and Research. https://doi.org/10.1080/08111146.2017.1295935.

Green, J., Newman, P., 2017b. Citizen utilities: the emerging power paradigm. Energy Policy 105, 283–293. http://www.sciencedirect.com/science/article/pii/S0301421517300800.

Grid-Wise Architecture Council (GWAC), 2019. GridWise Transactive Energy Framework Version 1.1. US Department of Energy pnnl_22946_gwac_te_framework_july_2019_v1_1(3).pdf.

IEA, 2021. Global Energy Supply Investment by Sector, 2019-2021. World Energy Investment 2021. https://www.iea.org/data-and-statistics/charts/global-energy-supply-investment-by-sector-2019-2021-2.

IPCC, 2021. IPCC Sixth Assessment Report. The Physical Science Basis. https://www.ipcc.ch/report/ar6/wg1/.

Kafle, Y., Mahmud, K., Morsalin, S., Town, G., 2016. Towards an Internet of Energy, pp. 1–6. https://doi.org/10.1109/POWERCON.2016.7754036.

Kuhn, T., 1996. The Structure of Scientific Revolution. University of Chicago Press, Chicago pp.37, 1441 139, 159.

Lazard, 2017. Summary Findings of Lazard's 2017 Levelized Cost of Energy Analysis [image] Available at: https://www.lazard.com/perspective/levelized-cost-of-energy-2017/. (Accessed 28 April 2021).
Lezama, F., Soares, J., Hernandez-Leal, P., Kaisers, M., Pinto, T., Vale, Z., 2019. Local energy markets: paving the path toward fully transactive energy systems. IEEE Transactions on Power Systems 34, 4081–4088.
Macsween, I., 2021. P415 'Facilitating Access to Wholesale Markets for Flexibility Dispatched by Virtual Lead Parties' - Elexon BSC [online] Elexon.co.uk. Available at: https://www.elexon.co.uk/mod-proposal/p415/. (Accessed 28 April 2021).
Ndlovu, V., Newman, P., 2020. Leapfrog technology and how it applies to trackless tram. Journal of Transportation Technologies 10, 198–213. https://doi.org/10.4236/jtts.2020.103013.
Newby, J., 2021. Climate Grief. New South Books, Sydney.
Newman, P., 2020a. Covid, cities and climate. Historical and Potential Transitions for the New Economy Urban Science 4 (3), 32. https://www.mdpi.com/2413-8851/4/3/32#abstract.
Newman, P., 2020b. Hope in a time of civicide: regenerative development and IPAT Sustainable. Earth 3, 13. https://doi.org/10.1186/s42055-020-00034-1.
Office of Energy Policy and Innovation, 2020. Participation of Distributed Energy Resource Aggregations in Markets Operated by Regional Transmission Organizations and Independent System Operators. Federal Energy Regulatory Commission, Washington.
Pflugmann, F., Ritzenhofen, I., Stockhausen, F., Vahlenkamp, T., 2019. Germany's Energy Transition at a Crossroads [online]. McKinsey & Company. Available at: https://www.mckinsey.com/industries/electric-power-and-natural-gas/our-insights/germanys-energy-transition-at-a-crossroads. (Accessed 28 April 2021).
REN21, 2021. Renewables 2020 Global Status Report [online]. Paris: Renewable Energy Policy Network for the 21st Century. Available at: https://www.ren21.net/wp-content/uploads/2019/05/gsr_2020_full_report_en.pdf. (Accessed 28 April 2021).
Roberts, M., 2020. Distributed Energy Resources Score Big Win with FERC Order 2222 [online]. Microgrid Knowledge. Available at: https://microgridknowledge.com/ferc-order-2222-distributed-energy/. (Accessed 28 April 2021).
Roser, M., 2021. Why Did Renewables Become So Cheap So Fast? Drawn from Lazard LOCE Analysis Version 13.0 Data. https://ourworldindata.org/cheap-renewables-growth.
RSPV Regulations, 2019. Uttar Pradesh Electricity Regulatory Commission.
Strielkowski, W., Streimikiene, D., Fomina, A., Elena, S., 2019. Internet of energy (IoE) and high-renewables electricity system market design. Energies 12 (24), 4790. https://doi.org/10.3390/en12244790.
The European Parliament and the Council of the European Union, 2018. Directive (EU) 2018/2001 of the european parliament and of the council. Office Journal of the European Union.
UPERC Uttar Pradesh Electricity Regulatory Commission Lucknow, 2021. Approval of ARR and Tariff for State Discoms for FY 2021-22, APR of FY 2020-21 and True-Up of FY 2019-20. https://www.uperc.org/App_File/Final_TariffOrderUPStateDISOCMsFY2021-22(29-07-2021)DigitallySigned-pdf729202113115PM.pdf.

Wacket, M., 2021. Germany's Energy Drive Criticised over Expense, Risks [online]. Reuters. Available at: https://www.reuters.com/article/germany-energy-audit-idUSL8N2LS2RC. (Accessed 28 April 2021).
Zuboff, S., 2019. Surveillance capitalism: the fight for a human future at the new frontier of power. PublicAffairs.

Further reading

British Virgin Islands Electricity Corporation (Amendment) Act, 2015, p. 1.
Desai, P., 1981. Estimates of Soviet Grain Imports in 1980-85. International Food Policy Research Institute, Washington, D.C.
Ellman, M., 1988. Soviet agricultural policy [online] Economic and Political Weekly 23 (24), 1208–1210. Available at: http://www.jstor.org/stable/4378606. (Accessed 28 April 2021).
Evans, S., 2015. Germany to close brown coal plants in effort to meet 40% emission cuts [online] Renew Economy. Available at: https://reneweconomy.com.au/germany-to-close-brown-coal-plants-in-effort-to-meet-40-emission-cuts-87307/. (Accessed 28 April 2021).
Green, J., Newman, P., Forse, N., 2020. Renew Nexus: Enabling Resilient, Low Cost & Localised Electricity Markets through Blockchain P2P & VPP Trading [online]. Perth. Available at: https://uploads-ssl.webflow.com/5fc9b61246966c23f17d2601/607e724f8dfb1a2d5928bbc0_renew-nexus-project-report.pdf. (Accessed 28 April 2021).
Morgan, J.P., 2020. Tenth Annual Energy Paper. Eye on the Market. [online] Amsterdam: J.P. Morgan Bank. Available at: http://vaclavsmil.com/wp-content/uploads/2020/09/JPM2020.pdf. (Accessed 28 April 2021).
Randall, T., 2015. Solar and Wind Just Passed Another Big Turning Point [online]. Bloomberg.com. Available at: https://www.bloomberg.com/news/articles/2015-10-06/solar-wind-reach-a-big-renewables-turning-point-bnef#footnote-1444106375369. (Accessed 28 April 2021).
Reconnect Energy, 2021. MERC Approves the 'Green Power Tariff' for the Consumers of All the Distribution Licensee of Maharashtra [online]. Reconnectenergy.com. Available at: https://reconnectenergy.com/blog/2021/04/merc-approves-the-green-power-tariff-for-the-consumers-of-all-the-distribution-licensee-of-maharashtra/. (Accessed 28 April 2021).
Tarantino, M., 2017. Analysis of Key Factors for Successful Auction Programs: Experiences outside of Europe [ebook]. Enel Green Power. Available at: https://www.irena.org/-/media/Files/IRENA/Agency/Events/2017/Mar/8/Enel-Analysis-of-key-factors-for-successful-auction-programs.pdf?la=en&hash=2FAB3BBA9BDCEE26623B0C6A776FBDD846B21779. (Accessed 28 April 2021).
Vbsolarexchange, 2021. Victoria Bitter - Solar Exchange [online]. Available at: https://www.vbsolarexchange.com.au/. (Accessed 28 April 2021).

5

Community inclusion currencies

William O. Ruddick[1,2]

[1] *Grassroots Economics Foundation, Kilifi, Kenya;* [2] *Initiative for Leadership and Sustainability (IFLAS), University of Cumbria, Carlisle, United Kingdom*

1. Introduction

The abuse of monopolistic currency systems has caused generations of economic trauma across the globe and fuels the destruction of our planet.

Historically and today being forced to use currencies created by people outside your community meant you are under a colonial power. I believe strongly in empowering communities to make their own economic systems and connect to others. Communities can create their own credit backed by their production and use it as a medium of exchange—as has been done for centuries prior to colonization.

The current global credit creation system is not able to serve the needs of the masses (Stein 2013) and foreign crypto currencies would gladly try to fill this space—while local economic systems and technology need support and regulation—and importantly economic liberty needs to be understood as a fundamental human right.

I am inspired by groups of women in rural Kenya that could not pay for labor and farm inputs and instead believed in the future production from their businesses and farms and created a credit against it. They issued this credit on small paper notes that could be used to pay for seeds, water, labor, and manure. The farmers could then use them to pay for school fees, health care, hair braiding, and child care. Those recipients could use them over and over knowing that when food was harvested from the women's group farm they could buy the produce with it—and the cycle continues again and again.

After starting in one village, for over 12 years now with Grassroots Economics Foundation (GEF), I have watched this technique known as Community Inclusion Currencies (CICs) evolve digitally, organically grow in refugee camps and hundreds of vulnerable

Intelligent Environments. https://doi.org/10.1016/B978-0-12-820247-0.00002-3

communities and become modularized by the Red Cross, World Food Program, GIZ, UNICEF, and other humanitarian organizations (Ruddick 2020). The techniques developed with GEF ride on a wave of historic and contemporary community currency initiatives, like WIR Banks, Canadian Tire Money, LETs, SELs, Bangla Pesa, Berkshares, Bristol Pound, Worgl Script, and many more.

1.1 Currency primer

A CIC is a divisible and tradable claim against payment for an issuer's goods and or services. It consists of three elements: an issuer or service provider —such as a community of businesses; a recorded claim against redemption; and a token or voucher that is a divisible and endorsable representation of this claim (Fig. 5.1). This is not very different from the way people view vouchers in general, yet when created against a claim rather than 100% collateral in national currency—a new source of credit has now been created.

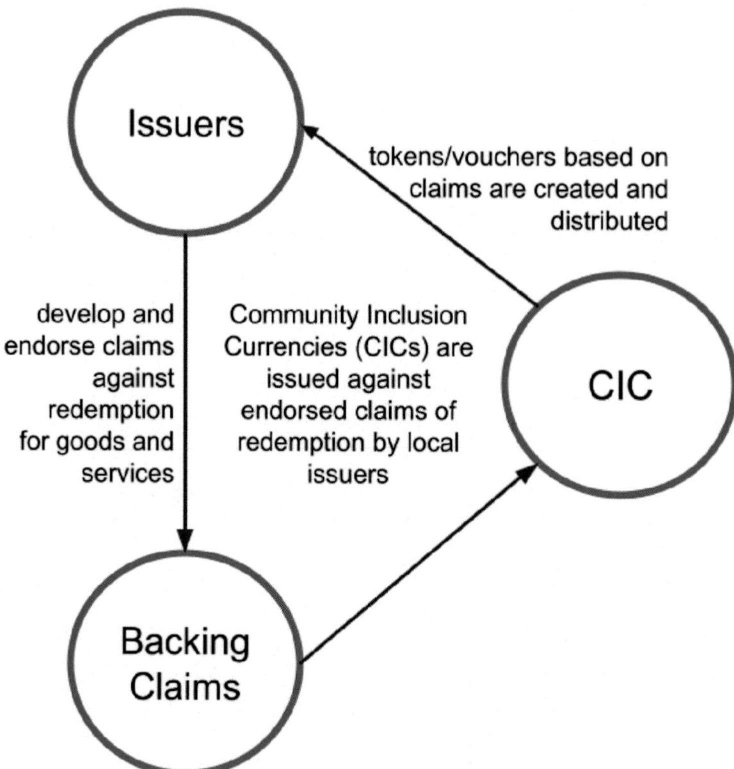

Figure 5.1 The basic building blocks of a community inclusion currency.

A good example for an issuer is the women's group mentioned in the introduction: 28 women who sell their labor, seeds, vegetables, restaurant meals, hair braiding, teaching, and so on. They can come together and create a claim—a written constitution—that specifies that they will redeem 10% of their annual sales in a voucher. Then create—mint—those vouchers and distribute them among themselves and as well community projects. The vouchers often have a holding tax—demurrage—that is collected by a common group account and voted on for redistribution. It's an extremely simple idea of creating money—credit—against future production with communal risk and reward.

2. Real world applications

2.1 Regenerative agriculture

I want to single out this application for CICs because it has profound implications. The degraded state of the world's food systems and the trajectory toward environmental collapse is staggering. There are solutions to this like; syntropic agroforestry—a distillation of permaculture that is extremely effective at creating Food Forests (2021)—which regenerate the soil, sequester carbon, and grow healthy food. This technique was developed by Ernst Götsch in Brazil and has been inspiring people around the globe (Götsch 1995). The main problem with this technique is that it requires a large amount of labor especially in arid climates and doesn't yield substantial financial returns for long periods. Environmentalists need a method to enable people to create their own form of credit against the future production of these farms—as a way to kick-start regenerative practices globally and maintain them economically.

Enabling communities to create a CIC against their future farm production and collective goods and services means that a farmer can get the credit she needs in advance and repay it without interest using the vegetables and other produce from her farm.

There are inputs that are hard to bootstrap in this way. Not everyone will provide farm inputs or work for *future carrots.* In the best circumstances, CICs are created by a whole group of businesses, so while your backing in future carrots might not be appealing, one could use them at the hair salon and maize mill as well. The network of backing institutions is really what makes these *vouchers* into a medium of exchange/currency.

Given that these syntropic agroforestry farms also sequester carbon in the soil and trees in ways that can be measured via

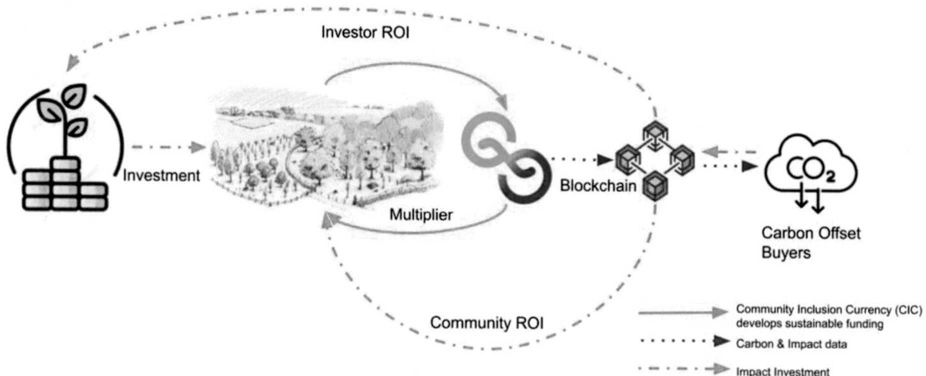

Figure 5.2 CIC usage in regenerative agriculture and carbon sequestration.

soil testing (Lal 2004)—there is carbon credit value beyond the carrots. In this vein of bootstrapping, an investor could pay for the inputs that the community can't and receive some of the carbon offsets in return (Fig. 5.2). While in the carbon example here investment payout can be measured, often those measurements are hard because the payouts are not always obviously profitable. Fortunately the impacts from CICs in developing stable economies can be indexed into nearly all the UN's Sustainable Development Goals. Meaning that the adjacency value of a CIC also includes impacts that humanitarian organizations are dedicated to supporting.

2.2 Humanitarian aid

CICs began as a humanitarian approach toward supporting vulnerable communities to tap into their own abundance. GEF began these programs by simply training and organizing community groups to issue a voucher against their own production and measuring the stability and increase to local trade and social cohesion as a result.

The Red Cross and other humanitarian organizations began to partner with GEF and picked up these concepts in 2019 (Fig. 5.3) and continued to use them for a variety of modalities such as:

- **Cash for Assets**—local asset development supported by humanitarian organizations. These can be both hard assets like farm equipment, cooperatives or soft assets such as education or a local market. The CIC in this case creates a web of support for that asset and ensures that it is a social enterprise.
- **Cash and Voucher Assistance**—The CIC transactional flows can identify where support is needed in vulnerable

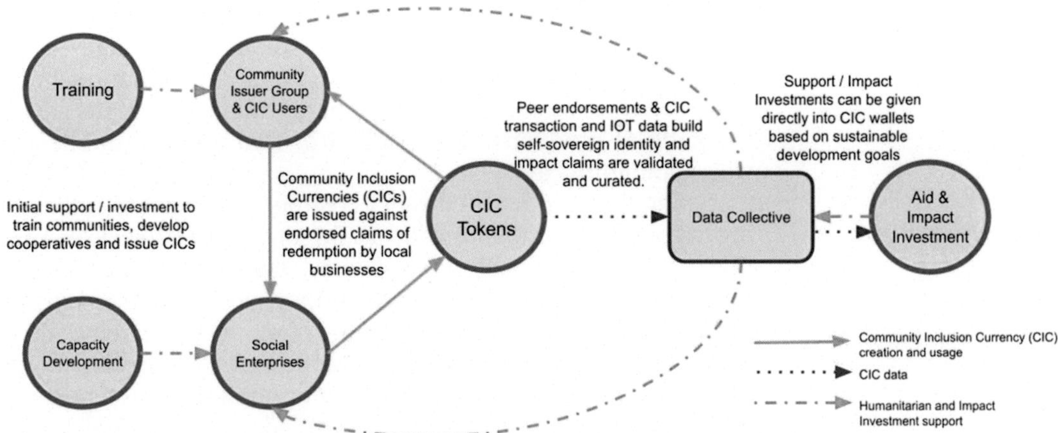

Figure 5.3 CIC usage in humanitarian support.

communities and enable humanitarian organizations to directly inject aid (Red Cross 2020).

Humanitarian aid is tasked with a huge amount of work and hampered by a paucity of funding. Crisis response is often limited to some form of air dropping of money or food. These inputs don't create stable economies and often leak away to major cities in a matter of days by the need to acquire goods and services from these urban centers. Instead of dropping money on communities—building sustainable assets with in-built local economies to support and maintain them is crucial for real and enduring change. While immediate crisis response is still needed in whatever form gets people out of their suffering, CICs plot a path toward recovery and resilience.

2.3 Taxation

This touchy topic is the last thing a lot of community currency designers often want to think about, yet the first question they are asked.

At the time of writing this chapter, a CIC is nothing more than a tradable voucher, in most regulatory regimes. Taxation on these vouchers is similar to trading any crypto currency—a gray area at best. When exchanging CCs or any crypto currency for National Currency is when formal tax regimes are being entered. I say "at the time of writing," because things change fast in this space and actively thinking about how taxes can or should be imposed, collected, and redistributed is extremely important. Below are some concepts on taxation of CCs that should be considered.

Community Currencies are about giving people the right to issue their own credit and use it as a medium of exchange—often filling the gaps left by low liquidity and hoarding of national currency. There is an obvious tension here with governments seeing CC trade as productive activity and/or utilization of public services, going untaxed.

Generally community currency creators don't want to end funding to governments that provide useful services but they do want to make sure people have a say in how taxes are spent! GEF, as nonprofit foundation, is trying to support people to live together without the constant fear and trauma of monetary scarcity.

Demurrage on currency is a simple concept: currencies should decay over time (i.e., negative interest or holding tax as a percentage deducted from all balances). This idea was created by the economist Silvio Gesell and first implemented Austrian town of Wörgl in 1932 with great success (Blanc 1998). It was created in order to reduce hoarding and encourage people to invest in local productive capacity—leaving currency as a medium of exchange and less of a form of savings. Rather than using paper currency and the purchase of stamps to keep your currency valuable, as was done in the 1930s communities and humanitarian organizations can use modern technology such as blockchain to create complete transparency and automation of tax collection (we will address technologies like blockchain further on). To use demurrage as taxation digitally today—this holding tax can be collected automatically using blockchain smart contracts and deposited into a public contract or Decentralized Autonomous Organization (DAO) (Fig. 5.4). Anyone holding the currency would have a right to vote on the DAO to determine where their demurrage goes. In pilots GEF is working with local Governments to regulate these DAO contracts to ensure a percentage goes to them—and they as well would be taxed on any unspent funds.

2.4 Municipal currencies and basic income

Besides simply taxing CICs local governments can also issue them. A municipality, town, or local administration is an ideal issuer and anchor for a CICs—the taxation of which can be used for government spending and redistributed as a basic/guaranteed income. Municipalities have the means to issue and back a CIC and the intention to build sustainable and thriving local markets—such a municipal CIC can in turn act as a growth medium and network token for other CICs which allow local groups and businesses to form strong local markets through network of connected CICs.

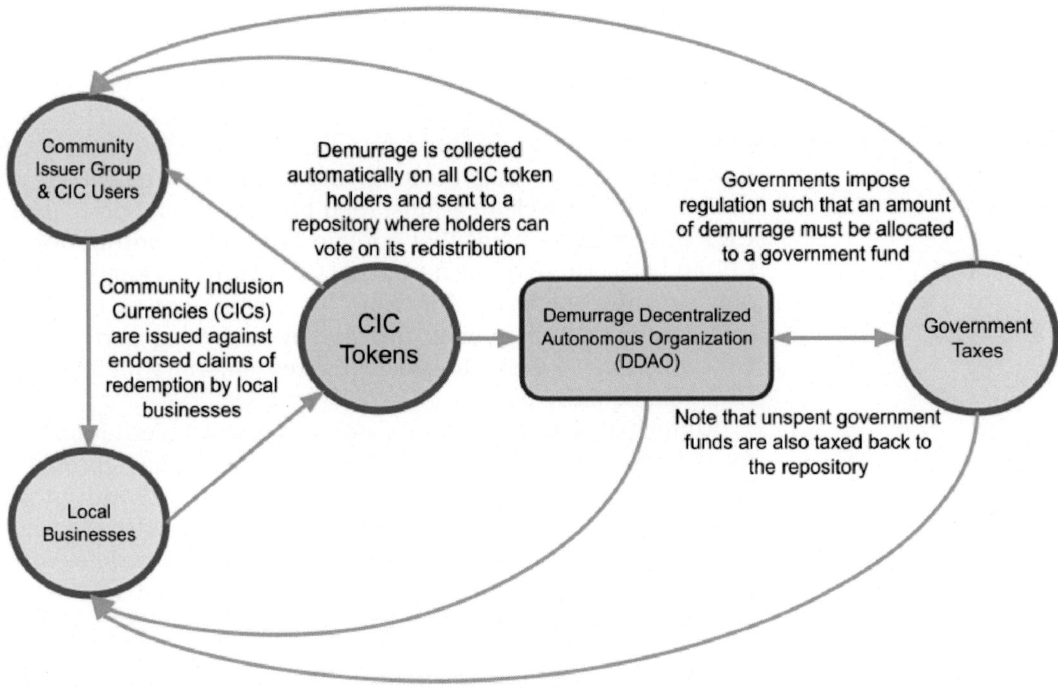

Figure 5.4 CIC usage in taxation.

In its simplest form a municipality creates a token that is distributed to residents and local projects—and taxed and redistributed as a basic income for those active in the network. This CIC would be backed by the holding tax itself and as well local services offered by the municipality, giving, for instance, 50% off public transport or health services. This is similar to Sarafu Network in Kenya which is taxed and redistributed. The tax and redistribution incentivizes trade and discourages hoarding and increases trade.

Businesses and groups of residents can create a CICs against their production—using some of them like vouchers in exchange for the municipality's CIC—in order to support the municipality. This is a tangible and measurable form of corporate social responsibility and social enterprise.

This approach being pilotted in Kitui Kenya allows business and communities to transparently and measurably connect their CICs to the greater social service network formed by the municipal CIC. Online marketplace features these supporting businesses as a way to drive traffic to them. The initial supply and taxes collected from holding fees on balances of the CIC are also used to support the village elders, aid community support networks and for local programs such as Food Forests (2021).

A municipality creating such a CIC creates a contract against its redemption as well as taxation and redistribution. This contract is voted on and signed and fixed to the CIC token on a blockchain. Supporting business networks can in turn create their own CIC as a claim against their production and place those CICs into liquidity pools that contain both their contribution of CIC and an amount of the municipal CIC in order to enable traceable exchange between the two. This means that people keep their municipal economies thriving by accepting and trading CIC which can be exchanged in limited amounts for business CICs (ala liquidity pools).

Municipality or local administrations are wonderful anchors for community health when they express their values through a CIC. The possibilities of municipal CICs combined with group created CICs are profound and life affirming. Consider the value in decentralized, municipally supported economies and networks of municipal CICs—building and supporting local as well as regional or national economies.

3. Currencies and blockchains

Up to this point, we skirted around the various technologies that enable CICs. We mentioned paper notes, riding on the backs of dozens of other techniques for ledger keeping, from cowry shells to chiefs keeping physical ledger books to keep track of reciprocal obligations. Since the introduction of a centrally issued currency as a colonial technique to employ and control the masses—countries like Kenya have lost many of the traditional practices of reciprocity. Indeed the concept of devising one's own ledger system or currency has become a lost art that is only now coming back into mainstream.

While community currencies have been around in various forms, such as cruciform ledgers, dating back to the earliest records of human history—the ability to create them has been fundamentally changed by the introduction of cryptographically secure distributed ledger technology (DLT)—blockchain-based systems.

Using a distributed ledger that allows people to run nodes that duplicate and validate the ledger means that the record keeping can be communalized into a public service. The tokens or currencies created on these ledgers have no bounds in numbers, which is both good and bad. Bitcoin for instance is based on a contract that issues tokens based on people running their computers nonstop for months and now years on end which is a massive waste of energy. It has been an eye opener for the world that a currency can be created outside a nation state, yet it has huge limitations and is again like many colonial currency systems, owned by the few and being imposed on the vulnerable.

Bitcoin and blockchains in general have opened peoples' eyes to the fact that currency is simply a measuring tool. I love to tell people the story of the construction worker who couldn't finish his job because he ran out of inches; People can't run out of currency or inches or any measuring tool. People simply define them—but the way they are defined them matters. Currencies can be defined using a contract just like they using a paper constitution. That contract can define the rules for issuance, taxation, backing, minting, voting rights, and so on. In fact, several contracts can work together to structure the entire currency system.

When designing contracts one must appreciate the differences and interplay between immutable algorithmic contracts versus mutable social contracts. This holds especially true when deploying on a blockchain which can provide a near-infinite memory capacity. Social materialism can result from rigid contracts as social structures versus social idealism from social contracts that can contain smaller immutable tools and rules, but are free to mutate and evolve.

DLTs can give us the potential for trustworthy communal ledgers and as well give us the tools to design social contracts-like currencies. Note that while the space around blockchain and crypto currencies is currently a minefield of hype, ponzi schemes, speculation, and consolidation, there are many programs that are seeing the opposite and looking at more peer to peer and communal architectures that can be used by anyone without extractive fees, rent seeking, and monopolies. For CICs, we've implemented them using Proof of Authority networks such as Bloxberg.org which are run by universities, and also Proof of Stake networks like Celo.org, but the technology can be implemented on any ledger system which can be on any network of trusted computers.

3.1 Claims and currencies

Global financial systems as well as humanitarian relief is based on claims of impact, but the current infrastructure especially in vulnerable communities is weak to nonexistent, which causes a lot of friction. The promise of a cryptographic approach to claims is that groups of smaller actors can now more easily erect authoritative and trustworthy infrastructure. These claims can be endorsed and backed-up by data and live in data-objects (such as NFT) owned by an individual or organization.

All consumers of information live in and have to navigate in a world of claims. One of the chief claims humans unknowingly deal with on a daily basis are claims against currency redemption; indeed, national currencies are valuable because they are claims against some form of redemption. Endorsements on those claims give us more and more confidence in currencies.

Governments along with banks issue national currencies, and claim that they will redeem them against taxes over time. This fiat bargain works as long as the issuance of more and more credit doesn't cause inflation and there isn't a loss of endorsement. Endorsements to build trust in national currencies are not always obvious but can come in many forms, such as circulation data, peer to peer business acceptance, as well as legal systems that uphold claims. This type of currency, being our standard medium of exchange worldwide, has many repercussions—namely, inequality as issuance is centralized and the lack resiliency when such massive systems fail.

Issuers, who are not nations or banks, with their own claims and tokens have popped up from time immemorial. The growth of nonnational currencies lies in their claims and endorsements and ability to integrate with other systems.

Canadian Tire Money are simple vouchers denominated in Canadian dollars and have been in circulation since the 1950s with only one business as the backing. Because their supply and circulation (liquidity) is low compared to the size of the community they operate in, they don't operate effectively as a medium of exchange—but for a village in Kenya or Cameroon they do, or when combined with producer credits from many other businesses they span entire regions and markets.

In a credit system like CICs there is an issuer and a claim of redemption and a token—which is a divisible and can change owner and can act as a broader medium of exchange given strong endorsement, for example, group of women in a village may create a CIC to use as a medium of exchange as a claim against the produce from their cooperative food forest. These CICs may be accepted outside of the group by a local hair salon because the local elders have endorsed them and people have been able to spend them on food from the cooperative.

The idea of taking such Producer Credits and combining them together into networks of CICs to build resilience in vulnerable communities works well as long as there are strong foundational issuers and strong endorsements, such as groups of businesses and leaders. Towns issuing their own script (currency) were immensely effective at supporting local economies during depression eras. Had these depression era systems been taxable/integrate-able by larger states they might still be in use today. Nowadays, communities have programmable tokens which can be taxed automatically (via demurrage/holding/Gesell taxes). Communities also have systems that can network together servers to create censor resistant and secure ledgers. Decentralized economic systems really change dynamics in areas with chronic shortage of money. Generally, brute force airdropping currency on a population doesn't create local ownership or stakeholders for good reason—because such a token is missing both: fundamental claims against redemption and endorsements.

3.2 Cryptographically endorsing claims

How does one trust claims as well as tokens issued against them? If you think of a digitized claim as a declaration held by an entity/issuer and endorsed with an encrypted signature (private key)—you can treat that data object like a noneditable and encrypted file on a computer (or decentralized ledger system/nonfungible token) that only the owner can choose to show to others. That claim can declare anything, such as what a currency is being issued and redeemed for and it can be cosigned as an endorsement using the private keys of people and institutions that believe that claim. The number of tokens created against that claim can be determined by the endorsements (in a DAO or old-school paper contract that is later scanned) as could the various parameters like demurrage and where the initial supply could go and linkages to other tokens or collateral. Finally, as someone looking to accept these tokens, I could look at the claim they are issued against as well as the entire supply and circulation history of those tokens on a ledger—as a form of peer to peer endorsement. These tokens could also be held in liquidity pools connecting them to other tokens and claims, meaning that even if the token issuer fails to redeem them there are other avenues for spending the tokens. You can even look at how these tokens circulate to get a lot of information about how they are distributed, how quickly they are redeemed and redistributed, and so on. This gives us a way to derisk and trust currencies not issued by governments or banks by inspecting claims as well as endorsements and associated data.

While you can look at currency through the lens of cryptographically endorsed claims, you can also look at all sorts of other claims, that is, I claim I live in Kenya, founded a nonprofit foundation and have a daughter. Just like a claim against redemption that claim can be digitized and endorsed directly by cosigners and as well by secondary data. Community Currencies when combined with other types of claims offer a huge amount of secondary data to support various claims about impacts and even identity.

Various claims can be supported using community currency data along with other survey or IoT data such as

1. Product offerings: how many people are buying those products and giving ratings on them.
2. Organic supply chains: following the purchases from farm to plate for specific foods.
3. Currency risk: how circular is the economy, velocity of the tokens, distribution of the token supply, connection to other currencies.
4. Identity claims: endorsements and transactions create a form of continuously verified identity, much better than current Know Your Customer requirements.

3.3 Rewarding verified claims

Frameworks and protocols for various types of endorsed claims that can be held self-sovereignty by individuals and groups (related to trade, demographics, impacts, and even carbon offsetting) as well as marketplaces that consume that information, are needed across sectors; from humanitarian organizations trying to measure and reward impacts against sustainable development goals, to people wanting to derisk an investment.

Consumers of endorsed claims (organizations that need trustworthy data) could include the UNICEF supporting SDGs, carbon offset purchasers, impact investors, loan and insurance providers, and so on. Rewards or payment related to such claims also need to support the system of endorsements (such as peer endorsements, web of trust and surveys), as well as the ledger systems that are holding those claims and providing data integrity and security. Such a claim market and reward system would promote people, institutions and even impact investors to seek out verified impacts. The same could also give people positive incentives for running servers (nodes) in order to validate data in order to mine impact rewards.

While Grassroots Economics is working to implement these concepts, the creation of open source frameworks and protocols for claim endorsement and rewards, is a vision held by many people and organizations. We're proud to join the ranks of inspiring humanitarian organizations like the Red Cross, UNICEF, World Food Program and GIZ who want to enable local resilience and measure and reward impact, as well as technical groups who are building open source application specific systems meant to give humanity the infrastructure to solve real problems and live in harmony while navigating a world of claims.

3.4 Connecting currencies

As communities create their CICs as a credit against their future production, projects, collateral, and excess capacity, they will begin to look at various ways to connect these tokens together and as well to other networks. Below I'll describe and contrast two approaches, namely, a Fixed versus Algorithmic Rate liquidity pools. But before that I just want to give a simple overview of what a liquidity pool is.

Blockchain and #defi readers are probably familiar with a Bonded Pool like you can find with Uniswap or in the Bancor Network, but let's start with its sibling the Static Pool—which simply is a contract holding two tokens that are exchangeable to each other (similar to a money changer on the side of the road in Mombasa). In the fixed exchange rate or static pool above, A community creating a CIC can decide to add some of their CIC A token supply to a common pool along with some tokens from another community B. The pool contains A and B tokens.

Someone holding A tokens pays some A tokens to someone holding B tokens, the pool accepts A tokens from A and gives B tokens to B. Now anyone can push in A tokens to that pool and get out B tokens with a 1:1 fixed exchange rate—that is, until there are no more Bs in the pool. At which point someone from community B would need to add some Bs to rebalance the pool before any more exchange is possible. This creates a simple way for community A and B to trade with each other with a limited amount of tokens in the pool.

Next let's talk about a Bonded pool—the kind you will find in decentralized exchanges like Uniswap or the Bancor Network. In the algorithmic exchange rate or bonded pool above, A community creating a CIC can similarly decide to add some of their CIC A token supply to a common pool along with some tokens from another community B.

Now if anyone wants to push in A tokens to that pool they can get out B tokens with an initial 1:1 exchange rate—but every time you add more A's you get less and less B's out. This can virtually go on forever until for each A added you only get 0.0000001 B's and so on.

This creates another way for community A and B to trade with each other with continuous liquidity but changing exchange rates. There can be a lot more added to the liquidity contracts, such as oracles that can adjust prices and investment shares that can grow based on exchange fees which are also options.

Communities could also create DAOs and vote on which pools are allowed into the network. But let's stick with the simple versions mentioned above and compare them a bit further:

While the Bonded Pool allows for continuous liquidity and a market price stabilization effect, it also creates a variable exchange rate that is often hard to deal with for regular commerce. In the extreme case, where many A's have been converted to B (changing the rate) and one CIC A user sends 10 tokens to buy tomatoes and they turn into only one B token—the tomato seller could demand more tokens—but this is quite cumbersome.

On the contrary with a Static Pool, one side of the pool could simply run out causing trade to stop until there is trade in the opposite direction. This could be equally frustrating for commerce and require the two communities to come up with a regular method of trade balance or to allow for multiple nonexchangeable tokens coexisting in their wallets.

If communities connect their CICs to a basic income or network token like Sarafu in a 1:1 Static Pool—all such CICs would automatically be exchangeable 1:1 with each other (Fig. 5.5). This is appealing because it creates a well defined common pool of tokens connected through a network token. This method combines the concept of a UBI with a credit system—described briefly here.

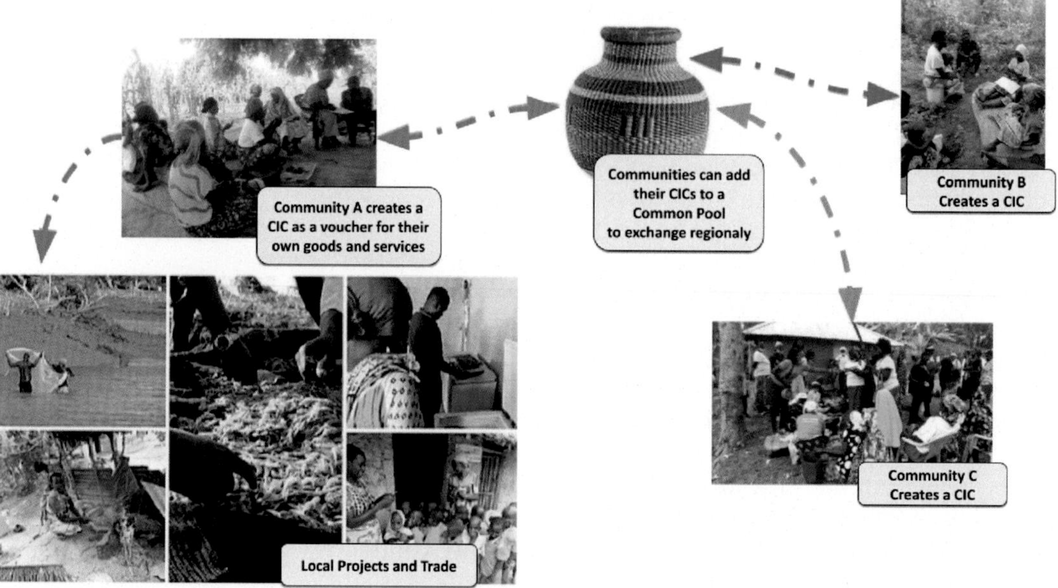

Figure 5.5 CIC connectivity.

Also note that both types of pools could be used to connect a CIC with some other nonCIC token (like BTC, Eth or DAI) who's value might be fluctuating or unknown relative to the CICs—in this case having market supply and demand to establish that price over time might be preferable using a Bonded Pool. Note that many such pools can coexist in the same network, connecting the same tokens. So connecting UBI and CICs on static pools while also connecting to non-CICs via bonded pools could allow for in-network 1:1 exchanges and variable/market rate exchanges against foreign tokens (e.g., Eth or stable coins).

4. Methodology

A CIC can be built in many ways that are suitable to different contexts. This section is designed to give you a feel for how CICs are implemented. You will find out more information about what a CIC is and what kind of community support is needed. This guide gives enough background for you to know if you need to go back to one of those steps, but it does not cover them in full. It also does not cover next steps or the technical requirements for implementing a CIC. Here you will find a list of general procedures in starting a CIC, followed by some exercises that you can do with a community looking at setting one up.

1. **Resource Mapping**—what is available locally? Looking to primary production, value addition and service sectors—as organizations that create their own value or source their inputs locally.
2. **Gathering Commitments and Support**—working with other businesses, faith based organizations, clubs, businesses, local governments, and so on to create a commitment to the backing and support of a local currency system.
3. **Auditing and Mediation**—ensuring that there are parties involved that will validate commitments to backing the CIC with goods and services or other forms of collateral and support dispute resolution. It's very important to create safeguards to deal with issues such as businesses failing and people left with unusable CICs.
4. **Contract Creation and Minting**—this involves creating the CIC as a physical or digital token such that its supply is known by all parties and can be queried in the future. GEF utilize DLT or blockchains to ensure that there is transparency and that no one can tamper with the ledger or supply. It's important that the ledgers (servers) are as possible to avoid rent seeking service fees.

5. **Sensitization and Circulation**—while the issuing group can begin trading the CIC for goods and services among themselves—generally they will want a broader community to accept them. GEF often uses the expression, "braiding" to denote the process of connecting two people together into a reciprocal relationship with a CIC, then adding another and another until you have strong braids/market linkages.
6. **Balancing Trade**—trade balance is extremely important. The more imbalanced the distribution of a CIC is over time, the less useful it is as a medium of exchange.
7. **Circulation**—the more effective or active the circulation is, the less supply of a CIC needs to be created. Methods to increase circulation and promote trade balance should take into account both high and low balances—community markets and gathering where people with high balances can use them and where people with low balances can sell goods or services allow for healthy flows. Taxation of balances (holding or Gesell taxes or demurrage) is extremely effective and can even act as a basic income when redistributed (Fukao 2005).

4.1 Learn by doing

Here CIC developers are probing our ability as humans to trust each other and to derisk that trust as a collective with surplus, collateral, and clear repercussions. The following are example exercises that can be done with aspiring community groups. Often the only way to really understand a local currency program is to try it—and a risk free game setting is a good starting point. Host a potluck, mixer, workshop, brai, barbecue—invite your friends, neighbors, clients and colleagues and your supply chain to a gathering where each of you brings something to the table.

4.1.1 Materials

- White Board/Chalkboard/Flipchart
- Chalk/Markers
- Small White slips of paper (These will represent stock of goods and services)
- Pen/Pencil for each participant
- Masking Tape (Or any tape to put something on the wall)

4.1.2 Set-up

Give each player the following materials:

- Pen/Pencil
- One A4 sized white paper

- Six medium sized white slips of paper (or numbers of your choosing)
- Beans = at least enough for 10 for each participant. These will have a value of 10 CICs

4.1.3 Exercise setup

Having a shared goal and shared projects are important success factors for CICs. In this exercise, you are going to understand your community better. The purpose of the exercise is to understand what you could use the CIC to do in your community.

Sometimes community currencies are printed like paper money, but today most community currencies are digital—because most people now know how to use mobile money on their phones. CIC will generally be mobile or digital money but you will use paper and beans to signify your CIC today. This allows us to see where the entire supply of CIC is at all times, so you can understand how the money flow works.

In this exercise, you are going to map our resources and needs. Then you will simulate trading with the paper and beans. At the end, you will take account and discuss what happened.

4.1.4 Step 1: Resource mapping

Needs: Identify all the needs people have in the community and trace their sources. What does the community import? (e.g., money, flour) What about needs like emotional support, tree planting?

- *Think about the needs of the community, including physical needs like petrol and flour. Also think of services like a Boda ride or childcare, and care needs such as tending to someone ill.*
- *Write down on the large piece of paper two or three of the needs and I will write them on the board here.*

Then collect the papers and write them on the board. Add a star each time the resource is repeated.

- *Which of these must be imported?*
- *What are the most common resources identified?*
- *Are there any "circular" trades or cycles where the money would stay within the community?*
- *What happens to the national economy when there are more imports than exports (Leaking bucket idea: There is more water flowing out than flowing in)?*

4.1.5 Step 2. What can I offer?

Now let's look at what the groups can offer. Take a look at this list or things we've made that others want in the community.

What services or items can you provide to help others fulfill their needs? If you don't have something right now, what could you provide in the future?

Please take the slips of white paper. Each paper will represent something you can sell to the community. On each piece of paper, write down something you are selling. Try to choose something that you can actually sell in the community. If you don't have something right now, you can just choose from the list so everyone can play the game. With a long rope or clothesline have the group stand in a circle and then have a starting person say what they have to offer and toss the rope to someone that would accept that offer and keep going until the rope is finished. This web is essentailly a map of the economy that could exist in the community. You can set this web down and move to the next excersise.

4.1.6 Step 3. Barter credit

In this exercise the group is going to trade in the beans, representing the CIC, for the goods they are trading, represented by slips of paper.

Remember, money is just an agreement between people. If the group agrees that beans are money, they can use them for trade. Imagine a trusted group of people in the community did the same: created a voucher for their goods which they could use for a currency.

You are now going to pretend that these beans are a kind of money. Each bean represents 10 CICs, and the CIC is equivalent to the national currency. I will now give everyone 10 beans, to represent 100 CICs. Make sure to count your beans so you all start out with the same number!

Give each participant 10 beans (you can choose the number and adjust). Have them count to make sure they got the same as everyone else.

Now, look at your white slips. On the back, write down a price for that item. It needs to be multiples of 10 shillings (or whatever national currency you are using), because you only have the beans for now (Ideally these white slips can add up to the value of all the beans you've given them.).

Give them time to write on the back of each slip. Also do some slips for yourself, including one for a Boda ride. On the back, write down 50, etc.

Now you are all ready to trade. For example, I have a Boda ride (hold up the paper) *and on the back I wrote 50 (flip and show the back). If you want the ride, you give me five beans. I give you the slip with the Boda ride and then take another white slip and write the same on the new slip, Boda ride on one side and 50 on the back. I still have the motorbike and can give someone else a ride. The same for your services. If you sell one, write up another slip. It's like a market so you can sell as many as you want of your items or services.*

Now go around to one another and buy things you would normally buy. Everyone should make at least five trades. After you make seven trades, sit down and let us know you are finished.

Play for 5–10 min and finish five trades.

4.1.7 Step 4. Community trade audit

Set up a chart on the board with everyone's name.

Let's find out what happened. Count your beans. If you think you have the most, say out loud what you have. Have the person with the most go and write their name and how much they have, and then so on with the next person who has the most.

Have people call out their bean totals, and write their names with the number of beans they had, in order of the most beans to the least beans, on the board.

Discuss in the group:

- *What is interesting about the amounts?*
- *The person at the top (name the name) has a trade balance surplus of ____ CIC. That means that she didn't spend so much in the community and sold a lot of her products or services. What could the community do to make sure she has more to buy?*
- *The people at the bottom (name the names) have trade debits of ____ (their starting amount minus their balance). This means they did not offer goods or services that were in demand enough in the community. What could you do about that?*

Listen for ideas like bringing in additional people into the circle, training people for new professions, reducing consumption of things that are not produced locally, etc.

Now, count what was purchased. You could do that by collecting slips or a raise of hands for what people bought.

Discussion questions:

- *What do these papers tell us about the trade in the community?*
- *What is interesting about the trades?*
- *With the columns in mind, reflect on the daily needs. Are some, most, or all daily needs being met by what was traded? Is there anything missing?*
- *How would someone restock inventory that came from outside needing national currency?*

Discuss and write down a list of challenges, such as

- Restocking
- Trust

- Distance between users
- People not knowing where to spend
- Holding too much CIC
- People changing CIC pricing
- Seasonal products
- Supplying a limited amount (100 CIC): advantages and disadvantages.

A lot more can be done in playing such a game but ideally it gives you a context in which to start considering what kind of agreements need to be created for a currency to be created.

4.2 Currency creation memorandum

What follows is a generic example of an agreement to create a CICs that could be created between a group, a municipality, and many other actors. Note that some third-party organization would review this application and audit the capacity of the group to fulfill their claims against redemption. While this memorandum would be an example of a group applying to a service provider (Sarafu Network) that is also providing auditing services, these functions can be held by various local parties.

1. **Preamble:** Sarafu Network is a network of people and organizations that seek to exchange goods and services using digital vouchers (also known as CIC) that represent designated goods and services of the members. We [Organization name] *(herein called the Applicant which includes members of the Applicant organization)* seek to join the Sarafu Network and develop our own voucher to support our local economy and community [Voucher Name][Voucher Symbol].
2. **Voucher Allocation:** Vouchers are allocated to the Applicant as digital points into an account (herein called the Group Account) provided by the Service Provider. The Applicant may use the vouchers and commits to redeem the vouchers for a specific quantity of goods and services *(See Applicant Group Membership Table).*
   a. **Allocation Limits:** The total amount of vouchers allocated to the *Applicant* will be no greater than 10% of the Applicant's audited annual sales capacity *(See Validator).*
3. **Voucher Value:** The Applicant must accept the vouchers at parity with national currency for their committed goods and services.
4. **Kenyan Law:** Using vouchers does not exempt users from paying taxes or any other Kenyan laws.

   a. Trades are to be agreed between a willing Buyer and a willing Seller under Kenyan law. Both parties must satisfy themselves that all trade is lawful.
5. **Accounts:** All accounts are made accessible through user phone numbers. Users must have a sim card and access to a phone to access their accounts.
   a. **Group Account:** The group account is designated as the voucher group holder for the purposes of initial allocation, fines, savings, and other group holdings. *(See Official Signatories)*
6. **Holding Fees:** Any user holding your voucher will be subject to a holding fee of 2% of their balance monthly. This fee will be deducted automatically from all accounts. Collected fees will go into the *Group Account* and are used by the group to promote the healthy flow of their vouchers and support community programs.
   For the sake of brevity, I will summarize the following sections as:
7. **Service Provider, Validator, Mediators and Dispute resolution, Duration and renewal of contract, Changing this agreement, Termination, Indemnification, Entirety, Notices**
8. **In WITNESS WHEREOF**, the duly authorized representatives of the Applicant, mediators, validator and Service Provider sign this agreement in two (2) originals for equal content and validity on the dates indicated below, and agree to abide by the terms stated in this agreement.
   a. **Group Membership Table:** The undersigned comprise the members of the Application and agree to acceptance of vouchers up to the value of commitments specified below.
      i. Full Name, Phone no., Committed Goods and Services, The value of the commitments to be accepted for vouchers. *, Date, Signature E.g Sally Kamau, 0727889961, water, $10,000/ = , June 20, 2021, XXXXX
   b. **Official Signatories** Should include the group leaders(chairperson, treasurer), Mediators, Auditors, Service Provider.
9. **Best Practices:** while this agreement establishes the relationship with the applicant, mediators and the service provider—it is recommended that the Applicant group have clear internal agreements and documentation on the following:
   a. **Distribution**: establish how the vouchers will be used by the Applicant, including the usage of fees and distribution and or loaning to members and for group projects.
   b. **Loans and Repayment:** if vouchers will be given out as loans, there should be a clear productive purpose for those loans, a repayment period and clear fines for delinquency.

c. **Trade Balance:** members should be required to accept as many vouchers as they spend in a timely manner and be subject to fines.
d. **Projects:** any group projects should be well planned and a designated manager put in charge (e.g. using vouchers as a community support fund for vulnerable households and community gardens).
e. **Yearly Cycle:** There should be an annual period where all vouchers should be returned to the Applicant group account, debts cleared, and vouchers reissued.
f. **Market/Meeting Days:** regular meeting and/or market days (e.g., weekly) should be mandatory—where members meet to trade, discuss and compare voucher balances openly and attempt to reduce high balances and increase low balances.
g. **Balance limits:** members should have clear limits to how many vouchers they will choose to hold at any given time in order to maintain their businesses and not accumulate too many vouchers. Generally voucher issuers will limit their balance to double the amount they were intially created.

5. Pay it forward

These ideas of currency creation, backing, taxation, and even exchange between currencies are all ancient and have been tried over and over with different iterations. While the technology has changed in some dramatic ways—CICs are largely social and political concepts. The will to implement them, is often driven by leaders and communities willing to come together to take on mutual risk and reward.

Believing in yourself, your business, your municipality, your community, and your larger network to be able to build consensus and take on mutual risk and reward is a huge step. Look for examples of this happening around the world and you will be amazed at how fast our socio-political-economic can change and is already.

Creating a credit against communal future production is simply one intervention in a long line of potential economic interventions. Designing systems of endorsements and certifications where reciprocity doesn't need a fungible token economy are possible, especially once you establish trusted flows of resources.

When faced with a countless number of tokens, currencies and ideas, ask yourself and your community what you represent and value and how you can ensure that you support one another and don't fall into the trap of dependence on externally created currencies. Our ancestors knew how to do this and we as a community can relearn it ourselves—create your own currency.

Glossary

CIC—A promissory note against future production developed and maintained by a community.

Cash and Voucher Assistance—A humanitarian response involving the distribution of national currency or vouchers backed with aid funds or products.

DLT or Blockchain—A collection of servers that replicate and validate a shared ledger.

GEF—Grassroots Economics Foudnation—A nonprofit organization based in Kenya with the mission to enable people, groups, and organizations to develop local economic systems, in order to trade, share, value, and support collective action.

IGA—Income Generating Activity.

Liquidity Pools—Algorithmic and decentralized systems that enable conversion between two or more tokens or currencies.

Acknowledgments

There are so many people that have made this work possible and contributed in a myriad of ways. I'm going to list a few here that deserve special recognition because of their dedication to the topic of community currencies over the years: Shaila Agha, Grace Rachmany, Adam Bornstien, Safia Verjeey, Roy Awaho, Njambi Njoroge, Emmanuel Mbui, Wilfred Chibwara, Janet Treezer, Joyce Kamau, Amina Godana, Thomas Greco, Matthew Slater, Eyal Hertzog.

References

Blanc, J., 1998. Free money for social progress: theory and practice of Gesell's accelerated money. American Journal of Economics and Sociology 57 (4), 469–483.

Food Forests, 2021. Syntropic Agroforestry with CICs. https://www.grassrootseconomics.org/food-forests.

Fukao, M., 2005. The effects of 'Gesell'(Currency) taxes in promoting Japan's economic recovery. International Economics and Economic Policy 2 (2), 173–188.

Götsch, E., 1995. Break-through in Agriculture. AS-PTA, Rio de Janeiro, p. 22p.

Lal, R., 2004. Soil carbon sequestration to mitigate climate change. Geoderma 123 (1–2), 1–22.

Red Cross (Kenya) CIC Program Survey, 2020. https://www.grassrootseconomics.org/post/red-cross-cic-pilot-survey-mukuru-kenya.

Ruddick, W.O., 2020. Community Inclusion Currency White Paper. https://gitlab.com/grassrootseconomics/cic-docs/-/blob/master/CIC-White-Paper.pdf.

Stein, P., Ardic, O.P., Hommes, M., 2013. Closing the Credit Gap for Formal and Informal Micro, Small, and Medium Enterprises.

6

Managing uncertainty/making miracles: understanding and strategizing for unpredictable outcomes in the implementation of intelligent government

Keith Guzik[1] **and Gary T. Marx**[2]

[1] *University of Colorado Denver, Denver, CO, United States;* [2] *Massachusetts Institute of Technology, Cambridge, MA, United States*

> *The new always happens against the overwhelming odds of statistical laws and their probability, which for all practical, everyday purposes amounts to certainty; the new therefore always appears in the guise of a miracle. The fact that man is capable of action means that the unexpected can be expected from him, that he is able to perform what is infinitely improbable.*
>
> **Hannah Arendt, The Human Condition.**

1. Introduction

If environments are to become more "intelligent," attention to research, planning, legislation, coordination, and implementation is necessary (Lopes, 2017). Intelligent environments can help government in many ways. They may do this by sustaining the natural and built environment, reducing the risks posed by environmental change, managing the industrial engines and artifacts of society, and increasing compliance with policy and law. Intelligent environments need to be created with humility and awareness of the factors that limit success and sometimes make things worse.

Given the complexity and complications of human societies, making any government more efficient is challenging. Democratic societies with their legitimate conflicting interests face even greater challenges. Consider, for example, making government

Intelligent Environments. https://doi.org/10.1016/B978-0-12-820247-0.00008-4

more intelligent through the adoption of advanced information and communication technologies (ICT). The World Bank (2016) estimates that only 20% of projects seeking to digitalize government organizations and operations are successful, even holding apart just what the criteria and measurements for success are. The difficulties primarily stem from the "large gap between the regulatory, political, management, process, and skill realities in government and the ambitions of e-government projects" (The World Bank, 2016: 165).

State efforts to employ technological means for control are frequently challenged by an "*uncertainty principle*" that applies to social as well as physical worlds. This refers to unwanted unpredictability or uncertainty operating at the individual, organizational, political, cultural, environmental, and technical levels of control projects (Marx and Guzik, 2017). The uncertainty principle helps us understand why government attempts, and organizational efforts more broadly, at technological control often fall far short of the ideal.

Yet, the abject failure, again holding apart the often multiple dimensions and measurements of failure, of digital or intelligent government is not a given. There are relative success stories. Studying these can help us better understand efforts to digitize the state, just as can the study of failures. This chapter discusses two case studies of successful digital governance: the first in the former Soviet republic of Estonia and the second in the United States. In examining these, we seek lessons for bolstering effective intelligent environments.

The chapter has three parts. The first considers the "uncertainty principle" as it applies to governance through technological means. The second covers the case studies of successful innovation. The third, drawing from the cases, offers some lessons that can inform the creation and functioning of intelligent environments.

2. The uncertainty principle

Obamacare, more formally known as the Affordable Care Act, extended health insurance coverage in the United States. In doing so, it illustrated many of the challenges of using digital technology to modernize service delivery. On October 1, 2013, the program's website was launched and on the first day of operations, only six people were able to sign up. Over the next 10 days there were more than 14 million unique visits to the website. But after 1 month, only 26,794 people had enrolled for coverage—90% fewer than the administration had projected.

President Obama acknowledged, "There's no sugarcoating it. The website has been too slow. People have been getting stuck during the application process. And I think it's fair to say that nobody is more frustrated by that than I am" (Lee and Brumer, 2017).

Subsequent inquiries identified reasons for the failure. First was the massive *scale* of the project. The HealthCare.gov architecture involved a transaction processing application able to interact in real time with existing federal agency databases and more than 170 insurance carriers. It also involved a data services hub allowing health insurance marketplaces to immediately validate applicants' personal information from that stored in federal databases and insurance companies across new and older legacy information systems (Chambers, 2014). Ultimately, over 50 separate contractors would work on the project (Chambers, 2014).

Such an effort required strong, clear *leadership*. Evaluations such as that by Lee and Brumer (2017) found such leadership lacking. Most blame was laid upon the Centers for Medicare and Medicaid Services (CMS), the agency charged with ensuring the website's development and operation. CMS failed to follow a range of basic program management practices. For instance, in terms of *cost management*, CMS signed cost-reimbursable contracts with software developers rather than fixed-price contracts. This ballooned the cost for website development from an expected $292 million to $2.1 billon (Lee and Brumer, 2017). This failure was tied to poor *requirements management*—the hardware and software requirements on the project changed seven times over the 10 months prior to deployment. These changing requirements impacted *schedule management*–features of the HealthCare.gov Website were modified only a week before the launch. A *lack of testing* was endemic to the project—end-to-end testing was conducted only in the final weeks before launch (Chambers, 2014). CGI Federal, the lead software developer on the project, had a poor track record for delivering on government contracts (Chambers, 2014). Subcontractors on the project called attention to negative aspects of CMS's *organizational culture*, as they did not feel accepted as equals or that their concerns about the project were heard (Lee and Brumer, 2017).

Given these factors, the project's size exploded. It was estimated that the initial HealthCare.gov site contained 500 million lines of code. Five million lines of this needed to be rewritten to correct the website's shortcomings. As a point of comparison, a large bank's suite of software applications is about one-fifth this size (Lee and Brumer, 2017).

The initial failure of the HealthCare.gov story underscores the importance of effective *management* in adopting ICT for government services. But a range of factors beyond (mis)management need consideration. In previous work, we identify complicating factors (Marx, 2016; Guzik, 2016). For instance, Guzik (2016) describes how the Mexican government attempted to adopt intelligent information systems to modernize its relationship with its citizenry as part of a larger strategy for combating insecurity. This included a national mobile phone registry to prevent and combat kidnappings; a national car registry to reduce arms trafficking and car thefts; and a national identity card to help track criminals and crime victims. Like HealthCare.gov, each of these efforts to varying degrees failed to live up to their promise.

Mismanagement played a role in these stories. But in the case of the mobile phone registry, *citizens actively resisted* by refusing to register their numbers with the government or registering with falsified data (such as the personal identification number of the then Mexican president). Eventually, the Mexican Senate voted to abolish the program. The national identity card was redundant with the Mexican national voting card, the de facto form of identification in the country. As a result, *government agencies at the federal and state levels sought to block* the implementation of the program. In the end, the scale of the identity card program was reduced to include only minors under the age of 18. And participation in the program was modest. The national car registry grew slowly in the country, taking root in those states run by governors from the same *political party* as the president, and today it serves as a functional federal database useful for verifying the legal status of vehicles up for sale or that the police encounter on the streets.

Such cases illustrate that the *uncertainty principle* is inherent to public and private efforts to manage society through technical or other means. To illustrate the basic points, we next connect five prominent components of the uncertainty principle to the problems of HealthCare.gov.

Agents and goals. The development and implementation of advanced ICT technologies in government is generally distributed across networks of *agents*, including federal officials and employees responsible for designing a program or protocol, private sector actors who deliver and maintain the software and hardware for programs, and state-level officials and employees who implement programs. However, these agents may not share the same goals, leading to challenges in modernizing government operations (Marx and Guzik, 2017). In the case of HealthCare.gov, the Obama administration officials in charge of overseeing the project were interested in obtaining a website to help fulfill the provisions of the Patient Protection and Affordable Care Act; the private firms developing software for the website were interested in generating revenue for their work with the government; and some state officials were actively opposed to the federal project. Adding to the complexity was the number of agents, over 50 private software firms, participating in developing the project. Such a cacophony of interests requires strong leadership and management. These were absent from HealthCare.gov.

Subjects and resistance. The intended recipients or subjects of state services can interrupt plans for making the state more intelligent through technology. Subjects are able to unfurl different modes of resistance against technological forms of social control, ranging from masking one's identity to avoid identification by the state to simply refusing to participate in an action or program (Marx, 2016, ch. 5; Marx and Guzik, 2017). There was little resistance to HealthCare.gov, and subjects generally welcomed it. In this case, the congruence between the goals of authorities and subjects facilitated acceptance. Yet, the five uncertainty sources can be independent and incongruities are often present. And it is important to note that governance is relational, involving the interactions of both governors and the governed.

Politics and Law. The legal and political contexts of government institutions and agencies bear on the outcomes of digital initiatives. For instance, federal systems of political power present unique challenges—federated states limit the reach of national government. States have constitutional guarantees for *not* participating in some national undertakings. Politics can further complicate the equation, when oppositional political parties view a program as detrimental to their own interests (Marx and Guzik, 2017). The difficulties launching HealthCare.gov are illustrative. The Patient Protection and Affordable Care Act was one of the more contentious pieces of legislation in recent US history, with Republicans aggressively opposing the Democratic legislation. Many states under Republican leadership, for their part, refused to participate in the program, which placed a greater burden and responsibility on the federal government, increasing the scale and difficulty of the federal government's work.

Culture. National and local cultural differences can weigh upon technical systems in unexpected ways. Past government failures and the reputation of state institutions can influence how citizens interpret new initiatives, regardless of how "intelligent" and "reasonable" they are. Popular skepticism around the Patient Protection and Affordable Care Act likely increased the pressure on the Obama administration to deliver a winning website, leading the CMS to rush the program without proper testing.

Technology and Environment. The technical design of digital systems impacts upon system outcomes. But so too do the design and material makeup of the elements that the systems look to govern. These vary in their material or digital make up in ways that make them more or less "sticky" in regards to efforts to control, track, and order them (Guzik, 2016). With HealthCare.gov, the redundancy and volume of unnecessary code complicated the operation of the website. Citizens' records were stored in different formats and in different locations (e.g., those of insurance providers vs. those from state agencies), complicating their integration into the federal website.

These factors underscore a central premise of the approach known as science and technology studies (STS). In the words of Andrew Pickering (1995), the world "is continually doing things, things that bear upon us not as observational statements upon disembodied intellects but as forces upon material beings" (Pickering, 1995:6). The world has agency—"material agency" (Pickering, 1995:6)—as exhibited by the challenges our natural environment continually presents us in the form of forest fires, rising seas, and deadly storms. However, notions of agency can also be applied to "things" like legal documents (Kahn, 2019; Latour, 2010) as they enable certain courses of action while discouraging or preventing others. These are structures or social facts that in some ways are equivalent to natural forces such as gravity or darkness.

The uncertainty principle encourages us to embrace and extend this way of thinking to projects of control such as those involving intelligent environments. Implementing an intelligent motorway or identity card is immensely challenging, not only because government officers and members of the public may resist it, but also because material objects like automobiles and human physiognomy have their own propensities that limit control efforts. Such "distributions of agency" (Pickering, 1995) have to be accounted for and managed (if not always subject to full control) to have success.

But while this complexity imposes some limits and serves to tilt solutions in particular directions, the certainty of uncertainty does not make intelligent government impossible. There are numerous examples of successful intelligent environment projects. In studying relatively successful outcomes, lessons for managing the uncertainty principle and increasing the chances for creating and implementing better outcomes can be identified. The next section reviews two such success stories —the development of digital democracy in the post-Soviet Baltic republic of Estonia and the successful modernization of departments of motor vehicles in the United States.

3. Case studies

3.1 Estonian digital democracy

Estonia, the tiny former Soviet republic of 1,329,000 people, is illustrative of how digital technology can transform the public sector and contribute to more intelligent government. Estonians are able to access essentially any public service, file taxes, vote, order prescriptions, and sign legal documents online without having to come face-to-face with state employees. Citizens take advantage of these opportunities, with nearly all personal income tax declarations and medical prescriptions done online. About 30% of votes in local and national elections are cast digitally as well. The digital government infrastructure is estimated to save 2% of annual GDP and significant working time for workers (Kattel and Mergel, 2018).

Estonia's digital success involves X-road, a secure data infrastructure platform for data exchanges, and a system for the digital identification of citizens. Almost all Estonians have a state-issued digital identity. And digital signatures can be used online for public and private transactions.

The success of Estonia as a digital democracy is all the more impressive considering where the country started from. Estonia gained independence from the collapsing Soviet Union in 1991, but maintains a land border with the Russia, with its history of invading neighboring countries. The bifurcated population is 70% ethnic Estonian and 25% Russian. Following independence, the country had a modest technological base and limited resources to build a digital infrastructure. It is surprising then that the country became a model of digital governance.

How did Estonia do it? Its drive to digitalization did not follow from a single foundational policy document or statement. Estonia did not create a central office to organize and manage its digital transformation. Nor has it legislated ICT innovation (Kattel and Mergel, 2018). For example, the Estonian state abides by a "once only" principle—citizens and business need provide identifying personal information to the state only once. Government offices subsequently requiring that information have access it to it through the X-road platform (Wimmer et al., 2017). "Once only" is intended to reduce the bureaucratic burden on citizens and state workers. But it is a principle, not a law.

Rather than legislative or organizational dictates, Estonia's success resulted from a combination of managerial, technical, cultural, political, and geopolitical factors (Kattel and Mergel, 2018). Estonia's embrace of digital government has followed general *principles*, chief of which has been for departments and agencies "to develop their own digital agendas" since they best know their needs. This honors decentralization and localism. Furthermore, initially lacking the resources to purchase market solutions from established vendors, the country came to embrace an "unspoken principle of frugality." But frugality was not interpreted to mean cheap or inferior, as another abiding principle for the nation has been to "leapfrog" the technology of the West (Kattel and Mergel, 2018).

Adherence to these principles had *technical* ramifications. First, digital solutions in Estonia have necessarily been "open-source" in order to save money. Second, allowing departments and agencies to develop their own solutions has created the need for a software layer permitting interoperability across distributed IT systems and databases in their data exchanges. This is the purpose and function of X-road, which serves as the secure data exchange for its distributed public IT systems and databases (Kattel and Mergel, 2018).

In terms of *organization*, without a central technology innovation office, agencies have relied on strong informal networks involving the public and private sectors in pushing digitization forward. For example, banks, with a clear interest in verifying personal identity, initially issued electronic identification materials to citizens. Some cybersecurity experts moved from banks to the government. This proved vital in responding to a Russian distributed denial of service (DDoS) attack in 2007 and paved the path for continuous personnel movement between sectors. These networks provide a regulative function usually fulfilled by the law or regulations. Groups that do not cooperate can be excluded from the network (Kattel and Mergel, 2018).

Banks have also been integral with another component of Estonia's success, *education*. They sponsored different educational initiatives to support IT education in schools and society in general, enabling citizens to use their online services. Estonia's legacy as a center for linguistic and communication research during Soviet times also bolstered its digital experiment. The country had a large number of highly educated and skilled ICT professionals when it was part of the Soviet Union.

Estonia's national *culture* was also a support. Digital development served as a symbol for leaving its Soviet past behind and as an indicator of Estonia's position relative to Europe and internationally. Kattel and Mergel (2018) label this sense of cultural and historical purpose as Estonia's "mission mystique." This mission transcends organizational institutions and strengthens the digital transformation networks. The mission mystique helps legitimize risk-taking and experimentation. It offers *political support* for the digitalization of society across political parties.

Estonia's cultural support for digitalization is clearly tied to its *history* and *geography*. The country's close proximity to Russia, which has invaded and ruled Estonia throughout history, provided motivation for undertaking measures, such as digitalization, that promised to strengthen independence. But also an important factor in building its ICT capacity is its proximity to Scandinavia. In 1991, the Estonian government reorganized the Ministry of Communications into two state-owned companies, Eesti Telekom and Eesti Post, decoupled them from Soviet telecommunication networks, and created a mobile joint-venture with Swedish and Finnish counterparts (Högselius, 2005:81). This move provided the country greater independence from its larger and stronger European and U.S. counterparts.

Finally, consider *scale*. Estonia is a small country with a population concentration in its capital city (almost one third of its 1.3 million inhabitants live in Tallinn). This smaller-scale facilitated the creation of socio-technical networks that have been vital to digital success.

Yet, Estonia is not without problems. Kattel and Mergel (2018) report that Estonia's digital project did not increase citizen engagement or digitally transform public services. While electronic identity and other innovations have improved the efficiency of public service delivery, the services themselves have largely stayed the same. And citizen satisfaction with such central services as health care and education has remained low. Finally, digitalization has not diminished inequality in the country, especially the segmentation of ethnic Russians into lower-quality jobs (Saar and Helemäe, 2017). These limitations reflect the fact that digital democracy in Estonia resulted from "a tight-knit elite network of politicians business leaders and civil servants" rather than through "co-creative processes with citizens" (Kattel and Mergel, 2018:13). These points notwithstanding, Estonia's experiences help us identify strategies for managing the uncertainty principle (considered in the final section).

3.2 U.S. department of motor vehicles

Transportation is intricately tied to the environment. The threat automobility poses to natural and human-made environments is well known. The resources required to fuel motor vehicles, the air and ground pollution they generate, and the quality of life issues they involve make automobile regulation central for governments (Guzik, 2016). Control over automobility generally rests with departments of motor vehicles (DMVs). DMVs carry much of the promise and responsibility for building intelligent transportation systems able to reduce threats from automobiles to natural and social environments.

In spite of their importance, DMVs in the United States are often subject to criticism. It is difficult to imagine a more universally scorned government agency in the United States than the DMV. They are synonymous with long lines and driver frustration. DMV agencies have even been ridiculed in popular song, with the rock band Primus singing in the 1990s: "I've been to hell. I spell it, I spell it DMV; Anyone that's been there knows precisely what I mean."

Why are DMVs perceived so poorly? The reasons are multiple. One is *scale*. DMVs in the United States register over 250 million cars and trucks and 12.5 million boats and license over 200 million drivers. Approximately 33 million US residents use DMV services each year. Service delivery for such a large number of people can create problems. Another problem is *technical*. Most DMVs were saddled with dated information systems coded in antiquated computer languages. Another challenge is *techno-cultural*. Given the now common place ease of hopping online and receiving goods with a single computer click, the experience of standing in long lines at the local DMV office is exasperating. The expectation of one-click convenience has been labeled the "Amazon effect" (Newcombe, 2018). Another issue is *legal*. Following the September 11 terrorist attacks, the federal government passed new requirements for driver's licenses and identity cards, termed Real ID. These required DMVs to use biometric identification and to verify that license applicants were legally in the country. That could not be done with the outdated technology then in place (Newcombe, 2018). Another problem is *managerial*. Efforts at modernizing the information systems at DMVs were not new. But instead of creating new efficiencies for licensing and registrations, solutions routinely failed by following "waterfall methodologies." This methodology plans out software solutions in steps before implementation (and thus can be brittle in the face of unanticipated challenges).

Yet, in spite of the challenges, DMVs in many places in the United States have been significantly transformed. Drivers can renew licenses, register cars and change addresses online at any time. Many DMVs have successfully moved from mainframes to open-source based environments permitting cloud data storage. The departments have even become sources of innovation, with mobile applications allowing for the conception of mobile driver's licenses, which would be kept digitally on one's mobile device rather than physically in one's pocket. It is for these reasons that industry observers have announced "redemption for the DMV" (Newcombe, 2018).

How did this change occur? *Technical innovation* played a role, as open source software and cloud storage made for more dynamic information systems. However, many states actually kept their existing technology, mainframe computers requiring outdated COBOL code for example, even though that technology was initially considered a problem (Newcombe, 2018). Ironically, the antiquated technology turned out to be beneficial. Mainframes, although dated, were built to last (Newcombe, 2018). Thus, in enhancing digitalization, many agencies were followed a strategy of "don't fix what isn't broke."

Public private partnerships were often important for these efforts. Some states used private vendors to host platforms for driver and vehicle services. Such outsourcing makes it likely that the technology will be regularly refreshed. Furthermore, it saves governments money, since they don't have to compete with the private sector to attract highly skilled IT workers (Newcombe, 2018).

Making the public–private partnerships work required rethinking *management* practice. One factor involved transitioning from the traditional waterfall method of software development, where vendors are expected to specify an entire product in advance and later deliver it, to an agile method, where vendors share finished steps with clients to ensure the software is serving its purpose. In addition, states have put into practice open and transparent contract bidding and award processes, where bidders are aware of the rules and the status of their applications throughout the process, including the reasons why their bids were rejected. These changes are believed to encourage more vendors to compete for contracts (Martin et al., 2018). As well, some states have institutionalized performance review processes, where customers at branch offices are routinely surveyed to measure their levels of satisfaction with DMV services—this feedback is then used to improve service (Martin et al., 2018).

In an ironic turn, the digitization of the DMV has also succeeded by not focusing only on technology. Successful states adopt a *holistic* approach targeting the organization, processes, and facilities of the office (Newcombe, 2018). One innovation has been to group various services into "super offices" or "one-stop shops," where drivers can access all DMV services at one location (Martin et al., 2018).

Finally, *law* has been a factor in the success stories. To encourage up-to-date records, states such as California introduced amnesty programs for drivers with licenses suspended for unpaid fines. Before 2015, the California DMV had over four million such cases. Amnesty programs offered automatic reinstatement of licenses and reduced outstanding fees for drivers participating in the program (California State Senate, 2015). By bringing drivers back into the system, the department has increased its ability to regulate driving behavior.

As with Estonian digital democracy, this success story has its drawbacks. On-line government services are imperfect and goals can conflict. For instance, state laws protecting the drivers' privacy may limit how much data can stored in proprietary cloud space. And long lines have not altogether disappeared (McQuillan, 2019). That said, obtaining a driver's license and registering a vehicle in the United States have become much easier and more efficient.

4. Lessons

In a recent meta-analysis, Gil Garcia and Flores-Zuniga (2020) identify factors related to successful intelligent government. Successful digital initiatives are defined by implementation by the state and adoption by citizens. For implementation, what matters is whether governments are able to follow through with their efforts, including the organizational power of the digitizing agencies; top-level leaders' commitment and political support for initiatives; appropriate skills for project operations among personnel; effective project management with an eye to realistic timelines, requirements, scope, and goals; and appropriate technical infrastructure, including data compatibility and information management. On the side of adoption, users' perceptions of security and privacy, trust of the government, access to technology, and awareness of the programs increase use.

This framework resonates with the sources of uncertainty we discuss. Implementation focuses on the actions of *agents*, while adoption on the behaviors of *subjects*. Successful implementation and adoption, in turn, depend upon *political, technical,* and *cultural* factors.

The case studies of healthcare.gov, Estonian digital democracy and U.S. departments of motor vehicles considered above offer a way of reducing uncertainty. To reduce the uncertainty surrounding the diversity of *agent* interests involved in project development, *leadership* is critical. Such leadership was notably absent in the case of HealthCare.gov, while Estonia benefitted from leadership continuity regarding the importance of digitizing the state and also the basic principles for doing that. To reduce the possibility of inadequate *technical* specification or glitches, effective *program management* is needed in specifying appropriate technology and minimizing glitches. Agile development has helped DMVs in the US succeed in their modernization efforts, while adherence to outdated approaches caused the scale of HealthCare.gov to balloon. To reduce the deleterious effects of *politics* upon project implementation, significant *political consensus* is needed. Both HealthCare.gov and the Affordable Care Act were highly politicized. This complicated the website's launch. In contrast, the nonpartisan nature of DMVs and the support for digital initiatives by Estonian political leaders informed their success.

These case studies also help us identify factors for managing the uncertainty principle. To return to the point made above, a challenge of realizing digital government, intelligent environments, or any other endeavor seeking control is "distributed agency" (Pickering, 1995). That is, not only do people have their own interests and inclinations that impact what happens, but influences also come from natural environments, material objects, and the law and culture. Building a national healthcare website, digitizing democratic government, or reforming departments of motor vehicles requires more than good technology, good government, and trusting citizens. This work, rather, involves "tuning" (Pickering, 1995) or "enrolling" (Callon, 1984) disparate agents, subjects, laws, technologies, environments, and cultures into a common strategy or program aware of their mutual, and often interactive, nature. The successes of Estonia and United States DMVs, and the challenges of HealthCare.gov, allow us to identify lessons for completing such tuning or enrollment work.

Table 6.1 summarizes lessons for managing uncertainty suggested by these three cases. We structure these lessons by the source of uncertainty. For instance, regarding *agents*, the case studies illustrate the importance of *public private* partnerships. The banking sector served as a key ally in developing digital identity verification systems in Estonia, as well as training the population on its operation. Companies in the US developed software to help incompatible data systems better communicate within DMVs. Such partnerships relieve the public sector of hiring such personnel in house.

Of course, HealthCare.gov's unexamined reliance on public–private partnerships weakened it, at least initially. This speaks to the need to balance organizational arrangements with appropriate work and management strategies. Not only must leadership be clear, but *agile* or iterative work strategies for collaborations are important. Under such arrangements, protocols and solutions evolve through the collaboration of developers

Table 6.1 Sources of uncertainty and their management.

Area of uncertainty	Source of uncertainty	Management strategy
AGENTS	Dissimilar goals and loyalties	Public—private collaboration; Clear leadership; Agile management; Targeting sectors;
SUBJECTS	Resistance	Incentives
LAW AND POLITICS	Constitutional and legal constraints; Party politics	Under-specification; Sovereignty
TECHNOLOGY	Wrong specifications; Quirks; Environmental challenges	Craft; Multi-functionality; Inter-operativity; Distributedness
CULTURE	Trust; Legitimacy	Letting go; Awareness of irrationality and surprise; Dream

and end users. The move from traditional waterfall strategies (where end solutions are defined from the start) to agile strategies proved critical for DMVs, while the absence of agility harmed HealthCare.gov. Developers working on the HealthCare.gov project felt excluded from the project. *Agile* management helps give voice to both developers and users, increasing commitment.

The challenge of coordinating *agents* on digitalization projects also requires attention to *sectors*. Rather than trying to bring change all at once across a broad swath of agencies, it is better to focus on particular sectors of the state or society. In the case of Estonia, the banking sector's concern and experience with personal identification techniques and data security made it an ideal ally in building the country's digital state.

Turning to *subjects*, the case studies from Estonia and the U.S. department of motor vehicles offer some insight on how to reduce resistance. Public participation in government initiatives cannot be assumed simply because they are valued by government. Users have to value them as well. *Incentives* condition that value. In Estonia, participation in the digital state offers citizens savings by circumventing time-consuming trips to government offices. For motorists in the United States, DMVs increased participation by re-instating licenses suspended and reducing fees for previous infractions.

Regarding *politics and law*, there are no easy answers for creating political consensus. But here, the Estonian experience provides some guidance. For one, tying the modernization of the state to *sovereignty* provided the country's digital initiatives with support across the political spectrum. In addition, Estonia's example offers the counterintuitive lesson that *under-specifying* legal requirements can be more successful than overspecifying them. States and governments are familiar with rules, decrees, and centralization of power as basic strategies for governing. Yet the Estonian success was predicated on the absence of foundational documents, rigid regulations on technology, and even a central organization to administer innovations. Instead, principles—of sovereignty, frugality, and convenience—served as broad guideposts for government agencies to develop their own solutions regarding digitalization.

The cases of Estonia and DMVs offer lessons regarding the *technical dimensions* of successful digitalization. For one, digital technology allows for enhanced *multifunctionality* within government operations. DMV "super-centers" in the United States or completely mobile services in Estonia permit a single agency to offer a multiplicity of transactional services. Digital technologies such as Estonia's X-road or the DMV modernization projects of proprietary data companies in the US enhance the *interoperability* of the state. This permits interactions between the data infrastructures of different state agencies, including legacy systems already in existence. The *distributedness* of data networks is also a common feature of success in Estonia and the United States. Whereas government data were previously stored either in physical files or digital mainframes within separate governmental offices, storing data in the cloud improves access for both bureaucrats and citizens.

These two case studies underscore the importance of being "*crafty*" (Guzik, 2016). Rather than starting digital projects from scratch, these projects built on existing strengths, with what was already being done well. Estonian cybernetics and linguistic studies were not simply seen as esoteric fields left over from the Soviet era. The legacy data infrastructures at the U.S. departments of motor vehicles were antiquated and could be seen as irrelevant and antithetical to the digital age. Yet, both were used to facilitate innovation and modernization.

Finally, consider *culture*, broadly defined. In discussing how agents, subjects, laws, and technology can be brought together to create intelligent environments, this chapter has embraced the importance of rational thought and planning. Agents of technological innovation may have a better chance of success by sharing the work of digitization across public and private agencies. Subjects of technological innovation can be brought into the fold through financial or temporal incentives. The politics of digital development can in general be best managed through a distanced approach built on broad principles, rather than on highly specified dictates. The technologies of intelligent governments can offer better service through multifunctionality, interoperability, and distributedness.

Yet as important and reasonable as such factors may be, they cannot fully account for the frequent distance between the circumstances in which digital futures are imagined and their eventual outcomes. For a small, recently liberated Baltic nation facing a technologically advanced world, there seemed few reasons to hope it could become technologically advanced. Is sovereignty from a larger and more aggressive neighbor a reasonable hope? Are aspirations to leap frog a technologically superior West reasonable? More simply put, where does reason lie and what can we expect from it?

In the epigram that opened the paper, Arendt (2013) notes that human inventiveness and courageous responses often occur in the face of rational analyses indicating why a problem cannot be solved. She notes, "The new always happens against the overwhelming odds of statistical laws and their probability," which makes the new "always appears in the guise of a miracle." Such mundane miracles are possible because, as Arendt (2013) notes, "man is capable of action." If we forget or neglect our ability to act in the world, even a world that is increasingly technological and seemingly beyond our reach, then our cause is surely lost. As the Italian theorist Gramsci observed in confronting challenging problems, "pessimism of the intellect, and optimism of the will" is often needed.

The efforts to create intelligent environments rest on the granite bedrocks of the enlightenment and the renaissance. Yet that heritage has an ironic message—rational analysis may suggest that little or nothing can be done, sustaining inaction. Such a belief feeds on itself in devouring hope. Fortunately, as the articles in this volume suggest, much can be done. A central message from Kant through Ortega y Gasset, Jaques Ellul, and Robert Merton involves avoiding the hubris of undue rationalism, particularly as it involves thought divorced from observation. Beyond offering a means forward, the systematic, empirical approach of science and technology can bring a humbling awareness of complexity and answers that lead to new questions. As Jaques Ellul (2005) suggests, technology can provide "us with cures for our ills by creating further ills."

Yet in spite of bouts of disillusionment and the need for some distance from the exaggerated claims of the rational project, it is our best shot in the tragedy of the human situation. Rational approaches can identify what needs to be done, as well as why doing it is so often incomplete and challenging. They offer a way to think about possibilities and limits in a world on the brink.

The best governance involves humility and hope—skepticism regarding solutions that are offered as perfect and cost free, but also regarding claims that nothing can be done. When things are done, they must be continually subject to analysis. As the man said, "things change" and the confounding forces are multiple. Fortunately, through rational analysis, rather than through blind faith in either ideology or technology, partial solutions may be found.

As with the carrot dangling in front of the donkey, seemingly forward steps may not ensure success, and, in a dynamic world, success may not last. Policy analysts and scholars must be jugglers and minefield-walkers in attending to both the hope and the despair from rational approaches. They need to simultaneously be skeptical, while not drowning in doubt, and hopeful, while not uncritically swimming in optimism. French theorist Bernard Charbonneau (Ellul and Chastenat, 2005:5) observed, "we live in a conflictual, incomplete, irrational world and it is precisely up to us to establish a little order even though this is difficult and provisional." Yet reason and miracles can combine in contributing to that.

References

Arendt, H., 2013. The Human Condition. University of Chicago Press, Chicago.

California State Senate Subcommittee on Modernizing Government, 2015. The DMV: A Case Study in Modernization. Available at: https://sgf.senate.ca.gov/sites/sgf.senate.ca.gov/files/background_informational_hearing_the_dmv-_a_case_study_in_modernization.pdf.

Callon, M., 1984. Some elements of a sociology of translation: domestication of the scallops and the fishermen of St Brieuc Bay. The Sociological Review 32 (1), 196–233.

Chambers, L., 2014. Case Study: Saving Obamacare. Chambers & Associates Pty Ltd. Available at: https://www.chambers.com.au/public_resources/case_study/obamacare/saving-obamacare-case-study.pdf.

Ellul, J., Chastenet, P.T., 2005. Jacques Ellul on Politics, Technology, and Christianity: Conversations with Patrick Troude-Chastenet. Wipf and Stock Publishers, Eugene, OR.

Gil-Garcia, J.R., Flores-Zúñiga, M.Á., 2020. Towards a comprehensive understanding of digital government success: integrating implementation and adoption factors. Government Information Quarterly 37 (4), 101518.

Guzik, K., 2016. Making Things Stick: Surveillance Technologies and Mexico's War on Crime. University of California Press, Berkeley, CA.

Högselius, P., 2005. The Dynamics of Innovation in Eastern Europe: Lessons from Estonia. Edward Elgar Publishing, Cheltenham.

Kahn, J., 2019. Islands of Sovereignty: Haitian Migration and the Borders of Empire. University of Chicago Press, Chicago.

Kattel, R., Mergel, I., 2018. Estonia's Digital Transformation: Mission Mystique and the Hiding Hand. UCL Institute for Innovation and Public Purpose Working Paper Series (IIPP WP 2018-09). Available: https://www.ucl.ac.uk/bartlett/public-purpose/wp2018-09.

Latour, B., 2010. The Making of Law: An Ethnography of the Conseil D'État. Polity, New York.

Lee, G., Brumer, J., 2017. Managing Mission-Critical Government Software Projects: Lessons Learned from the HealthCare.gov Project. IBM Center for the Business of Government. Available: http://www.businessofgovernment.org/sites/default/files/Viewpoints%20Dr%20Gwanhoo%20Lee.pdf.

Lopes, N.V., 2017. Smart governance: a key factor for smart cities implementation. In: 2017 IEEE International Conference on Smart Grid and Smart Cities (ICSGSC), IEEE, pp. 277–282.

Martin, J.B., Bhadury, J., Cordeiro, J., Waite, M.L., Amoako-Gyampah, K., 2018. Service operations in DMV (division of motor vehicles) offices of the USA - a comparative study. Management Research Review 4 (41), 504–523.

Marx, G.T., 2016. Windows into the Soul. University of Chicago Press, Chicago.

Marx, G.T., Guzik, K., 2017. The uncertainty principle: qualification, contingency and fluidity in surveillance outcomes. In: McGuire, M., Holt, T. (Eds.), The Handbook of Technology, Crime and Justice. Routledge, New York, pp. 481–502.

McQuillan, L., 2019. Driving Californians Crazy. Independent Institute Briefing. January 29. Available: https://www.independent.org/publications/article.asp?id=11705.

Newcombe, T., 2018. Redemption for the DMV. Government Technology. Available: https://www.govtech.com/computing/Redeption-for-the-DMV.html.

Pickering, A., 1995. The Mangle of Practice: Time, Agency, and Science. University of Chicago Press, Chicago.

Saar, E., Helemäe, J., 2017. Ethnic segregation in the Estonian labour market. In: Tammaru, T., Kallas, K. (Eds.), Estonian Human Development Report (EHDR) 2016/2017. Foundation Estonian Cooperation Assembly, Tallinn. Available: https://2017.inimareng.ee/en/immigration-and-integration/ethnic-segregation-in-the-estonian-labour-market/.

Wimmer, M., Tambouris, E., Krimmer, R., Gil-Garcia, J.R., Takeoka Chatfield, A., 2017. Once only principle: benefits, barriers and next steps. In: 18th Annual International Conference on Digital Government Research, Staten Island, NY, USA. Available: https://ro.uow.edu.au/eispapers1/559/.

World Bank Group, 2016. World Development Report 2016: Digital Dividends. World Bank Publications.

7

Geodesign to address global change

Carl Steinitz[1], Brian Orland[2], Tom Fisher[3] and Michele Campagna[4]

[1]Graduate School of Design, Harvard University, Cambridge, MA, United States; [2]College of Environment and Design, University of Georgia, Athens, GA, United States; [3]College of Design, University of Minnesota, Minneapolis, MN, United States; [4]Deparment of Civil Engineering, Environment & Architecture, University of Cagliari, Cagliari, Italy

1. Introduction: the global challenge

Three global trends inform this chapter: increased environmental and social risk, growing demands for and growing threats to democracy and public participation, and ubiquitous information technology. Each increasingly influences the practices of the design professions and geographically oriented sciences, and the ways in which their education and activities are organized toward influencing and carrying out environmental and social change. These trends are well known, but education and practice have not adapted fast enough to them. The third, information technology, may be an important key to solving the first and second.

Growing global population, rising global temperature, decreasing food production, increasing food prices, and declining air quality, fresh water and biodiversity all confront humankind, yet actions remain uncoordinated in a sufficient, timely, and globally effective way. That makes it difficult to mitigate their serious negative impacts, increasing environmental and social risk. Meanwhile, the rapid and easy spread of information increases the demand for participation in planning for the future, even as it disrupts democratic and legal processes with misleading or misguided social media. Immediately available data from the brief messages or ordinary movements of the cell phones of ordinary people, for example, can reveal impending disaster or emerging opportunities. Interaction with computing has developed in ways that are almost like interpersonal

Intelligent Environments. https://doi.org/10.1016/B978-0-12-820247-0.00016-3

relationships yet without the social conventions that enable users to recognize altruism or unreliability.

While global challenges loom ever larger, a generic problem remains: How shall the very beginning and strategic stages of planning for longer-term change in a large, multisystem, multiclient, relatively unpredictable and *contentious* context be organized and conducted … and ensure that the outcomes generate more winners than losers? Do planning methods fit the global challenges? Traditional discipline-by-discipline "silo"-based strategic planning is not appropriate for a digitally integrated world comprising multiple systems addressing global challenges operating at diverse regional and local levels (Pettit et al., 2019). Instead, an integrative design approach is needed, enabling rapid evaluation of system interactions and trade-offs, and accessible to users with diverse expertise, including citizen representatives. This is the central vision of geodesign, a structured design and planning approach based in systems thinking, implemented via linked evaluation and modeling within a geographic information system (GIS). Furthermore, to address global issues, designers and planners are constrained if they are not able to compare their plans with others, and thus increase the shared knowledge that will be the foundation of truly global design. This chapter describes the International Geodesign Collaboration (IGC), a formalized approach to geodesign that enables meaningful project–project comparison, consistent evaluation metrics, and a common framework for reporting project outcomes.

2. Geodesign and sustainable development

Implementing sustainable development requires both technological and social settings that are organized to ensure that human activities would not harm the capacity of the earth's ecosystem to absorb their impacts. In 1992, the United Nations' Rio Declaration on Environment and Development introduced 27 principles to achieve sustainable development, and the related Agenda 21 set an operational program to implement them. These actions led to development and adoption of 17 UNDP Sustainable Development Goals (SDGs) that transpose global principles into operational objectives and accompanying metrics, globally and locally. While the implementation of those principles and programs are yet to be fully achieved, most countries have acknowledged those principles to address issues such as climate change, food and water security, biodiversity conservation, and population migration.

To achieve sustainable development requires complex and multifaceted planning, and this is possibly why its holistic implementation is hard to achieve. Addressing the complex relationships between humans and the environment demands the intelligent management of natural resources, the reduction in pollution originating from human activities, and the movement toward social goals such as balanced distribution of wealth and broader participation in decision-making. The role of science and technology is acknowledged as a priority in supporting informed decision-making. The emergence of advanced technical systems, such as remote sensing, GIS, and big-data analytics, can help address global-scale challenges and prove effective in assessing current conditions and the impacts of potential paths forward. The benefits of big-data analytics to urban and regional management are real and serious; however, these tools are not sufficient when applied to longer-term planning. Almost all approaches to data analysis focus on a single system at a time; they assume that current spatial patterns of that system evolve, and that all others remain constant. Even when testing hypothetical changes such as a new highway link in a transportation network, they assume that the performance data of the old system and its analysis can be transferred to the new situation. They also fail to anticipate how a system might change as a result of disruptive external forces, such as COVID-19, or simply as a function of time. Changes in the management of housing and industrial development and consequent changes in mobility systems may be the effects of planning decisions made to accommodate future socio-cultural or political change, change processes inaccessible to big-data analytics.

Such changes can be anticipated by experts; judgments based on experience of physical and social settings are integral to change processes. The geodesign processes assume that participants, whether experts or "people of the place," express vital but intangible values through the political knowledge, thoughtfulness, judgment, and the implicit social contracts that they bring to the planning arena, combined with the will to negotiate and the means to look ahead, plan strategically, and make leaps forward rather than changing incrementally. This is where geodesign can play a central role in planning for larger, longer term, and potentially contentious future policies and projects.

3. Strategic planning for significant change

In order for serious societal and environmental sustainability aims to be pursued successfully, outcome-oriented planning for guided, intended change—planning by design—is inevitably a collaborative endeavor, with participants from various design professions and geographic sciences, linked by technology for rapid communication and feedback, and reliant on transparent communication with the people of the place who are also direct participants. The people of the place are not just the clients; they are the designers as well. Quoting Herbert Simon in his 1978 Nobel Prize lecture, "Everyone designs who devises courses of action aimed at changing existing situations into preferred ones (Simon, 1978)." However, it is highly likely that the conditions under which this objective would be met by 2050 will be substantially different from those of today. The likely direct and indirect impacts of projected climate change, demographic shifts, and technical innovation must be considered in relationship to current conditions. Coming to a politically acceptable planning strategy is inevitably a negotiation among the people of the place, aided by design professionals and geographic scientists, and supported by information technologists.

Geodesign is a design process that is normally organized for collaborative, negotiated decision-making (Steinitz, 2017). It is especially applicable to large, longer-term, complex, and contentious circumstances related to planning for the future. Fisher (2016) describes geodesign as "a geo-spatial approach to grand challenges ... allowing communities of people with common interests to find each other as well as to generate alternate ways of addressing a challenge." It enables different stakeholders to work together, and with scientists, design professionals and information technologists in a digitally supported process where the impacts of proposed designs are shown in real time. What makes geodesign interesting and innovative is that the process is geared toward negotiation among different stakeholders seeking to strike a compromise (Fig. 7.2). It attempts to shift the paradigm from a zero-sum game to a win-win situation.

Geodesign is strategic: Geodesign is most useful at the beginning of thinking about and deciding on the strategy of what to do. It does not normally produce a precise final product. Rather, "It could be ... or should be ... something like this."

Geodesign is complex: There are multiple systems and geographic scopes, and uncertainties. Geodesign methods should fit the context. Its technical support must be flexible, iterative, transparent, and rapid.

Geodesign is dynamic: Geodesign changes are sets of system-based policies and projects. Geodesign must rapidly move from infinite possible designs toward a socially, environmentally, and economically feasible set of decisions.

Geodesign is collaborative: The "natural language" of geodesign must be easily understood by all. The geodesign endgame must support informed negotiation.

Geodesign is iterative: The geodesign process involves a number of cycles of proposal, assessment, negotiation, decision, updating, review and critique, out of which the best solutions emerge.

4. Organizing geodesign

Geodesign is organized by a systems-oriented framework (Steinitz, 1990, 2012), which asks six relevant questions that apply to any geodesign circumstance and for which the answers are six model types (Fig. 7.1).

1. How should the state of the territory be described in content, space, and time? This question is answered by representation models, the data which the study relies upon.
2. How does the territory operate? What are the functional and structural relationships among its elements? This question is

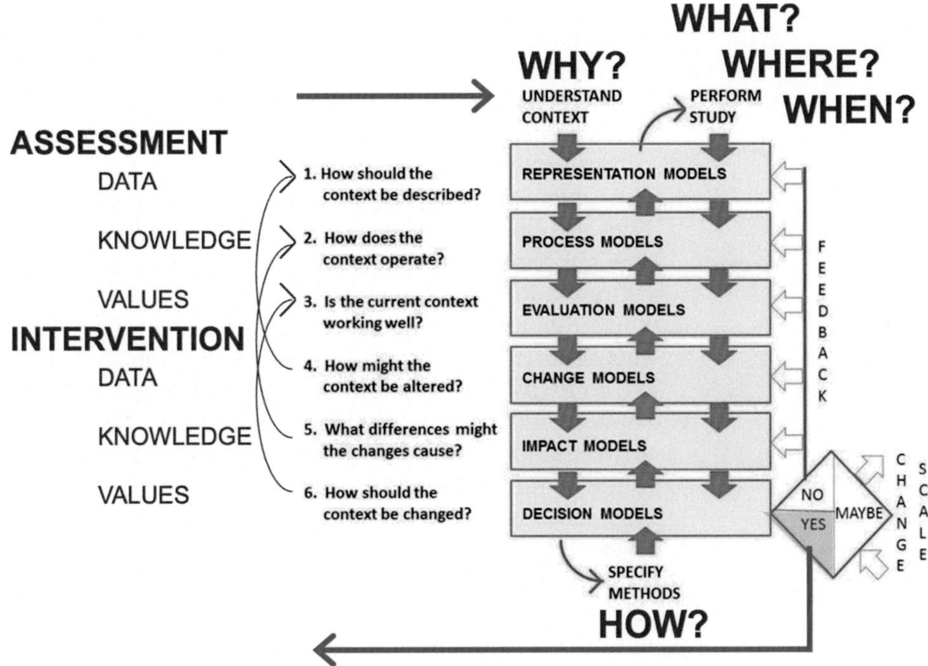

Figure 7.1 A framework for geodesign (Steinitz, 2012).

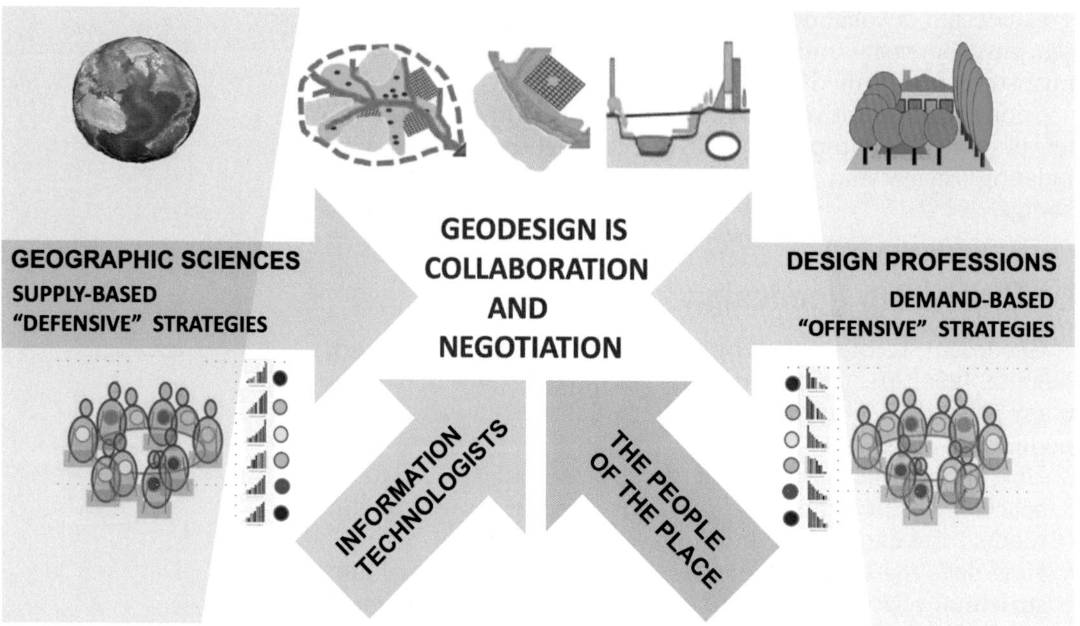

Figure 7.2 Geodesign is collaboration and negotiation (Steinitz, 2017).

answered by process models which provide knowledge for the several analyses that make up the content of the study.

3. Is the current state of the territory working well? This question is answered by evaluation models, which are dependent upon cultural values of the decision-making stakeholders.
4. How might the territory be altered—by what policies and actions, where and when? This question is answered by the change models which will be tested in this research and contain additional data.
5. What difference might the changes cause? This question is answered by impact models, which contain knowledge produced by the process models under changed conditions.
6. How should the territory be changed? This question is answered by decision models, which, like the evaluation models, are dependent upon the cultural values of the decision-making responsibilities.

Over the course of a geodesign study, each of the six questions and its subsidiary questions are asked three times: first to define the context and scope of the work (the WHY? questions); second to identify the methods of study (the HOW? questions), and third, to implement the study method (the WHAT, WHERE, and WHEN? questions).

Geodesign involves thinking globally while recognizing that the six geodesign model-types will vary locally, and while also seeking global comparisons, it requires a level of global technical coordination. As illustrated in Fig. 7.1, decision and evaluation models share the same values and language, impact and process models share the same information, and change and representation models share the same data. When all of these models are defined and made operational, they become the methodology for the geodesign study, and their outcomes will help determine the future of the particular geographical context.

Geodesign is never a linear process. While the framework potentially results in a very complex study, the same questions are posed again and again, whereas the various models, their methods, and their answers vary according to the context in which they are used (Hollstein, 2019).

5. Collaborative negotiation as a geodesign method

Geodesign has most frequently been applied to the initial planning stages of problems that are politically contentious, and these inevitably require negotiation to achieve consensus. The two most common circumstances are when the people of the place disagree among themselves about what the problem is and what should happen, and when those who are responsible for providing guidance in the form of a designed proposal work in separate "silos" rather than in direct collaboration, and disagree about what should be proposed. Negotiation is the most important method for arriving at political consensus regarding future change. When seen across a range of problem sizes and scales, collaborative negotiation in geodesign is especially applicable in this middle range (Fig. 7.2).

At a global scale, the geographic sciences provide guidance, and at the small, project scale, the design professions provide service. The mandate for collaboration especially occurs in the middle range, where the people of the place, who have the major political role in reaching agreement and activating change. Coming to a politically acceptable planning strategy is a collaboration among the people of the place, aided by geographic scientists and design professionals, and supported by information technologists. This is not easy to achieve, especially when thinking longer-term and globally. The geodesign framework provides the collaborators with a basis for understanding, communication, collaboration, and negotiation.

Collaborative negotiation as a geodesign method is different from the two most frequent ways of organizing design studies: commission and competition. In a commission, a brief is given to a design team and sequential presentations are made until a design is accepted by the client. In a competition, separate design teams work toward a series of designs from which one is selected. In both of these, the process is closed to others outside the client and the design team who are then assumed to "own" the ideas. In collaborative negotiation, alternative designs are made, but in a public environment in which all aspects of the design process are shared. The objective is that good ideas will gain support, regardless of source, in order to be part of the negotiated final design. In this approach, it is important that the process of negotiation be organized on the basis of either interteam similarity or symbiosis, and that a sequential process of negotiation lead to a final collaboratively agreed design (Ballal and Steinitz, 2015). Fig. 7.3 illustrates this process, in which separate designs are made representing competing constituencies with varied decision models, informal negotiated sharing of ideas occurs, and a formal negotiation process then develops the final design.

Geodesign as an integration of technologies: Geodesign draws upon a range of techniques and tools, each with its foundational technologies.

A systems-thinking framework: Systems thinking is embodied in GISs through the display of spatial relationships associated with thematic attributes within individual systems, interacting with other systems and layers, through the medium of map algebra.

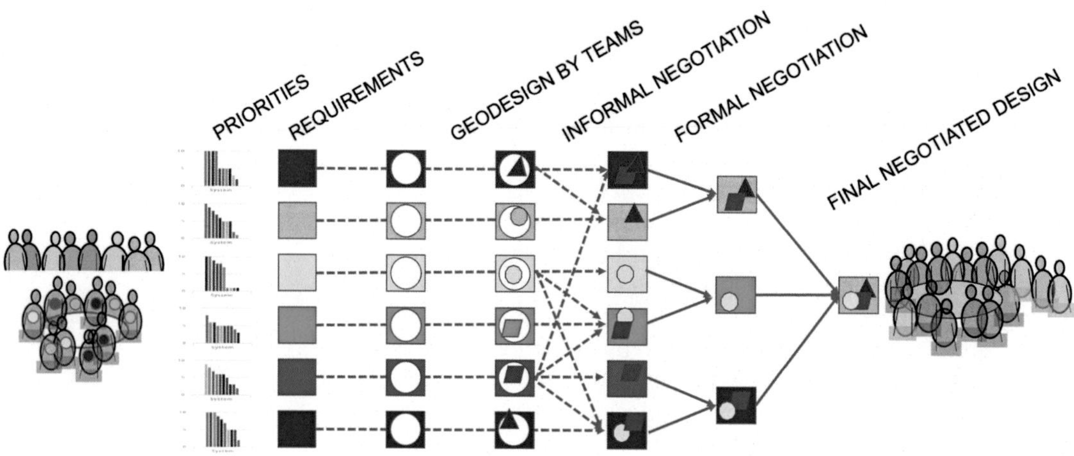

Figure 7.3 Collaborative negotiation to a final design (Steinitz, 2017).

Public participation: Rather than being passive recipients of designs created by others, the "people of the place" are key participants, able to propose design interventions, evaluate their impacts, and communicate their ideas in a common geodesign language accessible to all other participants, according to a transactive approach (Khakee, 1998) to planning and design.

Data-based decision-making: Design interventions are guided by data-driven and transparent evaluation models and are immediately incorporated into the base data so that subsequent iterations and adjustments start from a new origin point, not the original one. Participants can query anomalous outcomes by reference to the underlying data.

Iterations driven by impact assessments: Performance and impact assessments are continuously ongoing, requiring the enabling of immediate iteration supporting negotiation and adjustment of goals. Iteration is integral to the geodesign process and not a distraction delaying forward progress. It is central to the public, participatory intent of geodesign.

Visual communication of spatial relationships: The visualization foundations of geodesign are driven by the key questions: "How big will that be?", "How close or far away from me will it be?" "How badly will it affect me?" and "How will it change the world as I currently see it?" The language of visualization transcends differences in background, knowledge, and comprehension. The ability to compare before-and-after, and scenario A versus scenario B are essential to geodesign communication and the consequent understanding which is essential to negotiation and decision.

6. Technology in support of geodesign

Geodesign takes advantage of advances in technology both in procedural and substantial form. On the one hand, accelerating technology advances in data acquisition and management offer new possibilities to address urgent issues such as environmental risk, quality of life, and economic development, while, on the other hand, advances in the utility and accessibility of spatial-temporal geographic information and communication technologies offer unprecedented capabilities for supporting citizens and scientists in the geodesign process without the requiring prior training in GIS, remote sensing, etc. (Batty, 2013).

The formal development of a global data infrastructure and the rise of geographic Internet technologies, such as geobrowsers supported by the global diffusion of Global Positioning Systems in smartphones, have enabled the emergence of crowdsourced Volunteered Geographic Information and Social Media Geographic Information (SMGI) monitoring not only the physical environment but also social behaviors and dynamics (Campagna, 2016; Capineri et al., 2016).

Computing power also has dramatically increased in the last decade, enabling software development in GIS and related technologies to realize Planning Support Systems (PSS), that comprise "*a subset of computer-based geo-information instruments, each of which incorporates a unique suite of components that planners can utilise to explore and manage their particular activities*" (Harris, 1989, quoted in Geertman and Stillwell, 2004, p. 291). Since then, a number of full-fledged PSS have emerged, based first on desktop then web architecture (Brail et al., 2001; Geertman et al., 2015). To support the broader, inter-PSS collaboration required by geodesign has required that system designers address the inadequacies in PSS methods highlighted by Vonk et al., (2005). In response, tools specifically directed to geodesign have emerged, notably Esri's *Geoplanner* and *GeodesignHub* developed by Ballal (2015). Geoplanner is a web-based extension of the ArcGIS suite of tools, using the ArcGIS Online platform for data sharing. Geodesignhub utilizes state-of-the-art open-source geographic web technologies, basing the structure of the workflow on the Steinitz framework for geodesign (Steinitz, 2012).

The geodesign framework and its models guide the explicit knowledge building that is central to decision making in design. From the representation to the decision model, the spatial and temporal dimensions of geographic information are taken into account together with decision-makers' and stakeholders' values. Both Geoplanner and Geodesignhub augment traditional GIS operations with advanced visualization, forecasting, simulation, and multicriteria evaluation models and tools, which are commonly found in state-of-the-art PSS. Their web-based nature ensures that the "digital divide" is minimized. Recent experiences brought on by the Covid-19 pandemic forcing IGC workshops online has demonstrated the ability to connect communities' socio-technologically and thus enable socio-political process to be virtual. Geodesign methods and tools have proved to be successful supporting fully digital collaborative design, with participants ranging from teenagers in Brazilian favelas (Monteiro et al., 2018) to experienced planning experts in London.

7. Strategic planning for global change: the International Geodesign Collaboration

In response to the urgent need for global action, the IGC was organized in 2018. While it is principally academic, with members in 155 universities and 50 countries, its aim is to better understand, and then teach, how geodesign can address design challenges in settings that are widely dispersed and that differ widely in scale and in the extent of resources (skilled people and prepared data) available to find geodesign solutions. The IGC is driven by a specific and exceptionally complex problem: how to identify and share the lessons and practices developed by a globally dispersed array of experts so that the resulting knowledge can be leveraged to solve our most pressing societal needs? The solutions will call for deep integration across the traditional expertise residing in the physical, natural, and social sciences, but they will be articulated through the landscape- and city-shaping of planners, designers, and engineers. How will multidisciplinary teams in multiinstitutional and multinational groups consider and respond to the environmental, economic, and social impacts of development and change in natural and increasingly engineered systems. These include structural components such as cultural and governmental differences, but also the leadership skills of individuals, team construction, and communication (Orland and Steinitz, 2019). Fig. 7.4 indicates the global distribution of the participating universities.

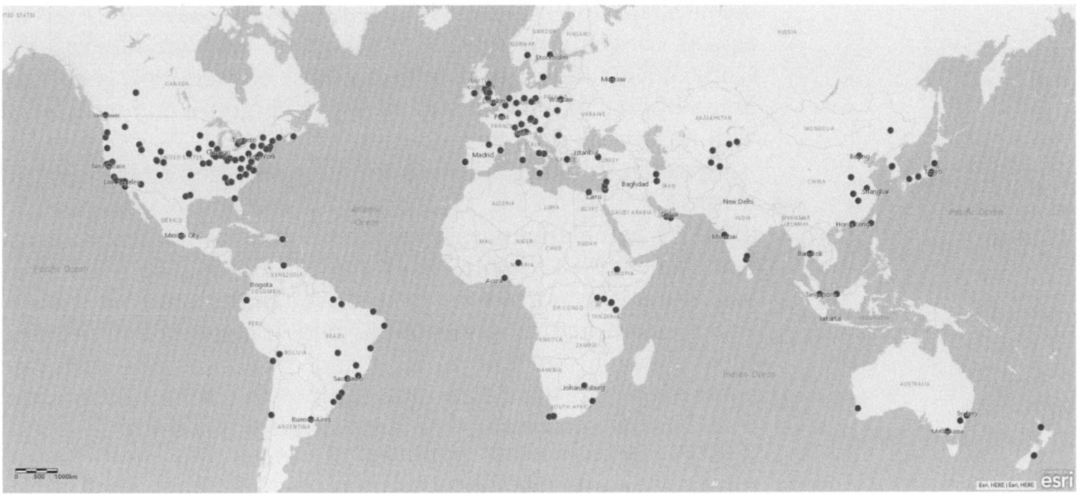

Figure 7.4 Participating university locations.

Almost every university in the world studies these issues and is potentially in a position to propose improvements to our normal everyday social and environmental practices. Yet every university and every unit of government acts in its own set of geographies and societies, and with its own content, definitions, methods, languages, color codes, and representation techniques. It is extremely difficult to compare across studies to learn from each other. The IGC proposes a radical increase in shared standardization. Finding the best solutions for complex problems requires identifying and evaluating alternate methods from disparate locations and having a means for sharing, comparison and mutual learning.

8. The IGC conventions: a common "language" for geodesign

To enable efficient and effective collaboration and to reveal comparable similarities and contrasts across studies, the IGC uses a common analytical, evaluative, and communication "language" (Kim, 2020). This is central to effective collaboration and eventual action, and key to public understanding of complex issues. And that communication can be done without professional jargon, artistic obscurity, and scientific myopia. Rather than ending with the quantitative and narrative explication of economic development or governmental policy, the IGC uses digital maps and plans to visually communicate the spatial-temporal implications of planned change. The IGC conventions described below shape the common IGC geodesign language; they are an agreed convention allowing comparison without limiting the scope of IGC studies. In developing these conventions, geodesign draws upon and integrates a range of techniques and tools, each with its foundational technologies.

Systems thinking: Systems thinking emerged in the work of Norbert Wiener in his 1948 book, *Cybernetics*. It developed in the 1970s as a planning approach for solving the multiple concurrent challenges of complex problems (Meadows, 2008), while proposing that the world is a series of overlapping systems, such as water infrastructure, agricultural, and transportation systems, each of which has its own logic and operations and each one interacting with the others operating at the same location and time. It is this complexity that causes strategic planning via geodesign to necessarily be imprecise in space and time. System thinking is embodied in GIS and it is applied in geodesign via diagrams of system-based policies and projects.

A common IGC geodesign workflow: The IGC workflow puts systems thinking into practice. Geodesign is normally a collaborative enterprise, so a geodesign study must be undertaken in a way that is understandable by all participants—especially by the people of the place. The basis for shared understanding includes the ability to conceive individual policies and projects and combine them into comprehensive designs. Any individual change, no matter how seemingly localized, affects the system as a whole and can influence what is subsequently feasible and preferable. Rapid design iterations are critical in geodesign, so there must be the ability to rapidly assess potential impacts and costs of design proposals. Given the amount of data and need for data updates, digital platforms for collaboration and communication usually form the basis of the geodesign workflow (Fig. 7.5).

Shared selection of global systems: The most challenging constraint imposed by the IGC was to limit the representational schema to facilitate comparison while accepting that for many projects that requirement would be onerous. IGC 2019-20 required teams to adopt eight common systems and enabled two flexible selections (Fig. 7.6). For many IGC studies, choice was used for the protection of cultural and historical assets. The

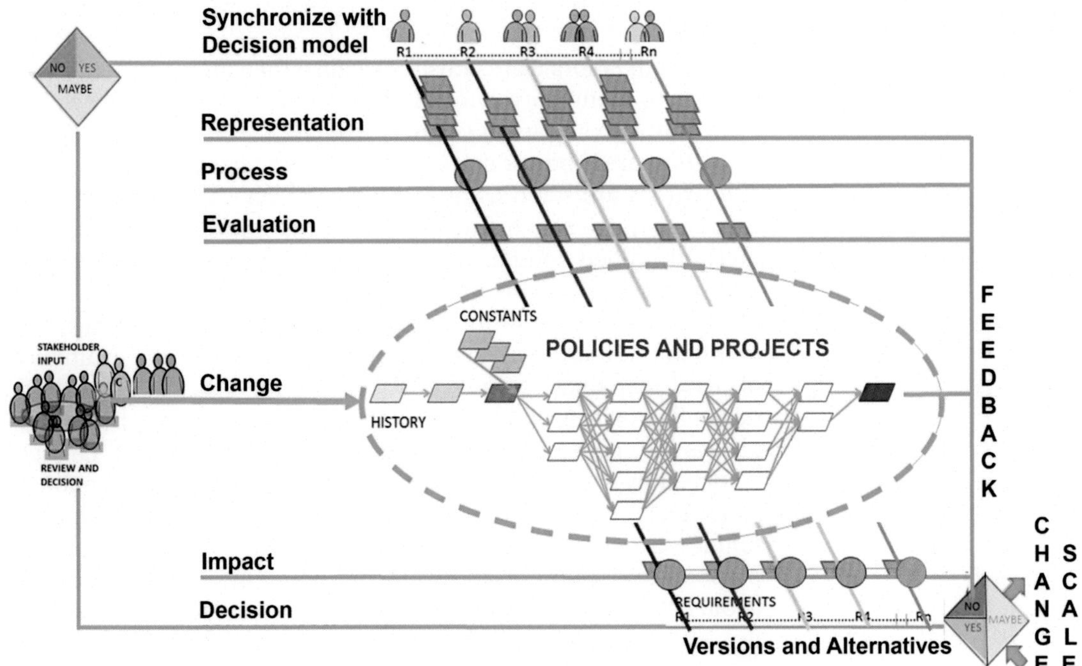

Figure 7.5 A geodesign workflow (Steinitz, 2017).

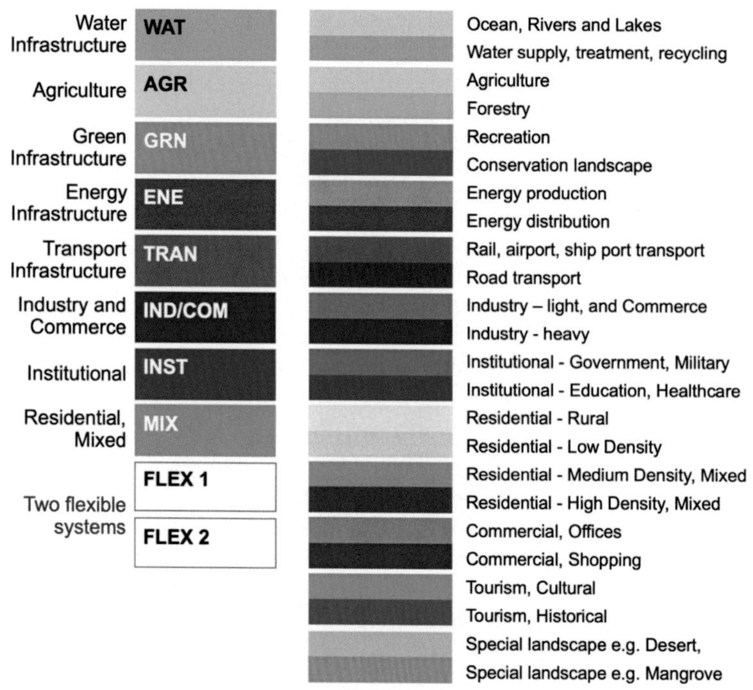

Figure 7.6 Eight required systems, and two flexible systems which may be chosen from the column on the right.

IGC system colors were chosen because they are commonly used globally to identify evolving land-use patterns across time as well as to enable comparisons across studies.

Study area boundaries, shapes, and sizes: environmental study areas are seldom square; however, the IGC's square study areas in a range of standard sizes achieves several ends: first, it enables simplified comparison of projects, whether using quantitative measures or visual comparison alone, and second, it compels the consideration of project context. Both of these issues relate to another advantage of square study areas: the evaluation of land capabilities and impacts should not be considered narrowly in terms of the immediate effects of a project, but should always be considered in terms of the incremental changes achieved by the project. For example, in evaluating the capability, suitability, or feasibility of a proposed project area, a community might want to see particular values extend beyond the immediate planned development, to reveal additional opportunities, and to avoid unnecessary redundancy. Impacts, similarly, must be put in context to understand if the designed benefits are proportional to the investment made, and if they are meaningful rather than trivial in the broader scope of potential changes in the area (Fig. 7.7).

Common scenarios and timeframes: Project-to-project comparison is only possible when they share common strategies and are reported at common timeframes. The three defining change strategies for IGC are:

- The early-adopter, where innovations are implemented immediately, and the changes tracked through time.
- The late-adopter scenario, which delays adoption of innovations, in most circumstances resulting in less overall change.
- The nonadopter scenario, often called "business-as-usual," which accepts that change will occur but not necessarily shaped by implementing any design or technology innovations. IGC specified the common reporting times of 2035 and 2050 (Fig. 7.8).

Common expectations for the future: Major international agencies and national governments recognize a range of global challenges to be faced, from population increase to poverty alleviation to pollution control. The IGC convened a panel of experts to identify 12 issues of global scope that would shape geodesign

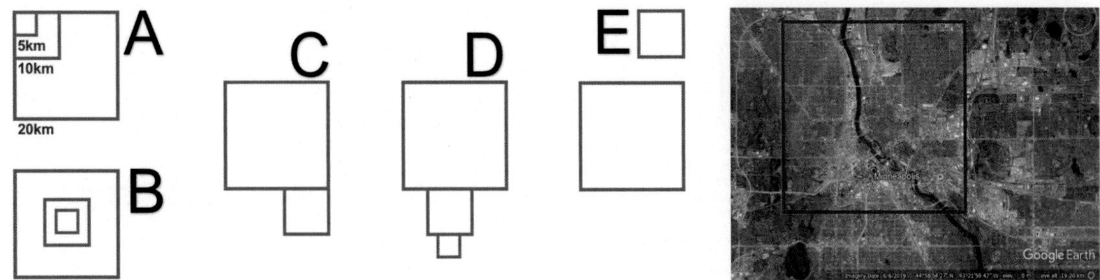

Figure 7.7 Study area boundaries: squares of 0.5 × 0.5, 1, 2, 5, 10, 20, 40, 80, 160 km, etc.

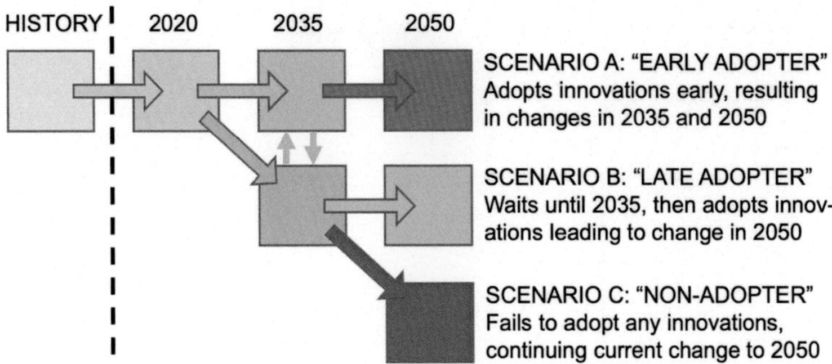

Figure 7.8 Three design scenarios in three time-stages. IGC studies have been assumed to start in 2020.

responses IGC participants and other experts might have to challenges at national, regional, and local scales IGC participants refer to the global assumptions when identifying project requirements (see Global Assumptions at https://www.igc-geodesign.org/global-systems-research) (Fig. 7.9).

A shared library of geodesign innovations: Innovation to address global challenges can occur in each of the systems identified in Fig. 7.3. For each of the nine required systems a panel of experts was asked to compile lists of design, planning, and technological innovations that may contribute to developing geodesign solutions; 187 were identified, spread across the nine required systems (see System Innovations at https://www.igc-geodesign.org/global-systems-research) (Fig. 7.10).

Common assessment metrics: A central basis of comparison among different circumstances and results of scenario-based designs are impact models. The IGC uses the UN SDGs as a basis for impacts assessment and comparison (https://www.un.org/sustainabledevelopment/). The content of this publication has not been approved by the United Nations and does not reflect the views of the United Nations or its officials or Member States. The SDGs are 17 global goals designed to be a "blueprint to

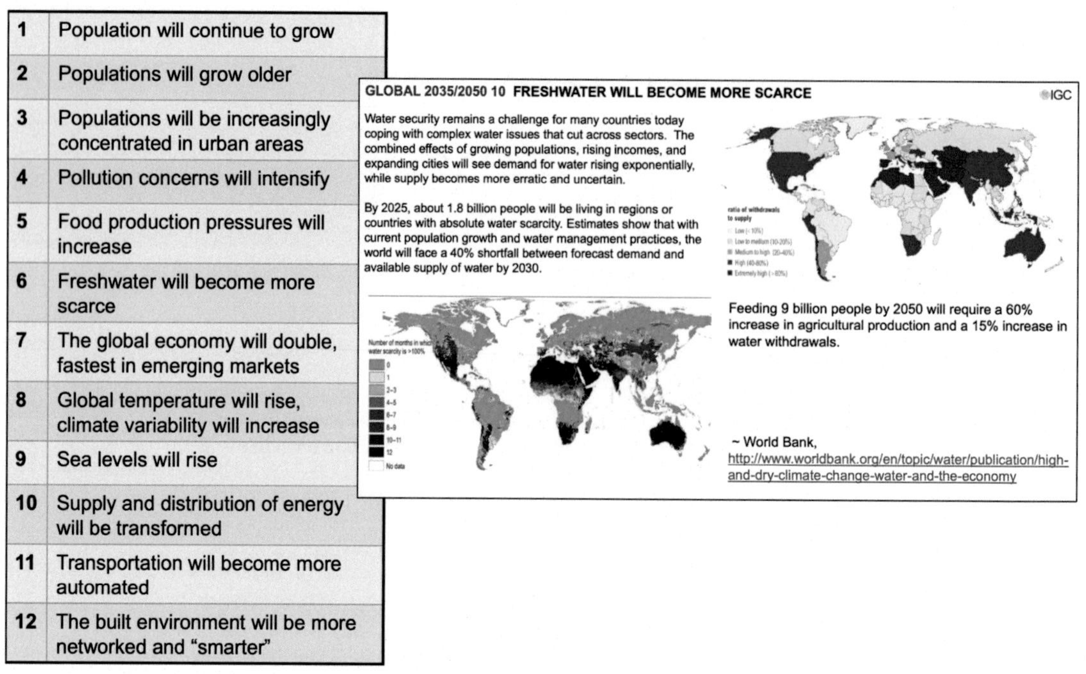

Figure 7.9 Global change assumptions — example: fresh water will become more scarce.

achieve a better and more sustainable future for all." The SDGs, set in 2015 by the United Nations General Assembly and intended to be achieved by the year 2030, are part of UN Resolution 70/1, the 2030 Agenda (Fig. 7.11).

IGC has developed a workflow to achieve summary assessments of SDGs (Fig. 7.12). These assessments require single, summary, positive-to-negative judgments to be made for each of the resource systems against each of the SDG goals that have design consequences, with a positive or negative score for each design. Impacts may have a range of values across the affected areas, they may be influenced by the spatial pattern of changes, and they may be influenced by conditions outside the square study area. Regardless, summary judgments enable comparisons within and among case studies, to inform and feed back into the design process. Fig. 7.12 shows the SDG judgments for alternate scenarios in the Wasatch Front Planning 2050 study by the IGC team from Utah State University. Full details of the workflow can be found at: https://www.envizz1.com/project-workflow.

Common reporting of outcomes and comparisons: Common reporting formats were designed by the IGC for posters and PowerPoint presentations. In each case, about half of each format was required for purposes of comparison and half was flexible to

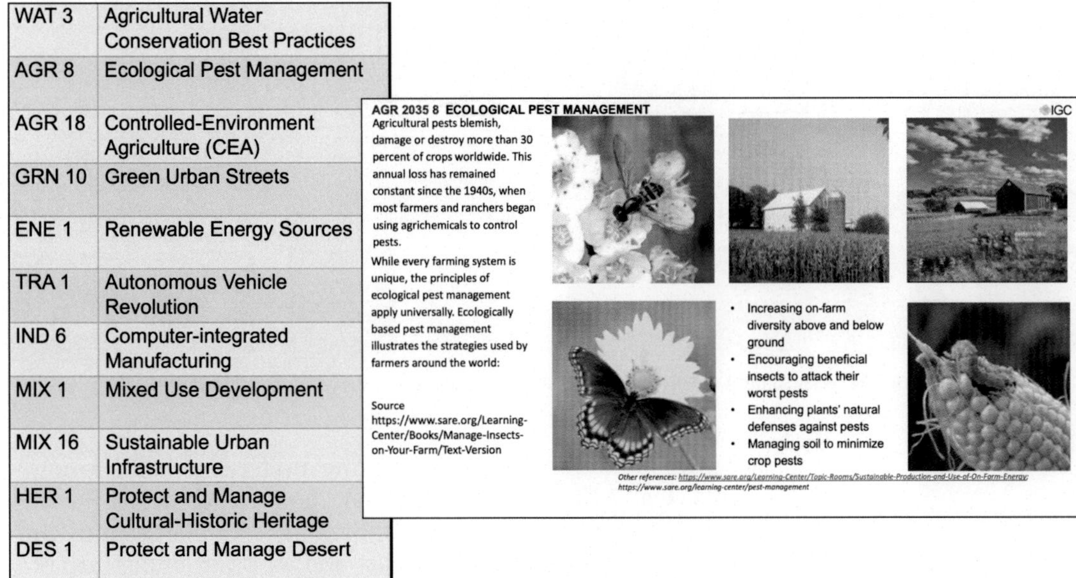

WAT 3	Agricultural Water Conservation Best Practices
AGR 8	Ecological Pest Management
AGR 18	Controlled-Environment Agriculture (CEA)
GRN 10	Green Urban Streets
ENE 1	Renewable Energy Sources
TRA 1	Autonomous Vehicle Revolution
IND 6	Computer-integrated Manufacturing
MIX 1	Mixed Use Development
MIX 16	Sustainable Urban Infrastructure
HER 1	Protect and Manage Cultural-Historic Heritage
DES 1	Protect and Manage Desert

Figure 7.10 Innovations selected for Al Ain, United Arab Emirates — example: ecological pest management.

Figure 7.11 17 UN sustainable development goals (United Nations General Assembly, 2015).

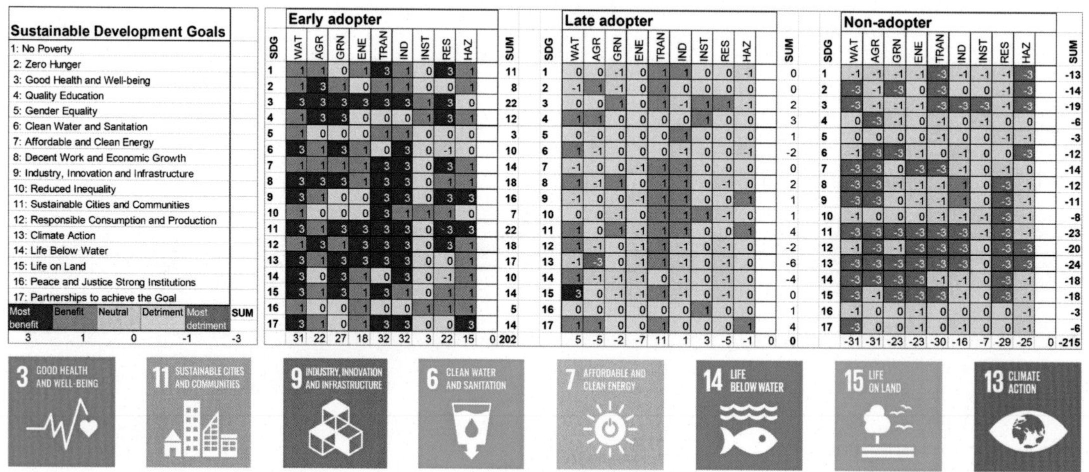

Sustainable Development Goals					
1: No Poverty					
2: Zero Hunger					
3: Good Health and Well-being					
4: Quality Education					
5: Gender Equality					
6: Clean Water and Sanitation					
7: Affordable and Clean Energy					
8: Decent Work and Economic Growth					
9: Industry, Innovation and Infrastructure					
10: Reduced Inequality					
11: Sustainable Cities and Communities					
12: Responsible Consumption and Production					
13: Climate Action					
14: Life Below Water					
15: Life on Land					
16: Peace and Justice Strong Institutions					
17: Partnerships to achieve the Goal					
Most benefit	Benefit	Neutral	Detriment	Most detriment	SUM
3	1	0	-1		-3

SDG	Early adopter WAT	AGR	GRN	ENE	TRAN	IND	INST	RES	HAZ		SUM
1	1	1	0	1	3	1	0	3	1		11
2	1	3	1	0	1	1	0	0	1		8
3	3	3	3	3	3	3	1	3	0		22
4	1	3	3	0	0	0	1	3	1		12
5	1	0	0	0	1	1	0	0	0		3
6	3	1	3	1	0	3	0	-1	0		10
7	1	1	1	1	3	3	0	3	1		14
8	3	3	3	1	3	3	0	1	1		18
9	3	1	0	0	3	3	0	3	3		16
10	1	0	0	0	3	1	1	1	0		7
11	3	1	3	3	3	3	0	3	3		22
12	1	3	1	3	3	3	0	3	1		18
13	3	1	3	3	3	3	0	0	1		17
14	3	0	3	1	0	3	0	-1	1		10
15	3	1	3	1	3	1	0	1	1		14
16	1	0	0	1	0	0	1	1	1		5
17	3	1	0	1	3	3	0	0	3		14
	31	22	27	18	32	32	3	22	15	0	202

SDG	Late adopter WAT	AGR	GRN	ENE	TRAN	IND	INST	RES	HAZ		SUM
1	0	0	-1	0	1	1	0	0	-1		0
2	-1	1	-1	0	1	0	0	0	0		0
3	0	0	1	0	1	-1	1	1	-1		2
4	1	1	0	0	0	0	1	0	0		3
5	0	0	0	0	0	1	0	0	0		1
6	1	-1	0	0	0	-1	0	0	-1		-2
7	-1	0	0	-1	1	1	0	0	0		0
8	1	-1	1	0	1	1	0	-1	0		2
9	-1	0	0	-1	1	1	0	0	1		1
10	0	0	-1	0	1	1	1	-1	0		1
11	1	0	1	-1	1	1	0	0	1		4
12	1	-1	0	-1	1	-1	0	-1	0		-2
13	-1	-3	0	-1	1	-1	0	-1	0		-6
14	1	-1	-1	-1	0	-1	0	-1	0		-4
15	3	0	-1	-1	1	-1	0	-1	0		0
16	0	0	0	0	0	0	1	0	0		1
17	1	1	0	0	1	0	0	0	1		4
	5	-5	-2	-7	11	1	3	-5	-1	0	0

SDG	Non-adopter WAT	AGR	GRN	ENE	TRAN	IND	INST	RES	HAZ		SUM
1	-1	-1	-1	-1	-3	-1	-1	-1	-3		-13
2	-3	-1	-3	0	-3	0	0	-1	-3		-14
3	-3	-1	-1	-1	-3	-3	-3	-1	-3		-19
4	0	-3	-1	0	-1	0	-1	0	0		-6
5	0	0	0	0	-1	0	0	-1	-1		-3
6	-1	-3	-3	-1	0	-1	0	0	-3		-12
7	-3	-3	0	-3	-3	-1	0	-1	0		-14
8	-3	-3	-1	-1	-1	1	0	-3	-1		-12
9	-3	-3	0	-1	-1	1	0	-3	-1		-11
10	-1	0	0	0	-1	-1	-1	-3	-1		-8
11	-3	-3	-3	-3	-3	-3	-1	-3	-1		-23
12	-1	-3	-1	-3	-3	-3	0	-3	-3		-20
13	-3	-3	-3	-3	-3	-3	0	-3	-3		-24
14	-3	-3	-3	-3	-1	-1	0	-3	-1		-18
15	-3	-1	-3	-3	-3	-1	0	-3	-1		-18
16	-1	0	0	-1	0	0	0	0	-1		-3
17	-3	0	0	-1	0	-1	0	0	-1		-6
	-31	-31	-23	-23	-30	-16	-7	-29	-25	0	-215

Figure 7.12 Assessment matrix for SDGs, showing judgments for alternate scenarios.

accommodate varied local reporting preferences and requirements. Fig. 7.13 shows the template and posters from the IGC teams at University of São Paulo, Brazil and Chulalongkorn University, Thailand. The IGC formats and all prior studies are presented in the IGC web site https://www.igc-geodesign.org/.

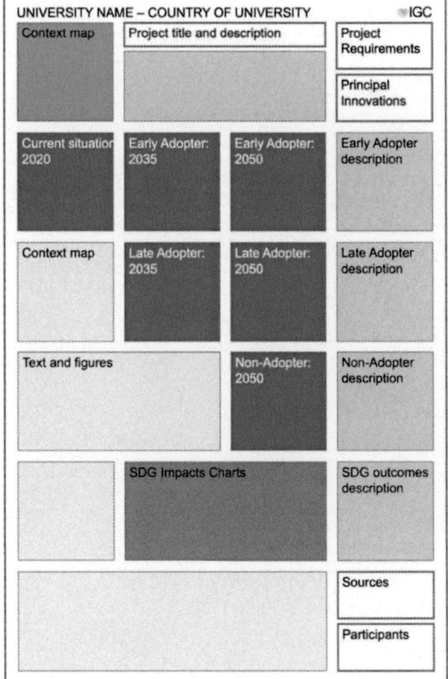

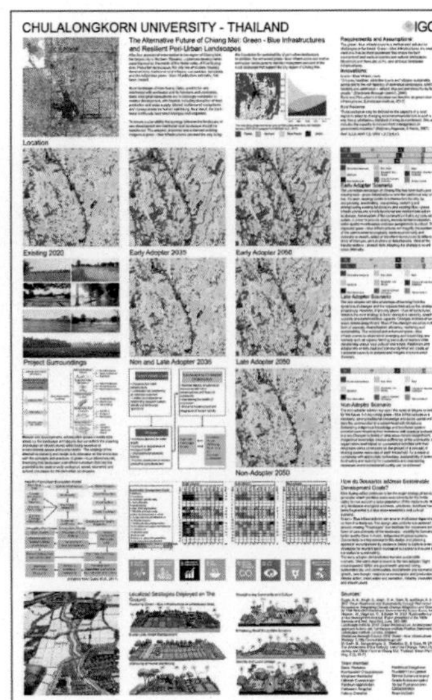

Figure 7.13 Common reporting templates.

9. Two IGC case studies

Here are two case studies showing how the IGC process and formats work while being varied: The CAMKOX Corridor: rethinking the growth of the London region, and The Minneapolis Green New Deal: the effect of policy on place. Both involve growth and change and are in relatively well-planned and well-funded countries. Both relate to a major city, yet one is expanding a major city, while the other is remaking a central city. One seeks a negotiated final design, while the other recommends a vision for change.

10. The CAMKOX corridor: rethinking the growth of the London region

The Cambridge—Milton Keynes—Oxford (CAMKOX) Corridor, is the fastest growing region in the United Kingdom. The UK National Infrastructure Commission (NIC) report from 2017, *Partnering for Prosperity: A new deal for the Cambridge–Milton Keynes-Oxford Arc,* set out a policy-driven vision and approach to infrastructure-led development linked to the housing challenge in the region. It proposes to add a new east-west expressway and a re-established railway, as well as 780,000 housing units and 1,450,000 people to the existing CAMKOX population of around 3,300,000 (Fig. 7.14). A 2-day workshop was

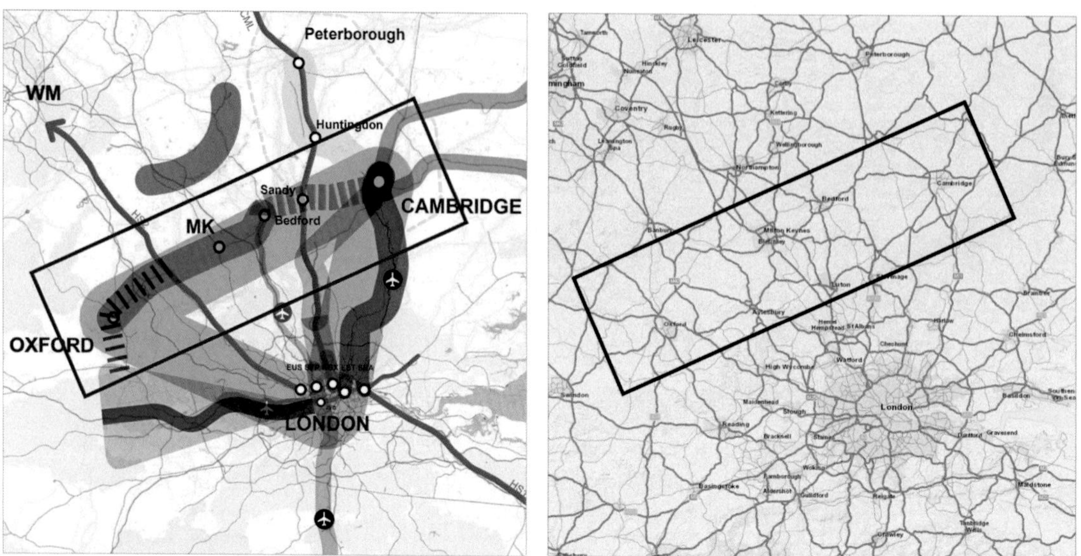

Figure 7.14 (A) The national infrastructure commission greater London growth strategy (Neuman et al., 2018), (B) CAMKOX study area, Cambridge, Milton Keynes and Oxford (CASA/University College London).

organized by The Center for Advanced Spatial Analysis (CASA) of University College London to reconsider this proposal. The participants were 20 professional planners and academics with experience in the region and its issues.

The CAMKOX Corridor comprises 30 Councils which have local planning responsibility for the region. It forms the northern fringe of the greater London city region to which it is profitably tied, just north of the London Green Belt. Traversing the corridor from south to north is the proposed high-speed rail line HS2 and other proposed transport links. Taken together, these are intended to enhance connectivity, mobility, and productivity across the region. Other impacts of growth also need to be addressed, such as last mile connectivity and multimodal transport, social inequities, land consumption of agriculture and forests, greater flood risk, pollution, and loss of ecological function and the visual integrity of this historical landscape region including its villages and towns (Fig. 7.15). These impacts need to be addressed by an assessment of alternative growth scenarios and their impacts, and in advance of major infrastructure projects.

There are important complications: the HS2 high-speed train project does not connect with the CAMKOX Corridor's currently proposed train, and it is not planned and will not be built to do this. The right-of-way of the prior train linking Cambridge with

Figure 7.15 CAMKOX corridor scenes—clockwise from top left: Uffington White Horse and Dragon Hill by Chris Andrews is licensed under CC BY-SA 2.0; the town Bridge, Bedford by Dave Hamster is licensed under CC BY 2.0; Christ Church—College & Oxford Cathedral Aerial View by John D Fielding is licensed under CC BY 2.0; Stowe House, Buckinghamshire by Rictor Norton & David Allen is licensed under CC BY 2.0.

Bedford (and to Milton Keynes and Oxford) was sold when the train line closed in the 1980s. It is now substantially developed and no longer available for a train. There is considerably more travel demand from CAM, MK, and OX to London, and into CAM, MK, and OX from their immediate subregion, than from CAM to MK to OX or the reverse. The London policy to maintain its greenbelt is under pressure from many proposed developments, and the availability and price of housing in London is a major political issue. There is highly organized opposition to the proposed development of the region.

The National Infrastructure Commission hosted a CAMKOX design competition in 2017 (Malcolm Reading Co., 2017) (Table 7.1). From 58 entries, four teams were shortlisted to expand their first stage proposals into development growth strategies appropriate to the CAMKOX corridor. The public were invited to

Table 7.1 Requirements.

- •Add 780,000 units of housing for 1.45 million people.
- •Double industry and commerce.
- •Protect cultural landscapes.
- •Protect or expand greenbelt and green infrastructure.
- •Improve institutional cores.
- •Reduce flooding, retain water.
- •Intensify agriculture, conserve prime soils.
- •Increase local production of energy.
- •Increase transportation efficiency in CAMKOX corridor.

comment. Diagrams of policies and projects were derived from the competition winners and additional selected IGC innovations (Table 7.2) and were entered into Geodesignhub software workshop as initial elements for the geodesign workshop's designs.

The workshop was structured by the conventions of the IGC (IGC, 2018; Orland and Steinitz, 2019). It adopted the eight required IGC systems as the basis for design, for example, green infrastructure, transportation, energy infrastructure, etc., and added low-density housing and historic-cultural protection as flexible systems. It applied the three scenarios of early-, late-, and nonadopters of systems policy and project innovations, it

Table 7.2 Selected innovations for early and late scenario adoption.

WAT 2 Water retention
AGR 4 Carbon farming
AGR 18 Controlled environment (greenhouse) agriculture
GRN 1 Resilient landscape infrastructure
ENE 1 Renewable energy sources
TRA 8 EAV cars disrupt rail industry
IND 2 Industrial robotics
IND 5 Mass customization
IND 14 Web-distribution robotics
MIX 10 Defining high density locally
FLEX 1 Protect historic places
FLEX 2 Protect cultural landscapes

reported the impacts at three time-steps, 2020 (existing), 2035, and 2050, and it comparatively assessed the three final 2050 designs according to the United Nations Sustainability Development Goals, SDGs.

The workshop was organized and managed in Geodesignhub software (Ballal and Steinitz, 2015). Geodesignhub is a cloud-based, free and open access, open platform software built by Hrishi Ballal (2015, 2020). It is designed to link with other tools and models via an application programming interface (API), rather than to contain its own complex data, models, and visualization tools (Fig. 7.16). It is used to manage geodesign for large, complex, politically contentious projects and studies in their early conceptual and strategic phases when the process is at its most dynamic. It is designed to support collaboration and negotiation. Geodesignhub aims to be as simple as possible: easy to learn, set up, use, and (most importantly) easy to understand. The tool allows participants to easily change their proposed plans as they work through several reiterations of their designs in response to evaluations related to the characteristics of the study area. Further changes resulting from collaboration and negotiation with other participants can be made quickly and directly evaluated. It includes tools to support comparison among designs and negotiation toward agreement. These aspects of Geodesignhub were the focus of the CAMKOX case study.

Geodesignhub is a cloud-based, free and open access, open platform software built by Hrishi Ballal in cooperation with Carl Steinitz and Stephen Ervin. It is designed to link with other tools

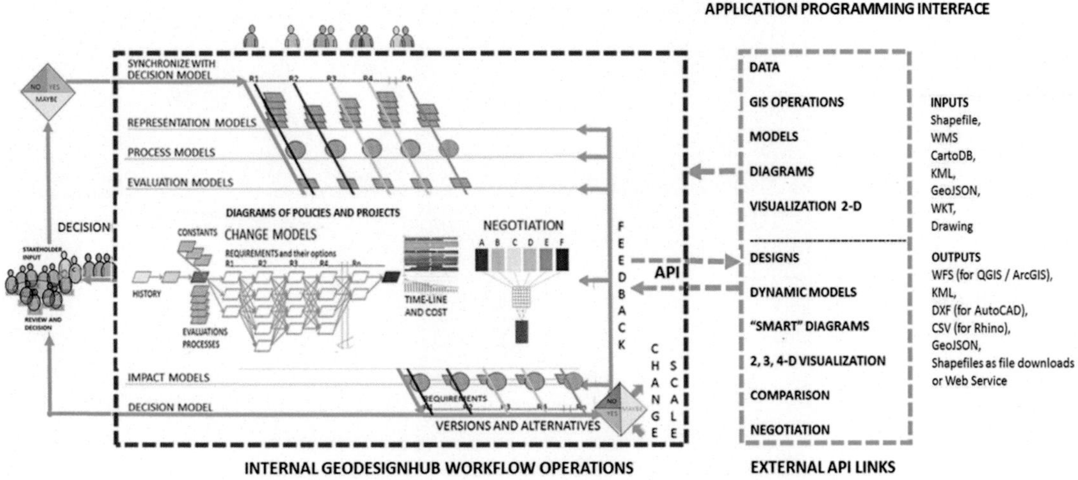

Figure 7.16 Geodesignhub—a digital workflow for geodesign

and models rather than to contain complex substantive algorithms itself. It is used to manage geodesign for large, complex, politically contentious projects and studies in their early conceptual and strategic phases when the process is at its most dynamic. It is designed to support collaboration and negotiation toward agreement.

Six geodesign teams edited and added to the initial diagrams to reflect the Innovative policies and projects, made designs for 2035 and 2050, Each team selected, added, or edited policy and project diagrams to generate its Version one proposals for 2030 and 2050. These were assessed for their impacts and costs and revised at least once, for Version two and again assessed. The paired scenerio-based teams then negotiated consensus designs to 2050 and negotiated a final recommended design (Fig. 7.17).

The Early Adopter teams first introduced conservation policies for prime soils, water, agriculture and the historic-cultural landscape. They retained the regional greenbelts while promoting a new and linked CAMKOX national park network. They designated nonprime soils for conversion to industrial, controlled environment agriculture, the purple polygon in Fig. 7.18. Urban development was focused on mixed higher density residential and service uses concentrated along the CAMKOX corridor, including a new urban center at a new connection with HS2. Most transportation will rely on future multimodal transport on roads while retaining

DAY 1
INTRODUCTION, THE PROBLEM, DIAGRAMS OF POLICIES AND PROJECTS, SYNTHESIS: GEODESIGN FOR 2035

DAY 2
SYNTHESIS: GEODESIGN FOR 2050, PRESENTATION, COMPARISON, NEGOTIATION TO A FINAL DESIGN

Figure 7.17 The 2-day geodesign workshop Photos by Tess Canfield.

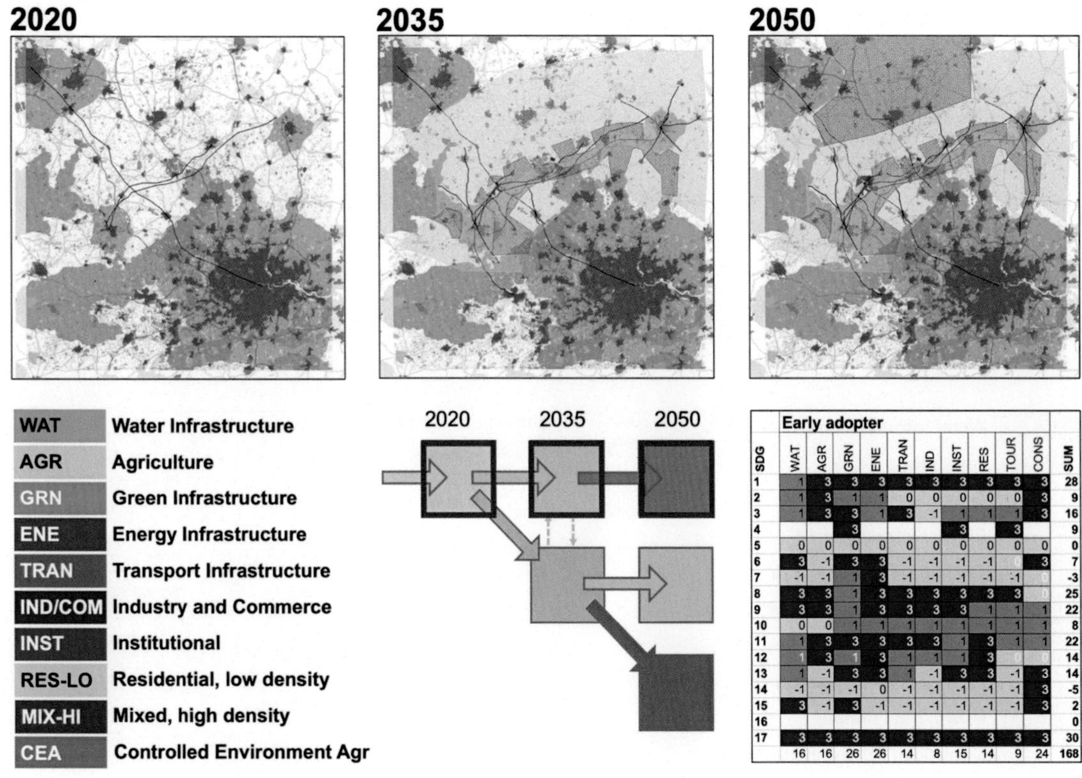

	Early adopter										
SDG	WAT	AGR	GRN	ENE	TRAN	IND	INST	RES	TOUR	CONS	SUM
1	1	3	3	3	3	3	3	3	3	3	28
2	1	3	1	1	0	0	0	0	0	3	9
3	1	3	3	1	3	-1	1	1	1	3	16
4			3				3		3		9
5	0	0	0	0	0	0	0	0	0	0	0
6	3	-1	3	3	-1	-1	-1	-1	0	3	7
7	-1	-1	1	3	-1	-1	-1	-1	-1	0	-3
8	3	3	1	3	3	3	3	3	3	0	25
9	3	3	1	3	3	3	3	1	1	1	22
10	0	0	1	1	1	1	1	1	1	1	8
11	1	3	3	3	3	3	1	3	1	1	22
12	1	3	1	3	1	1	1	3	0	0	14
13	1	-1	3	3	1	-1	3	3	-1	3	14
14	-1	-1	-1	0	-1	-1	-1	-1	-1	3	-5
15	3	-1	3	-1	-1	-1	-1	-1	-1	3	2
16											0
17	3	3	3	3	3	3	3	3	3	3	30
	16	16	26	26	14	8	15	14	9	24	168

Figure 7.18 Early adopter scenarios for 2020, 2035, 2050: SDG score = 168.

the highly dispersed pattern of villages and towns and associated technical-oriented industry (Fig. 7.18).

The Late Adopter teams adopted the expressway and train plans of the NIC by 2035 and the preferred dispersed, lower density development patterns, and distributed growth among the many Councils in the region. The exception is Milton Keynes' plan for higher density mixed development by 2026. They conserved agriculture and its associated landscapes. After 2035, Policies change. An HS2 link and innovative policies and projects promote mixed higher density development, and a new urban center develops around the connection with HS2. Continued landscape conservation is focused on special protection for the most traveled tourism zone (Fig. 7.19).

The nonadopter teams continued the preferred lower density pattern and distributed growth in the region, adopting the NIC expressway and train plans for 2035. The exception is Milton Keynes, which plans higher densities by 2026. Conservation

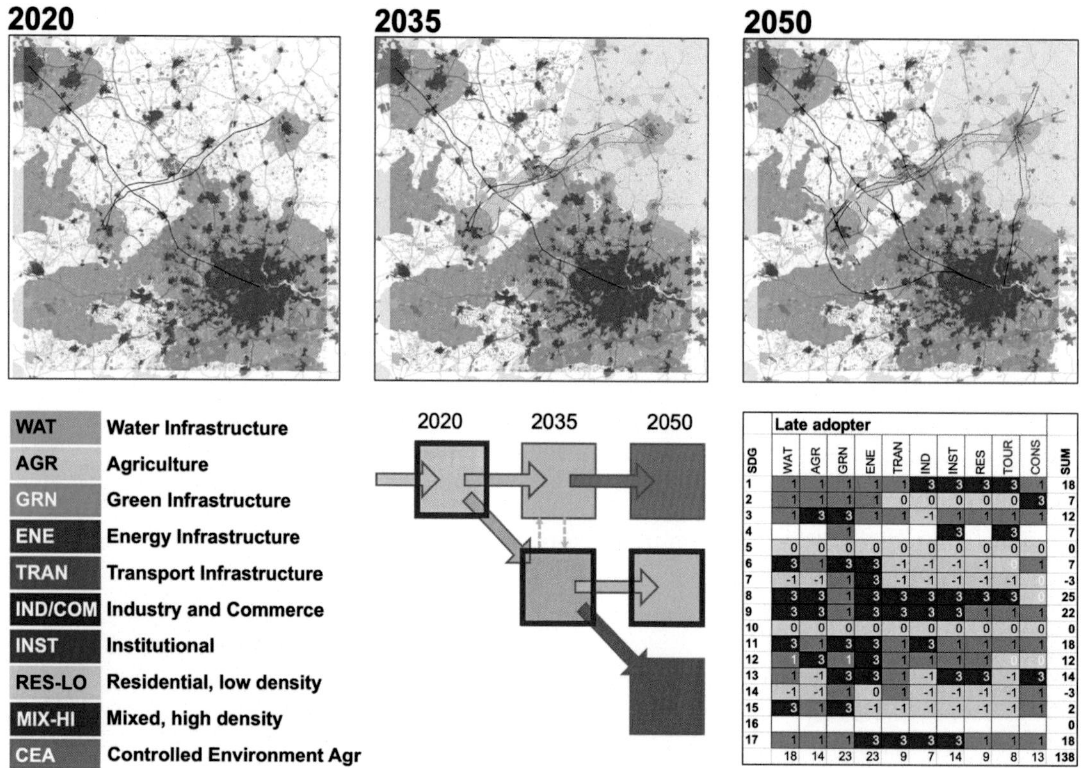

SDG	Late adopter WAT	AGR	GRN	ENE	TRAN	IND	INST	RES	TOUR	CONS	SUM
1	1	1	1	1	1	3	3	3	3	1	18
2	1	1	1	1	0	0	0	0	0	3	7
3	1	3	3	1	1	-1	1	1	1	1	12
4			1				3		3		7
5	0	0	0	0	0	0	0	0	0	0	0
6	3	1	3	3	-1	-1	-1	-1	0	1	7
7	-1	-1	1	3	-1	-1	-1	-1	-1	0	-3
8	3	3	1	3	3	3	3	3	3	0	25
9	3	3	1	3	3	3	3	1	1	1	22
10	0	0	0	0	0	0	0	0	0	0	0
11	3	1	3	3	1	3	1	1	1	1	18
12	1	3	1	3	1	1	1	1	0	0	12
13	1	-1	3	3	1	-1	3	3	-1	3	14
14	-1	-1	1	0	1	-1	-1	-1	-1	1	-3
15	3	1	3	-1	-1	-1	-1	-1	-1	1	2
16											0
17	1	1	1	3	3	3	3	1	1	1	18
	18	14	23	23	9	7	14	9	8	13	138

Figure 7.19 Late adopter scenarios for 2020, 2035, 2050; SDG score = 138.

projects focused on retaining agriculture and its associated landscapes and villages. These policies and projects were continued to 2050, enlarging the distributed lower density development pattern. People could live how and where the market was strongest, but at the cost of an impacted cultural-historic landscape (Fig. 7.20).

The early adopter scenario achieves greater SDG benefits in green infrastructure, transportation, and mixed-use development than the late adopter scenario, which initially benefits lower density housing and decentralized industry. The nonadopter design which focuses on distributed lower density housing changes the most land into urban uses, with the most detrimental impacts and the least SDG benefits.

The CAMKOX study was organized to negotiate a single proposed alternative to the NIC proposal. The final negotiation had to consider the feasibility of immediate initiation of innovative policies and projects aimed at 2050, while reconsidering the

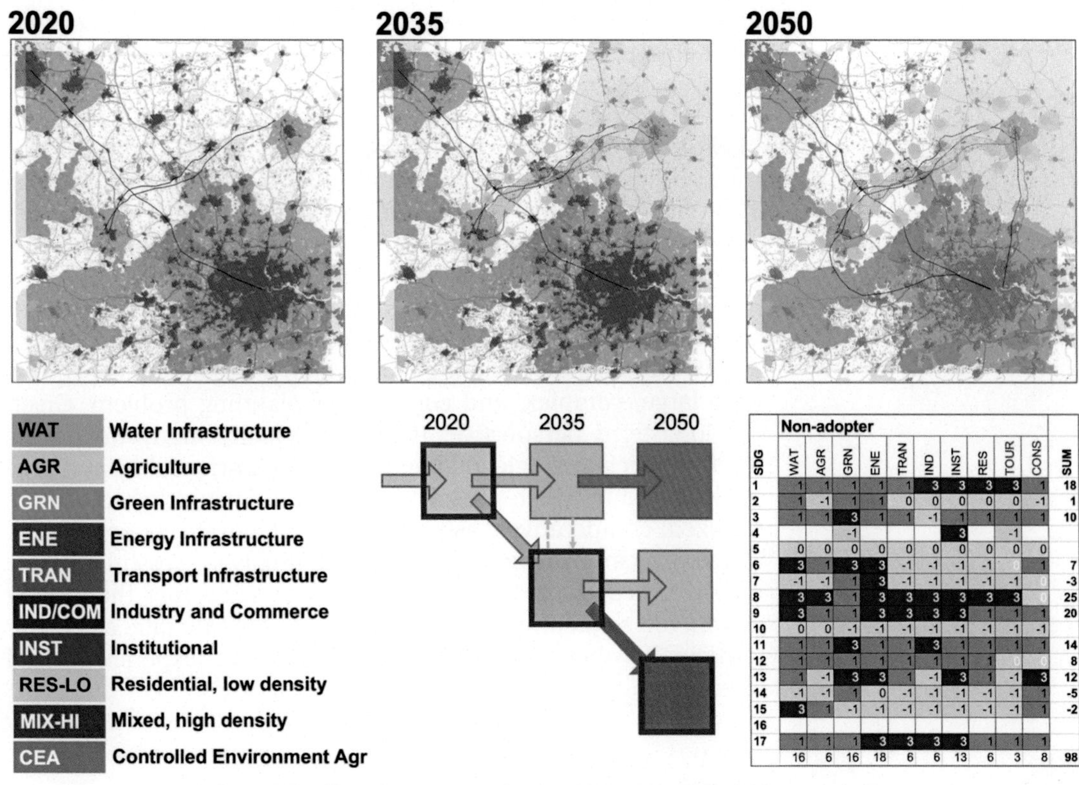

SDG	Non-adopter										SUM
	WAT	AGR	GRN	ENE	TRAN	IND	INST	RES	TOUR	CONS	
1	1	1	1	1	1	3	3	3	3	1	18
2	1	-1	1	1	0	0	0	0	0	-1	1
3	1	1	3	1	1	-1	1	1	1	1	10
4			-1				3		-1		
5	0	0	0	0	0	0	0	0	0	0	
6	3	1	3	3	-1	-1	-1	-1	0	1	7
7	-1	-1	1	3	-1	-1	-1	-1	-1	0	-3
8	3	3	1	3	3	3	3	3	3	0	25
9	3	1	1	3	3	3	3	1	1	1	20
10	0	0	-1	-1	-1	-1	-1	-1	-1	-1	
11	1	1	3	1	1	3	1	1	1	1	14
12	1	1	1	1	1	1	1	1	0	0	8
13	1	-1	3	3	1	-1	3	1	-1	3	12
14	-1	-1	1	0	-1	-1	-1	-1	-1	1	-5
15	3	1	-1	-1	-1	-1	-1	-1	-1	1	-2
16											
17	1	1	1	3	3	3	3	1	1	1	
	16	6	16	18	6	6	13	6	3	8	98

Figure 7.20 Nonadopter scenarios for 2020, 2035, 2050: SDG score = 98.

policies and projects developed in the scenario-based designs. In the final negotiation process of the workshop, it became clear that the negotiating participants favored the innovative policies and projects of the Early Adopter teams. Yet one of its central early policies was not accepted. The controlled environment agriculture (CEM) development policy had been located in the most productive grains-producing region, and this was counter to what was seen as a long-term national need.

The negotiated final design initially adopts the innovative policies and establishes an expanded and connected green and blue infrastructure. Despite the market favoring lower densities these were principally related to favoring the innovative higher rather than lower densities for the CAMKOX corridor, but not to the total exclusion of some concentrated areas of lower density. After considerable discussion, the negotiating participants placed great emphasis on growing the existing settlements along the major transport corridor spine. They did this with an emphasis on automated private vehicles in a new highway designed for efficient linking into "trains," rather than an emphasis on rebuilding the train network that formerly existed. The major reason for this was the existing and highly distributed location of industries and institutions throughout the region and the need for the existing transport system to have additional links to these many locations. The final negotiated design achieves substantial environmental and housing benefits while expanding development in this key growth region of the United Kingdom (Fig. 7.21).

The CAMKOX workshop is an example in which knowledgeable experts who are also stakeholders agreed to use geodesign and its supporting technology to develop a negotiated consensus on a large, complex, and contentious planning problem. Given the long-term perspective, they were clearly many unknowns around which strategic judgment based on current data and projections and in which prospective innovations needed to be synthesized, comparatively assessed, and collaboratively negotiated. These workshops were perceived to be highly successful because they were conducted as "live" collaborations rather than being conducted sequentially in many separate bureaucratic silos. The participants brought their multidisciplinary experience and

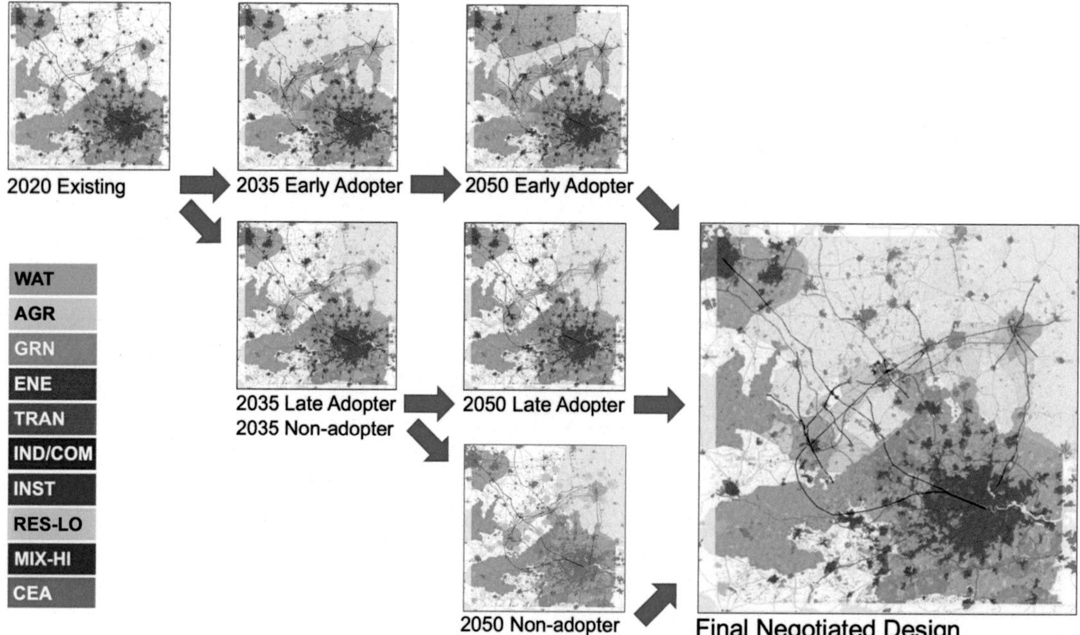

Figure 7.21 Negotiation to a final 2050 design.

expertise, and a central reason for success was their collaboration toward a prospective solution supported by an effective framework and effective digital technology.

11. The Minneapolis Green New Deal: the effect of policy on place

The Green New Deal (GND) is a resolution in the United States House of Representatives (2019) that calls for a 10-year national mobilization to achieve the following 10 goals (Tables 7.3–7.7).

This study was organized by the University of Minnesota Design Center. It studied how those 10 goals would affect a section of Minneapolis, which straddles the Mississippi River in a metropolitan area of three million people (Fig. 7.22).

Table 7.3 The 10 green new deal goals.

1."Guaranteeing a job with a family-sustaining wage, adequate family and medical leave, paid vacations, and retirement security to all people of the United States."
2."Providing all people of the United States with—(a) high-quality health care; (b) affordable, safe, and adequate housing; (c) economic security; and (d) access to clean water, clean air, healthy and affordable food, and nature."
3."Providing resources, training, and high-quality education, including higher education, to all people of the United States."
4."Meeting 100% of the power demand in the United States through clean, renewable, and zero-emission energy sources."
5."Repairing and upgrading the infrastructure in the United States, including... by eliminating pollution and greenhouse gas emissions as much as feasible."
6."Building or upgrading to energy-efficient, distributed, and 'smart' power grids, and working to ensure affordable access to electricity."
7."Upgrading all existing buildings in the United States and building new buildings to achieve maximal energy efficiency, water efficiency, safety, affordability, comfort, and durability, including through electrification."
8."Overhauling transportation systems in the United States to eliminate pollution and greenhouse gas emissions from the transportation sector as much as is technologically feasible, including through investment in—(a) zero-emission vehicle infrastructure and manufacturing; (b) clean, affordable, and accessible public transportation; and (c) high-speed rail."
9."Spurring massive growth in clean manufacturing in the United States and removing pollution and greenhouse gas emissions from manufacturing and industry as much as is technologically feasible."
10."Working collaboratively with farmers and ranchers in the United States to eliminate pollution and greenhouse gas emissions from the agricultural sector as much as is technologically feasible."

Table 7.4 System geodesign goals.

1.Water infrastructure: Provide water and sanitation to all (SDG 6), Conserve freshwater (SDG 14), Provide access to clean water (GND 2d), Upgrade buildings for efficient use of water (GND 7)
2.Agriculture: Sustainable food production (SDG 2), Ensure healthy lives (SDG 3). Responsible consumption and production (SDG 12), access to affordable food (GND 2d), Reduce pollution and greenhouse-gas emissions from agriculture (GND 10)
3.Green Infrastructure: Build resilient and innovative infrastructure (SDG 9), Promote renewable energy (SDG 13), Restore natural ecosystems (GND 2d), Upgrade infrastructure to reduce pollution (GND 5)
4.Energy Infrastructure: Provide affordable, reliable, sustainable and modern energy for all (SDG 7), Use clean, renewable, and zero-emission energy sources (GND 4), Build smart power grids (GND 6)
5.Transport Infrastructure: promote inclusive and sustainable industrialization (SDG 9), Overhaul transportation system to reduce pollution and greenhouse-gas emissions (GND 8)

6.Industry & Commerce: end poverty (SDG 1), generate employment through industry innovation (SDG 9), promote clean manufacturing (GND 9)
7.Institutional: ensure quality, inclusive education (SDG 4), promote gender equality (SDG 5), reduce inequality (SDG 10), provide high-quality education to all (GND 3)
8.Mixed use residential: build sustainable cities and communities (SDG 11), create affordable, safe, and adequate housing (GND 2b)

Table 7.5 Project assumptions.

•The city and metropolitan area's population will continue to grow
•Energy supply will need to be increasingly renewable and local
•Transportation will become electrified and more automated
•The built environment will become more networked and smarter
•Climate variability and food production pressures will grow

Table 7.6 Five GND goals that seemed most pertinent to Minneapolis.

1.Reduce inequality and expand economic opportunities
2.Transition to a green economy, helping displaced workers
3.Achieve full employment with community-defined projects
4.Adapt to climate change with re-purposed infrastructure
5.Switch to 100% renewable energy and water recycling

Table 7.7 Innovations for early and late scenario adoption.

WAT 2: Water retention
AGR 11: Urban agriculture
GRN 9: Connected green infrastructure
GRN 15: Climate change adaptation
ENE 1: Renewable energy sources
TRA 1: Autonomous vehicle revolution
IND/COM 16: Reinvented small business
MIX 3: Citizen—responsive smart cities
MIX 4: Emerging public/private spaces

Figure 7.22 A green new deal for Minneapolis, study area in North and Northeast Minneapolis.

Minneapolis has a long history of progressive politics, most recently eliminating single-family zoning in order to increase the density and affordability of housing, and this project carried on that tradition by looking at how a national policy like the GND would affect neighborhoods immediately adjacent to downtown Minneapolis, which contain some of the wealthiest and poorest districts in Minnesota (Fig. 7.23).

The project team categorized the 10 GND goals and the 17 SDG goals according to the IGC's eight systems:

The Minnesota Design Center at the University of Minnesota organized and hosted the study. Participants included community members, faculty, staff, practitioners, and students. The workshop attendees used Esri ArcGIS for the data and Esri GeoPlanner as the analytic platform. Touch-screen monitors enabled more interactive conversations among the three subgroups (Fig. 7.24) exploring either the early adopter, late adopter, or non-adopter scenarios which follow.

12. Early adopter scenario

The early adopter scenario responds to increased flooding along the Mississippi River, replacing an existing industrial area with open space able to accommodate flood water (Fig. 7.25). The rise of autonomous vehicles by 2035 leads to the repurposing of highways by 2050 into connected green space, with adjacent mixed-use affordable housing and community-based businesses.

Figure 7.23 Four Minneapolis views. Photos: Peyton Chung, licensed under Flickr CC BY 2.0.

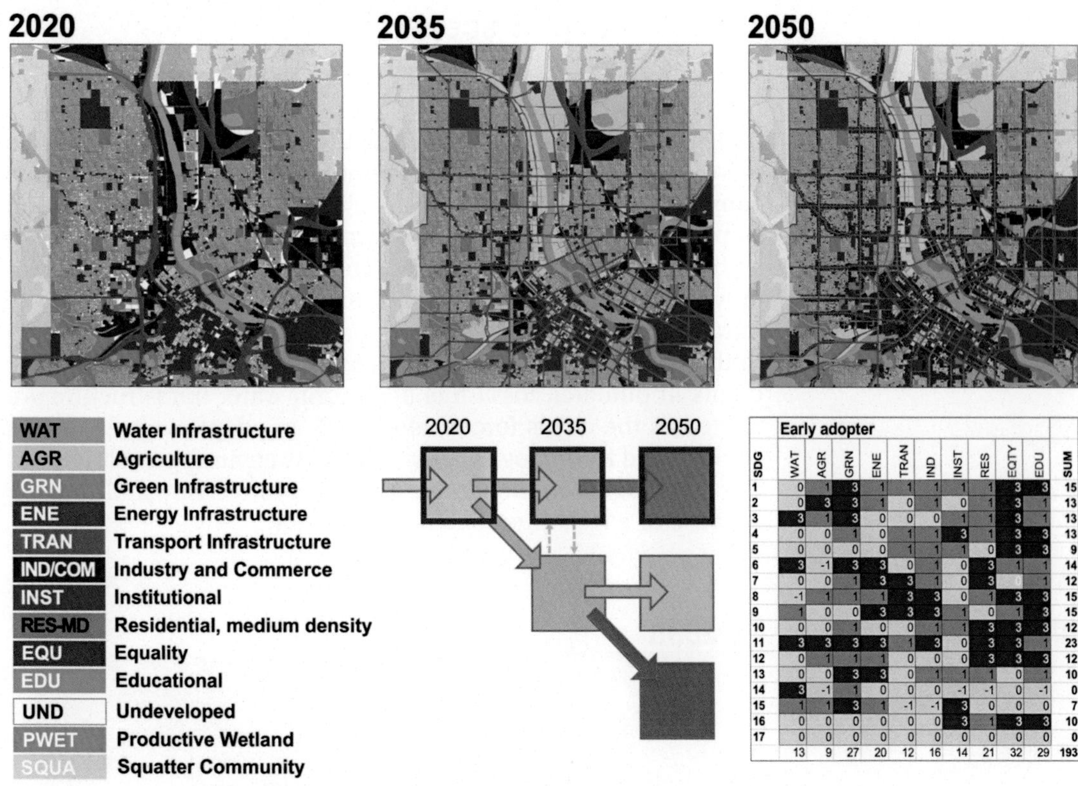

	Early adopter										
SDG	WAT	AGR	GRN	ENE	TRAN	IND	INST	RES	EQTY	EDU	SUM
1	0	1	3	1	1	1	1	1	3	3	15
2	0	3	3	1	0	1	0	1	3	1	13
3	3	1	3	0	0	0	1	1	3	1	13
4	0	0	1	0	1	1	3	1	3	3	13
5	0	0	0	0	1	1	1	0	3	3	9
6	3	-1	3	3	0	1	0	3	1	1	14
7	0	0	1	3	3	1	0	3	0	1	12
8	-1	1	1	1	3	3	0	1	3	3	15
9	1	0	0	3	3	3	1	0	1	3	15
10	0	0	1	0	0	1	1	3	3	3	12
11	3	3	3	3	1	3	0	3	3	1	23
12	0	1	1	1	0	0	0	3	3	3	12
13	0	0	3	3	0	1	1	1	0	1	10
14	3	-1	1	0	0	0	-1	-1	0	-1	0
15	1	1	3	1	-1	-1	3	0	0	0	7
16	0	0	0	0	0	0	3	1	3	3	10
17	0	0	0	0	0	0	0	0	0	0	0
	13	9	27	20	12	16	14	21	32	29	193

Figure 7.24 Early adopter scenarios for 2020, 2035, 2050: SDG score = 186.

Urban agriculture occupies most lawns and boulevards, as water retention and recycling strategies recharge the aquifer. Microgrid renewable energy production also occurs in neighborhoods, using distributed networks of building-mounted solar arrays. A major emphasis is on community-based economic development, with accessible retraining opportunities and full employment of everyone capable of working. Green infrastructure connects neighborhoods currently separated from the river and offers linked habitat corridors as well as multi-model transportation corridors. With an intensive investment in the Green New Deal, Minneapolis may have a greater chance of achieving socially equity, economically prosperity, and environmental resilient, and be better prepared as a destination city for environmental refugees.

13. Late adopter scenario

Because of its late start after 2035, the city is not as well prepared for the disruptions that climate change and environmental refugees will bring. The infrastructure is not as ready to handle increased flooding and while autonomous vehicles have become common by 2035, resistance to changing the infrastructure in response to them leads to a lot of wasted investment in outmoded highways and parking structures. This scenario also results in a lot of wasted human potential as unemployment and a lack of retraining opportunities prevent many people from contributing to the economy and their communities. At the same time, investments in outdated fossil-fuel and storm-water infrastructure are wasted as the city is forced, after 2035, to adapt more quickly to climatic and technological disruptions. As environmental refugees start arriving, accommodating them is more costly and difficult because of a lack of preparation (Fig. 7.25).

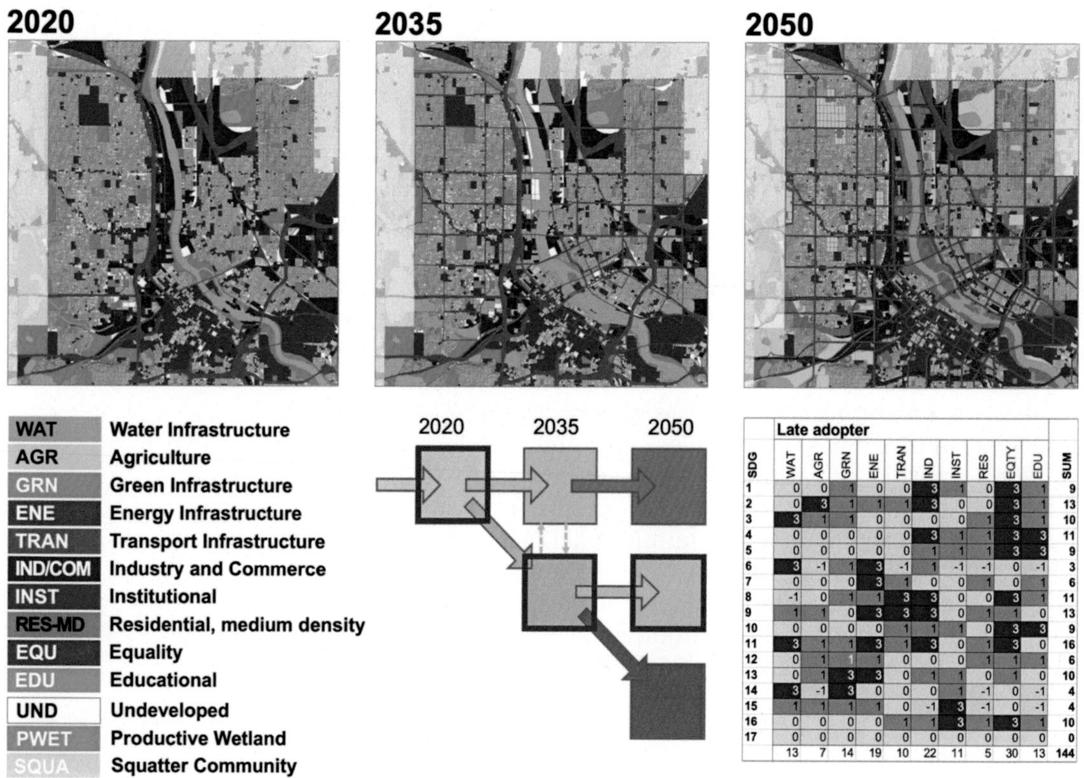

SDG	Late adopter WAT	AGR	GRN	ENE	TRAN	IND	INST	RES	EQTY	EDU	SUM
1	0	0	1	0	0	3	1	0	3	1	9
2	0	3	1	1	1	3	0	0	3	1	13
3	3	1	1	0	0	0	0	1	3	1	10
4	0	0	0	0	0	3	1	1	3	3	11
5	0	0	0	0	0	1	1	1	3	3	9
6	3	-1	1	3	-1	1	-1	-1	0	-1	3
7	0	0	0	3	1	0	0	1	0	1	6
8	-1	0	1	1	3	3	0	0	3	1	11
9	1	1	0	3	3	3	0	1	1	0	13
10	0	0	0	0	1	1	1	0	3	3	9
11	3	1	1	3	1	3	0	1	3	0	16
12	0	1	1	1	0	0	0	1	1	1	6
13	0	1	3	3	0	1	1	0	1	0	10
14	3	-1	3	0	0	0	1	-1	0	-1	4
15	1	1	1	1	0	-1	3	-1	0	-1	4
16	0	0	0	0	1	1	3	1	3	1	10
17	0	0	0	0	0	0	0	0	0	0	0
	13	7	14	19	10	22	11	5	30	13	144

Figure 7.25 Late adopter scenarios for 2020, 2035, 2050: SDG score = 136.

14. Nonadopter scenario

The nonadopter scenario shows how resistance to change can lead a prosperous and progressive city to become impoverished, provincial and partisan (Fig. 7.26). This scenario results in growing inequality, leading rich and poor neighborhoods, physically very close to each other in the city, to become embattled. This scenario also sees growing climate change denial, and a refusal to plan for it. That, in turn, leads to ever-more expensive and catastrophic weather-related events, as people abandon low-lying parts of the city and infrastructure and building repair cannot keep up. As environmental refugees arrive, they squat on all available open space, occupying public golf courses and the city's extensive park system. This also leads to a deteriorating natural environment, declining public health, and overwhelmed water and food systems, pushing the city toward bankruptcy.

The workshop did not develop a final design, but instead, laid out three different scenarios for policy makers to consider. The

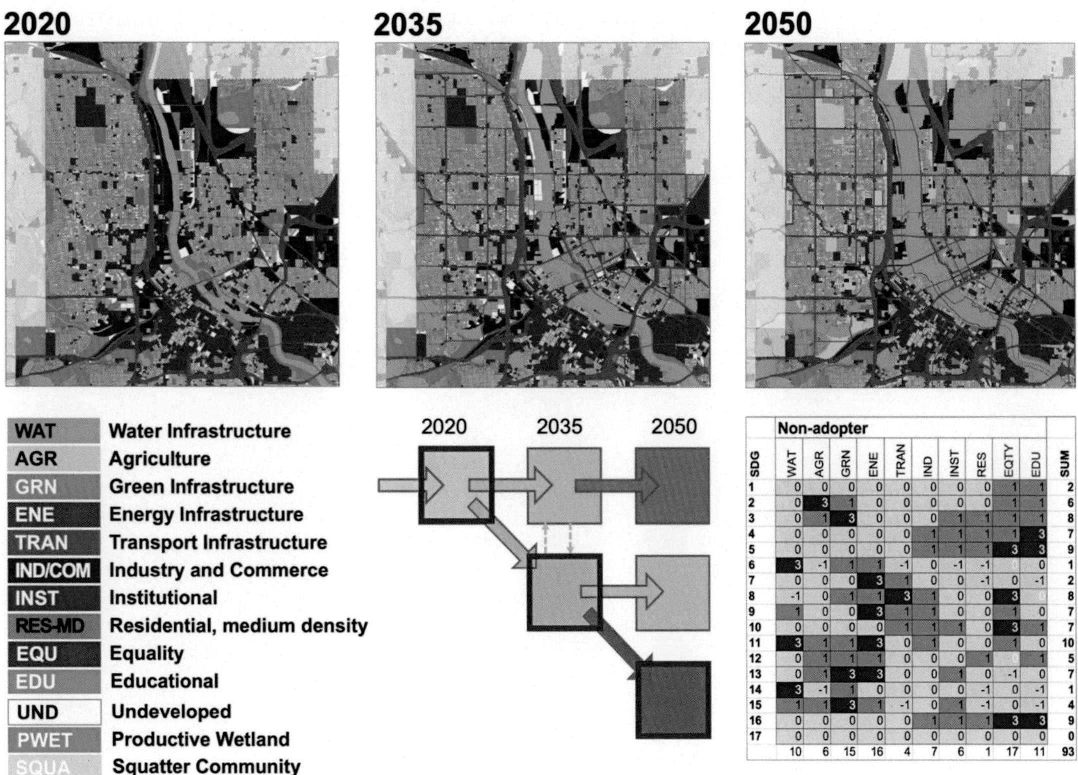

SDG	WAT	AGR	GRN	ENE	TRAN	IND	INST	RES	EQTY	EDU	SUM
	Non-adopter										
1	0	0	0	0	0	0	0	0	1	1	2
2	0	3	1	0	0	0	0	0	1	1	6
3	0	1	3	0	0	0	1	1	1	1	8
4	0	0	0	0	0	1	1	1	1	3	7
5	0	0	0	0	0	1	1	1	3	3	9
6	3	-1	1	1	-1	0	-1	-1	0	0	1
7	0	0	0	3	1	0	0	-1	0	-1	2
8	-1	0	1	1	3	1	0	0	3	0	8
9	1	0	0	3	1	1	0	0	1	0	7
10	0	0	0	0	1	1	1	0	3	1	7
11	3	1	1	3	0	1	0	0	1	0	10
12	0	1	1	1	0	0	0	1	0	1	5
13	0	1	3	3	0	0	1	0	-1	0	7
14	3	-1	1	0	0	0	0	-1	0	-1	1
15	1	1	3	1	-1	0	1	-1	0	-1	4
16	0	0	0	0	0	1	1	1	3	3	9
17	0	0	0	0	0	0	0	0	0	0	0
	10	6	15	16	4	7	6	1	17	11	93

Figure 7.26 Nonadopter scenarios for 2020, 2035, 2050: SDG score = 87.

Early Adopter Scenario fully embraces the SDG's and the GND goals, both of which focus on clean energy (SDG7), job creation (SDG 8), a green economy (SDG 9), and resilient communities (SDG 11). The GND goals also align with SDG 1, 2, 3, 4, and 5, in which the entire population would be gainfully employed, well nourished, in good health, with educational opportunities for all.

The Late Adopter Scenario has these same goals, but because of their adoption 15 years later, there are more obstacles to overcome, such as the loss of nearly an entire generation to unequal opportunities, inadequate education, and poorer health outcomes. This scenario achieves some of the early adopter ones, but later and to a lesser extent. The nonadopter scenario shows what happens when the forces resisting change prevail, with ever greater inequality among communities and genders, increasingly expensive environmental damage that causes disruptions to the lives of growing numbers of people, and the growing socioeconomic segregation of the city. It is a scenario that no one would want for their children (Fig. 7.27).

The recommended scenario shows how former industrial land along the river would be better used for urban agriculture and

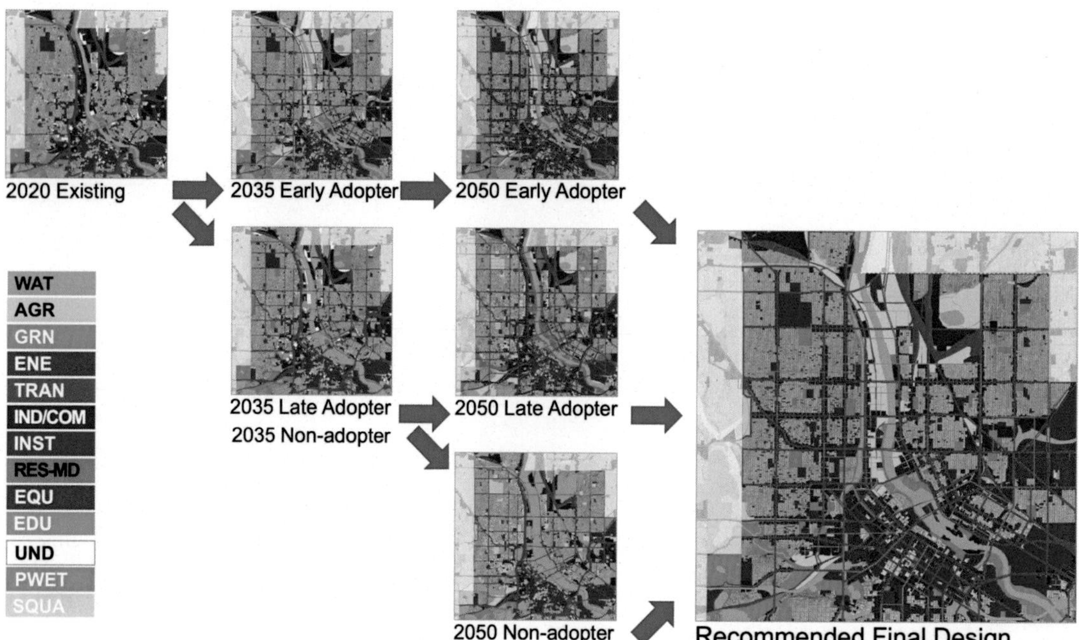

Figure 7.27 The recommended design for 2050.

park space, how highways offer opportunities for renewable energy production and how commercial corridors could also serve as business incubators. That scenario also shows that, despite the claims of some who oppose the Green New Deal because of its short-term costs, the long-term costs of not acting are far greater. Leadership at the city level—influenced, in part, by this study—has discussed enacting a local version of the Green New Deal.

There are important lessons to be drawn from the two studies above. They demonstrate the range of issues that major global cities will face by 2050. The CAMKOX study focused on regional growth toward an environment that combines aggressive conservation and major newly built infrastructure with multiple higher density urban centers. The Minneapolis study focused on rebuilding the central part of an extensive metropolitan area, with major planning in support of its social infrastructure to accommodate new and different residents. Many other global cities will need to grow, many will need to rebuild, many will have similar populations and many will have new populations .... and most will have all of these. Environmental management will be paramount. Innovations in energy and transportation and in infrastructure management are likely inevitable. What is clear from these and other IGC scenarios is that not responding to likely needs and expected innovations will produce far worse outcomes as seen in their SDG assessments than thinking forward and planning ahead. The financial costs will be high. Perhaps the most important lesson from these two case studies is that neither the negotiated design for the CAMKOX corridor nor the recommended design for Minneapolis follows current trends in the private development market. The processes of implementing change will also need to be transformed.

15. How IGC studies have applied geodesign globally

Achieving plans that address global issues has three fundamental requirements. First, it must rely heavily on understanding and learning from precedents. To be effective, then, designers and planners must be able to understand solutions tried and tested elsewhere and be able to learn from those precedents. Second, the designs or plans implemented in one region inevitably affect the operation of systems in the adjacent ones. Even if they remain incompatible, similarities and differences can only be identified if trans-boundary comparisons can be made, requiring that each plan be translated, or—preferably—created in a common representational system. Third, while systems thinking seeks to illuminate how decisions are made by enabling the interrogation of each step in the development of a plan, large plans addressing numerous simultaneous issues inevitably have complex system structures, and each system has its own complex logic. Faced with such an array of issues, achieving meaningful public participation and even expert-to-expert communication is difficult. The IGC framework uses a set of conventions, a language of communication, to bring structure and organization to system thinking that enables scenario outcomes to be meaningfully compared and with lessons drawn that enable people in quite different situations to communicate with one another. Our applications of the IGC framework, through the projects of the IGC network, illustrate the power of using such a disciplined approach to design.

Consistent systems: By using a common set of colors for geodesign systems and thus revealing their patterns of development, three high-latitude urban-regional projects display similar goals in consolidating cores and creating green—belt conservation zones to achieve efficiency and resulting reductions in greenhouse gas production and improved water management. Fig. 7.28 shows urban project comparisons from (A) Manchester, UK (University of Manchester) (B) Munich, Germany (Hochschule Weihenstephan-Triesdorf) and (C) Xi'an, China (Peking University).

Scales and sizes: By arraying three projects at similar scales (Fig. 7.29), it is possible to see the designer's intentions as well as how the designer's intentions are shaped by, left-to-right, the influence of topography in Japanese settlement patterns, the expansive large-area planning required for a new airport in

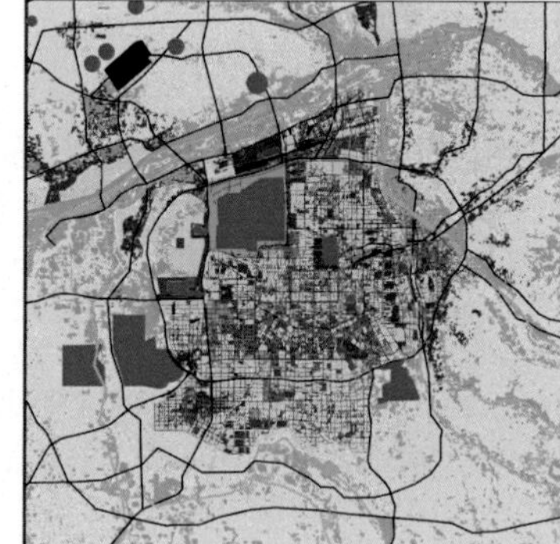

Figure 7.28 Urban project comparisons.

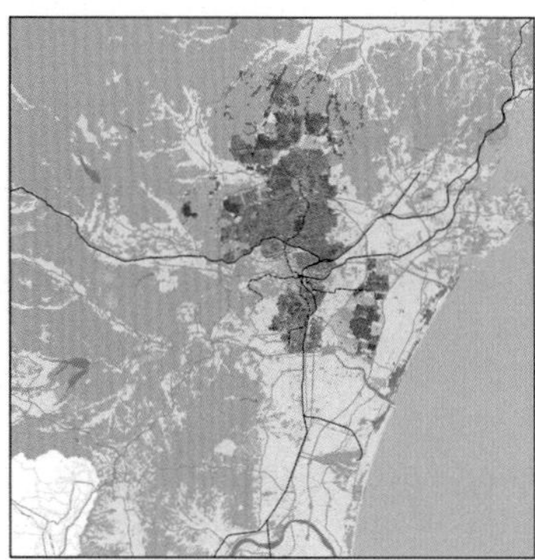
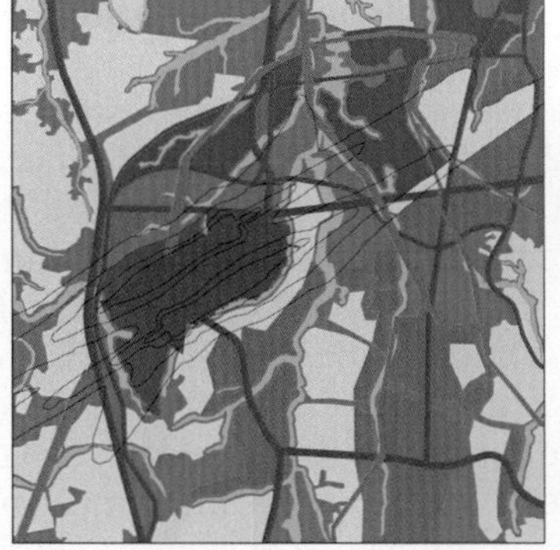

Figure 7.29 20 × 20 km projects reveal land use texture.

Australia, and the granular development dictated by a topographically varied rural landscape with strong land-use and ownership traditions in Taiwan (A) Sendai, Japan (Tohoku University), (B) Sydney, Australia (University of New South Wales), (C) Tamsui, Taiwan, (National Sun Yat-Sen University).

Conversely, three dense urban projects, each looked at through a 5 km × 5 km square lens for comparability, demonstrate common strategies of reinforcing transportation corridors for commercial and mixed development while identifying and protecting green urban corridors for stormwater management, habitat preservation and for passive recreation to relieve the human pressures of urban living. Fig. 7.30 shows urban design strategies common to (A) Mexico City (Universidad Autonoma Metropolitana) (B) Mumbai, India (School of Environment and Architecture-Mumbai), and (C) São Paulo, Brazil (University of São Paulo).

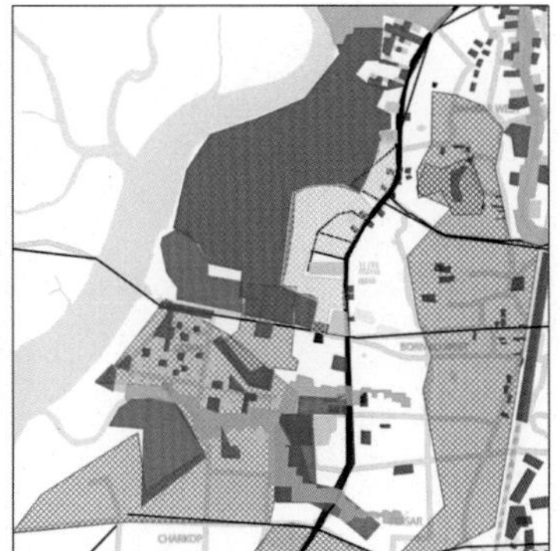
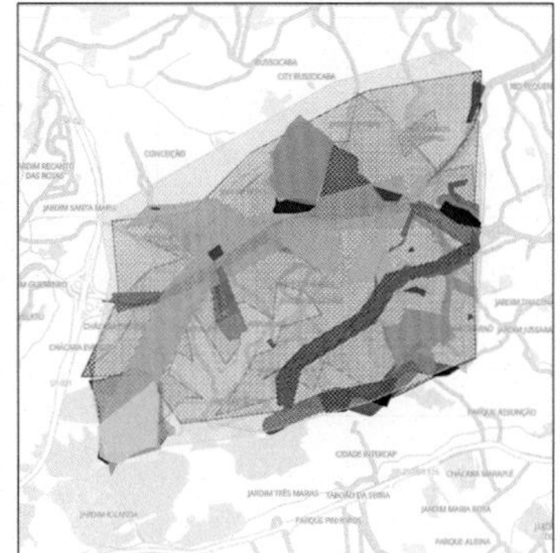

Figure 7.30 5 × 5 km projects reveal common urban design strategies.

Shared scenarios and timeframes: The impact of time passing is revealed, not only for a single project but through side-by-side comparison with others, designers can discern how time impacts design development under different organizational, climatological, economic, etc. regimes, in this case the organic expansion of mixed-use development along a transportation corridor. Fig. 7.31 shows progression through time in (A) 2020 (B) 2035 (C) 2050 in Winneba, Ghana (University of Virginia).

Similarly, the consistent array of design scenarios enables the comparison of three design scenarios: continue plans already in place, wait and see and implement changes in the future, or initiate innovative designs immediately, not only for a single project but through the adoption of common means of representation the effects of those changes can be compared with other design settings with different characteristics and constraints This case from Utah shows the alternative geodesign strategies (A) Early adopter, (B) Late adopter, (C) Nonadopter, of design innovations in Salt Lake City and The Wasatch Front, USA (Utah State University). the Early adopter plan emphasizing mixed use development in order to reduce urban sprawl, versus the nonadopter plan where low-density housing is allowed to expand the urban footprint (Fig. 7.32).

Assumptions and expectations about the future: In Fig. 7.33 below from USA (University of Georgia), Turkey (Harran University), and Nigeria (Ahmadu Bello University), each study has listed its starting assumptions about the future. Similarities between the items chosen suggest areas of shared global priority, and differences indicate areas where regional differences might be a significant factor in responding to global change.

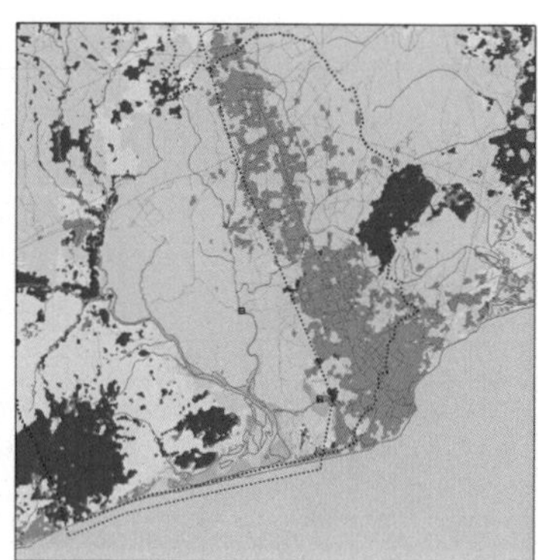
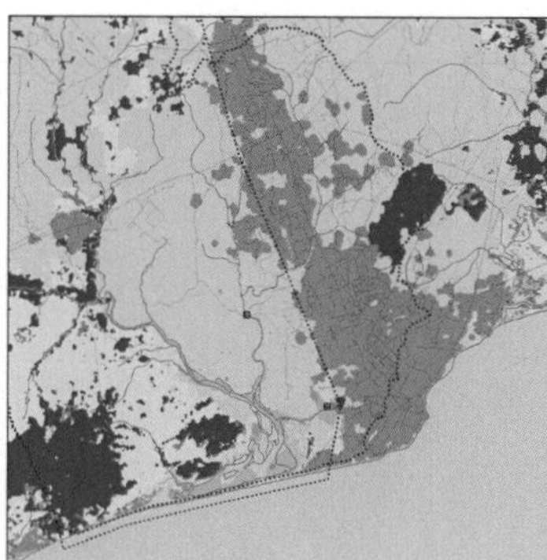

Figure 7.31 Geodesign progression through time (A) 2020 (B) 2035 (C) 2050.

Figure 7.32 Alternative geodesign strategies (A) early adopter, (B) late adopter, (C) non-adopter, of design innovations.

	Georgia coast counties, USA		Şanlıurfa, Turkey		Zaria, Nigeria
1	Population: 320,000 new people in the region.	1	Convert squatter settlements creating new homes for 250,000 inhabitants.	1	Green infrastructure: Correct deforestation and land degradation through green policies and programmes.
2	Housing: 190,000 new housing units needed.	2	Design new neighborhoods to avoid heat islands.	2	Governance: The right caliber of leadership to ensure continuity of policies and projects.
3	Population displaced by sea level rise (NOAA 3 ft projection): 95,000 .	3	Replace uncontrolled irrigation and fertilizing with precision farming.	3	Renewable energy: Generate renewable energy and encourage household clean energy.
4	Commercial: 2,700 acres of new commercial development.	4	Build tourism based on archaeology and religion.	4	New housing: 213,706 new housing units will be needed, most in urban and sub-urban areas.
5	Industrial: 15,400 acres of new industrial development.	5	Model service sector on UK's Wiltshire, home of Stonehenge.	5	Agriculture and industrial revitalization: Provide employment while expanding rural economy and food security.

Figure 7.33 Local/regional project requirements respond to global assumptions.

Adoption of innovations: Fig. 7.34, from Ghana (University of Virginia), Germany (Leibniz University-Hannover), and Japan (Ritsumeikan University), shows the varying patterns of innovation adoption into the designs. Some are adopted by multiple projects and thus potentially suitable for global adoption, AGR 5—Agritourism and GRN 1—Resilient landscape infrastructure are examples in Fig. 7.34. Others, frequently the majority, represent the variety within the 187-innovation IGC library and may be specific to more limited conditions.

Common evaluation metrics: To refine project-to-project comparisons requires simple metrics or descriptors that track and articulate how designs evolve over time—from 2020 to 2035 to 2050, did the situation improve or decline? Between the early adopters of innovations, through the late adopters to the nonadopters, did the innovations results in improvements? Fig. 7.35 shows a matrix assessing performance of each system against

Winneba Lagoon, Ghana		Lahn River, Germany		Yosano, Japan	
WAT 3	Conserve agricultural water by adopting best practice.	WAT 2	Water retention	AGR 2	Robots fight weeds
WAT 8	Constructed wetlands to retain water and treat waste water.	AGR 1	Organic agriculture	AGR 5	Agritourism
AGR 4	Improve agricultural practices and productivity.	AGR 3	Rewilding, let nature take its course	AGR 15	Drones in agriculture
AGR 5	Agritourism.	GRN 1	Resilient landscape infrastructure	GRN 9	Connectivity and elements
AGR 13	Aquaponics.	GRN 2	Resilient landscape infrastructure for rural communities	TRA 1	Automated transportation infrastructure
GRN 1	Resilient landscape infrastructure.	GRN 13	Regaining the riparian ecosystem	TRA 13	Redefining biking with bike shares
GRN 17	Green infrastructure for coastal resilience.	GRN 15	Adaptation to climate change	IND/ COM 13	Internet-based commerce
GRN 18	Mangroves for coastal resilience.	ENE 1	Renewable energy sources	MIX 1	Mixed use development
MIX 10	Increase urban density for new development by 50%.	TRA 17	Transportation network with sustainable energy infrastructure	IND/ COM 8	Technical singularity
INS 6	Improve environmental education.			INS 4	The future home health care

Figure 7.34 Three primarily agricultural areas in different geographies, with different innovations and designs.

each SDG for IGC projects of three sizes. In some systems, early innovation has more impact than in the others, but in general, early innovation designs are superior in the SDG assessments. The examples in Fig. 7.35 are for three different project sizes—Seoul, South Korea, 3.5 × 3.5 km (University of Seoul), Virginia Beach, USA, 10 × 10 km (Virginia Tech. University), Al Ain, United Arab Emirates, 80 × 80 km (United Arab Emirates University).

Common reporting of outcomes and comparison: A series of related page layouts have been developed for poster, book, and projected slide display. The consistent use of these layout enables project-to-project comparison by various themes—project size, project climate, urban-rural location, developed versus less-developed nations (Fig. 7.36). Each of these comparisons, enabled by the shared IGC geodesign language, represents a valuable learning opportunity for participants whether students, experienced designers, public officials, or citizens of the place.

16. Conclusion: Geodesign in global public practice

While the geodesign approach has been extensively applied in research and educational settings by a growing community of adopters around the world, geodesign methods are robust and have been applied in varied but comparable circumstances many times with public officials and private participants. In addition to the CAMKOX and Minneapolis case studies above, the three additional, albeit brief, geodesign studies are examples of

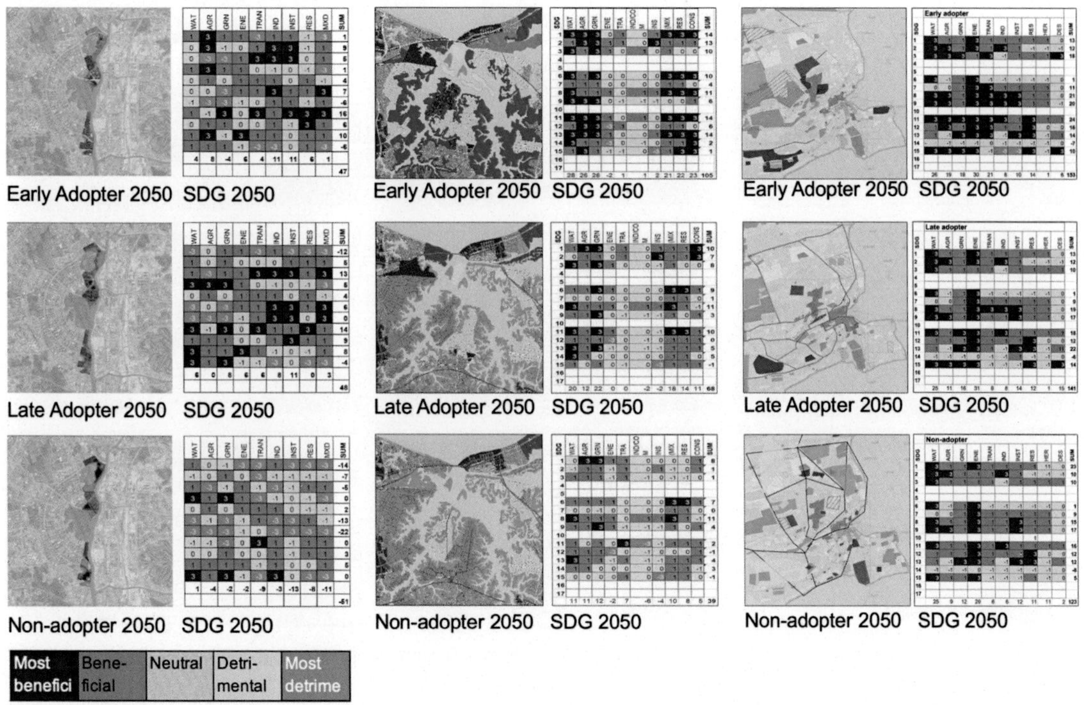

Figure 7.35 SDG judgment matrices for early- versus late-versus nonadoption of geodesign innovation for three project sizes.

many in which the participants were diverse people who advise and make these kinds of strategic decisions.

Among the first and most complex examples is the Georgia (USA) Coastal study (Rivero et al., 2015, 2017) involving 10 Counties with planning responsibility and the coordinating Coastal Regional Commission of Georgia. The 2-day workshop was requested after the US National Oceanic and Atmospheric Administration forecast the potential zone of sea level rise caused by projected climate change. The study was coordinated by the IGC team from the University of Georgia. It was organized so that each County and the Coastal Commission was represented and had its own geodesign team responsible for designing for growth and change to 2050. The regional commission was responsible for negotiating intercounty relationships and a final negotiated regional plan which acknowledged expected coastal sea rise and demographic changes (Fig. 7.37).

Moura et al. (2017) at the Federal University of Minas Gerais, Brazil, supported the public authorities in Belo Horizonte (Monteiro et al., 2018; Patata et al., 2018) in geodesign workshops

Figure 7.36 An array of summary IGC figures, comparable within a row.

Figure 7.37 The Georgia, USA, coastal study. Photos by Tess Canfield.

directly involving the residents in participatory geodesign, making their own design for the provision of a regulated plan for public services in their informal settlement (Fig. 7.38). This approved strategy has subsequently been applied in other favelas in Belo Horizonte.

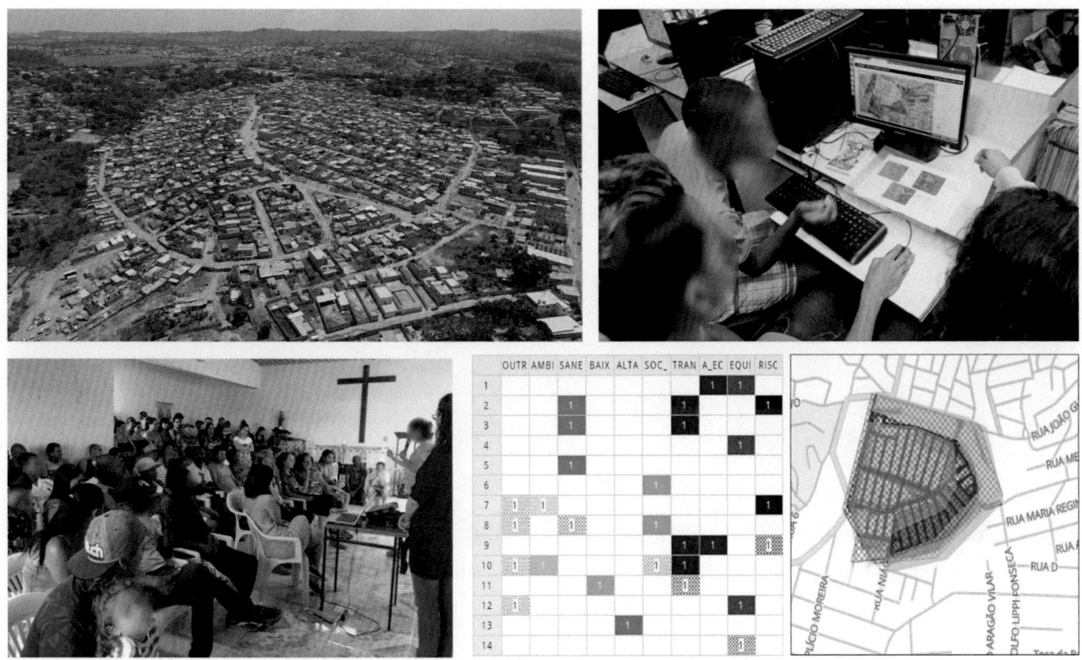

Figure 7.38 A regularization plan for Dandara, Belo Horizonte, Brazil.

The study "Envisioning Sydney's urban future" was organized on behalf of the City of Sydney, Australia, by the team from University of New South Wales. Participants were from the relevant city and metropolitan public agencies, the two municipalities, and private consulting firms. One objective of the 2 day workshop was "breaking down the silos through geodesign" (Pettit et al., 2019). The task for the geodesign study was to double the population of the city's oldest and fully developed suburban area by 2050, and also improved its water and green infrastructure. In addition, the city's major hospital complex and the University of New South Wales would double (Fig. 7.39).

At the end of this workshop, Professor Roderick Simpson, Environment Commissioner of the Greater Sydney Commission and Professor of Planning at the University of Sydney said: "The geodesign approach is most effective in dealing with complexity and emergence of the city in the context of the city as a mosaic of places - this is an approach that is gaining currency at the Greater Sydney Commission. Place-based planning allows a wide range of factors to be considered concurrently by reducing the scale not the scope. It also allows a contextually specific response which geodesign supports." "The selection process and

Figure 7.39 Envisioning Sydney's urban future. Photos by Tess Canfield.

negotiation in the geodesign process could be considered a form of emergence, particularly if emergence is seen to be a pattern or an idea that gains prominence. This is through the negotiation process and consensus - which is where the geodesign process adds significant value."

The number of experiences applying geodesign in support of real-world planning processes around the world is steadily growing. The appreciation of decision-makers and practitioners is usually high to very high (Pettit et al., 2019). The results of collaborative geodesign initiatives are positively influencing the way participants work toward introducing innovation toward global sustainability objectives and are bringing substantial procedural improvement in the planning and administration of local spatial development.

The IGC continues in its mission of education and research in geodesign and welcomes all university teams to join https://www.igc-geodesign.org/joining-igc. The lessons of the first IGC iteration are summarized in *The IGC: Geography by Design* (Steinitz, Orland and Fisher et al., 2020). The IGC studies in the first and second iterations are shown in https://www.igc-geodesign.org/. The technological underpinnings of IGC are supporting a global network with a global to local to global perspective, conducting coordinated geodesign studies while educating people and building capacity in geodesign (Fig. 7.40). This has been

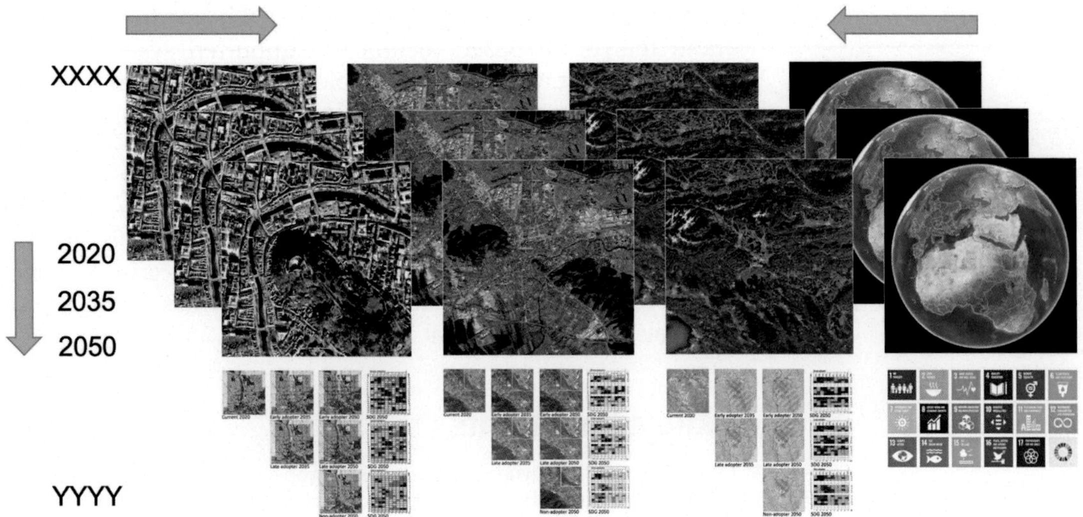

Figure 7.40 Geodesign with a global to local to global perspective.

enhanced in a series of IGC teaching-workshops conducted by international teams collaborating in real time with geodesign support technology and entirely via the internet, and shown in https://www.igc-geodesign.org/geodesign-workshops.

There are three major conclusions from the work to date. IGC studies have been highly coordinated, yet the innovative scenario-based designs were more different than similar. Clearly, pursuing even one system's strategy globally, and based on one set of innovations, results in outcomes that are shaped by regional and local expectations and will vary widely. Variations based on geography, climate, culture, and economic development likely will continue to guide future change. This should not be seen as a failing of the approach but a success. By providing a consistent structure for creation and communication of geodesign studies, the variations that emerge become the key substance of the global-to-local-to-global negotiations, iterations, and accommodations that are essential to forward progress.

While it may be seen as self-fulfilling prophecy, the early selection and adoption of integrated systems innovation in almost all IGC studies to date resulted in better outcomes than late adoption, and considerably better than nonadoption of locally selected innovation. Furthermore, the ability to demonstrate the emergence of positive design outcomes and to trace them back to their origin system policy and project components and their attributes, provides the greater transparency desired in all geodesign studies. The close-coupling of the geodesign framework to analytically based, technically supported, system evaluations and impact assessments, enables the informed negotiation necessary for the reconciliation of locally varied objectives with global goals.

Building on these lessons, and on our continuing improvement of geodesign processes and supporting guidance as shown herein, the IGC will continue to provide a framework for coordinating different efforts to understand impacts on critical global systems and to ensure that geodesign activities bring about high levels of environmental improvement.

Acknowledgments

We thank the CAMKOX workshop participants who shall remain anonymous, and the professional firms whose diagrammatic ideas were used as the initial basis for the geodesign study.
We thank the University of Minnesota Design Center staff and community affiliates who participated in the Minneapolis geodesign study: Carly Anderson, Jonee Brigham, Bob Close, Remi Douah, Thomas Fisher, Tim Griffin, Joseph Hang, Mathias Hughey, Bruce Jacobson, Ursula Lang, Aaron Parker, and Emily Stover.
We thank the many participants and institutions which made the IGC studies which we have included in this publication.

References

Ballal, H., 2015. Collaborative Planning with Digital Design Synthesis. Ph.D. Dissertation. Centre for Advanced Spatial Analysis, Faculty of the Built Environment, University College, London, United Kingdom.

Ballal, H., 2020. Geodesignhub. https://www.geodesignhub.com/.

Ballal, H., Steinitz, C., 2015. A workshop in geodesign synthesis. In: Buhmann, E., Ervin, S., Pietsch, P. (Eds.), Digital Landscape Architecture. Herbert Wichmann Press, Germany, pp. 400–407.

Batty, M., 2013. Defining geodesign (= GIS + design?). Environment and Planning B: Planning and Design 40 (1), 1–2.

Brail, R.K., Klosterman, R.E., 2001. Planning Support Systems: Integrating Geographic Information Systems, Models, and Visualization Tools. ESRI Press.

Campagna, M., 2016. Social Media Geographic Information: why social is special when it goes spatial?. In: European Handbook of Crowdsourced Geographic Information https://doi.org/10.5334/bax.d.

Capineri, C., Haklay, M., Huang, H., Antoniou, V., Kettunen, J., Ostermann, F., Purves, R. (Eds.), 2016. European Handbook of Crowdsourced Geographic Information. Ubiquity Press, London. https://doi.org/10.5334/bax.

Fisher, T., 2016. An education in geodesign. Landscape and Urban Planning 156, 20–22.

Fisher, T., Orland, B., Steinitz, C., 2020. The International Geodesign Collaboration. Esri Press, Redlands CA, USA.

Geertman, S., Stillwell, J., 2004. Planning support systems: an inventory of current practice. Computers, Environment and Urban Systems 28 (4), 291–310. https://doi.org/10.1016/S0198-9715(03)00024-3. ISSN 0198-9715.
Geertman, S., Ferreira, J., Goodspeed, R., Stillwell, J., 2015. Planning support systems and smart cities. In: Lecture Notes in Geoinformation and Cartography, vol 213. Kluwer Academic Publishers.
Harris, B., 1989. Beyond geographic information systems. Journal of the American Planning Association 55 (1), 85–90. https://doi.org/10.1080/01944368908975408.
Hollstein, L.M., June 2019. Retrospective and reconsideration: the first 25 years of the Steinitz framework for landscape architecture education and environmental design. Landscape and Urban Planning 186, 56–66.
International Geodesign Collaboration, 2018. http://www.geodesigncollab.org.
Khakee, A., 1998. Evaluation and planning: inseparable concepts. Town Planning Review 69 (4), 359–374.
Kim, M., 2020. The natural language of geodesign. In: Fisher, T., Orland, B., Steinitz, C. (Eds.), The International Geodesign Collaboration. Esri Press, Redlands CA, USA, pp. 149–153.
Malcolm Reading Co. https://competitions.malcolmreading.co.uk/cambridge oxfordconnection/news/2017/national-infrastructure-commission-reveals-gallery-of-final-design-concepts.
Meadows, D., 2008. Thinking in Systems. A Primer, Earthscan, London, p. 95.
Monteiro, L.D.O., Moura, A.C.M., Zyngier, C.M., Sousa De Sena, Í., De Paula, P.L., 2018. Geodesign facing the urgency of reducing poverty: the cases of Belo Horizonte. DISEGNARECON 11 (20), 6.1–6.25. Available in: http://disegnarecon.univaq.it/ojs/index.php/disegnarecon/article/view/362.
Moura, A., Carsalade, F., Palhares, R., Zyngier, C., 2017. Geodesign in Pampulha cultural and heritage urban area: Visualization tools to orchestrate urban growth and dynamic transformations. Rozwoj Regionalny i Polityka Regionalna 35, 73–87.
Neuman, M., Tchapi, M., Sharkey, M., Gelgota, A., Itova, I., 2018. East West Arc: Re-thinking Growth in the London Region. University of Westminster, London.
Orland, B., Steinitz, C., 2019. Improving our global infrastructure: the international geodesign collaboration. Journal of Digital Landscape Architecture 4, 213–221. Wichmann.
Patata, S., Lisboa de Paula, P., Moura, A.C.M., 2018. The application of the Geodesign in a Brazilian illegal settlement. Participatory planning in Dandara occupation case study. In: Leone, A., Gargiulo, C. (Eds.), Environmental and Territorial Modelling for Planning and Design. FedOAPress, Naples, Italy, pp. 673–685. https://geoproea.arq.ufmg.br/publicacoes/2018/the-application-of-geodesign-in-a-brazilian-illegal-settlement-participatory-planning-in-dandara-occupation-case-study.
Pettit, C.P., Hawken, S., Ticzon, C., Steinitz, C., Ballal, H., Canfield, T., Leal, S.Z., Lieske, S.N., Afrooz, A.E., 2019. Breaking down the silos through geodesign – Envisioning Sydney's urban future. Environment and Planning B: Urban Analytics and City Science 1–18. https://doi.org/10.1177/2399808318812887.
Rivero, R., Smith, A., Ballal, H., Steinitz, C., 2015. Promoting collaborative geodesign in a multidisciplinary and multiscale environment: coastal georgia 2050, USA. In: Digital Landscape Architecture.
Rivero, R., Smith, A., Orland, B., Calabria, J., Ballal, H., Steinitz, C., Perkl, R., McClenning, L., Key, H., 2017. Multiscale and multijurisdictional geodesign: The Coastal Region of Georgia, USA. Landscapes 19 (1), 42–49.

Simon, H., 1978. Rational Decision Making in Business Organizations. Nobel Prize Lecture. https://www.nobelprize.org/uploads/2018/06/simon-lecture.pdf.
Steinitz, C., 1990. A framework for theory applicable to the education of landscape architects (and other environmental design professionals). Landscape Journal Fall 136–143.
Steinitz, C., 2012. A Framework for Geodesign. Esri Press, Redlands, CA, USA.
Steinitz, C., 2017. Geodesign Negotiation with Four Case Studies. https://youtu.be/QERJbL9J1Xw.
United Nations General Assembly, 2015. UN Resolution 70/1, the 2030 Agenda, the UN Sustainable Development Goals.
109 United States House of Representatives, February 7, 2019 (The Green New Deal).
Vonk, G., Geertman, S., Schot, P., 2005. Bottlenecks blocking widespread usage of planning support systems. Environment and Planning A. https://doi.org/10.1068/a3712.

Further reading

Campagna, M., Di Cesare, E.A., Matta, A., Serra, M., 2018. Bridging the gap between strategic environmental assessment and planning: a geodesign perspective. International Journal of E-Planning Research 7 (1), 19. https://doi.org/10.4018/IJEPR.2018010103.
ESRI ArcGIS. https://www.esri.com/en-us/arcgis/about-arcgis/overview.
ESRI GeoPlanner. https://www.esri.com/en-us/arcgis/products/arcgis-geoplanner/overview.
Geodesignhub.com, https://www.geodesignhub.com/.
Moura, A.C., 2018. The application of Geodesign in a Brazilian illegal settlement: participatory planning in Dandara occupation case study. In: INPUT Conference, Viterbo Italy. https://www.researchgate.net/publication/327446994.

8

Smart working and flexible work arrangements: opportunities and risks for sustainable communities

R. Roberto[1], M. Penna[2], B. Felici[2] and M. Rao[3]

[1]*ENEA (Italian National Agency for New Technologies, Energy and Sustainable Economic Development), Energy Technologies Department, C.R. Saluggia, Italy;* [2]*ENEA (Italian National Agency for New Technologies, Energy and Sustainable Economic Development), Studies, Analysis and Evaluations Unit, Sede Legale, Rome, Italy;* [3]*ENEA (Italian National Agency for New Technologies, Energy and Sustainable Economic Development), Department of Fusion and Technology for Nuclear Safety and Security, C.R. Frascati, Italy*

1. Introduction

Over the last few decades, new working models, enabled by digital technologies, have spread throughout the labor markets. These approaches follow the shift in economic development from employment in manufacturing to services and knowledge-based jobs enabled by information and telecommunications (Gschwind and Vargas, 2019), where work arrangements do not necessarily require the worker to be present at the workplace. Nevertheless, even though the relationship between work and digital technologies has grown, creating favorable conditions for breaking the link between worker and workplace, the speed of this transformation has been very slow, due to the presence of cultural and organizational barriers. More recently, several studies are exploring the potential of an emerging smart management approach based on trust, cooperation, flexibility and delegation, to improve the performance and resilience of businesses and institutions. This "smart working" approach "through a combination of flexibility, autonomy and collaboration, which does not necessarily require the worker to be present in the workplace or in any pre-defined place enables them to manage their own working hours, while nevertheless

Intelligent Environments. https://doi.org/10.1016/B978-0-12-820247-0.00001-1

ensuring consistency with the maximum daily and weekly working hours laid down by law and collective agreements" (European Parliament, 2016). Smart working is a flexible way of working that focuses on results and the enhancement of skills, in which the old business logic disappears, and workers are freed from rigid schedules and mandatory presence in the office. It is becoming increasingly clear that a key to the success of remote work lies in a paradigm shift, i.e., in transforming work models so that they take into account people's well-being and their "capability" (Stiglitz et al., 2009) to choose the conditions under which they perform their work activities. It is, therefore, necessary to intervene on organizational models in a broad sense, involving the various actors, according to a team organization in which autonomy, accountability, and collaboration among workers are valued. Preparatory phases through staff training and information actions at all levels are an essential part of the process. Experiences all over the world in public and private companies that have adopted this approach have already shown positive results. Organizational change is also proving useful for driving sustainable change in urban systems through adoption of integrated models for developing liveable, equitable and inclusive communities.

The COVID-19 emergency, which emerged abruptly in 2020, prompted a transformation of work practices, forcing a major experiment in working from home to ensure business continuity. This was a large-scale test to explore the opportunities and critical issues of flexible work organization and showed the priorities that need to be addressed to capitalize on this experience and foster an increasingly conscious use of digital technologies. It should be noted that the experience of moving work activities into homes in the COVID-19 period has nothing to do with remote work and the various forms it has taken over the years and in different work and cultural contexts.

The following pages will discuss some of the main features of new models of work organization functional to company and worker purposes, as long as the impact of smart working on mobility, urban environment, territorial development, liveability, and socio-relational aspects. The paper aims to provide some reflections on how changes in work organization can have cascading effects on the organization of cities, influencing people's quality of life and the quality of the environment more generally. This paper is based on the evidence and body of work available at the end of 2020. The transition to what has been called a "new normal" at the end of the pandemic could lead to configuring radical changes compared to the pre-pandemic period. The results of the analysis of experiences during the post-pandemic period should therefore be carefully analyzed.

2. Telework and smart work: definitions and main features

2.1 Telework and other TICTM forms

"Telework and ICT-based mobile work (TICTM) is any type of work arrangement where workers work remotely, away from an employer's premises or fixed location, using digital technologies such as networks, laptops, mobile phones and the internet. It offers workers flexibility in where they work and when they work" (Eurofound, 2020a). Telework refers to a form of organizing and/or performing work in the context of an employment contract, as defined in the European framework agreement on telework (Eurofound, 2020b). The main objective of these approaches is to enable employees to work remotely. A wide range of concepts has been used to describe remote work, with a greater or lesser degree of flexibility, in terms of place and time of work, and with several differences in the innovation of work arrangements. These include telecommuting, smart work, agile work, remote work, mobile e-work, telework, and ICT-based mobile work. The latter can be defined as the use of information and communication technologies, such as smartphones, tablets, laptops and/or desktops, for work performed outside the employer's premises. Regulatory and cultural differences in working time and workplace flexibility, as well as in ultra-broadband networks, have a strong impact on the characteristics, effects, intensity, and results of telework and ICT-based mobile work (Eurofound, 2020b). In Europe, for example, Nordic countries combine generous social security for parents and the elderly with a regulatory framework and work culture that allow for a good work-life balance. Southern and Eastern countries, on the other hand, are characterized by a lower level of formal flexibility and an emphasis on presenteeism, while Central countries fall in between those two poles (Gschwind and Vargas, 2019; Chung et al., 2007; Eurofound, 2012).

2.2 Smart work

During the last decade, a new and peculiar organizational approach adopted by several private and public organizations has been labelled in different ways, such as "smart work", "agile work", "modern and flexible work" and "dynamic work". The objectives of these programs tend to be similar, and there is a general consensus toward the label "smart work", which we will therefore use to describe this approach.

The basic intuition behind smart working is to strengthen competitiveness by acting on innovation in work organization in addition to product and process innovation. Thus, the core of this approach is a radical innovation of work, characterized by a high degree of flexibility in work organization and empowerment of workers. It is achieved by adopting the main principles and tools of the knowledge economy and investing to enhance human capital (Tronti, 2015). Human capital is defined here according to the Organization for Economic Cooperation and Development as the knowledge, skills, competencies and attributes embodied in individuals that facilitate the creation of personal, social and economic well-being (OECD, 2001). As we will see in detail below, this particular approach is the key factor for success in changing large-scale commuting patterns. Unlike telework - a work-life balance tool that concerns a limited group of a company's employees - the innovation in work organization pursued by smart working involves all employees with no distinction. It does not mean that all people have to work remotely all the time, but that they have the opportunity to choose times and places that suit their work objectives and their own needs and preferences. The key features of the smart working approach are the organization of work activity by cycles, phases, and objectives, management by results, a culture base ond, high levels of autonomy, flexibility in time and workplace, technological equipment, new tools and work environments, reduced dependence on physical resource,s and openness to continuous change.

Two meaningful definitions of *smart working* have been proposed by the Smart Working Observatory of the School of Management of the Politecnico di Milano and by Flexibility.co.uk Ltd. The first one underlines the holistic approach that distinguishes this new working model: "*a new management philosophy founded on a return to people being given flexibility and autonomy in choosing their spaces, their working times and the tools they use, against a backdrop of taking more responsibility for the outcome*" (Smart Working Observatory). The second emphasizes how to improve business performance through new ways of working: "*Smart Working is a business-focused approach to flexible working that delivers more efficiency and effectiveness in work organisation, service delivery and organisational agility, as well as benefits for working people*" (Lake, 2015).

3. Moving from tackling life-work balance toward a novel work organization

3.1 Telework

The term "telework" was first introduced by Nilles (1988) to indicate home-based work implemented in companies and agencies in the United States (US). Telework and the subsequent ICT-based modes of remote work emerged in response to societal developments. For decades, they were mainly adopted as a work-life balance measure and to reduce commuting time and costs. Their application has varied considerably across countries and organizations and over time, as a result of the changing regulatory and cultural context. There is an extensive literature on teleworking, from the first generation of telework, which focused primarily on the home-office mode, to the second and third generations, which deal with the evolution toward more flexible organization of work and the three key elements: technology, location, and organization (Nilles, 1998; Kurland and Bailey, 1999; Ryan and Kossek, 2008; Peters et al., 2009; Tooran, 2011 Boell et al., 2013; Greer et al., 2014; Bloom et al., 2015; Gschwind and Vargas, 2019). Positive as well as negative aspects have been observed in the application of telework, which are highly variable and closely related to the strategies and arrangements of each organization. There is evidence that the adoption of teleworking positively influences firms' productivity, although this may not occur for all TICTM arrangements. Specifically, productivity improvements are not observed in companies that do not use remote work to pursue a more efficient or effective organizational design (Neirotti et al., 2012).

The culture of welfare also plays a fundamental role in determining the success of teleworking arrangements. Very poor results occur in a company when no welfare programs are adopted and teleworking is identified as the least demanding tool, from an economic and organizational point of view. In such cases, the rigid vision of working from the office/workplace continues to be dominant, and teleworking is seen only as the possibility to work from an alternative location, often not adequately supported by organizational procedures and appropriate IT tools. This attitude has led to the development of remote working arrangements designed to discourage workers from requesting them, apart from the few driven by compelling needs. This approach often has implications for employees with disabilities, as companies try to avoid making adjustments in the workplace (Moon et al., 2014). Under such conditions, the choice of teleworking is the consequence of the lack of other options and exposes people to the risk of isolation, loneliness and social exclusion, with negative effects on workers (Houseman and Polivka, 2000). More frequently, teleworking has been implemented within welfare programs, at the request of the worker, to improve autonomy, flexibility and work-life balance, or at the request of the employer, for organizational reasons, or as an agreement between the parties.

The European Foundation for the Improvement of Living and Working Conditions (Eurofound) and the International Labor Organization analysed the effects of teleworking and TICTM on work organization, work-life balance, health, performance and workers' prospects. They also provided an overview of the relevant legislation at European level and mapped the regulations in Member States related to improving the work-life balance of TICTM workers (Eurofound, 2020a). The findings show that TICTM has advantages for both employers and employees in terms of quality of work and life. Some potential disadvantages are also reported. In particular, the report discusses an emerging and less intuitive situation, which is the opposite of other well-known side effects, such as the risk of isolation. High levels of flexibility in time and place of work, when combined with high levels of demands in terms of performance and rediness, can lead to increased work loads and longer and non-routine working hours. In the absence of care management, an undesirable new pattern of working time may emerge, in which it is more difficult to distinguish working time from non-working time and workplace from non-workplace. As several studies have shown, an important precondition for effective and efficient remote working is also that remote workers have access to their company's communications systems and can exchange information with colleagues and their managers, regardless of time and location (Eurofound, 2015). Such arrangements are essential to prevent the risk of isolation, loneliness, and social exclusion.

Very often the introduction of teleworking has stimulated a more general innovation in the workplace in the form of organizational changes, flexibility, online learning and new forms of cooperation. Thus, in innovation-friendly cultural contexts, the implementation of remote working has become an opportunity to rethink work, questioning traditional obligations related to the workplace and schedules, and giving people more autonomy in defining ways of working centered on results-based responsibilities. Teleworking has an inherent limitation that prevents deep organizational innovation. Even when organizations have good policies to allow people to work flexibly, flexibility is still managed as an exception. That is, there is a predefined "normal" way of working and people can ask for a different working model. The "right to request" is generally governed by specific regulations and practices within each private and public organization, and limits are often set on the total number of teleworkers per company/division. Moving beyond this approach, as discussed below, paves the way for smart working.

3.2 Smart work

Scholars started talking about smart working when numerous private and public organizations were involved in achieving "flexibility as the norm". Many pilot cases have provided concrete examples for policymakers. At the base was the intuition that in order to strengthen competitiveness it is not enough to work on product and service innovation, but it is necessary to act on processes and organizational models. In several countries, these experiences have been monitored to deepen the success stories and to support private and public companies in understanding the benefits and in their paths toward a new organizational model of work (Osservatory.net, 2014a,b, 2016a,b,c, 2017a,b, 2018a,b, 2020; AXA Group; Virgin Group; Smart Working at Wokingham Council; Imperial College London; Tech Research Asia; CIPD, 2019).

According to these models, work takes place at the most appropriate times and places for the activities involved: it is only about the activities involved, not about changing the working model for a whole role. The way in which the most appropriate times and locations are assessed involves taking into account the needs of the company, the customer, cost-effectiveness, collaboration needs, available tools and the preferences of the individual. So it is about managing by results rather than presence, and engaging employees in a work culture based on trust. Universities, consultancies and service companies with expertise in developing smart working models played a relevant role in supporting businesses, the public sector and nonprofit organizations to implement comprehensive and strategic approaches to modernizing working practices and workplaces. Several models have been developed to estimate "smart working maturity" of organizations and to plan strategic and integrated pathways for a comprehensive and successful smart working program. An example of a Smart Working Maturity Model, reporterted in Lake (Lake, 2015), outlines the main stages of change that organizations go through in their journey to implement smart working in a strategic and integrated way.

The training of workers and managers is central to the success of smart work. It is not just a matter of acquiring digital skills—which are also necessary to ensure basic use of technologies - or of developing new technical skills, but of developing a participatory, motivated and aware path, favorable to the evolution of relational and managerial skills. In particular, dedicated training courses have been decisive in preventing the side effects that can affect high-involvement practices.

The results of these experiments affected both companies, in terms of improved productivity, reduced absenteeism, reduced costs for physical spaces, and others, and individuals, in terms of improved work-life balance, reduced costs for travels, greater satisfaction and well-being. Work organization is known to have an influence on work commitment and skill development (Bakan et al., 2011; Craig and Pinder, 2008; Cooper-Hakim and Viswesvaran, 2005; Jaros, 2007; Khan et al., 2010; Riketta, 2002; Robbins and Judge, 2007; Schappe, 1998; Sempane et al., 2002: Sinclair et al., 2005). A Eurofound study found that workplaces, where employee engagement is high, are more successful in developing workers' capacity for high performance and showed that these key factors are mutually reinforcing (Eurofound, 2020c). As noted above, the teleworking approach focuses on single objectives, mainly on work-life balance, less frequently on reducing operating costs. Smart working, on the other hand, promotes organizational practices that simultaneously increase the well-being of workers, the competitiveness of companies/efficiency of public administration, and cost savings. Creating organizational conditions for employees to perform at their best is at the core of this approach. The centrality of the individual and of knowledge and learning processes derives from the practices of the "knowledge-based economy" and the "learning organization", which stimulate participation through the application of intelligence and creativity to work (cognitive participation). In fact, a "learning organization" considers knowledge, acquired individually by people within organizations, as common capital and intentionally uses learning processes to learn about itself and its potential (Argyris and Schön D., 1978). Learning becomes a lever to change the way the organization operates, with a view to its continuous development.

Participatory management processes also draw attention to the development of internal and external communication systems aimed at involving and creating convergence among the various stakeholders. Three strategic elements come into play: ICT, engagement, and flexibility. The most influential recommendations emphasize the importance of involvement of employees, who are expected to make decisions about their work and have the opportunity to contribute to the organization's strategic plans. This means that the choice to work remotely or from the office is an option or facilitator, and not a condition for accessing or keeping a job. In "smart working" agreements work-life balance remains a pillar belonging to the sphere of "job satisfaction". In fact, job satisfaction is not limited to the development of professional satisfaction but also aims to make workers perceive a positive transformation in the context of their private lives. For this purpose, smart working training courses also address the issue of separation of work and private life and the so-called *right to disconnect.* In short, it refers to the right of employees to disconnect from their work and not to receive or respond to work-related e-mails, calls, or messages outside normal working hours.

The smart working approach is in line with the guiding principles of the labor policies of the European institutions, aimed at improving growth and competitiveness on the one hand and strengthening social rights and personal well-being on the other. As acknowledged by the EU Council "Conclusions on well-being at work" (Council of the European Union, 2020a), the wellbeing of individuals and economic growth are interdependent and mutually reinforcing (see Box - Main legislative initiatives supporting smart working arrangements). An approach based on flexible work organization helps to reduce stress, burnout, depression and other psychosocial risks at work, which are costly to employers, employees and society as a whole. The OECD estimates that these costs exceed 4% of the GDP of European Countries (OECD/EU, 2018). The Commission's communication on a New Industrial Strategy for Europe recommends that industries, national authorities, social partners and other stakeholders sign up to a Skills Pact to unlock public and private investments in upskilling and reskilling the workforce (Council of the European Union, 2020b). In some cases, governments have supported and promoted the adoption of smart working through guidelines.

In Italy, smart working was introduced by Law n. 81/2017, with the aim of encouraging employers to introduce spatial and temporal flexibility in their organizations by adapting - and assuring compliance with - general labor rules, such as working time, workplace safety, controls, and more, in the new framework (Council of the European Union, 2020b). To support organizations in implementing smart working principles, the United Kingdom developed a code of practice which covers changes in working practices, culture, work environments and associated technology. It provides recommendations for good practices in the implementation of smart working, against which organizations can be benchmarked (see Box - Main legislative initiatives supporting smart working arrangements).

Main legislative initiatives in support of smart working arrangements in Europe

European Union

Directive 89/391/EEC on occupational safety and health

The Directive 89/391/EEC on occupational safety and health envisaging measures to directly protect the safety and health of workers, describes how employers and organizations should ensure "*information, consultation and balanced participation*" in implementing the principles of worker protection. These principles include "*adapting the work to the individual, especially as regards the design of work places, the choice of work equipment and the choice of working and production methods, with a view, in particular, to alleviating monotonous work and work at a predetermined work rate and to reducing their effect on health*" and "*adapting to technical progress*".

Council conclusions on enhancing well-being at work N.8688/20—June 8, 2020

The European Council conclusions on well-being at work, published in June 2020, recognise the link between employee engagement, well-being and performance. Involving employees in decision-making processes, particularly with regard to their workplace, improves satisfaction and personal development, increases overall well-being at work and productivity. It also leads to greater commitment and motivates workers to make full use of their skills and improve them.

Council conclusions on Reskilling and up-skilling as a basis for increasing sustainability and employability, in the context of supporting economic recovery and social cohesion N. 8682/20—June 8, 2020

In 2020, the European Council adopted conclusions on reskilling and up-skilling as a basis for increasing sustainability and employability, in the context of supporting economic recovery and social cohesion. The outbreak of COVID-19 in 2020 highlighted the crucial role of digital skills and competencies in ensuring business continuity as well as in providing remote education and training. In this context, the Council invited Member States to ensure that recovery plans include a strategic approach to reskilling and up-skilling, as well as measures to adapt education and training based on lessons learned from the COVID-19 crisis.

United Kingdom

UK smart working - code of practice (standard PAS 3000:2015)

PAS 3000 provides a strategic framework for modernizing working practices. It was developed in support of the *UK Civil Service Reform Program*, based on the Cabinet Office document The Way We Work—A Guide to Smart Working in Government (Lake, 2015) and on the Smart Working Handbook (Lake, 2015). It gives recommendations for establishing good practices in the implementation of Smart Working, against which organizations can be benchmarked. It covers changes to work practices, culture, work environments, and associated technology.

Main legislative initiatives in support of smart working arrangements in Europe—Cont'd

Italy

Italian law May 22, 2017, n. 81, measures for the protection of non-entrepreneurial autonomous work and measures to encourage flexible adaptation as to times and places of subordinate [i.e., non-autonomous] work

Chapter II of the Italian law n. 81/2017 set out a soft legislative framework for helping companies and public administrations to adopt a managerial approach by enhancing workers' autonomy and flexibility and asking them to be accountable for results. The law affirms fundamental rights of workers, such as the right to disconnection, equal pay and continuous training, It establishes the necessary precautions to ensure that activities are safeguarded and carried out safely. It does not introduce a new type of contract, but a free and reversible agreement between employers and employees aimed at mutual benefit.

Finland

New working hours act of Finland March 13, 2019

Finland's new Working Hours Act of March 13, 2019 was adopted with the aim of better addressing current working arrangements. It replaces the concept of "workplace" with a more neutral concept of "working place". In the new context, working hours are not tied to a specific workplace, but rather working time is defined as time spent working. The Act also includes provisions related to working hours banks and facilitates the formation of agreements, as employers and employees are allowed greater freedom to deviate from the relevant Collective Bargaining Agreements.

The expected benefits of adopting new ways of working are related to the possibility of developing integrated policies. According to Underdal (Underdal, 1980), the basic requirements for integrated policies are:

- comprehensiveness (recognizing the purpose and consequences of policies in terms of time, space, actors and issues);
- aggregation (a minimum extent to which policy alternatives are evaluated from a global perspective);
- consistency (a minimum extent to which a policy penetrates policy levels and governmental sectors).

There are many calls for greater integration of policies, one of the most prominent of which is the environment, where integration is frequently recognized as crucial for sustainable development. In this regard, smart working shows several appealing characteristics, as it encompasses a wide range of areas (corporate, personal and community levels) including environmental effects.

The literature on remote working shows potential to reduce congestion, air pollutants and greenhouse gas emissions (see the section on *Energy consumptions and smart working*). This potential stems from the evidence that, in a very large number of cases, daily office communting is a pattern of behavior based on regulatory standards and cultural legacies, rather than on organizational and economic convenience. The large-scale application of flexible work arrangements in 2020, after the COVID-19 epidemic, to entire classes of workers who previously had limited or no access to this work option, is consistent with evidence indicating that previous arrangements were largely driven by factors related to regulations, work culture and management culture (Sostero et al., 2020).

However, some controversial aspects of smart working need to be taken into account. The first is the danger of fads and false attributions. Formal imitations of the paradigm illustrated have little or no benefit in return. The value of smart working derives from the changing socio-technical context. Therefore, if the organization remains committed to the role rather than the task, to the individual rather than the team, to the assignment rather than the leverage of professional skills, marginal or no value is generated. The benefit increases in proportion to the motivation and conviction of the actors involved. Formal imitations also entail the risk of worse working conditions due to over-involvement practices. With regard to the false attribution, it is imperative to stress that smart working is something different from moving work activities from the office to the home and that flexibility in the choice of the workplace does not necessarily imply working from home.

Smart working requires a dynamic redesign of work organization. As well as careful preparation and periodic monitoring processes aimed at identifying the occurrence of any critical issues. Monitoring is part of the strategy to manage the increased complexity. It helps to understand and meet new needs and to implement corrective actions. Virtual teams, multitasking conditions, mobile working, expectations of being available constantly and the need for support in adapting to and learning new digital tools can expose employees to new risks, related to mental workload and information overload.

Leadership that promotes health can help to prevent technostress and other critical outcomes. However, the key tool to manage the "dark side of the technology" is an inclusive and participative approach. With smart working, a system of widespread participation is established, in which the worker becomes a key player in workplace safety. The development of new risks and new prevention techniques must therefore be followed by a dynamic and specular knowledge from the worker throughout a continuous training process including occupational safety and health issues. Exemplary of the side effects of working remotely in the absence of adequate work organization is what happened in 2020, when the need to contain the COVID-19 infection and maintain physical distance during the pandemic forced people to work from home, without training or adequate space and equipment. This forced work-from-home accommodation had positive aspects but at the same time negative impacts, which were highly unequal between and within countries and social groups, exacerbating existing inequalities (Adams-Prassl et al., 2020).

The second risk is even more insidious and linked to generational, territorial, economic and social gaps. Indeed it is crucial to ensure that the digital transition does not create new conditions for social gaps. Aiming at digitalization requires vigilance so that the different opportunities for using the network and the new communication and collaboration tools do not lead to a classification of people's 'value' according to their different degrees of access to the network and to services.

4. Contribution of smart working to the quality of the urban environment

After considering the transformative potential of smart working on the quality of life and the professional sphere, this section aims to highlight the potential positive impact on the environmental quality of urban systems.

Making cities and human settlements inclusive, safe, resilient, and sustainable is one of the Sustainable Development Goals agreed in 2015 by the United Nations (UN) to create a better world by 2030. According to UN projections (IRP, 2018), the urban population is expected to double between 2010 and 2050, with about 68% of the world's population living in urban areas. Developing countries, in particular, are undergoing a rapid transformation from rural to urban economies. Good urban planning represents a great potential source of savings, in terms of resources, energy, emissions, and wastes (IRP, 2018), and can also lead to positive effects on equality and social inclusion. The global economic future is intertwined with the way urban challenges will be addressed, and international bodies and teams of experts from different disciplines are working to promote a transition to sustainable models of urban development. Although the priorities to be addressed and the characteristics of urban areas differ across world regions, they are facing common challenges. They include the complex interrelationships between cities and wider ecosystems, urban population growth and demographic change, spatial change and development, infrastructure planning and implementation, mobility, pollution, congestion and resource flows. As assumed by urban theories, the organization of urban space and social organization are mutually contingent and any social change will transform cities (Tooran, 2009). Scholars suggest the adoption of a sustainable mobility approach to design cities of high quality accessibility and environment (Banister, 2008). As will be discussed, the mobility aspects are intimately linked to the organization of work. A paradigm shift, based on a new model of work organization, is needed to ensure that new mobility practices and urban fabric organization are possible and replicable on a large scale.

Sustainable and smart development of communities may be achieved through integrated and multi-sectoral approaches, capable of connecting the diverse elements that constitute human settlements and pursuing more efficient, more competitive and more inclusive collective and personal solutions. An effective urban governance proposal goes in the opposite direction to sectoral approaches, which aim to meet the multiple needs of urban communities separately and entrust the balancing of competing interests to subsequent compromises.

The Urban Agenda for the European Union (European Commission; European Commission, 2016), highlighting the many interconnections existing in urban areas, considers cities as centers for driving positive change and development, supporting the transition to a sustainable society. This policy initiative put multi-level governance into action for urban areas and indicated the priority themes for the Urban Agenda for Cities, which can be traced to the main areas covering: the environment, the economy, socio-political aspects, culture and territory. Although the work dimension is not explicitly indicated, the organization of work is a key element in defining the main social and territorial structures (Mumford, 1968). It has a significant impact on the quality of life of people and families, the economy of the city, the demand for mobility of citizens, their consumption behavior, their social relations and urban development as a whole. Smart working as a new model of work organization can play a role in supporting the new approach to the way cities and urban areas are designed and lived, due to the central role that works plays in people's daily life.

Rethinking new models of work organization with greater flexibility, autonomy, and responsibility of the worker, as highlighted in the previous paragraphs, implies a paradigm shift that is by no means obvious, in which work is no longer the element to which people's lives and the organization of the territory must adapt. The EU Urban Agenda suggests an interconnected vision among the different parts of the urban system, whereby a change produces a transformative effect on the whole system. While the issues of sustainable development in urban areas have been the subject of reflection and political debate for decades, much work still needs to be developed both in theoretical terms and in terms of empirical investigations. The transformative effects of new models of work organization and the possibility of understanding and managing the complexity of the urban system and the set of connections and relationships among the different dimensions involved (among them: mobility, energy, environment, culture, relations) need further study and experimentation.

A model for analyzing the demand for mobility is proposed in the section *Smart working and mobility models*, while the section *Energy consumption and smart working* deals with energy consumption and emissions.

4.1 Smart working and mobility patterns

Based on this integrated, multilevel vision of the sustainability transition, the effect of unlocking work from traditionally fixed times and places can be a key factor that can lead to multiple effects in the areas shown in Fig. 8.1, particularly on quality of life and the environment, some of which will be illustrated in the following paragraphs. The triangle on the left in Fig. 8.1 shows the relationship between the dimensions of work, community, and territory in the traditional work system (in the absence of smart working): the organization of work imposes its own rules, determining the adaptation of people's behavior and habits to its requirements and exerting pressure on the territory, which often results in vehicle congestion and environmental stress. The triangle on the right illustrates the effects of change due to the adoption of more flexible forms of work organization through smart working, which make it possible to overcome the limits of a one-way vision and offers greater scope for dynamic interaction between all the dimensions involved. In relation to the urban system, unlocking the hitherto fixed dimension of work can trigger a number of related changes, enabling wider adoption of sustainable, user-centered models for mobility, urban design, housing planning, and land use.

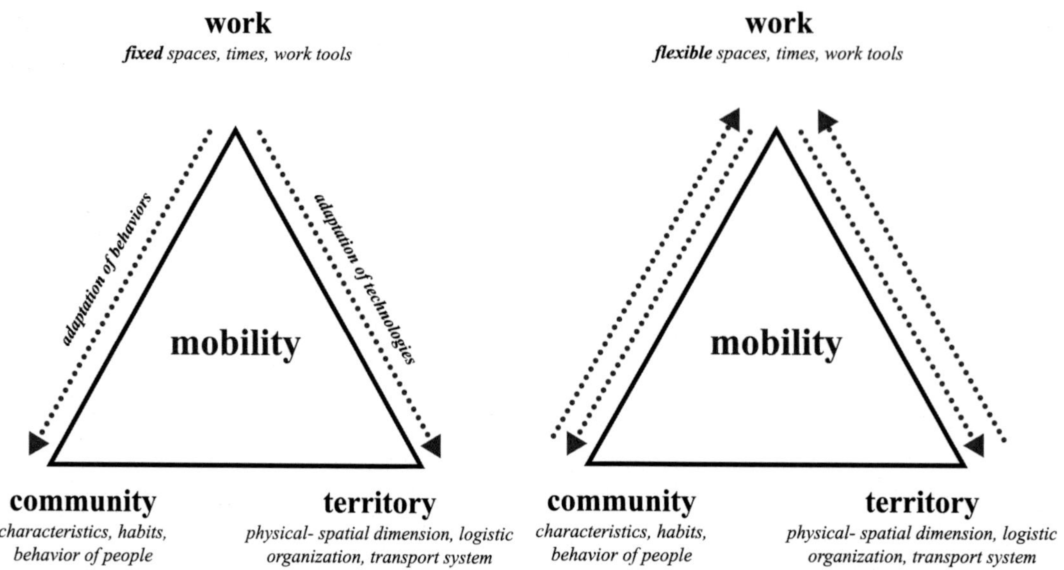

Figure 8.1 Models of work organization and urban policy: traditional (left) and the new model (right).

Mobility is among the greatest challenges for the future of cities, with important social, health, environmental and economic impacts. The critical issues of mobility are mainly addressed by sectoral policies that focus on the offer of mobility services and on transport infrastructures rather than operating upstream, that is, on the real reasons and needs for travel. These are mainly technical and regulatory measures aimed at containing urban pollution and fuel consumption and reducing congestion. These interventions have physical as well as economic limitations and showed limited impact, as reported in the Special Report on Urban Mobility of the European Court of Auditors on June 2020 (European Union, 2020). The report points out that, although cities have implemented a number of initiatives, "on the basis of audit work at the Commission and eight different cities in Germany, Italy, Poland and Spain, we found no indication that EU cities are fundamentally changing their approaches and that there is no clear trend toward more sustainable modes of transport".

The increasing number of vehicles in circulation exacerbates traffic congestion in cities and limits the emission reductions achieved by new engines and technical measures. Regulatory measures, including traffic restrictions, zoning, and congestion charges, are also being adopted that prohibit or inhibit the circulation of private vehicles in limited areas and at specific times. Governments and agencies also promote nonregulatory (or "soft") measures that focus on changing individual behaviors of citizens toward more sustainable choices. Evidence supports the conclusion that regulatory and nonregulatory measures used in isolation are often not effective (Tooran, 2009; Barr and Prillwitz, 2014) and that the solutions for sustainable mobility need to be framed through integrated policies that address underlying the social and economic contexts for current practices. Indeed, unsustainable mobility patterns are intricately intertwined with social and consumption practices and are linked to the structure and organization of physical environments. The case of Copenhagen (European Union, 2020), where urban mobility planning is combined with urban planning, is noteworthy. For example, offices and workspaces with more than a given number of employees can only be established in close proximity to a major public transport station.

Behavior and social practices of people, therefore, become fundamental to determining the success of public policies.

An emerging, interdisciplinary field of research, known as Mobility Studies, proposes a different approach to the analysis of mobility that also considers the level of social interactions and the way in which urban environments are organized.

Some authors (Sheller and Urry, 2006) talk about a new mobility paradigm through which a "fluid interdependence" is recongnized between material and immaterial dimensions capable of maintaining social connections. Other scholars use the concept of "mobility biographies", to refer to "at certain moments in individual's life the daily travel patterns, the car ownership or other mobility characteristics change to an important degree" (Lanzendorf, 2003)

Kaufmann attributes to new forms of mobility the joint action of transforming the labor market, the characteristics of territory as well as the transport and communication networks (Kaufmann, 2011). This is a very interesting line of studies, including from a methodological point of view, to understand what is reported below.

The elements that contribute to the definition of mobility policies can be traced back to three main domains: the *work* and its organizational model; the *community*, intended as a group of individuals and families, whose socio-demographic characteristics determine habits, behaviors and lifestyles; the *territory*, seen in its physical and spatial characterization, which determines its logistical organization, and therefore the transport system (Fig. 8.1). The model is represented schematically as a system in which mobility is placed at the center of a triangle with the three domains indicated above as vertices. The work dimension, a pillar of the organization of our societies, traditionally conditions the other dimensions (see Fig. 8.1, image on the left), contributing to imbalancing effects in terms of the quality of people's lives and the quality of the natural and urban environment.

It is evident that as long as most wokers are forced to use the same busy routes, at the same time and every day, effort to meet sustainability goals become huge. Considering the bigger questions about why we travel and the ways in which mobility practices develop over time and space, it appears how changing perspectives on mobility issues, considering whether it is possible to act on the portion of daily travel determined by cultural legacies, norms and practices, can offer solutions.

The change in work arrangements through the use of smart working and the use of ICT and the Internet of Things (IoT) allows also the development of mobility management tools to contain risks and inconveniences for the population in the event of particular events, such as:

- scheduled critical events (strikes, sports or social events that attract important flows of people, adoption of traffic reduction measures made necessary by exceeding the air quality limit values, and more);
- consequences of important weather events (flooding, snowfall, landslides, and more);
- high probability of incurring nonprogrammable events (forecast of weather events, risk of terrorist attacks, ...).

Following the attacks of 11 September 2001 in the United States, remote working, introduced by the Telework Enhancement Act of 2010 (US Government, 2010), drew attention as a key element in the development of emergency plans for government agencies to cope with extreme weather events, natural disasters and terrorist attacks. As a result, teleworking was included in the Federal Government's Continuity of Operations Plans (COOP) and was part of the U.S. Office of Personnel Management's evaluations of the human resource management programs adopted by agencies. The latest report to Congress on the application of the Telework Enhancement Act (US Office of Personnel Management, 2017) shows that the use of remote work to ensure continuity of operations during emergencies has become a normal practice for several federal agencies, which has drastically reduced weather-related delays and closures. It also appears that agencies did not just meet the minimum legal requirements, but were able to strategically exploit teleworking in support of critical objectives. To this end, the possibility of complementing stable telework has proved particularly useful.

Another example of the use of teleworking for the management of potentially critical events is that of London where, on the occasion of the 2012 Olympic Games, in order to mitigate traffic and overcrowding of public transport expected in view of the exceptional influx of people, a city plan was used to promote the use of teleworking in public and private companies (UK Government, 2013; METI, 2017).

Some considerations on the use of remote working during the emergency due to COVID-19 are given in the chapter *Smart-working in the context of pandemic and post-pandemic scenarios.*

4.2 Smart working, urban environments, and territorial development

A redefinition of the work organization model not only allows action to be taken on the demand for mobility and in the related aspects of traffic, congestion, air quality and energy consumption. It allows, in fact, to "unlock" other sectors, where so far it has only been possible to introduce solutions and technologies aimed at improving the liveability and sustainability of urban environments to a limited extent. The COVID-19 pandemic crisis in 2020 forced the public and private sectors to accelerate procedural changes and technological innovation in the workplace. After the remote working experience during the lock-down periods, companies started to question the need for large, expensive and centrally located offices in favor of territorial offices and mixed solutions using smart working. At the same time, architects and urban planners were asked to rethink the idea of workspace in order to have spaces that are protected, healthy and able to guarantee business continuity. Richard Sennett, an expert in urban planning, explains that more flexible buildings are needed, capable of adapting to short-terms need for greater social distance but also to economic changes that seem to be leading to a multifunctional use of space, with offices that can become entertainment venues, shops or even homes. "What we have built now are fixed, immobile structures that only serve one purpose" (BBC, 2020).

Regarding changes in behavior and living habits that may be accelerated in certain historical phases, the reorganization of the logic of home-to-work travel becomes a relevant issue in the renovation of urban areas and the development and use of urban suburbs. It is therefore possible to influence the transformation of local structures, especially those characterized by high commuting and the contrast between congested neighborhoods, where work activities are concentrated, and other neighborhoods. These areas are often degraded and lacking in services and identity precisely because they have traditionally been used as dormitory districts. While some positive effects of smart working in urban suburbs have already been noted through studies on urban regeneration (Bloomberg et al., 2018), the future of the central business district where offices and services have traditionally been located, is less clear. The decentralization of services and production activities and services can lead to a significant urban transformation in which the relationship between the central business district and the periphery changes. The risk of depopulation and unemployment of economic sectors such as transport and food services located in the central business district can be avoided by formulating an integrated urban policy.

Liveable functionally and socially mixed-use neighborhoods are an efficient and functional method of renovation and use of urban areas (IRP, 2018; Kawai, 2008). They are a form of development that combines residential and commercial use and provides amenities at the neighborhood, block and building level to guarantee proximity to services in residential areas. Renovation projects with mixed-use neighborhoods can attract more people if smart working approaches become a common practice, also enabling the exploitation of "soft" mobility options at the city/neighborhood level.

Urban renewal initiatives

The relationships between urban sustainability and societal transformation and the potential associated with the organizational transformation of work through the adoption of remote working have been investigated by several scholars (Portney, 2002; Kellert, 2005; Kawai, 2008). The shift from potential to measurable transformations in cities and communities is still ongoing. For its realization, it is necessary to implement integrated multi-sectoral policies, and results from case studies are not yet available in the literature, although pilot cases have been launched and are shortly illustrated below.

Successful examples of renovation and redevelopment projects combining mixed-use zoning, people-centered urban planning, and sustainable mobility options have been implemented in some cities and pilot areas. Among the others, the Hammarby Sjöstad area, in Stockholm (IRP, 2018), and the Superblocks urban model (Mueller et al., 2020), were constructed or approved for construction in several Spanish cities.

Redevelopment initiatives should include coworking centers and arrangements for the presence of company branches and they engaged multiple stakeholders. The existing initiatives have not been conceived with a direct reference to smart working, however, it appears evident that its adoption can also have repercussions on urban regeneration and their replication potential. In fact, when urban renovation initiatives respond to people's needs - the possibility of access to services, workplaces, recreational and residential places within the same neighborhood - thus being not only addressed to specific categories of people and upper classes, they can be replicated on a larger scale, thus supporting sustainable development of cities.

The example of Milano (Italy)

The municipality of Milan has been implementing initiatives for improving the quality of life and supporting urban transformation and renovation projects that include smart working. It has signed a memorandum of understanding with the representatives of labor, culture, university, research, trade unions, and professional associations for the creation of territorial synergies, and developed actions aimed at introducing smart working approaches in public administrations and private companies. In 2014 it launched the "Agile Work Day" and in 2017 the "Agile Work Week". 53,000 workers were involved in the 2019 edition, and over 44 companies joined the different editions one or more times (Comune di Milano, 2017a). Isola and Garibaldi-Repubblica neighborhoods have been identified as the first areas of analysis and testing within the project Smart Lab Milano Concilia 4.0, aimed at creating an integrated model

Urban renewal initiatives—Cont'd

of work-life balance and corporate welfare (Comune di Milano, 2017b). The actions were coordinated with other existing corporate welfare and smart working projects, especially in the context of the Milano Concilia 4.0 Alliance, to provide information and recommendations to be extended to further areas of the city. The actions carried out so far include chronotopic analyses of data on the location, timetables, and characteristics of the available services and of the resident and temporary populations of the Isola-Garibaldi; field observation for the detection of mobility flows; interview to coworking users present in the trial area; redefinition of the territorial plan of Milan timetables and to initiatives aimed at improving the well-being of the populations. The replication potential is high, and the project intends to replicate the activities and the chronotopic analysis in other neighborhoods in Milan. The actions initiated led in 2020 to the project MIRE (Milan on the net - from welfare to rediscovered time), run in synergy with the city's Time and Timetable Plan (Comune di Milano, 2020a). Among the challenges posed: is the harmonization of temporal rhythms, as factors for improving the quality of life and the protection of health.

Thanks to the actions taken and the previous introduction of smart working within the municipal administration, in Milan during the COVID-19 pandemic in a very short time the administration activated smart working for more than 6000 municipal workers, ensuring continuity and quality of the services provided and bringing to light the need for a transformation of the ways and times of work already in place. Especially in consideration of the change in the lifestyles of those who live, work, consume and move around the city due to the persistence of the COVID-19 emergency, a path of sharing has been undertaken, aimed at improving the strategy on the basis of a broad public-private dialogue with categories, associations, and citizens. Many of the initiatives put in place by the City of Milan devote particular attention to micro, small and medium-sized enterprises, to promote the development of more agile organizations and support over time the organizational flexibility actions undertaken to cope with the pandemic.

The actions described have laid the foundations for the development of strategies aimed at the redevelopment of some urban areas and a reorganization of the city according to the "15-minute city" model described in the following paragraph (Comune di Milano, 2020b).

The "15-minute city"

Several cities are experimenting with the idea of a 15-minute city, a concept developed by Carlos Moreno inspired by the work of Jane Jacobs and other authors (Moreno, 2016; Moreno et al., 2021). The "15-minute" idea is based on research into how city dwellers' use of time could be reorganized to improve both living conditions and the environment. "We don't want to oblige people to stay in the 15-minute district," Moreno says. "We don't want to recreate a village. We want to create a better urban organisation." Paris in the first place, and other cities like London and New York are considering the transformation of some areas according to the 15-minute city model.

The 15-minute city consists of decentralized mini-hubs where everything residents need can be reached in 15 min on foot or by bicycle. The concept, initially proposed to increase the quality and sustainability of life in cities, is designed to guarantee access to six essential functions within a short perimeter - living, working, providing, taking care, supporting, and recreating. As more employees can work without going to the office, this concept will be able to meet the needs of more people and allow for a better quality of life in urban environments.

This approach, which can support the envisioning of a comprehensive urban design strategy, is gaining momentum in 2020, also in the perspective of supporting a deeper and resilient recovery from the COVID-19 pandemic, by fostering a more local and healthy way of life for their citizens (Forbes, 2020; C40 Cities Climate Leadership Group, 2020; Financial Times, 2020; Moreno et al., 2021).

Greater flexibility in the choice of residential location is possible, if people no longer have to live within a limited distance from their place of work. A wider choice for residential location introduces nascent opportunities for decentralized urban models to attract workers, complex and diverse models of suburban employment, and for playing productive roles in the new economy. In this regard, we recall, among others, the experience of an Italian public administration, the Autonomous Province of Trento (Penna et al., 2020), which introduced smart working for its employees to respond to the organization of its territory, consisting of distant valleys. Rethinking work in a delocalized way compared to traditional offices becomes an opportunity to address the territorial and social asymmetries of communities and to revitalize territories far from the areas of greatest presence of production activities and services. The opportunities and challenges posed by the transformation of the relationship between work and place for cohesion policies in Europe's internal areas came to the attention after initiatives for the repopulation of villages (thanks to economic concessions, such as the so-called "1-euro houses, or tax concessions) and since 2020, following the COVID-19 pandemic and phenomena such as the Italian "south-working". In the South Working® project and other initiatives smart working is a concrete tool for promoting economic, social and territorial cohesion. It can change people's lives and affect the demographic dynamics and cohesion of territories, contributing to reducing the gap that currently exists between territories with different levels of development, according to the principles of the Treaty on the Functioning of the European Union. With the same purpose, in the United States, the Agency of Commerce and Community Development's of Vermont established the Remote Worker Grant Program in 2018, which provides funds to individuals to offset the cost of relocating to Vermont as an incentive to move and work in the state. The program aims to meet the need for more workers in Vermont, as well as to promote remote workers and remote work arrangements. Between January 2018 and January 2020, 224 new Vermont remote workers were granted, increasing Vermont's population by almost 400 people and 100 families (Agency of Commerce and Community Development, 2019, 2020).

4.3 Energy consumption and remote working

Reducing the need to travel is a key element of sustainable travel planning. In this regard, smart working shows interesting characteristics for the implementation of integrated urban policies aimed at maximizing positive effects on the organization of cities and controlling possible side effects.

Teleworking has often been associated with environmental benefits. Appeals to the environmental aspect of remote working have been made when motivating the promotion of teleworking in local agendas or organizational policies to mitigate mobility demand (European Platform on Mobility Management, 2018). However, the impact of remote working on mobility trends was barely perceived until the COVID-19 pandemic occurred in 2020, which forced teleworking to a completely new level, with a significant impact on several environmental sectors and fuel demand. Due to extreme changes in human behavior, there has been a drastic reduction in mobility (IEA, 2020), which has contributed to an improvement in air quality worldwide in 2020 with a strong reduction in main pollutants, especially in large cities (Berman and Ebisu, 2020; Viteri et al., 2021; He et al., 2020; Dantas et al., 2020; The World Bank, 2020). Forecasts on the widespread of remote working as a permanent feature of the future work environment (OECD, 2020b) motivated the International Energy Agency – IEA to reduce its diesel and petrol forecasts (IEA, 2020).

So far, a large number of studies have been conducted on the environmental effects of remote working, but these have suffered from the lack of a unified perspective in analyzing and measuring the effects directly and indirectly induced by its adoption. The context is very complex and each person may adopt a number of different behaviors in many different areas (travel habits, reasons for traveling, energy efficiency choices in the home/work environment, and so on). In existing studies, there is great variability in key aspects of the assessment, from the structure of the population samples used to the methodology adopted in the calculation (i.e., the modeling approach to retrieve data in real-time), and the parameters under consideration may vary from one study to another, depending on the focus of the survey. The impacts of remote working on energy and emission savings highlighted in the various studies are ambiguous, as multiple factors not strictly related to work organization can significantly influence the results. Giovanis explored the relationship between teleworking, air quality, and traffic in Switzerland concluding that "teleworking can be a promising tool for urban planning and development, focusing at the traffic volume reduction, and the air quality improvement" (Giovanis, 2018). Anyway, mobility experts agree that communication technologies and new work models have conflicting impacts on travel behavior. For example, Mokhtarian found that telework may reduce vehicle miles traveled by eliminating commute trips, although teleworkers may at the same time offset the time savings of commuting with additional or longer leisure travels (Mokhtarian et al., 1995). Furthermore, workers who only need to travel to the office 1 or 2 days per week may decide to move further away from the workplace to enjoy lower housing costs or a larger house, which may offset any travel savings due to teleworking (Horner et al., 2016). Teleworking leads to a reduction in the number of commuter trips, resulting in fuel and emission savings and positive effects in terms of reduced urban congestion and traffic at peak hours.

Since the 1970's, many researchers have studied diverse aspects of remote working, achieving progress in understanding key issues but also, at times, divergent, conflicting, and counter-intuitive outcomes (Allen et al., 2015). Problems of definition and methodology, implicit assumptions and conceptualizations of remote working among different researchers have contributed to conflicting results and inconsistencies. Other problems may be related to the diversity of remote work research: researchers come from a wide range of disciplines including psychology, urban planning, transport studies, management, labour law, information and communication systems, and others (Allen et al., 2015; Bailey and Kurland, 2002; Golden, 2012; Ikezoe, 2013; Ozcelik, 2010; Wellman et al., 1996). In addition, several key factors that influence the potential benefits of adopting flexible working models have also changed. They can be clustered around the four areas that form the cornerstones of this research: environment, economy, technology and social-organizational aspects.

There is no consensus on the energy and environmental benefits of teleworking, so there is a lack of coordinated promotion of remote working as a means of supporting low-carbon energy transition programs: this is true for both governments and companies. In this context, Hook et al. (Hook et al., 2020) provide a systematic review of the current state of knowledge on the energy impacts of teleworking and smart working. The energy balance includes the energy savings from reduced commuting and the energy consumption associated with changes in (a) non-work travels of the teleworker and other family members; (b) the size and occupancy of the workplace; and (c) the location and occupancy of employees' homes. The aim is to identify the conditions in which teleworking can lead to a net reduction in overall energy consumption and the circumstances in which the benefits of teleworking are not offset by unintended impacts, commonly referred to as "rebound effects" (Berkhout and Hertin, 2004; Hook et al., 2020), such as increased frequency and/or length of private trips and other increases in energy consumption. Regarding the results, most of the works (26 out of 39) suggest that remote working (both from home and in telecentres) leads to a net *reduction* in energy consumption and/or emissions: only five studies report a net increase. These benefits mainly result from the elimination of commuting, the reduction of congestion, the concomitant reduction of vehicle emissions, and reductions of energy consumption in offices.

The possibility that remote working reduces overall energy consumption is linked to the impact it has on many areas, including commuting, non-work travel and the use of energy in the office and in the workplace. The main problem we have found in most studies is their limited scope: the impact on well-being in the workplace, work-life balance, reduced travel times. A more organic and flexible modelling framework and possibly real-time analysis, e.g. of mobile phone patterns, will be needed to fully assess the net energy consumption associated with large-scale smart-working adoption in the urban context in order to estimate these effects.

Some of the literature on ICT and energy suggests that an increase in remote working may lead to higher energy consumption at home (Chapman, 2007). Several studies show that, even taking into account an increase in home energy consumption, teleworking could result in overall energy savings, as it reduces office space per capita (e.g., through hot-desking) and potentially means that offices no longer need to be heated or cooled to the same level or for the same period. The overall reduction in energy consumption and emissions depends on a number of factors, related to the methods of energy management (heating and cooling) in the premises used to carry out work activities at the employee's location and in remote offices, and the employesss' travel habits for personal, family and leisure activities, possibly modified by remote working. As with the benefits of reduced commuting, these potential gains depend on a number of factors, including the extent to which companies downsize or close their offices as the number of teleworkers increases.

To improve the reliability and accuracy of the estimation of the net effects of smart working on the energy, environmental and mobility dimensions, it is therefore necessary to systematize the research methodology. Large-scale experiments and systematized analysis methodologies could provide indications as to wheter the positive effects of smart working on mobility demand and energy consumption can be maximised.

ICT and related energy consumptions and GHGE

Information and Communication Technologies (ICT) are becoming more and more relevant in people's lives, and are often associated with a reduction in CO_2 emissions. But is this true?

The Information and Communication Industry, did not receive much attention in the Paris Agreement, since it is often praised for enabling efficiencies that help reduce the footprint of other industrial sectors. In 2018 a detailed and rigorous analysis of the global ICT carbon footprint was performed (Belkhir and Elmeligi, 2018), including both the production and operational energy of ICT devices and the operational energy for the ICT infrastructure support. The results show that, if unchecked, the relative contribution to green gas emissions of ICT could account by 2040 worldwide for more than half of the relative contribution of the whole transportation sector in 2016.

In 2020, a systematic investigation on the effect of digitalization on energy consumption, from a methodological point of view, was carried out (Lange et al., 2020). Four effects are investigated: (1) direct effects from the production, use and disposal of ICT; (2) increase in energy efficiency from digitalization; (3) economic growth from increased productivity in labor and energy and (4) sectoral change/outsourcing from increased ICT services. The results indicate that effects 1 and 3 tend to increase energy consumption, while effects two and four tend to decrease it. The work reveals that the two increasing effects prevail, so that, overall, digitalization appears to increase energy consumption. These results were explained by four insights from ecological economics: (a) physical capital and energy are complements in the ICT sector; (b) energy efficiency increases lead to rebound effects; (c) ICT cannot solve the difficulty of decoupling economic growth from energy; (d) ICT services are relatively energy-intensive and add. In the future, digitalization can only boost sustainability if it fosters effects two, and four without promoting effects 1, and 3.

Moving to real-case applications, in light of the increasing role of finance in the global economy (Arshad et al., 2020), estimate the effect of ICT, trade, economic growth, financial development, and energy consumption on carbon emissions in South and Southeast Asian (SSEA) region for the period of 1990–2014. Results show that financial development and ICT have deteriorated the quality of the environment in the SSEA region, suggesting that ICT goods and services are not energy-efficient in both emerging and advanced countries and that most financial investments were made in unfriendly environmental projects in emerging countries. On the contrary, in advanced countries, financial development mitigates CO_2 emissions. Findings showed bidirectional causality between CO_2 emissions and energy consumption as well as unidirectional causality one-way causation from trade, economic growth, financial development, and ICT to CO_2 emissions.

Recommendations for policy-makers lead to a greater awareness of the impact of ICT on energy consumption and to better regulation of their production to facilitate the integration of energy efficiency into user routines.

It seems reasonable to consider that the actions needed to mitigate and curb the explosive GHGE footprint of ICT go through a combination of renewable energy use, tax policies, managerial actions, and alternative business models.

4.4 Contribution of smart working to the quality of life

Regarding the sustainability of urban systems, as outlined in the previous section, a new model of work organization has effects on mobility demand, transport, air quality and more generally on the entire urban system and its relations with neighbouring rural environments. To complete the argument, which concerns people's quality of life more generally, this section briefly addresses studies on the relationship between remote working and motivational aspects, which are essential for sociotechnical transition. The investigations conducted by scholars illustrate the difficulty of identifying a clear and direct relationship between many factors, some of them objective, such as the characteristics of one's family structure, and others concerning personal desires and motivations.

Work-life balance, a welfare-related issue discussed in the paragraph "*Moving from tackling life-work balance toward a novel work organization*", plays a fundamental role in the choice of remote working when the family has to face the needs of young children or the difficulties of one of its members. In this case, remote working could contain or reduce potential conflicts due to taking on both work and family tasks (Allen et al., 2015). Work-family conflict arises when the worker is not able to manage the pressure from family or work (Allen, 2012). The conflict is termed WIF when *work interferes with family*, or FIW when *family interferes with work* (Greenhaus and Beutell, 1985). The risk of family interference is greater for women, who are more likely to be overburdened by family work. According to the European Institute for Gender Equality, the disproportionate amount of time women spend on caring and housework has an impact on their participation in work and opportunities for social, personal and civic activities, reinforcing gender segregation in education and the labor market (European Institute for Gender Equality, 2019). Studies show that work-family conflict decreases with increasing adaptation to a new work organization (Gajendran and Harrison, 2007) or with training in a better division of family and work time (Penna et al., 2020).

Regarding "job satisfaction", workers are more satisfied when the amount of remote work is not very high. When a certain threshold is exceeded, satisfaction does not increase, but the feeling of social isolation and the lack of face-to-face interactions with colleagues grows (Golden and Veiga, 2005; Virick et al., 2010). Remote work, satisfaction, and stress are closely linked both in working life and in the personal sphere. The autonomy of remote workers produces less stress and more satisfaction thanks to the degree of autonomy in the execution of tasks, times and working methods with increased performance and productivity (Sardeshmukh et al., 2012; Gajendran et al., 2014). Data collected during the "Agile Work Week" initiatives in Milan by the city administration in collaboration with the Municipal Agency of Mobility, Environment and Territory and the Bocconi School of Management indicated that, in addition to the time gained for private life, smart working increased efficiency, motivation and productivity.

Commuting has a negative effect on well-being, especially on long journeys from home to work, on mental stress and, in general, on workers' health (Morikawa, 2018). The choice to work remotely, with reduced daily communting, improves the quality of life of the worker who can free up time and energy to pursue personal interests and improve family and social relationships.

The results described above are also found in the study on teleworking and smart working conducted in Italy among public sector workers (Penna et al., 2020). The evaluation of workers' personal experience carried out through the use of a semantic map, a visual representation model of the answers to open-ended questions, made it possible to identify the strong relationship between time and remote working. The map shows four clusters of respondents based on the different levels and types of satisfaction:

- area of personal satisfaction (appreciation for the freedom of choice in managing recovered time);
- area of family satisfaction (appreciation for the time they were able to dedicate to better management of family commitments);
- area of professional satisfaction area (appreciation for the time they were able to devote to better work performance);
- area of dissatisfaction or criticality (feelings of isolation and stigma).

The lexical analysis showed the centrality of the term 'time' as the most frequently used lexical form. The multifaceted associations with other terms referring to the plurality of options on how and why teleworking has been experienced suggest that workers appreciate the value of "time" enriched by the qualitative dimension. The time freed by the avoided home-work commute is reconfigured according to needs and desires. It can open up unexpected changes and possibilities. In some cases, remote work becomes an opportunity to release energies and motivations, giving individuals autonomy in managing their time. In positive experiences, workers perceive, in particular, the possibility of choise, self-determination that frees up space in any direction, improving family relationships or making work activities more efficient. In the answers that fall in the "area of dissatisfaction", the negative effects of prejudices, feelings of isolation and concern about possible limited carreer advancement were reported. But the fear of losing the teleworking option and time flexibility was also reported.

5. Smart-working in the context of pandemic and postpandemic scenarios

With over 100 countries having gone into lockdown, the COVID-19 pandemic spread worldwide in the spring of 2020 and triggered at that time third and greatest economic, financial, and social shock of the 21st century, after September 11, 2001, and the global financial crisis of 2008. The COVID-19 crisis made it possible to study resilience and emergency response capacity. It offered the opportunity to rethink cities with a long-term planning perspective, based on a new approach to urban spaces, able to take better into account the diverse needs, revisiting public spaces, and moving from a logic of mobility to one of accessibility to comfort and basic services. Before the COVID-19 outbreak, only about 2% of U.S. employees worked remotely all the time. At the peak of the lockdown in March–May 2020, this rose to 40%–50%, according to various surveys. The percentage in Europe was similar. The U.S. National Bureau of Economic Research, using data from the prepandemic era, has estimated the share of jobs that can be done from home. It ranges from just 5% in Mozambique to 53% in Luxembourg. They also noted a strong correlation between GDP per capita and a country's teleworking potential (Bartik et al., 2020).

The COVID-19 emergency has brought the world's attention to the value of remote work. The exceptional nature of the event provided the context for large-scale experimentation of the potential of teleworking while keeping in mind that, in most cases, the situation that occurred was not smart working but working from home in very particular and stressful conditions. During the pandemic, the needs of patients with chronic diseases risked being overlooked, due to the reduced opportunities for routine clinic visits. Where the telemedicine system was available, these patients have adopted various telehealth services such as video conferencing and remote monitoring (Liu et al., 2020). The outbreak of the COVID-19 pandemic required a quick and adaptive response. Countries had to adapt the functioning of their public governance systems, agencies, and public services, by massively switching to teleworking as the new modus operandi. Governments reorganized the way they meet and make decisions. Public service delivery continued but was often limited to the urgent needs of citizens and businesses and largely dependent on the capacities of digital government (Sigma, 2020). Sectors where a high percentage of the workforce was not able to work remotely have experienced significant greater declines in employment, even greater reductions in expected revenue growth, worse stock market performance and a higher probability of expected default.

Remote work and study have become the norm for a large part of the population following lockdown and physical distancing measures. Many companies made an effort to adapt work and mobility models to a "new normal" in which employees, where appropriate and possible, work remotely. The impact of teleworking on mobility seems to have helped to give cities an impetus to rethink their approach to urban spaces and support new options. In many cases, cities started to adapt mobility and urban planning, with the aim of recovering public spaces for citizens, rethinking the position of essential urban functions to guarantee easier access to urban services and structures, and ensuring the safety and health of people (OECD, 2020a).

However, employees and places are unequal when it comes to remote working in the form that it was experienced during the pandemic crisis. The digital divide is one of the many inequalities confirmed by COVID-19, but other inequalities and issues have had a significant impact on remote work experience. Our homes and the environments in which we work may not be suitable, in terms of size, separation of living spaces and safety. Many people have had to work, study and carry out daily activities in situations that are neither facilitating nor suitable. Several experiences gathered during the first year of the COVID-19 pandemic period also report that, while struggling with a forced work-from-home mode, women also had to take on a disproportionate share of the workload at home and for family care (Eurofound, 2020d; Blaskó et al., 2020). The decline in employment linked to the economic crises in many sectors and to physical distancing measures had a strong impact on sectors with high female employment rates (Alon et al., 2020). Other inequalities cannot be attributed to the COVID-19 emergency, for example, those depending on the type of work performed (smart working is suitable for categories of workers who perform jobs typically associated with a higher level of education/specialization), on the development of the country and network infrastructure, and more.

Remote working, if properly planned and applied according to the smart working model, is an essential tool for maintaining the operation of our health, social and economic systems. Due to a very stressful situation, the results from the large-scale experimentation of remote working methods in emergency conditions need therefore to be analyzed carefully and with a multidisciplinary perspective.

6. Perspectives on the transformative potential of smart working

From the discussion in the previous sections, the effects of smart working on different individual and collective spheres are highlighted. It is becoming clear that the significant transformative potential of smart working can only be fully exploited by using integrated, multi-sectoral and inter-disciplinary approaches.

Smart working, understood as a model based on flexibility and autonomy in the choice of workspace, time and tools in a context of greater employee responsibility for results, represents a significant change in the organization of work, enabling managers and employees to work according to new logics and approaches. This process can generate radical changes within companies and institutions, as well as important transformation of personal and family life. The outcomes of new work and life styles on social and productive arrangements, as well as on mobility and on the shape of cities, open interesting perspectives on which to reflect. The question is how societal practices change over time, including in relation to technology, and to what extent policies can drive this change toward beneficial outcomes for the whole community.

Today, 55% of people live in urban areas, a figure that is expected to reach 68% by 2050 (IRP, 2018). Further increases in population and activities in urban environments can have disruptive effects on the quality of the environment and sustainability issues in general. Current mobility schemes have shaped citizens' lifestyle and the layout of our cities, resulting in impacts on sustainable land use in urban areas and their hinterlands. Urban congestion is a growing problem worldwide. Motor vehicle use is also growing rapidly. Commuting, mainly due to rigid schedules and high dependence on private vehicles, heavily influences congestion. Therefore, it can be expected that urban dynamics can be positively influenced by desynchronizing schedules and reducing the need to travel. Despite the fact that the EU has allocated 16.3bn€ through the European Structural and Investment Fund between 2014 and 2020 to change the way people move in cities and an additional €200m has been provided to larger cities by the Connecting Europe Facility, there is no evidence of a trend toward more sustainable modes of transport. In addition, greenhouse gas emissions from transport have continued to rise and congestion has increased in most of the cities analyzed (European Court of Auditors, 2020). Traditionally, congestion has simply been accepted as one of the problems associated with transport, and infrastructure has been built to solve it. However, as explained in a report on the results of U.S. research on so-called "induced demand", "*If you expand people's ability to travel, they will do it more. [...] Making driving easier means that people take more trips in the car than they otherwise would*" (Duranton and Turner, 2009). This increase in travel offsets any extra capacity that infrastructure improvements might provide. As a result, traffic levels and congestion remain constant.

Evidence shows that technological changes toward sustainability are inadequate without changes in social practices (Shove and Walker, 2007). The massive penetration of smart working allows for new tools, based on the possibility of modifying people's behavioral models in a noncoercive way. Some scholars report that the use of remote work in creating sustainable communities has begun to be recognized at the level of urban and regional policies and that urban strategies that adopt remote work approaches to reshape urban form and mobility patterns should be developed (Kawai, 2008; Tooran, 2009). Regarding how flexible work organization measures have a positive effect on urban congestion, several studies are underway. Among them, an Australian study on alternative ways to ease congestion identified flexible working as a possible solution (Hopkins and McKay, 2019). In the United States, several travel demand management experiments were analyzed that included telework as one of the measures, suggesting remote working as strategic niche management from a multi-level perspective[1] (Stiles, 2020).

[1]The multi-level perspective (MLP) is aconcept for understanding how complex systems undergo change, based on the interactions between the "landscape layer", a "regime layer", and "niche innovations" (Geels, 2002; Smith et al., 2010). Regime change can result from different combinations of top-down landscape pressures such as broad changes in socio-economic conditions, and the bottom-up acceptance of niche innovations. The multilevel perspective focuses attention on how activities within niches may eventually lead to regime-level transitions. Although niche-level progress may not be sufficient for bringing about sustainability transitions, such progress is surely necessary for any transition in dominant regimes that organize production and consumption processes for the principal constituents of inclusive well-being (Anadon et al., 2016). Strategic niche management is an explicit effort to support the development of emerging technologies that present a more sustainable alternative to existing technological regimes (Kemp et al., 2007).

There is consensus that to have more effective sustainable lifestyle policies and practices, it is critical to understand the reasons for consumption choices and what shapes related behavior. This context-specific understanding can be derived through three interlinked underlying lifestyle factors: (1) *motivations*; (2) *drivers*; and (3) *determinants*. These should be at the core of policies, institutional frameworks, programs, and infrastructure when influencing lifestyle design (United Nations Environment Programme, 2016).

Remote working measures, intended as a work-life balance measure (telework), represent good practice, but they are not able to trigger a socio-technical transition, given the small audience among employees. Smart working, as a new management approach, has a wider transformational potential that affects the personal and collective dimensions. By improving the quality of life and work, the benefits can involve corporate and institutional economic interests, as well as workers, strongly influencing "motivations", "drivers" and "determining". The innovation of smart working is not purely technological or related only to the choice of an alternative workplace. Technologies offer tools and cause rapid upheavals in production structures, but without participatory planning new ways of working, coherent with sustainable lifestyles, have no chance.

Pursuing a participative approach has a strong link to the "Stiglitz-Sen-Fitoussi" Commission's proposal (Stiglitz et al., 2009) aimed at measuring economic performance and social progress through quality of life and well-being. In the context of this discussion, it means a shift from the economic and social effects of technologies to joint and participatory planning. From the worker's point of view, greater participation corresponds to the recognition of one's own attitudes, personal history, and work experiences, which are decisive in articulating the time, mode, and consequently the success of work performance. The voluntary dimension of choice, with a perspective of flexibility and responsibility over times and places of work, reduces the risk of alienation of workers, especially when the process is accompanied by training actions aimed at building trust between worker and employer, and within teams, to increase autonomy, responsibility and collaboration.

The emergency measures of the COVID-19 crisis related to work activities implemented in 2020 have shown the transformative potential of smart working despite the conditions imposed. Based on the evidence available at the time of the preparation of this paper, it is believed that the crisis may have acted as an accelerator of social transformation, capable of bringing about positive and lasting change. For this change to occur, a number of key conditions are necessary: acting to remove cultural, organizational and political resistance that keeps remote working at a niche scale, and implementing integrated, long-term strategies involving multilevel, multi-sectoral policy planning.

References

Adams-Prassl, A., Boneva, T., Golin, M., Rauh, C., 2020. Inequality in the Impact of the Coronavirus Shock: Evidence from Real Time Surveys, IZA Discussion Paper n.13183.

Agency of Commerce and Community Development, 2019. Remote Worker Grant Program Annual Report. https://accd.vermont.gov/sites/accdnew/files/documents/DED/Remoteworker/2019RemoteWorkerReport.pdf. last accessed 2020-12-20.

Agency of Commerce and Community Development, 2020. Remote Worker Grant Program Annual Report. https://accd.vermont.gov/sites/accdnew/files/documents/Remote%20Worker%20Report%20Oct%202020.pdf. last accessed 2020-12-20.

Allen, T.D., 2012. The work-family interface. In: Kozlowski, S.W.J. (Ed.), The Oxford Handbook of Organizational Psychology. Oxford University Press.

Allen, T.D., Golden, T.D., Shockley, M., 2015. How effective is telecommuting? Assessing the status of our scientific findings. Psychological Science in the Public Interest 16 (2), 40–68.

Alon, T., Doepke, M., Olmstead-Rumsey, J., Tertilt, M., 2020. The Impact of Covid-19 on Gender Equality. National Bureau Of Economic Research Working Paper No. 26947 JEL No. D10, E24, J16, J22.

Anadon, L.D., Chan, G., Harley, A.G., Matus, K., Moon, S., Murthy, S.L., Clark, W.C., 2016. Making technological innovation work for sustainable development. Proceedings of the National Academy of Sciences of the United States of America 113 (35), 9682–9690.

Argyris, C., Schön, D., 1978. Organizational Learning: A Theory of Action Perspective. Addison-Wesley, Reading.

Arshad, Z., Robaina, M., Botelho, A., 2020. The role of ICT in energy consumption and environment: an empirical investigation of Asian economies with cluster analysis. Environmental Science and Pollution Research 27.

AXA Group, Smart Working: Flexwork and agile working, available online https://www.axa.ch/en/about-axa/jobs-career/what-axa-stands-for/work-models.html, last accessed 2021-01-13.

Bailey, D.E., Kurland, N.B., 2002. A review of telework research: findings, new directions, and lessons for the study of modern work. Journal of Organizational Behavior 23, 383–400.

Bakan, I., Büyükbee, T., Erahan, B., 2011. An investigation of organizational commitment and education level among employees. International Journal of Emerging Sciences 1 (3), 231–245.

Banister, D., 2008. The sustainable mobility paradigm. Transport Policy 15 (2), 73–80.

Barr, S., Prillwitz, J., 2014. A smarter choice? Exploring the behaviour change agenda for environmentally sustainable mobility. Environment and Planning C: Government and Policy 32, 1–19. https://doi.org/10.1068/c1201, 2014.

Bartik, A.W., Cullen, Z.B., Glaeser, E.L., Luca, M., Stanton, C.T., 2020. What Jobs Are Being Done at Home during the Covid-19 Crisis? Evidence from Firm-Level Surveys. National Bureau Of Economic Research Working Paper No. 27422 JEL No. J01, J24, M5, O3.

BBC, 2020. Coronavirus: how can we make post-pandemic cities smarter? https://www.bbc.com/news/technology-53192469 last accessed 2020-10-20.

Belkhir, L., Elmeligi, A., 2018. Assessing ICT global emissions footprint: trends to 2040 & recommendations. Journal of Cleaner Production 177, 2018.

Berkout, F., Hertin, J., 2004. De-materialising and re-materialising: digital technologies and the environment. Futures 36 (Issue 8).

Berman, J.D., Ebisu, K., 2020. Changes in U.S. air pollution during the COVID-19 pandemic. Science of The Total Environment 739, 2020.

Blaskó, Z., Papadimitriou, E., Manca, A.R., 2020. How Will the COVID-19 Crisis Affect Existing Gender Divides in Europe?, EUR 30181 EN. Publications Office of the European Union, Luxembourg, ISBN 978-92-76-18170-5, p. JRC120525. https://doi.org/10.2760/37511, 2020.

Bloom, N., Liang, J., Roberts, J., Ying, Z.J., 2015. Does Working from Home Work? Evidence from a Chinese Experiment. The Quarterly Journal of Economics Stanford University, pp. 165–218, 2015.

Bloomberg, Shearmur, R., Pajević, F., 2018. Work Habits Are Changing: Cities Need to Keep up. https://www.bloomberg.com/news/articles/2018-08-31/what-does-work-sprawl-mean-for-urban-planning. last accessed 2020-12-20.

Boell, S.K., Campbell, J., Cecez-Kecmanovic, D., Cheng, J.E., 2013. Advantages, challenges and contradictions of the transformative nature of telework: a review of the literature. In: Proceedings of the Nineteenth Americas Conference on Information Systems, Chicago, Illinois, August 15-17, 2013.

C40 Cities Climate Leadership Group, 2020. How to Build Back Better with a 15-minute City. https://www.c40knowledgehub.org/s/article/How-to-build-back-better-with-a-15-minute-city?language=en_US. last accessed 2020-12-20.

Chapman, L., 2007. Transport and climate change: a review. Journal of Transport Geography 15 (5), 354–367.

Chung, H., Kerkhofs, M., Ester, P., 2007. Working Time Flexibility in European Companies. Office for Official Publications of the European Union, Luxembourg.

CIPD, 2019. Enabling Flexible Working, Cross-Sector Case Studies and Practice Highlights, 2019 available online. https://www.cipd.co.uk/Images/flexible-working-case-studies_tcm18-58762.pdf. last accessed 2021-01-13.

Comune di Milano, 2017a. La settimana del lavoro agile 22-26 maggio 2017. Esiti. https://www.comune.milano.it/documents/20126/995550/Esiti++Settimana+Lavoro+Agile+-+anno+2017+.pdf/790601ba-5b90-b544-ede7-0da2291784b9?t=1555424499281. last accessed 2021-04-20.

Comune di Milano, 2017b. http://economiaelavoro.comune.milano.it/progetti/smart-lab-milano-concilia-40 last accessed 2021-01-13.

Comune di Milano, 2020a. http://economiaelavoro.comune.milano.it/progetti/mire-milano-rete-dal-welfare-al-tempo-ritrovato last accessed 2021-01-13.

Comune di Milano, 2020b. Milano 2020 Strategia di adattamento. https://www.comune.milano.it/documents/20126/95930101/Milano+2020.++Strategia+di+adattamento.pdf/c96c1297-f8ad-5482-859c-90de1d2b76cb?t=1587723749501. last accessed 2021-01-13.

Cooper-Hakim, A., Viswesvaran, C., 2005. The construct of work commitment: testing an integrative framework. Psychological Bulletin 131 (2), 241–259.

Council of the European Union, 2020a. Council Conclusions on Enhancing Well-Being at Work N.8688/20 - 8 June 2020.

Council of the European Union, 2020b. COM(2020) 102 Final Communication from the Commission to the European Parliament, the European Council, the Council, the European Economic and Social Committee and the Committee of the Regions. A New Industrial Strategy for Europe.

Craig, C., Pinder, 2008. Work Motivation in Organizational Behaviour. Psychology Press.

Dantas, G., Siciliano, B., Boscaro França, B., da Silva, C.M., Arbilla, G., 2020. The impact of COVID-19 partial lockdown on the air quality of the city of Rio de Janeiro, Brazil. Science of The Total Environment 729.

Denworth, L., 2020. The Biggest Psychological Experiment in History Is Running Now. What can the pandemic teach us about how people respond to adversity? Science 323 (1), 39–45.

Duranton, G., Turner, M.A., 2009. The Fundamental Law of Road Congestion: Evidence from US Cities NBER Working Paper No. 15376, JEL No. L91, p. R41.

Eurofound, 2012. Organisation of Working Time: Implications For Productivity and Working Conditions – Overview Report.

Eurofound, 2015. New Forms of Employment. Publications Office of the European Union, Luxembourg.

Eurofound, 2020a. Telework and ICT-Based Mobile Work: Flexible Working in the Digital Age, New Forms of Employment Series. Publications Office of the European Union, Luxembourg.

Eurofound, 2020b. Regulations to Address Work–Life Balance in Digital Flexible Working Arrangements, New Forms of Employment Series. Publications Office of the European Union, Luxembourg.

Eurofound, 2020c. How Does Employee Involvement in Decision-Making Benefit Organisations?, European Working Conditions Survey 2015 Series. Publications Office of the European Union, Luxembourg.

Eurofound, 2020d. Living, Working and COVID-19, COVID-19 Series. Publications Office of the European Union, Luxembourg.

European Commission, 1, https://ec.europa.eu/futurium/en/urban-agenda , last accessed 2020-10-20.

European Commission, 2016. Urban Agenda for the EU. Pact of Amsterdam. https://ec.europa.eu/futurium/en/system/files/ged/pact-of-amsterdam_en.pdf. last accessed 2020-10-20.

European Court of Auditors, 2020. Sustainable Urban Mobility in the EU: No Substantial Improvement Is Possible without Member States' Commitment, Special Report 06/2020.

European Institute for Gender Equality, 2019. Gender Equality Index 2019. Work-Life Balance.

European Parliament, 2016. European Parliament Resolution of 13 September 2016 on Creating Labour Market Conditions Favourable for Work-Life Balance (2016/2017(INI)).

European Platform on Mobility Management, 2018. Mobility Management Strategy Book. Intelligent Strategies for Clean Mobility towards a Sustainable and a Prosperous Europe.

European Union, 2020. Special Report - Sustainable Urban Mobility in the Eu: No Substantial Improvement Is Possible Without Member States' Commitment.

Financial Times, 2020. Whittle N., Welcome to the 15-minute City. https://www.ft.com/content/c1a53744-90d5-4560-9e3f-17ce06aba69a. last accessed 2020-12-20.

Forbes, 2020. Reid C, Every Street in Paris to Be Cycle-Friendly by 2024 Promises Mayor last accessed 2020-12-20. https://www.forbes.com/sites/carltonreid/2020/01/21/phasing-out-cars-key-to-paris-mayors-plans-for-15-minute-city/#230470886952.

Gajendran, R.S., Harrison, D.A., 2007. The good, the bad, and the unknown about telecommuting: meta-analysis of psychological mediators and individual consequences. Journal of Applied Psychology 92 (No. 6).

Gajendran, R.S., Harrison, D.A., Delaney-Klinger, K., 2014. Are telecommuters remotely good citizens? Unpacking telecommuting's effects on performance via I-deals and job resources. Personnel Psychology 68 (2). May 2014.

Geels, F.W., 2002. Technological transitions as evolutionary reconfiguration processes: a multi-level perspective and a case-study. Research Policy 31 (8).

Giovanis, E., 2018. The relationship between teleworking, traffic and air pollution. Atmospheric Pollution Research 9 (1), 1–14.

Golden, T., 2012. Altering the effects of work and family conflict on exhaustion: telework during traditional and non-traditional work hours. Journal of Business and Psychology.

Golden, T.D., Veiga, J., 2005. The impact of extent of telecommuting on job satisfaction: resolving inconsistent findings. Journal of Management 32.

Greenhaus, J., Beutell, N., 1985. Sources and conflict between work and family roles. The Academy of Management Review 10 (No. 1).

Greer, T.W., Payne, S.C., 2014. Overcoming telework challenges: outcomes of successful telework strategies. The Psychologist-Manager Journal 17 (No. 87–11), 2014.

Gschwind, L., Vargas, O., 2019. Telework and its effects in Europe. In: Telework in the 21st Century, ISBN 9781789903744.

He, G., Pan, Y., Tanaka, T., 2020. The short-term impacts of COVID-19 lockdown on urban air pollution in China. Nature Sustainability 3, 1005–1011, 2020.

Hook, A., Court, V., Sovacool, B.K., Sorrell, S., 2020. A systematic review of the energy and climate impacts of teleworking. Environmental Research Letters 2020 15 (9), 093003.

Hopkins, J.L., McKay, J., 2019. Investigating 'anywhere working' as a mechanism for alleviating traffic congestion in smart cities. Technological Forecasting and Social Change 142, 258–272. May 2019.

Horner, N.C., Shehabi, A., Azevedo, I.L., 2016. Known unknowns: indirect energy effects of information and communication technology. Environmental Research Letters 11 (10).

Houseman, S.N., Polivka, A.E., 2000. The implications of flexible staffing arrangements for jobsecurity. In: Neumark, D. (Ed.), On the Job: Is Long-Term Employment a Thing of the Past? Russell Sage Foundation, NewYork.

IEA, 2020. IEA - International Energy Agency, 2020, Oil Market Report.

Ikezoe, H., 2013. Diversification of the "workplace" and problems with labor law. Japan Labor Review 10 (3).

Imperial College London, Business Case for Smart Working, available online https://www.imperial.ac.uk/admin-services/ict/about-ict/smart-working-at-imperial/smart-working-toolkit/smart-working-for-managers/business-case-for-smart-working/, last accessed 2021-01-13.

IRP, 2018, The Weight of Cities: Resource Requirements of Future Urbanization. Swilling, M., Hajer, M., Baynes, T., Bergesen, J., Labbé, F., Musango, J.K., Ramaswami, A., Robinson, B., Salat, S., Suh, S., Currie, P., Fang, A., Hanson, A. Kruit, K., Reiner, M., Smit, S., Tabory, S. A Report by the International Resource Panel. United Nations Environment Programme, Nairobi, Kenya.

Jaros, M., 2007. Meyer and Allen Model of Organizational Commitment: Measurement Issues. Southern University College of Business, USA.

Kaufmann, V., 2011. Rethinking the City. Routledge and EPFL Press.

Kawai, Y., 2008. Work/life community by telework – possibilities and issues in the case of Loma Linda. Journal of Green Building 3 (2), 128–139.

Kellert, S.R., 2005. Building for Life: Designg and Understanding.

Kemp, R., Schot, J., Hoogma, R., 2007. Regime shifts to sustainability through processes of niche formation: the approach of strategic niche management. Technology Analisys and Strategic Management 10 (2).

Khan, M.R., Ziauddin Jam, F.A., Ramay, M.I., 2010. The impacts of organizational commitment on employee job performance. European Journal of Social Sciences 15 (3), 292–298.

Kurland, N., Bailey, D., 1999. Telework: the advantages and challenges of working here, there, anywhere and anytime. Organizational Dynamics 53–68.

Lake, A., 2015. The Smart Working Handbook, second ed. Flexibility.co.uk.

Lange, S., Pohl, J., Santarius, T., 2020. Digitalization and energy consumption. Does ICT reduce energy demand? Ecological Economics 176.

Lanzendorf, M., 2003. Mobility biographies. A new perspective for understanding travel behaviour. In: 10th International Conference on Travel Behaviour Research, 2003.

Liu, N., Huang, R., Baldacchino, T., Sud, A., Sud, K., Khadra, M., Kim, J., 2020. Telehealth for non critical patients with chronic diseases during the COVID-19 pandemic. Journal of Medical Internet Research 22 (8).

METI, 2017. Nationwide Teleworking Campaign Project in Light of the 2020 Tokyo Olympic and Paralympic Games. https://www.meti.go.jp/english/press/2017/0724_002.html. last accessed 2021-04-20.

Mokhtarian, P.L., Handy, S.L., Salomon, I., 1995. Methodological issues in the estimation of the travel, energy, and air quality impacts of telecommuting. Transportation Research A: Policy and Practice 29 (4), 283–302.

Moon, N.W., Linden, M.A., Bricout, J.C., Baker, P.M.A., 2014. Telework rationale and implementation for people with disabilities: considerations for employer policymaking. Work 48 (1), 105–115.

Moreno, C., 2016. La Ville du Quart D'heure: Pour un Nouveau Chrono-Urbanisme available online: https://www.latribune.fr/regions/smart-cities/la-tribune-de-carlos-moreno/la-ville-du-quart-d-heure-pour-un-nouveau-chrono-urbanisme-604358.html. last accessed 2021-0420.

Moreno, C., Allam, Z., Chabaud, D., Gall, C., Pratlong, F., 2021. Introducing the "15-minute city": sustainability, resilience and place identity in future post-pandemic cities. Smart Cities 4, 93–111. https://doi.org/10.3390/smartcities, 2021.

Morikawa, M., 2018. Long Commuting Time and the Benefits of Telecommuting, RIETI Discussion Paper Series 18-E–025.

Mueller, N., Rojas-Rueda, D., Khreis, H., CirachM, Andrés, D., Ballester, J., Bartoll, X., Daher, C.D.A., Echave, C., Milà, C., MárquezS, Palou, J., Pérez, K., Tonne, C., Stevenso, M., Rueda, S., Nieuwenhuijsen, M., 2020. Changing the Urban Design of Cities for Health: The Superblock Model, vol 134. Environment International.

Mumford, L., 1968. The City in History: Its Origins, its Transformations, and its Prospects. Mariner Books, ISBN 9780156180351 (first published April 1961).

Neirotti, P., Paolucci, E., Raguseo, E., 2012. Telework configurations and labour productivity: some stylized facts. International Journal of Engineering Business Management 4.

Nilles, J.M., 1988. Traffic reduction by telecommuting: a status review and selected bibliography. Transportation Research A: General 22 (4), 301–317.

OECD, 2001. The Well-Being of Nations: The Role of Human and Social Capital. OECD Publications.

OECD, 2020a. Cities policy responses. available online. https://www.oecd.org/coronavirus/policy-responses/cities-policy-responses-fd1053ff/. last accessed 2021-04-21.

OECD, 2020b. Productivity gains from teleworking in the post COVID-19 era: how can public policies make it happen? available online. https://www.oecd.org/coronavirus/policy-responses/productivity-gains-from-teleworking-in-the-post-covid-19-era-a5d52e99/. last accessed 2021-04-21.

OECD/EU, 2018. Health at a Glance: Europe 2018:State of Health in the EU Cycle. OECD Publishing, Paris. https://doi.org/10.1787/health_glance_eur-2018-en.

Osservatorynet, 2014a. Heineken Business Case 2014. https://www.osservatori.net/it/prodotti/formato/business-case/lo-smart-working-in-heineken-migliorare-la-produttivita-attraverso-il-telelavoro. last accessed 2021-01-13.

Osservatorynet, 2014b. Unilever Business Case 2014. https://www.osservatori.net/it/prodotti/formato/business-case/unilever-progetto-agile-working. last accessed 2021-01-13.

Osservatorynet, 2016a. Barilla Business Case 2016. https://www.osservatori.net/it/prodotti/formato/business-case/smart-working-in-barilla-un-nuovo-modo-di-lavorare-per-uno-stile-di-vita-equilibrato-e-sostenibile. last accessed 2021-01-13.

Osservatorynet, 2016b. Tetra Pak, Business Case Smart Working last accessed 2021-01-13. https://www.osservatori.net/it/prodotti/formato/business-case/sviluppare-il-lavoro-in-ottica-smart-l-esempio-vincente-di-tetra-pak.

Osservatorynet, 2016c. Siemens Business Case Smart Working last accessed 2021-01-13. https://www.osservatori.net/it/prodotti/formato/business-case/smart-working-siemens-business-case.

Osservatorynet, 2017a. Axa Italia Business Case 2017 last accessed 2021-01-13. https://www.osservatori.net/it/prodotti/formato/business-case/axa-italia-ripensa-il-lavoro-nel-settore-assicurativo-non-solo-spazi-ma-anche-una-cultura-smart.

Osservatorynet, 2017b. Mars Italia Business Case Smart Working 2017 last accessed 2021-01-13. https://www.osservatori.net/it/prodotti/formato/business-case/smart-working-2-0-il-caso-mars-italia.

Osservatorynet, 2018a. Università di Trento Business Case Smart Working last accessed 2021-01-13. https://www.osservatori.net/it/prodotti/formato/business-case/universita-di-trento-smart-working.

Osservatorynet, 2018b. Mercedes Business Case Smart Working last accessed 2021-01-13. https://www.osservatori.net/it/prodotti/formato/business-case/smart-working-in-mercedes.

Osservatorynet, 2020. ENEL Business Case Smart Working 2020. https://www.osservatori.net/it/prodotti/formato/business-case/lo-smart-working-in-enel. last accessed 2021-01-13.

Ozcelik, Y., 2010. The rise of teleworking in the USA: key issues for managers in the information age. International Journal of Business Information Systems 5 (issue 3).

Penna, M., Felici, B., Roberto, R., Rao, M., Zini, A., 2020. Il tempo dello Smart Working. La PA tra conciliazione, valorizzazione del lavoro e dell'ambiente. ENEA.

Peters, P., Bleijenberg, I., Oldenkamp, E., 2009. The telework adoption process in a Dutch and French subsidiary of the same ICT-multinational: how national culture and management principles affect the success of telework programs. The Journal of E-Working 3 (2009), 1–16.

Portney, K.E., 2002. Taking sustainable cities seriously. Economic Development, the Environment, and Quality of Life in American Cities.

Riketta, M., 2002. Attitudinal organizational commitment and job performance: a meta-analysis. Journal of Organizational Behavior 23 (3), 257–266.

Robbins, S.P., Judge, T.A., 2007. Organizational Behavior, 12th. Ed. Prentice Hall.

Ryan, A.M., Kossek, E.E., 2008. Work-life policy implementation: breaking down or creating barriers to inclusiveness. Human Resource Management 47 (2), 295–310, 2008.

Sardeshmukh, S.R., Sharma, D., Golden, T.D., 2012. Impact of telework on exhaustion and job engagement: a job demands and job resources model. New Technology, Work and Employment 27.

Schappe, S.P., 1998. The influence of job satisfaction, organizational commitment, and fairness perceptions on organizational citizenship behaviour. The Journal of Psychology 132 (3), 277–290.

Sempane, M., Rieger, H., Roodt, G., 2002. Job satisfaction in relation to organizational culture. Journal of Industry Psychology 28 (2), 23–30.

Sheller, M., Urry, J., 2006. The new mobilities paradigm. February 2006, Environment and Planning A 38 (2), 207–226.

Shove, E., Walker, G., 2007. Caution! Transitions ahead: politics, practice, and sustainable transition management. Environment and Planning, A 39 (4).

Sigma, 2020. Public Administration: Responding to the COVID-19 Pandemic, Mapping the EU Member States' Public Administration Responses to the COVID-19 Pandemic (For EU Enlargement and Neighbourhood Countries last accessed 2020-12-20. http://www.sigmaweb.org/publications/SIGMA-mapping-public-administration-response-EU-members-coronavirus-COVID19.pdf.

Sinclair, R.R., Tucker, J.S., Cullen, J.C., 2005. Performance Differences among four organizational commitment profiles. Journal of Applied Psychology 90 (6), 1280–1287.

Smart Working at Wokingham Council, available online http://www.flexibility.co.uk/cases/Wokingham-Council-Smart-Working.htm, last accessed 2021-01-13.

Smart Working Observatory, https://www.osservatori.net/en/research/active-observatories/smart-working, last accessed 2020-10-20.

Smith, A., Voß, J.P., Grin, J., 2010. Innovation studies and sustainability transitions: the allure of the multi-level perspective and its challenges. Research Policy 39 (4).

Sostero, M., Milasi, S., Hurley, J., Fernández-Macías, E., Bisello, M., 2020. Teleworkability and the COVID-19 Crisis: A New Digital Divide? European Commission, Seville, p. JRC121193.

Stiglitz, J., Sen, A., Fitoussi, J.P., 2009. Report of the Commission on the Measurement of Economic Performance and Social Progress.

Stiles, J., 2020. Strategic niche management in transition pathways: telework advocacy as groundwork for an incremental transformation. Environmental Innovation and Societal Transitions 34.

Tech Research Asia, BlueWork: The American Express Workplace Strategy, available online http://techquarterly.asia/node/23, last accessed 2021-01-13.

The World Bank, 2020. Air Pollution: Locked Down by COVID-19 but Not Arrested July 2, 2020. https://www.worldbank.org/en/news/immersive-story/2020/07/01/air-pollution-locked-down-by-covid-19-but-not-arrested. last accessed 2021-01-13.

Tooran, A., 2009. Urban design in the digital age: a literature review of telework and wired communities. Journal of Urbanism: International Research on Placemaking and Urban Sustainability 2 (3).
Tooran, A., 2011. Urban implications of telework: policy gap in Sydney metropolitan planning?. In: Proceedings 3rd World Planning Schools Congress, Perth (WA), 4-8 July 2011.
Tronti, L., 2015. Economia della conoscenza, innovazione organizzativa e partecipazione cognitiva: un nuovo modo di lavorare, in Economia & Lavoro, n. 3 (2015).
UK Government, 2013. Department for culture, media and sport, report 5: post-games evaluation. Meta-Evaluation of the Impacts and Legacy of the London 2012 Olympic Games and Paralympic Games. ECONOMY EVIDENCE BASE Post-Games Evaluation Summary Report, July 2013.
Underdal, A., 1980. Integrated marine policy: what? Why? How? Marine Policy 4 (3).
United Nations Environment Programme, 2016. A Framework for Shaping Sustainable Lifestyles.
US Government, 2010. Public Law No: 111-292 (12/09/2010), p. 124. STAT. 3165.
US Office of Personnel Management, 2017. Status of telework in the federal government. Report to the Congress.
Virgin Group, Proof that flexible working works, available online https://www.virgin.com/branson-family/richard-branson-blog/proof-flexible-working-works, last accessed 2021-01-13.
Virick, M., Da Silva, N., Arrington, K., 2010. Moderators of the curvilinear relation between extent of telecommuting and job and life satisfaction: the role of performance outcome orientation and worker type. Human Relations 63 (1).
Viteri, G., Díaz de Mera, Y., Rodríguez, A., Rodríguez, D., Tajuelo, M., Escalona, A., Aranda, A., 2021. Impact of SARS-CoV-2 lockdown and de-escalation on air-quality parameters. Chemosphere 265, 2021.
Wellman, B., Salaff, J., Dimitrova, D., Garton, L., Gulia, M., Haythornthwaite, C., 1996. Computer networks as social networks: collaborative work, telework, and virtual community. Annual Review of Sociology 22 (1), 39–45.

9

Intelligent spatial technologies for gender inclusive urban environments in today's smart cities

Sophia German[1], Graciela Metternicht[1,3], Shawn Laffan[1] and Scott Hawken[2]

[1]*Earth & Sustainability Science Research Centre, University of New South Wales, Sydney, NSW, Australia;* [2]*School of Architecture and Built Environment, University of Adelaide, Adelaide, SA, Australia;* [3]*School of Science, Western Sydney University, Sydney, NSW, Australia*

1. Introduction

Safer cities for women is an aspiration of the 2030 United Nations Sustainable Development agenda and is also supported by the New Urban Agenda from 2016 and various other recent global initiatives such as the *Safe Cities and Safe Public Spaces for Women and Girls* (UN Women, 2019), which builds on the *Safe Cities Free of Violence against Women and Girls* report (UN Women and ICRW, 2012).

Such aspirations have emerged to address the widespread violence against women in urban spaces. According to the World Bank Group (2020), gender-based violence is "a global pandemic" that affects as many as one in three women in their lifetime. Gendered violence is both explicit and implicit and inflicted through gendered crimes but also through systemic cultural norms that control and shape how women move through space. As the world becomes increasingly urbanized it is essential that such inequity is addressed within cities. Around the world, cities are structured in ways that expose women and girls to actual and perceived threats of violence. Together actual and perceived threats of violence combine to dissuade and exclude women from navigating certain areas of cities.

Intelligent Environments. https://doi.org/10.1016/B978-0-12-820247-0.00012-6

The connection between urban landscape and social behavior has been investigated since the 1960s. Landscape architecture plays an important role in shaping how people perceive their environment, and also where crime is likely to occur. The theory of Defensible Space as a way to deter crime through architectural design was introduced by Oscar Newman (1972), based on the work of Jane Jacobs (1972) on creating environments with natural surveillance. The basis of these ideas was that architecture should reflect a safe and friendly living environment to eliminate the conditions for crime to take place. This idea created the foundations for Crime Prevention Through Environmental Design (CPTED), spearheaded by Jeffery (1971). Along with Space Syntax—the geometrical study and analysis of urban spaces as networks that influence use, walkability, and safety from crime—introduced by Bill Hillier and Julienne Hanson (1984), these seminal works have laid the foundations for urban safety and crime prevention.

Shaw (2013) (p.188) writes that evaluation of urban safety has typically been "largely gender blind in failing to take account of how risk is gendered in relation to victimization, offending and public/private spaces." However, this is changing. Understanding how perceptions of safety are formed and manifested through space and time has become an increasingly important global issue related to gender equality and sustainable cities. As critical urban scholar Saskia Sassen (2015) suggests "The last decade has seen a proliferation of movements by and for women aimed at a critical confrontation with the gendered city and at securing the right to safety in the city."

Smart cities and geospatial technologies have been promoted as a way to address and confront the challenge of gendered cities (Hawken et al., 2020b). These emerging technologies are able to source, capture, record, and analyze new streams of information that can challenge the status quo (Hawken et al., 2020a; Han and Hawken, 2018; Hawken et al., 2020a). Geospatial technologies fall within the umbrella of intelligent systems that enable location-based analytics and the application of a "systems perspective" of social and environmental issues at different scales—from local to global (Li et al., 2020). Geographic information systems (GIS) (Jakobi and Pődör, 2020), crowdsourcing platforms (Pánek, 2018; Viswanath and Basu, 2015), phone or web-based applications to collect location-based, and in some cases, real-time data (Solymosi et al., 2020; Chataway et al., 2017) coupled with qualitative approaches (Boschmann and Cubbon, 2014) are some technologies that have been used in recent research in the field of perceived safety. Research applying such approaches shows that the extent of female concern about safety in urban spaces differs as a function of several factors—who you are, where you are, what you are doing, time of day, who is around, and how the surrounding area appears (Yates and Ceccato, 2020). Each factor that contributes to this feeling of safety is often manifested in how a woman engages with her surroundings (Vera-Gray, 2018; Rahm et al., 2021).

The aim of this chapter is to provide a synthesis of the state-of-the-art on applications of intelligent spatial technologies for understanding factors that influence women's perception of safety in urban environments, evaluating the strengths and weaknesses of current research approaches through a systematic review of literature —including relevant initiatives driven by practice—and drawing from these lessons on modes of data collection, analysis, and synthesis that can be recommended for moving the research agenda forward. To this end, we first introduce concepts of gender-inclusive cities and how these standards and ideals fit in a global context. Secondly, we delve into the importance of considering women's perception of safety as a measure of accessibility, pulling apart the specific factors that comprise a perception. Thirdly, we explore and discuss spatial technologies and data-driven approaches and what they can offer in the realm of safety perception, followed by a discussion and conclusion on the need for gender-inclusive spaces and the role of geospatial technologies in the design of such spaces.

1.1 Gender inclusive public spaces: concepts and state of the art

According to the Handbook for Gender-Inclusive Urban Planning and Design (World Bank, 2020, p.10) gender-inclusive cities can be defined as those, which actively include the voices of women; promote citizen-city relationship building involving women; meet the needs of women; seek out and sharing robust, meaningful new data on gender equity; enhance the capacity and influence of underrepresented groups in key decisions, and commit the necessary finances and expertise to deliver on intentional gender equity goals. More commonly and concisely it has been defined as the role gender plays with regard to access, mobility, and safety in public areas. The need for cities that are fit-for-all arises from the fact that experiences in urban space are gendered, and many of the contemporary planning principles stem from patriarchal ideas (Dymén and Ceccato, 2011; Beebeejaun, 2017). In Fig. 9.1 we combine several of these definitions to formulate an example cityscape that incorporates these aspects.

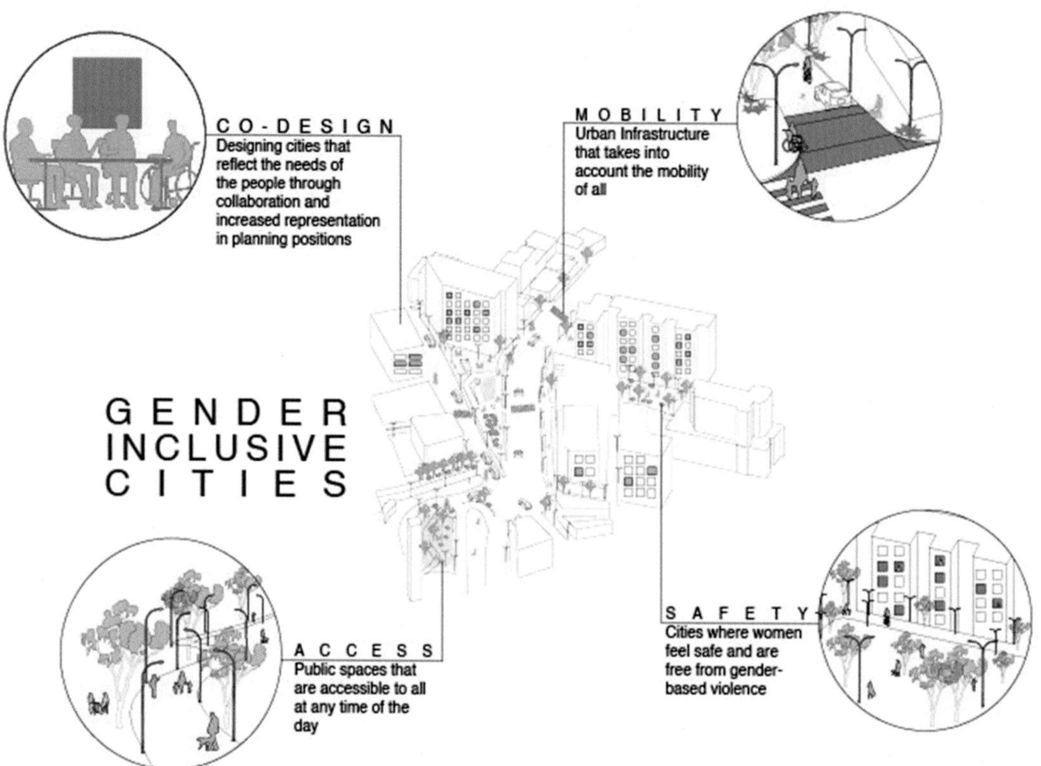

Figure 9.1 The four principles of gender-inclusive cities, designed according to the concepts of UN Women (2011), ICLEI and UITP (2020), UN Habitat (2012), World Bank Group (2020).

An example of how noninclusivity is manifested is explored in the *Free to Be* project (Tanner et al., 2020). Through crowdsourcing "safe" and "unsafe" spots from women and girls below the age of 30 in five cities, this initiative captured the extent of gender-based violence and street harassment faced by many in Lima, Madrid, Sydney, Dehli, and Kampala. The myriads of ways women and girls are socially excluded were manifested in their descriptions of why they deemed a place to be safe or unsafe. For example, a woman aged 25 in the Sydney central business district in the evening reported that the spot was "*poorly lit, few people around. Have been catcalled and leered at by men on many occasions. Used to work nearby, and would take a longer route when dark after work*" (Committee for Sydney, 2019). A woman aged 16 reported at Avenida Tomas Valle, Lima, that "*it is very common to go through this area as I have to take bus/combi every day to go to study, rudeness, offensive and sexist comments, sexual slang, every day! I really got used to this abuse and living with fear is my day to day! When I return safely to my house it is a miracle and I thank God for that*" (Plan International, 2018). These are just a snapshot of the measured ways women and girls consider their safety in public spaces.

Research and policy recognize the need for gender-inclusive cities (UN Women, 2011; ICLEI and UITP, 2020; UN Habitat, 2012; World Bank Group, 2020), noting its impact on aspects of planning related to codesign, accessibility, mobility, and safety (Fig. 9.1). More to the point, Fig. 9.1 illustrates the importance of: a) designing urban spaces and transport options to meet those outcomes such as better lighting, well-kept vegetation, and clean streets (Box 9.1), b) listening to the stories of women from various cultural and socio-economic backgrounds and those from gender minorities, and c) increasing representation in planning positions by way of gender mainstreaming. Despite this recognition, research shows that most cities are yet to be gender inclusive. The prevalence of gender-based violence and fear of attack are among the many reasons driving social exclusion in public spaces (Beebeejaun, 2017; Vera-Gray and Kelly, 2020; Koskela and Pain, 2000).

Perception of safety has a significant impact on accessibility to, and movement through, public spaces (Mellgren et al., 2018; Vera-Gray, 2018), regardless of previous victimization (Logan and Walker, 2017; Abbott and McGrath, 2017). It affects how people behave, access, and move through cities (Curtis, 2012), both spatially and temporally. In that way, avoidance of places, route choices, access to services, transport options, nightlife, physical activity, the choice to live in an area, where one works, and how one dresses are all connected to the notion of gendered experience on safety. There is therefore a need to understand what drives these perceptions to improve the accessibility of women to cities' infrastructure, and thus city livability.

Gender-inclusive design can enhance women's safe access to public spaces as shown in cities of Colombia that introduced aerial cable cars in 2004, as an alternative transit option to increase citizen safety when traveling through low-income neighborhoods. A study led by Heinrichs and Bernet (2014) assessed the accessibility and safety of this transit option to identify women's perception and use of cable cars. They found that: (a) women felt more secure with this option above all other public transport options; and (b) travel time and costs were reduced, increasing overall mobility, safety, and accessibility.

1.2 Relevance of women's perception in understanding "safety" and "fear" in public spaces

Perception of safety is linked to the study of fear of crime, a longstanding and ongoing area of research that aims to understand the reasons behind the fear of being victimized by crime (Lagrange et al., 1992; Ferraro, 1995; Hale, 1996; Jackson, 2005; Franklin and Franklin, 2009; Ceccato, 2016). The importance of understanding fear of crime comes from the notion that liveability is reduced when someone changes their behavior to avoid such emotions (Doran and Burgess, 2012), which could possibly be manifested through the choice of where to live or what areas to avoid. It is both a social and physical problem, and several papers have investigated the notion of disorder and incivilities (Roman, 2008; Doran and Lees, 2005; Lagrange et al., 1992; Wyant, 2008).

Until recently, research on fear in public spaces was mostly qualitative and nonspatial. Pain (1997), Lagrange and Ferraro (1989), and Doran and Burgess (2012) describe some of the limitations associated with measuring fear of crime in this way, and these concepts are summarised in Table 9.1.

Table 9.1 Common limitations associated with fear of crime studies based on qualitative, non-spatial methods.

Problem	Associated limitations
Recalling information in an interview	The brain tends to either overcomplicate or oversimply the events that occurred, and specific features of the surrounding environment that may cause fear can be hard to recall.
Questions asked by the interviewer	Interviewer bias can occur through leading questions that increase fear in the participant.
Spatial scale: neighborhood versus street-level analysis	Fear can dissolve as soon as one turns the corner; neighborhood fear of crime is not indicative of a fear of crime within each subarea of that neighborhood.
Gender, culture, socio-economic status, etc. are not considered	Experiences of fear are gendered, requiring data to be gender disaggregated; this is also true of cultural factors, socio-economic status, and/or expectations of gender roles across race and culture.
Comparing gendered fear of crime with crime rates	Although women's fear might be more prevalent than men's, some studies have found that more crimes were directed at men. Unfortunately, this is difficult to compare as crimes against women are less often reported, and men may be putting themselves into harm's way more often, perhaps due to a lack of fear.

To address these limitations the fields of women's fear of crime, and place-based and/or real-time analyses have emerged (Chataway and Hart, 2019; Pain, 1997; Doran and Burgess, 2012). The former is a field specific to sexual assault and/or street harassment in public spaces. Women's safety audits, first established in Canada (Whitzman et al., 2009), were the first to recognize that a women's safety differs from men's.

To understand what contributes to a perception of safety in women, the concept of perception and how it is formed needs to be introduced. The subjective nature of emotions as one observes and moves through a city landscape, and its subsequent inequitable nature was introduced by Kevin Lynch (1960) in his book "The Image of the City". He noted that city design, social disorder, and temporal factors can exclude groups of people and thus reduce women's "right to the city" (Beebeejaun, 2017). Socio-economic status, age, gender identity, sexual orientation, physical ability, race, or previous experience of victimization are other key factors that influence the formation of fear, characterized as either personal or psychological vulnerabilities that imply that fear is not equally experienced across groups of people (Franklin and Franklin, 2009; Dymén and Ceccato, 2011). Feeling in control is another contributing element to the perception of safety (Dymén and Ceccato, 2011), often manifesting through choice and availability of transportation. The influence of the media and reported incidents of crime also impact an individual's perception of safety (Kalms et al., 2018), that perception is likely to vary across communities. More to the point, fear is not experienced equally across communities (Yates and Ceccato, 2020), hence the need to focus on specific groups of people when considering urban design and planning for equal access to space, regardless of age, gender, socio-economic status, culture, and religion.

A variety of social, temporal, and environmental factors contribute to a person's perception of safety in public space. These factors can be tied to locations such as a specific street, green space, or transport node, or can exist over broader spatial extents such as suburbs and neighborhoods (Yates and Ceccato, 2020). Socially, perception can be influenced by the presence of people, diversity of gender usage, the familiarity of the place, pre-existing ideas of neighborhoods, and social dynamics (Gargiulo et al., 2020; Kalms et al., 2018; Viswanath and Basu, 2015). "Unpredictable people" such as the homeless, people under the influence of alcohol, and teens can also contribute to the perception of safety, as a manifestation of social disorder (Committee for

Sydney, 2019). Temporally, perception of safety can be influenced by time of day, days of the week, or by season. Although fear of crime is often associated with night fall and darkness, other times also seem to have an impact—dawn, dusk, or even during daylight hours (Boessen et al., 2017). Day of the week influences, for example, the frequency and availability of public transport services (Chowdhury and Van Wee, 2020), and the number of people engaging in drinking, all of which can influence the perception of safety (Kalms et al., 2018). Seasonal impacts can include the climate and how that might affect the presence of people, or the timing of holidays when people are not working. One's perception of environmental safety can be influenced by the amount of lighting in an area (Boomsma and Steg, 2014; Rahm et al., 2021), the openness of the space, land use (Gargiulo et al., 2020), vegetation (Mouratidis, 2019), visibility of the space (Li et al., 2015), quality of infrastructure (Yates and Ceccato, 2020), landscape design (World Bank Group, 2020), pedestrian mobility (Golan et al., 2019), and proximity to public transport (Gargiulo et al., 2020; Viswanath and Basu, 2015). The notion of environmental disorder is often associated with perceived safety and actual rates of crime (Wyant, 2008). Feeling in control is another contributing element to the perception of safety (Dymén and Ceccato, 2011), often manifesting through choice and availability of transportation.

Prior research using place-based analyses (Solymosi et al., 2020; Ristea and Leitner, 2020; Glas et al., 2019; Doran and Burgess, 2012) have helped address physical and temporal attributes contributing to the feeling of fear; what remains is further investigation into how gender and place can be incorporated into fear of crime studies using geospatial technologies.

1.3 Understanding perception through spatial technologies

Spatial technologies can help understand, measure, and analyze perceptions through the acquisition and manipulation of spatially explicit data. Remote sensing, Global Positioning Systems (GPS), or Geographic Information Systems (GIS) technologies are examples of ways that spatial data can be acquired. GIS is essentially the culmination of geography and science, allowing for the analysis of complex data to identify spatial patterns that might not otherwise have been noticed. GIS helps planners in understanding how people interact with their environment, especially with the increased popularity of Internet of Things technology (IoT) and Big Data (Li et al., 2020; Tao, 2013; Williams,

2020). The geospatial revolution has in many ways democratized knowledge by making access to knowledge more accessible but also by empowering the collection of data through participatory methods. For example, data collection has conventionally been carried out by those with the resources to pursue what was a very intensive and painstaking activity. Today the tool to collect and collate and interpret data have been put into the hands of citizens everywhere in the form of smart phones and mobile computers (Williams 2020, Hawken et al., 2020a)

There is a lack of agreement about the essential subjective variables necessary to measure perception. Whilst some research has focused on areas that participants deem "safe" or "unsafe" (Solymosi et al., 2015; Tanner et al., 2020; Pánek et al., 2019), others are interested in the "why" aspect of perception—amount of lighting (Boomsma and Steg, 2014), vegetation (Sreetheran and Van Den Bosch, 2014), visibility of the space (Li et al., 2015), proximity to public transport (Ceccato, 2017; Gardner et al., 2017), or surrounding land use (Viswanath and Basu, 2015). Prior research has also focused on how perceptions of surroundings might impact the choice to engage in physical activity (Pérez Tejera, 2012; Gargiulo et al., 2020), or mobility limitations based on perceived safety (Gauvin et al., 2020; Loukaitou-Sideris, 2006). The temporal nature of perception has been explored as well (Solymosi et al., 2015; Chowdhury and Van Wee, 2020). As such, a range of qualitative and quantitative geospatial approaches have been adopted to measure these variables (Table 9.2), many as part of mixed methodology frameworks.

Oftentimes, the utility of variables that measure perception depends on spatial scale. This means that the specific variables used can be too localized to then be applied in another place, while others are too broad scale and may not provide useful information on specific streets or land use types. Previous research (Jakobi and Pődör, 2020) has addressed this by undertaking the same analysis on more than one city; creating a safety rubric that can be applied in different contexts and scales (Viswanath and Basu, 2015a); or testing the same variables across different land uses such as transport nodes and parks (Pérez Tejera, 2012).

Generally, variables that are relevant across space—or proven to impact safety feelings, such as lighting—seem to lack the complexities associated with gendered perception. In that way, there is potential to ask different questions to help planners design safer cities. It is then pertinent to question why we lack common ways to measure perception. If safety audits exist to measure

Table 9.2 Qualitative and quantitative approaches used with geospatial technologies used to analyze perception of safety.

Data	Methodology
Qualitative	Go-along interviews
	In-depth interviews
	Crowdsourcing qualitative data through phone or web-based platforms
	Focus groups
	Sketch maps
	Questionnaires
Quantitative	Real-time place-based questionnaires
	Spatio-temporal analysis
	Mobile platforms that record GPS location
	GPS tracking to understand route choice
	Ecological momentary assessments
	Hot spot analyses
	Crowdsourcing quantitative data through phone or web-based platforms

safety across space, a similar audit for the perception of safety that considers gendered experiences should exist too.

2. Methodological framework

A review method that integrates (1) literature-focused review with (2) practice-based review was adopted for this work. This two-part approach brings together the strengths of both peer-reviewed sources and emerging practice-based knowledge production. The approach, therefore, acknowledges the importance of the rapidly developing action-based research now taking place around the world in establishing any state-of-the-art review.

The methodological framework was designed to enhance understanding of how geospatial technologies can help characterize perceived safety in the context of gender by exploring and reviewing relevant sources pertaining to either peer-reviewed literature or initiatives driven by practice. Peer-reviewed literature appraised current approaches that research has adopted to understand the perception of safety using GIS as a repeatable, science-based method. Initiatives driven by practice reviewed projects and apps that enable important work on the gender-based perception of safety; without necessarily being "scientific" they provide an important evidence-base to this field.

2.1 Literature-based review: methodological selection of research on geospatial research on women's safety

Literature was reviewed to identify common trends, strengths, and limitations among research papers that use geospatial technologies to map gendered perceptions of safety in urban spaces. A systematic search, screening, and data extraction from a set of peer-reviewed literature that met predefined inclusion and exclusion criteria were undertaken. Scopus, Web of Science, and ProQuest were chosen as they are three commonly used multidisciplinary databases, using a time frame of 1990 to November 2020, and only papers written in English were considered. The conceptual framework guiding the initial searching process consists of four steps (Fig. 9.2).

Having defined the research question, the overarching themes were recognized as: (a) GIS (b) Women (c) Safety (d) Perception, and (d) Urban space. The multidisciplinary nature of this field means that keywords used to identify publications may vary substantially. Although this was flagged as an issue implying that we may find a limited number of papers, we endeavored to use search terms capturing the essence of relevant publications that

Figure 9.2 Conceptual framework identifying the steps used to guide the search process.

met our criteria. In any case, citation chaining was used to help find more publications to counteract the impact of search term bias. Citation chaining is the process of sourcing useful and relevant references from a good research publication that is aligned with a research topic.

Inclusion and exclusion criteria were guided by the conceptual framework (Fig. 9.2), and did encompass:

a. Publications incorporating geospatial technologies, spatial analysis, or spatially acquired data. Emphasis on this was important for determining the varied nature of geospatial approaches available to researchers. Although spatial data can be more robust if temporal data is collected with it, we deemed it to not be a necessary criterion.

b. Publications elucidating how perception can be measured and analyzed using spatial concepts. In that way, publications that focused on capturing the perception of space or social influences (such as fear of crime) through a set of variables (e.g., lighting, social disorder) or binary measures (e.g., safe, or not safe) were considered.

c. Publications that collect gender-disaggregated data. This acknowledges that gender is a factor influencing the perception of safety.

Because we were interested in perception, publications that used GIS to record and map incidents of gender-based violence (GBV) were excluded. Narrowing the scope of our search to only include fear/perception as opposed to incidents of GBV was important to identify specific environmental parameters controlling perception and potential consequent behavior. Furthermore, research about fear or violence in private spaces was excluded, also where the methodology was not transparent.

The screening process involved two steps: all papers found through searching were organized by their titles to determine their likelihood of relevance to our study. Papers deemed relevant were included in the next step that focused on reviewing the abstract to see if they met the inclusion and exclusion criteria and if they were primary research. Papers remaining from these steps were analyzed in-depth to extract information relevant to this research (Table 9.3).

2.2 Practice-based review: selection of geospatial practices focused on women's safety

Geospatial methods have been incorporated into the selected projects for a variety of reasons such as to improve city safety,

Table 9.3 Information extracted from selected research papers and justification for extraction.

Information	Justification for extraction
Geographical scope	To detect any spatial patterns among the location of study areas
Keywords	To identify the varied use of keywords across disciplines
Target group	To identify the gender, age, economic, or cultural qualities noted among participants of each study
Number of participants	To identify the number of participants involved or data entries obtained
Data collection approach	To analyze the scope of methods used to collect data
How perception was measured	To analyze the scope of variables and techniques used to measure perception
Analytical approach	To analyze the scope of methods used to visualize and/or analyze data
Strengths	To identify common strengths associated with scope, spatial analysis, and data across papers
Limitations	To identify common limitations associated with scope, spatial analysis, and data across papers
Future research recommendations	To identify common future research recommendations according to each paper

increase awareness, or provide a story-telling platform for urban experiences without necessarily being driven by research. We found that such initiatives are often government-funded and therefore increasingly important policy influencers for developing gender-inclusive cities.

The initiatives selected to use a phone or web-based platform to gather, collate, visualize, or analyze spatial data relating to the perception of safety or incidents of gender-based violence. Although this chapter is about perceptions of safety, there are lessons that can be learned from these initiatives, even if their focus is to create awareness of gender-based violence incidents.

Initiatives were identified using word of mouth, browsing google, through papers in the literature review, or recommended by experts in the field. Initiatives were analyzed to determine their effectiveness with regards to their data collection methods, analysis approaches, and visualization techniques. Elements extracted are described in Table 9.4.

Table 9.4 Information extracted from selected initiatives and justification for extraction.

Information	Justification for extraction
Status	To indicate if the initiative is currently active, or has been suspended
Topic	To identify the focus of the initiative as gathering information on gender-based violence or safety feeling
Geographical scope	To detect any spatial patterns among the location of initiatives, and identify what is available to users globally
Target group	To identify the target group of the initiative
Real-time data	To determine the inclusion or exclusion of real-time data collection
How perception was measured	To analyze the scope of variables and techniques used to measure perception
Transparency of methodology	To determine the transparency of the methodology used to collect, analyze, and distribute data
Completeness of data	To identify the extent of disclosing whilst gathering data
Platform	To note if the initiative exists on a phone or web-based platform

3. Results: literature and practice-based

The two sets of results presented are our findings from the literature search and practice-based review based on their inclusion criteria (see the section on the methodological framework).

A total of 381 papers were found through the initial literature search. Of these, 82 were relevant to our study, of which 18 passed the inclusion criteria. A further three papers were sourced through citation chaining, giving a total of 21 publications (Table 9.5).

A set of 12 relevant practice-based—or in some cases evidence-based—initiatives that have been used to gather similar data, whether based on perceived safety or incidents of gender-based violence, were identified to have met the inclusion criteria.

3.1 Literature based results

As a growing field of research, past literature reviews have focused on the use of place-based analysis for fear of crime studies (Solymosi et al., 2020), mapping gendered experiences of the city (Datta and Ahmed, 2020; Priya Uteng et al., 2019), how specific urban environments can cause emotional distress (Gong et al., 2016), using qualitative methods to analyze fear of crime (Curtis, 2012), and the benefits and limitations associated

Table 9.5 Peer-reviewed literature that met the criteria for inclusion.

Paper	Citation	How perception was measured	Data collection approach	Analytical approach
Gender Mainstreaming in Urban Planning: The Potential of Geographic Information Systems and Open Data Sources	Carpio-Pinedo et al. (2019)	Visibility; capacity of seeing and being seen in public space	"Active network": Calculating the proximity (at most 80m) to a shop or metro station through network distance	Quantitative GIS (network analysis) and overlaying and intersecting open source (OS) data
The safe city: Developing of GIS tools for gender-oriented monitoring (on the example of Kharkiv City, Ukraine)	Fesenko et al. (2017)	State of the curb, walking path, access to community services, women's refuges, and lighting	Web-based safety audit completed via phones that collected data on 3 separate maps: mobility features, social infrastructure, and lighting	Survey123 and ArcGIS Online. Visualization of safety audit information across the three maps.
Women's safety perception assessment in an urban stream corridor: Developing a safety map based on qualitative GIS	Gargiulo et al. (2020)	Four spatial indicators for safety index values: lighting, vegetation density, visibility, and land use	14 in-depth interviews (map based and go-along) with women who use this green environment to identify influencing factors on perceived safety	Sequential mixed model of interviews and geo-data analysis (land use, land cover, imagery, DEM) to create a safety map
Gendered walkability: Building a daytime walkability index for women	Golan et al. (2019)	Crime, street cleanliness, parking lots, type of businesses, traffic, parks and open space, curb ramps, graffiti, and slope	Focus groups to identify the weighting of variables: what is considered most important for their walking	Mixed methodology: focus groups and density analysis on weighted variables to obtain a GIS-based walkability index
The shrinking world of girls at puberty: Violence and gender-divergent access to the public sphere among adolescents in South Africa	Hallman et al. (2015)	Asked to indicate specific areas and rate them on a scale of extremely safe to extremely unsafe	Primary and secondary school groups draw area to represent their community on a satellite image. Data was gender disaggregated to compare exposure to physical and social environments	The calculated average extent of areas perceived to be safe using participatory mapping and group discussions

Continued

Table 9.5 Peer-reviewed literature that met the criteria for inclusion.—*continued*

Paper	Citation	How perception was measured	Data collection approach	Analytical approach
Safer cities for women: Global and local innovations with open data and civic technology	Hawken et al. (2020b)	Urban specific parameters: lighting, public transport, openness, visibility, and walking path	Open Data of safety score for Bogota as calculated by SafetiPin used to establish safety-related metrics	Statistical analysis to see how urban parameters affect perceived safety, and an open interactive map
A Geospatial Mixed Methods Approach to Assessing Campus Safety	Hites et al. (2013)	Focus groups discuss safety concerns and mark "very dangerous", "dangerous", or "cause for concern", on maps	Students selected by stratified convenience sampling to ensure diversity in gender, ethnicity, academic status, and academic major	Mixed methods: focus groups and geospatial statistics (kernel density hotspot analysis) and campus crime data
GIS-Based Statistical Analysis of Detecting Fear of Crime with Digital Sketch Maps: A Hungarian Multicity Study	Jakobi and Pődör (2020)	Participants indicate areas as "Safe" or "Unsafe" by drawing polygons on the digital sketch map	Digital sketch maps and existing crime data. Online or web application promoted via social media channels. 41% female, 59% male	Digital sketch maps and statistical GIS. Created a grid-based model to compare results of cities
Bringing emotions to time geography: the case of mobilities of poverty	McQuoid and Dijst (2012)	Participants use photos and diaries whenever surroundings spark fear, e.g., on dark streets in the early hours of the day	Preliminary interviews with low-income single women along with photo and travel diaries to note emotions in time and space	Mixed methods: qualitative interviews, auto-photography, and travel diaries
The impact of urban tree cover on perceived safety	Mouratidis (2019)	Safety evaluated as "very low" to "very high". Socio-demographic data noted	Perceived safety, socio-demographic data, GIS data of canopy cover, and Oslo municipality data to create neighborhood deprivation index	Neighborhood deprivation index is used to analyze safety. GIS for buffer zones and to measuring the distance to a city

Table 9.5 Peer-reviewed literature that met the criteria for inclusion.—*continued*

Paper	Citation	How perception was measured	Data collection approach	Analytical approach
Analyzing the relationship between perception of safety and reported crime in an urban neighborhood using GIS and sketch maps	Ogneva-Himmelberger et al. (2019)	Respondents indicate on sketch map areas they feel unsafe and indicate why. Gender, age, and time spent living in the area are noted for comparison	Police reported crimes (point data) and perceptions of unsafe areas (polygon data). Perception data from door-to-door surveys. The location was chosen as deemed "persistent violent crime hotspot"	Geospatial analysis of crime perception data according to gender and length of residency AND comparison of crime data with perception
Comparing Residents' Fear of Crime with Recorded Crime Data-Case Study of Ostrava, Czech Republic	Pánek et al. (2019)	Points on the map marked where they feel unsafe. Type of crime and social disorder noted.	Police reported crimes and perception of unsafe areas. Perception data gathered through an online questionnaire	Spatial auto-correlation analysis: Moran's I and cluster mapping to compare fear of crime with recoded crimes
Mapping Emotions: Spatial Distribution of Safety Perception in the City of Olomouc	Pánek et al. (2017)	Place-points marked where they feel unsafe day and night. Gender, age, place of residence, frequency of visits to unsafe places and reasons are noted	Paper-based questionnaire on the street by trained interviewers and web-based crowdsourcing tool that authors created (PocitoveMapy.cz)	Spatial density analysis via hexagonal aggregation for geovisualization. Use of Spearman's rank correlation to analyze relationships among unsafe feelings
Spatial and Temporal Comparison of Safety Perception in Urban Spaces. Case Study of Olomouc, Opava and Jihlava	Pánek et al. (2018)	Places marked as feeling unsafe day and night. Gender, age, residence, frequency of visits, and reasons noted	Paper-based questionnaire by interviewers, web-based crowdsourcing tool that the authors created (PocitoveMapy.cz), and in-situ interviews	Geovisualization by hexagonal aggregate-ion. Cities compared to identify land uses and time related to feelings of unsafety
Gender differences in a walking environment safety perception: A case study in a	Rišová and Sládeková Madajová (2020)	3 cells on the map that feel unsafe day and night, and cells that are	Adolescents (13—16 yrs) that went to different schools within the same	Activity mapping to show areas deemed unsafe and/or unwalkable by

Continued

Table 9.5 Peer-reviewed literature that met the criteria for inclusion.—*continued*

Paper	Citation	How perception was measured	Data collection approach	Analytical approach
small town of Banská Bystrica (Slovakia)		inconvenient to walk in at day and night are selected	district. Large map of the area known as "the ward" was split into cells of 200 × 200m and was provided to each adolescent	gender and time of day. Gender differences tested through inferential statistics
Mapping fear of crime as a context-dependent everyday experience that varies in space and time	Solymosi et al. (2015)	App tests level of worry, "very worried"- "not at all worried". Public transport use and specific crime that is feared is noted	Participants from a university setting test app prototype that sends notifications to complete the survey or a report can be filled postevent	Experience sampling method and follow-up interviews to see if the app is good for place-based and real-time fear of crime
Disruption and design: Crowdmapping young women's experience in cities	Tanner et al. (2020)	"Good" or "Bad" spots on the *Free to Be* app, with an option to explain why	*Free to be* captures harassment events and perceived safety of young women in their cities	Online crowdsourcing tool and analysis of comments to reveal the extent of fear
SafetiPin: an innovative mobile app to collect data on women's safety in Indian cities	Viswanath and Basu (2015)	Rubric-based survey on light, walk path, gender usage, security, openness, public transport, visibility, and feeling	SafetiPin was launched to perform safety audits. Trained auditors and volunteers use App to collect safety information in various Indian cities	Visualization of safety scores per area calculated by fixed-effects regression model to see the influence on safety feeling
Exploring the Role of Transportation in Fostering Social Exclusion: The Use of GIS to Support Qualitative Data	McCray and Brais (2007)	Issues on public transport, places they go regularly, places they would like to go but cannot access, and personal safety	Low-income women participate in focus groups and self-mapping exercises of individual space	Spatio-temporal access analyzed via data coding. Standard distance spatial model to measure regular/occasional activities
Children's perception of their city center: a qualitative GIS methodological investigation in a Dutch city	Alarasi et al. (2016)	Stickers used for liked or disliked places, and photos taken of positive or negative places on guided tours	Children do participatory mapping, focus groups, guided tours, and interviews to identify physical and social reasons for liking or not liking places	Cluster mapping and coding of language to identify themes. A semantic differential scale used to aggregate perceptions

Table 9.5 Peer-reviewed literature that met the criteria for inclusion.—*continued*

Paper	Citation	How perception was measured	Data collection approach	Analytical approach
Visualizing geographies of perceived safety: an exploration of Muslim women's experiences in public space	Richter (2014)	A line was drawn for city/campus routines. Areas marked as safe, unsafe, neutral, or with an "x". Impact of wearing or not wearing a hijab on perceived safety. Photos taken of safe/unsafe areas	Women who work or go to school in Columbia were recruited to do surveys, sketch maps, a photography exercise, and follow-up interviews	Grounded theory coding to identify themes. Inverse distanced weighted interpolation for sketch map data

with the increased uptake of personal safety apps (Gstrein and van Eck, 2018). The results presented hereafter show a wide range of methodologies and analyses have been used to understand gendered perception, whether in the literature or through initiatives driven by practice.

Target groups were varied, with differences in gender, age, income, and cultural background. One-third of the papers focused solely on women, whilst the other two-thirds collected data that analyzed men and women, usually to compare the difference (Fig. 9.3). None of the papers focused on trans or gender-diverse groups. Age varied among target groups, ranging from young adolescents to middle-aged adults, whereas some papers used survey data, and age among participants was unclear. Income and culture were explored in some papers, but this changed depending on the focus of the paper. Physical disabilities were considered in one paper.

Keywords were highly varied across papers (Fig. 9.4). The main keywords relating to spatial criteria concepts included "GIS", "Geographic Information System", "Geovisualisation", "Crime mapping", and "Emotional mapping", whilst fear or perceived safety revealed that "Fear of crime", followed by "Subjective data", and "Emotional mapping" were the most consistently

Figure 9.3 A comparison of gender differences explored in a. publications and b. initiatives.

Figure 9.4 Word cloud showing the frequency of keywords used from the literature search. Place names were excluded. An "*" indicates that the word had similar outputs and was combined, e.g., "Adolescent" and "Adolescents". This figure was created using the word cloud resource, www.wordclouds.com.

used keywords to describe these studies. Gender-specific terms include "gender", "women", and "girls".

Some papers are inspired by high levels of crime within an area, while others focus on activity spaces such as green environments, public transport, university campuses, neighborhoods, or entire cities (Table 9.5).

Table 9.5 summarizes the variables assessed modes of data collection, and analytical approaches identified in the papers. Variables chosen to assess perceived safety were either focused on safe and unsafe locations or a set of variables related to the physical and social environment. Among these, some papers considered sociodemographic factors of participants, and how these might relate to perceived safety, while others were interested in sociodemographic features of the area in which the study took place.

The temporal aspect was not explored in all papers (Table 9.5), but some took into consideration the difference between day and night (Rišová and Sládeková Madajová, 2020) or collect their data in real-time (Solymosi et al., 2015; Pánek et al., 2018). Data was collected through digital means (crowdsourcing, apps, etc.), in-person with researchers (questionnaires, focus groups, sketch maps, etc.) or in their own time (routine activity diaries, photo journals, etc.). Sometimes secondary data sources were referenced to aid analysis, including aggregated data from government-issued household surveys, land use data, and local crime statistics. Analytical approaches were either quantitative, qualitative, or part of a mixed methodology. Depending on the aim of the paper, some were interested in visualizing data, while others engaged in data synthesis through geostatistical analyses.

3.2 Practice-based results

Our analysis of the set of 12 relevant phone or web-based platforms (Table 9.6) contrasted with the findings of the literature review in several ways. Unlike the peer-reviewed literature, the experience of trans, gender diverse, and members of the LGBTQ + community were recorded on two platforms (Fig. 9.3), She's a Crowd and Safecity. Since some of the platforms were not borne out of gender-based violence, data was not always gender disaggregated. Participants had options with regards to completing all fields in a survey, and behaviors or avoidance post-incident could also be noted. Some initiatives presented shortcomings in terms of transparency of the methodologies applied. Output and communication of results were common around those that had reports describing the usage of data. A common feature observed was that data is not available to users in nonaggregated forms (unless it is specifically requested, or a collaboration occurs).

Many active initiatives boast global accessibility, including SafetiPin, She's a Crowd, HarassMap, HollaBack!, and Safecity, while others may have been active in multiple cities, such as

Table 9.6 Initiatives of interest. The "×" means that the initiative does not require, does not have, or has no publicly available information about that aspect within its features.

	Active	Type of data	Where	Real-time	Variables measured	Postevent	Method	Completeness of data entry	Platform
SafetiPin (https://safetipin.com/)	Yes, launched in 2013	Safety feeling	Global; Began in India	Survey in real-time	Lighting, openness, visibility, walk path, people, security, public transport, gender usage, feeling	×	Available	Users must complete all fields	Phone and web-based
She's a Crowd (https://shesacrowd.com/)	Yes, launched in 2018	Safety feeling; GBV	Melbourne and Sydney, Australia	×	"Good" or "Bad" experience, land use, surroundings, time of day, year, incident, age, sexuality, and ethnicity	Personal impacts postincident	×	Not required	Web-based
Free to Be, Plan International (https://www.plan.org.au/you-can-help/join-the-movement-for-girls-rights/free-to-be/)	No, the study of 2016—18	Safety feeling; GBV	Sydney; Lima; Dehli; Melbourne; Madrid; Kampala	×	"Good" or "Bad" spot, followed by the opportunity to describe the experience	Events that ensued incident	Available	Not required	Web-based
HarassMap (https://harassmap.org/en/)	Yes, launched in 2012	GBV	Cairo, Egypt	×	Self or observed experiences of sexual harassment	×	Available	Not required	Web-based
Hollaback! (https://www.ihollaback.org//)	Yes, launched in 2013	GBV	Global; Began in the United States	×	Self/observed sexual harassment, followed by the type of harassment, and type of location, e.g., at school	×	×	Not required	Phone and web-based
Safecity (http://www.safecity.in/about/)	Yes, launched in 2012	GBV	Global; Began in India	×	Self or known incidents, age, time, date, and type of harassment	×	×	Users must complete all fields	Phone and web-based

Fear of Crime App, (Solymosi et al., 2020)	No, the study of 2011	Safety feeling	London, England	Survey in real-time	The scale of worry in being a victim of crime and type of crime, "not at all worried" to "very worried"	×	Available	Users must complete all fields	Phone-based
GeoBAT, (Jeantete, 2019)	No, the study of 2019	Safety feeling	Albuquerque, United States	Survey in real-time	Perceived safety through the Likert scale, "Feel safe" to "Unsafe", and on surroundings or people	Avoidance of area postevent	Available	Users must complete all fields	Phone-based
Safety App, (Deshmukh et al., 2020)	Yes, launched in 2020	Safety feeling	Mumbai, India	×	The scale of lighting, walk path, visibility, security, and transport	×	Available	Users must complete all fields	Phone-based
Geography of crime fear, (Chataway et al., 2017)	No, the study of 2017	Safety feeling	Gold Coast, Australia	Survey in real-time	Scale for frequency of worry, likelihood, control, a consequence of victimization, and on surroundings or people	×	Available	Not required	Phone-based
PocitoveMapy.cz (https://www.pocitovemapy.cz/)	Yes, launched in 2015	Safety feeling	Olomouc, Opava and Jihlava, Czech Republic	×	"Safe" or "unsafe" areas as points and/or polygons during the day and at night	×	Available	Users must complete all fields	Web-based
Safe and the City (https://safeandthecity.com/)	Yes, launched in 2019	GBV	London and Berlin	×	Self or observed experiences of unsafety used to predict safety throughout the city	×	×	Not required	Phone-based

Free to Be, and PocitoveMapy.cz. Cities in India, Australia, and the United States have had the most initiatives (see Table 9.6).

4. Discussion

This chapter set out to identify if and how intelligent spatial technologies are being used to capture gendered perceptions of safety in urban space and time; and if so, the extent of current uptake and the type of applications—both in the literature and in praxis. Our findings suggest that such tools can provide more detailed information that can be used to inform policy and, in turn, be used to develop gender-inclusive spaces according to three main themes. Firstly, current approaches highlight gender but do not always adopt a critical approach to gendered experiences. Secondly, geospatial technologies have only partially addressed safety perceptions, and thirdly, there is wide scope for future research and recommendations for policy. The themes affirm current practice-based approaches but also challenge them in particular ways. We, therefore, conclude with a series of recommendations for practice and have summarized these in Box 9.2.

4.1 Deepening dimensions of gender-inclusive spaces

Our first finding is that whilst the various dimensions of gender-inclusive spaces have been radically expanded through recent research and practice there remain gaps for underdeveloped dimensions also in the way such dimensions relate to space

(1) Gender diversity: broaden and deepen dimensions of gendered safety perceptions. Gendered perceptions of safety in city spaces are diverse and need to be studied in more holistic ways. Future work must include the experiences of women, trans, nonbinary, and gender-diverse individuals.

(2) Novel geospatial methods: innovation with emerging mobile geospatial methods and technologies. Geospatial technologies offer a myriad of spatially sound analyses that can be used to understand trends in perceptions of safety across space and time.

(3) Authentic research: codesign and integration of users in research and data collections and interpretation. This engages with communities that are generally marginalized or not represented in decision-making positions.

and time. The adoption of gender-responsive approaches means considering principles of a gender-inclusive city and how these can be embedded into planning, but also a deeper understanding of how and why space is experienced differently. Whilst our review highlighted the myriad of ways gendered experiences of safety have been explored (Tables 9.5 and 9.6), we note knowledge gaps remain in; identifying how the intersection of age, ethnicity, and socioeconomic status among other factors affect these gendered perceptions; how the spatiality of mobility constraints across time are manifested; and how the inclusion of LGBTQ+ and gender-diverse experiences are best addressed. These varying dimensions of gendered safety intersect in important ways and we have presented this in Fig. 9.5.

Publications focused on gendered accessibility to urban spaces explored how: (a) school-aged students access their neighborhoods at different developmental stages (Hallman et al., 2015), (b) women in lower socio-economic situations utilized public transport systems (McCray and Brais, 2007), (c) university-aged students access their campus (Hites et al., 2013), and (d) adult women engage with green environments (Mouratidis, 2019; Gargiulo et al., 2020) (Table 9.5). Each of these papers focuses on a specific group of people based on age, education, ability, and socioeconomic status, and doing so acknowledges that perceptions can differ based on these identities. The intersection of these variables, however, is yet to be geo-spatially explored. Going that

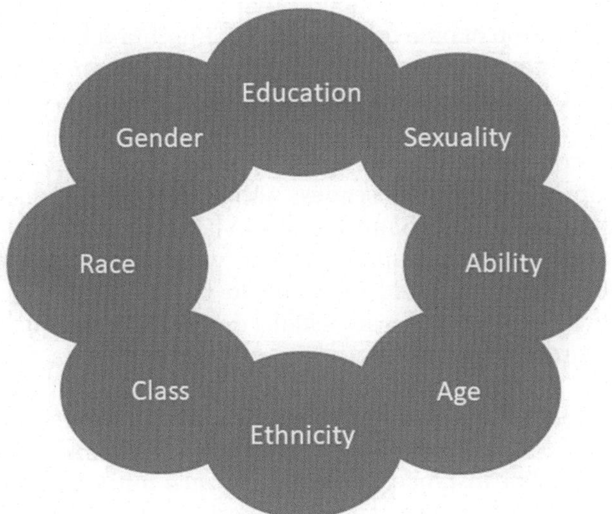

Figure 9.5 Visual representation of intersectionality.

further step means that each aspect of a person's identity is engaged in a meaningful way to understand how this may shape fear and perception of space (Fig. 9.5). This is especially true in social research, as is the case for urban planning (Cho et al., 2013). The relationship between people and their environment is complex and being able to understand social and personal variables driving the inclusion or exclusion of people across space must be considered.

Safety through design is another relevant aspect of gender-inclusive spaces (Fig. 9.1). Although gender-based violence is a social phenomenon, there are certain environments that increase fear (Koskela and Pain, 2000; Loukaitou-Sideris and Fink, 2008) and where crime is more likely to occur (Ceccato, 2016). Gargiulo et al. (2020) and the practice-based initiative *SafetiPin* are both examples of how data can be collected on these aspects to understand how specific landscape features can be experienced differently. Gargiulo et al. (2020) applied spatial analysis to four GIS-based variables (lighting, vegetation density, visibility, and land use) recognized to affect women's perception of safety in an urban stream corridor of Barcelona. Their research shows that routes used by women were based on these perceptions, and thus specific areas were avoided. It also exemplifies how such variables can be very much localized to specific environments. On the other hand, the extensive database—both spatially and temporally—of *SafetiPin* is based on safety audits carried out in more than 20 cities worldwide. Their phone-based platform "MySafetiPin", enables users to input their age and gender, and complete a rubric-based questionnaire that gathers information about their perception of nine parameters: lighting, openness, visibility, walk path, people, security, public transport, gender usage, and safety feeling (Viswanath and Basu, 2015). The report is completed in real-time and is geotagged. This data is used to make safety scores that can be used by planners and policy makers to improve urban landscapes. Although *SafetiPin* does well in collecting large data volumes that can be easily repeatable across different geographic spaces, other variables triggering "fear"—such as those explored by Gargiulo et al. (2020)— are not considered. Those variables are usually derived through qualitative analysis can help understand more localized factors that may be limiting access and mobility. Asking questions about specific localities helps to identify what urban spaces limit access, especially when people have the option to say if and how they avoid such areas. For instance, the *She's a Crowd* initiative asks participants if their experience happened in private, such as being at someone's house, at their workplace, or at home, or if their experience happened in public such as when they were walking, cycling, at school or university, in transit, or in a public space.

Our results indicate that avoidance of area is linked with mobility, and there is scope and potential for advancing understanding of how perception impacts this. Gauvin et al. (2020) present a model for understanding gender differences in mobility using Big Data. Their research use call records to determine patterns of movement, locations visited and duration of stay in a place, disaggregated by gender, as a proxy of perception. It exemplifies the way large-scale data can be used to recognize gendered spatio-temporal trends in mobility, indicating the interest and potential such technologies offer to understand access inequities, especially considering the increasingly relevant notion of Smart Cities (Singh, 2019).

Our review shows the broad aspects of "mobility": in the context of walkability (Rišová and Sládeková Madajová, 2020), access to services (Fesenko et al., 2017), physical activity(Gargiulo et al., 2020), public transport (McCray and Brais, 2007), and general movement throughout a city (McQuoid and Dijst, 2012; Carpio-Pinedo et al., 2019). McCray and Brais (2007) show the negative consequences of designing a public transport network in Quebec without gender considerations. More to the point, women's perceptions are that these networks do not cater to them, especially if they have children or if they need to move from place to place to access certain services. These findings highlight that transport networks must consider the fact that routines and responsibilities differ among people and should hence cater to those to avoid social exclusion. Drawing on the stories of these women helps paint a picture of mobility needs across groups of people, and since the perception of safety does limit women when they move through urban places, such experiences can provide the information required for urban change to account for gender diversity. This is becoming increasingly important when considering such a concept as the 30-minute city (Levinson, 2020), where the perception of safety has not been considered an important factor with regard to smart mobility.

Further complications arise when cis- and heteronormative assumptions are applied to the collection and analysis of data. This phenomenon is evident in the research analyzed, which either focused only women's experiences or compared male versus female (Fig. 9.3, Table 9.5). Only a third of the research focused on women's experiences —and made little to no inquiry as to how their gender affected that experience— but instead analyzed this as an independent variable. Moreover, none of the papers focused on gender-diverse, trans, nonbinary, or genderqueer experiences. LGBTQ + experiences were also not considered. Whilst there is a growing body of research about gender-diverse experiences across space (Doan, 2007, 2010; Lubitow et al., 2017, 2020; Browne et al., 2010), we struggled to find publications that engaged with this in a spatially explicit way. Two out of 12 initiatives collect data on gender-diverse individuals, but only one of those considers the impact of belonging to the LGBTQ + community.

Current tech approaches are not critical enough. They highlight gender disparity rather than focusing on the implications of this within women's lives. To address this, codesign, the fourth principle of a gender-inclusive city (Fig. 9.1), requires that we listen to the voices and stories of those who are marginalized (Sanders, 2000; Michiel de and Martijn de, 2013), to include more women, trans, and gender diverse individuals through community engagement (Bawden and Edwards, 2018). Giving a voice to women of all sociodemographic backgrounds, and those who exist outside the gender binary spectrum is important to understand how to cater to their needs. In this regard, our review shows that data is not often collected with marginalized groups in mind. The Committee for Sydney (2019) in collaboration with Plan International Australia and Monash University XYX Lab presents an example of using crowdsourcing data, and the integration of women and girls in focus groups to brainstorm ways design could include them.

Lastly, all research publications in this analysis fail to consider gender that exists outside the binary. *She's a crowd* addresses this discrepancy by collecting stories of women, trans, gender diverse, and from members of the LGBTQ + community. All forms of gender-based violence and safety perception are noted—sexual assault is as valid as street harassment, intimidation, or general lack of comfortability in a place. It is vital that urban design reflects such principles, that marginalized voices are being heard, and that there is increased representation in policy and planning sectors.

Geospatial methods inform future research on perceptions of urban gender safety.

Whilst research and practice have identified a range of ways that gender-inclusive spaces can be defined, how these can then be mapped remains a challenge across a number of fronts including resolution, scale, time, and accuracy of attributes and inclusive dimensions.

Geospatial analysis approaches varied throughout publications. Whilst all use spatial data, only 14 out of 21 papers performed spatial analysis using their data. Some of these analyses include spatial statistics, spatial autocorrelation analyses, network analyses, kernel density estimations, hotspot analyses, spatio-temporal analyses, spatial interpolation, standard distance spatial modeling, and spatially weighted summation.

Capturing the complex nature of perceptions and emotions through geospatial approaches has its challenges, and our findings suggest there is potential for more inquiry into how to use these to measure perception. All research publications and practice-based initiatives analyzed have different ways of understanding and measuring perception, and it is not clear how to assess the effectiveness of the approaches used. Table 9.7 lists

Table 9.7 Elements of research when using geospatial approaches to address social problems.

Element	Relevant questions
Spatial scale	Should I do a neighborhood or city-level analysis? Will my analyses be localized or repeatable across space? Should I analyze a specific land use?
Spatial data	Should I collect data in point, polygon, or line form, or use a mix of all three? How should I convert qualitative data into spatial layers?
Variables	To assess perception, is it best to analyze "safe" and "unsafe" spots, a set of environmental parameters, or identify common themes in interviews?
Temporal scale	Should I collect real-time data, ask about perception during the day and night, or ask participants to recall stories from the past?
Social value	Is it best to collect data that is socially rich? Should I compare the experience of men, women, trans, and gender-diverse people? Is intersectionality important?
Participants	How many participants should I include in my research? Should they belong to the same social setting, e.g., a university?
Research method	Should my research be qualitative, quantitative, or part of a mixed methodology framework?
Analysis	Should I use density, network, or data coding analysis? How can I present the data in a meaningful way with geovisualization?
Data completion	How important is it that participants answer all elements of a survey? Should data be reflective of more people or be consistent and comparable?
Post-event	Is it important to collect data on how participants interact with space after an experience they have had?
Policy	Should I create a product that can be used by planners or implemented in policy? What kind of data is needed to do so?
Platform	Should I use a phone or web-based platform? Should it be crowdsourced from the general population, or from a specific sample of people?

elements and some relevant questions identified in the literature and reports reviewed. Two research projects reviewed (Box 9.3) exemplify the huge variability in accessibility, collection of temporal data, sampling size, and data completeness.

The elements in Table 9.7 can guide the stages of research design and implementation. Each choice entails benefits and limitations, and there is not a "one size fits all approach", as evidenced by the results of the literature review. One trade-off previously discussed seems to be if data is socially rich, then it is likely to not be spatially rich. Good spatial data will usually be linked to both space and time, complete (i.e., every question in a survey answered), and easily comparable and thus repeatable. Often when data is spatially rich, it lacks the complexity relating to perception, especially with regard to the variety of experiences faced by many in urban space, such as the evidence obtained from *She's a Crowd,* which considered gender diverse experiences. Some research papers compare gendered perception to crime rates against women and men (Jakobi and Pődör, 2020; Pánek et al., 2017). Though results can be easily compared and spatially sound, associating this to gendered fear presents issues. It is known that crimes against women, especially with regard to gender-based violence are underreported (Australian Bureau of

Solymosi et al. (2015) present a prototype of a phone-based app that can be used to detect fear of crime in a robust way that considers time and place and recruit six university students for its piloting. The questionnaire collects the level of worry about the fear of crime in real-time or after the fact, mode of transport, and the type of crime that they are fearful of. Whereas capturing geolocation data that is tagged with the participant's perceived safety at the moment is a clear benefit for analysis and modeling, the app does not collect gender-disaggregated data, nor does it ask for an explanation as to why the participant was fearful, aside from identifying the type of crime they were fearful of.

Tanner et al. (2020) describe the methodology and results of the *Free to Be* project, a web-based platform launched in Sydney, Kampala, Delhi, Lima, and Madrid after an initial pilot in the city of Melbourne. The aim was to capture the extent of street harassment faced by young women and their experiences of feeling safe or unsafe through an open and accessible crowdsourcing tool. While on the web-based platform, participants can anonymously geotag a location as a "good" or "bad" spot and can describe their experience if they wish. The experiences could be recent, or from a long time ago. Large sums of data are collected, but due to the nature of accessible platforms, a lot of useless data was generated that need to be cleaned. Regardless, data was comparable across all five cities (21,200 valid pins). One of the issues with this data was its lack of completeness—a spot could be noted as "good" or "bad", but we cannot infer any reasons unless we have more information.

Statistics, 2016), and hence, unrepresentative with regard to reported crimes. Such comparisons may also propagate a culture where women are fearful for no reason.

The ability to capture data in real-time is very useful for geospatial analysis (Solymosi et al., 2020) including the opportunity to use spatio-temporal analyses and modeling. Creating tools that can do so allows for analysis of factors associated with perception at the moment, as opposed to recalling an event, which has been known to cause issues in fear of crime research in the past (Table 9.1). Having the option to complete a report after the fact, is good for promoting safe reporting. If an incident occurs that causes someone to be severely concerned about becoming a victim of crime, it is more important to remove themselves from that situation (if possible), than it is to stand there and report the level of fear. Not all platforms allow for this, such as the case for *SafetiPin*, meaning that reports made at the moment might not be representative of the extent of fear within an area that causes high levels of fear. The *Free to Be* platform does not require participants to time-tag an experience (Tanner et al., 2020), and this optional, rather than the default, the inclusion of temporal elements, and challenge analysis. Although geospatial approaches such as an analysis of spatial autocorrelation can help identify how and if data are related in space, completeness of data can very quickly become a limiting factor. Regardless, the stories that are written hold a lot of depth in language that can be used to understand the underlying social, physical, and temporal factors that impact fear in young women, and arguably, the nonforceful manner is better equipped for capturing sensitive data. The accessible nature of the *Free to Be* platform also targeted young women across five cities and was primarily interested in showcasing the extent of street harassment, sexual assault, and a sense of fear that was not uncommon among young people, regardless of where they are in the world. Being able to compare these experiences across cities is very useful and can say a lot about gender-inclusivity.

4.2 Integrating gender with geospatial technologies for an inclusive planning future

Fear of crime, GIS, and gendered experiences in cityscapes are very detailed areas of research but are not linked in the geospatial world. Our findings evidence the potential gains and benefits from better linking them for advancing the agenda of gender-inclusive spaces. Publications reviewed point to ongoing research needs around a range of aspects but also highlight a lack of integration between them.

Linking the perceived landscape to the physical landscape to discern spaces of vulnerability warrants discussion. This is essentially how geospatial technologies can be used in the future to delve deeper into how this phenomenon persists over space and time. For example, fuzzy logic could be used to represent and model the gray area of what is perceived to be a safe or unsafe space. A finer detailed analysis following the detection of hotspots could be done to find these areas that cause fear. To that end, the focus on specific urban spaces such as parks, transport nodes, schools, universities, etc. would also prove useful for planners when designing any of those public spaces. Further consideration of the importance and weighting of physical, social, and temporal factors affecting perception is also needed. The spatial nature of social exclusion behaviors due to mobility or accessibility constraints is another interesting topic.

Many of the above concepts are to do with the complexity of perception, and the importance of intersectionality and community consultation. The personal, subjective, and sensitive aspects of gender make its study complex. Our final finding is that there is a need for better and more authentic ways to capture and integrate data. Such integration can come through participatory approaches as several papers (Fesenko et al., 2017; Gargiulo et al., 2020; Hawken et al., 2020b) and practices (Tanner et al., 2020) suggest. Using participatory approaches in this way can aid in the codesign of spaces (Shaw, 2016), and in collecting data with the right level of detail to implement change. The most powerful initiatives link data to evidence-based action with government agencies and planning projects. Such tech approaches include *She's a Crowd* and *HarassMap,* which engage constituents meaningfully through data activism and education. The accessibility of initiatives (and their reach to marginalized communities) should be combined with research-backed analyses. We need stronger geospatial data that meets the criteria for detail that local government and planners require to write policy and develop the built environment, but also needs to incorporate that sensitive element to be more reconciled. The success of all initiatives relies on making them more authentic with their subject groups. This information can be used to humanize Smart Cities approaches. The potential to analyze this data geospatially is infinite.

5. Conclusion

This chapter explored how the application of geospatial technologies—both in data collection and analysis—can be used to measure and understand women's perception of safety and subsequently help to build an evidence base to develop gender-inclusive spaces. The gendered power imbalance and inequity that exists within cities requires us to have a deeper understanding of how city design and other environments are contributing to this.

Current approaches to map the perception of safety in open spaces highlight gender but do not always adopt a critical approach to gendered experiences. Gender safety, and its perception, in city spaces, needs to extend beyond women, to include the trans, nonbinary, and gender-diverse community. Including the voices of those who are marginalized through codesign will improve cities for all making them safer and building stronger communities.

There is potential for increased uptake of geospatial technologies to understand women's perceptions of safety, and to draw lessons on a standardized set of variables that can be measured across space and time. In that way, geospatial technologies have only partially addressed safety perceptions. There are challenges associated with measuring perception, including but not limited to the variables used to represent this, or which personal factors such as age or income are important to consider. The world of GIS is vast, and so too is the potential to use these tools to understand the gendered perception of space. Our research suggests various ways forward and highlights the following gaps. In that way, determining the most effective ways of using geospatial technologies to understand the safety perception of public spaces from the perspective of gender requires further inquiry.

Here it is helpful to remind ourselves that "gender equality is not only a fundamental human right, but a necessary foundation for a peaceful, prosperous and sustainable world" (UN, 2015). As innovative centers of commerce and wealth generation, cities present profound opportunities to address gender-based inequity that remains so entrenched in cities around the world. In this chapter, we have outlined emerging and promising ways to address such inequalities through geospatial approaches. Such geospatial approaches are not simple technical approaches but rely on the careful and dedicated development of intelligent socio-technological systems that are developed by social entrepreneurs and the communities with which they collaborate.

References

Alarasi, H., Martinez, J., Amer, S., 2016. Children's perception of their city centre: a qualitative GIS methodological investigation in a Dutch city. Children's Geographies 14, 437–452.

Australian Bureau of Statistics, 2016. Personal Safety, Australia: Statistics for Family, Domestic, Sexual Violence, Physical Assault, Partner Emotional Abuse, Child Abuse, Sexual Harassment, Stalking and Safety. Australian Bureau of Statistics. Available from: https://www.abs.gov.au/statistics/people/crime-and-justice/personal-safety-australia/latest-release#experience-of-violence. (Accessed 30 March 2021).

Bawden, G., Edwards, A., 2018. Pride of place: Co-design, community engagement and the victorian pride centre. Fusion Journal 43–63.

Beebeejaun, Y., 2017. Gender, urban space, and the right to everyday life. Journal of Urban Affairs 39, 323–334.

Boessen, A., Hipp, J.R., Butts, C.T., Nagle, N.N., Smith, E.J., 2017. Social fabric and fear of crime: considering spatial location and time of day. Social Networks 51, 60–72.

Boomsma, C., Steg, L., 2014. Feeling safe in the dark: examining the effect of entrapment, lighting levels, and gender on feelings of safety and lighting policy acceptability. Environment and Behavior 46, 193–212.

Boschmann, E.E., Cubbon, E., 2014. Sketch maps and qualitative GIS: using cartographies of individual spatial narratives in geographic research. The Professional Geographer 66, 236–248.

Browne, K., Nash, C.J., Hines, S., 2010. Introduction: towards trans geographies. Gender, Place & Culture 17, 573–577.

Carpio-Pinedo, J., De Gregorio Hurtado, S., Sánchez De Madariaga, I., 2019. Gender mainstreaming in urban planning: the potential of geographic information systems and open data sources. Planning Theory & Practice 20, 221–240.

Ceccato, V., 2016. Public space and the situational conditions of crime and fear. International Criminal Justice Review 26, 69–79.

Ceccato, V., 2017. Women's victimisation and safety in transit environments. Crime Prevention and Community Safety 19, 163–167.

Chataway, M.L., Hart, T.C., 2019. A social-psychological process of "fear of crime" for men and women: revisiting gender differences from a new perspective. Victims & Offenders 14, 143–164.

Chataway, M.L., Hart, T.C., Coomber, R., Bond, C., 2017. The geography of crime fear: a pilot study exploring event-based perceptions of risk using mobile technology. Applied Geography 86, 300–307.

Cho, S., Crenshaw, K., McCall, L., 2013. Toward a field of intersectionality studies: theory, applications, and praxis. Signs 38, 785–810.

Chowdhury, S., Van Wee, B., 2020. Examining women's perception of safety during waiting times at public transport terminals. Transport Policy 94, 102–108.

Committee for Sydney, 2019. Safety after Dark: Creating a City for Women Living and Working in Sydney. Commitee for Sydney, Sydney.

Curtis, J.W., 2012. Integrating sketch maps with GIS to explore fear of crime in the urban environment: a review of the past and prospects for the future. Cartography and Geographic Information Science 39, 175–186.

Datta, A., Ahmed, N., 2020. Mapping gendered infrastructures: critical reflections on violence against women in India. Architectural Design 90, 104–111.

Deshmukh, A., Banka, S., Dcruz, S.B., Shaikh, S., Tripathy, A.K., 2020. Safety App: Crime Prediction Using GIS. 2020 3rd International Conference on Communication System, Computing and IT Applications (CSCITA).
Doan, P.L., 2007. Queers in the American City: Transgendered Perceptions of Urban Space, vol. 14, pp. 57–74.
Doan, P.L., 2010. The tyranny of gendered spaces – reflections from beyond the gender dichotomy. Gender, Place & Culture 17, 635–654.
Doran, B., Burgess, M., 2012. Putting Fear of Crime on the Map: Investigating Perceptions of Crime Using Geographic Information Systems. Springer, New York.
Dymén, C., Ceccato, V., 2011. An international perspective of the gender dimension in planning for urban safety. In: The Urban Fabric of Crime and Fear. Springer Netherlands.
Ferraro, K.F., 1995. Fear of Crime: Interpreting Victimization Risk. State Univ. of New York Press, Albany.
Fesenko, T., Fesenko, G., Bibik, N., 2017. The safe city: developing of GIS tools for gender-oriented monitoring (on the example of Kharkiv City, Ukraine). Eastern-European Journal of Enterprise Technologies 3, 25–33.
Franklin, C.A., Franklin, T.W., 2009. Predicting fear of crime. Feminist Criminology 4, 83–106.
Gardner, N., Cui, J., Coiacetto, E., 2017. Harassment on public transport and its impacts on women's travel behaviour. Australian Planner 54, 8–15.
Gargiulo, I., Garcia, X., Benages-Albert, M., Martinez, J., Pfeffer, K., Vall-Casas, P., 2020. Women's safety perception assessment in an urban stream corridor: developing a safety map based on qualitative GIS. Landscape and Urban Planning 198, 103779.
Gauvin, L., Tizzoni, M., Piaggesi, S., Young, A., Adler, N., Verhulst, S., Ferres, L., Cattuto, C., 2020. Gender gaps in urban mobility. Humanities and Social Sciences Communications 7, 1–13.
Golan, Y., Wilkinson, N.L., Henderson, J., Weverka, A., 2019. Gendered walkability: building a daytime walkability index for women. Journal of Transport and Land Use 12, 501–526.
Gong, Y., Palmer, S., Gallacher, J., Marsden, T., Fone, D., 2016. A systematic review of the relationship between objective measurements of the urban environment and psychological distress. Environment International 96, 48–57.
Gstrein, O.J., van Eck, G.J.R., 2018. Mobile devices as stigmatizing security sensors: the GDPR and a future of crowdsourced 'broken windows. International Data Privacy Law 8, 69–85.
Hale, C., 1996. Fear of crime: a review of the literature. International Review of Victimology 4, 79–150.
Hallman, K.K., Kenworthy, N.J., Diers, J., Swan, N., Devnarain, B., 2015. The shrinking world of girls at puberty: violence and gender-divergent access to the public sphere among adolescents in South Africa. Global Public Health 10, 279.
Han, H, Hawken, S, 2018. Introduction: innovation and identity in next-generation smart cities. City, Culture and Society 12, 1–4. https://doi.org/10.1016/j.ccs.2017.12.003.
Hawken, S., Han, H., Pettit, C., 2020a. Introduction: Open Data and the Generation of Urban Value. Open Cities, Open Data: Collaborative Cities in the Information Era.

Hawken, S., Leao, S., Gudes, O., Izadpanahi, P., Viswanath, K., Pettit, C., 2020b. Safer Cities for Women: Global and Local Innovations with Open Data and Civic Technology. Open Cities | Open Data.

Heinrichs, D., Bernet, J.S., 2014. Public transport and accessibility in informal settlements: aerial cable cars in Medellín, Colombia. Transportation Research Procedia 4, 55–67.

Hillier, B., Hanson, J., 1984. The Social Logic of Space. Cambridge University Press, Cambridge.

Hites, L.S., Fifolt, M., Beck, H., Su, W., Kerbawy, S., Wakelee, J., Nassel, A., 2013. A geospatial mixed methods approach to assessing campus safety. Evaluation Review 37, 347–369.

ICLEI, UITP, 2020. Promoting Safe and Sustainable Cities with Public Transport for the SDGs. ICLEI - Local Governments for Sustainability, Brussels.

Jackson, J., 2005. Validating new measures of the fear of crime. International Journal of Social Research Methodology 8, 297–315.

Jacobs, J., 1972. The Death and Life of Great American Cities. Harmondsworth, Penguin.

Jakobi, Á., Pődör, A., 2020. GIS-based statistical analysis of detecting fear of crime with digital sketch maps: a Hungarian multicity study. ISPRS International Journal of Geo-Information 9, 229.

Jeantete, B.A., 2019. GeoBAT: crowdsourcing dynamic perception of safety data through the integration of mobile GIS and ecological momentary assessments. In: Master of Science (Geographic Information Science and Technology). University of Southern California.

Jeffery, C.R., 1971. Crime Prevention Through Environmental Design 14, 598-598.

Kalms, N., Condliffe, Z., Matthewson, G., Salen, P., Edwards, A., Bawden, G., 2018. Girl Walk: Identity, GIS Technology and Safety in the City for Women and Girls. SOAC 2017 Australian Cities Research Network.

Koskela, H., Pain, R., 2000. Revisiting fear and place: women's fear of attack and the built environment. Geoforum 31, 269–280.

Lagrange, R.L., Ferraro, K.F., 1989. Assessing age and gender differences in perceived risk and fear of crime. Criminology 27, 697–720.

Lagrange, R.L., Ferraro, K.F., Supancic, M., 1992. Perceived risk and fear of crime: role of social and physical incivilities. Journal of Research in Crime and Delinquency 29, 311–334.

Levinson, D., 2020. The 30-minute City: Small Decisions for Big Gains. I Move Australia. Available from: https://imoveaustralia.com/thoughtpiece/30-minute-city/>. (Accessed 30 March 2021).

Li, W., Batty, M., Goodchild, M.F., 2020. Real-time GIS for smart cities. International Journal of Geographical Information Science 34, 311–324.

Li, X., Zhang, C., Li, W., 2015. Does the visibility of greenery increase perceived safety in urban areas? Evidence from the Place Pulse 1.0 Dataset 4, 1166–1183.

Loukaitou-Sideris, A., 2006. Is it safe to walk? Neighborhood safety and security considerations and their effects on walking. Journal of Planning Literature 20, 219–232.

Loukaitou-Sideris, A., Fink, C., 2008. Addressing women's fear of victimization in transportation settings: a survey of U.S. transit agencies. Urban Affairs Review 44, 554–587.

Lubitow, A., Abelson, M.J., Carpenter, E., 2020. Transforming mobility justice: gendered harassment and violence on transit. Journal of Transport Geography 82, 102601.

Lubitow, A., Carathers, J., Kelly, M., Abelson, M., 2017. Transmobilities: mobility, harassment, and violence experienced by transgender and gender nonconforming public transit riders in Portland, Oregon. Gender, Place & Culture 24, 1398–1418.

Lynch, K., 1960. The Image of the City. The M.I.T. Press, Massachusetts.

McCray, T., Brais, N., 2007. Exploring the role of transportation in fostering social exclusion: the use of GIS to support qualitative data. Networks and Spatial Economics 7, 397–412.

McQuoid, J., Dijst, M., 2012. Bringing emotions to time geography: the case of mobilities of poverty. Journal of Transport Geography 23, 26–34.

Mellgren, C., Andersson, M., Ivert, A.-K., 2018. It happens all the time": women's experiences and normalization of sexual harassment in public space. Women & Criminal Justice 28, 262–281.

Michiel de, L., Martijn de, W., 2013. Owning the City: New Media and Citizen Engagement in Urban Design, vol. 18. First Monday.

Mouratidis, K., 2019. The impact of urban tree cover on perceived safety. Urban Forestry & Urban Greening 44, 126434.

Newman, O., 1972. Defensible Space: Crime Prevention through Urban Design. Macmillan.

Ogneva-Himmelberger, Y., Ross, L., Caywood, T., Khananayev, M., Starr, C., 2019. Analyzing the relationship between perception of safety and reported crime in an urban neighborhood using GIS and sketch maps. ISPRS International Journal of Geo-Information 8, 531.

Pain, R.H., 1997. Social geographies of women's fear of crime. Transactions of the Institute of British Geographers 22, 231–244.

Pánek, J., 2018. Emotional Maps: Participatory Crowdsourcing of Citizens' Perceptions of Their Urban Environment, vol. 91. Cartographic Perspectives.

Pánek, J., Ivan, I., Macková, L., 2019. Comparing residents' fear of crime with recorded crime data—case study of Ostrava, Czech Republic. ISPRS International Journal of Geo-Information 8, 401.

Pánek, J., Paszto, V., Marek, L., 2017. Mapping emotions: spatial distribution of safety perception in the city of Olomouc. In: Ivan, I., Singleton, A., Horak, J., Inspektor, T. (Eds.), Rise of Big Spatial Data.

Pánek, J., Paszto, V., Simacek, P., 2018. Spatial and temporal comparison of safety perception in urban spaces. Case study of Olomouc, Opava and Jihlava. In: Ivan, I., Horak, J., Inspektor, T. (Eds.), Dynamics in Giscience.

Pérez Tejera, F., 2012. Differences between users of six public parks in Barcelona depending on the level of perceived safety in the neighborhood. Athenea Digital Revista de pensamiento e investigación social 12, 55.

Plan International, 2018. Free to Be in Lima. Plan International, United Kingdom.

Priya Uteng, T., Singh, Y.J., Lam, T., 2019. Safety and daily mobilities of urban women-Methodolgies to confront the policy of "invisibility. In: Measuring Transport Equity. Elsevier.

Rahm, J., Sternudd, C., Johansson, M., 2021. In the evening, I don't walk in the park": the interplay between street lighting and greenery in perceived safety. Urban Design International 26, 42–52.

Richter, C., 2014. Visualizing Geographies of Perceived Safety : An Exploration of Muslim Women's Experiences in Public Space.

Rišová, K., Sládeková Madajová, M., 2020. Gender differences in a walking environment safety perception: a case study in a small town of Banská Bystrica (Slovakia). Journal of Transport Geography 85.

Sanders, E.B.-N., 2000. Generative Tools for Co-designing. Springer London, London, pp. 3–12.

Sassen, S., 2015. Built Gendering. Design Magazine. Available from: http://www.harvarddesignmagazine.org/issues/41/built-gendering. (Accessed 31 March 2021).
Shaw, M., 2013. How do we evaluate the safety of women? In: Whitzman, C. (Ed.), Building Inclusive Cities Women's Safety and the Right to the City. Routledge, New York.
Shaw, M., 2016. Women as Actors in Community Safety: Taking Action Worldwide. Women and Children as Victims and Offenders: Background, Prevention, Reintegration. Springer International Publishing.
Singh, Y.J., 2019. Is smart mobility also gender-smart? Journal of Gender Studies 1–15.
Solymosi, R., Bowers, K., Fujiyama, T., 2015. Mapping fear of crime as a context-dependent everyday experience that varies in space and time. Legal and Criminological Psychology 20, 193–211.
Solymosi, R., Buil-Gil, D., Vozmediano, L., Guedes, I.S., 2020. Towards a Place-Based Measure of Fear of Crime: A Systematic Review of App-Based and Crowdsourcing Approaches. Environment and Behavior, 001391652094711.
Sreetheran, M., Van Den Bosch, C.C.K., 2014. A socio-ecological exploration of fear of crime in urban green spaces – a systematic review. Urban Forestry & Urban Greening 13, 1–18.
Tanner, S., Kalms, N., Cull, H., Matthewson, G., Aisenberg, A., 2020. Disruption and design: crowdmapping young women's experience in cities. IDS Bulletin 51, 113–128.
Tao, W., 2013. Interdisciplinary urban GIS for smart cities: advancements and opportunities. Geo-spatial Information Science 16, 25–34.
UN, 2015. Goal 5: Achieve Gender Equality and Empower All Women and Girls. United Nations. Available from: https://www.un.org/sustainabledevelopment/gender-equality/. (Accessed 30 March 2021).
UN Habitat, 2012. Gender Issue Guide: Urban Planning and Design. United Nations Human Settlements Programme, Nairobi.
UN Women, 2011. Building Safe and Inclusive Cities for Women: A Practical Guide.
UN Women, 2019. Ending violence against women: creating safe public spaces. Available from: https://www.unwomen.org/en/what-we-do/ending-violence-against-women/creating-safe-public-spaces. (Accessed 30 March 2021).
UN Women, ICRW, 2012. Safe Cities Free from Violence against Women and Girls. UN Women.
Vera-Gray, F., 2018. The Right Amount of Panic: How Women Trade Freedom for Safety. Policy Press.
Vera-Gray, F., Kelly, L., 2020. Contested gendered space: public sexual harassment and women's safety work. International Journal of Comparative and Applied Criminal Justice 44, 265–275.
Viswanath, K., Basu, A., 2015. SafetiPin: an innovative mobile app to collect data on women's safety in Indian cities. Gender & Development 23, 45–60.
Williams, S., 2020. Data Action: Using Data for Public Good. MIT Press.
World Bank Group, 2020. Handbook for Gender-Inclusive Urban Planning and Design. World Bank Group, Washington DC.
Wyant, B.R., 2008. Multilevel impacts of perceived incivilities and perceptions of crime risk on fear of crime. Journal of Research in Crime and Delinquency 45, 39–64.
Yates, A., Ceccato, V., 2020. Individual and spatial dimensions of women's fear of crime. International Journal of Comparative and Applied Criminal Justice 265–288.

10

Toward an intelligent mobility regime

Stephen Potter, James Warren, Miguel Valdez and Matthew Cook
School of Engineering and Innovation, The Open University, Milton Keynes, United Kingdom

1. Overview

This chapter adopts a framework based on the multilevel perspective (Geels, 2010, 2011). It begins by exploring the socio-economic factors behind personal transport trends (these are within the *socio-technical landscape* in the diagram below). The chapter then moves to the level of the *socio-technical regime* to discuss transport policy and planning, arguing that the way in which this operates lags behind the shifts in the mobility forming factors and behaviors of the socio-technical landscape. This analysis shows that current transport policy is attuned to the requirements of a past landscape, and this conceptualization is embedded in obdurate transport planning structures, approaches, and professional skills. Intelligent environment developments are thus applied in a 20th century manner that consigns digital mobility thinking and practices to a subsidiary supporting role (such as information and booking apps or a "last mile" add on to existing public transport systems). The transformative potential of intelligent mobility is being bottled up within a late 20th century mindset, practices, and institutional structures (Fig. 10.1).

To explore the practical implications of this misalignment for intelligent mobility developments, the chapter focuses on a case study of the design of the public transport system, examining the different ways in which intelligent mobility technologies are being applied. These are structured into a four-category typology. Some of these applications (types 1 and 2) assign intelligent mobility technologies to a supporting role for the existing regime by augmenting existing transport policy regime approaches,

Intelligent Environments. https://doi.org/10.1016/B978-0-12-820247-0.00020-5

whereas others (types 3 and 4) represent a potential regime transformation approach. The chapter ends by exploring how practitioners can mold new technology trials and niche experiments to lead toward greater transformative impacts. It concludes that the transport policy regime needs to align to the new socio-technical landscape and the emergence of intelligent mobility technologies could develop such a transformation.

2. Transport's sustainability challenge

Our globalized world depends on a high level of connectivity and the application of digital technologies. Reconciling this with the need to significantly lower environmental and climate change threats is one of the major challenges in this century. While many other economic sectors have successfully reduced negative environmental impacts, transport has shown little overall improvement. It remains a major contributor to poor city air quality and transport's CO_2 emissions continue to grow. In Europe, by 2015, transport's CO_2 emissions were 26% above their 1990 levels (European Environment Agency, 2018). Globally the growth in transport's CO_2 emissions is even higher; the International Energy Agency (2019) reported that, in 2016, transport's global CO_2 emissions were 71% higher than in 1990 and accounted for one-quarter of total CO_2 emissions.

The growth of vehicle ownership is faster in developing economies than in the developed economies of the "north"

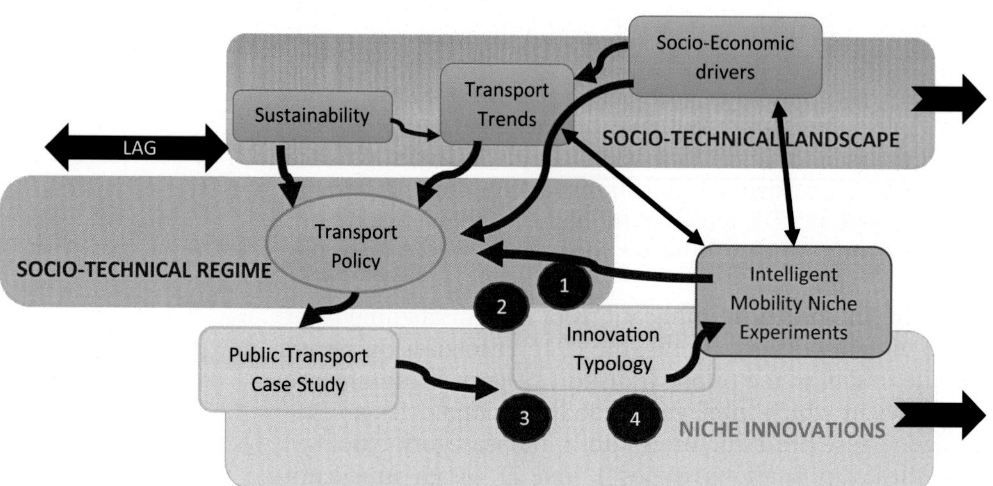

Figure 10.1 A multilevel perspective of the chapter. Based on Geels, F.W., 2010. Ontologies, socio-technical transitions (to sustainability), and the multi-level perspective. Research Policy, 39(4), 495–510, Geels, F.W., 2011. The multi-level perspective on sustainability transitions: responses to seven criticisms. Environmental Innovation and Societal Transitions, 1(1), 24–40.

(Table 10.1). However, vehicle ownership in the latter (and consequent CO_2 emission per person) are considerably higher than in the emergent developing economies.

More detailed UK data provide an indication of what is behind the failure to cut transport's greenhouse gas emissions. The UK is committed to achieving net zero CO_2 emissions by 2050 (Department for Business, Energy and Industrial Strategy, 2019a), which requires at least a 3%–4% CO_2 reduction per annum. Between 2000 and 2015, the UK's average fuel consumption of petrol cars improved by 32% and by 28% for diesel cars. This has been coupled with the introduction of low carbon hybrid and electric vehicles (Rietmann and Lieven, 2019). But in aggregate, although from 1990 to 2018 the UK's end-user greenhouse gas emissions dropped by 44%, those from transport were reduced by only 3% (Department for Business, Energy and Industrial Strategy, 2019b). As a result, transport's share of emissions increased from 21% in 1990 to over 33% in 2018. Rather than a 3%–4% CO_2 reduction per annum, the transport sector has barely managed a 1% reduction per decade.

Table 10.1 Vehicles per 1000 people in selected countries/regions, 2007 and 2017.

Country/Region	Vehicles per 1000 people	
	2007	2017
India	36.3	121.3
Africa	24.0	38.4
Indonesia	32.8	90.6
Asia, Far East	63.4	112.0
Asia, Middle East	101.4	149.9
China	30.3	156.3
Central and South America	128.3	176.0
Brazil	132.0	210.3
Mexico	224.3	331.6
Europe, East	270.8	373.3
Europe, West	587.5	611.9
Pacific	541.1	629.7
Canada	609.4	669.4
United States	844.5	831.2

Source of data: Davis, S and Boundy, R (2019). Transport Energy and Data Book, Edition 37, Oak Ridge National Laboratory, https://tedb.ornl.gov/wp-content/uploads/2019/03/TEDB_37-2.pdf, Table 3.6

In all economies, transport is a sector that, from an environmental perspective, remains deeply problematic. Applying new technologies to vehicles has improved fuel efficiency and cut emissions per vehicle km. but, as noted by Frey (2018) among others, fuel economy improvements have been more than counterbalanced by wider socio-economic factors increasing car use and transport dependency. In the UK these underlying socio-economic factors include, for example, employment being less stable than in the past, which, together with spatial differences in housing costs, leads to more long-distance trips, multiple trips for child care, and new behaviors such as the emergence of super-commuters who swap their daily commute for weekly or fortnightly travel to faraway homes (Budden, 2014). Social networks are also increasingly fluid—they have changed as our 24/7 society has developed and, despite the growth in social media (or possibly because of it), people travel more and further for social purposes.

These long-term underlying factors are reflected in a number of figures on travel behavior. For example, Table 10.2 shows changes in travel purposes in Britain.

In Britain, over the last 40 years the distance traveled peaked in the early 2000s and has subsequently decreased by 7%. Metz (2019) argues that, at least in highly motorized countries, travel time, distances, and trips are now static. But within this overall trend, there has been a significant drop in commuting (12%),

Table 10.2 Average kilometers traveled per person/year in Britain by journey purpose.

	1995	2005	2018
Commuting	2322	2250	2056
Business	1185	1148	913
Education	304	336	343
Escorting	784	932	943
Shopping	1438	1389	1198
Personal business	771	824	725
Visiting friends	2268	2339	1950
Entertainment and sport	737	797	848
Holiday and day trips	1439	1544	1539
Total[a]	11,246	11,563	10,513

[a]Allowing for rounding and conversion from miles.

Source: Department for Transport (2019). National Travel Survey 2018, Trip Purpose. UK National Statistics https://www.gov.uk/government/statistical-data-sets/nts04-purpose-of-trips.

Business (23%) and shopping trips (17%), while escort trips (i.e., the school run and other trips to take another person somewhere) have increased by 20%, entertainment by 15% and holiday/day trips by 7%. Overall, travel has shifted to involve more complex movements, to be less local - and hence walk trips have substantially dropped - and to be more geographically dispersed. In contrast to the predictable commutes of the 20th century, transport now increasingly shifts to dispersed patterns of behavior.

Switching to cleaner fuels, like measures to increase fuel efficiency has been promoted via vehicle-level actions linked to the decarbonization of electricity generation and, in the longer term, the potential for decarbonizing hydrogen production. The uptake of electric vehicles (EV) has been encouraged within the user-owner paradigm, and many countries provide purchase subsidies, tax incentives, and grants for recharging infrastructure. But even in Norway, where substantial tax subsidies reduce the capital and running costs of EVs to below the cost of internal combustion engine cars (Figenbaum, 2017), half of car sales are still for internal combustion engine vehicles. Even with major incentives and actions, the transition to less carbon intensive forms of automobility can be lengthy and incomplete.

3. Key structural trends behind travel behaviors

Transport and environmental policy actions have generally failed to recognize the mobility impacts generated by deeply embedded changes in the economic and social practices of our urban environments. Economies are increasingly service and consumer focused and travel behaviors have shifted to reflect this long-term structural change. Mobility patterns have become increasingly complex and dispersed in several ways. They are increasingly dispersed in time, as '24/7' becomes the norm for services and behaviors; there is geographical dispersal and also dispersal across functions (less work, business and shopping travel and a growth in social trips). There has also been a dispersal across demographics—the retired and elderly travel more, while independent travel for children and the young is more constrained. These structural changes mean that contemporary patterns of travel are hard to accommodate using public transport outside of major city centers and conurbations.

Transport planning has traditionally focused on workplace journeys, but in Britain (as shown in Table 10.2), these now constitute only 15% of all trips (19% of distance traveled) and business travel represents only 3% of trips (7% of distance) (Department for Transport, 2019). As noted in the report *All Change?* (Marsden et al., 2018), the major areas of travel growth are in social and leisure-related purposes. Geographically, the strongest growth has not been along major corridors to city centers but in suburban, urban fringe ("peri-urban") and rural areas (Hall, 2013). The nature of our urban environments has changed and consequently so too has our mobility behavior.

The change in travel by demography was noted in the report *On the Move* (Headicar and Stokes, 2016) and in *All Change?* (Marsden et al., 2018). For the elderly, driving license ownership has markedly increased, but among "millennials" (people under 35 years in age) it dropped from 80% in 1995 to 60% in 2016. It appears that the young, IT-savvy millennials are buying into new behaviors, with car ownership less of a priority compared with other lifestyle aspects. In a study of millennial travel behaviors in the USA, UK, and Australia, Delbosc (2019) noted they drive less, tend to be city-oriented, use urban public transport and the emerging IT-based cab services such as Uber, Kapten, Bolt, and Ola. However, there are significant variations. In some cities there are fewer alternatives to driving and people's desires to adopt a millennial lifestyle with reduced car use cannot readily be achieved.

We are only just beginning to see how intelligent city technologies will influence, accelerate and redirect changes in urban mobility. A range of digital technologies are interacting to provide "the most significant technological trend faced globally" (Leviäkangas, 2016). These include instrumented sensor networks, mobile devices and consumer electronics combined with integrated telecommunication infrastructure and advanced programming algorithm methodologies. These not only affect transport technologies and methods but are instigating further structural changes in the nature of employment, leisure, social activities and shopping. There is an emerging "time of unprecedented change in the transport system" (GOfS, 2019) which will see digital and autonomous technologies "completely disrupt" the mobility ecosystem (KPMG, 2019).

4. Realizing the potential of intelligent mobilities

Having reviewed the intelligent-mobilities challenge at a strategic socio-technical landscape level, the question emerges as to how the transport practitioner takes this into account in terms of policies, service designs, and practices. The challenge is how might a transition path to a viable and sustainable mobility system develop amidst increasingly ubiquitous intelligent technologies.

To do this, we focus down on the crucial example of urban public transport. Enhancing the attractiveness of public transport systems to effect a major shift away from private car use is a crucial part of transport policy in most developed countries. Yet this has only been achieved to a significant extent in high density city contexts, while elsewhere private motorized travel is burgeoning.

Traditional transport policy has tended to be built around the fading pattern of 20th century travel behaviors, with a focus on commuting trips along busy corridors from suburbs into city centers. This traditional approach has been complemented with initiatives for low carbon fuels (principally electric traction). Typically, actions to promote public transport focus on the construction of metro or tram lines and the provision of improved and subsidized bus services intended to encourage motorists to leave their car at home when commuting. Urban planning policies have followed this corridor system design, seeking to make places as much like big cities as possible, with settlements and facilities clustered along high-density corridors radiating from city centers (Fig. 10.2). Such high-density urban forms can be controversial and contested as socially undesirable, but are favored by many urban planners as there are historical statistical correlations between low car use with high population and employment density.

In his comprehensive review of this and other approaches, Banister (2005) cites case studies of cities that have achieved a 10% cut in car use through approaches utilizing planning controls and public transport development.

Since the 1980s, the researchers Paul Newman and Jeffrey Kenworthy have compiled a series of influential statistical studies on the energy intensity of travel in world cities. In a study of energy use in transport in 44 major cities across the globe, Kenworthy (2018) showed that transport energy per capita ranged from under 10,000 MJ to over 50,000 MJ per annum and that large capacity rail-based public transport systems produced the lowest energy use per passenger kilometre. The key statistical conclusions were:

- Lower energy use is associated with higher density of population and jobs and higher centralization of jobs in a Central Business District;

Figure 10.2 High-density suburban development clustered along a metro system in Hong Kong. Source: S. Potter.

- Fuel prices are less significant in reducing transport energy use than physical planning layout and density;
- Higher road traffic speeds and less congestion reduce fuel use per vehicle, but increase overall fuel use as these involve sprawling car-dependent cities with poorer public transport and low cycle and walking access;
- Car use and GDP has become decoupled in more developed cities.

It is notable that this and most other studies concentrate on urban layouts that enhance the use of large capacity, fixed track, public transport systems for work journeys, although the metrics used do relate to energy use in all travel. Significantly, these studies see the effect of intelligent city technologies as subsidiary to the major historical trends determining city layouts. Kenworthy seems to view new vehicle technologies as applying only to the private car and dismisses recent policy initiatives around such technologies as simplistic panaceas "*with little appreciation for the complex array of factors in the way that cities function*" (Kenworthy, 2018 p 201). He argues that the more important task is creating less automobile dependent cities within which "new vehicles technologies can be applied to make the remaining car use less energy consumptive and damaging to the broader life of cities" (Kenworthy, 2018 p 202).

The need for more sustainable and less automobile dependent cities is crucial. But there is a danger of not fully recognizing that radically new technologies are interacting with cities and their structures to create and mold socio-economic behaviors that will produce significant shifts in travel patterns. It is not a matter of slotting in 21st century technologies into a city structure optimized on 20th century behaviors.

Furthermore, intelligent technologies could be the key to transforming all types of public transport—not just high-capacity corridor systems for commuters. Intelligent technologies will initially be applied within the existing transport regime, but will soon begin to change it. There is a fundamental lag in the whole infrastructure of transport policy and planning. The conceptualizing of transport policy still seems to relate to a past landscape, and this conceptualization is embedded in transport planning structures, approaches, and professional skills.

If cities are to become less automobile dependent, how might intelligent technologies transform public transport for it to become not just suitable for traditional commuting flows? Intelligent technologies will impact the whole array of complex behaviors and functions in the emerging socio-technical landscape of the city.

5. A multi-level perspective analysis

In the overview of this chapter, it was noted that use is made of the multi-level perspective framework. It has already been argued that the socio-technical regime lags behind changes in the socio-technical landscape—and that results in intelligent mobility technologies failing to be used in a transformative manner. To address this situation requires us to shift down the Multi-level perspective.

A generic diagram of the multilevel perspective MLP is shown in Fig. 10.3 (and from which Fig. 10.1 was derived). This comprises three levels of socio-technical systems, differentiated by the speed at which variables associated with these change. “Higher” levels are more stable than “lower” levels in terms of the number of actors and degrees of alignment between the elements.

We began at the top level of the socio-technical landscape and factors determining trends in the mobility landscape and then noted the way that transport policy and practices in the next level (the socio-technical regime) have lagged behind shifts in the landscape. The regime level is of primary interest in the MLP because transitions are defined as shifts from one regime to

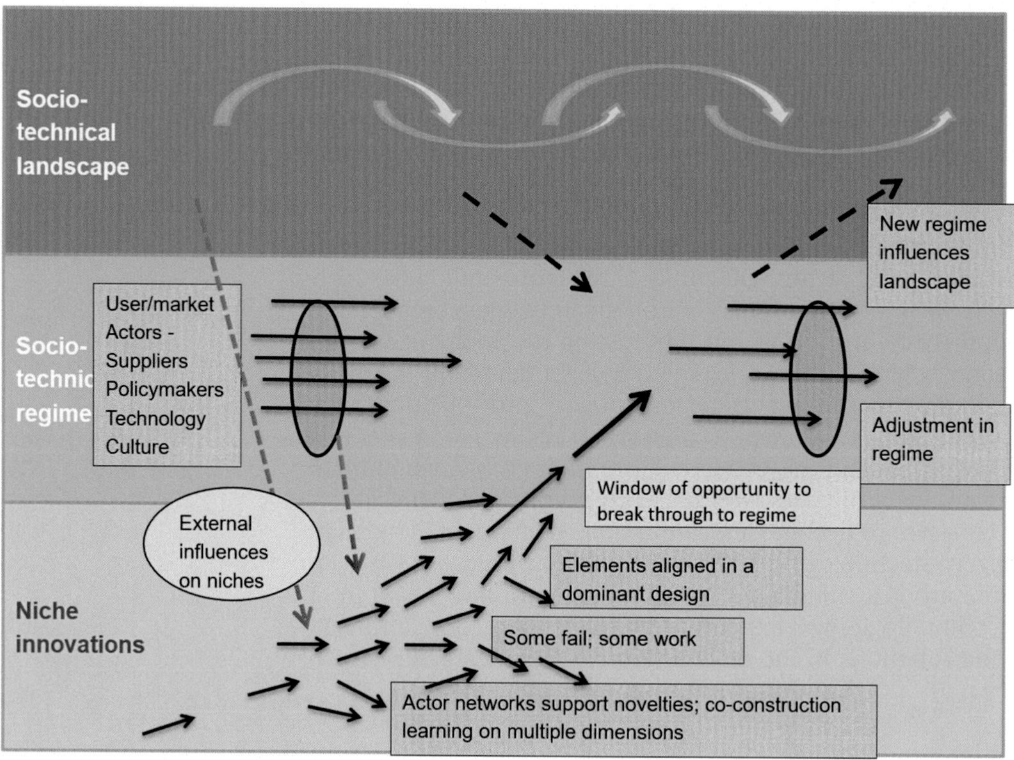

Figure 10.3 The multilevel perspective. Based on Geels, F.W., 2010. Ontologies, socio-technical transitions (to sustainability), and the multi-level perspective. Research Policy, 39(4), 495–510, Geels, F.W., 2011. The multi-level perspective on sustainability transitions: responses to seven criticisms. Environmental Innovation and Societal Transitions, 1(1), 24–40.

another regime (Geels, 2011). However, regime change may be more readily initiated at a smaller and less stable level, namely, the niche.

Niche environments are found in specific places, applications, markets and experiments where actors are prepared to accept the challenges, higher costs and instabilities associated with new technologies and ways of doing things. Niches provide protective, nurturing environments where new configurations that are not commercially viable can be improved, until eventually the new way of doing things is ready to compete head-on with the dominant option in a part of its market. This is where intelligent mobilities develop and find their place. Niche applications provide opportunities for the development of novel socio-technical practices and the formation of supportive actor networks. Some may fail, others succeed—while many will depend on windows of opportunity to break into the mainstream.

According to the MLP, a new regime for sustainable mobility will involve a transition from the current socio-technical transport regime to another more sustainable one. Such transitions are not simply about the development and uptake of new, perhaps more sustainable, technologies but about changing the obdurate set of socio-technical practices which are based on both technologies and, crucially, user behaviors. Here both new technologies and associated new user practices are needed. Further, whether we are concerned with public or private transport, firms and business systems will be key players in such processes, implying that new business models will be required.

Parts of the regimes may be destabilized as novel practices and technologies enter the regime and change it in fundamental and far-reaching ways. Docherty et al. (2018), for example, uses the MLP to explore governance aspects of transport's socio-technical regime, arguing for regime-level changes to effect a transition to Smart Mobility. But we presently seem to be in a situation where, as noted in the discussions above, some regime actors see intelligent mobilities technologies as something that will transform the mobility regime, whereas others see it as only providing a peripheral role, with a regime transformation built around more conventional policy actions. Niche actions are impacting on the mobility regime and a struggle is emerging around the type of regime change desired.

6. Niche innovations and regime change in public transport

Today, transport practitioners find themselves engaging with innovative intelligent mobility technologies as niche experiments and trials. They are also challenged as to how these applications can be incorporated into their "business as usual" or how these innovative technologies might change "business as usual" into something new. These practitioner challenges are about the interactions that take place between niche experiments and the actors, institutions and practices within the urban mobility socio-technical regime.

This situation impacts all aspects of transport systems, but for the key sustainability challenges identified at the beginning of this chapter, an important issue is whether intelligent mobility systems can reinvigorate public transport systems to help move the transport sector toward a more sustainable future. The declining relevance of corridor-based public transport systems has its origins in deep structural changes at level of the socio-technical landscape. As already noted, traditional transport/land use policies seek sustainability by requiring people to conform to the technical operational needs of high-capacity corridor rail systems, with cities and suburbs reconfigured around high-density corridors. But could intelligent mobility technologies provide a different approach toward a sustainable regime transformation?

A first stage in applying intelligent mobility systems would be to enhance traditional corridor public transport systems. This is already under way with electronic ticketing, integration with credit cards, timetable, and trip planning apps all coming into use. But a further stage is when intelligent mobility systems can also start to improve the quality and reach of public transport networks themselves. As noted by Kenworthy (2018), modern rail and urban tram systems (light rapid transit, LRT) have emerged as a clean and attractive public transport system for many cities and have a substantially lower environmental impact than travel by car. But in terms of contemporary patterns of travel, such high-capacity corridor systems can only serve a minority of transport needs. They work well for large volume commuting trips to a city and subregional centers but are ill-suited to the highly dispersed travel behavior that now characterizes life today. Furthermore, such high-capacity rail-based systems are expensive to build, their routes are fixed and are very prone to cost and timescale overruns. In Edinburgh, a three-line tram network costed at £375 m ended up as only one line, opening years late at a cost of £776 m excluding loan interest charges (edinburghtraminquiry.org). Among the reasons for this were unexpected issues in underground service diversions and archaeological remains found on the route. However, once opened, the Edinburgh tram has proved very popular, with passenger numbers exceeding the forecasts leading to the system moving into an operating profit within 2 years of opening.

Ways to extend the reach of metro-type systems have included the development of guided buses (such as in Cambridge, Eindhoven and Adelaide), together with mass transit busway systems such as in Curitiba in Brazil, but these largely depend on diesel bus technology and generally have not provide a step-change quality of service (Hodgson et al., 2013). People still opt for cars when they can. Guided buses are widely perceived both by users and policy makers as inferior to a modern electrified tram light rail service (Hensher et al., 2015).

Exploiting emerging intelligent technologies to the full could change this situation. Rapid charging for electric buses using advanced automotive batteries is now economically viable, both using pantographs and inductive charging plates (Miles and Potter, 2014). A combination of these EV technologies and electronic guidance means that enhanced-quality battery electric vehicles can now fulfil the function of trams without the need for costly and inflexible track and overhead line infrastructure. This considerably reduces the cost and time taken to introduce a high-quality public transport system. Such designs are also amenable to autonomous operations as technology advances; autonomy could be applied partially (e.g., first on segregated sections) and then, as autonomous driving in mixed traffic is proven, it can be applied more generally. This is a niche development that is beginning to transition towards becoming part of the public transport regime.

An example, which was implemented remarkable quickly, is the Chinese automated rapid transit (ART) service (Newman, 2018). These battery-powered electric vehicles provide the capacity, passenger comfort, ambiance and performance of a modern tram (Fig. 10.4). They are charged every 3 km at station stops, and use optical, GPS, and Lidar guidance rather than rails. The elimination of steel rails is an important benefit, as diversion of services under new tram lines is a major cost and source of project delay (Knowles, 2007). At present the ART vehicles are manually driven, but are designed to be upgraded to autonomous operation as the technology becomes available. ART trials took place in 2017 and it entered operational service in Zhuzhou in 2018. Within a year ART services were also running in other Chinese cities. In 2019, an ART operated a trial in Qatar (Anon, 2019).

In the UK, Cambridge is planning a 142 km. ART-type metro system, the *Cambridge Autonomous Metro* (CAM) by

Figure 10.4 An automated rapid transit vehicle on trial in Zhuzhou. Source: CRRC Zhuzhou.

redeveloping its guided busway and constructing a 12 km city center tunnel (Paton, 2019). The £4 billion scheme has lines running out to suburbs and nearby towns, including a substantial city center tunnel. This aims to provide a high-capacity commuter service using large battery-electric inductively charged tram-like vehicles. In early 2020, Milton Keynes announced proposals to use similar vehicles, but for a more urban 140 km network (Fig. 10.5). This would not require tunnels, and so is costed at a modest £1.1 billion (Milton Keynes Council, 2020). The autonomous vehicles under consideration for both are very similar to the Chinese ART.

In December 2019, a trial hydrogen powered rapid transit vehicle, the Fébus, was introduced in the provincial French city of Pau (Randall, 2019). This provides an express bus service to the city center using a tram-style vehicle, but is manually driven and guided. Hydrogen fuel cell vehicles remain expensive but, by eliminating the need for on street chargers, could in the longer term become viable.

The crucial thing in the design of these emerging ART-style systems is that, as well as the vehicles being designed around key intelligent mobility technologies, the quality and image of the vehicles and the service offering seeks to distance them from conventional buses and align user perceptions with that of a high-tech modern metro service. To do this, as Hodgson et al. (2013) showed, requires a high level of route segregation from other traffic to ensure reliability. To achieve this in places like Cambridge, some major infrastructure is needed (i.e., the

Figure 10.5 Artist impression of the proposed Milton Keynes rapid transit vehicles and stop. Source: Milton Keynes Council, 2020. Milton Keynes Strategy for 2050: Draft for Engagement. Milton Keynes Council, January.

city center tunnel), which raises costs considerably if large tram-scale vehicles are involved. In places like Milton Keynes, Pau, and Zhuzhou, there is scope to reallocate roadspace and use dedicated lanes on existing highways and road edge reserves, which substantially reduces infrastructure costs.

7. The four types of intelligent mobility innovation

The above examples show ways in which intelligent mobility concepts have progressed from augmenting existing public transport systems to one that provides a response to the trends in the mobility landscape through a redesign of transport systems themselves.

The development of new technologies, including inductive charging of modern automotive batteries, electronic guidance and autonomous driving, presents the opportunity to provide new metro quality services where previously the cost of building a conventional tram line could not be economically justified. Intelligent technologies can be the key to providing a wider reach for high quality corridor public transport services—both in developed and in the developing economies. There is much obduracy in the public transport network, not only in the more obvious obduracy of existing infrastructure, but in existing institutions, regulatory systems and mindsets. Despite this, there are indications that real change is possible, as shown by the emergence of designs like ART and the Pau Fébus.

Niche developments such as ART map well onto the existing socio-technical regime. They provide an opportunity to extend high quality corridor services into a wider range of urban environments. This represents an approach of using intelligent environment initiatives to augment the existing public transport regime's business model of big vehicles operating on fixed corridor routes. In most cases, these developments still focus upon the fading patterns of 20th century travel behavior. The Fébus, for example, is specifically intended to provide an express commuter service, as is the Cambridge CAM system. The Milton Keynes proposal, however, is more about providing an urban network of services, which relates more closely to modern patterns of dispersed travel demand.

However, such enhancements, although they could address some of the shifts in the new mobility landscape, do not tackle the key point that the design of the traditional public transport regime itself is ill suited to the contemporary landscape of travel demand. Rather than being used to augment and optimize the existing transport system regime, intelligent technologies should be seen as the starting point for a system redesign: only in this way sustainable transformations can occur.

How niche experiments relate to the existing regime and the actors within that regime varies from being broadly compatible (as in the case of ART) to being extremely disruptive. When considering an innovation, it is important to be aware of its relationship to the actors and institutions of the regime in which it will be introduced. Who will be excited by, welcome and embrace a niche experiment? Who will view it as a threat to be contained and controlled? Who will want to constrain an innovation to their particular viewpoint and expectations?

The type of niche experiment and how it relates to a regime is clearly important. A useful way to categorize the types of niche experiment is provided by the Product Service System (PSS) innovation literature. PSS research particularly explores the sustainability of different service designs, arguing that the more advanced and disruptive designs would yield the highest improvements in sustainability. Drawing on a PSS typology presented in Cook et al. (2006), a four-fold typology has been developed here to represent contrasting relationships between an intelligent cities niche development and the public transport regime. The four types are shown in Box 10.1:

Because the public transport regime involves long-life fixed physical infrastructures, institutional structures, practices, and ways of operating, plus regulatory systems built around existing business models, there are significant challenges in introducing innovations that do not map onto these regime elements. Type 1 (Augmentation) innovations present relatively few structural difficulties, but from then on there are increasingly serious obstacles. Type 2 map well onto the business model, but not the established skills, professional approaches and processes of traditional initiatives such as metro, tram, and bus developments. Type 3, Intelligent Service Redesign, might initially be viewed as a "last mile" solution to a conventional public transport system, but could eventually be substantially disruptive if it led to a system and business model redesign.

It is perhaps no surprise that attempts at the Type 4 concept of MaaS have failed to achieve more than occasional partial, small scale highly subsidized applications (Pangbourne, 2018). There is also an issue that MaaS is limited by the business model in which it operates. MaaS would work best when linked to a Type

1. **Intelligent augmentation**: where digital enhancements are added to an existing PSS, such as a city's public transport services. This would include e-ticketing and digital informational systems provided for public transport users.

2. **Intelligent product redesign**: where a key product used in delivering a service is redesigned around the capabilities of new smart technologies. The ART trackless tram is an example of the progression to this innovation stage.

3. **Intelligent service redesign**: where new smart technologies are used to redesign the transport service itself such as a mobility service provided by demand responsive minibuses or small autonomous pods.

4. **Intelligent mobility service:** where the *function* of mobility is provided through integrative intelligent technologies. People would use a digital service platform to request travel from A to B, which would then be provided and paid for by the service drawing on a portfolio of transport services. This fourth stage relates to the emerging concept of Mobility as a Service (MaaS), although that is presently conceptualized as within existing transport services (Transport Systems Catapult, 2016).

3 service redesign, but applied to the existing service design and business model of public transport, MaaS seems likely to have only a limited impact. There is a danger in introducing an advanced intelligent interface for an outdated service. Unless the core services meet mobility needs, then an integrative MaaS-type interface is only likely to disappoint users.

These four types of intelligent mobility development can also be identified in other transport sectors. For example, for the car, Type 1 (augmentation) would be where there are GPS, semiautomation and other digital enhancements to internal combustion engine cars. Type 2 might be where electric vehicles and autonomous driving are introduced but the system of private vehicle ownership remains (the product is redesigned but not the system). Type 3 could be where car mobility services would be provided (as in a car club), with Type 4 being again where the *function* of mobility being provided in a MaaS-like manner. There would be increasing convergence between the public and private transport systems in the final two types.

This kind of analysis helps us to understand and categorize the different ways in which niche innovations in smart digital technologies could develop, and each of these would have different impacts on the mobility regime and the subsequent environmental impacts produced, with the greater environmental benefits likely from Type 2 onwards.

8. Getting from A to B—a framework for systemic transformation

This four-type categorization of intelligent mobility niche developments can help to identify the benefits and issues involved with each, but (as we have just noted), there are increasingly significant challenges in moving to the more radical innovation stages. Historically, incremental changes and exploration of novel designs in specialist applications are often the way that innovative ways of working develop, in which learning and adaptation occur and they then move toward becoming mainstream.

How the regime changes through the interactions between intelligent transport configurations and a complex network of existing and new actors could produce a wide mix of potential outcomes. It is possible that resultant urban mobility behaviors could move toward a reduction in the environmental and social impacts of transport, while other outcomes would lead toward worsening congestion and environmental impacts. The level of uncertainty involved is substantial, as noted by Lyons (2016), with there being not just gaps in knowledge but a divergence of views on both outcomes and policy responses all playing out amidst an extremely complex web of socio-technical relationships.

9. Think big, start small—niche seeds of a system redesign

So, where does that leave the practitioner as they become increasingly aware of a whole range of intelligent technologies coming into the transport sector? There is a danger of ad hoc responses producing no more than a high-tech drift into an unsatisfactory future. It is necessary to think big and have a vision for regime transformation, using this to start small in the way niche experiments are constructed and used.

Using the MLP as a framework can be useful for practitioners, users and policymakers to explore and analyze the various emergent intelligent mobility technologies, the niches in which they are developing and their impact on the incumbent regime. In terms of niche applications of relevance to our public transport system case study, there are a variety of examples. One of these has come to be seen more by city authorities as a problem rather than a transformative opportunity; this is the appearance in the taxi and private hire (minicab) market by new businesses from the digital economy world.

As travel has become increasingly dispersed, the only existing public transport mode that could fit this pattern has been the taxi. However, the taxi is a mode of transport with a regime design legacy of its own, built around a 19th-century business model of street hailing, taxi ranks and high fares. But, by using new IT tools, organizations such as Uber, Lyft and Ola have developed new service models that cut costs and fares (Boeckel et al., 2012), thus challenging the incumbent 19th-century taxi model. These new operators have a business model involving a user-friendly booking and payment app, crowdsourced owner-drivers, plus highly efficient scheduling and back-office software. Together, this service redesign can outperform incumbent minicab operators on price and performance and leaves the old taxi model standing (if not redundant).

The rapid appearance of digital invaders in the taxi market has invoked the politically powerful wrath of the taxi industry in cities around the world. The digital invader has been resisted and a number of city authorities have supported the existing cab regime by constraining or banning the lead operator, Uber, and in at least one case have even jailed their executives (Groden, 2015). Yet, despite its business practice defects, the Uber-style model is a configuration that matches the current mobility landscape. Indeed, many conventional cab operators have subsequently adopted app-based booking and management systems to optimize vehicle operations, cut costs, and increase competitiveness.

The entry of a new taxi model does not in itself represent a transformative public transport system. In terms of our four-category intelligent mobility model, this is intelligent augmentation with some elements of intelligent service redesign. However, these elements, if developed and configured could move more strongly in the direction of intelligent service redesign. For example, both Uber and Lyft introduced a ride sharing facility, but it has not proved attractive to most of their users. Situations have occurred where the second passenger was not at the pickup point leading to major delays for the first passenger. Both Uber and Lyft suspended their pool facility when the COVID-19 pandemic hit in 2020 and it may not be reinstated.

This suggests that, rather than adapting a cab model optimized for individual bookings, a business model specifically designed for shared vehicle use could be more successful. The design of a ride-sharing service from scratch that is rooted in modern ICT tools could be a significant step toward the digital taxi sector entering the mainstream public transport regime. This is what the Mercedes-backed company Via (previously named ViaVan) has done. Rather than a generic taxi service, ViaVan's model represents a fusion of taxi and bus elements. They use shared eight-seater vehicles (Fig. 10.6) to provide point-to-point services within a defined service area (ViaVan Technologies, 2019). It is not a door-to-door service, but users

Figure 10.6 A ViaVan vehicle in Milton Keynes. Source: AM Valdez.

are taken directly between local pickup/drop off points at times booked via an app, and share trips with other users en route. Its business model includes flexible vehicle rental for drivers, cashless payments, app booking, and scheduling software to ensure a driver's income, or drivers are actual employees with a set salary. This fusion between the business model of a taxi and bus service makes for operational efficiency and results in a fare roughly half-way between that of a bus and taxi. It is presently based on manual driving, but the business model is designed for a transition to autonomous driving when available for use in mixed traffic. With drivers representing over half of total costs, autonomy would further reduce fares closer to that of buses - and that would be for a 24/7 service of a consistent quality.

Local transport services are only just starting to be touched by the regime-restructuring power of the digital revolution. In the long term, for some locations (particularly peri-urban and rural) and time periods (evenings and night-time) Uber- or Via-style systems and their autonomous successors are set to become the public transport of the digital age.

New partnerships are beginning to emerge between these new digitally based players and other transport practitioners. For example, in 2020 the city authority of Milton Keynes contracted Via to replace one subsidized conventional bus service with Via's demand responsive service at a normal bus fare. In 2021, it moved on to replace all subsidized bus services on a similar demand responsive basis (Potter et al., 2022). A Type 3 service redesign is taking place.

Once autonomous driving is added to such a service redesign, as is being explored through developmental projects such as the LUTZ Pathfinder pods (Transport Systems Catapult, 2019), then a further service redesign transformation comes into place. The potentially transformative impact of "small autonomous vehicle/small infrastructure" public transport is that, rather than people needing to adjust their behavior to the schedules and routes of a bus or metro, they can travel directly, whenever they want, on services that can operate 24 h a day, 7 days a week. Crucially, the level of service can be maintained at times of low demand, thus overcoming the poor quality of infrequent evening, night and Sunday public transport services experienced today. This is a service system design that matches the socio-technical landscape of the 21st-century city—not one requiring 21st-century society to conform to a 19th-century transport system architecture (Fig. 10.7).

So, initial niche experiments can develop experience and understanding, lead to identifying market sectors in which they can

Figure 10.7 The LUTZ Pathfinder pod. Source: Connected Cities Catapult.

best operate and then be applied and transition into mainstream applications with the potential to transform the regime as a whole. The above maps out a possible transition path, but a key question is how and who molds the direction of the regime transformation and the criteria used in that process.

In terms of environmental impacts, small-vehicle, on-demand, public transport systems could cut energy use through operating vehicles only when needed and at a good vehicle occupancy. This energy and emission reduction would be greatly enhanced should the service quality lead to a lowering of car dependence. Given the trend of millennials to defer car ownership in present cities, such a potential could be considerable. It is such regime level changes that has the potential to deliver significant energy and sustainability gains together with greater social inclusion and economic benefits.

A shift to a public transport service system of this type has major implications for transport and urban planning. At the moment, such new intelligent mobility services are largely seen as a "last mile" solution to extend the reach of conventional corridor public transport systems. The actors in the existing regime can only conceive of such new service concepts in this way. But such an initial application could be an important niche in which learning and understanding develop for both the users and providers of local demand responsive transport services.

In the longer term, although conventional corridor big-vehicle systems can continue to serve the market for which they are suited, the key benefits will be from the emergence of small-vehicle noncorridor systems that can provide a viable alternative to private car use in suburban and urban fringe situations. For public authorities, the infrastructure costs of developing such demand responsive services are relatively low and possibly could be subsumed within a commercially viable package. Such a service would complement and strengthen the position of existing corridor services and also of long-distance sustainable transport services like rail, allowing a corridor design to serve more varied travel demands.

In this transformation several threads possibly combine to produce a new intermeshed system of public transport services, with the potential to deliver a more sustainable pattern of travel behavior. Quite how these threads will combine - and what others may join the melee - is still unclear. An ideal might be a vision in which intelligent mobility technologies are applied to high-capacity rail-based systems along heavily trafficked corridors (including intercity travel), coupled with other medium-density routes operated by ART-type vehicles. These would work alongside area-based demand responsive vehicle services as well as shared bike and other personal transport vehicles. Together with appropriate Type 4 information, booking, and payment systems this could produce a public transport regime suited to emerging urban mobility needs.

10. Exploring and supporting transition paths

This chapter has argued that the scale of the sustainable transport challenge demands a regime-changing approach: new patterns of transport technologies and practices are needed. A window of opportunity for such a reconfiguration is provided by the increasing pace at which ICT and pervasive computing technologies are woven into urban environments and embedded in networked and increasingly autonomous vehicles. We have explored the four niche innovation types through which an intelligent mobility regime might emerge, with the presence of a variety of pathways that could lead toward a new and more sustainable transport regime.

But will this actually happen? Often industry and policymakers present a somewhat deterministic technological roadmap of moving from one stage to the next until a desired state is achieved. This is far too naive an approach for the complexities and rival set of expectations among key participants in our transport regime. What is required is an adaptable development and exploration of technologies and applications together with enabling socio-economic infrastructures that have a transformative potential. There is a severe danger of locking intelligent environments into a roadmap defined by the structure and behaviors of the existing regime. However, it is necessary to identify niches and initial applications within the existing regime (types 1 and 2 of the of intelligent mobility development model), but with the flexibility and potential to transform the regime itself (types 3 and 4).

Niche experiments and trials need to develop understanding and experience to help direct a transition to a more sustainable and socially inclusive regime. Some key features of such a program might be:

- Identify test-bed opportunities where early stage technologies have the best chance of success, even if this may not eventually be the main sector for their impact. - but:
- Avoid locking intelligent city developments into the old regime. A key trap is seeking a solution for a past and fading regime.
- Seek actions to meet challenges, not to procure a particular solution.
- City and public authorities need to learn how to partner with network actors to facilitate positive developments.
- Ensure learning by providers and users takes place and is shared.
- Provide actions that allow behaviors and practices to adapt and change.
- Don't see only threats in the way the digital sector is moving into the transport sector. Identify markets and sectors where a partnership with the new systems adds particular value. This might include specialist transport for people with disabilities and the elderly, peri-urban development areas, supporting people back into work, etc.
- Identify what would provide value to operators to develop services that support low carbon public transport services and systems.
- Find ways to develop concepts in flexible stages—not an all-or-nothing system that cannot adapt to change.
- Identify the role of appropriate regulation (air quality could be a key issue here) and what are appropriate incentives.

Weber et al. (1999) and Caniëls and Romijn (2006) provide more generic details on planning niche experiments and trials.

There is a role here for public policy, which itself needs to evolve to operate in a new manner. As Kane and Whitehead (2018) point out, it is very easy to imagine emerging transport disruptions leading to "a series of nightmare scenarios and poorer transport systems unless we have sensible and informed public policy to avoid this." There is a need for policy to favor the development of niche innovations which ultimately have the potential to create more sustainable transport systems. In such instances, urban, regional, and national government plays a key role. This is not simply a case of picking winners but of observing trends in promising innovations which would benefit from further specific investments such as challenge funds and public procurement. It is also not just about technology development; the financial, social and business model transition paths need as much - if not more - attention than technology. Financial risk sharing and reduction, enabling commercial value to be realized and protecting the interests of partners are all part of facilitating innovative developments to take place. There is a crucial role here for a public-authority-led process in partnership with commercial and other actors. But, for public policy to be effective in such endeavors, it must be clear and stable so as to create an environment in which firms feel sufficiently confident to invest.

The way in which the public sector does transport policy needs to change as much as any other actor in transport's socio-technical regime. As Docherty et al. (2018) noted, given the profound impacts of the automobility transition on the economy, the environment and society, there is no time to be lost in beginning the task of thinking through how state action and public policy will need to change to take account of the implications of the transition to a "Smart Mobility" future.

There is a real danger of public sector policy initiatives relying on the way it worked in the old regime which, despite landscape pressures for change, has proved to be obdurate. This existing transport policy regime has a focus on controlling funding and managing infrastructure together with regulatory and subsidy measures. Such interventions will remain necessary but need a new policy structure in which to operate. The intelligent mobilities world is one where transport policy is done in a less hierarchical way with interventions to develop, manage and shape networks and identify windows of opportunity that fit into a broad and flexible innovation approach. Such enabling governance demands very different sorts of skills, practices and understanding by governments such as city authorities. The networks may act as a conduit for applications to public funds, but this is only within the partnership enabling model of governance. As Hill and Lynn (2005) noted in their review of empirical practice in a U.S. context, this form of enabling governance is within a system of constitutional authority that is necessarily hierarchical. However, such enabling forms of governance are being increasingly used and seem to be particularly appropriate to the role of shaping innovation and transitions. Seen in this way, the role of the public sector is not to pick technological "winners," fund and provide them, but to stimulate niche development and proliferation that support public policy objectives.

There is a valuable public sector role in shaping the development of niches. This may challenge *how* local authorities currently operate to become effective innovation enablers. The public sector must not be sidelined, but there is a danger that could happen if they do not understand the new role needed (Giddens, 2008). There is a growing case for partnership models in which city authorities, rather than taxing to fund public sector projects, instead adopt an innovation management role. This is likely to require entrepreneurial skills that may be quite different to those usually associated with transport planning. It is perhaps only through such a governance approach that radical transport innovations can be managed to make the transition between niche and regime without incurring high costs, disruption, or important innovations being constrained to limited applications.

Enormous opportunities emerge for the development of a transformative, sustainable intelligent mobility regime and its associated service systems. The danger is that a transition to a sustainable intelligent mobility regime could be stifled if intelligent mobility only operates within the institutional structures of the existing socio-technical regime.

References

Anon, 2019. China's Self-Driving Trackless 'Rail Bus' Starts First Overseas Run. China Daily.com. July 16th. https://www.chinadaily.com.cn/a/201907/16/WS5d2d4057a3105895c2e7dab7.html.

Banister, D., 2005. Unsustainable Transport. Taylor and Francis, London, UK.

Boeckel, M., Sprunger, B., Smith, K., Work, E., 2012. Uber—How a Technology Firm Is Changing the Traditional Transportation Model. Kellogg School of Management, Northwestern University, Evanston, IL, USA.

Budden, R., 2014. The Brave World of Super-commuters. Worklife, bbc.com, 19 November. https://www.bbc.com/worklife/article/20141118-the-worlds-longest-commutes.

Caniëls, M., Romijn, H., 2006. Strategic Niche Management as an Operational Tool for Sustainable Innovation: Guidelines for Practice. Eindhoven Centre for Innovation Studies. The Netherlands Working Paper 06.07.

Cook, M.B., Bhamra, T.A., Lemon, M., 2006. The transfer and application of Product Service Systems: from academic to UK manufacturing firms. Journal of Cleaner Production 14, 1455–1465.

Davis, S., Boundy, R., 2019. Transport Energy and Data Book, 37. Oak Ridge National Laboratory. https://tedb.ornl.gov/wp-content/uploads/2019/03/TEDB_37-2.pdf.

Delbosc, I., Mc Donald, N., Stokes, G., Lucas, K., Circekka, G., Youngsung, L., 2019. Millennials in cities: comparing travel behaviour trends across six case study regions. Cities 90, 1–14.

Department for Business, 2019a. Energy and industrial Strategy. UK Becomes First Major Economy to Pass Net Zero Emissions Law, News Release. June 27, DBEIS. https://www.gov.uk/government/news/uk-becomes-first-major-economy-to-pass-net-zero-emissions-law.

Department for Business, 2019b. Energy and Industrial Strategy, 2018 UK Greenhouse Gas Emissions: Statistical Release, UK National Statistics, 28 March.

Department for Transport, 2019. National Travel Survey 2018, Trip Purpose. UK National Statistics. https://www.gov.uk/government/statistical-data-sets/nts04-purpose-of-trips.

Docherty, I.M., Anable, J., 2018. The governance of smart mobility. Transportation Research Part A 115, 114–125.

European Environment Agency, 2018. Greenhouse Gas Emissions from Transport. European Environment Agency, Copenhagen, Denmark.

Figenbaum, E., 2017. Perspectives on Norway's supercharged electric vehicle policy. Environmental Innovation and Societal Transitions 25 (December), 14–34.

Frey, H.C., 2018. Trends in on road transportation energy and emissions. Journal of the Air & Waste Management Association 68 (6), 514–563.

Geels, F.W., 2010. Ontologies, socio-technical transitions (to sustainability), and the multi-level perspective. Research Policy 39 (4), 495–510.

Geels, F.W., 2011. The multi-level perspective on sustainability transitions: responses to seven criticisms. Environmental Innovation and Societal Transitions 1 (1), 24–40.

Giddens, A., 2008. The Politics of Climate Change. Policy Network, London.

Government Office for Science, 2019. The Future of Mobility. Foresight, Government Office for Science, London, 31 January. https://www.gov.uk/government/publications/future-of-mobility.

Groden, C., 2015. Two Uber Executives Arrested in France. Fortune.com. http://fortune.com/2015/06/29/uber-executives-arrested. (Accessed 20 June 2019).

Hall, P., 2013. Refreshing the parts that other transport cannot reach. Town and Country Planning 121–132. March.

Headicar, P., Stokes, G., 2016. On the Move. Independent Transport Commission, London, UK.

Hensher, D.A., Mulley, C., 2015. Modal image: candidate drivers of preference differences for BRT and LRT. Transportation 42 (1), 7–23.

Hill, C., Lynn, L., 2005. Is hierarchical governance in decline? Evidence from empirical research. Journal of Public Administration, Research and Theory 15 (2), 173–195.

Hodgson, P., Potter, S., Warren, J., Gillingwater, D., 2013. Can bus really be the new tram? Research in Transportation Economics 39 (1), 158–166.

International Energy Agency, 2019. CO2 Emissions Statistics. International Energy Agency, Paris, France. https://www.iea.org/statistics/co2emissions.

Kane, M., Whitehead, J., 2018. How to ride transport disruption—a sustainable framework for future urban mobility. Australian Planner 54 (3), 177–185.

Kenworthy, J.R., 2018. Reducing passenger transport energy use in cities: a comparative perspective on private and public transport energy use in American, Canadian, Australian, European and Asian Cities. In: Droege, P. (Ed.), Urban Energy Transition Renewable Strategies for Cities and Regions. Elsevier, pp. 169–204. Ch.2.1.

Knowles, R., 2007. What future for light rail in the UK after ten year transport plan targets are scrapped? Transport Policy 14 (1), 81–93. January.

KPMG, 2019. Mobility 2030, 19 February. https://home.kpmg/uk/en/home/insights/2017/04/mobility-2030.html.

Leviäkangas, P., 2016. Digitalization of Finland's transport sector. Technology in Society 47, 1–15.

Lyons, G., 2016. Transport analysis in an uncertain world. Transport Review 36 (5), 553–557.

Marsden, G., Dales, J., Jones, P., Seagriff, E., Spurling, N., 2018. All Change? the Future of Travel Demand and the Implications for Policy and Planning. Commission on Transport Demand, London, UK.

Metz, D., 2019. Driving Change: Travel in the Twenty-First Century. Agenda Publishing, Newcastle.

Miles, J., Potter, S., 2014. Developing a viable electric bus service: the Milton Keynes demonstration project. Research in Transportation Economics 48, 357–363.

Milton Keynes Council, 2020. Milton Keynes Strategy for 2050: Draft for Engagement. Milton Keynes Council, January.

Newman, P., 2018. Why Trackless Trams Are Ready to Replace Light Rail. EconoTimes. https://www.econotimes.com/Why-trackless-trams-are-ready-to-replace-light-rail-1433854.

Pangbourne, K., Stead, D., Mladenović, M., Milakis, D., 2018. The case of mobility as a service: a critical reflection on challenges for urban transport and mobility governance. In: Marsden, G., Reardon, L. (Eds.), Governance of the Smart Mobility Transition. Emerald Publishing, UK, pp. 34–46.

Paton, G., 2019. £4bn 'trackless Tram' to Reduce Congestion in Cambridge. The Times. London March 19.

Potter, S., Valdez, M., Enoch, M., Cook, M., 2022. Demand-responsive transport returns to Milton Keynes - lessons for a bus industry in crisis? Town and Country Planning 91 (5), 319–329.

Randall, C., 2019. World's First Hydrogen BRT Launches in France, Electrive. Dec 18. https://www.electrive.com/2019/12/18/worlds-first-hydrogen-brt-launches-in-france/.

Rietmann, N., Lieven, T., 2019. A comparison of policy measures promoting electric vehicles in 20 countries. In: Finger, M., Audouin, M. (Eds.), The Governance of Smart Transportation Systems. Springer, Berlin, Germany.

Transport Systems Catapult, 2016. Mobility as a Service. TSC, Milton Keynes.

Transport Systems Catapult, 2019. Self-driving Pods. TSC, Milton Keynes. https://ts.catapult.org.uk/innovation-centre/cav/cav-projects-at-the-tsc/self-driving-pods/.

ViaVan Technologies, 2019. What Is ViaVan? https://support.viavan.com/hc/en-us/articles/360003169292-What-is-ViaVan.

Weber, M., Hoogma, R., Lane, B., Schot, J., 1999. Experimenting with Sustainable Transport Innovations. A Workbook for Strategic Niche Management. Twente University, Enschede.

11

Autonomous mobility in the built environment

Nimish Biloria[1,2]

[1] *Faculty of Design, Architecture and Building, University of Technology Sydney, Sydney, NSW, Australia;* [2] *Department of Urban and Regional Planning, University of Johannesburg, Johannesburg, South Africa*

1. Introduction

Cities are inherently complex ecosystems, embodying interactions between people, technology, environments, and economics. It is critical to understand the correlation between these counterparts of the city and find value in services that can provide equitable access while acquiring an empathic quality. Empathy, herein, implies the feeling of identification and responsiveness from something or someone, in this case, mobility and modes of transport. Mobility drives critical economic factors such as productivity, economic expansion, movement of goods and services, and influences social inclusion to compete in an increasingly connected global context (Ecola et al., 2014; Rodrigue et al., 2019). Since before the horse carriage to the private car to the airplane, humankind's attempts to enhance modes of transport have evolved significantly, with transportation and mobility becoming one of the largest and rapidly evolving economic and innovation sectors in the world over the past century (Cornet et al., 2012). However, with the increase in our ability to choose different transport modes, growth in vehicle manufacturers and service providers, and an increase in both private ownership and shared transportation, we also witness the adverse impacts of this surge in transport options. Pervasive reliance on the major motorized mobility driver fossil fuel has not only resulted in depleting the earth of its resources but has also contributed to an increase in air pollution levels and greenhouse gas emissions, resulting in climate emergencies globally. Still 95% reliant on petroleum, global transportation has only begun to make small shifts to the electrification of vehicles (Rodrigue, 2020).

Intelligent Environments. https://doi.org/10.1016/B978-0-12-820247-0.00007-2

An increase in ride-sharing services, such as Lyft and Uber, has also resulted in an increase in road congestion (Hiltzik, 2020). This again results in congestion, increased vehicle miles traveled as well as resultant wear and tear of infrastructure and break dust associated particulate matter—PM2.5 and PM10 discharge in the air we breathe. Besides this, transport linkages also govern urban growth and are decisive in strengthening, maintaining, or weakening social connectivity as well as an equity dimension to how, where, and who can be physically connected. Thus, it is particularly crucial that mobility, as an integral part of the city's ecosystem, evolve from a holistic understanding of social, economic, technological, and context-aware underpinnings. This means facilitating the efficient integration of technology with contextually embedded and customer-centric services. Such services tend to be inclusive irrespective of the citizen's physical and mental vulnerabilities and diverse socioeconomic backgrounds. It is thus unsurprising that transport researchers undertake extensive research on pertinent aspects of mobility. These range from consumer attitudes affecting travel choices (Ye and Titheridge, 2017) to sustainable and smart mobility (Berger et al., 2014; Grant-Muller and Usher, 2014; Papa and Lauwers, 2015) to emerging technologies, such as autonomous vehicles (Burns, 2013; Shladover, 2018), automated road systems (Ioannou, 1997; Madigan et al., 2017), and integrated transport systems (ITS) (Grant-Muller and Usher, 2014; Menouar et al., 2017), mobility—urban fabric linkages (Newman et al., 2018) to name a few.

2. Overview of the autonomous vehicle sector

2.1 Understanding automation within the context of autonomous vehicles

The transport sector has received much attention as one of the most important enablers of mobility over the last decade. Self-driving cars or autonomous vehicles (AVs), a concept that has lingered in the transportation sector since the late 1920s, have once again taken center stage in the 20th century. It was as early as the 1920s that inventors started experimenting with remote-controlled radio systems, which subsequently resulted in General Motor (GM) showcasing the 1939 Futurama exhibit at the New York World Fair. This was the first time that a vision of autonomous electric cars driving through crowded city centers was communicated to millions of visitors of the world fair. The vision incorporated electric cars powered by circuits embedded in the road surface that could be controlled by radio waves. A 3d mock-up exposed visitors to a futuristic city center with traffic flow of radio-controlled electric automobiles (Fig. 11.1A and B). Futurama presented an ingenious vision that not only put forth the idea of autonomous driving, but also laid the foundation for smart infrastructure and vehicle to infrastructure communication. This vision was further adopted by the Central Power and Light Company in 1956 for developing inspired advertisements in leading newspapers outlining their vision of embedding electronic devices in roads to develop electric super-highways to aid autonomous vehicles.

Such visions were also tested in reality in 1958 and the 1960s, just before and after World War II. In 1958, the Nebraska Department of Roads prototyped 400 feet long stretch of a public highway outside Lincoln to allow demonstrating autonomous vehicles in collaboration with Radio Corporation of America and General Motors. Two Chevrolet vehicles with embedded radio receivers, and audible and visual warning devices that could activate the car's steering, braking, and acceleration communicated with embedded radio impulses to guide the vehicle movements successfully. In the 1960s, similarly witnessed testing of a Citroen DS car by the United Kingdom's Transport and Road Research Laboratory by means of magnetic cables embedded in road surfaces of a dedicated test track. However, considering that embedding intelligence within road infrastructure would be an

a

b

Figure 11.1 A. The mock-up used for the GM presentation at the 1939 World Fair, New York; B. public viewing areas designed to get an overview of the mock-up for the 1939 New York World Fair. (A) Norman Bell Geddes, Available at: https://en.wikipedia.org/wiki/File:Street_intersection_Futarama.jpg. (B) Norman Bell Geddes, Available at: https://velocetoday.com/self-drive-cars-and-you-a-history-longer-than-you-think/.

expensive affair, a transition to developing smart devices that could be directly fitted to existing cars. Much of this research and development has paved the way to actualizing multiple dynamic driving tasks and security systems of today. 1987–95 saw flourishing activities with this mode of automation under generous funding from the European Commission's Eureka/Prometheus initiative. Vision-based robotic guidance system as well as the world's first autonomous vehicle developed under the guidance of Ernst Dickmanns in Munich, called VaMP and the VITA-2 (Fig. 11.2), which drove autonomously on the dual lane motorway to the Paris Charles de Gaulle airport in France for more than a 1000 km, are prized achievements of this funding initiative. This success was furthered in 1996 by Professor Bianco and Alberto Broggi at the University of Parma, Italy, with their development of ARGO, a technology that incorporated two low-cost black and white video cameras and stereoscopic vision algorithms that allowed an autonomous car to understand its surroundings in real-time.

Contemporary AVs, armed with this background of technical research, embody one to several aspects of the dynamic driving task performed by automated systems without any human intervention, through its ability to sense its surroundings (Lutin et al., 2013; Report et al., 2015; Anderson et al., 2016; Lyon et al., 2017; Zmud and Reed, 2018). A fully autonomous vehicle can steer in a road network, detect objects in its surrounding, and drive safely without human intervention. Connected autonomous vehicles

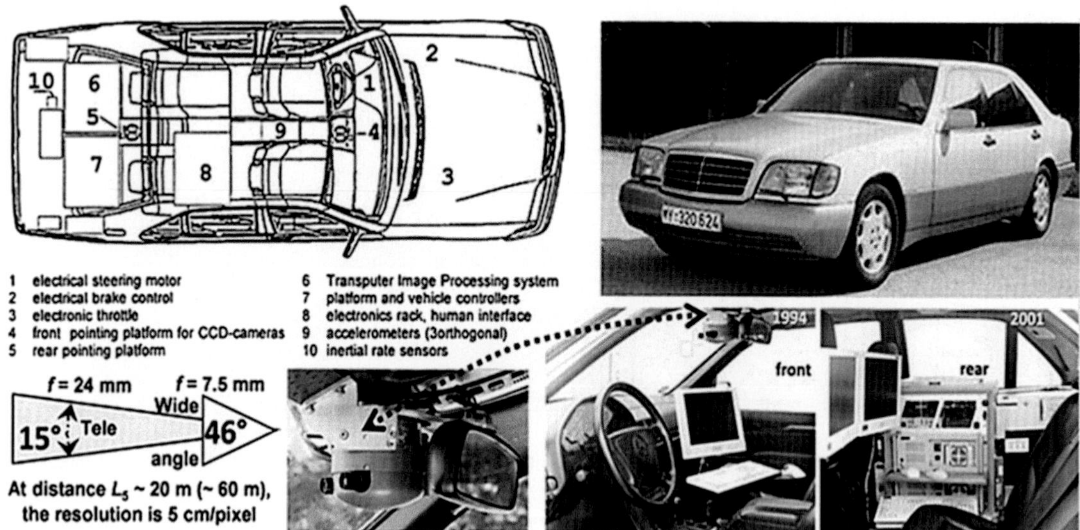

Figure 11.2 The VaMP driverless car developed as a part of the PROMETHEUS funding initiative developed under the guidance of Ernst Dickmanns in Munich, Germany. Ernst D. Dickmanns, Available at: https://en.wikipedia.org/wiki/VaMP.

(CAVs) can additionally communicate with the surrounding road infrastructure and other vehicles with what is called vehicle-to-infrastructure (V2I) and vehicle-to-vehicle (V2V) technology (Lyon et al., 2017; Zmud and Reed, 2018). They use a range of communications, electronics, and computing technologies. Depending on the context, they collect and transmit real-time traffic data and information to infrastructure networks such as ramp signals and dynamic lane control signs. Improving traffic flows on motorways by using advanced traffic signals that dynamically adjust in response to traffic conditions, to other connected vehicles, and in some cases to pedestrians through variable message signs.

The Society of Automotive Engineers (SAE) outlines five levels of autonomous functionality (SAE, 2018) (Fig. 11.3). These categorizations of automation can be classified within three scenarios: evolution, revolution, and transformation (Fraedrich et al., 2015). The evolution scenario constitutes technological innovations that help reach automated driving goals such as adaptive cruise control, lane-keeping assist, parking assist, and emergency braking assist and is of primary interest to automobile manufacturers. The revolution scenario involves innovations in ITS that combine data systems, AI, GPS-based mapping technologies, etc. and is of primary interest to ICT companies. The transformation scenario involves innovations wherein personal mobility is integrated with public transportation—autonomous shuttles, robo-taxis, etc., that cater to on-demand mobility and first-and-last mile connectivity, which is of primary interest to service companies and transportation departments. Fully autonomous evolution and revolution-based systems—Level 3 and above—are yet to enter the market and ply in actual traffic conditions (Shladover, 2016; Kyriakidis et al., 2019). However, automated public transportation such as metros, trains, and trams are already in service around the world (Fraszczyk and Mulley, 2017; International Association of Public Transport (UITP), 2018, 2011; Wang et al., 2016; Yin et al., 2017, etc.), but these require specialized supporting infrastructure.

It is asserted that these technologies have the potential to reduce accidents and thus improve travel safety (Fagnant and Kockelman, 2015; Prioritising the Safety Potential of Automated Driving in Europe, 2016), ease traffic congestion, and reduce emissions (Fagnant and Kockelman, 2015; Anderson et al., 2016); save time taken to travel (Steck et al., 2018); unlock valuable real-estate for other purposes (Pearce, 2017; Steck et al., 2018); and improve public transport effectiveness (Clements and Kockelman, 2017). Simultaneously, these technologies are hoped to improve social

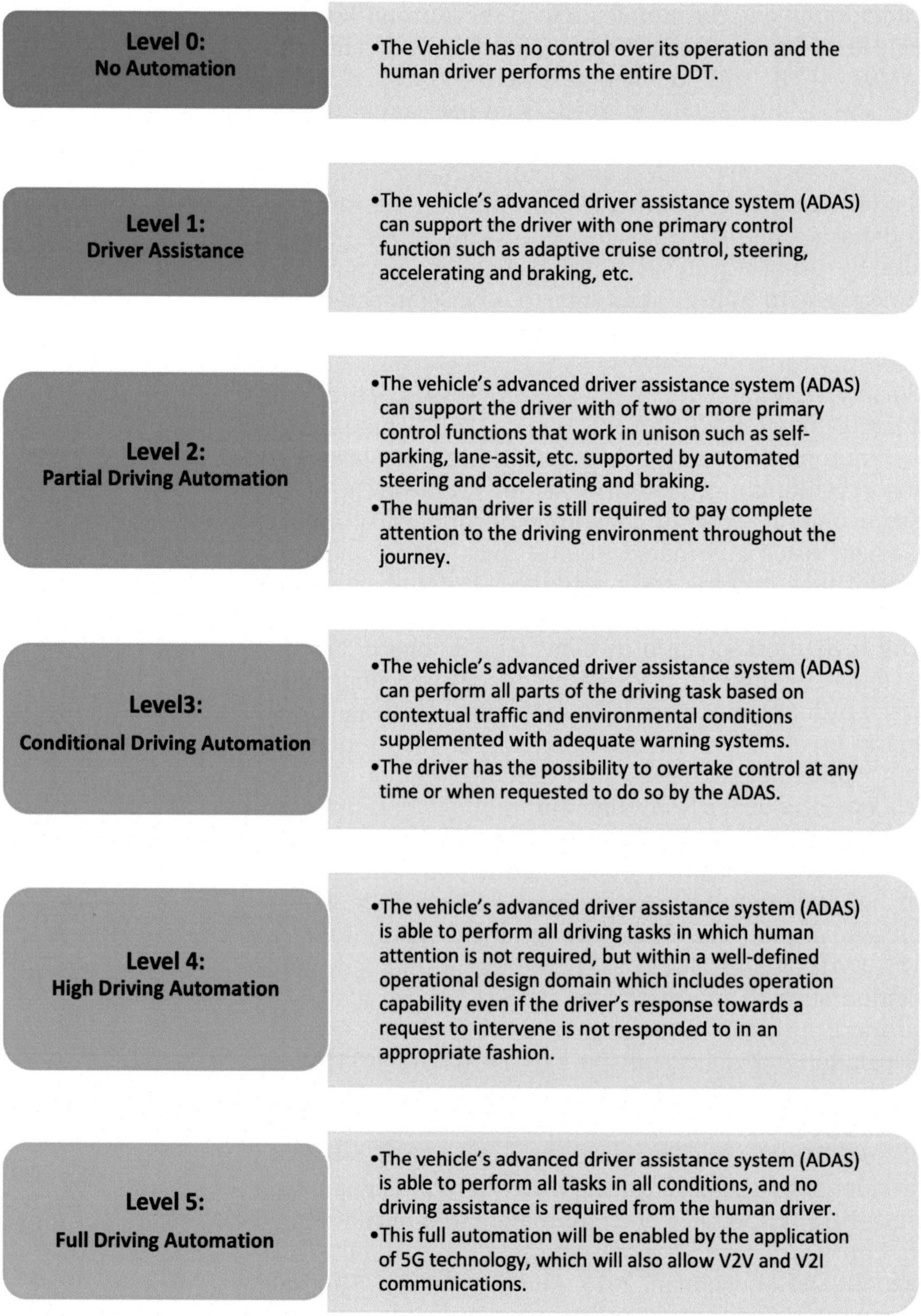

Level 0: No Automation	•The Vehicle has no control over its operation and the human driver performs the entire DDT.
Level 1: Driver Assistance	•The vehicle's advanced driver assistance system (ADAS) can support the driver with one primary control function such as adaptive cruise control, steering, accelerating and braking, etc.
Level 2: Partial Driving Automation	•The vehicle's advanced driver assistance system (ADAS) can support the driver with of two or more primary control functions that work in unison such as self-parking, lane-assit, etc. supported by automated steering and accelerating and braking. •The human driver is still required to pay complete attention to the driving environment throughout the journey.
Level3: Conditional Driving Automation	•The vehicle's advanced driver assistance system (ADAS) can perform all parts of the driving task based on contextual traffic and environmental conditions supplemented with adequate warning systems. •The driver has the possibility to overtake control at any time or when requested to do so by the ADAS.
Level 4: High Driving Automation	•The vehicle's advanced driver assistance system (ADAS) is able to perform all driving tasks in which human attention is not required, but within a well-defined operational design domain which includes operation capability even if the driver's response towards a request to intervene is not responded to in an appropriate fashion.
Level 5: Full Driving Automation	•The vehicle's advanced driver assistance system (ADAS) is able to perform all tasks in all conditions, and no driving assistance is required from the human driver. •This full automation will be enabled by the application of 5G technology, which will also allow V2V and V2I communications.

Figure 11.3 SAE automation levels. Adapted from Society for Automotive Engineering International SAE J3016. Author: Nimish Biloria.

and economic inclusion (Howard and Dai, 2014; Fagnant and Kockelman, 2015; Zmud and Reed, 2018), also for population segments with limited access, for example, elderly, special-needs individuals, and low-income groups. But, while there are several projected benefits, there is still a dearth of information and understanding concerning the requirements for fully autonomous motorized transport. Studies on consumer laws, insurance, and liability (Clayton Utz, 2016), data security and privacy (Clayton Utz, 2016), and rules and regulations (Shladover, 2018) concerning AVs are still very limited. Besides this, there has been very less debate and conclusive regulation developed based on recent accidents and resulting property and physical damage—including death caused by AVs. For instance, Waymo One, the robo-taxi service of Waymo since its launch in 2018 has had 18 accidents involving pedestrians, cyclists, drivers, and other objects while experiencing 29 separate incidents where a driver had to take control of the vehicle to prevent an accident (Wiggers, 2020). Similarly, 2 people were killed in a driverless Tesla car crash in 2021. This happens during a time when The National Highway Traffic Safety Administration is still investigating nearly two dozen crashes involving Teslas where they could have been using auto-pilot mode (Pietsch, 2021). Despite these incidents, no plausible response from these big corporations has yet been received with Tesla having disbanded its public relations team and Waymo as of 2021 has still not agreed to sign on agreements such as Safety First for Automated Driving, which describes a framework for the development, testing and validation of safe autonomous vehicles.

2.2 Operation models for AVs

The AV sector's operational models for can be broadly categorized as the following:

1. **Personal autonomous vehicles:** these are privately owned vehicles for personal use and come with benefits such as high level of convenience, freedom to perform activities within the vehicle without any restrictions, and convenience to leave personal belongings at will. This mode of ownership could benefit people who do not know how to drive, people who tend to travel regularly, people who reside in areas with limited mobility options, and people who prefer privacy and comfort. However, there are also flaws such as the cost of ownership, the possible inability to change or upgrade vehicles easily, and the added conundrum of promoting private vehicle use instead of public and shared modes of transport to reduce congestion.

2. **Shared autonomous vehicles:** these are self-driving taxi fleets owned by commercial service providers and are particularly appealing to people who incur low annual mileage while providing them with a choice to hire different vehicular typologies to suit their needs. This model's benefits include door-to-door services or dedicated pick-up zones while adding some level of social interaction. However, the disadvantages could range from inconvenience in terms of wait time, inability to ensure the vehicle's safety and cleanliness, and nonassistance if loading luggage or communications during emergency times. These disadvantages are also largely dependent on the commuters' civic behavior and the strict adherence to servicing regulations and general maintenance by the service provider.
3. **Shared autonomous rides:** these are primarily self-driving shuttles, vans, buses, etc. primarily mass-transit services to be aimed at improving first-and-last mile connectivity, inter-transit connectivity short-haul connectivity to shopping malls, schools, etc. Such services, akin to existing bus services, tend to be the least expensive owing to their shared nature but at the same time tend to be the least convenient as regards comfort, speed, and flexibility of the service itself, as opposed to on-demand services. Toyota's unveiling of the e-Palette ride sharing AVs at the 2018 CES show is a promising step toward the development of modular platforms that can be customized to suit various purposes such as public ridesharing, office and school transportation, and delivery vehicles. The cost aspect holds a promise for mass uptake of such mode of transport. Some researchers have investigated the relevance of shared autonomous services concerning costs incurred by customers as $1/km for a taxi to $0.25/km for other modes of shared AVs and the annual rate of return-on-investment as 13% for a fleet of 2118 AVs (Burns et al., 2013; Chen et al., 2016.; Fagnant and Kockelman, 2015). However, the impact of introducing shared AVs in addition to existing services is also bound to add to the congestion of today's overflowing infrastructure. Clever strategies for replacing conventional ride-sharing modes of transport in a phased manner by developing strategic roadmaps for the introduction of shared AVs thus need to be considered by transportation authorities globally.

Trackless Trams, a hybrid between a bus, a tram, and a light rail does show a promising alternative to smaller shared AVs for deploying large-capacity autonomous public transport. Apart from being able to tackle transporting a large number of people at one time—therefore reducing the total volume of cars on the road, trackless trams are able to operate electrically with batteries that have the capacity to recharge within 30 seconds at each station/stop or within 10 minutes at the end of the line. Equipped with an autonomous optical system, guided via GPS and Lidar technologies, and operating on rubber wheels, an important aspect of trackless trams is the complete absence of the need to lay physical tracks on existing infrastructure. This aspect not only speeds up the process of deployment of trackless trams, but also tremendously reduces deployment costs while creating minimal disruptions for laying new infrastructure (Newman et al., 2018). At the urban development front, similar to Light Rail, the potential for land development and associated property appreciation are benefits that such connectivity at minimal infrastructural costs could bring about. However, as is true for all transportation projects, the role of the government to support and assist in potential urban regeneration, community engagement, and financial support would be much needed to support such autonomous transport initiatives.

4. **Service and security vehicles:** Autonomous vehicles have also entered the service as well as the security sector. Services such as freight delivery, garbage collection, parcel, and postdelivery services within both urban and regional areas are all promising markets for driverless autonomous vehicles. Volvo, with its research and development in the vehicle automation sector, has already developed and tested autonomous electric vehicles that are wirelessly connected to a transport center and have demonstrated safe and efficient transport of goods in 2018. The vehicle, an autonomous tractor named VERA can be controlled and monitored via intelligent control center that is capable of monitoring the battery charge, load and location at any point in time and is able to maintain the efficient operation of an entire fleet accordingly. The Volvo group has also partnered with Aurora Innovation Inc. to develop and commercialize autonomous trucks to move cargo between different cargo hubs. Similarly, promising strides have been made within the autonomous waste collection trucks by Volvo. In a collaboration with Swedish waste and recycling specialists Renova in 2017, Volvo tested their autonomous refuse truck within urban areas. The use of preprogrammed routes and continual sensor-based monitoring and safety control for providing enhanced safety are some of the critical features of such autonomous service-oriented mobility.

In the defense sector, a study by the RAND Corporation (McKay et al., 2020) focused on the safety of military convoys (Fig. 11.4). RAND states that fully autonomous driverless vehicles

Figure 11.4 An example of a fully autonomous military vehicle: the mission master autonomous vehicle developed by Rheinmetall Canada. The vehicle incorporates an eight-wheel drive, skid-steer, electric, unmanned platform that ca n be operated in robotic, semi, or fully autonomous driving modes. Rheinmetall Defense, Available at: https://www.rheinm etall-defence.com/en/rheinmetall_defence/systems_and_products/unbemannte_fahrzeuge/mission_master/index.php.

would reduce the number of service members needed to operate large convoys in sensitive areas of operation and estimates that 78% fewer soldiers would be at risk as compared to current practices in 2020. Military concepts are being developed, from fully autonomous vehicles with the capacity to be completely unmanned; the partially unmanned, wherein a lead vehicle that is manned is followed by autonomous or slave vehicles; and minimally manned, wherein one person controls each AV to overlook the autonomous operations and the driving environment. According to RAND as opposed to the 78% risk reduction with the introduction of fully autonomous convoys, the partially autonomous convoy would put 37% fewer soldiers at risk, and a minimally autonomous convoy would put 28% fewer soldiers at risk. According to RAND, the partially unmanned concept is the one gaining maximal traction and will be deployed within the defense sector from 2019 onward. The minimally manned concept is already in operation and can be deployed in urban and highway environments.

Besides the automation perspective, research on the human component still needs to be conducted. According to RAND, the psychological pressure on soldiers who are manning the autonomous convoys could be extremely high owing to the sense of responsibility for the unmanned convoy that is following their vehicle. The need to be extremely agile and highly efficient in multi-tasking could also imply the hiring of experienced drivers only, thus creating a disadvantage for entry-level aspiring drivers. Pros and cons of vehicle automation in the military services thus need to be weighed from a safety, human as well as efficiency perspective simultaneously.

2.3 Business models for supporting AV operations

However, operational models cannot be sustained unless underpinned by sound economic feasibility and innovative business models. Interestingly, the aforementioned operational models can also be seen from the perspective of three general categories of business models (Berrada et al., 2017): "Product" based; "Service" based; and "Function" based business models. The Product model is linked with the production and sale of products wherein economic profitability depends on the unit's sale. The economic value of the product is thus connected to its future exchange value. This scenario directly relates to the "Personal autonomous vehicles" operational model wherein the provider not only sells the product but is also responsible for selling all associated maintenance, software, training, components, equipment, etc. connected with the AV. Thus, these business models require large investments and face strong competition among several national and international market participants to build personalized AVs.

On the other hand, service-based business models are primarily concerned with providing nontransferrable technical and intellectual services. Their primary feature is the interaction between the service provider and the customer, in this case, the commuter in the AV. According to Lovelock (Lovelock, 2014), the transport of persons and/or transport of goods supplemented by supporting services, such as skills and training services for stakeholders, and virtual and experimental platforms, are some of the business models for services catering to AVs. The "shared autonomous vehicles" operational model, which will primarily be owned and run by commercial service providers, can thus be classified under this business model. These models are relatively easier to deploy and are relatively low risk, provided that the service offered caters to customer demand and provides added value to the customer.

Function-based business models, also termed as a "product service system model," can be seen as a hybrid of the "product" model and the "service" model with the primary aim of fulfilling customer needs from the perspective of functioning units delivered to the customer. As customer satisfaction becomes key to such models' success, it is critical to optimize the product - in this case, the AV, its safety, utilitarian value, reliability, and service offering to enhance the willingness to use the AV. The "Shared autonomous rides" operational model falls into this category. It includes AV shuttles and similar mass-transit-oriented offerings and thrives on the direct association between the service provider and the successful uptake of the service by citizens, Such models are described as socially responsible and operating as sustainable business ventures (Roy, 2000; Beuren et al., 2013).

The concept of "shared mobility," which is presently gaining prominence via a plethora of car-pooling, ride-sharing, and public transport services, holds an exciting opportunity to reshape the operational and business models for the AV sector. The "Shared autonomous vehicles" and the "Shared autonomous rides" operational models associated with the corresponding "Service" and "Function" based business models will undoubtedly undergo further transformations as we reach levels of full automation. Models based on vehicle ownership criteria such as the Business-to-Consumer Service model, Peer-to-Peer Service model, and Hybrid Business/Individuals service model, in conjunction with network operation criteria, shall need to be carefully explored (Stocker and Shaheen, 2017). The future of AVs and their successful adoption in different countries rests on how relations between the individual/owner, the service provider/operator, the vehicle type, and the service models materialize. The business models' profitability and successful uptake will depend upon the hybridization of business models, critical aspects such as technology advancements, policy structures, legislation and regulations, customer engagement and satisfaction, including travel behavior preferences, and Avs' economic impact.

2.4 Commercial opportunities and availability of AVs

Despite the ongoing debates and decision-making processes to legalize and safely deploy AVs, Gartner (Rimol, 2019) predicts that more than 740,000 autonomous-ready vehicles will be added to the global market in 2023 (Table 11.1). This is a change of more than 400% from 2018, which was a modest 137,129. The primary reason for this increase is due to regulations and legislation currently being developed in Europe, China, and North America. The units, in this case, do not necessarily demonstrate the sale of physical units but point toward the net change in the total number of vehicles that are autonomous-ready, that is, vehicles with

Table 11.1 Autonomous-ready vehicles net additions, 2018–23 (Rimol, 2019).

Use case	2018	2019	2020	2021	2022	2023
Commercial	2407	7250	10,590	16,958	26,099	37,361
Consumer	134,722	325,682	380,072	491,664	612,486	708,344
Total	**137,129**	**332,932**	**390,662**	**508,622**	**638,585**	**745,705**

enhanced software and hardware such as cameras, radars, lidars, integrated navigation, and computerized vehicle monitoring software, which can make them capable of achieving a higher level of autonomy. Interestingly, early adopters have differing views on this expected growth, that is, whether it is privately owned AVs or shared AVs or shared public rides.

Another point of interest is the market-growth forecast to 2026 when the personal AV market, which was valued at USD 27.09B globally in 2017, has a projected compound-annual-growth rate (CAGR) of 41.50%. This implies that the AV market is expected to reach USD 615.02B globally by 2026 (Business Wire, 2019). This is fueled by the increasing need for restructuring and improving mobility infrastructure and decreasing car ownership, and transition toward shared mobility initiatives, aiming to reduce traffic density and congestion.

A transition toward Mobility-as-a-Service (MaaS) holds the key to this expected market growth with a significant focus on various forms of passenger vehicles. Allied Market Research (2019) suggests that the hardware segment will dominate this market growth and account for nearly three-fifths of the total market revenue. The services segment will also naturally gain momentum at both private and public sector levels and is expected to grow at a CAGR of 46.17%. In line with this projection, the robotaxi segment will witness the highest CAGR of 49.17%. Considering that the development of AV technologies and legislation and policies will result in a gradual change in the acceptability of Level 4 and 5 SAE-rated AVs by 2030, it would be safe to assume that maximum growth will be at the Level 2 and 3 modes of automation.

Though promising, the AV segment's projected market growth trends are still hinged upon fundamental technological development, governmental policy, laws and regulations, and customer demand and acceptability. However, the most critical threat to the AV market is associated with the software, quintessentially cyber-attacks, which, imply safety issues, data privacy, and loss of personalized control (Sheehan et al., 2019). Information networks that connect AVs containing information on financial networks, distributed sensor networks embedded within the infrastructure, traffic control and regulation networks (Lin, 2017), and V2V communication networks—in the case of CAVs (Elliott et al., 2019), are crucial but are prone to data breaches. This, in the long run, can result in disruption of traffic services, cause accidents, as well as result in data theft. Technological advancements will prove futile unless a foolproof cybersecurity protocol is put into practice to make it impossible for hackers and terrorist organizations alike to overtake AVs' control.

Apart from this technological vulnerability, the other associated risk to markets comes from this technology's very consumers. This risk in the form of psychological fear concerning safety factors comes in various forms: data theft and privacy concerns (Raiyn, 2018); lack of confidence in the AV's ability to operate safely in mixed traffic conditions (Othman, 2021); fear of automation failure and inability to take back control of the AV (Cunningham and Regan, 2015); feeling unsafe owing to the absence of driver/operator, etc. Thus, customer willingness to adopt the AV wave is critical to gain an audience for the AV revolution and uphold the projected market growth.

2.5 Customer insights

Recent incidents such as the self-driving Uber Volvo crash in Tempe, Arizona in 2018, which killed a pedestrian, and the Tesla Model X, which, while operating on autopilot hit a highway divider and burst into flames in 2018, have, for a good reason, tainted the confidence levels of customers with regards to AVs. Besides these issues concerning the safety of AVs, one of the biggest challenges stems from user trust in the system and the attitude toward technology, both crucial factors for gaining support and acceptance. Most studies focusing on these challenges are primarily opinion-based surveys and identify several perceptions and acceptance parameters that are mainly psychological, sociodemographic, functional, and economical. Most user knowledge is perception-based and is influenced by factors such as reports of AV crashes, technology biases, and general lack of knowledge on AVs. A major limitation of these studies is the lack of experiential information on user acceptance and trust in AVs by individuals with first-hand experience riding in an AV. Besides, studies that do test user interaction while riding in partially or highly automated AVs have been in artificially simulated environments and with manual controls where the driver can take back control from the vehicle (Merat and Jamson, 2009; Strand et al., 2011; Koustanaï et al., 2012; van den Beukel and van der Voort, 2017; Cramer and Klohr, 2019; Lodinger and DeLucia, 2019). Studies testing user perception, experience, and acceptance of autonomous shared rides as part of public mass transit are minimal, for example, The European CitiMobil2 trial, the DTU Lyngby Campus trial in Denmark, the Sydney Olympic Park Autonomous Shuttle Trial in Sydney.

Experience is key to how users feel about AVs. The opportunity to interact with AV technology and experience how the technology works can bridge the gap between perception and reality, remove some of the fears associated with AVs, and lead to greater acceptance. Capturing first-hand user experience and sentiments riding in AVs provides first-hand data concerning current capabilities and future requirements and improves our knowledge and understanding of the interactions between autonomous technology, road users, roadside infrastructure, and other vehicles. This knowledge will assist governments and policymakers in understanding existing perceptions, concerns, and acceptance levels and, in turn, will allow them to devise appropriate regulatory frameworks, policies, and governance structures to ensure a smooth transition toward a holistic autonomous mobility future.

3. Autonomous vehicles and sustainability

3.1 Principles of sustainable transport

Greenhouse gas emissions from global transport are a staggering 14% (IPCC, 2014), three-quarters of which is due to ground vehicular transport. These emissions are on the rise at a rate of 2.5% per year and are projected to double by 2050 (IEA, 2017). Besides this, the cost of traffic congestion alone was $124 billion in 2013, and this number is expected to reach $186 billion by 2030 (INRIX, 2014). Transport is seen as a key to addressing these issues. Sustainability is universally understood as creating constructive conditions for social, economic, and environmental welfare (Meadows, 1998; Rode and Burdett, 2011). Social equity, economic efficiency, and environmental responsibility have been three fundamental principles of sustainability. These three principles, when applied to transportation, acquire novel dimensions. For instance, environmental responsibility is directly connected with the discourse on clean and energy-efficient modes of travel that can positively impact the built environment and enhance health and well-being. Economic principles are directly connected with the earlier discourse on service and business models while embodying a socially responsible yet economically efficient structure that is cost-effective and inherently adaptive to changing customer needs. On the social front, transportation can ideally be more responsible for addressing issues such as enabling mobility that enhances people's well-being while uplifting their standard of living equitably. Some of the vital contributions could be addressing optimal coverage of neighborhoods, addressing the unique needs of varied demographics, such as the elderly, women, and differently abled, and structuring context-sensitive service offerings such as time and frequency of service.

Given this context of sustainable transport, the dominant perspective is that increasing efficient public mass transit will be the only key to attaining this sustainable vision. However, various other models such as car-sharing and car-pooling services and the new-entrant—self-driving or autonomous vehicles are being introduced. However, a generational divide, more specifically the Millennials and Gen Z as opposed to the Baby Boomer and Gen X generation, pertaining to the allure of personal car ownership still persists. For the Baby Boomers and Gen X generation, personal car ownership is deeply connected with social, cultural, and financial independence and stature. Apart from contributing to the convenience factor, it contributes to the psychological conditioning of how one thinks and portrays oneself (Sheller and Urry, 2000). On the contrary, Millennials and Gen X tend to favor car "access" over car "ownership" (Eliot, 2019). Car sharing, only next to public transport, has thus become the preferred mode of transportation for this generation. Zipcar's study comprising a sample set of 1045 adults over the age of 18 outlined in the Smart Cities Dive network (EMBARQ Network@WRIcities, 2017) of the personal transportation and car ownership behavior among the 18—34 years of age bracket revealed that almost 55% of the millennial population in the United States consciously decided to drive less. Environmental concerns tend to be the primary reason behind such a decision, coupled together with the cost of single ownership as opposed to the benefits of collaborative consumption initiatives, thus contributing to the sharing economy.

AVs on the other hand, from an environmental perspective, reap the benefits of automation for the practical application of eco-driving principles that allow for reduction of fuel consumption by 20% (Igliński and Babiak, 2017) while in-turn reducing greenhouse gas emissions. This ability of AVs is particularly beneficial for urban driving where traffic congestion is an everyday occurrence. However, such a scenario or for that matter even better scenarios can be attained if AVs become the predominant mode of transport since the collective operation of AVs will aid in eradicating human errors that impact the level of congestion. AVs owing to their in-built control systems are prone to follow speed limits and road regulations while negotiating and coordinating routes with other AVs and reducing the need for constant acceleration, thus ensuring a lower level of fuel consumption. AVs could also contribute toward the reduction of Greenhouse gas emissions from the built environment. This is specifically connected with the vast areas needed for building car parks. It is estimated that urbanized areas invest as much as 15% of urban space for building car parks (Ben-Joseph, 2012). The ability of AVs to be programmed to perform other services such as ridesharing during the time they are not being used by the original owner, as well as their ability to navigate on their own to find parking in places where the demand for space and thus cost of building is lower, allows for an overall decreased need for parking spaces in already overburdened urban settings. This can result in the reduced consumption of resources for building, reduced emission of greenhouse gas during the construction phase in addition to the reduction in large financial expenditure within urban areas with overpriced real estate. Given such environmental benefits for the future of accepting AVs in the built environment, one must not forget that the cost of AVs will become a deciding factor for their adoption. With costs almost 4 to 5 times that of conventional vehicles, the adoption of AVs might even result in an economic divide and ownership will become more of a status symbol rather than serving the original cause of being environmentally efficient while being equitable at the same time. Considering the aforementioned generational trend of aversion to ownership, rideshare options in the form of autonomous taxi fleets as well as autonomous public transport vehicles could hold a promising future. The rebound effects of this mode of sharing would imply higher traveled kilometers per vehicle and thus the lower life expectancy of the vehicle per se. However, it is expected that newer, more energy-efficient AV models with better end-of-life recyclability will replace them. This, in any case, would be a better option than using older more polluting cars or public transit vehicles as replacements—meeting Euro 6 or above standards. Additionally, the increasing efforts to produce better performing, lesser polluting, and more reliable engines, in conjunction with the electric car revolution, are all pointing toward this desire to contribute to the vision of sustainable transport.

Changing human behavior while at the same time being cognizant of the needs and demands of people at large, and generational trends are thus crucial while adopting AVs within the broader context of sustainable transport. It is also vital to consider the time and scale aspects of the various components of sustainable transport. For instance, in the case of AVs, components such as developing infrastructure, upgrading or changing policy, and introducing new modes of transport versus the rate of technological development, have different timelines of research, development, and implementation, different economic structures aiding or restricting them, differing scalability potential, and differing rates of social acceptance. These differences need careful consideration by local governments, AV manufacturers, AV service providers as well as analysts and researchers before proposing or making autonomous transport-oriented decisions. Coordinating such diverse components and successfully achieving the major dimensions of sustainable transport—environment, economy, and society (Fig. 11.5)—is not only a

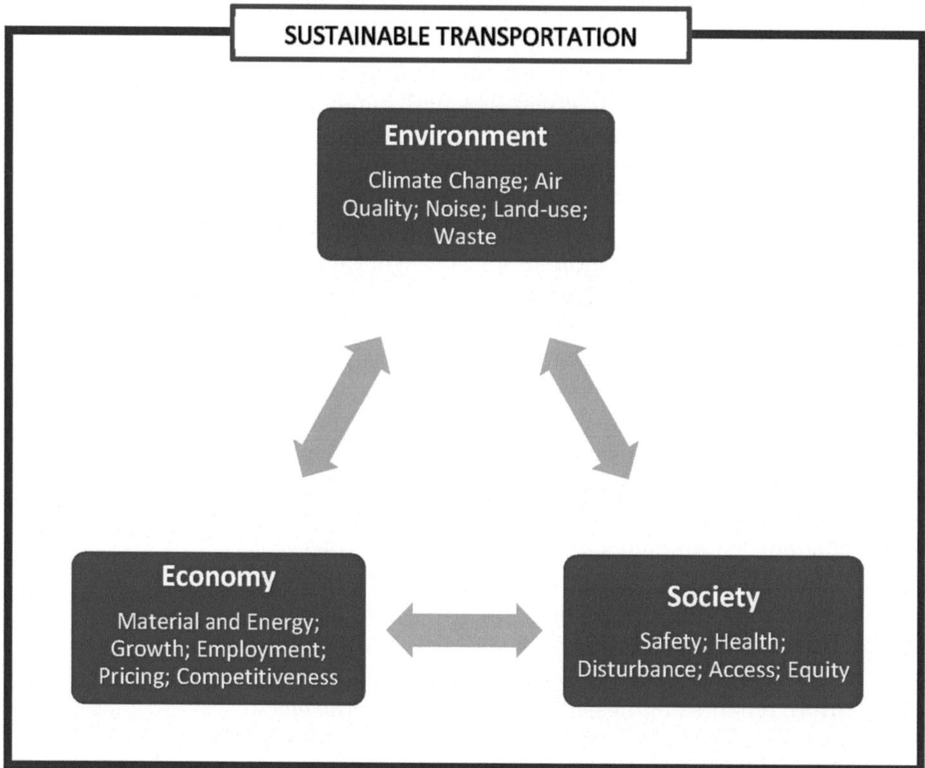

Figure 11.5 Three fundamental dimensions of sustainable transport. Author: Nimish Biloria.

challenging task for the aforementioned stakeholders but could result in flawed assumptions pertaining to the success of the sustainable transport vision by overplaying the achievements of one dimension over the other.

For instance, despite the equal importance of the three dimensions, the most prominent discussions concerning sustainable transport still tends to circulate around the environmental impacts of transport and consequently around mitigation measures relating to the same. These measures also tend to focus specifically on addressing greenhouse gas emissions and particulate pollution. The environmental equity dimension and its association with sustainable transport often take a back seat. The environmental equity dimension spans across concerns such as urban growth and environmental protection from the perspective of intergenerational equity as well as intragenerational equity (Feitelson, 2002). Intergenerational equity in this case concerns the intertemporal usage of natural resources to maintain a balance between use and recycling of resources to maintain a healthy balance between each societal generation. The intragenerational equity on the other hand concerns the fair use of global natural resources by the current generation. What should also be considered is the physical and social displacement that at times happen owing to new infrastructure developments. Encroachment of land, decentralization of activities, and the resulting relocation of existing functions on greenfield sites often result in equity concerns at a spatial and environmental scale, let alone the constriction of arterial routes owing to resulting urban connectivity requirements. The introduction of AVs and the associated ease of long-distance commutes in an efficient manner is bound to result in urban growth with people wanting to move to affordable locations. Resulting interconnections between existing arterial routes and the new urban settlements would thus need to be carefully planned while providing equal consideration to environmental equity. Responsible urban growth could also result in the development of polycentric models of cities that would result in the reduction of longer distance commutes while providing equitable opportunities for economic growth.

Given this context of sustainable transport and AVs, the following section dives deeper into the pros and cons of AVs as a sustainable mode of transport.

3.2 Are autonomous vehicles a sustainable mode of transport?

AVs have the unique ability to process contextual information faster than humans as they can exchange information using V2V and V2I communication technologies in real time. This aspect of AVs contributes to the economic efficiency principle of sustainable transport, increases road capacity, and organizes traffic flows optimally by reducing distances between each vehicle and can maintain lanes and spatially navigate in an informed manner to reduce or eliminate roadblocks and congestion (Kane and Whitehead, 2018). This organized behavior of traffic can thus significantly decrease road accidents by eliminating human error—a significant factor in road accidents. Besides this, owing to its ability to analyze its operational performance and engine health, AVs can manage maintenance and other associated services such as minor repairs by self-navigating to the nearest designated repair station (Hörl et al., 2016). This can drastically reduce road congestion due to vehicular breakdowns and better service efficiency by ensuring on-time arrival and departure rates. These calculated or rather quantified traffic behavior analytics and the resultant benefits have been rigorously tested via simulating AVs and their behavior in urban settings (ITF, 2014).

There are several advantages and disadvantages that need consideration. For instance, on the positive side, with the efficiency of travel that AVs bring with them, the demand for mobility increases, resulting in higher vehicle occupancy rates and thus reduction of energy consumption per passenger. However, this also implies that overall traffic volume, as well as road usage, will increase. This increase is owing to increased efficiency, potential for nondrivers and nonlicense holders to travel independently, and the rise in low-density peripheral developments due to ease of access, ultimately resulting in an increase in traveled kilometers (Lee and Kockelman, 2019). Apart from personal AVs, shared AVs, which in principle would expand services such as carpooling to service offerings developed by private enterprises. Convenience and ease of access aside and the possibility of such vehicles driving empty to reach their next passenger would also result in increased energy use and kilometers traveled. Also, having got rid of the arduous task of driving, interregional and interurban travel is deemed to increase, thus adding to the increase in energy use. Technical advancements and the associated increase in sensing, control, and automation enabling computations required to keep AVs operational also result in consuming more energy than conventional vehicles. Gawron et al. (2018) speculate a 4%

increase in emissions as compared to nonautomated vehicles over their lifetime. Mitigation measures for reducing energy consumption can range from customizing the design and size of shared AVs for task-specific goals; investment in electric and hybrid electric powertrains; on-demand dynamic ride sharing; vehicle-to-vehicle platooning, to name a few (Lee and Kocleman, 2019).

From a social equity perspective, AVs open up the mobility market to population segments that either do not know how to drive or have limited mobility options, for instance, the elderly, disabled, neighborhoods with limited mobility options, etc. This increase in accessibility results in creating an inclusive and equitable society as regards the provision of access. The possibility of AVs serving as a means for first-and-last mile connectivity further aids this demographic in securely traveling to various locations. However, the digital-heavy nature of AV services—in the form of digital platforms for service requests, etc., can also be a hurdle for the digitally illiterate or in areas with poor internet or mobile-service connectivity. Furthermore, AVs' positive impact on health and well-being due to reduced risk of accidents and increased accessibility and connectivity (Crayton and Meier, 2017) have been speculated. The increased reliance on AVs owing to ease of access could also lead to a sedentary culture due to decreased active means of travel such as walking and cycling.

From an environmental perspective, AVs and their associated organized behavior-oriented benefits can reduce carbon emissions with lesser fuel consumption and optimized routing increase the possibility of an electric future. However, these depend on multiple factors such as the rate of uptake, precision, and efficiency of the route guidance software, especially within hybrid environments where AVs and traditional vehicles cotravel. Electrification of vehicle drivetrains holds a promise toward reducing environmental pollution caused by vehicular transport. A 4.2% share of all passenger cars globally have promisingly shifted in the favor of electric vehicles and plug-in hybrids. This 1.7% increase from 2019 already shows a favorable level of interest within the electric vehicle segment. According to a Statista report compiled from ACEA, CAAM, and EV-Volumes, Norway, Iceland, and Sweden are global leaders in electric vehicle adoption with 74.8% of all vehicles being electric in 2020. In Europe, Germany reported an increase of 263% with respect to the sale of plug-in hybrids and electric vehicles in 2020. China, with a growth of 15% and a total of 1.2 million electric passenger cars sold in 2020 still leads the world in the electric and hybrid vehicle uptake. Given this tendency to harness electric-powered vehicles—which might become the ideal drivetrain for AVs, it is vital to consider the sources used for energy generation to holistically cater to the charging requirements for electric AVs. Investments within the renewable energy sector such as wind and solar farms as opposed to nonrenewable sources such as coal thus need to be increased significantly to promote a truly energy-conscious future.

After having elaborated upon the nature of sustainable transport and the pros and cons associated with the induction of AVs within the built environment, the following section elaborates upon four critical urban pillars that need to be addressed for paving an autonomous transport future.

4. Four urban pillars for defining a sustainable future with autonomous vehicles

The discussion so far covered issues ranging from automation, operation and business models, commercial viability and opportunities, customer insights, and relating the AV future to that of sustainable transport. No singular dimension can be held purely accountable for changing mobility behavior, leading to the wide-scale acceptance of this technology. All showcased a level of interdependence and projected simulated scenarios that will involve a redesign of our infrastructure, technology, and policies to ultimately impact mobility behavior.

What is evident, though, is the inherent interconnection between four key components constituting the urban context: Infrastructure: both physical and digital; Technology: hardware, software, communication, and data security; Customer: mobility behavior, service, and business model innovation from a person-centered perspective; and Policy: concerning liability, legislations, and universal standards. For instance, for customers, developing trust in the technology—operational safety and reliability, being certain about personal travel data privacy, and being assured that AVs will not become active targets of cyber-attacks are viable concerns. These are equally important concerns for technology developers, policymakers, and governments. Simultaneously, clarity regarding how innovative service models are beneficial, customizable, and equitable, apart from being economical, safe, and reliable, is equally important to customers, service providers, and associated technology developers.

Similarly, apart from enabling AVs' operation, the infrastructure component is also responsible for generating innovative land-use solutions and ensuring citizens' safety and well-being. It is thus of crucial importance to governments, technology providers, and vehicle manufacturers alike. Furthermore, automation will slowly but surely remove the need for drivers and necessitate effective safety legislation and regulations to be enforced. These also need to be ethical and equitable not only for owners/drivers/passengers of AVs but also for pedestrians and other vehicles. The four urban pillars of infrastructure, technology, customer, and policy will thus need to be critically understood to realize an autonomous future. These criteria will govern the chosen pathway to attain either "Augmented Mobility," incorporating AVs and nonautonomous vehicles, or "Full Autonomy" implying fully autonomous vehicles, including V2V and V2I communications. The following sections elaborate upon these urban pillars from the perspective of sustainable autonomous mobility.

4.1 Infrastructure

Historically, land-use patterns are planned around the type of mobility culture—such as automobile based versus mass-transit based versus active mobility based—and the urban theories that have shaped city development (Alonso, 1964; Getis and Getis, 1966; Thunen and Heinrich, 1966). For instance, the Bid-rent urban theory, developed in 1826, promotes an ideology wherein nearness to the city center or the commercial business district and its associated mixed-use nature, which facilitate everyday needs, have a higher value. Suburbia and urban sprawl are thus conditions where land value is lower but with a higher cost of transportation. To date, we seek a trade-off between land costs versus transportation costs to make decisions about where we live or work. Urban growth is often an outcome of such ideologies where expensive high-density city centers are often surrounded by less expensive medium-density and subsequently by cheaper low-density urban fabric in the form of urban sprawl.

An intricate relationship exists between infrastructure and transport connectivity, city planning theories, and the economic underpinnings of choice about living and working locations. The ease of access to interregional and interurban regions will propel urban growth. People's tendency to live further away and the gradual rise of polycentric cities subsequently impacts novel land use, and necessiates the need for informed urban planning. Such developments within the urban planning domain can result in positive changes to our living and working conditions and can impact our well-being and enhance our liveability while diminishing everyday costs—including costs associated with car ownership, maintenance, fuel, and travel time. However, as mentioned in 3.2, the overall increase in energy consumption, as well as the total kilometers traveled, are also foreseeable negative impacts of the inevitable urban sprawl. Mitigation measures suggested in 3.2 should thus be taken into account while developing future roadmaps for autonomous Vehicles and their varied service offerings.

From a place-making perspective, AVs will also directly impact everyday physical infrastructure, such as parking spaces, traffic intersections, pathways, street signals, and existing roads. For instance, V2I communication technologies that enable AVs to operate seamlessly require upgraded road networks with sensing and information relaying capabilities, excellent surface conditions without potholes, cracks or other irregularities lane divisions with retroreflective surfaces, and high-quality signages with good visibility. These would also need to be streamlined to enable safe driving conditions and seamless V2V and V2I communications. Furthermore, the communication between infrastructure maintenance/management companies and satellite and mapping companies would need to be much more accurate and real-time to inform the AVs of every possible spatial alteration that might affect their movement. Finally, the dynamic growth of automation technology, sensing, computational prowess, and AI and machine-learning capabilities would enable AV service providers, transportation researchers, and IT support teams to develop predictive analytics and maintenance capabilities to reduce operational costs and develop better safety standards. However, these technological advancements and integration efforts within existing urban infrastructure will also result in increased cost of construction and associated maintenance. Feasibility modeling and careful weighing of costs versus benefits, not only from an economic perspective but also from a social equity perspective, thus need to be conducted rigorously to arrive at informed decision-making.

One other urban element that could change would be parking—vertical, on-street, and dedicated parking lots. Presently, parking spaces consume enormous real estate, especially in dense city centers, considering that an average car is typically parked for 95% of its running life (David, 2016). AVs' ability to serve as a pick-up and drop-off service, which is projected to reduce car ownership and encourage car-pooling and ridesharing, could drastically reduce parking real estate and allow them to be relocated to peripheral areas. Apart from car-pooling and ride-sharing services, private AV owners could also program their vehicles to return home after dropping off other passengers instead of letting the vehicle sit idle at home. Researchers at the University of Toronto have simulated the effects of various parking layouts for AV-specific parking lots. Their findings suggest a 62%–87% more autonomous cars can be parked in the same parking lot as opposed to conventional cars. This can potentially lead to smaller parking lots and aid in freeing up urban space (Nourinejad et al., 2018). However, consider a scenario where private owners would not want to pay for parking, and thus program their vehicles to roam freely on the urban streets till a pickup is requested. This could also have repercussions such as increased congestion on the streets owing to the quantum of AVs occupying existing infrastructure. At the same time user tendencies, specifically of private owners wanting their vehicles to be available within a few minutes. This could unlock premium city-center real estate for other activities that do not compromise density and are conducive to health and well-being, such as active Mobility—walking, cycling, sports, etc., green spaces, and public spaces. However, governments would need to be strategic about how these changes impact their revenues—loss of parking revenue, fuel tax, etc. They will need to develop innovative partnerships with commercial stakeholders such as infrastructure companies, ICT companies, telecom and mobility service providers, and companies invested in better health and well-being to ensure a steady infrastructure budget.

Infrastructure networks, in the case of sustainable autonomous transport systems, imply physical and digital networks that will aid in AV operations. Physical infrastructure such as motorways and other large-scale fixed assets tends to be long-term initiatives and are cost-intensive and complex to build and alter. Furthermore, the rapid pace of technological change and the adoption of new trends and behaviors by society, at times, outpace the time frame within which new physical infrastructure projects are erected. This could lead to discontinuities in catering to changing infrastructure needs down the line. Thus, investment in infrastructure upgrades and new projects must be efficient and agile and gradually build up capacity while incorporating a level of flexibility and nimbleness to absorb evolving needs and trends. AVs, including driverless trains, freight operations, light rail/metro services, allow for platooning or automated distance maintenance between each vehicle, and real-time information communication to increase the network's capacity. However, at the same time, carrying capacity—autonomous public shared vehicles versus autonomous private cars, and the physical spaces these occupy should also be considered. Thus, the decision-making process surrounding the development of infrastructure networks should be synchronous with contextual needs. A calculated consideration of the aforementioned capacity versus infrastructure footprint occupancy, and generational trends needs to be carefully considered. Equally crucial is the understanding and design of road and street environments based on land use and demographic. Thus, considering the complexity of handling a vast number of variables alongside rapid technological growth within the AV sector, it is deemed desirable that government departments of transport, urban planning, and sociocultural policymakers operate as a team. This will aid in developing strategic planning frameworks, support, evaluation toolkits, and operating plans.

Digital infrastructures, such as those embedded within our physical networks to support autonomous transportation, should become a priority while retrofitting or upgrading existing infrastructure and as a standard for all new infrastructure projects. Intelligent management centers that collate, process, and analyze large datasets to inform intelligent congestion management systems—automated ramp signals, dynamic lane control signs, dynamic traffic signals, variable message signs for pedestrians, etc, and to communicate with AVs should become an inherent capability of contemporary infrastructure initiatives. This should be equally applicable to freight services, optimizing routes, reducing congestion, and supply chain timelines while maintaining high safety standards. However, the impact of this digital revolution should not only be limited to the digitally literate but should filter through to information imparting public infrastructure facilities such as bus stop displays and electronic signages and, if possible, should integrate with conventional news media to have a far-reaching and inclusive outlook to benefit commuters.

Additionally, data from smart roads and motorways with advanced vehicle tracking capabilities, embedded sensors, and safety monitoring systems should, in combination with contextual data sensed by the AVs, be harvested in real time and subjected to machine learning and analytics. These would aid in discovering congestion and accident patterns and resolving these in real-time, extracting information related to travel time and maintenance schedules, communicating these with customers in real-time to help them plan their travel, and predicting road maintenance schedules. However, one should not forget the pace of technological development, and thus digital networks should have the flexibility to adapt and scale. An excellent way to do this would be to establish partnerships between governments, technology sectors, and vehicle manufacturers to collectively understand the challenges, limitations, and opportunities presented by the digital infrastructure.

Aspects of sustainable development that enhance human health and well-being reduce the burdens of ownership, use infrastructure more efficiently, and provide back to society by enhancing liveability are some of the benefits that can be attained by redefining our infrastructure. However, to advance AVs as a sustainable mode of transport, recognizing and understanding the present and future challenges, and accordingly developing inherently adaptable infrastructure networks, allowing for the reuse of existing assets, amplifying capacity, and supporting innovative service provisions is quintessential. Breaking down siloed thinking and engaging in a future where data sharing and multi-criteria optimization for improving the performance of our infrastructure and enhancing place-making attributes of our cities should become the ultimate goal of redefining infrastructure.

4.2 Technology

Telematics play a crucial role in the real-time transfer of data to and from an AV. Both fully automated data capture—using infrastructure embedded sensing, in-car sensing, GPS systems, and data relayed from transportation authorities, as well as automation combined with human data input, for instance, mobile applications such as Waze, enrich geospatial and spatiotemporal datasets, which aid in the seamless performance of AVs. Thus, advances in telematics are of prime importance to reliably communicate the actual state of the context to and from the vehicle, including geospatial mapping, physical location mapping, and communication of the state of the infrastructure at any given time. Technologies that support V2V and V2I communications, for instance, licensed dedicated short-range communication (DSRC), sensor visualization, etc., irrespective of the presence of internet services or failure of sensors in vehicles, will allow for continuity of data communication (Anderson et al., 2016). Additionally, secure and fast data communication via telematics could also be harnessed for both operating system updates and allied web-associated content services, for instance emailing, web conferences, Netflix, etc. within AVs.

However, successively reaching a scenario wherein seamless data communication would become the norm requires an iterative approach. This implies harvesting the power of current 4G LTE and 5G networks for data transfer and communication, but this depends on how local governments, AV service providers, and IT infrastructure providers make wireless services available and accessible using secure pathways. Establishing mutual contracts between telecommunication providers, vehicle manufacturers, service operators, and governmental bodies should thus be encouraged to test the feasibility, speed, and reliability of such modes of communication. Trials involving existing or purpose-built real traffic scenarios with embedded V2V and V2I communication infrastructure should also be extensively tested to generate confidence within the average citizen and push for technology acceptance. While it is highly contested whether the use of independent communication systems approaches, such as onboard sensors only, DSRC only, and Wi-Fi/Bluetooth only, would suffice. Anderson et al. (2016) state that a preference for a combinatorial approach using a mix of these technologies could produce highly beneficial and trustworthy communication protocols.

Among the most significant points of mistrust and fear toward the adoption of AVs are data security and privacy (Pype et al., 2017) and the ownership of the data (of the vehicle, its owner, and/or passenger) (Von Solms and Van Niekerk, 2013; Petit and Shladover, 2015; López-Lambas, 2018), especially since customization and personalization within service models, could become the norm in the future. Being people-centric and catering to individual needs without mining individual travel behavior while building robust security protocols across many automakers is indeed a daunting technical challenge. The need for fail-proof security measures, which prevent any hijack of the AV's operating system that allows a third party to take vehicular operations, is extremely critical without which an autonomous future is highly unlikely to prevail. Both digital cyberattacks that can compromise visual information and road infrastructure-related information and physical attacks aimed at faltering the hardware need to be considered equally seriously (Lima et al., 2016). Vehicle communication data such as the time of usage of the vehicle and geolocation and parking locations of the vehicle are equally susceptible datasets that are prone to cyberattacks. AV manufacturing companies themselves carry a huge burden to ensure security and have strict regulations and safety checks for products procured from suppliers (Parkinson et al., 2017) and ensure that installed microcontroller chips within the vehicle's hardware are able to signalize cyberattacks. Stavova et al. also argue for enhancements of in-vehicle user interfaces to allow for frequent updating of the cybersecurity enhancement options (Stavova et al., 2018).

Furthermore, in-vehicle platforms, which continually gather operational performance data, also gather passenger/owner data, for instance, in-vehicle camera and GPS systems such as Tesla's sentry mode. While a boon during insurance and liability claims or during security and regulatory-related scenarios such as accidents and theft, the very availability of this data poses a challenge. Issues of data ownership and personal data privacy and the right to reveal the same is a highly contested territory (Lee, 2017). Travel and behavioral patterns, when harnessed for analytics, could create unfair benefits for insurance companies—creating unfair behavioral and character opinions based on visits to certain geo-locations such as pubs/bars, brothels, restaurants, and casinos and cross-referencing it with their age, race, gender, and sexual preferences. This could be used as a base while calculating insurance premiums and credit ratings or during insurance and liability claims (Rannenberg, 2016). To build a sustainable pathway for AVs, such technical yet very human concern needs urgent attention, and if not catered to, can create an environment of inequality and social discrimination. One way to address these issues would be to anonymize personal data, limit data storage timelines, and highlight only personal behavior trends that affect vehicular performance. Thus, a balance between corporate ownership of data for economic gains and personal, but anonymous, optimized service provision would be desirable from both customer and policy perspective.

4.3 Customer

Customer-centric design and customer experience are vital to attracting customers to the AV segment, especially concerning service offerings. While in-vehicle connectivity and media-oriented packages would become prime features for attracting customers, customer feedback-driven service offerings should be of prime importance. Furthermore, to be sustainable—from the economic, social and environmental front simultaneously, there needs to be a mix between improving customer experience and accomplishing goals and visions set forth by governments and service providers alike. Thus, as opposed to developing a plethora of mobile applications with one-sided service offerings, a cocreation approach must be initiated wherein governments, industry, and customers work together to shape efficient autonomous operations. Instead of this, three criteria should always be the cornerstones of cocreation strategies: (1) connecting communities in an equitable, ethical, and safe manner; (2) transforming service delivery models through technology; and (3) enriching customer experience through personalized and customized service offerings.

Apart from pick-up and drop-off services, service offerings should aid in first-and-last mile connectivity, include integrated payment systems, and, most importantly, provide customers with real-time travel information such as traffic conditions, best modes of transport, travel times, and prices. Thus, the effective use of geospatial and spatiotemporal datasets, collected by vehicles and people, would become defining elements for customer interfaces and associated customization options of the future.

MaaS, which is inherently inclusive and equitable, would benefit from such open-data communication platforms that keep customers informed in real time. Networked and connected AVs including busses, taxis, car-pooling/car-sharing cars, trams, freight, and ferry could become the medium for exchanging real-time data, especially pertaining to the best mode of travel and transport connections to reach one's destination at any given time. Additionally, integrating spatial and commercial datasets could provide other on-demand delivery to customers while providing commercial opportunities to local businesses. Thus, customer input via participatory interfaces could become the next medium for understanding user needs, opinions, and demands. This is of particular value to sustainable autonomous mobility (SAM)—from a social learning perspective, since it can provide opportunities for AI and machine learning systems to learn and enrich personalized service provision and provide seamless on-demand Mobility.

This mode of customer-centric mobility implies that governments would need to initiate regulatory mechanisms of open data and change the top-down, centralized control over current mobility options. Governments would also need to rethink regulations that hamper innovative service model experiments including aspects of data security and privacy while allowing for a competitive marketplace approach to emerge. Though technological giants like Google, after acquiring Waymo, have entered the AV market, the driverless vehicle market is already being heavily explored by individual car manufacturing companies like Tesla, Volvo, Ford, and Mercedes to name a few. This multiplicity of players within the driving automation sector seems promising for breeding a competitive market at the commercial front. It remains to be seen if companies like Waymo, who primarily are engaged with developing sophisticated AI and Machine Learning applications to enable autonomous driving, under Google's management diversify and specialize in distributing advanced control systems to other car manufacturers. Enabling large-scale pilot projects involving AVs, digital platforms for services, and experience-based feedback from customers should in any case become much more widespread. The outcomes of such experiments, once analyzed, would facilitate inventive collaborations between the government and the private sector while at the same time allowing successful service providers to operate and deliver customer-centric outcomes. Contributing to a shared economy while maintaining ethical competitiveness and addressing customer needs could become a vital step in achieving SAM.

Other essential sets of SAM criteria are equity and safety. Personal safety and the safety of pedestrians and other vehicles are critical to customers within the AV context. The development of advanced driver assistance systems is currently geared toward eliminating human error by developing capabilities of advanced perception of context by the vehicle itself (Hayashi et al., 2012; Shim et al., 2012; Lee et al., 2014; Li et al., 2014; Naranjo et al., 2016). Given this safety parameter, social equity, as a critical aspect of sustainable and empathic cities, will need to be critically assessed. The proposed service offerings and economic conditions built around the AV ecosystem should also cater to the most vulnerable such as poor, elderly, and disabled by assisting them in performing everyday tasks efficiently and becoming more participative and economically independent.

Furthermore, AVs' cost when they are first released, and the availability and accessibility of economically affordable service offerings should also be addressed at the onset. The autonomous revolution's impact could be undesirable if comparable pricing and connectivity options are currently available and are of better value in the autonomous ecosystem and only available to the wealthy and able-bodied population. Catering to issues such as limitations in accessibility due to physical ailments, such as vision impairment, wheelchair-bound, etc., nonownership of a vehicle, or nonaccessibility of mobility options due to low economic status, age, and health ailments that prevent mobility should become critical issues for sustainable autonomous mobility. Another critical factor, from a social equity perspective, is to highlight and communicate the value of automation as it regards the distribution of the human workforce. This is vital from a social acceptance perspective wherein the benefits of an autonomous future in terms of safety—reduced accidents and technical failures, and efficiency—predicting failures and enabling agile response systems, need to be balanced versus the possible loss of jobs to automation. Innovative models addressing new job creation and upskilling that enable the coexistence of technology and human jobs—managing systems, customer services, etc., should be adopted to ensure widespread social acceptance of autonomous mobility.

With an increase in refining electric and hybrid vehicle platforms as well as the ever-increasing advances in AI that AVs could potentially adopt, the possibilities for reducing pollution levels, noise levels, traffic accidents, travel time, etc. can be substantially mitigated. Furthermore, freed-up real estate, owing to the reduction of parking spaces, could potentially be repurposed to benefit society. Developing affordable housing or spaces for active mobility—running, cycling, walking, etc. or green spaces that could become the city's lungs that help reduce pollution could be some such innovative repurposed functionalities. Naturally, government willingness and financial support in conjunction with maintaining a healthy competitive market are essential to develop such evidence-based approaches that redefine mobility. However, as was discussed in earlier sections, issues surrounding added costs for enhancing infrastructure for V2I communication, their maintenance and upkeep, costs of AVs themselves and the lack of user confidence in safety and personal data security, are all areas of concern. This context, without the development of suitable financial incentives from the Government to encourage the uptake of AVs, are all factors that could hamper the growth of this innovative sector. The impact of SAM with respect to its embedded social, environmental, and economic value thus needs to be carefully weighed. This exercise is deemed essential for rethinking our cities and for offering a sustainable social paradigm.

4.4 Policy: standards, regulations, and liability

The establishment of government and industry standards—engineering criteria pertaining to technology design and communication—and public regulations—codes of law, are critical for a sustainable autonomous transport future. However, owing to the relative novelty of the AV technology and the long timeframes involved in developing and delivering regulations and standards, progress at these fronts is relatively slow. Rapid technological evolution and breakthroughs (Wees and Kiliaan, 2004) are factors that need to be considered by regulators and standards development bodies globally. The feasibility of standards needs to be evaluated through prototyping, testing, and assessment before developing strict regulations. Meta-regulations, such as setting out strict measures for testing new technologies that are ethical and unharmful to people and other road users, should be established, facilitating unbiased testing and trialing before strengthening said regulations. Reaching consensus with AV stakeholders and considering the economic feasibility of new standards is another factor that could hamper the standardization of technology. However, adhering to similar technology principles—common principles of safety and security, driving performance, data privacy, etc., and weighing their physical performance rates could become a basis for applying equitable standards across different industrial sectors.

In order to inspire customer confidence the development of new trials and technology should be made transparent, and findings should be made public. Consensus about safety issues such as collision avoidance, object recognition, and situation awareness should be strictly monitored by safety regulators as well as vehicle manufacturers and service providers. Testing and evaluating new standards should also consider the population's diversity concerning understanding, retaining, and responding to the AV system's directions. A sustainable vision of an equitable and unbiased understanding of both internal and external system interactions, their performance concerning human-machine interaction, and the performance of sensors and control systems in varied environmental conditions (Milakis et al., 2017) should thus become the norm.

Interconnected with the standards and regulations component, the liability component is equally important for building trust and determining the economic efficiency of the concerned parties—the passenger/owner/driver, the insurance provider, and the manufacturer. The dissociation of the driver from a fully autonomous vehicle—levels 4 and 5, puts the onus of liability on the manufacturer of the autonomous technology. Although a projected autonomous future will eradicate human error (Kane and Whitehead, 2018) and thus reduce accidents, the burden of designing and developing robust technological operations, which are less likely to falter increases exponentially for the manufacturer. This implies that manufacturers would become cautious about releasing their AVs and/or accompanying guidance and data harvesting and communication systems in the market. Another area of impact would be the cost of AVs. Due to liability issues, manufacturers could build in liability-related economic costs within the overall product cost, making the vehicle itself expensive and thus not economically affordable for all (Priest, 1985). Besides this, the level of safety standards, which could be improved with technological development, could also be a point of contention concerning the risk that the manufacturer is willing to take, which has direct implications on the physical risk posed to the user of the AV. Liability connected with the level of communication and intuitive comprehension afforded by in-vehicle communication systems would imply extensive testing and understanding of human behavior before a manufacturer decides to deploy their AVs. These added responsibilities, as well as the financial risks, could very likely propel most manufacturers toward weighing the benefits of service offerings such as robotaxis and car fleets versus private AVs for which they are liable.

5. Conclusion

Redefining transportation for an autonomous future is a complex task that requires technological progress coupled with economically feasible service models and requires a deeper understanding of changing customer demands/needs supported by robust standards and regulations. This implies that the mobility sector needs to adopt a more adaptive, flexible, and agile system that acknowledges the rapidly changing nature of technology and its influences at the sociocultural and planning levels. The one-model fits all approach needs to be rethought. Understanding the city as a mosaic of cultural, economic, and demographic mix with differing needs must be considered for developing customized service, pricing, and operation models. This chapter not only identified the nested value of the pillars of infrastructure, customer, technology, and policy within the bigger discourse on sustainable autonomous transport but has also tried to present their implications on sustainable urban development. Through the lens of an AV revolution, the notion of mobility will have direct implications on how our urban environment and its nested infrastructure lifelines—both physical and virtual, will impact social, economic, and environmental sustainability. Besides this, it is also clear that if our cities need to embrace empathic and responsive service offerings cognizant of citizens' needs and demands, then service models and associated business operations need to become innovative and embrace customer-driven solution space. While doing so, it is also vital to respect the essence of sustainable development with its three fundamentals of equity, economics, and environment. These three aspects of sustainability and their intricate relationship constantly feature in the urban pillars elaborated upon in this paper. The links between equitable accessibility, elevated living standards, physical and mental well-being due to responsive service provisions, and technological and associated environmental benefits are amply evident throughout the discourse. What has also come to the fore is the need for both governments and industry—both corporates and service providers, to change their outlook from core profit-making to a socially beneficial approach as the accepted mode of operation.

From a technology perspective, AVs are inherently data collecting, data processing, and data communication entities. AVs' capacity to optimize routes, reduce congestion, reduce pollution, increase accessibility, and yield economic benefits can potentially result in building a sustainable and healthy future. However, we should not take this at face value but rather be strategic in weighing the pros and cons of the widespread use of AVs in our everyday life and its impact on the built environment. For instance, on the mobility front, AVs can increase urban densification, reduce travel time, and make land value equitable. However, it can also give rise to urban sprawl, promote AV dependency, increase the total number of vehicles on the road, and increase door-to-door deliveries that reduce active mobility levels, thus adversely affecting health and wellbeing.

Furthermore, while AVs could reduce the burden of car ownership, it could also increase undesirable competition between public transport versus shared mobility versus private vehicles. Similarly, on the social front, AVs could free-up prime real estate due to a lesser need for parking spaces, which could be used for active mobility, affordable housing, green spaces, and/or other similarly innovative and beneficial models. However, these could also be used for building profit-making, socially undesirable ventures. Other positive social impacts could be a decrease in congestion; increase in road safety; reduction in travel costs; and better accessibility for all. At the same time, AVs could negatively impact employment, be inequitable for the digitally nonliterate, give rise to premium services that increase costs, and render misuse of personal data and preferences not only by hackers but also by insurance companies and corporates alike. Governments, policymakers, manufacturers, and software developers must be cognizant of such opposing ramifications and conduct extensive research via active collaboration with all impacted stakeholders to verify and weigh such pros and cons before developing and implementing standards, regulations, and policies.

Additionally, these regulations and policies, especially concerning liabilities, should ensure a democratic playing ground and be equally applied to all people, manufacturers, vehicle operators/service providers, and governments. Opportunities for prototyping, testing, trialing, and educating both human and AI/machine learning processes should be encouraged while allowing for flexibility and adaptability within regulatory frameworks. Similarly, regulations and policies concerning ownership of data, anonymizing data sets, and storage timeframes of data sets should be tackled at the onset amicably and inclusively. It is therefore crucial to establish a coalition between the government, the customer, the private sector, and the research community to capture ground realities and become strategic and proactive in delivering equitable and feasible autonomous mobility solutions.

Policymakers and researchers who provide evidence-based data to policymakers should take cognizance of the fact that current operational scenarios for AVs are not modeled on the basis of an overall change in the activity patterns of users. These changes that will be brought about by the integration and uptake of AVs in the near future will impact workplace and living locations, resulting in the need for new connecting infrastructure, and an increase in public space as a by-product of the reduced need for parking. Modeling autonomous transport systems to forecast and equitably accommodate a changing society should thus become a prominent backbone of any policy development concerning AVs in the built environment. Another issue that policymakers need to take heed of is the fact that integrating AVs in the built environment is an inherently multi-disciplinary task. Typical trends of portfolio-based siloed policy-making within the Government sector thus need to be revisited in favor of multi-disciplinary decision-making committees that can holistically make informed decisions. Implications on urban growth, infrastructure development, social equity, demographics as well as regulations and transportation policies thus need to be understood from a relational perspective before generating policies and legal frameworks concerning AVs.

On the industry front, a bigger picture understanding of material ecosystems and the employment market needs to be considered as well. For instance, concerns over job losses for delivery—food as well as goods, the role this plays in both formal and the informal market, and the simultaneous increase in demand for mining ores to meet the requirements of building microchips and associated control system hardware, need to be considered as integrated challenges that need to be addressed. Besides ensuring healthy competition within the AV market, one also needs to be cautious about fair workforce regulations and the impact of automation within the manufacturing sector that AV manufacturers deploy. It is equally important to consider issues surrounding circularity and end-of-life implications with respect to the materials used and how they are resourced and recycled to cultivate a truly sustainable outlook for the AV industry. The AV industry could also take up tasks of the upskilling workforce that would be otherwise made redundant owing to the increasing use of automation in construction and find ways of reintegrating them within the industry.

Land use planners also need to consider and project potential urban growth implications due to the advent of AVs. Urban growth owing to the ease of commute, navigational efficiency, and organized traffic flow will allow for both people and workplaces to be located in further off locations. Reorganizing land use and the development of connecting infrastructure in an equitable and efficient manner is thus a critical issue to be considered. At the same time, investment in the development of intelligent infrastructure as well as the integration of pick-up locations for shared autonomous services, and redevelopment of public infrastructure services, etc. all fall under land-use development initiatives. Besides this, the integration of the AV network with the energy network prepares for a future where electric vehicles take up a large share of the AV market. Similarly, initiatives such as optimal integration of wireless 4 and 5-g network infrastructure with existing and new roads should be simultaneously conducted to prepare for a connected autonomous vehicle future.

Data providers specifically need to pay attention to the usage of data that will be generated by AVs. Commercial use of private data, hacking into data portals as well by illegal entities as well as the use of sold data by marketing companies to name a few, are all issues that the AV sector and more specifically data providers should be addressed. The issue of protection of privacy or in other words data generated by privately owned AVs and shared AV service providers is still a big question that is left unanswered by potential data providers such as Google, Amazon, and Lyft. Sylvia Zhang, in her article titled *Who owns the data generated by your smart car?* (Zhang, 2018), issues a word of caution by Amnon Shashua—cofounder of Mobileye—to companies such as Google and Uber to take privacy concerns extremely seriously to ensure a smooth uptake of AVs in the near future. A scenario where data privacy, consent-based data usage, and similar practices in conjunction with the user/owner of AVs become an ethical practice should thus be aimed for. In conjunction with this, legal rights and regulations around ownership of AV data need to be developed at a faster pace to avoid scenarios where ownership and rights over all user data become the property of AV companies. A high level of transparency should be maintained around this critical issue surrounding data privacy to inspire confidence among potential AV aspirants.

Questions, such as wether computer-driven autonomous cars will be safer, or wether we will feel psychologically secure in a driverless vehicle at all times, are still to be addressed and proven. A more prominent and reflective issue however is the AV movement's desire to solve how we use cars rather than focusing our attention on how to reduce the amount of car usage itself. The immense number of cars on the road and the excessive reliance on motor vehicles are the central issues that needs addressing if targets of efficiency, convenience, and environmental sustainability are ever to be reached. In the business-as-usual scenario where human-driven cars are still the majority in the 2020s, it is impossible to reach or even assume the full efficiency and associated benefits of an autonomous future, which at best are projected calculations when autonomous transport would become the norm. Platooning scenarios associated with AVs are also most likely beneficial for long-singular direction inter-city travel—which, in any case, are usually less congested zones, as opposed to the real problem: shorter trips with frequent stoppage at intersections to allow for multi-directional traffic flow within urban settings. Martin Daum—CEO of Daimler, Germany, in 2018, after having conducted dedicated platooning trials for freight trucks not only hinted that Platooning might not be the solution that everyone was hoping for but also eventually canceled the entire program altogether (Roberts, 2018). The other fear associated with increasing travel efficiency via AVs is their distribution on local/interior routes, which normally tend to be quieter, people friendly, and relegated to low-speed travel, to meet the target of congestion reduction on primary routes. Compensating for such diversion would be eventually met via adding traffic volume and increasing speed limits on streets that were otherwise quiet and socially active. It is yet questionable if AVs hold the key to answering critical urban issues such as traffic congestion, reduction of car usage, and reduction of environmental pollution or will the development of electrically powered efficient public transport networks for large-scale human movement suffice as a sustainable mode of urban transport.

Finally, it must be noted that issues raised in this chapter are aimed at raising awareness and creating a backdrop for governments, policymakers, manufacturers, service providers, built environment specialists, and citizens to help them make informed decisions regarding sustainably adopting AV technology. Extensive research on social, technical, spatial, and regulatory fronts is needed to establish a context-aware, sustainable path toward this autonomous mobility revolution.

References

Allied Market Research, 2019. Global Autonomous Vehicle Market Is Expected to Reach $556.67 Billion by 2026. Available at: https://www.globenewswire.com/news-release/2019/07/03/1877861/0/en/Global-Autonomous-Vehicle-Market-is-Expected-to-Reach-556-67-Billion-by-2026.html.

Alonso, W., 1964. Location and Land Use: Toward a General Theory of Land Rent. Harvard University Press, Cambridge.

Anderson, J., et al., 2016. Autonomous Vehicle Technology: A Guide for Policymakers, Autonomous Vehicle Technology: A Guide for Policymakers. RAND Corporation. https://doi.org/10.7249/rr443-2.

Ben-Joseph, E., 2012. ReThinking a Lot: The Design and Culture of Parking. The MIT Press, p. 7.

Berger, G., et al., 2014. Sustainable mobility—challenges for a complex transition. Journal of Environmental Policy and Planning 16 (3), 303–320. https://doi.org/10.1080/1523908X.2014.954077.

Berrada, J., Leurent, F., Christoforou, Z. 2017. Which business models for autonomous vehicles? ITS Europe, Strasbourg.

Beuren, F.H., Ferrrira, M.G.G., Miguel, P.A.C., 2013. Product-service systems: a literature review on integrated products and services. Journal of Cleaner Production 47, 222–231.

Burns, L.D., 2013. Sustainable mobility: a vision of our transport future. Nature 497, 181–182.

Burns, L., Jordan, W., Scarborough, B., 2013. Transforming Personal Mobility. New York, NY.

Business Wire, 2019. Global Autonomous Vehicles Market Outlook to 2026—Market Is Expected to Reach $615.02 Billion by 2026, Growing at a CAGR of 41.5%—ResearchAndMarkets.Com | Business Wire. Available at: https://www.businesswire.com/news/home/20190719005370/en/Global-Autonomous-Vehicles-Market-Outlook-2026–. Accessed: 1 March 2020.

Chen, T.D., Kockelman, K.M., Schoch, E.P., 2016. Management of a Shared, Autonomous, Electric Vehicle Fleet: Implications of Pricing Schemes 2 3.

Clayton, U., 2016. Driving into the Future: Regulating Driverless Vehicles in Australia. Available at: https://www.claytonutz.com/articledocuments/178/Clayton-Utz-Driving-into-the-future-regulating-driverless-vehicles-2016.pdf.aspx?Embed=Y. Accessed: 10 December 2019.

Clements, L.M., Kockelman, K.M., 2017. Economic effects of automated vehicles. Journal of the Transportation Research Board 2606, 106–114.

Cornet, A., et al., 2012. Mobility of the Future Opportunities for Automotive OEMs.

Cramer, S., Klohr, J., 2019. Announcing automated lane changes: active vehicle roll motions as feedback for the driver. International Journal of Human–Com puter Interaction 35 (11), 980–995. https://doi.org/10.1080/10447318.2018.1561790.

Crayton, T., Meier, B.M., 2017. Autonomous vehicles: developing a public health research agenda to frame the future of transportation policy. Journal of Transport and Health 6, 245–252.

Cunningham, M., Regan, M.A., October 2015. Autonomous vehicles: human factors issues and future research. In: Proceedings of the 2015 Australasian Road Safety Conference, vol 14.

David, Z.M., 2016. Available at: https://fortune.com/2016/03/13/cars-parked-95-percent-of-time/.

Ecola, L., et al., 2014. The Future of Driving in Developing Countries:, RAND Corporation. RAND Corporation. Available at: https://www.rand.org/pubs/research_reports/RR636.html. Accessed: 29 February 2020.

Eliot, L., 2019. The reasons why Millenials aren't as car crazed as baby bookers, and how self driving cars fit it. Forbes. Available at: https://www.forbes.com/sites/lanceeliot/2019/08/04/the-reasons-why-millennials-arent-as-car-crazed-as-baby-boomers-and-how-self-driving-cars-fit-in/?sh=70fd375b63fc.

Elliott, D., Keen, W., Miao, L., 2019. Recent advances in connected and automated vehicles. Journal of Traffic and Transportation Engineering (English Edition) 6 (2), 109–131.

EMBARQ Network@WRIcities, 2017. Available at: https://www.smartcitiesdive.com/ex/sustainablecitiescollective/new-study-millennials-prefer-car-access-over-ownership/32723/.

Fagnant, D.J., Kockelman, K., 2015. Preparing a nation for autonomous vehicles: opportunities, barriers and policy recommendations. In: Transportation Research Part A: Policy and Practice, vol 77. Elsevier Ltd, pp. 167–181. https://doi.org/10.1016/j.tra.2015.04.003.

Feitelson, E., 2002. Introducing environmental equity dimensions into the sustainable transport discourse: issues and pitfalls. Transportation Research Part D: Transport and Environment 7 (2), 99–118.

Fraedrich, E., Beiker, S., Lenz, B., 2015. Transition pathways to fully automated driving and its implications for the sociotechnical system of automobility. European Journal of Futures Research 3 (1), 11. https://doi.org/10.1007/s40309-015-0067-8.

Fraszczyk, A., Mulley, C., 2017. 'Public perception of and attitude to driverless train: a case study of Sydney, Australia', urban rail transit. Springer Berlin Heidelberg 3 (2), 100–111. https://doi.org/10.1007/s40864-017-0052-6.

Gawron, J.H., Keoleian, G.A., De Kleine, R.D., Wallington, T.J., Kim, H.C., 2018. Life cycle assessment of connected and automated vehicles: sensing and computing subsystem and vehicle level effects. Environmental Science & Technology 52 (5), 3249–3256.

Getis, A., Getis, J., 1966. Christaller's central place theory. Journal of Geography 65 (5), 220–226. https://doi.org/10.1080/00221346608982415.

Grant-Muller, S., Usher, M., 2014. Intelligent Transport Systems: the propensity for environmental and economic benefits. Technological Forecasting and Social Change 82 (1), 149–166. https://doi.org/10.1016/j.techfore.2013.06.010.

Hayashi, R., et al., 2012. Autonomous collision avoidance system by combined control of steering and braking using geometrically optimised vehicular trajectory. ', Vehicle System Dynamics 50, 151–168.

Hiltzik, M., 2020. What can cicties do about congestion from ridesharing', Government Technology. Available at: https://www.govtech.com/fs/transportation/what-can-cities-do-about-congestion-from-ridesharing.html#:~:text=Recent%20studies%20have%20found%20that,devastate%20the%20local%20taxi%20industry.&text=Start%20with%20congestion.

Hörl, S., Ciari, F., Axhausen, K.W., 2016. Recent Perspectives on the Impact of Autonomous Vehicles. Arbeitsberichte Verkehrs-und Raumplanung, p. 1216.

Howard, D., Dai, D., 2014. Public Perceptions of Self-Driving Cars: The Case of Berkeley. California, Washington DC.

IEA, 2017. World Energy Investment 2017. Available at: http://www.iea.org/publications/wei2017/.

Igliński, H., Babiak, M., 2017. Analysis of the potential of autonomous vehicles in reducing the emissions of greenhouse gases in road transport. Procedia Engineering 192, 353–358.

INRIX, 2014. Americans Will Waste $2.8 Trillion on Traffic by 2030 if Gridlock Persists. Kirkland, WA, USA.

Ioannou, P., 1997. In: Ioannou, P. (Ed.), Automated Highway Systems. Springer.

IPCC, C.C., 2014. 'Mitigation of Climate Change', Contribution of Working Group III to the Fifth Assessment Report of the Intergovernmental Panel on Climate Change.

ITF, 2014. Urban Mobility System Upgrade: How Shared Self-Driving Cars Could Change City Traffic. Paris. Available at: https://www.itf-oecd.org/sites/default/files/docs/15cpb_self-drivingcars.pdf. Accessed: 4 December 2019.

Kane, M., Whitehead, J., 2018. How to ride transport disruption—a sustainable framework for future urban mobility. Australian Planner 54, 177–185.
Koustanaï, A., et al., 2012. Simulator training with a forward collision warning system: effects on driver-system interactions and driver trust. Human Factors 54 (5), 709–721. https://doi.org/10.1177/0018720812441796.
Kyriakidis, M., et al., 2019. A human factors perspective on automated driving. In: Theoretical Issues in Ergonomics Science, vol 20. Taylor and Francis Ltd., pp. 223–249. https://doi.org/10.1080/1463922X.2017.1293187, 3.
Lee, C., 2017. Grabbing the wheel early: moving forward on cybersecurity and privacy protections for driverless cars. Federal Communicaton Law Journal 69, 25–52.
Lee, J., Kockelman, K.M., 2019. Energy implications of self-driving vehicles. In: 98th Annual Meeting of the Transportation Research Board, Washington DC, vol 1.
Lee, J., et al., 2014. Lane-keeping assistance control algorithm using differential braking to prevent unintended lane departures. Control Engineering Practice 23 (1), 1–13.
Li, K., Juang, J.C., Lin, C., 2014. Active collision avoidance system for steering control of autonomous vehicles. IET Intelligent Transport Systems 8 (6), 550–557.
Lima, A., Rocha, F., Völp, M., Esteves-Verissimo, P., 2016. Towards safe and secure autonomous and cooperative vehicle ecosystems. In: Proceedings of the 2nd ACM Workshop on Cyber-Physical Systems Security and Privacy, Vienna, pp. 59–70.
Lin, Y.Y., 2017. Integrated Traffic Regulation and Data Networking for Autonomous Transportation Systems. Doctoral dissertation. UCLA.
Lodinger, N.R., DeLucia, P.R., 2019. Does automated driving affect time-to-collision judgments?. In: Transportation Research Part F: Traffic Psychology and Behaviour, vol 64. Elsevier Ltd, pp. 25–37. https://doi.org/10.1016/j.trf.2019.04.025.
López-Lambas, M., 2018. The socioeconomic impact of the intelligent vehicles: implementation strategies. In: Intelligent Vehicles. Elsevier, New York, USA.
Lovelock, C., 2014. Marketing des services. Pearson s. 1.
Lutin, J.M., Kornhauser, A.L., Lerner-Lam, E., 2013. The revolutionary development of self- driving vehicles and implications for the (July). ITE Journal 5. Available at: https://pdfs.semanticscholar.org/bb99/0b9d9ce60abe30db69f3510c1389d8b3af17.pdf?_ga=2.148253109.326413842.1564706728-981934300.1561380294.
Lyon, B., et al., 2017. Automated Vehicles - Do We Know Which Road to take.Pdf - OneDrive. Infrastructure Partnerships Australia. Available at: https://onedrive.live.com/?authkey=%21AvzqEYKzqY2NnW8&cid=334BDC500F44704D&id=334BDC500F44704D%2189712&parId=334BDC500F44704D%2186336&o=OneUp.
Madigan, R., et al., 2017. What influences the decision to use automated public transport? Using UTAUT to understand public acceptance of automated road transport systems. Transportation Research Part F: Traffic Psychology and Behaviour 50 (August), 55–64. https://doi.org/10.1016/j.trf.2017.07.007.
McKay, S., Boyer, M.E., Beyene, N.M., Lerario, M., Lewis, M.W., Stanley, K.D., Giglio, K., 2020. Automating Army Convoys, Technical and Tactical Risks and Opportunities. RAND ARROYO CENTER SANTA MONICA CA SANTA MONICA United States. https://www.rand.org/pubs/research_reports/RR2406.html.
Meadows, D.H., 1998. Indicators and information systems for sustainable development. In: The Earthscan Reader in Sustainable Cities. Earthscan.

Menouar, H., et al., 2017. UAV-enabled intelligent transportation systems for the smart city: applications and challenges. In: IEEE Communications Magazine, vol 55. Institute of Electrical and Electronics Engineers Inc., pp. 22–28. https://doi.org/10.1109/MCOM.2017.1600238CM, 3.

Merat, N., Jamson, H.A., 2009. How do drivers behave in a highly automated car. In: Proceedings of the Fifth International Driving Symposium on Human Factors in Driver Assessment, Training and Vehicle Design.

Milakis, D., Van Arem, B., Van Wee, B., 2017. Policy and society related implications of automated driving: a review of literature and directions for future research. Journal of Intelligent Transportation Systems 21, 324–348.

Naranjo, J.E., et al., 2016. Application of vehicle to another entity (V2X) communications for motorcycle crash avoidance. In: Journal of Intelligent Transportation Systems: Technology, Planning, and Operations Planning, and Operations. Advance online publication.

Newman, P., Mouritz, M., Davies-Slate, S., Jones, E., Hargroves, K., Sharma, R., Adams, D., 2018. Delivering Integrated Transit, Land Development and Finance–a Guide and Manual: with Application to Trackless Trams. Sustainable Built Environment National Research Centre (SBEnrc).

Nourinejad, M., Bahrami, S., Roorda, M.J., 2018. Designing parking facilities for autonomous vehicles. Transportation Research Part B: Methodological 109, 110–127.

Othman, K., 2021. Public Acceptance and Perception of Autonomous Vehicles: A Comprehensive Review. AI and Ethics, pp. 1–33.

Papa, E., Lauwers, D., 2015. Smart Mobility: Opportunity or Threat to Innovate Places and Cities? May Real Corp 2015, pp. 543–550. https://doi.org/10.13140/RG.2.1.4084.7527.

Parkinson, S., Ward, P., Wilson, K., Miller, J., 2017. Cyber threats facing autonomous and connected vehicles: future challenges. IEEE Transactions Intelligent Transportation System 18, 2898–2915. https://doi.org/10.1109/tits.2017.2665968.

Pearce, D., 2017. How Autonomous Vehicles Will Support the Unstoppable Rise of the City, pp. 4–5. Available at: https://www.minterellison.com/articles/how-autonomous-vehicles-will-support-the-unstoppable-rise-of-the-city.

Petit, J., Shladover, S., 2015. Potential cyberattacks on automated vehicles. IEEE Transactions: Intelligent Transport Systems 16, 546–556.

Pietsch, B., 2021. 2 Killed in Driverless Tesla Car Crash, Officials Say. New York Times. Available at: https://www.nytimes.com/2021/04/18/business/tesla-fatal-crash-texas.html.

Priest, G.L., 1985. The invention of enterprise liability: a critical history of the intellectual foundations of modern tort law. In: The Journal of Legal Studies, vol 14. University of Chicago Press, pp. 461–527. https://doi.org/10.1086/467783, 3.

Prioritising the Safety Potential of Automated Driving in Europe, 2016.

Pype, P., et al., 2017. Privacy and security in autonomous vehicles. In: Automated Driving. Springer, Berlin/Heidelberg, Germany, pp. 17–27, 2017.

Raiyn, J., 2018. Data and cyber security in autonomous vehicle networks. Transport and Telecommunication 19 (4), 325–334.

Rannenberg, K., 2016. Opportunities and risks associated with collecting and making useable additional data. In: Autonomous Driving. Springer, Berlin/Heidelberg, Germany, pp. 497–517.

Report, I., et al., 2015. Connected vehicles: are we ready. Available at: https://www.mainroads.wa.gov.au/Documents/ConnectVehiclesWeb.RCN-D15%5E23413758.PDF.

Rimol, M., 2019. Gartner Forecasts More than 740,000 Autonomous-Ready Vehicles to Be Added to Global Market in 2023. Gartner. Available at: https://www.gartner.com/en/newsroom/press-releases/2019-11-14-gartner-forecasts-more-than-740000-autonomous-ready-vehicles-to-be-added-to-global-market-in-2023.

Robert, J., 2018. Dai,ler's Daum: Platoooning May Not Be the Holy Grail. Available at: https://www.truckinginfo.com/313900/daimlers-daum-platooning-may-not-be-the-holy-grail.

Rode, P., Burdett, R., 2011. Cities: investing in energy and resource efficiency. In: Towards a Green Economy: Pathways to Sustainable Development and Poverty Eradication. United Nations, Nairobi, Kenya.

Rodrigue, J.-P., 2020. Transportation and energy. In: The Geography of Transport Systems. Routledge, New York, ISBN 978-0-367-36463-2.

Rodrigue, J.-P., Comtois, C., Slack, B., 2019. Transportation and the Spatial Structure. The Geography of Transport Systems, pp. 49–94. https://doi.org/10.4324/9781315618159-2.

Roy, R., 2000. Sustainable product-service systems. Futures 32 (3–4), 289–299.

SAE, 2018. J3016B: Taxonomy and Definitions for Terms Related to Driving Automation Systems for On-Road Motor Vehicles. SAE International. Available at: https://www.sae.org/standards/content/j3016_201806/.

Sheehan, B., Murphy, F., Mullins, M., Ryan, C., 2019. Connected and autonomous vehicles: a cyber-risk classification framework. Transportation Research Part A: Policy and Practice 124, 523–536.

Sheller, M., Urry, J., 2000. The city and the car. International Journal of Urban and Regional Research 24 (4), 737–757.

Shim, T., Adireddy, G., Yuan, H., 2012. Autonomous vehicle collision avoidance system using path planning and modelpredictive-control-based active front steering and wheel torque control. Proceedings of the Institution of Mechanical Engineers, Part D: Journal of Automobile Engineering 226 (6), 767–778.

Shladover, S.E., 2016. The Truth about "Self-Driving" Cars. Scientific American, December.

Shladover, S.E., 2018. Connected and automated vehicle systems: introduction and overview. In: Journal of Intelligent Transportation Systems: Technology, Planning, and Operations, vol 22. Taylor and Francis Inc., pp. 190–200. https://doi.org/10.1080/15472450.2017.1336053, 3.

Stavova, V., Dedkova, L., Matyas, V., Just, M., Smahel, D., Ukrop, M., 2018. Experimental large-scale review of attractors for detection of potentially unwanted applications. Computer Security 76, 92–100. https://doi.org/10.1016/j.cose.2018.02.017.

Steck, F., et al., 2018. How autonomous driving may affect the value of travel time savings for commuting', transportation research record. In: Journal of the Transportation Research Board, vol 2672. SAGE Publications, pp. 11–20. https://doi.org/10.1177/0361198118757980, 46.

Stocker, A., Shaheen, S., 2017. Shared Automated Vehicles: Review of Business Models. Available at: www.itf-oecd.org. Accessed: 1 March 2020.

Strand, N., et al., 2011. Interaction with and use of driver assistance systems: a study of end-user experiences. In: 18th World Congress on Intelligent Transport Systems, (May 2014). Available at: http://publications.lib.chalmers.se/cpl/record/index.xsql?pubid=148309.

Thunen, V., Heinrich, J., 1966. In: Hall, P. (Ed.), The Isolated State. Pergamon Press.

UITP, 2011. Metro Automation Facts, Figures, and Trends. UITP, Brussels.

UITP, 2018. World Report on Metro Automation 2018. UITP, Brussels.
van den Beukel, A.P., van der Voort, M.C., 2017. How to assess driver's interaction with partially automated driving systems – a framework for early concept assessment. Applied Ergonomics 59, 302–312. https://doi.org/10.1016/j.apergo.2016.09.005.
Von Solms, R., Van Niekerk, J., 2013. From Information Security to Cybersecurity, vol 38. Computer Security, pp. 97–102.
Wang, Y., et al., 2016. Survey on driverless train operation for urban rail transit systems. In: Urban Rail Transit, vol 2. Springer Berlin Heidelberg, pp. 106–113. https://doi.org/10.1007/s40864-016-0047-8, 3–4.
Wees, V., Kiliaan, A.P.C., 2004. Vehicle safety regulations and ADAS: tensions between law and technology. IEEE International Conference on Systems, Man and Cybernetics 4, 4011–4016.
Wiggers, K., 2020. Waymo's driverless cars were involved in 18 accidents over 20 months. Venture Beat. Available at: https://venturebeat.com/2020/10/30/waymos-driverless-cars-were-involved-in-18-accidents-over-20-month/.
Ye, R., Titheridge, H., 2017. Satisfaction with the Commute: The Role of Travel Mode Choice, Built Environment and Attitudes, vol 52. Transportation Research Part D: Transport and Environment, pp. 535–547. https://doi.org/10.1016/j.trd.2016.06.011.
Yin, J., et al., 2017. Research and development of automatic train operation for railway transportation systems: a survey. In: Transportation Research Part C: Emerging Technologies, vol 85. Elsevier Ltd, pp. 548–572. https://doi.org/10.1016/j.trc.2017.09.009.
Zhang, S., 2018. Who owns the data generated by your smart car. Harvard Journal of Law & Technology 32, 299.
Zmud, J.P., Reed, N., 2018. Socioeconomic impacts of automated and connected vehicles. In: Brussels: Synthesis of the Socioeconomic Impacts of Connected and Automated Vehicles and Shared Mobility. Paper Presented at the Sixth EU–US. Transportation Research Symposium, Conference Proceedings 56. Available at: https://www.nap.edu/catalog/25359/socioeconomic-impacts-of-automated-and-connected-vehicles.

12

Smart building and district retrofitting for intelligent urban environments

Borragán Guillermo[1,2], Verheyen Jan[1,2], Vandevyvere Han[1,2] and Kondratenko Irena[1,2]

[1] *Vito, Belgium;* [2] *EnergyVille, Belgium*

1. Current scope of smart retrofitting

The built environment has emerged as a major domain of intervention on the path to a low-carbon society. Two complementary strategies can be put to work: reducing the energy demand of buildings on the one hand; filling in the remaining energy needs with sustainable and renewable sources on the other hand. The potential for increasing the energy efficiency of existing buildings is still underexploited (IEA, 2019), whereas the uptake of renewable energy for the generation of energy from sustainable sources has performed better. This lagging position already turns urban retrofit into a particular endeavor. The intermittent behavior of renewable energy sources adds another challenge: the need to use energy storage and deploy digital energy support systems. In addition to digital metering and building management that measures and optimizes the functioning of a building functioning and including users interaction, smart operation of energy resources requires a well-interconnected grid that maximizes the use of locally generated energy. Through the additional mechanism of sector coupling, exchange between the thermal and electric pillar of the energy system, and between stationary, mobile, residential, industrial, and transport systems have emerged as well, increasing the range of the energy management spectrum even more.

Buildings play an important enabling role in this energy paradigm shift, moving from unresponsive and highly energy-demanding elements to highly efficient, potentially energy autonomous microenergy hubs embedded in the wider urban

Intelligent Environments. https://doi.org/10.1016/B978-0-12-820247-0.00011-4

energy system: consuming, producing, managing, storing, and supplying energy in an intelligent way, potentially making the system more flexible and efficient. This involves building owners and users centrally. It implies a second smart component: informing the building owner about the preferred retrofit options and supporting the building user in performing the best possible energy management. The benefits of smart retrofit are then not only to be reaped in terms of energy and carbon savings. Better health, comfort and quality of life, less energy dependency, and increased real estate value are just some of the additional value propositions that can be identified (Building Renovation: A kick-starter for the EU Recovery, Renovate Europe; Study (BPIE, 2020)). Assessing these benefits will greatly enhance the case for smart retrofitting. Better quantification of these multiple gains is therefore needed to prove both the viability of the enhanced business case and the better quality of life for building users that are ultimately being realized.

Last but not least, the construction sector undergoes increasing digitalization and is progressively moving toward an Industry 4.0 model (European Parliament, 2015). The Fourth Industrial Revolution (or Industry 4.0) is the ongoing automation of traditional manufacturing and industrial practices, using modern smart technology. Large-scale machine-to-machine communication and the internet of things (IoT) are integrated for increased automation, improved communication and self-monitoring, and production of smart machines that can analyze and diagnose issues without the need for human intervention. With regard to building retrofit, the possibilities of customized industrial production are rather promising. For example, it allows to handle existing buildings of which none is identical to another in an optimized manner, by providing prefabricated retrofit packages that are custom made, based on a laser scanning of the building. This enables productivity gains and reduces error margins. The construction sector's Industry 4.0 transformation does not come without challenges, however. To start with, the sector is facing capacity problems both in terms of size and training of its workforce (SCIS, 2020). Fully integrated and digitally supported supply chains are needed. Furthermore, the lack of uniformity in the building stock remains a substantial barrier for industrialized and automated processes, leading to the sustained need for deep customization.

1.1 Zooming-in on the building retrofit challenge

Residential buildings account for approximately 40% of the EU's total energy consumption, and for 36% of the greenhouse gas emissions from energy (European Commission, 2020). The European Commission estimates that around 75% of the EU residential stock is energy inefficient, yet almost 80%–95% of today's buildings will still be in use in 2050 (European Commission, 2020). The renovation of buildings can lead to significant energy savings and play a key role in the clean energy transition. To reach the 55% emission reduction target compared to 1990 levels, by 2030 the EU should lower buildings' greenhouse gas emissions by 60%, their final energy consumption by 14%, and energy consumption for heating and cooling by 18% (European Commission, 2020).

Renovation concerns the improvement of the conditions of residential buildings in terms of energy performance and involves replacement or upgrade of building elements that have a strong bearing on energy use (e.g., heating systems, ventilation and air-conditioning, boiler replacement, wall insulation, etc.) as well as the installation of self-sufficient energy sources (e.g., solar photovoltaic or thermal generation).

Different types of refurbishment are possible depending on the energy savings achieved and the estimated costs per m^2. The "*Comprehensive study of building energy renovation activities and the uptake of nearly zero-energy buildings in the EU,*" prepared for the European Commission (Ipsos Belgium and Navigant, November, 2019) proposes different renovation depths: below threshold ($x < 3\%$ savings); light renovations ($3\% \leq x \leq 30\%$ savings); medium renovations ($30\% < x \leq 60\%$ savings); and deep renovations ($x > 60\%$ savings). The study shows achieved renovation rates in residential buildings for the period 2012–16. The annual weighted energy renovation rate is estimated to be close to 1% within the European Union. The annual amount of deep renovations in the EU has been found to be very low, only around 0.2%, with relatively small variation when looking at individual Member States. Similar to residential buildings, the study finds that the weighted energy renovation rate in nonresidential buildings is estimated to be close to 1% within the EU. The study results highlight the insufficient progress in the building sector across the EU in terms of moving toward a decarbonized building stock despite the vast potential.

The renovation potential in the EU is quite significant with 110 million buildings considered in need of renovation; and a policy objective to at least double the annual energy renovation rate of residential and non-residential buildings by 2030 and to foster deep energy renovations (Claeys et al., 2019).

While some experts argue that one of the major problems is the lack of sufficient capacities within the construction industry, the reality is that there is little awareness on energy efficiency measures among homeowners as well. More importantly, the cost-optimized level for building refurbishment is often limited to energy efficiency paybacks, ignoring some other relevant aspects of renovation such as benefits for health and comfort or reduced environmental impact.

Higher energy efficiency performance of the building stock is much better achieved through medium or deep renovations, which is also beneficial to accommodate for the use of renewable energy sources, providing thermal and electrical energy to the building. In recent years, the cost of renewable sources such as solar and wind energy has become financially more than competitive in comparison to fossil fuels (REN21, 2022).

Energy efficiency improvements in buildings require a comprehensive view: evidence suggests that relying on isolated energy efficiency efforts alone is risky. For example, the British Energy Saving Trust evaluated the capacity of different packages of insulation measures such as cavity wall or loft insulation to decrease the use of energy (Energy Saving Trust, 2008). Real metering data consumption was recorded before and after renovation in a sample of more than 1500 buildings. Results revealed that the different insulation measures triggered comparable reductions in consumption of around 14% with respect to prerenovation levels. This figure represents half of the theorized energy savings estimated to occur during the renovation planning. Similar discrepancies between expected values and real consumption have been observed across other countries at the level of residential and nonresidential buildings. This gap is often referred in the literature as the "performance gap" and is characterized by large variations within the theorized energy distribution confidence intervals. While high-energy efficiency buildings (i.e., low kWh/m^2 consumption) tend to consume more energy than expected, inferior buildings (i.e., high kWh/m^2 consumption) consume indeed less.

This phenomenon is often described as a problem to generate good energy-consumption predictions and some professionals directly account for it in their calculations. More precisely, the performance gap can be subdivided in two opposed phenomena referred to as "the rebound" and the "prebound" effects. The "rebound effect" has been associated with increases in consumption driven by improvements in the energy performance of the dwelling. In other words, when new components are installed to save energy at the building level, the probability of the occupants to adopt new inefficient habits rises (e.g., heating the whole house, leaving windows open, etc.). Rebound effects have been estimated quite significantly ranging between 10% and 30% of the heating costs.

On the contrary, the "pre-bound effect" illustrates how occupants living in energy-inefficient buildings tend to use less energy than expected (potentially at the expense of comfort). Under this perspective, energy efficiency retrofit is only half as good as expected if the rebound and the pre-bound effects are not handled, a fact which might eventually lead to only realizing half the benefits of renovation for energy reduction and decreased CO_2 emission.

2. Will energy digitalization and data services foster smart renovation?

The idea of using constant data flows to improve services and processes refers to the popular terminology "smart" and is applicable to a vast number of domains from communication to industry, agriculture, or governance (Greeven et al., 2017). Since its popularization in the 1980s, digitalization has come to generally be seen in helping optimize, transform, and develop new business models in a large variety of fields.

The European Green Deal (Claeys et al., 2019) striving for Europe to become the first climate-neutral continent is addressing climate change and environmental degradation through an integrated policy package. One of the Green Deal's main pillars is the Renovation Wave, intended at improving the state of repair and energy efficiency of the EU's building stock. Given the complex present context, digitalization opens a promising opportunity to contribute to both mitigation of the COVID-19 pandemic effects on society as well as to boost Europe's actions across different sectors of the economy toward a clean and circular economy, with the Renovation Wave as one of its spearheads.

The energy refurbishment and improvement of the building stock are critical to a wider decarbonized and clean energy future, promising to improve people's well-being and to boost the economy at the same time. The construction and building renovation sectors account for around 13% of the world's GDP but they also have a long record of poor productivity. Many projects have cost overruns and are delivered late (McKinsey Global Institute, 2017). A recent report from the European Joint Research Center suggests that this might be in part explained by the low uptake of the digital transformation within the sector, especially when compared to other areas such as telecommunications (Desruelle et al., 2019) or mobility (Bellini and Nesi, 2018). The potential incorporation of digital technologies into the renovation market represents a promising way to generate competitive advantages and its recent application is already bringing positive results such as the unitized building process (Evans-Greenwood et al., 2019).

Centralized calculations fed by data could help to identify buildings requiring renovation and to categorize them accordingly to the type of renovation they require, thus helping to set better energy efficiency targets. Modeling data are already used to estimate the monetary costs that a group of buildings need to reach a specific energy efficiency level, facilitating the deployment of coordinated renovation programs at a district level.

An important factor to consider when it comes to building renovation is setting up a high ambition target, for example, as an Energy Performance Certificate (EPC) median value of category "A" for the building stock by 2050 (Vlaamse Regering, 2020) risks on having a low cost-efficiency. While the deep renovation is critical for buildings that have poor energy performance levels (Artola et al., 2016), digitalization and dynamic data technologies could fill in the cost-efficiency gap by improving the energy efficiency of buildings having better EPC labels (such as B and C). For instance, the use of digital data streams fed by smart metering inputs allows the grids and the buildings to develop a highly adaptable behavior adjusting their current demands (Lawrence et al., 2016). This can lead to a higher degree of grid decentralization, foster energy savings and independency, and create local value. However, the cost and maintenance of such systems must be considered.

2.1 Algorithms for occupants: "knowing for doing"

Conventionally, the profitability of building renovation is calculated as the investment payback time resulting from the subsequent energy savings. Consequently, other relevant benefits such as health improvements or increased property value are disregarded, eventually underestimating the real value of renovation (Ferreira et al., 2017). While the reason for this approach is defendable by the complexity to assess objectively the impact of these "cobenefits," the reality is that the lack of knowledge about them makes renovation less interesting in the eyes of citizens. It is indeed suggested that the lack of awareness about these benefits and the renovation burden associated with the intervention might be, in some cases, more important than the financial costs (Klöckner and Nayum, 2016).

In an increasingly digital world, computer data-driven technologies are opening new opportunities (Niesen et al., 2016). New calculations driven by algorithms offer an enormous potential to obtain high-value information facilitating and optimizing on-site interventions. For instance, the availability of accurate data is supporting citizen's tailored recommendations for building renovation, improving the suitability of the intervention while at the same time allowing for more precise follow-up and calculation of optimized intervention timing.

While an algorithm must not be understood as an all-knowing entity, its capacity to link or predict events exceeds to some extent the human one. When it comes to renovation, algorithms for machine learning can be used to scale up in a cost-efficient manner, the best output "renovation-behavior" for each dwelling, making on-site expertise accessible to a larger number of households.

Furthermore, this level of digital customization represents an advantage to reduce assessment costs and burden for end-users during the decision and renovation phases, eventually boosting building and district renovation, that is, facilitation. Moreover, monitoring can provide facility managers with precise information about the building state and actual performance, giving them not only the capacity to anticipate future events but also indications to adjust the type of intervention, that is, optimization.

This approach reflects a change from the traditional standardization in which identical measures are proposed to a group of buildings as a way to reduce costs, leading to the generation of data increasing exponentially (SINTEF, 2013). Digitalization has the potential to make building renovation switch from a *service-centered* approach in which providers compete to propose the best market services to occupants, to a user-centered one in which automatic and accessible algorithms are used to communicate their specific needs (Fig. 12.1). From selling personal data (being an important driver for "data driven" society) to receiving free-of-charge advice, this new "data-citizen" model could potentially lead to citizens' empowerment. However, it is worth pointing out that the full consequences resulting from this new power to make choices and exert influence are still unknown and difficult to predict (Lammi and Pantzar, 2019).

For an effective user-focused model to take place, three pillars are required. Firstly, the exchange of information needs to be secure, protecting privacy rights as a basis for deserving trust while promoting the participation of citizens (European Commission, 2020). Secondly, the information needs to be subjected to good analytics as data only acquires value once it is processed for use, and

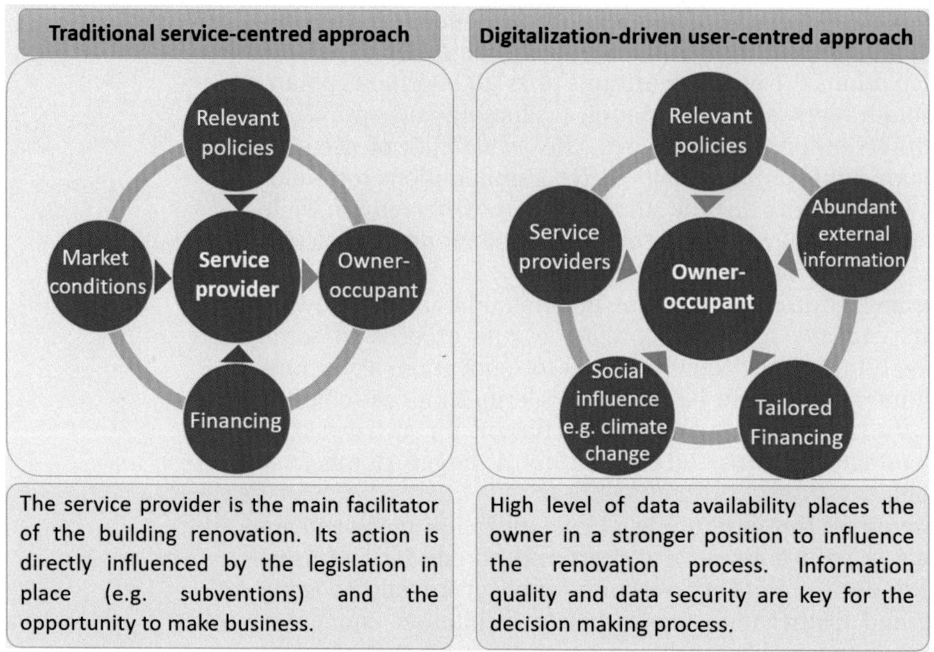

Figure 12.1 User-focused model in the building renovation market. Borragán, G (2020).

thirdly, citizens must have sufficient clear and trustworthy information to make the best use of the potential benefits it offers.

For the service-oriented sectors of the economy, transitioning into a competent digital society is a large-scale challenge that involves all actors in a value chain, not only end-users. As digitalization is changing the market rules, services are more and more interconnected and all actors within the renovation industry, from small SMEs to global manufacturers, have the opportunity to derive optimal value from digitalization.

2.2 Upscaling renovation: a new digital value chain prompted by industry 4.0

Digital technologies are changing the face of industry by bringing data directly into the productive chain in the so-called Fourth Industrial Revolution: Industry 4.0 (Rojko, 2017). The second and third industrial revolutions were characterized by the automation of human and machine manufacturing processes respectively. In contrast, the industry 4.0 cluster of technological trends redesigns this idea of mass production and uses data and connectivity to go back to a certain degree of product customization while maintaining low production costs. As mentioned earlier, this is done due to a high degree of connectivity between the actors and the capacity to acquire and process relevant data rapidly. As a result, the boundaries between final consumers, intermediates, and production industries are less defined, with more frequent digitalization of services and reallocation of production.

New organizational capacities triggered by digital technology, such as collaborative innovation, integration of supply chains, and the connection of production resources, lead to the specialization of the value chain (Luz Martín-Peña et al., 2018). The particularities of the renovation industry with a relatively long value chain involving many different actors imply it is well positioned to benefit from this new way of structuring the offer of services. As a consequence, the number of start-ups in the construction domain that rely on digital technology to offer their services has increased during the last years and research shows that their funding is growing exponentially (Sekai, 2017).

Digitalization contributes to simplifying the decision-making process, facilitating collaborative approaches, optimizing the coordination between installers, enhancing the customization of retrofit interventions, and reducing production costs. In this regard, the concept of a One-Stop-Shops (OSS) has been gaining relevance over recent years. One-stop-shops have been advocated by the European Commission through the "Smart financing for smart buildings" initiative and through the energy performance of buildings directive (EPBD) as part of the Directive 2018/844/EU, whereby the Member States are required to facilitate access to appropriate mechanisms for accessible and transparent advisory tools, such as one-stop-shops for consumers and energy advisory services, on relevant energy efficiency renovations and financing instruments (European Commission, 2018). Digitalized OSS services are tools that simplify the renovation process by gathering relevant information and expertise in one place. Their efficacy relies on their capacity to guide the user through the whole renovation journey, from benchmarking the available intervention options, to finding the best materials providers and installers and also by easing the access to financing options and tools to follow up the renovation process. The exploratory review of case studies of past and ongoing OSS (Boza-Kiss and Bertoldi, 2018) has shown how an OSS is able to bridge the gap between the fragmented supply and demand side in a building renovation.

Furthermore, other digitalized technologies such as building information modeling (BIM) and digital twins have improved some specific segments of the building renovation sector. For example, cloud-based BIM coupled with digital building duplicates can be useful to reduce renovation costs since they facilitate coordination of the different actors involved in the renovation chain (Volk et al., 2014). Furthermore, the generation of digital documentation offers updated information including geometric and semantic references that can be used by different professionals to make decisions about the renovation characteristics, such as luminance, acoustics, lifecycle of materials, and ventilation simulations, or to improve the design and aesthetics. Besides this, the use of digital models and 3D visualizations displaying real data can act as a catalyzer of the renovation as they promote new business models and facilitate stakeholder engagement (Stojanovic et al., 2018). Last but not least, the use of big data analytics relying on the information contained in the digital twin model can benefit from AI and machine learning classification approaches to detect, for instance, nonoptimized indoor structures or to aggregate buildings with the same kind of renovation needs (Stepup project, 2020).

A novel concept, developed and referred as "cognitive renovation" in the ELISIR project (Rinaldi et al., 2020), proposes the gathering of building-use information through real-time sensor data as a way to add a cognitive layer that infers with the user's behavior to progressively reduce user's intervention. As occupant needs are predefined before the renovation takes place, this approach allows to define a priori the smart components that will be installed, thus reducing costs by avoiding a fully automated and connected home. Moreover, during the postrenovation facility management phase, the use of lot sensors can be used to infer user's behavior and progressively reduce user's intervention, which in turn leads to energy savings and improved comfort.

Data can also be used as a prevention strategy, identifying the presence of risks compromising the health of the occupants and anticipating renovation needs. For instance, levels of humidity and/or oscillations of temperature in a room could be used as a marker indicating the need to replace the windows or to improve ventilation.

Experts have pointed toward the need to deal with a lack of a qualified labor force to be able to respond to the increasing renovation demands (i.e., the European aim to double the current renovation rate), as well as to the capacity of the construction sector for Industry 4.0. Professional education must be enhanced to respond to the needs of the sector. For example, training on energy efficiency and the use of digital technologies in building renovation, offered through online, e-learning methods, opens

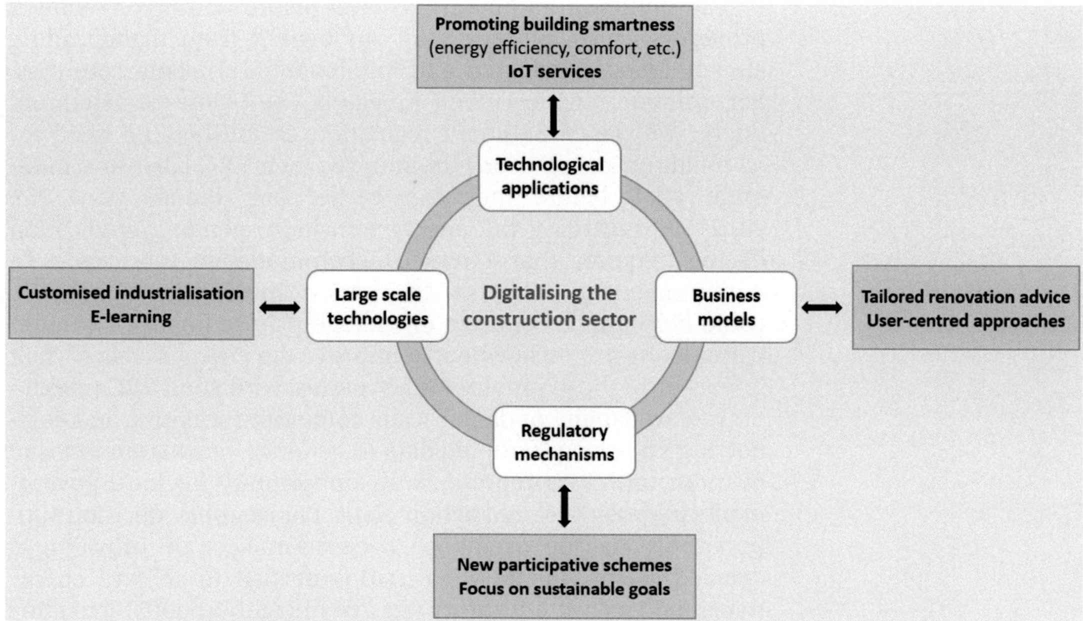

Figure 12.2 Different aspects of digital technology applications in retrofitting buildings.

up opportunities to create a better prepared and a more inclusive labor market (Fig. 12.2).

2.3 E-governance for e-renovation

With building renovation gaining importance to mitigate the effects of climate change and as a means to trigger local economic activity, policy schemes setting building renovation targets are being widely used. The *European Energy Performance of Buildings Directive* (2015), the *Australian Energy Efficiency Policy Handbook* (2016), the Canadian "*Alterations to Existing Buildings*" scheme (2019), or the energy efficiency policies identified within "*China's national Thirteenth Five Year Plan*" (2016–20), all consider digital innovation to be indispensable as a way to create new market value and to accelerate the renovation rate of the old inefficient building stock. Also, existing data observatories, such as the European Building Stock Observatory, the Energy Poverty Observatory, or the West-African ECOWAS observatory for Renewable Energy and Energy Efficiency (ECOWREX), are already available options that provide statistical information for policymakers.

The minimum required EPC level before renting or selling a property is also an area that can benefit from digitalization, already being considered and implemented in some countries. For example, in the United Kingdom, the Domestic Minimum Energy Efficiency Standard regulation establishes the need for all buildings rating G or F to improve their EPC label to a minimum of E before they can be let out. France (Law No. 2015–992 regarding the energy transition, pending application decree) requires that a rented accommodation must meet "a minimum energy performance criterion" In addition, digital tools could help public actors to encourage private financers to offer better loans to homeowners to improve the energy levels of their homes or to those purchasing properties with good EPC rates.

The availability of digital scans combining scientific and engineering knowledge with big data to generate renovation maps of districts and cities represents an opportunity for local governments to design tailored action plans. For example, decision support tools can be useful for decision-makers by providing a detailed set of simulation scenarios needed to achieve energy transition goals at a territory (e.g., city neighborhoods) including energy savings, CO_2 emission reductions, renewable energy production increases, as well as insights into possibilities for an upscaling strategy that defines high energy performance at the district/neighborhood rather than at the individual building level.

2.4 Conclusions and caveats of digitalization

Digital technologies allow the construction industry and the renovation market to reinvent themselves with new business models, and economic players to become more engaged and to improve economic resilience and competitiveness. The digitalization opportunity for the renovation market requires coordinated participation of the whole value chain. Ensuring an optimized digital transition should consider the following rules:

1. Digital structures must always guarantee a safe data exchange among citizens, stakeholders, industries, and governments. Data compliance needs to be considered as a civil right and should always take precedence over any kind of potential added value. This is essential not only to offer fair digital services but also to ensure citizen's trust in the processes. A beneficial digital society is one where citizens are owners of their personal data and have the capacity and knowledge to decide what to do with them. General data protection regulations are a "must" for all public and private organizations.

2. There must be awareness about the risk of digitalization upon the polarization of the labor market. As anticipated by some authors, the digitalization of work could exert pressure on those with middle-level skills who might see their employments downgraded or becoming obsolete (Blix, 2017). Flexible employment legislation incentivizing the upgrading of worker skills through professional education within the work environment could help to address this challenge.
3. It is important to set operating limits for digital technologies. Although new data-driven approaches can be very useful to facilitate decision-making processes, it is important to have in mind that they are just algorithms composed of lines of code incapable of considering the whole picture. For this reason, they should be interpreted as advisory tools or decision facilitators while leaving room for human factors to step in before the final decision is made.

3. Building renovation impact on cities' sustainability and resilience: a step toward a healthier urban environment

3.1 Multiple benefits of building renovation and urban regeneration

Building renovation implies the reuse of parts of the building, thereby reducing the amount of new materials used and waste produced in the course of a building's lifetime. However, material use associated with renovation activities still adds, to a significant extent (Heeren et al., 2015), to the environmental impact of the building including associated CO_2 emissions and resource depletion.

In recent decades and driven by EU directives, the focus within the building value chain actors has been on optimizing new building design in terms of energy efficiency and the use of energy from renewable sources. Although existing buildings are also subject to these directives, it appears difficult to obtain the needed renovation rate both in terms of quantity and of energy performance level at a pace required to reach the decarbonization targets by 2050.

Barriers have been identified that could explain this lack of progress (Ipsos Belgium and Navigant, 2019; EU Smart Cities Information System, 2021). One of these barriers usually can be found at the very core of the decision-making process in which energy saving and energy generation measures are evaluated solely considering energy and financial costs, neglecting all other important multiple cobenefits arising from undertaking building renovation. The widespread adoption of such a narrow evaluation approach systematically undervalues the full impact of energy-related renovations relevant to the individual but also to society as a whole. If the right approach is chosen, energy renovations can lead to a range of benefits both at individual, at district or urban level, and at wider societal level (Fig. 12.3).

3.2 The role of the built environment in health and well-being

The built environment impacts human health in two ways. On the one hand, people spend nearly 90% of their time in indoor environments for a variety of activities. The indoor environmental quality of buildings (with its four main aspects: thermal comfort, indoor air quality, acoustical comfort, and lighting), deeply impacts the health of building users (Mujan et al., 2019). Energy efficiency measures in renovation can improve comfort levels and thereby productivity as well as the physical and mental health of the building users (IEA, 2019; Smith et al., 2014).

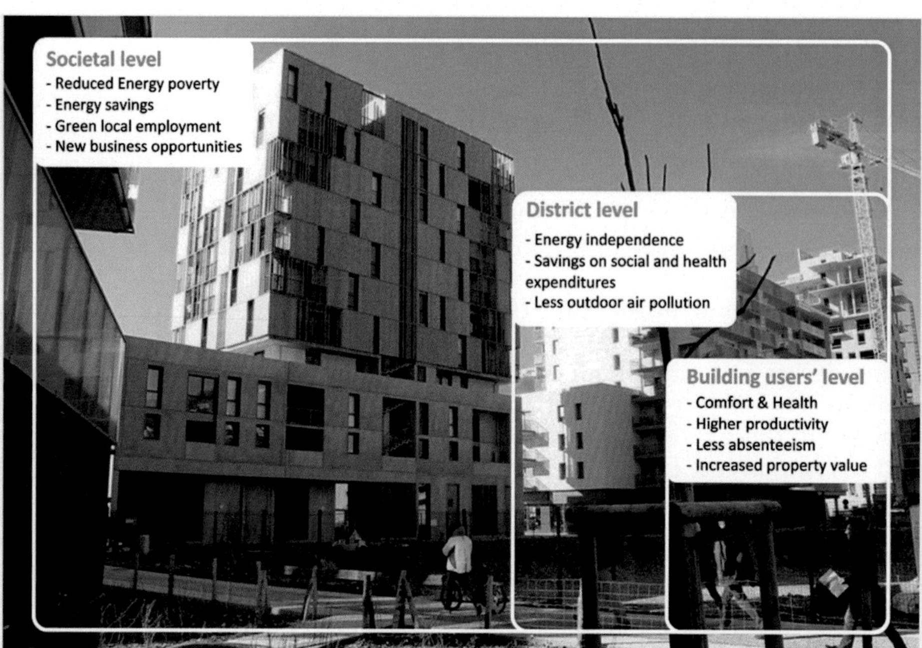

Figure 12.3 Multiple benefits of renovation over the whole building ecosystem.

Essential prerequisites to achieve this potential are adequate building and HVAC design and their commissioning and the use of very low-polluting building materials. However, adverse effects on health and wellbeing after renovation have also been observed (Ferreira and Almeida, 2015; Yu and Kim 2010) in cases where these prerequisites have not been respected or in cases of suboptimal operation, maintenance or presence of specific indoor activities such as smoking.

On the other hand, production of construction materials, building design, construction, use, renovation, and demolition have also a significant impact on the environment. This impact contributes to global climate change and increased outdoor air pollution. Climate change has an overwhelmingly negative effect on overall health as it undermines essential ingredients of good health, such as clean air, safe drinking water, sufficient food, and secure shelter (WHO; 2018). Reducing the emissions of greenhouse gases and other air pollutants from buildings will substantially contribute to climate change mitigation and improved health (IEA, 2019).

As stated earlier, humans stay nearly 90% of their lives indoor, with more than 56% of this time spent at home and 37% at work. Research on housing and health has shown that the physical features of the building have a significant impact on occupant's performance (Miller et al., 2009) and physical and mental health (Evans, 2003). Also, thermal comfort and health appear to be more important than economic drivers to trigger decision-making toward renovation (Klöckner and Nayum, 2016). Moreover, housing structural quality, maintenance, and upkeep are associated with better levels of restoration from stress and fatigue as it has been reported that tenants are willing to pay a premium of 5%–10% for healthier buildings (Miller et al., 2009).

People living in poor housing and indoor environments are more prompted to experience safety issues (e.g., heating system regulators, water boilers, etc.) and lack balanced thermal comfort situations (e.g., larger variations of temperature, cold, etc.). Similarly, poorly insulated buildings contribute to the presence of higher levels of noise, especially in high-density areas. Noise is detrimental to health in several aspects including mood alterations, sleep disturbances, psychophysiological impairments, cardiovascular disease, and negative effects on fetal development. Along the same line, the use of inadequate building materials and inefficient ventilation is associated with indoor pollution issues, dampness, or mold that can lead to asthma, allergies, or respiratory diseases. For instance, the presence of radon at home has been associated with lung cancer (Gray et al., 2009) and the concentration of harmful particles coming from indoor tobacco smoke, excess moisture, and other volatile organic compounds (such as the ones coming from cooking) have gained more attention.

Other particularities of buildings such as lighting or ergonomics and aesthetics are also factors influencing the comfort, well-being, and health of occupants. Daylight has direct effects on vision and the regulation of circadian rhythms with implications for sleep/wake states, alertness, mood, body temperature, and behavior (Webb, 2006). Ensuring good illumination levels in indoor areas has been associated with increased levels of performance (Aries et al., 2015), and there is also evidence suggesting that the structural design and configuration of the building have an impact on people's activity (Codinhoto et al., 2009).

The World Health Organization (WHO) estimates that inadequate housing related to the previously cited issues accounts for over 100,000 premature deaths per year in Europe alone. Energy efficiency upgrades of households can thus contribute to the alleviation of energy poverty and reduction of the CO_2 footprint of the building sector, and also promote positive changes in people's homes and lives (Underhill et al., 2019).

3.2.1 Benefits of renovation at the building users' level

The benefits for building users that add to reduced energy consumption and CO_2 emissions include higher comfort and a healthier indoor climate, reduced energy poverty, less absenteeism and higher productivity in working environments, and an increased property value with better futureproofing.

However, it is unclear how the presence of "greener elements" in a building affects its final value (Morri and Soffietti, 2013). Sustainability assessment schemes such as BREEAM or LEED claim that there is a direct impact of the sustainability level of a property on its liveability (including health and performance) and its value (Dermisi, 2009; Soulti and Leonard, 2016). For example, several studies on residential buildings applying hedonic regression have investigated the relation between a property's energy performance (as measured by the EPC) and its value. Results showed overall positive relationships between energy efficiency label and property sales value (e.g., in Austria + 8%, Belgium + 5.4%, France (Marseille) + 4.3% (or Lille) + 3.2%, and Ireland + 2.8%) (Bio Intelligence Service et al., 2013). However, there were also some exceptions to this tendency in cities such as Oxford where it appeared to be a negative correlation, and in Paris where the trend was not visible at all (Heijmans and Loncour, 2017). These results suggest that other parameters such as the geographical location or the building history may have a more significant impact than improvements associated with EPC.

An important benefit associated with renovations is thus the quantification of the increased sales value of the property (Klöckner and Nayum, 2016). Hereby, renovation offers more than energy savings to a real estate as it also promotes benefits (i.e., increased property value, reputation and marketability, etc.), and positive effects on risks (reduced risk of losing value due to functional, economic, or physical obsolescence, of losing tenants and investors due to availability of sustainable buildings in future markets, etc.). It also limits negative risks (such as the need for new specialized service providers, exposure to natural degradation, etc.). Besides, building renovation also helps counteracting potential uncertainties inherent to the status quo (e.g., uncertainty associated with expected legislation, rent, health and productivity, energy prices or future interest rates, and inflation) (Bozorgi, 2015).

As a general rule, renovations requiring legal permits will increase the value of the property. For these reasons, it is suggested that indicators such as the savings-to-investment ratio are obsolete to estimate the real value in case of energy efficiency retrofit and it is recommended to include other variables, such as the level of the building's elements deterioration (lifetime index), the cost of borrowing money (when needed), or benefits associated to the installation of new technologies such as solar panels (Martinaitis et al., 2004).

The cost of conserved energy takes into account the lifetime of the measures and the cost of borrowing money but it does not include some unspecific factors such as the perceived market value, which can strongly vary across countries, regions, geographical areas, or people's awareness. An example is properties with electricity-generating solar panels, for example, in Arizona, which showed increased transaction prices of 17% when compared to equivalent buildings (Qiu et al., 2017). However, some of these positive impacts were not found in a study in England in which the presence of solar panels did not necessarily translate into higher appreciation of the value of the property (Morris-Marsham and Moor, 2011).

3.2.2 At the district or urban level

Additional benefits associated with the renovation can be reaped from adopting a district- or city-scale approach in the renovation, rather than working on a building-by-building basis.

Embedded in strategies of sustainable urban and spatial development, wider benefits include reduced energy dependence, savings on social and health expenditures, less outdoor pollution, safer and healthier living environments, more green local employment, and less traffic congestion.

Urban regeneration can include rolling out sustainable district energy systems, inserting green-blue networks throughout the urban tissue, or supporting the modal shift to sustainable transport modes by providing the appropriate infrastructures. This will often imply taking space from the car and giving it to citizens for walking, biking, and public transport; measures that may also add to the overall quality of the public space. The fear of using public transport for health reasons, notably during the COVID-19 pandemic, could be turned into an incentive to additionally promote (e-) biking and walking—and improving citizen's fitness in one move. For example, local authorities in Brussels, Milan, and Paris have already grasped the opportunity to speed up the realization of their soft mobility plans.

The use of district energy systems may result in both economic and environmental surplus value compared to an approach that works on a building-by-building basis. This is because the optimal balance between reduction of the energy demand (e.g., insulation of the building envelope), sustainable energy supply (e.g., heat pumps or sustainable district energy systems), and smart energy management (e.g., demand response or building energy management systems) differ between building level and district level. Such a tailored approach implies a modeling exercise to point out which measures are most appropriate according to the building types, and this in relation to their (urban) environment (e.g., where excess heat from nearby industry is available). The modeling provides insights on the impact of chosen measures through various energy (total energy consumption, total renewable energy production, etc.), environmental (CO_2 emission level), and financial (investment costs, return on investments, payback time, etc.) indicators.

First assessments as part of a modeling exercise done in a series of Belgian urban and suburban districts indicate that reductions of up to one-third of the CO_2 abatement cost can be obtained by a differentiated, context-sensitive approach for retrofit compared to setting one unique performance level target for all buildings (Vandevyvere et al., 2020).

3.2.3 At the wider societal level

An abundant literature has described the many positive effects of building energy retrofit as a way to create local economic value and positive societal impact. A large macroeconomic study conducted by the EC found that the most relevant impact of energy efficiency retrofit was a significant reduction in the number of households in energy poverty (Alexandri et al., 2016). Energy poverty is a relatively extended problem across EU countries, affecting all member states, and has a strong effect on the health of citizens (Thomson et al., 2017). As such, fighting energy poverty has become an important subject for many political organizations at national and/or international level (comparable to the access to health or education), as a way to promote equality among citizens.

While measures of energy retrofit are essential to fight inequalities to the access of energy, they often reach low cost-efficiency levels if only future energy savings are considered. A study conducted in Croatia investigating the impact of energy retrofit of residential and public buildings for the period 2015–20 concluded that energy savings alone were clearly insufficient to justify owner's investments in energy efficiency measures. However, when overall benefits for society including economic growth, employment, and protection of the environment were included, retrofit measures became very profitable (Mikulić et al., 2016). The authors predicted that besides decreased national dependence on imported energy, economic activity prompted by energy retrofit would exceed the government's grand rate level (determined at 40% of the building retrofit works). In other words, energy retrofit policies will act as a catalyzer for new economic activities that will increase public tax revenues in the long run.

Similar conclusions were drawn in an economic impact analysis of a large American energy retrofit initiative, the "Better Buildings Neighborhood Program (BBNP)." The authors estimated that created value associated with positive impacts on new jobs, energy savings, personal and local business generation, among others, included multiplying each dollar invested in the program (~508$ million) by a factor of 2.6 (1.3$ billion) (Vine et al., 2015). Even greater figures were estimated as the result of the Pan-Canadian Framework on Clean Growth and Climate Change ("PCF"), a Canadian plan to improve energy efficiency across the country between the period 2017 (Dunsky Energy Consulting, 2018). The program anticipates a net increase in GDP of $356 million (1%), which translates into $7 of GDP for every $1 spent on efficiency programs. It should be noted that both American and Canadian programs included all building typologies and not only residential buildings.

3.3 Assessment methods to account for the multiple benefits of building renovation

A more holistic evaluation approach is needed to account for the full potential of renovation interventions by integrating the cobenefits in the traditional cost–benefit analysis. However, accurate quantification of cobenefits is often difficult (Skumatz, 2009; International Energy Agency (IEA), 2012) or nearly impossible (Ferreira et al., 2017). Although hard to measure, it is still preferable to perform an analysis including ranges or order of magnitude values over excluding the impacts altogether (Skumatz, 2009).

Monetized estimates of cobenefits that are relevant from a private (individual) perspective include an increase in building value, as experienced by the individual, attributable to the implementation of renovation measures. This increase in value can only be estimated through surveys in which individual respondents are asked to state the value of the benefits they experience directly resulting from the implemented energy retrofit measures. These methods are referred to as contingent valuation and willingness to pay (WTP)/willingness to accept surveys. This can be done by directly asking for the estimated value, by estimated surplus value in relation to a base reference, or by ranking cobenefits or measures.

Methods to quantitatively account for the health effects of climate change and air pollution are widely available. However, methods for the monetary valuation of health effects from improved indoor environmental quality are less widespread (Alexandri et al., 2016). Namely, annual energy reductions can be translated per fuel source to emission reductions for greenhouse gasses (CO_2, CH_4, and N_2O) and air pollutants (particulate matter, SO_2, and NO_X), and can consecutively be translated to climate and health cobenefits, for instance by applying the social cost of carbon (SCC) and social cost of atmospheric release (SCAR) methods. The outcomes of the SCC and SCAR methods represent the monetary value of the health cobenefits (MacNaughton et al., 2018). WTP is also used for the valuation of health impacts (Desaigues et al., 2011). It corresponds to the monetary value one is willing to pay to avoid certain health impacts.

Last but not least, the WHO uses the DALY metric (disability-adjusted life years) (WHO, 2018) expressing the number of years lost due to ill health, disability, or early death. For instance, WHO uses the metric to quantify the environmental burden of disease (sum of DALYs across the population) related to inadequate housing in Europe for selected housing risks (WHO, 2018).

Health cobenefits are very much location dependent and variable over time. Current methods to quantify costs and benefits do not deal well with the geographical, social, or temporal distribution of impacts (Alexandri et al., 2016), leaving the vast potential for ICT technologies to further improve the quality of the assessment methods.

4. Perspectives and recommendations

Building construction has traditionally been not known for rapid innovation. Now signs emerge that digital systems have begun to transform the entire building renovation supply chain. Data-driven approaches are becoming relevant, from the early assessment of the existing building stock's renovation potential, deep into the execution and delivery process of retrofit works, and further up to postoccupancy management, monitoring processes, and the assessment of the wider societal benefits of upscaled building renovation.

At the same time, smart algorithms enable all involved stakeholders to profit from better decision support tools and enhanced building and energy management interfaces. "Smartification" also implies that buildings become active energy agents in wider peer-to-peer, renewable source-based energy communities. Proper scale integration becomes a paramount requirement for this endeavor: smart buildings only make sense when they fulfill their specific role within the smartly sustainable (energy) networks of the future.

But smart does not mean intelligent or wise: smart tools remain no less, no more than means to achieve sustainability and a better quality of life. This implies that the proper governance structures must be put in place to enable all of these transformations. Here, major bottlenecks must be addressed like the lack of capacity, both in numbers and in quality, within the construction sector, or the behavioral routines of building owners and users preventing them to embark on a path of profound change.

One element that may help to overcome these human rather than technical bottlenecks is to confront stakeholders with the right arguments. Here again, the role of good data and appropriate assessment methods becomes clear: although they do not provide the ultimate convincing power toward changed behavior and alternative investment decisions, they do increase awareness and inform better decisions with less effort for assembling the arguments. Especially, when such informing methods are combined with appropriate governance—nudging, networking, peer-to-peer exchanging, and the like we just may see the sustainability of the existing building stock improve dramatically.

References

Alexandri, E., et al., 2016. The Macroeconomic and other Benefits of Energy Efficiency, p. 138. Available at: https://ec.europa.eu/energy/sites/ener/files/documents/final_report_v4_final.pdf.

Aries, M.B.C., et al., 2015. Daylight and health: a review of the evidence and consequences for the built environment. Lighting Research and Technology. https://doi.org/10.1177/1477153513509258.

Artola, I., et al., 2016. Boosting building renovation: what potential and value for Europe? Directorate general for internal policies. Policy Department A: Economic and Scientific Policy 12. https://doi.org/10.2861/331360. PE 587.326.

Bellini, E., Nesi, P., 2018. Exploiting Smart Technologies to Build Smart Resilient Cities.

Bio Intelligence Service, Lyons, R., IEEP, 2013. Energy Performance Certificates in Buildings and Their Impact on Transaction Prices and Rents in Selected EU Countries, p. 151. Available at: http://eur-lex.europa.eu/legal-content/ET/TXT/HTML/?uri=CELEX:32010L0031&from=EN.

Blix, M., 2017. The effects of digitalisation on labour market polarisation and tax revenue. CESifo Forum 18 (4), 9–14.

Boza-Kiss, B., Bertoldi, P., 2018. One-Stop-Shops for Energy Renovations of Buildings, p. 69. Available at: https://e3p.jrc.ec.europa.eu/sites/default/files/documents/publications/jrc113301_jrc113301_reportononestopshop_2017_v12_pubsy_science_for_policy_.pdf.

Bozorgi, A., 2015. Integrating value and uncertainty in the energy retrofit analysis in real estate investment—next generation of energy efficiency assessment tools. Energy Efficiency 8 (5), 1015–1034. https://doi.org/10.1007/s12053-015-9331-9.

BPIE, 2020. Building Renovation: A Kick-Starter for the EU Recovery, Renovate Europe. http://www.renovate-europe.eu/wp-content/uploads/2020/06/BPIE-Research-Layout_FINALPDF_08.06.pdf.

Codinhoto, R., et al., 2009. The impacts of the built environment on health outcomes. Facilities. https://doi.org/10.1108/02632770910933152.

Claeys, G., Tagliapietra, S., Zachmann, G., 2019. How to make the European Green Deal work. Bruegel, Brussels, Belgium.

Dermisi, S.V., 2009. Effect of LEED ratings and levels on office property assessed and market values. The Journal of Sustainable Real Estate 1 (1), 23–47. Available at: http://www.josre.org/wp-content/uploads/2009/12/effect-of-leed-ratings-and-levels-on-office-property-assessed-and-market-values.pdf.

Desruelle, P., et al., 2019. Digital Transformation in Transport, Construction. Energy, Government and Public Administration. https://doi.org/10.2760/689200.

Desaigues, B., Ami, D., Bartczak, A., Braun-Kohlová, M., Chilton, S., Czajkowski, M., Farreras, V., Hunt, A., Hutchison, M., Jeanrenaud, C., Kaderjak, P., Máca, V., Markiewicz, O., Markowska, A., Metcalf, H., Navrud, S., Nielsen, J.S., Ortiz, R., Pellegrini, S., Rabl, A., Riera, R., Scasny, M., Stoeckel, M.-E., Szántó, R., Urban, J., 2011. Economic valuation of air pollution mortality: A 9-country contingent valuation survey of value of a life year (VOLY). Ecological indicators 11 (3), 902–910.

Dunsky Energy Consulting, 2018. The Economic Impact of Improved Energy Efficiency in Canada, p. 44.
Energy Saving Trust, 2008. Disaggregation of the Energy Savings Achieved from Insulation in EESOP 3 and the Energy Efficiency Commitment. Energy monitoring company final report.
European Commission, 2020. Renovation Wave Communication, COM/2020/662 Final.
European Parliament, 2015. Industry 4.0 Digitalisation for Productivity and Growth. Available at: https://www.europarl.europa.eu/RegData/etudes/BRIE/2015/568337/EPRS_BRI(2015)568337_EN.pdf.
Europen Commission, 2018. Directive (EU) 2018/844 of the European parliament and the Council of 30 May 2018 Amending Directive 2010/31/EU on the Energy Performance of Buildings and Directive 2012/27/EU on Energy Efficiency. Available at: https://eur-lex.europa.eu/legal content/EN/TXT/PDF/?uri=CELEX:32018L0844&from=EN.
Evans, G.W., 2003. The built environment and mental health. Journal of Urban Health 80 (4), 536–555. https://doi.org/10.1093/jurban/jtg063.
Evans-greenwood, P., et al., 2019. Digitalizing the Construction Industry A Case Study in Complex Disruption. Deloitte Insights.
EU Smart Cities Information System, 2021. Upscaling Urban Residential Retrofit for the EU'S Low Carbon Future: Challenges and Opportunities Empowering Smart Solutions. SCIS/SCM Policy paper.
Ferreira, M., Almeida, M., 2015. Benefits from energy related building renovation beyond costs, energy and emissions. Energy Procedia 78, 2397–2402.
Ferreira, M., et al., 2017. Impact of co-benefits on the assessment of energy related building renovation with a nearly-zero energy target. Energy and Buildings 152, 587–601. https://doi.org/10.1016/j.enbuild.2017.07.066. Elsevier B.V.
Gray, A., et al., 2009. Lung cancer deaths from indoor radon and the cost effectiveness and potential of policies to reduce them. BMJ (Online). https://doi.org/10.1136/bmj.a3110.
Greeven, C.S., et al., 2017. Enterprise collaboration systems: addressing adoption challenges and the shaping of sociotechnical systems developing offshore outsourcing practices in a global selective outsourcing environment -the IT supplier's viewpoint change management lessons learn. International Journal of Information Systems and Project Man Agement 5 (1), 63–77. Available at: http://www.sciencesphere.org/ijispm/archive/ijispm-0501.pdf#page=67.
Heeren, N., et al., 2015. Environmental impact of buildings - what matters? Environmental Science and Technology. https://doi.org/10.1021/acs.est.5b01735.
Heijmans, N., Loncour, X., 2017. Impact of the EPC on the Property Value, pp. 1–6 (H2020 Project No 692447).
International Energy Agency (IEA), 2012. The Multiple Benefits of Energy Efficiency Improvements.
International Energy Efficiency (IEA), 2019. World Energy Efficiency Outlook.
Ipsos Belgium and Navigant, 2019. Comprehensive Study of Building Energy Renovation Activities and the Uptake of Nearly Zero-Energy Buildings in the Eu Final Report, p. 87. Available at: https://ec.europa.eu/energy/sites/ener/files/documents/1.final_report.pdf.
Klöckner, C.A., Nayum, A., 2016. Specific Barriers and Drivers in Different Stages of Decision-Making about Energy Efficiency Upgrades in Private Homes, pp. 1–14. https://doi.org/10.3389/fpsyg.2016.01362.

Lammi, M., Pantzar, M., March 2019. The data economy: how technological change has altered the role of the citizen-consumer. Technology in Society 59, 101157. https://doi.org/10.1016/j.techsoc.2019.101157. Elsevier Ltd.

Lawrence, T.M., et al., 2016. Ten questions concerning integrating smart buildings into the smart grid. Building and Environment 108, 273–283. https://doi.org/10.1016/j.buildenv.2016.08.022.

Luz Martín-Peña, M., et al., 2018. The digitalization and servitization of manufacturing: a review on digital business models. Strategic Change 27 (2), 91–99. https://doi.org/10.1002/jsc.2184.

MacNaughton, P., et al., 2018. Energy savings, emission reductions, and health co-benefits of the green building movement review-article. Journal of Exposure Science and Environmental Epidemiology. https://doi.org/10.1038/s41370-017-0014-9.

Martinaitis, V., et al., 2004. Criterion to evaluate the "twofold benefit" of the renovation of buildings and their elements. Energy and Buildings 36 (1), 3–8. https://doi.org/10.1016/S0378-7788(03)00054-9.

McKinsey Global Institute, February 2017. Reinventing Construction: A Route to Higher Productivity. McKinsey & Company, p. 20. https://doi.org/10.1080/19320248.2010.527275.

Mikulić, D., et al., 2016. The economic impact of energy saving retrofits of residential and public buildings in croatia. Energy Policy 96 (2016), 630–644. https://doi.org/10.1016/j.enpol.2016.06.040.

Miller, N., et al., 2009. Green buildings and productivity. The Journal of Sustainable Real Estate 1 (1), 65–89. Available at: http://ares.metapress.com/content/6402637N11778213.

Morri, G., Soffietti, F., 2013. Greenbuilding sustainability and market premiums in Italy. Journal of European Real Estate Research. https://doi.org/10.1108/JERER-06-2013-0011.

Morris-Marsham, C., Moor, G., 2011. The impact of solar panels on the price and saleabilityf. Opticon 11 (11), 1–7.

Mujan, I., Anđelković, A.S., Munćan, V., Kljajić, M., Ružić, D., 2019. Influence of indoor environmental quality on human health and productivity-A review. Journal of cleaner production 217, 646–657.

Niesen, T., et al., 2016. Towards an integrative big data analysis framework for data-driven risk management in industry 4.0. In: Proceedings of the Annual Hawaii International Conference on System Sciences. https://doi.org/10.1109/HICSS.2016.627.

Qiu, Y., et al., 2017. Soak up the sun: impact of solar energy systems on residential home values in Arizona. Energy Economics 66, 328–336. https://doi.org/10.1016/j.eneco.2017.07.001. Elsevier B.V.

REN21, 2022. Renewables 2022 Global Status Report. REN21. https://www.ren21.net/reports/global-status-report/ (Accessed 30 November 2022).

Rinaldi, S., et al., 2020. A cognitive-driven building renovation for improving energy effciency: the experience of the elisir project. Electronics (Switzerland) 9 (4). https://doi.org/10.3390/electronics9040666.

Rojko, A., 2017. Industry 4.0 concept: background and overview. International Journal of Interactive Mobile Technologies. https://doi.org/10.3991/ijim.v11i5.7072.

Sekai, M., 2017. Industrial digitalisation in Europe: the growth of start-ups and the transformation of established firms. Mitsui & Co. Global Strategic Studies Institute Monthly Report.

SINTEF, 2013. Big Data, for Better or Worse: 90% of World's Data Generated over Last Two Years'. ScienceDaily.

Skumatz, L.A., 2009. Lessons Learned And Next Steps In Energy Efficiency Measurement And Attribution: Energy Savings, Net To Gross, Non-energy Benefits, and Persistence Of Energy Efficiency Behavior. Prepared for CIEE Behavior and Energy Program).

Smart Cities Information System/Smart Cities Marketplace, 2020. Upscaling Urban Residential Retrofit for the EU's Low Carbon Future: Challenges and Opportunities. Available at: https://smart-cities-marketplace.ec.europa.eu/insights/publications/upscaling-urban-residential-retrofit-eus-low-carbon-future-challenges-and.

Smith, K., Woodward, A., Campbell-Lendrum, D., Chadee, D., Honda, Y., Liu, Q., Olwoch, J., Revich, B., Sauerborn, R., Aranda, C., BERRY, H., BUTLER, C, 2014. Human health: impacts, adaptation, and co-benefits. In: Climate Change 2014: impacts, adaptation, and vulnerability. Part A: global and sectoral aspects. Contribution of Working Group II to the fifth assessment report of the Intergovernmental Panel on Climate Change. Cambridge University Press, pp. 709–754.

Soulti, E., Leonard, D., 2016. The Value of Breem A Review of Latest Thinking in the Commercial Building Sector. Bre Global ltd. Available at: http://www.breeam.com/filelibrary/Briefing Papers/BREEAM-Briefing-Paper——The-Value-of-BREEAM–November-2016——123864.pdf.

StepUP project, 2020. Using Digital Twins to Optimise Renovations and Drive Zero-Carbon'stepup-project.Eu. Available at: https://www.stepup-project.eu/2020/10/digital-twins-to-optimise-renovations-and-drive-zero-carbon/.

Stojanovic, V., et al., June 2018. Towards the generation of digital twins for facility management based on 3D point clouds. In: Proceeding of the 34th Annual ARCOM Conference, ARCOM 2018, pp. 270–279.

Thomson, H., Snell, C., Bouzarovski, S., 2017. Health, well-being and energy poverty in Europe: a comparative study of 32 European countries. International Journal of Environmental Research and Public Health 14 (6). https://doi.org/10.3390/ijerph14060584.

Underhill, L.J., et al., 2019. Simulation of indoor and outdoor air quality and health impacts following installation of energy-efficient retrofits in a multifamily housing unit. Building and Environment 106507. https://doi.org/10.1016/j.buildenv.2019.106507. Elsevier Ltd.

Vandevyvere, H., De Groote, M., 2020. Position Paper: Post COVID Recovery: Boosting the Economy through Large-Scale Renovation for Better and Healthier Buildings. EnergyVille Press. Available at: https://vito.be/en/news/boosting-economy-through-large-scale-renovation-better-and-healthier-buildings.

Vine, E.L., et al., 2015. Better Buildings, Better Economy: An Economic Impact Analysis of a Federal (August 2020).

Vlaamse Regering, May 2020. Long-term Strategy for the Renovation of Flemish Buildings, Performance, Energy Directive, Buildings.

Volk, R., et al., 2014. Building Information Modeling (BIM) for existing buildings — literature review and future needs. Journal Automation in Construction 38, 109–127.

Webb, A.R., 2006. Considerations for lighting in the built environment: non-visual effects of light. Energy and Buildings. https://doi.org/10.1016/j.enbuild.2006.03.004.

WHO, 2018. Climate Change and Health: Fact Sheet. Retrieved on 13 03 2021 from: https://www.who.int/news-room/fact-sheets/detail/climate-change-and-health.

Yu, C.W.F., Kim, J.T., 2010. Building pathology, investigation of sick buildings—VOC emissions. Indoor and Built Environment 19 (1), 30–39.

Further reading

Bashir, 2016. Warm Homes Oldham Evaluation: Final Report.

BPIE, 2011. Europe's Buildings Under The Microscope, Buildings Performance Institute Europe, Buildings Performance Institute Europe (BPIE), ISBN 9789491143014.

Dallasega, P., et al., 2018. Industry 4.0 as an enabler of proximity for construction supply chains: a systematic literature review. Computers in Industry. https://doi.org/10.1016/j.compind.2018.03.039.

European Comission, 2020a. White Paper on Artificial Intelligence - a European Approach to Excellence and Trust. COM(2020) 65 final. Available at: https://www.cambridge.org/core/product/identifier/CBO9781107415324A009/type/book_part.

European Comission, 2020b. Energy efficient buidlings. Available at: https://ec.europa.eu/energy/topics/energy-efficiency/energy-efficient-buildings_en?redir=1.

Miller, E., Buys, L., 2008. Retrofitting commercial office buildings for sustainability: tenants' perspectives. Journal of Property Investment and Finance. https://doi.org/10.1108/14635780810908398.

Mørck, O., et al., 2016. Shining examples analysed within the EBC Annex 56 project. Energy and Buildings. https://doi.org/10.1016/j.enbuild.2016.05.091.

Moseley, P., 2016. Practical Approaches to the Building Renovation Challenge. European Commission EASME, p. 13. https://doi.org/10.1016/j.energy.2004.04.055.

Runde, T., Thoyre, S., 2010. Integrating sustainability and green building into the appraisal process. Journal of Sustainable Real Estate. https://doi.org/10.5555/jsre.2.1.8241450318476wk0.

Sørensen, B.T., 2018. Digitalisation: an opportunity or a risk? Journal of European Competition Law & Practice 9 (6), 349–350. https://doi.org/10.1093/jeclap/lpy038.

13

Scale matters: exploiting cross-scale interactions for a smart and sustainable built environment

Ahmed Khoja
Faculty of Architecture, Munich University of Applied Sciences, Munich, Germany

1. Introduction

From the 1972 United Nations Conference on the Human Environment up to the Paris Agreement and the launch of the United Nations Sustainable Development Goals in 2015, the world is engaged in a long and continuous deliberation on finding the best sustainable development path to avert the looming climate changes. Today, there is an agreement that to keep global warming within the 2°C limit, the global greenhouse gas emissions must be halved by 2030 and reduced to zero by 2050 (United Nations Secretary-General, 2020). For the building sector, this would mean avoiding 50% of projected energy consumption growth (European Environment Agency, 2019). Given the fact that the majority of the existing building stock was built before the introduction of formal energy performance requirements and that over 75% of these inefficient buildings will still be in use post-2050 (Clarke et al., 2015; Filippidou and Jiménez Navarro, 2019), the deep energetic renovation of the existing building stock to the current state of the art net-zero energy buildings (NZEB) is regarded as the most cost-effective path to reach the climate goals of 2050 (Bruel et al., 2013).

To ensure the viability of the NZEB standard, or any other energetic renovation target, as a tool to avert the negative impacts of climate change, it is important to link the energetic goals with the greater holistic sustainability targets. Actually, with the absence of such holistic consideration, the deep energetic renovation of the

Intelligent Environments. https://doi.org/10.1016/B978-0-12-820247-0.00018-7

existing building stock to the NZEB standard can be equally harmful to the environment as other low-energy or traditional buildings (Paleari et al., 2013; Thiel et al., 2013; Passer et al., 2016; Tumminia et al., 2017). Moreover, due to the large upfront investment and associated high maintenance costs of NZEB, it is not yet economically viable for a large number of the existing buildings to reach the zero energy balance without heavy governmental subsidies (Vrijders and Wastiels, 2013; Esser et al., 2019).

The poor economic and environmental performance of the NZEB is primarily due to the lack of holistic sustainable consideration in building renovations. Sustainability is a complex and dynamic concept that interlinks several temporal and spatial scales and domains (Grosskurth and Rotmans, 2005). Incorporating the sustainability issues in the building sector requires a fundamental change in the temporal and spatial scales used in designing, constructing, and operating buildings. Otherwise, we run the risk that the new energetic renovations to NZEB standards will meet the same fate of previous efforts that tried to halt and reduce the adverse effects of buildings on the environment and brought minimal improvements (Clarke et al., 2015).

This chapter will debate the importance of adopting a holistic, cross-scale approach that integrates many topics and stakeholders across several temporal and spatial scales to realize a new generation of buildings that are healthy, smart, and sustainable. Moreover, it highlights the multiple benefits that can be achieved by combining sustainable design thinking and smart building technologies. Finally, the chapter will present the results of a pioneering international research project that applied a set of comprehensive and novel tools and design methodologies, aiming at paving the way for overcoming the cross-scale transition barriers.

2. Cross-scaling: exploiting the benefits of multiscale considerations in building renovations

Climate change and sustainability issues are not bound to a certain space or time. Actions taken at a smaller local scale such as a building can have an ever-lasting impact on a greater scale such as a neighborhood, a city or a nation and vice versa. Hence the maxim: global thinkinglocal actions. The traditional planning process hinders the application of such cross-scale consideration as it handles buildings individually and treats the time dimension as a linear quantity constrained between the building's start and finish date (Van Wyngaard et al., 2012). In reality, however, buildings do not stand in isolation, they are rather an integral part of a greater social and technical network that maintains and supports their function. Moreover, buildings cannot be treated as finished or constant due to the various adjustment cycles a building goes through throughout its lifetime. In this sense, the existing linear planning process that follows the triple constraints paradigm is ill-suited to address the interconnected, dynamic, and multiscale issues of sustainability. To incorporate sustainability in the planning process and to bridge the temporal and spatial gaps, a shift toward a holistic, multidimensional, and circular planning process is inevitable (Fig. 13.1). Bridging the temporal scale requires, on the one hand, broadening the time scope of the project beyond its operational life, embracing the circular motion of time viewing its past and future as a part of one cycle, and on the other hand, dictates the inclusion of several time resolution units that span from second to decades as per the specifics of each sustainability domain and subject.

Sustainability issues (society, ecology, economy) are dynamic, intertwined, and complex and cannot be properly treated using a single time unit. For example, the social sustainability issue of indoor thermal comfort dictates balancing the room operational temperature with the internal loads, the indoor and the cyclical outdoor climate. Due to the interaction between these parameters, thermal comfort planning must be done dynamically across several time resolution units spanning from minutes, days to months. With the help of modern smart building systems, even finer time resolution units of seconds and less can be utilized to optimize the performance of the building systems.

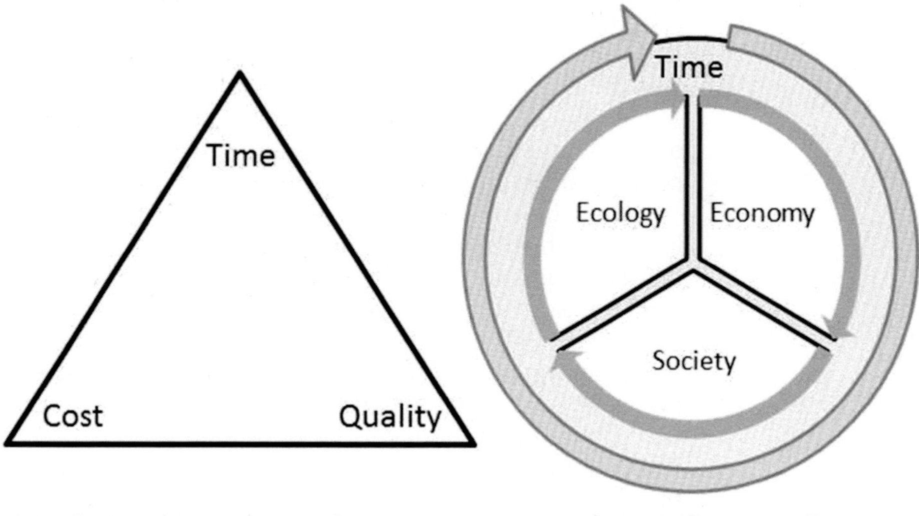

Figure 13.1 Triple constraint paradigm versus sustainability paradigm.

From the ecological perspective, a life cycle assessment (LCA) method is needed to assess the environmental impact of the passive and active building systems used to reach the desired indoor thermal comfort to avoid achieving one sustainability target at the expense of the other. After all, it is estimated that over 70% of all the materials extracted are used in cities and buildings (Kibert, 2007). The LCA assessment is done using long-time spans that stretch from years to decades. Hence, a different time resolution is needed from an ecological perspective than the ones used to assess the same topic from the social sustainability perspective. The same is also true for assessing the financial viability of the used systems following a life cycle cost approach.

Surely, the realization of a sustainable building would require covering a much larger and complex list of issues than the ones provided in this example. Nevertheless, the purpose of the example is to demonstrate the interdependency between sustainability and time as well as the importance of varying the time resolution to properly address sustainability issues in the building sector.

Thanks to the great advancements in the Information and Communication Technologies (ICT), it is possible to unlock the benefits of automated decision-making in near real time. The constant inflow of information from the smart-enabled active building systems such as lighting, heating ventilation, and cooling (HVAC) and renewable energy systems allows for commencing adjustments in the performance parameters of each system to optimize the performance of the whole with minimal user interference. Moreover, the ICT systems are able to integrate machine learning and forward-looking capabilities to preadjust the system performance parameters to accommodate possible changes in weather and/or user behavior patterns. Therefore, the ICT system can, on the one hand, improve building performance and, on the other hand, reduce equipment failures as well as the burden of complex decision-making (Hilty et al., 2014).

Smart building systems' exchange of information is not limited to the building parameter. Information can be exchanged between buildings. This transforms the building's role in the grid from a passive to an active one, in which excess energy and resources can be exchanged between buildings as well as with the greater grid. This broadens the spatial scale at which buildings are planned and operated and paves the way to the realization of the "global thinking and local action" slogan.

In the urgent case of decarbonizing the existing building stock, the insights that the ICT system provides about the cross-scale exchange of information and resources between the buildings and each other is vital for the wide-scale integration of renewable energy systems necessary to achieve the zero-carbon building stock target. The ICT systems allow for exploiting the synergies between the buildings. This optimizes the utilization of the generated energy and improves the energy performance of buildings and subsequently, their environmental and economic performance. Indeed, it was demonstrated that via cross-scaling the energy generation systems and coupling it with a targeted renovation of the building stock, an improvement of the primary energy balance by 30% can be attained over a standard single building renovation (Conci and Schneider, 2017).

The importance of integrating multiple spatial scales when renovating the building stock is rather more evident in the case of NZEB renovations. As shown in Fig. 13.2, a typical zero energy building usually exhibits a discrepancy between its energy generation and its energy consumption profiles. The load matching, that is, the degree of overlap between energy generation and load in net zero energy buildings hardly goes over 28% annually (Voss et al., 2010). This load mismatch increases the burden of the grid operation as well as increases the pressure on the energy storage facilities tasked with storing the surplus energy during light load periods, to provide it again during the peak load (Malin, 2010). Buildings that are fitted with the ICT systems can play a

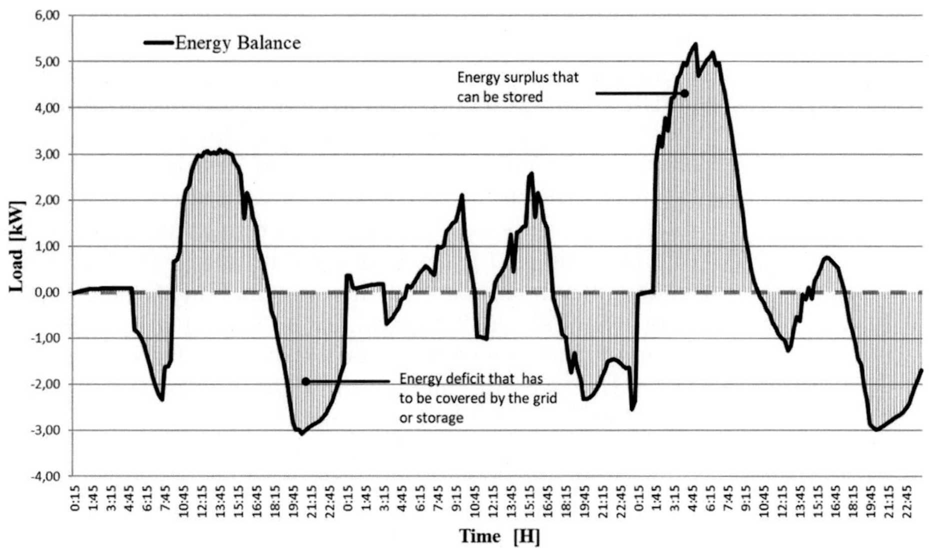

Figure 13.2 A typical energy balance profile of zero energy building.

pivotal role in overcoming this challenge by establishing a common energy system that takes advantage of the mutual utilization of energy production capacities (Marique et al., 2013; Organisation for Economic Co-operation and Development, 2013; Scognamiglio et al., 2014; Polly et al., 2016). For instance, the ICT systems used in the LEED-certified campus of King Abdullah University of Science and Technology in Saudi Arabia are able to save about 4% of the campus energy consumption by exploiting the diversity of energy loads alone (Malin, 2010).

Due to technical and/or legal barriers, buildings do not have an equal chance to achieve the NZEB state. This problem was investigated in a study carried out by the US Department of Energy. The study analyzed the technical potential of US nonresidential buildings to achieve net-zero energy using technologies that are expected to be widely available in 2025. The study revealed that under the most favorable conditions no more than 60% of the buildings can achieve the NZEB status (Griffith et al., 2007). Therefore, connecting the existing building stock into a common global energy system via ICT technologies would allow challenged buildings to have access to excess renewable energy production from other neighboring buildings. The realization of NZEB through connecting buildings to each other in a global energy system is more cost-effective over single-building NZEBs even in locations with the most favorable conditions for local renewable energy generation (Fernandez et al., 2009).

The previously mentioned examples show clearly the benefits of tackling the decarbonization of the building stock at various temporal scales that extend beyond the building's operational life and highlighted the importance of fully embracing the circular motion of the building in time. Moreover, these examples debated the multiple economic and environmental benefits of achieving the NZEB state at larger spatial scales beyond the single building level. Actually, due to this cross-scale relation between the building and its greater surrounding, it is argued that it is generally not possible to define sustainability at the building scale (Bourdic et al., 2012; Berardi, 2013). Such a cross-scale consideration dictates the wide utilization of smart building and ICT systems. However, the integration of these systems into the existing building stock would not automatically result in achieving the sustainability objectives (Hilty et al., 2014). After all, sustainability cannot be achieved through the switch of a button. It rather requires a rigorous and holistic assessment of the impact of these systems on the overarching social, ecological, and economic performance of the buildings using varying time units. Therefore, the deployment of ICT systems in the building stock to reach the climate targets should always be treated with vigilance.

In conclusion, it is safe to say that both smart building systems and sustainable building thinking across multiple temporal and spatial scales hold the key for the realization of the next generation of decarbonized and healthy buildings that are good for their users, community, and the globe.

3. Overcoming the cross-scale transition barriers: from theory to practice

The previous chapters demonstrated the importance of combining multiple temporal and spatial scales in building renovations to reach the 2030 and 2050 climate targets. Admittedly, the realization of such approach is quite challenging due to a number of practical and technical reasons such as the absence of compatible design processes and the lack of integrated design processes that address the complexity of cross-scale decision-making and the management of a large number of involved parties (owners, planners, funding agencies, tenants, etc.). Another challenge that hinders the adoption of the cross-scale approach is the data scarcity and weak reliability of the available data about the existing building stock. Moreover, applying the cross-scale approach introduces new interoperability requirements between building information modeling (BIM), building performance simulation tools, and geographic information systems (Wetter et al., 2013) as shown in Fig. 13.3.

The past decade has witnessed a great surge in research that aims to overcome the challenge of a multiscale approach in renovation projects. One of these research projects is the EU-funded applied research project of NewTREND (New integrated methodology and Tools for Retrofit design towards the next generation of ENergy efficient and sustainable buildings and Districts). The NewTREND project ran from 2015 to 2018 with the participation of over 30 researchers with various scientific backgrounds representing 13 European public and private research institutions from seven European countries (Finland, Germany, Hungary, Ireland, Italy, Spain, and the United Kingdom). The objective was the development of an integrated retrofit design methodology (IDM) supported by an online-based integrated decision support system (IDS) to facilitate the participatory design and decision-making in cross-scale retrofit projects. The NewTREND IDS consists of a series of interdependent software services that empower the stakeholders of the value chain with the ability to

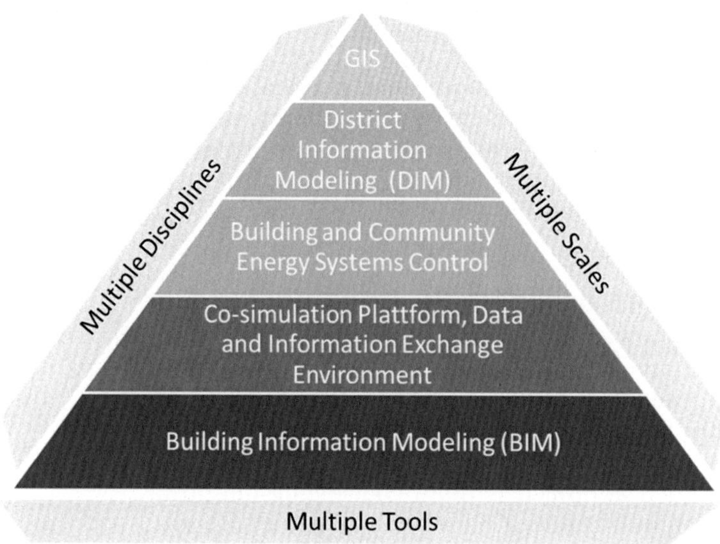

Figure 13.3 Interoperability requirements for cross-scale performance tools.

identify, select, and implement the most suitable sustainable energy retrofitting strategy for a single or multiple buildings.

To ensure the fulfillment of the project's ambitious targets, the research team was composed of an international multidisciplinary team covering a wide array of disciplines such as social and environmental sciences, building physics and mathematics, civil and mechanical engineering, public policy, economics, urban planning, architecture, computer and software programming, and IT technologies. This multidisciplinary team worked together as a cohesive entity to outline, develop, test, and validate the developed IDS system in real renovation projects. The case study sites in Hungary, Finland, and Spain have been selected with specific criteria to provide a homogenous picture of European cities and their characteristics, covering several European climate conditions, urban patterns, construction styles, and functions.

The Hungarian demo site consisted of 14 publicly owned buildings used for leisure and administrative proposes. The buildings are located in Bókay Garden, that is, situated in the 18th district of Budapest. A nearby historical elementary school shown in Fig. 13.4B was included in the test phase. The school buildings date back to the 1880s and have historical and cultural significance. The Finnish pilot neighborhood is located in the city of Seinäjoki at the north of the country. The demonstration site was made up of 15 buildings that date back to the 1930s and are part of a former hospital campus, as seen in Fig. 13.4A.

Figure 13.4 (A–C) An arial view of the former hospital campus in Seinäjoki (left), the primary school building in Budapest (center), and the apartment block in Sant Cugat del Vallèsn (right) (Google Maps 2021a,b,c).

Within the NewTrend project, the four largest buildings of the site were chosen for the pilot testing of the IDS. The chosen buildings are occupied by three main tenants: Seinäjoki University of Applied Sciences (SeAMK), Music School of Southern Ostrobothnia and a dental clinic. The Spanish demo site comprised several municipality-owned buildings, spread across three separate locations in the city of Sant Cugat Del Vallèsn in northern Spain. It included a set of three linked apartment blocks rented by young tenants at a subsidized rate illustrated in Fig. 13.4C and a state school in a secluded part of the city and two private houses in a neighborhood that mainly comprise single-family housing. The publication of Orova et al. (2018) provides a more detailed description of the project demo sites.

NewTREND's integrated design methodology dictated the inclusion of a wide array of stakeholders from each demonstration site to allow for participatory project management. Any person, group, or organization that can influence or is influenced by the renovation project is treated as a stakeholder. Therefore, the list of the involved stakeholders in each project included local municipalities, building users and planners, facility managers, neighborhood residents, and, when possible, local associations. These stakeholders were actively involved in the development and testing of the research project outcomes. Moreover, to link

Figure 13.4 cont'd.

these outcomes with the specific demand of the local market of each participating partner, seven local advisory teams (LAT) were established. The LAT is composed of representatives of the target groups, that is, the NewTREND tool end users from both the public and private side. The LATs acted as a professional support for the project and provided advice from the end user's point of view regarding the project results

For the successful integration of the stakeholders' interests and perspectives, participatory codesign methods were developed and implemented at several stages of the three- year research project. In the early project stages, sensors were installed in each demonstration building to collect data about the building's energy and thermal performance. The building users were asked to document their day-to-day experiences with the building over the period of a week. They were asked to document these regarding topics that cannot be measured through the installed sensors. The topics covered were maintenance level, access to the natural environment, outdoor spaces, and other social and

Figure 13.4 cont'd.

sensory design topics. The report done by Sweeney et al. (2018) provides more insights into the applied participatory codesign methods in each demo site.

In the later stages, the NewTREND researchers visited the sites in person to collect measurements and to hold interviews with the participants to better understand what they have documented in their diaries. Workshops were conducted to inquire about the stakeholders' needs and anticipation of the planned renovation works.

The results of these interviews and workshops proved vital for the development of the renovation solutions and the NewTREND planning tools as the researchers obtained detailed insights about the occupants' behaviors and preferences. For instance, occupants that have potted plants or vegetable boxes showed a strong preference for balconies, deep windowsills, roof gardens, good solar orientation, and outward or top-half opening windows. Integrating these items in the renovation can have an impact on solar gain, thermal bridging, infiltration, and purge ventilation and the overall performance of the building. Knowing such preferences and habits is not possible through simple site visits and sensor-based data collection. Actually, the codesign approach, especially the diary process, proved to be a successful form of engagement for design and was the most informative and constructive for the research. Although disrupting traditional power structures in design processes, the resulting data were also far richer and deeper than would have been possible with only a survey or hosting a large public meeting or pursuing a retrofit based on technical data alone. It enabled the research team to reposition the human component in building renovations putting it center-stage.

In parallel with the development of the participatory design methods, the development of the NewTREND IDS platform was underway. The IDS consists of a series of interdependent software services that operate at various spatial and temporal scales and provides the project team with the necessary framework for the data collection, information exchange, collaboration, evaluation, and implementation of the retrofitting work. To facilitate the usability of the platform a dedicated interactive manual was developed (Khoja et al., 2017). The manual guides the user through a series of steps and processes into finding the most effective energy retrofitting solutions for their project.

The platform is made up of three front-end tools that the user can interact with, supported with two back-end tools. The three front-end tools of the platform are the collaborative design platform (CDP), the data manager (DM), and the Technologies library. The two components forming the back end of the tool are the district information modeling server (DIM) and the Simulation and Design Hub. Fig. 13.5 illustrates how the front-end and back-end tools of the platform interact with each other.

The DIM Server is an interoperable, distributed, multimodel data exchange server that links the building with the district. The DIM server stores, exchanges, and translates various file formats between the CDP, the Simulation and Design Hub, and the DM and creates associations between them so that the information can be analyzed as the sum of the parts.

The Simulation and Design Hub is the second back-end tool and it retrieves relevant project information from the DIM server to carry out hourly dynamic simulations and calculations. The simulation results are then sent back to both the DIM server for storage and to the CDP for visualization and postprocessing.

The CDP is the project cockpit and the user's main landing point. The CDP provides an online environment for initiating the project, sharing its data and visualizing the simulation results. Moreover, the CDP can be used to post news about the project and create questionnaires and polls to engage the building users and other stakeholders in the renovation process. As cross-scale retrofitting project may consist of a very complex and large stakeholder configuration, the access rights to the CDP functions are constrained based on the specific role of each stakeholder in

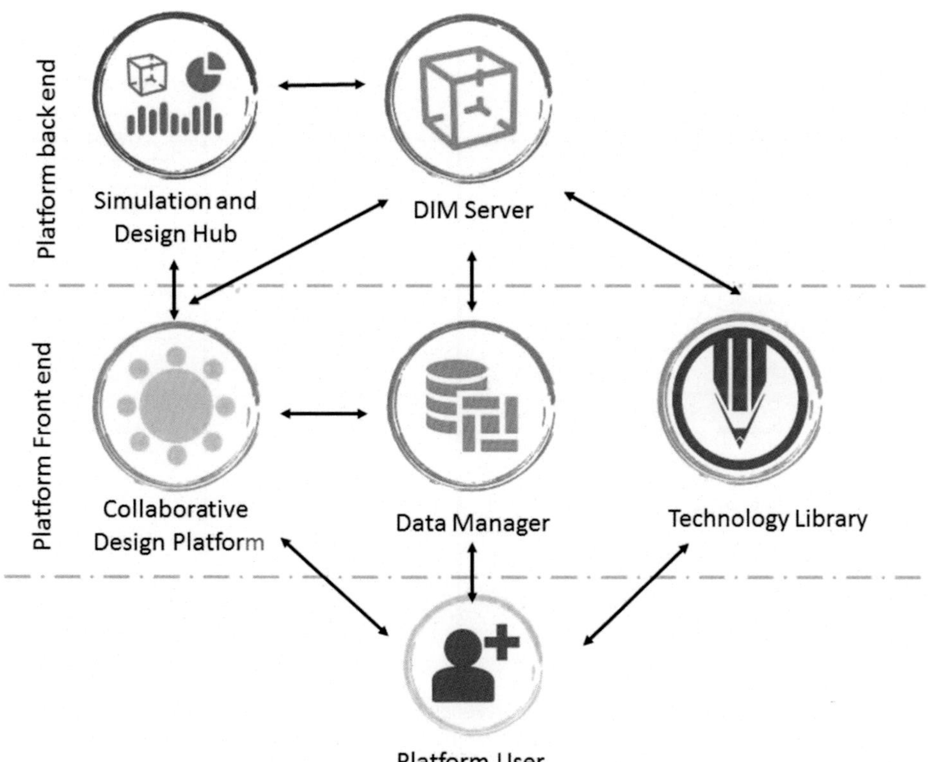

Figure 13.5 The interaction between the front- and back-end tools of the NewTREND IDS platform.

the project. Fig. 13.6 gives an example of how the project stakeholders can be assigned to project roles in the CDP.

To create a project in the CDP, the project raw CityGML and Industry Foundation Classes (IFC) files need to be uploaded to the platform. These files are stored in the DIM server and can be accessed through the DM to be edited and complemented with relevant information to populate the BIM model for each building.

The performance of the used BIM models can be simulated and when needed supplemented with intervention measures to create various renovation scenarios. At this stage, the technology library module can be used to help the planner and the end user alike finding the most suitable interventions. The booklet of Barbagelata et al. (2017) gives an overview of the functionality of the technologies library. To ensure the positive impact of the used renovation technologies on the sustainability performance of the project, a set of comprehensive sustainability key performance indicators (KPIs) that operate at both the single building and the larger urban scale was developed (Barbano et al., 2016).

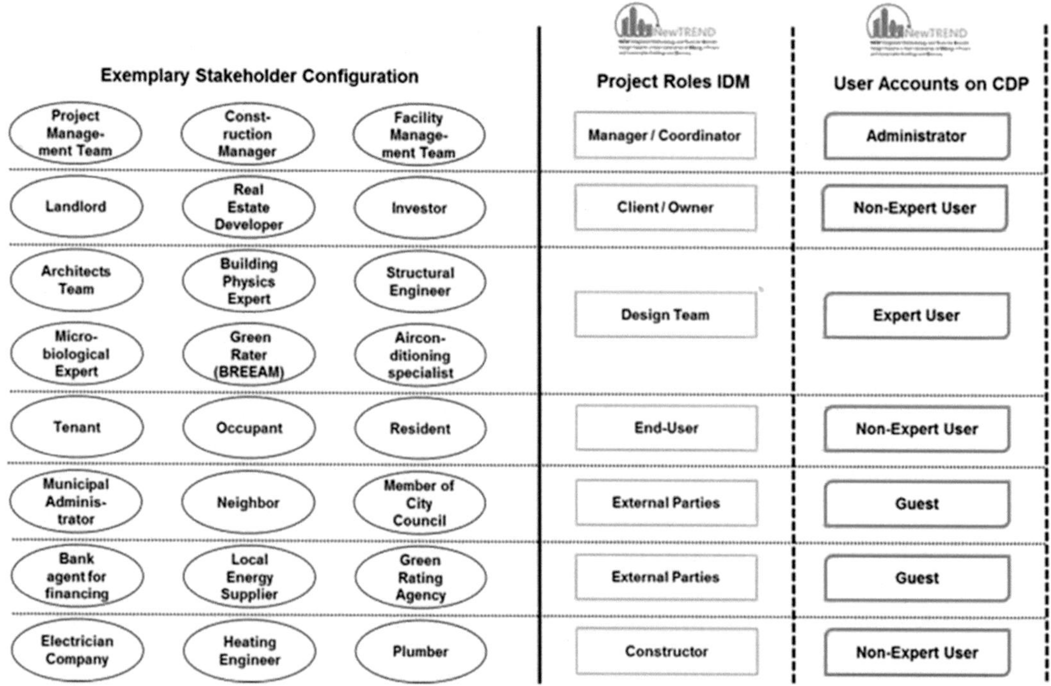

Figure 13.6 An example of assigning different stakeholders with project roles in the NewTREND IDS.

To overcome the data scarcity challenge as well as the time and effort needed to collect that building data, the CDP and DM platforms operate based on a novel progressive modeling framework that couples the BIM level of development (LoD) with CityGML level of detail (LOD).

The progressive modeling framework subdivides the data collection and consequently the building performance simulation scope into three modes of operation (Basic, Advanced, and Premium). Each operating mode lists the minimum data the planning team needs to collect via the Data Manager module to ensure that the used BIM models are of comparable maturity. In essence, each of the three operating modes requires a geometric model of the building and/or the neighborhood that is further enriched with semantic data. However, the main difference between the three modes lies in the amount and the degree of accuracy of the geometric along with the semantic data of the building/neighborhood as displayed in Fig. 13.7 and Table 13.1.

The planning team can progress between previously mentioned three modeling modes as per the available resources and the goal of the data collection process. Therefore, at the

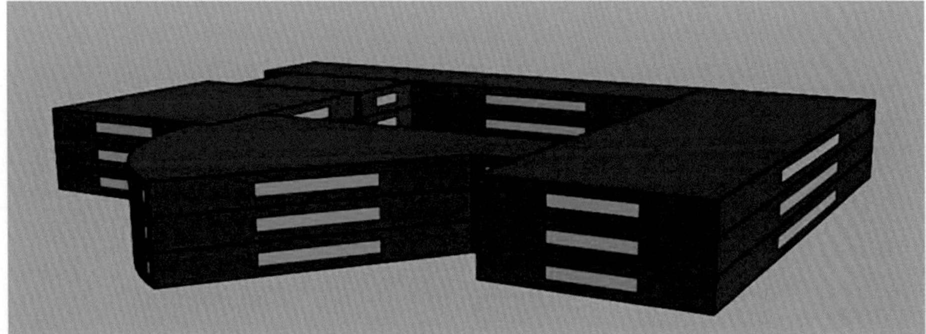

Figure 13.7 The application of the progressive modeling framework on a real case study showing the progressive maturity of the building BIM model in basic and advanced mode (Khoja et al., 2019).

Figure 13.7 cont'd.

beginning of each data collection cycle, the user is to set via the CDP the platform mode of operation. Consequently, the Data Manager would highlight the type of data that is to be collected for the project. This division of the data complexity, in turn, has a direct influence on the quantity and quality of the outputs the Simulation and Design Hub is able to offer and sustainability KPIs that can be evaluated (Fig. 13.8).

The Basic mode takes advantage of the 20/80 Pareto principle; hence, a fair degree of performance or accuracy can be obtained using a limited amount of resources or information. As a result, operating the platform in the Basic mode is most suitable in the early stages of the project when data availability is limited.

Table 13.1 An overview of the progressive simulation framework type of information, simulation scope, and project phases.

	Basic mode	Advanced mode	Premium mode
Geometry model	CityGML LoD 2	CityGML LoD 4	CityGML LoD 4
Extensivity of the model information	BIM LOD200 (AIA specification)	BIM LOD300 (AIA specification)	BIM LOD500 (AIA specification)
Main semantic information source	Default values from regulations and statistics	Working drawings, reports, user and owner questionnaires	Real-time measured values
Analysis objectives	Estimate the technical, economic, and environmental performance of the project	Estimate the social, technical, economic, and environmental performance of the project	Assess the actual social, technical, economic, and environmental performance of the project
Application scope	One or more building	Single building	One or more building
Most suitable phase of application	Early design phase-preretrofit	Design development	In use

The building geometry in the Basic mode is simple and approximated and handled as a single unit. Thanks to the wide coverage of Google maps, Google street view, and OpenStreetMap, the collection of building geometry data can be done remotely as a part of desktop research. Moreover, with the absence of more comprehensive information about the building's HVAC and electrical systems, as well as thermal and physical specifications of the building envelope, the DIM server uses information from local building statistics databases to fill in the data gaps. The DIM database contains local and regional information about the most prevailing building construction material and HVAC system for each building as per its use and year of construction.

Given the limited data requirements of the Basic mode, the practical usage of operating the CDP in this mode is constrained to predicting the building energy performance in a rough manner and subsequently its running costs and associated carbon

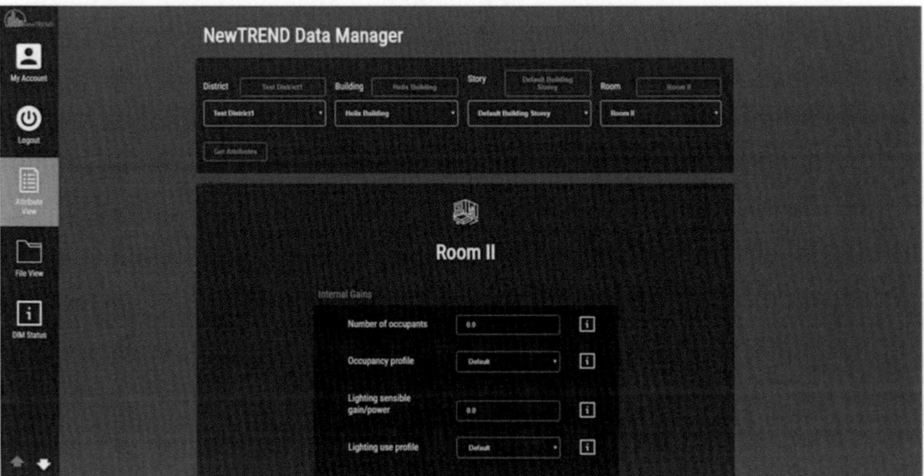

Figure 13.8 An illustration of the data manager user interface (Ntimos, 2018).

emissions. The actual testing of the Basic mode in the demo sites returned very good and promising results. Using the basic mode, the platform overestimated the annual thermal and electrical energy consumption of the Finnish demo site buildings by about 11% in comparison to the metered values. The same values were underestimated by about 1% and 8% in both the Hungarian and the Spanish cases, respectively (Maile et al., 2018). These good predictions can be attributed to the fact that the demo site buildings hosted unified and simple uses. Moreover, the demo cities had a well-maintained and updated digital representation of their buildings as well as an updated and detailed database about the typical construction and building systems used in the area. Nevertheless, in further testing, it was demonstrated that the accuracy and reliability of the simulation results of the Basic mode could be further improved by utilizing sensitive analysis methods (Khoja et al., 2019). These findings are also in line with the finding obtained by the ENTRANZE research project (Policies to Enforce the Transition to nearly Zero-Energy Buildings in the EU-28) that adopted a similar simulation approach (Zangheri et al., 2014).

The application of the Basic mode proved to be very helpful to support the decision-makers, building owners, and investors in prioritizing the buildings that need to undergo deep renovation (Maile et al., 2018; Khoja et al., 2019). Moreover, the results generated from the Basic mode provide the design team or the investor with a first impression about the amount of emissions reduction that can be achieved and the investments needed to reach it. In addition, the Basic mode can be used to model the energy performance of neighboring buildings which the planning team might not have access to. Therefore, the energy flow in the neighborhood and possible synergies potential between the buildings can be analyzed. Hence, each building can be viewed as a part of a global energy system. This feature of the Basic mode was tested in the Hungarian demo site of Bókay garden to evaluate whether it is more suitable to supply the park buildings with power from a central Combined heat and power plant (CHP) or through Photovoltaics (PVs) arrays installed on the rooftop of the park buildings. As the CHP plant require a high number of running hours to operate efficiently, the analysis showed that due to the low demand on heating by the analyzed buildings and the high agreement between the generated energy and the power demand, the PV installation deemed more suitable from a holistic technical, financial, and environmental standpoint (Maile'et al., 2018).

In comparison to the Basic mode, operating the platform in Advanced mode is far more demanding in terms of data acquisition and building geometry. Actually, the utilization of the Advanced mode is indispensable in the later stages of the planning process to generate detailed construction drawings and have a more reliable estimation of the building behavior. The DM module requires that building geometry used in this mode to be on par to a CityGML LOD4 (Gröger et al., 2012) and LoD300 BIM model (Kensek, 2014). Moreover, all other nongeometry data related to the building's active systems as well as thermal and physical properties need to be very detailed and verified onsite. As such, in comparison to the Basic mode, operating the platform in the Advanced mode enables the Simulation and Design Hub to offer a wider range of simulation outputs with superior accuracy and great detail. Indeed, with careful simulation and rigorous data acquisition, the simulated building energy performance in the advanced mode can be very close to that of the real one (Khoja et al., 2019). The generated simulation results can be viewed for each room of the building independently giving important information about the indoor thermal, visual, and acoustic comfort and indoor air quality.

From a practical point of view, the planning team can utilize the advantages of both the Basic and Advanced modes to model the existing neighborhood, in which the more accurate but more demanding advanced mode is reserved for the actual building that is undergoing renovation and the less accurate but quick Basic mode is used to model other neighboring building in a "local action and global thinking" approach.

The last and most comprehensive mode for operating the CDP is named the Premium mode. This mode is actually intended to be used by the owner or facility manager in the postrenovation phase to monitor the actual performance of the renovated building(s). The Premium mode is operated using the real-time inflow of automatically recorded data from the building's smart systems and sensors. Moreover, the BIM model used in the Premium mode is to be equal to that of a LoD500 BIM model (Kensek, 2014), that is, an actual as-built model. This enables the planner's team to monitor the building performance in near real time and to intervene when needed, thus closing the gap between actual and designed building performance. Moreover, the building facility manager and planners can update the building BIM model whenever a change in the building takes place to keep track of these changes.

Having high-quality and constantly updated high-resolution data provided by the building smart systems coupled with a "live" building BIM model as per the Premium mode should be listed as one of the targets of any renovation project. As mentioned before, buildings go through various changes during their life time. Keeping track of these changes and constantly observing the building performance in all the sustainability domains is a prerequisite for reaching the climate and sustainability targets of 2030 and 2050. The benefits of having real-time information about the building performance were demonstrated in the demo school buildings in both Spain and Hungary. The monitoring of the indoor air quality performance in both buildings showed unacceptable and unhealthy concentration levels of CO_2 in some of the classrooms (Maile et al., 2018). Therefore, advanced ventilation systems were incorporated as a part of the renovation work in both cases. Given the fact that adaptive user behavior and purge ventilation can be equally effective in solving the indoor air quality problem, tailored training programs that cater to the specific needs of the teachers and the students were developed in tandem with the installation of the ventilation and monitoring systems.

In conclusion, the real application of the progressive modeling framework in the demo cases proved the merits of each of the three operating modes. Today, an energy simulation is usually conducted at a late stage of the project life to verify the building design compliance with certain targets or codes (Reinhart and Fitz, 2006; Tupper and Fluhrer, 2010). The progressive modeling framework redefines the role of building energy simulation by putting it at the heart of each step of the project and by integrating several sustainability aspects to facilitate holistic and well-informed decision-making. The modes reflect the natural circular motion of the project in time and enable the project team to set and adjust the project targets as the project progresses and monitor its performance during its actual use. The application of these progressive models in everyday planning practice opens the doors widely for the realization of the much-needed new generation of the smart and sustainable building stock. The Basic mode balanced the effort with accuracy and proved to be very useful in the decision-making process conducted in the early phases of renovation projects providing a global view of the energy flow within the neighborhood. The use of the Advanced mode was inevitable for the development of detailed planning and construction documents. The wealth of information collected through the platform in the Premium mode allowed to shift the planning process from a linear into a circular continuous one. The research project results showed the urgent need for a similar integrated and holistic platform that can bridge both temporal and spatial planning scales and put the end user at the core of the renovation process. A platform that allows viewing the project beyond its completion and handover date and treats it as an evolving dynamic and active element of the built environment is very much required in today's construction practice to allow for a multidimensional cross-scale consideration of the built environment.

4. Discussion and outlook: finding a scale to fit

The renovation of the existing building stock to NZEB is a cornerstone for fulfilling the climate targets of 2050 and beyond. As demonstrated in the previous chapters, to ensure the viability of the NZEB renovation of the existing buildings in the climate battle, multitemporal and special scales are needed. The paper demonstrated that a win–win situation for all the stakeholders engaged in the renovation process can be achieved when the temporal and spatial scales are broadened and the stakeholders are actively engaged in the renovation process. The art is in finding the correct temporal and spatial scales and in gauging the optimal level of stakeholder engagement for each project. Incorporating the sustainability paradigm in the planning practice dictates escaping from the linear planning process into a circular, holistic multiscale one. Ssmart buildings can play a decisive role in the realization of a new generation of NZEB that are not just smart but sustainable as well. The smart system's ability to exchange and share information across various spatial and temporal scales is a key enabler for such a transformation. Nevertheless, the contribution of these smart building systems to reaching the climate targets must always be evaluated under a holistic sustainable lens. The existing sustainability rating systems still lack the proper integration of smart building and holistic user well-being dimensions (Berardi, 2013; Khoja and Danylenko, 2020). Moreover, the widely used sustainability rating systems still treat the building and its greater urban setting as two separate entities (Bourdic'et al., 2012). Cross-scale renovation requires an assessment system that can address the bidirectional causal relationship between the building and the larger urban context.

The NewTREND research project demonstrated the ability of incorporating various file formats and software solutions to generate a detailed and accurate picture of the built environment. Furthermore, it highlighted the importance of utilizing the full spectrum of BIM planning methods throughout the renovation project as BIM "offers the best solution for data management and flow throughout a retrofit project from the survey to the building site" (Larsen et al., 2011).

The progressive modeling framework discussed earlier facilitates the gradual integration of district-level information with building information in renovation projects by coupling the CityGML, IFC, and BIM files. Moreover, the framework takes advantage of the wealth of existing information; databases and smart systems to create a detailed holistic look of the built environment that extends beyond the project spatial boundaries and completion date.

The early adoption of BIM in an IDM similar to the one developed in the NewTREND project, results in shifting the effort of the project team from the more detailed design stages to the early phases of the project. This, in turn, empowers the project team with the ability to adjust the project performance targets early on in the project life and avoid costly design changes at later stages as displayed in Fig. 13.9.

The benefit of having a single platform that evolves with the building and is able to incorporate information from both the building smart systems and as-built BIM model can stretch far beyond disrupting the construction and building facility management sector. An integrated, dynamic and multiactor platform that is fed by near real-time data about the building stock can be an integral part of a larger smart city platform. This creates the conditions for a demand-driven market for energy, sustainable and smart buildings. Moreover, by integrating multiple stakeholders and information sources, the platform can eventually act as a digital one-stop shop that ties the "distributed" building information such as energy performance certificates and sustainability ratings in a single virtual place. The wide public availability of this

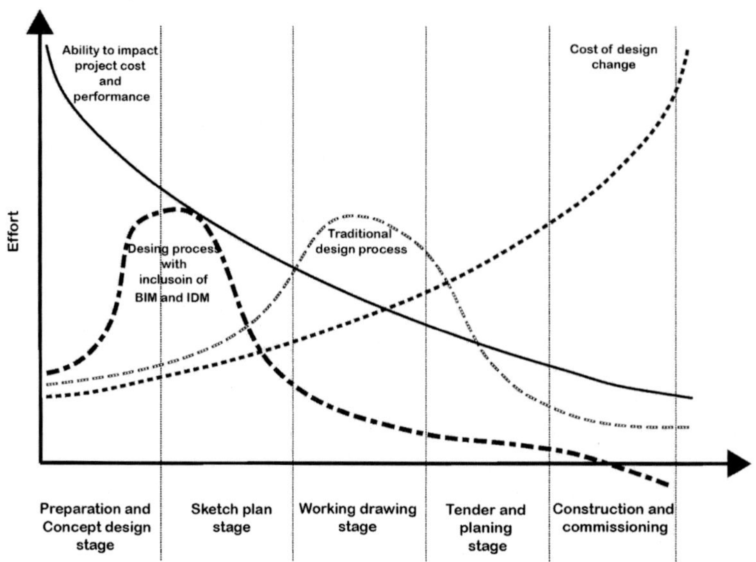

Figure 13.9 IDM coupled with BIM planning process versus traditional planning process.

information increases the transparency of the sector and ease the burden of decision-making for the tenants, owners, investors, and funding agencies. Moreover, it allows public policymakers to track the fulfillment of the climate target and create tailored made policies to correct the course when desired.

Today, the rapid digitalization process, the bitter lessons learned from the COVID-19 pandemic and the urgent global need for decarbonizing the building stock have strengthened the demand for a new generation of buildings that are sustainable, smart, and healthy (Esser et al., 2019; Khoja and Danylenko, 2020). The increasing public interest coupled with the great advancements in the design software and rapid proliferation of smart building systems and renewable energies presents a golden opportunity to realize these new generation of buildings.

Acknowledgment

The Author wishes to acknowledge the valuable contribution of NewTREND research colleagues, including, but not limited to: Birthe Klebow, Dimitrios Ntimos, Nick Purshouse and Valeria Ferrando (Integrated Environmental Solutions), Andras Reith, Ida Kiss, Melinda Orova, Réka Tóth and Viktor Bukovszki (ABUD Mernokiroda KFT), Falko Kiedaisch, Felix Stiller and Uli Jakob (Dr. Jakob Energy

Research), Andrea Moro, Giulia Barbano and Elena Bazzan (iiSBE R&D), Francisco David Gallego and Jara Feliu Gómez-Salcedo (REGENERA LEVANTE SL) Davor Stjelja, Ken Dooly and Tuomas Laine (Granlund), Judith McRae, Niall Dunphy, Paul O'Connor and Rosemarie MacSweeney (University College Cork), James O'Donnell, Paul Beagon and Walter O' Grady (University College Dublin), Johannes Steidl, Natalie Eβig and Paul Mittermeier (Munich University of Applied Sciences), Gerard Riba and Victor Martinez (Ajuntamiento De Sant Cugat Del Valles), Carlos Morales, Derek Bunn and Lucia Fuselli (London Business School), Guilia Barbagaleta, Marco Barbagelata, Paolo Musso and Tommaso Zerbi (STAM), Federico Seri, Gian Marco Revel and Marco Arnesano (Universita Politecnica Delle Marche), and the municipal staff that participated in the project. The NewTREND project received funding from the European Union's Horizon 2020 research and innovation program under the grant agreement no. 680474.

References

Barbagelata, M., Jakob, U., Stiller, F., 2017. Booklet 3: Retrofit Technologies from. http://newtrend-project.eu/documents/.

Barbano, G., Essig, N., Mittermeier, P., Orova, M., Beagon, P., Claudi, L., Gómez-Salcedo, J.F., Kiedaisch, F., 2016. Definition of Sustainable Key Performance Indicators from. http://newtrend-project.eu/documents/.

Berardi, U., 2013. Clarifying the new interpretations of the concept of sustainable building. Sustainable Cities and Society 8, 72–78.

Bourdic, L., Salat, S., Nowacki, C., 2012. Assessing cities: a new system of cross-scale spatial indicators. Building Research & Information 40 (5), 592–605.

Bruel, R., Fong, P., Lees, E., 2013. A Guide to Developing Strategies for Building Energy Renovation. Buildings Performance Institute Europe.

Clarke, L.E., Jiang, K., Akimoto, K., Babiker, M., Blanford, G.J., Fisher-Vanden, K., Hourcade, J.-C., Krey, V., Kriegler, E., Loschel, A., 2015. Assessing transformation pathways. In: Climate Change 2014: Mitigation of Climate Change. Contribution of Working Group III to the Fifth Assessment Report of the Intergovernmental Panel on Climate Change, Pacific Northwest National Lab.(PNNL), Richland, WA (United States).

Conci, M., Schneider, J., 2017. A district approach to building renovation for the integral energy redevelopment of existing residential areas. Sustainability 9 (5), 747.

Esser, A., Dunne, A., Meeusen, T., Quaschning, S., Wegge, D., Hermelink, A., Schimschar, S., Offermann, M., John, A., Reiser, M., 2019. Comprehensive Study of Building Energy Renovation Activities and the Uptake of Nearly Zero-Energy Buildings in the EU. Final Report, European Commission: Brussels, Belgium.

European Environment Agency, 2019. Progress on Energy Efficiency in Europe from. https://www.eea.europa.eu/data-and-maps/indicators/progress-on-energy-efficiency-in-europe-3/assessment.

Fernandez, N., Katipamula, S., Brambley, M.R., Reddy, T., 2009. Economic Investigation Of Community-Scale Versus Building Scale Net-Zero Energy.

Filippidou, F., Jiménez Navarro, J., 2019. Achieving The Cost-Effective Energy Transformation Of Europe's Buildings.

Google Maps, 2021a. Apartment Block in Demo Site in Sant Cugat Del Vallèsn, 20.03.2021, from. https://www.google.com/maps/place/Carrer+Mar+de+la+Xina,+08173,+Barcelona,+Spain/@41.4580111,2.

0768603,99m/data=!3m1!1e3!4m5!3m4!1s0x12a4972601afe931:0xe289f1a7a4df6bbb!8m2!3d41.4582051!4d2.0771471.

Google Maps, 2021b. Bókay Primary School, 20.03.2021, from. https://www.google.com/maps/place/B%C3%B3kay+%C3%81rp%C3%A1d+%C3%81ltal%C3%A1nos+Iskola/@47.4387074,19.1806193,166m/data=!3m1!1e3!4m5!3m4!1s0x4741c24177bbeaeb:0x7130736cb680e9df!8m2!3d47.4386547!4d19.1810372.

Google Maps, 2021c. Seinäjoki Former Hospital Campus, 20.03.2021, from. https://www.google.com/maps/place/Sein%C3%A4joki+University+of+Applied+Sciences+-+SeAMK/@62.7897236,22.8260098,448m/data=!3m1!1e3!4m5!3m4!1s0x4687cb95a158f2ff:0x4084164f765c30e1!8m2!3d62.7895954!4d22.8218403.

Griffith, B., Long, N., Torcellini, P., Judkoff, R., Crawley, D., Ryan, J., 2007. Assessment of the Technical Potential for Achieving Net Zero-Energy Buildings in the Commercial Sector. National Renewable Energy Laboratory (NREL), Golden, CO.

Gröger, G., Kolbe, T.H., Czerwinski, A., 2012. Candidate OpenGIS® CityGML Implementation Specification (City Geography Markup Language). Open Geospatial Consortium, Inc., OGC 06-057r1, 2006.

Grosskurth, J., Rotmans, J., 2005. The scene model: getting a grip on sustainable development in policy making. Environment, Development and Sustainability 7 (1), 135–151.

Hilty, L.M., Aebischer, B., Rizzoli, A.E., 2014. Modeling and Evaluating the Sustainability of Smart Solutions. Elsevier.

Kensek, K.M., 2014. Building Information Modeling. Taylor & Francis.

Khoja, A., Danylenko, O., 2020. Real estate 5.0: synthetizing the next generation of buildings. On Research 5 (5).

Khoja, A., Mittermeier, P., Essig, N., 2017. Manual Describing The Conduct Of The Developed Collaborative Design System from. http://newtrend-project.eu/documents/.

Khoja, A., Stjelja, D., Jämsén, T., Essig, N., 2019. Urban retrofitting: a progressive framework to model the existing building stock. In: IOP Conference Series: Earth and Environmental Science, IOP Publishing.

Kibert, C.J., 2007. The Next Generation of Sustainable Construction. Taylor & Francis.

Larsen, K.E., Lattke, F., Ott, S., Winter, S., 2011. Surveying and digital workflow in energy performance retrofit projects using prefabricated elements. Automation in Construction 20 (8), 999–1011.

Maile, T., Orova, M., Ntimos, D., Stjelja, D., MacSweeney, R., Barbagelata, M., Asens, P., Bazzan, E., 2018. Application Of The Methodology And Tool from. http://newtrend-project.eu/documents/.

Malin, N., 2010. The Problem with Net-Zero Buildings (And the Case for Net-Zero Neighborhoods). Building Green.

Marique, A.-F., Penders, M., Reiter, S., 2013. From Zero Energy Building to Zero Energy Neighbourhood. PLEA.

Ntimos, D., 2018. NewTREND Data Manager Integrated Environmental Solutions.

Organisation for Economic Co-operation and Development, 2013. Transition to Sustainable Buildings: Strategies and Opportunities to 2050. OECD.

Orova, M., Várnagy, S., Martinez, V., Asens, P., Riba, G., Dooley, K., Stjelja, D., 2018. Booklet 5: Pilot Projects. Retrieved 11.03.2021, from. http://newtrend-project.eu/documents/.

Paleari, M., Lavagna, M., Campioli, A., 2013. Life Cycle Assessment and Zero Energy Residential Buildings. PLEA.

Passer, A., Ouellet-Plamondon, C., Kenneally, P., John, V., Habert, G., 2016. The impact of future scenarios on building refurbishment strategies towards plus energy buildings. Energy and Buildings 124, 153–163.
Polly, B., Kutscher, C., Macumber, D., Schott, M., Pless, S., Livingood, B., Van Geet, O., 2016. From zero energy buildings to zero energy districts. In: Proceedings of the 2016 American Council for an Energy Efficient Economy Summer Study on Energy Efficiency in Buildings, Pacific Grove, CA, USA: 21-26.
Reinhart, C., Fitz, A., 2006. Findings from a survey on the current use of daylight simulations in building design. Energy and Buildings 38 (7), 824–835.
Scognamiglio, A., Garde, F., Røstvik, H.N., 2014. How net zero energy buildings and cities might look like? New challenges for passive design and renewables design. Energy Procedia 61, 1163–1166.
Sweeney, R.M., Lennon, B., Dunphy, N., 2018. Engagement of Stakeholders (Including Occupants) from. http://newtrend-project.eu/documents/.
Thiel, C.L., Campion, N., Landis, A.E., Jones, A.K., Schaefer, L.A., Bilec, M.M., 2013. A materials life cycle assessment of a net-zero energy building. Energies 6 (2), 1125–1141.
Tumminia, G., Guarino, F., Longo, S., Mistretta, M., Cellura, M., Aloisio, D., Antonucci, V., 2017. Life cycle energy performances of a Net Zero Energy prefabricated building in Sicily. Energy Procedia 140, 486–494.
Tupper, K., Fluhrer, C., 2010. Energy modeling at each design phase: strategies to minimize design energy use. Proceedings of SimBuild 4 (1), 48–55.
United Nations Secretary-General, 2020. No Excuse Not to Meet Net-Zero Emission Target by 2050. UN, New York, UN.
Van Wyngaard, C.J., Pretorius, J.-H.C., Pretorius, L., 2012. Theory of the triple constraint—a conceptual review. In: 2012 IEEE International Conference on Industrial Engineering and Engineering Management, IEEE.
Voss, K., Sartori, I., Napolitano, A., Geier, S., Gonçalves, H., Hall, M., Heiselberg, P., Widén, J., Candanedo, J.A., Musall, E., 2010. Load matching and grid interaction of net zero energy buildings. In: EUROSUN 2010 International Conference on Solar Heating, Cooling and Buildings.
Vrijders, J., Wastiels, L., 2013. Nearly Zero Energy Renovation of houses: life cycle costs and environmental impact. In: International Sustainable Building Conference.
Wetter, M., van Treeck, C., Hensen, J., 2013. New Generation Computational Tools for Building and Community Energy Systems, vol 60. IEA EBC Annex.
Zangheri, P., Armani, R., Pietrobon, M., Pagliano, L., Boneta, M.F., Müller, A., 2014. Heating and Cooling Energy Demand and Loads for Building Types in Different Countries of the EU. Polytechnic University of Turin, end-use Efficiency Research Group 3.

14

Ontologically streamlined data for building design and operation support

Ardeshir Mahdavi[1] and Dawid Wolosiuk[2]
[1] *Institute of Building Physics, Services, and Construction, Faculty of Civil Engineering Sciences, TU Graz, Austria;* [2] *Department of Building Physics and Building Ecology, Faculty for Architecture and Planning, TU Wien, Austria*

1. Introduction

Information and communication technology (ICT) has the potential to support various aspects and phases of the design, construction, and operation of intelligent and sustainable built environments. Thereby, the fruitful application of ICT depends on a genuine understanding of the criteria that characterize built environments' intelligence. An inclusive definition of such intelligence must be arguably be both multidomain and multiscale. The former attribute pertains to the multiple dimensions of environmental quality, covering not only functional, technical, ecological aspects, but also psychological and social ones. The latter attribute suggests that such aspects apply at different scales, from building components, to building zones, to whole buildings, neighborhoods, districts, and entire urban settings. Intelligent ICT support for designing and operating intelligent environments must thus cover an extensive and rich information space expanding over multiple domains and scales. This requirement highlights the critical importance of efficient and effective collection, storage, and processing of potentially vast amounts of data from multiple sources over multiple streams. Evidence-based methods for building design and operation support must rely on multiple streams of data obtained via monitoring and/or computational modeling. However, the heterogeneous nature of these data, as well as the multiplicity of deployed software-relevant formats and templates, represents major obstacles toward the efficient use of such data in the delivery and

Intelligent Environments. https://doi.org/10.1016/B978-0-12-820247-0.00003-5

management of intelligent built environments. To address the related challenges, further progress is needed, particularly concerning development and application of versatile data ontologies. In a nutshell, intelligent ICT support for design and operation of intelligent building environment requires advanced data monitoring and processing methods, which in turn requires appropriate ontologies.

Ontologies are developed and deployed to enhance knowledge and data exchange in a specific field or domain (Gruber, 1993). For instance, building industry benefits from well-structured ontologies such as Industry Foundation Classes (ISO, 2018a) or green building XML (Green Building, 2020) that drive Building Information Modeling software (ISO, 2018b). Efforts in building performance specification and assessment too can benefit from well-structured ontologies and data schemas. Toward this end, a recently introduced building performance data (BPD) ontology (complemented with BPD schema) attempts to identify, categorize, and capture the complexities of building related performance data and their attributes (Mahdavi and Taheri, 2018; Mahdavi and Wolosiuk, 2019a,b). As such, there are many different types of data related to built environments, representing a challenge in view of developing robust, comprehensive, and scalable ontologies. In case of BPD originating, for instance, from sensors or simulations, this process of data ontologization involves (i) preprocessing, (ii) categorical identification, (iii) supplementation of the relevant attributes, and (iv) encoding in a proper file format. Only then is such ontologized data ready to be used in various downstream applications. This chapter describes such an ontologization process as applied to large real-world building-related datasets. Specifically, building-related data are first processed in terms of fidelity and quality to be subsequently ontologized and delivered to a number of building performance assessment applications.

2. Building performance data (BPD)

Building performance assessment procedures require access to BPD, including as performance variables - or performance indicators - that involve multiple domains, scales, aspects, and degrees of resolution. Use cases of BPD are diverse (Mahdavi and Taheri, 2018; Mahdavi and Wolosiuk, 2019). These include, among other things, building quality assessment, compliance demonstration with building code requirements, specification of building attributes in certificate-type documents, comparison and ranking of building design alternatives, intelligent building operation, and smart grid applications. However, despite the critical role of BPD, there have been very few attempts to compose an explicit BPD ontology. The present contribution addresses this gap via the introduction of a systematic and comprehensive BPD ontology, which can offer multiple benefits. As such, ontologies can help structure the conceptual and semantic constituents of a domain and thus improve the efficiency of communication processes and developmental work therein. Whether obtained via measurement or simulation, the values of ontologically well-formed BPD can support visualization, optimization, and other decision support scenarios relevant to intelligent environments. A versatile BPD ontology can add to the clarity of building performance requirements specifications, advance the understanding of building performance principles in educational and training settings, and provide a solid foundation for the development of comprehensive data visualization engines (Mahdavi et al., 2005, 2016, 2017, 2018).

The development of the proposed original BPD ontology relied on an extensive review of common building performance indicators (BPIs) in thermal, air quality, visual, and acoustical domains, as well as various streams of building related data originating from monitoring systems and modeling applications. For each domain, categorical classification schemes were established and, for each category, concrete instances of common BPIs were considered. The ontology's structural core involves a systematic specification of the generic attributes of building performance variables. The general applicability of the ontology was demonstrated in that it was tested against a sample of BPIs from different domains.

3. Building performance indicators

The performance of buildings can be characterized through an extensive list of BPIs pertaining to multiple domains. These span from ones that assess strictly technical systems performance to those that are relevant to the "habitability" aspects of the building, including human health, comfort, and satisfaction (Mahdavi, 1998, 2011). A recent effort attempted to compile, review, and categorize a large number of BPIs. These were organized into topical domains, including energy efficiency, hygrothermal performance, thermal comfort, air quality, visual environment, and acoustical environment (Constantinou, 2017). Based on this effort, a general scheme of BPI categories was proposed as per Fig. 14.1. Therein, the main domain categories are

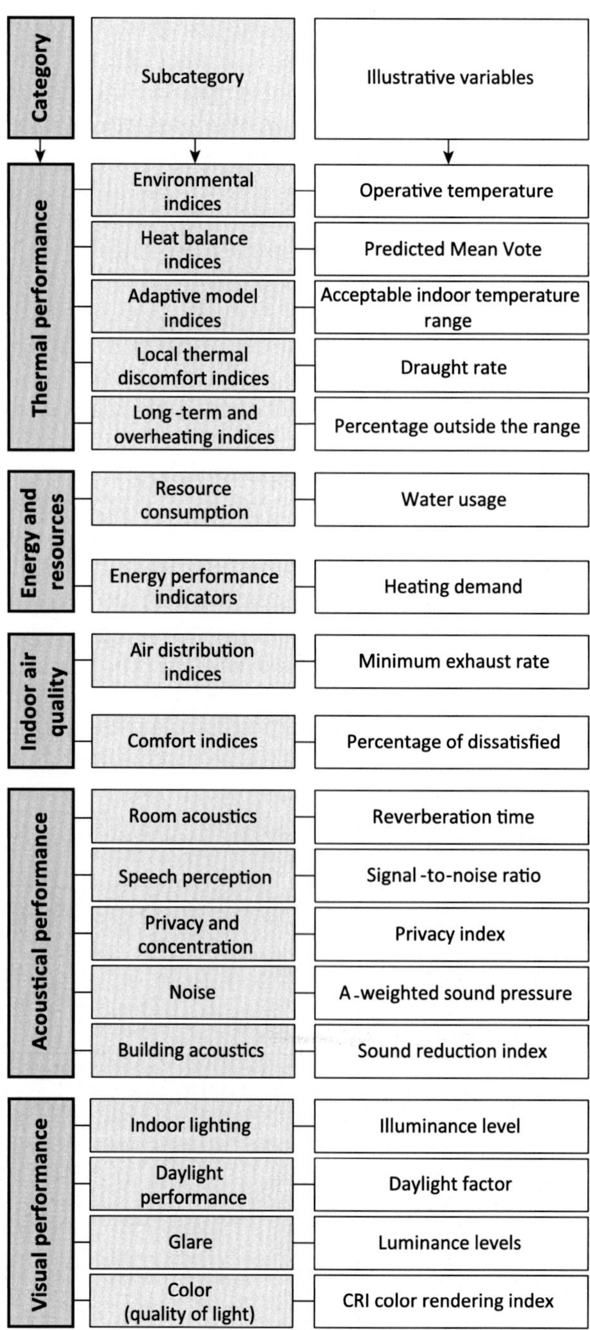

Figure 14.1 An overview of five building performance domains with subcategories and illustrative performance indicators examples.

mapped to relevant subcategories, exemplified by illustrative indicator instances.

The aforementioned review of BPIs facilitated a key observation. Despite their diversity, most indicators can be either directly mapped back to a measurable variable or are derived based on algorithmic manipulation of one or more of such variables. As such, the essential attributes of a BPI are similar to (or can be derived from) those applicable to measurable variables. Frequently, a primary (directly measured) variable, such as indoor air temperature itself, can act as a BPI (in this case, in the thermal performance category).

Aggregation (or other types of statistical treatment) of the values of such a variable over time and space can lead to more complex BPI definitions. Likewise, multiple, variously measured, calculated, estimated, or simulated variables can be synthetized into a compound BPI. A classic example of such a compound indicator would be predicted mean vote, whose definition requires the inclusion and algorithmic processing of values of variables pertaining to environmental conditions (air temperature, radiant temperature, air flow speed, air relative humidity) and occupants' personal factors (metabolic rate, clothing resistance) (Fanger, 1970). Guided by this observation and our previous experiences with performance data ontologies, we suggest that the essential ontological schema for BPIs can be obtained based on a previously introduced ontology of the primary building performance variables (Mahdavi and Taheri, 2018).

4. Ontological schema for building performance data

Utilizing the general map of indicators presented in Fig. 14.1, and considering additional aspects and requirements of measurable performance variables (Mahdavi and Taheri, 2018), a schema is proposed to capture the essential, ontologically relevant characteristics of BPD (see Table 14.1). This schema can be shown to fulfill key requirements of both measurable performance variables and BPIs, be those primary variables with actual values or compound variables with derived values. Each variable under consideration is mainly identified by its domain category and subcategory. The primary content of the schema is the variable's value. It carries a number of attributes and properties. The variable's type mainly specifies if its values are continuous or discrete. Each variable value is assumed to have a magnitude and, in certain cases, a direction vector. A relevant unit should be

Table 14.1 General schema for BPD.

Category			
Subcategory			
Variable	Name		
	Value	Type	
		Magnitude (size)	
		Direction (vector)	
		Unit	
		Spatial domain	Point
			Plane
			Volume
			Topological ref.
			Aggregation method
			Grid size
		Temporal domain	Time stamp
			Duration
			Time step
			Aggregation method
		Frequency domain	Range
			Band (filter)
			Weighting
			Aggregation method
	Agent		ID
	Notes	Data sources	Category
			ID/name
		Derivation method	Details (formula, link, etc.)

Modified based on Mahdavi and Taheri (2018).

specified for valid data interpretation and processing. Variable's category determines a number of additional properties that are specified in three domains. Spatial domain properties allow to associate a variable with a specific point in a Cartesian coordinate system or with a topologically specified location (for instance, via a room tag). Temporal domain properties can be expressed in the schema via a time stamp (e.g., for a sensor reading).

A time step denotes recurrent temporal intervals to which measured or simulation data could be assigned (e.g., hourly heating loads). Duration denotes the overall time frame to which a given variable value corresponds (e.g., annual cooling load). As such, time step and grid size can specify the discretization resolution of pertinent temporal and spatial continua. The frequency domain attributes are relevant to measured or simulated values that display wave characteristics such as electromagnetic radiation (including visible light) and sound.

If relevant, an agent ID attribute can be used to assign a given variable to a specific entity. Notes category pertains to additional relevant information addressing, for instance, the indicators' derivation background. In case of a monitored variable, notes could include a unique ID of a meter or sensor. In case of derived and compound indicators, notes could point to the pertinent computational procedure, such as applicable formulas, algorithms, and associated links and resources.

To illustrate the potential and robustness of the proposed ontology, three exemplary variables from different domains were selected pars pro toto (see Table 14.2). Thereby, categories, subcategories, and attributes of a given variables are indicated.

5. From data to application

Conceiving robust ontological schemata is not a trivial task. A comprehensive approach is required to encompass domain-specific features, details, or elements. A well-designed ontology with a well-structured schema should facilitate the process of identifying attributes, classes, and relations of its instances. Ontology implementation is where the theoretical concepts are put into practice. Depending on a domain or a field of interest that an ontology pertains to, the implementation process might include a list of specific challenges. Some of the relevant implementation questions are as follows:

1. What type of data is to be semantically enriched and where does the data originate from?
2. Should the data be preprocessed in any way (aggregation, segmentation, quality check)?
3. How can attributes be attached to the data in an efficient manner?
4. What is the best storage method for the ontologized data?

These questions exemplify the challenges related to the transformation of raw data to ontologized information that is ready to be processing in building performance assessment applications. As alluded to in the introduction, we focus in this chapter on a structured process (see Fig. 14.2), whereby building-related measured or simulated raw data is "ontologized" toward subsequent utilization in various building performance assessment applications. The following sections discuss in detail the different stages in this process.

Table 14.2 Illustrative representation of three exemplary BPIs following the structure of the proposed ontology.

Category				Energy and resources	Thermal performance	Visual performance
Subcategory				**Energy performance indicator**	**Heat balance indices**	**Indoor lighting**
Variable	Name			Heating load	Predicted mean vote	Illuminance levels
	Value	Type		Derived, Ratio	Derived, Interval	Primary, Ratio
		Magnitude		50	−0.13	463
		Direction		—	—	[0,0,1]
		Unit		$kWh.m^2$	—	lx
		Spatial domain	Point	—	[1.00,4.50]	[1.00,4.00,0.85]
			Plane	—	—-	—-
			Volume	Building A	—	—
			Topological reference	Building A	Office_012	Office_012
			Aggregation method	—	—	—
			Grid size	—	—	—
		TemporalDomain	Time stamp	—	June 11, 2018 09:00:00	December 01, 2018 12:40:00
			Duration	Annual	—	—
			Time step	1 h	1 h	5 min
			AggregationMethod	ArithmeticSummation	ArithmeticAverage	ArithmeticAverage
		Frequency domain	Range	—	—	—
			Band	—	—	—
			Weighting AggregationMethod	—	—	—
	Agent		ID	—	Occupant_4	—
	Notes	Data sources	Category	Simulation	Sensor	Sensor
			ID/name	Sim_20180729_1	Tem_3, Rh_3, airV_1,occ4_met, occ4_clo, ...	lux_4
		Derivation method		-	https://www.iso.org	-

Modified based on Mahdavi and Taheri (2018).

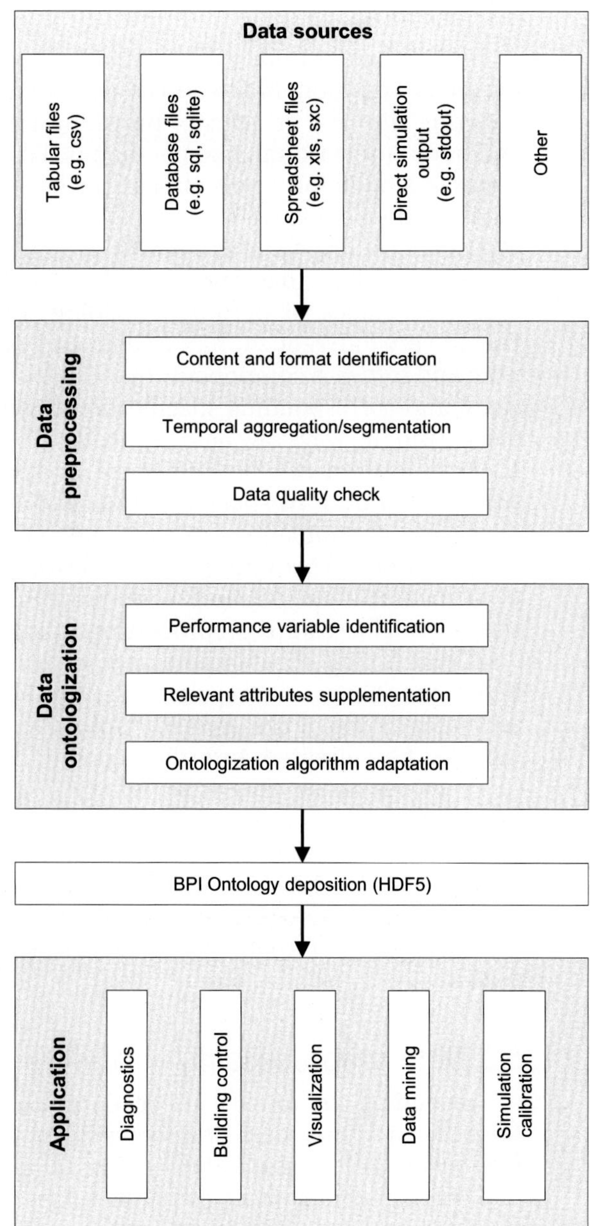

Figure 14.2 Schematic process overview for transformation (preprocessing, ontologization, storage) of performance data for use in various down-stream applications.

5.1 Sources of data

BPD can stem from various heterogeneous sources. Some of the most common BPD sources are building control systems, metering devices, or sensors providing information on indoor and outdoor environmental conditions. Likewise, computational building simulation applications can generate relevant performance data pertaining to, for instance, the thermal, visual, or acoustical conditions in the building. Similarly, "virtual" sensors can deliver data that are derived using both simulated and measured values of pertinent building performance variables. Due to very different sources of data and the multitude of hardware and software components (e.g., sensors and data logging devices) and corresponding specifications involved, there is a large diversity in the ways raw data are acquired and stored. The acquisition procedure can be influenced by specific manufacturers' standards or even by specific decisions of clients.

In case of simulation sources, often specific output formats are prescribed. This multiplicity of possible formats largely impacts the rest of the ontologization process as data from different sources might require preprocessing to match a common standard concerning the temporal nature of the data (i.e., event-based recordings vs. regular interval data) or its structural attributes. Some of the common output formats applied to BPD include: (i) delimited text files containing tabular data (e.g., CSV); (ii) database files (e.g., MySQL); (iii) spread sheet files (e.g., XLS); and (iv) direct simulation output (e.g., stdout).

In the process of ontological data structuring, sources of data might have to be handled individually. For instance, semantically different and heterogeneously structured data can be stored in the same output format. This issue is discussed in the following section.

5.2 Data preprocessing

Depending on the nature of data source and/or potential target applications, data preprocessing methods should be carefully taken into consideration before supplementing properties and storing performance variable values in a repository. The need for preprocessing is primarily related to the amount and quality of data. In this context, data sets (usually time series of measured or simulated performance values) should be examined in terms of data point sampling. As such, there are two common sampling strategies for data recording, namely event based and frequency based. In the event-based method, a measured value is only recorded when it indicates a meaningful change in the observed variable (e.g., indoor temperature changes above sensor's accuracy or above fixed threshold) or there is a change in state of a device (e.g., open/close window). This type of sampling is of interest due to the growing number of wireless and low energy monitoring solutions and the need for an energy-efficient monitoring regime.

The frequency sampling method is based on a fixed time period between recordings of measured values. This type of sampling might seem more straightforward, nonetheless the sampling frequency can vary from device to device. For this reason, both methods face an application-related data usability challenge as follows: Many analysis scenarios involving data streams from multiple sources require a common temporal base (i.e., uniform intervals) for relevant data analysis operations. Instances of such operations include, for example, correlation analysis, data aggregation, or multivariate statistical investigations. Depending on the application at hand, different temporal resolution levels of data samples might be required. Theoretically, the temporal resolution could be kept at a very high level. However, this could lead to data redundancy and unnecessarily high computational loads especially when processing large sets of data. As such, it might be appropriate to follow common practices in a domain and/or application scenario, when deciding about the desired level of data resolution. For example, in case of typical analysis scenarios involving indoor thermal environment, 15-minute time intervals have been found sufficient. Whereas electrical power quality monitoring might require much shorter time intervals due to rapid spikes, in the measured variable that would otherwise remain undetected.

The process of sensor-based data collection is prone to errors. Data quality control is a common practice that involves detection of flaws in a dataset to assure its validity and usefulness in future applications. There are a number of common quality-related challenges concerning data streams from monitoring devices. For instance, outliers are anomalous data points in a population of observations. Approaches to detect and mitigate outliers span from empirical methods (based on value range limits) to those rooted in descriptive statistics such as Tukey's fences test for detection (Tukey, 1977) or moving median for outlier removal.

Gaps in data represent another common problem. Here again, there are several strategies for filling missing data points. In case of small data gaps resulting from the removal of outliers, one commonly used method is the previously mentioned moving median or mean. In case of larger data gaps, a collection of data interpolation methods can be used. The source of such quality issues might be related to sensor malfunctions, temporal power supply interruptions, voltage drops due to a discharging battery, errors in communication with logger or gateway, and other external events.

All of the mentioned preprocessing elements need to be considered when preparing ontologized data for storage, especially when data are to be shared or archived. Hidden flaws and inconsistencies in data sets that are not detected and rectified during the preprocessing phase might hinder reliable utilization of data by future users.

5.3 Identification of categories and supplementation of attributes

The purpose of implementing an ontology-based schema is to give data a meaning and context. The ontology that is based on an empirical study of a domain (or a field of interest) outlines the categories, naming convention, and collection of attributes. As with many other cases, also in the case of BPD, the properties of data collections pertaining to performance variables or indicators need to be identified individually. This could become a cumbersome task that potentially involves manual processing of multiple variables, each requiring multiple properties to be identified. Depending on the case at hand, some properties might be available for scraping from the output files of the data sources (e.g., file name, header's content, column name, etc.). Nonetheless, in such an instance, strategies for information extraction need to be developed, resulting in additional efforts. This could be beneficial, but only when processing well-structured data sets. BPD, particularly data coming from monitoring systems, often lacks in particular categorical or spatial details. These details need to be supplied by a system designer or individually obtained. As such, the process of assigning relevant properties to data might be prone to human error, especially given the inherent diversity of diverse BPD.

5.4 Ontologized data deposition

Enriched BPD must be serialized in a format that meets several requirements characteristic for ontologies in general, as well as particular requirements pertaining to a specific domain. Such a format must be able to map the structure of hierarchical categories and their relations as specified in an ontology definition. It should also allow for assigning properties (detailed in schema) to categories, subcategories, and variables. What characterizes the BPD ontology is that it typically applies to large sets of time-oriented data. The storage format must not only allow for an effective access to categorical data attributes, but also—and more importantly—support efficient queries concerning time-dependent values of relevant variables. This condition excludes some of the simple text-based serialization solutions and requires some form of data base incorporation or data-specific file format utilization.

6. BPD ontology implementation

The BPD ontology and proposed schema were tested as part of a workflow, in which data from multiple sensors, monitoring indoor and outdoor environment, were processed into ontologically structured data. The data reported by each sensor are stored in an individual database file in a systematic manner. The naming convention for the source files and the internal data base structure were standardized, so as to mitigate future conversion processes. However, there are some examples of performance relevant data sets with a nonstandard format or source file content that requires individual treatment. In the present implementation effort, an example of such a data source is a sky-scanner. Data from this sensor come in a form of multiple csv files (one file per each day of recording) containing uniquely structured readings that need processing before being stored in an ontologically consistent manner.

Given the fairly well-structured output files generated by the main data source (sky-scanner) considered in this illustrative implementation, only a modest level of initial preprocessing (as described in the previous section) was necessary. However, not only the sky-scanner data but also data from other sources (e.g., indoor environmental sensors) were categorized and relevant attributes in the temporal, spatial, and frequency domains were organized in the form of a csv tabular file. Several functions written in the Python (Python, 2020) programming language were created to (i) transform performance data, (ii) supplement it with relevant properties, and (iii) serialize it in a HDF5 (HDF, 2019) file. HDF5 file format is a flexible scientific data format designed for storage of high volume of complex data. It is capable of storing data structures in a hierarchical manner. It is also capable of storing attributes assigned to the elements of structure. Such semantically enriched data were then tested in a series of applications. An instance of an advanced application is presented in the following section.

To illustrate how the ontologically structured data, deposited in a HDF5 file, can potentially be used in a performance analysis, an interface between populated BPD ontology and Ladybug Tools (Roudsari and Pak, 2013) was created. Ladybug Tools is a collection of free and open source environmental design applications built on top of simulation engines such as Radiance (Ward, 1994) and EnergyPlus (Crawley et al., 2001). It is integrated with the Rhino (McNeel, 2020b) 3D modeling software, which supports it in spatial context generation and results visualization. The interfacing is enabled through Grasshopper (McNeel, 2020a)—a visual programming language and environment for Rhino.

Originally designed for 3D algorithmic modeling and parametric design, Grasshopper includes a number of predefined components in various categories that serve this purpose. It also allows for creation of custom components such as Ladybug Tools that can be integrated in its visual programming environment. Grasshopper supports a number of programming languages that can be used to create general purpose or task-specific components. A number of custom components written in the Python programming language were created to enable utilization of the BPD ontology with selected Ladybug elements.

In general, the created components take the selected performance variable (extracted from HDF5 file based on attribute filtering) as an input, and process it (according to specified input parameters) to produce desired output in a format conforming to Ladybug's requirement. Fig. 14.3 presents one of the developed custom interface components used for extraction and conversion of monitored data (in this case, measured solar radiation data via a sky-scanner) to generate input required by Ladybug's *Radiation Analysis* element.

The illustrative case of incident solar radiation studies.

For this particular interfacing component instance (Fig. 14.3), the aim was to use detailed sky radiation data collected by a sky-scanner and direct solar radiation data (derived from global and

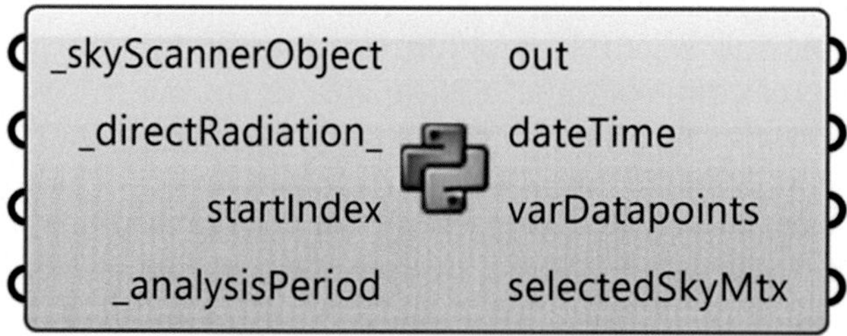

Figure 14.3 A custom component interface between BPD ontology and Ladybug's radiation analysis component.

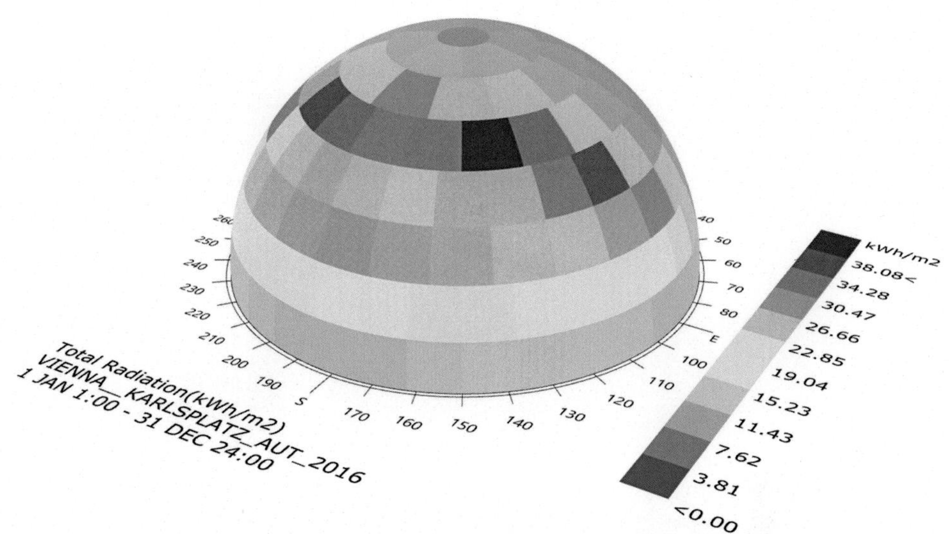

Figure 14.4 Visualization of total solar radiation generated from sky-scanner measurements in Vienna, Austria.

diffused solar irradiance measurements) toward solar radiation studies. Sky-scanner regularly measures, for a specific location, luminance and radiance of the sky hemisphere, represented as 145 segments or patches. A custom component was created to extract ontologically structured solar radiation data from BPD repository and process it in terms of the input format of the Ladybug's *Sky Dome* element. The *cumulativeSkyMtx* output is an array of aggregated total, direct, and diffused radiation values per sky patch for a selected time period. Fig. 14.4 presents a visualization of the annual diffuse sky radiation based on the data collected in 2016.

The same structured (*cumulativeSkyMtx*) output can be used as the input for the Ladybug's *Radiation Analysis* component. This component calculates the amount of solar energy falling on specific surfaces or on a group of selected surfaces. It calculates the incident solar radiation on a surface within a selected time period. It also allows for visualizing the results directly on the 3D model. Fig. 14.5 presents the result of such a study of an existing building in Vienna. The *Radiation Analysis* results can be used in solar heat gain studies or support solar energy systems design.

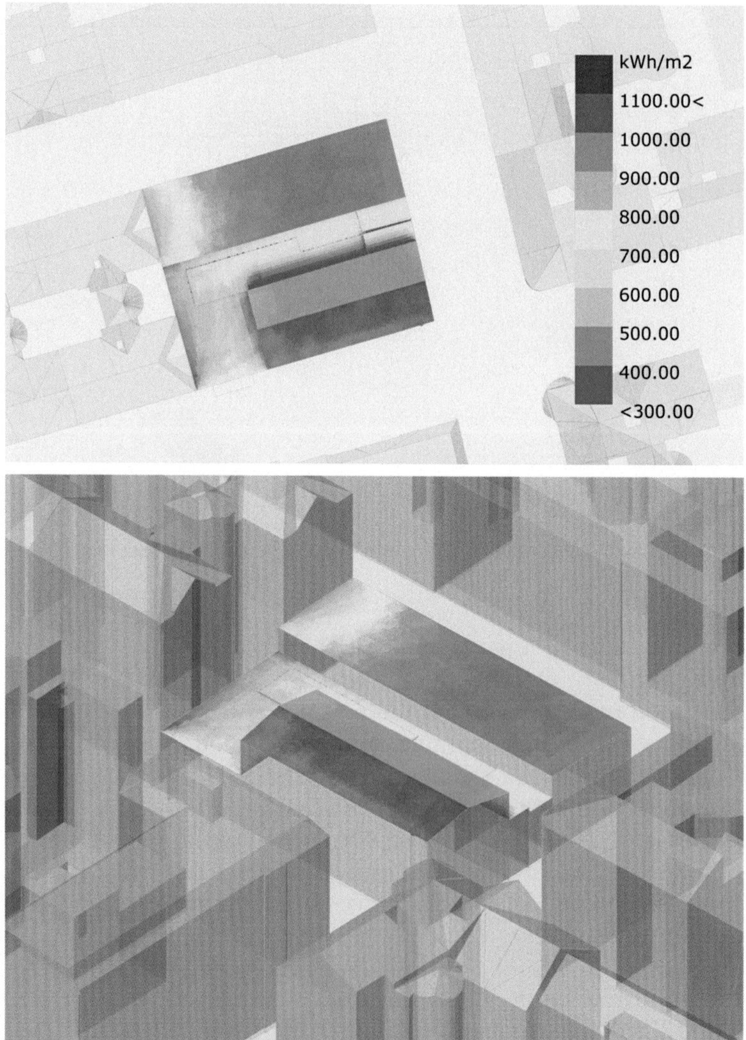

Figure 14.5 Illustration of a building performance assessment scenario (visualization of incident solar radiation density distribution across a complex roof configuration of an existing building); top supported by ontologically streamlined monitoring-based data.

7. Sustainably technology configuration support: an illustrative case study of ontologized data utilization

In the previous sections of this contribution, we described the technologies and processes by which heterogenous sources of data can be ontologically streamlined and thus be made amenable to, among other things, effective evidence-based design approaches. In the present section, we consider in more detail an instance of a technical application that illustrates the utility of ontologized data for practical purposes. Specifically, we consider a topic in the category of renewable energy utilization, namely the optimal configuration of PV (photovoltaic) panel installations. Our objective thereby is not to discuss general knowledge on PV panel production and installation, given the large body of literature in this subject (McEvoy et al., 2011; Lotsch et al., 2005; Krauter, 2006). Rather, we focus on the utility of a web-based computational application to respond to various design and configuration queries concerning the optimal configuration of building-integrated PV installations. Note that there are numerous scenarios with regard to the modalities and objectives of PV installations. One possible mode of classification of such scenarios pertains to the question of electricity import, export, and storage options (see Table 14.3). A project might be focused on application of PV mainly to cover a facility's base load, hence involving neither an electricity export to grid option not a local storage option. In a "powerplant" application scenario, the entire

Table 14.3 Summary listing of the variety of PV installation differentiated according to energy import (from the grid), export (to the grid), and local storage options.

Iconic illustration of scenarios	Electricity			Remarks
	Import from grid	Export to the grid	Local storage	
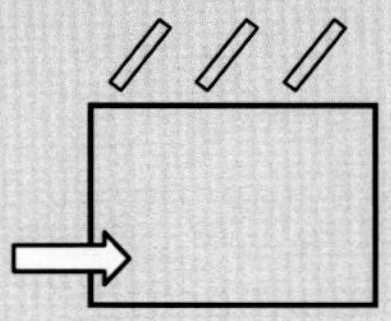	Yes	No	No	Main use case: coverage of base load
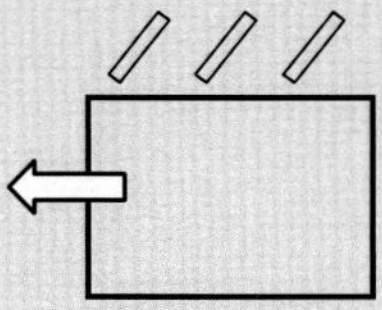	No	Yes	No	Power plant use case

Continued

Table 14.3 Summary listing of the variety of PV installation differentiated according to energy import (from the grid), export (to the grid), and local storage options.—*continued*

Iconic illustration of scenarios	Electricity			Remarks
	Import from grid	Export to the grid	Local storage	
	No	No	Yes	Fully autarkic use case
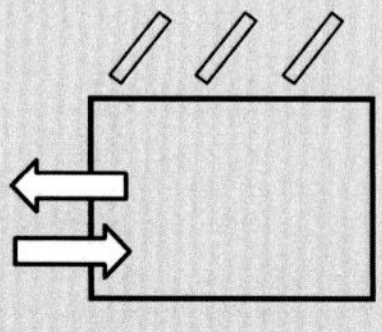	Yes	Yes	No	Configuration: Function of economy and regulations
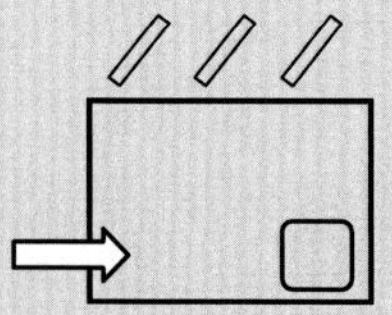	Yes	No	Yes	
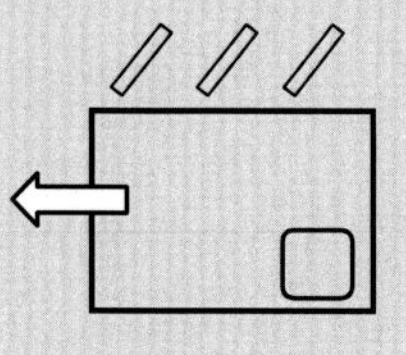	No	Yes	Yes	
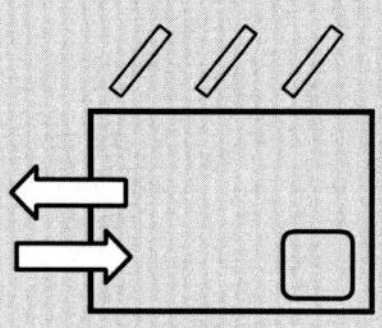	Yes	Yes	Yes	

electricity generated by PV panels is meant to be supplied to the grid. On the other hand, a fully autarkic (off-grid) application generates, stores, and uses energy entirely locally. Other scenarios may involve both energy import and export options with or without local storage. Specifically, in such scenarios, economic (i.e., the cost of installation and the cost of energy) and regulatory constraints must be taken into consideration in order to identify the optimal solutions. All these PV application and configuration scenarios can benefit from computational support. To this end, a truly extensive scope of information is required to optimally support the design and configuration of building-integrated PV installations. Roughly speaking, we may distinguish four categories of needed information:

1. Microclimatic data on the target location: Solar radiation data are obviously the most essential piece of information. However, other microclimatic variables (e.g., ambient temperature, humidity, wind speed, precipitations) may be also of interest.
2. Building and site-related information: To arrive at the proper size, location, and orientation of a building-integrated PV installation, detailed information on the building is needed, including shape and geometry, structure, and construction. Further essentially needed high-resolution (dynamic) data regarding the building's electrical energy demand profile.
3. Technical information on the components of the PV installation. Needless to say, detailed information is needed regarding the type and performance of PV panels, inverters, batteries, and other technical components of the installation.
3. Economic and regulatory information: As with other types of installation, economically relevant data (cost of design, installation, and maintenance of PV system as well as purchasing cost and exporting revenues of electricity) represent a key factor in decision-making. Similarly, procedural, administrative, and regulatory considerations constrain the space of possible solutions and must be thus addressed in the optimization process.

The aforementioned web-based computational platform for supporting the design and optimization of PV installations must be supplied with data from all the above categories. The efficiency of the process by which such heterogenous sources of data are brought to bear can significantly benefit from the previously described data ontologization approach. The developed computational platform for PV systems design support, benefits from the provision of ontologized data from all four information categories mentioned above. We have already exemplified in detail the data ontologization process using the solar irradiance computation and visualization process as a case in point (see Section 6). Though not identical in all cases, the ontologization process is similar in principle for the data types. We thus focus, in the following, on the demonstration of the utility of the computational environment in responding to a number of illustrative use cases.

The interactive web-based computational application for PV configuration support application largely utilizes the *pvlib* library (Holmgren et al., 2018) for the Python programming language that implements models and methods developed in the Sandia National Laboratories (SNL, 2020). The package offers several PV systems modeling approaches and support tools needed for PV systems benchmarking. We augmented these capabilities with Python, using the Dash framework for building web applications (Plotly, 2015). Thereby, a user interface for input specification as well as output visualization was developed. The visualization of the results of the user queries involves two main types. The first visualization is a contour plot of variables such as incident solar radiation on the PV panels, generated AC power by the PV panels, and annual financial balance (difference between system investments and energy cost savings over a predefined period of time). These values are plotted as a function of the panels' orientation (tilt and azimuth). The second implemented visualization option compromises a line graph representing, for a given building, given panel/inverter type, and given electricity price scheme, the accumulated (annual) cost balance as a function of the PV panel count and panel orientation.

To utilize the application, the user needs to provide some basic input data, including the applicable time period for analysis, a source for local solar radiation (and other relevant microclimatic) information, as well as information concerning PV module products (SNL, 2020) and associated inverter products (CEC, 2020). Depending on the nature of the query, further information may be also required with regard to the module count and the time horizon for financial analysis. Moreover, all queries involving local storage of electricity or electricity import/export from/to the grid necessitate the electrical energy load profile of the building hosting the PV installation. Table 14.4 provides a summary of the input assumptions relevant specifically to the three following PV configuration support scenarios.

7.1 The first illustrative use case

The query at the center of the first use case is as follows: Given specific PV panel and inverter technologies (see Table 14.4) installed in a specific location (Austin, Texas, USA), what

Table 14.4 Summary of the specific input information relevant to the three PV configuration use cases.

Input item	Source/value
Solar radiation data source	Typical Meteorological Year 3 (TMY3) (Wilcox, 2008)
Solar panel	Sandia module database (SNL, 2020)
Inverter	California energy commission database (CEC, 2020)
Analysis duration	Annual
Panel count	Cases 1 and 2:10 Case 3: Varying from 5 to 50
Investment cycle	Cases 2 and 3: 25 years
Load profile source	Cases 2 and 3: Commercial and residential hourly load profiles for all TMY3 locations in the United States (DOE, 2020b)
Energy import price	Cases 2 and 3: 0.15 EUR.kWh^{-1}
Energy export price	Case 2: 0.07 EUR.kWh^{-1} Case 3: Variable
System cost function	Cases 2 and 3: Based on Schrack Technik (Schrack, 2020)

cumulative electrical energy magnitudes can be generated over the period of a typical year given a quantity of 10 panels? The task is to compute and visualize the respective values as a function of the panel's azimuth and tilt. Fig. 14.6 displays the application's output, in terms of isolines of generated cumulative electrical energy in kWh. Whereas the strict optimum orientation is computed to be specified at an azimuth and tilt of 165 and 30 degrees respectively, the visualization also illustrates the potential flexibility in a range of orientations that would offer a similar level of performance.

7.2 The second illustrative use case

The query in the second illustrative use case pertains to the cost balance analysis of a building-integrated PV installation consisting of 10 specific PV panels (see Table 14.4). Further assumptions are as follows. The analysis is to be conducted for an investment cycle of 25 years. The purchase and installation cost of the installation is to be considered. The assumption is that if the building's electricity demand (see Fig. 14.7 for the relevant demand profile) is not covered by the PV installation, electricity must be purchased from the grid (at a price of 15 cents per kWh). On the other hand, if the installation produces more

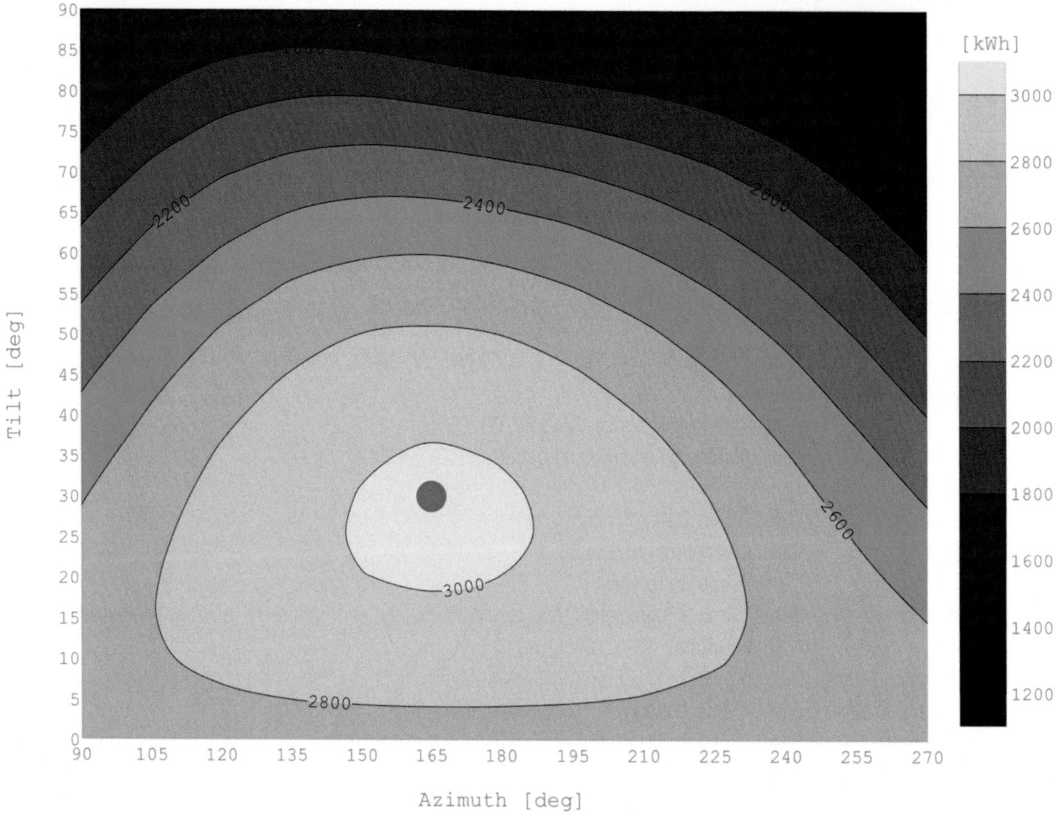

Figure 14.6 Isolines depicting computed cumulative electrical energy generated over a 1-year period (10 PV panels installed in Austin, Texas, USA) as a function of the panels' orientation (azimuth and tilt).

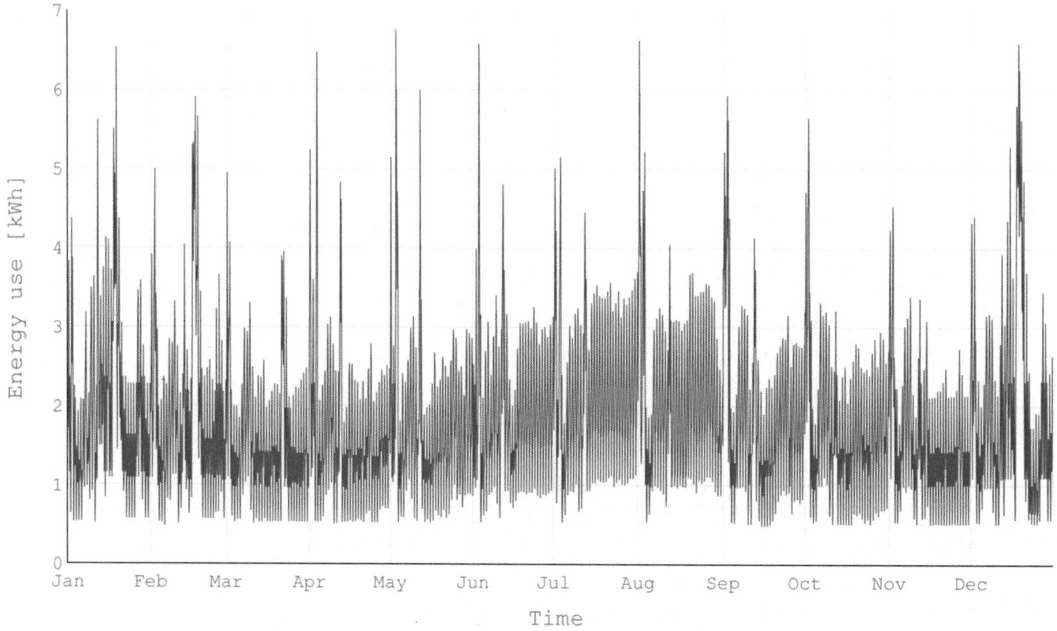

Figure 14.7 Assumed electricity use profile (hourly values over the course of 1 year) of the building in use cases 2 and 3. U.S. Department of Energy (2020b).

electricity than needed, the excess amount can be exported to the grid (generating an income of 7 cents per kWh of exported energy). The balance calculation thus considers the expenses for energy import as well as the income from exporting PV-based electricity to the grid. The results of this cost balance exercise are depicted in Fig. 14.8 in terms of isolines of annual cost balance (in euros), that is the difference between total cost of installation and energy purchase expenses over a 25-year period minus income due to electricity export to the grid over the same time period. Note that, given the illustrative nature of this (and the following) use case, the cost balance calculation has the character of a simple payback analysis. Specifically, the dynamics of energy prices and capital interests are not taken into consideration. However, these parameters can be readily included in the financial analysis component of the computational procedure.

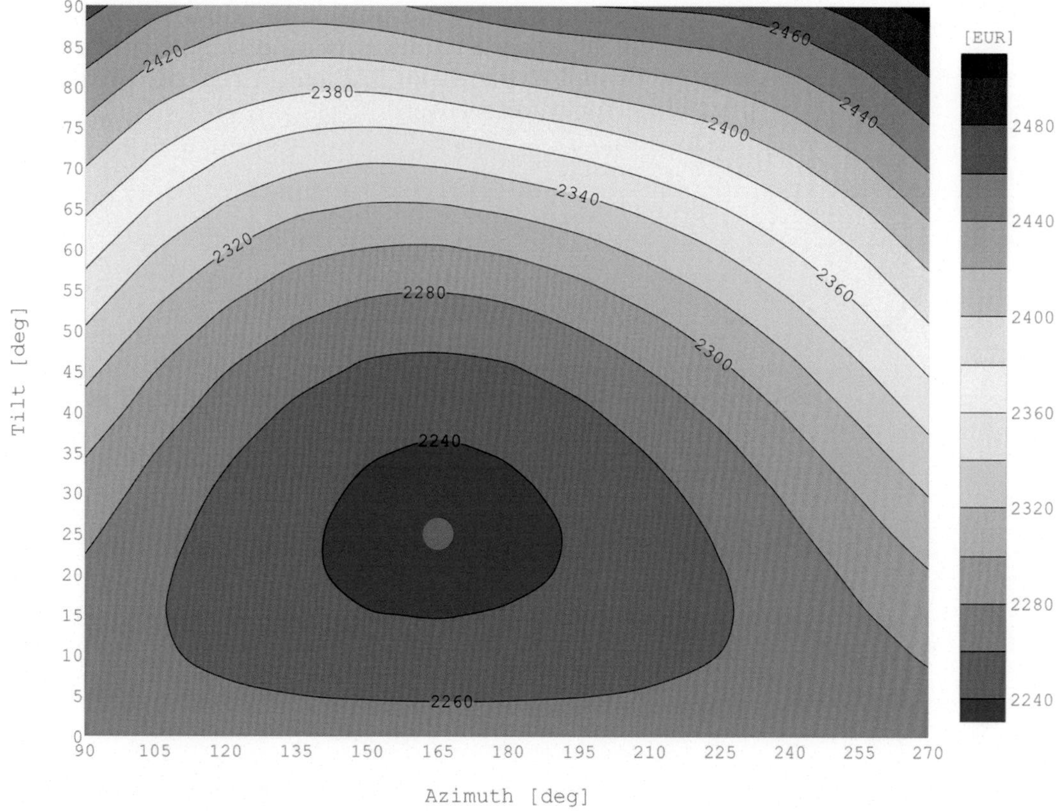

Figure 14.8 Isolines depicting computed annual balance pertaining to a building-integrated PV installation (building's electricity demand profile as per Fig. 14.7, location: Austin, Texas, USA) consisting of 10 PV panels. Expenses include installation cost as well as purchased energy from grid over a period of 25 years. Income pertains to the exported electricity to the grid over the same period. The visualization shows the annual balance in euros as a function of the panels' orientation (azimuth and tilt).

7.3 The third illustrative use case

The third illustrative scenario seeks to identify the optimal number of PV panels (of a given type) for an installation in the same location as the two previous cases (Austin, Texas, USA). As with the previous case, the objective of the optimization is to minimize the net annual system cost (the sum of the installation and electricity import expenses minus the income due to electricity export to the grid, calculated over a period of 25 years). The computational application allows to consider various orientations of the panels as well as different assumptions concerning the electricity import and export prices. To exemplify the results of the computations, Fig. 14.9 focuses on just one panel orientation (i.e., azimuth of 180 degrees south, tilt of 30 degrees) and a fix electricity purchase (import) price (15 cents per kWh). This figure suggests that, up to a minimum electricity export price (i.e., around 4 cents per kWh), every increase in the number of panels translates into lower annual costs. However, below this price threshold, a specific number of panels emerge as optimum (e.g., 30, 25, and 20 panels for 3, 2, and, 1 cent per kWh export price of electricity, respectively).

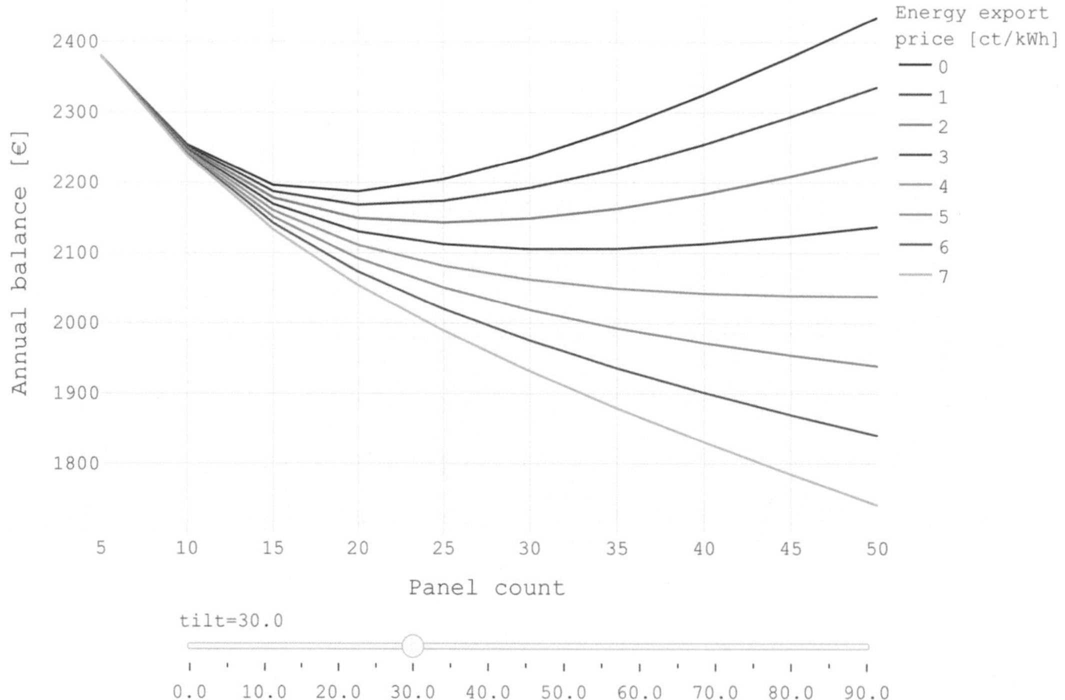

Figure 14.9 Computed annual balance as a function of the PV panel count (azimuth 180 degrees south, tilt 30 degrees, electricity purchase price 15 cents per kWh) and electricity export price pertaining to a building-integrated PV installation (building's electricity demand profile as per Fig. 14.7, location: Austin, Texas, USA).

8. Conclusions

Increasingly larger sets of BPD are needed for the efficient and effective deployment of ICT toward supporting the design and management of intelligent and sustainable built environments. Given the heterogeneous nature of the data (in terms of sources, types, and formats) needed by the ICT applications operating across multiple domains and multiple scales, it is critical to develop—and exploit the potential of—versatile and robust ontologies. This contribution presented such a BPD ontology. Moreover, it described the process and challenges concerning the transformation of primary BPD data into an ontologically structured format for use in advanced building performance assessment scenarios.

Specifically, using the illustrative example of monitored sky radiance data, we described a process whereby measured raw data are "ontologized" toward subsequent utilization for meaningful performance analysis purposes. Note that the process of ontologization has the potential to streamline the input data provision not just to a single instance of analysis tools but to a wide range of building performance applications that require structurally similar data types. As a result, the proposed process has the potential to provide effective support specifically in multidomain integrative and collaborative engineering applications pertaining to intelligent built environments.

To illustrate this potential, we presented the utility of an original application, developed to support the configuration of building-integrated PV installations. To supply this application with required input information, data from diverse sources are ontologized. These data sources pertain, among others, to the building (available collector area, electricity demand profile), location (solar radiation and other microclimatic data), PV technology (specifications of panels and inventers), and economics (installation costs, price schemes for electricity import and export). Having access to readily ontologized data, the application can be effectively deployed to respond to various practical queries. To demonstrate this capability, we use three exemplary use scenarios. Thereby, we illustrated how technically and financially optimal features of a building-integrated PV installation (e.g., type, orientation, and number of PV panes) can be derived given input information on the candidate building, its location, and technical and financial information about the PV and inverter technology options as well as pertinent pricing schemes for electricity import and export.

The ultimate potential for the systematic and pervasive integration of the introduced IT-supported methods, techniques, and tools depends to a large degree on the efficiency and effectiveness of the processes by which various kinds of information can be obtained by and shared among stakeholders and decision makers. Needless to say, such tools and methods do not lead, by themselves, to the adaptation of more sustainable practices in the building delivery process. As with many other domains, the building sector too requires major societal developments and policy-related measures, if the prioritization of sustainability-centric approaches is to become the norm. Nonetheless, once adapted as a matter of principle, sustainability-oriented approaches to the design, construction, and operation of built environments can significantly benefit from IT-supported ontologically systematized information acquisition, sharing, and processing methods.

References

California Energy Commission, 2020. Solar Equipment Lists. https://www.energy.ca.gov/programs-and-topics/topics/renewable-energy/solar-equipment-lists/ (accessed 28.08.2020).

Constantinou, N., 2017. A Comprehensive Multi-Domain Building Performance Indicator Catalogue. Master thesis. Department of Building Physics and Building Ecology, TU Wien, Vienna (Austria).

Crawley, D.B., Lawrie, L.K., Winkelman, F.C., et al., 2001. EnergyPlus: creating a new-generation building energy simulation program. Energy and Buildings 33 (4), 319–331.

Fanger, P.O., 1970. Thermal Comfort Analysis and Applications in Environmental Engineering. Mcgraw-Hill, New York.

Green Building XML schema, Inc, 2020. The gbXML Schema. https://www.gbxml.org/ (accessed 01.09.2020).

Gruber, T., 1993. Toward principles for the design of ontologies used for knowledge sharing. International Journal of Human-Computer Studies 43 (5–6), 907–928.

Holmgren, W., Hansen, C., Mikofski, M., 2018. Pvlib Python: a python package for modeling solar energy systems. Journal of Open Source Software 3 (29), 884.

International Organization for Standardization, 2018a. Industry Foundation Classes (IFC) for Data Sharing in the Construction and Facility Management Industries — Part 1: Data Schema. ISO 16739-1:2018).

International Organization for Standardization, 2018b. Organization and Digitization of Information about Buildings and Civil Engineering Works, Including Building Information Modelling (BIM) — Information Management Using Building Information Modelling — Part 1: Concepts and Principles (BS EN ISO 19650–1:2018).

Krauter, S.C.W., 2006. Solar Electric Power Generation – Photovoltaic Energy Systems. Springer, Berlin/Heidelberg/New York.

Lotsch, H.K.V., Goetzberger, A., Hoffmann, V.U., 2005. Photovoltaic Solar Energy Generation. Springer, Berlin/New York.

Mahdavi, A., 1998. Steps to general theory of habitability. Human Ecology Review 5 (1).

Mahdavi, A., Bachinger, J., Suter, G., 2005. Toward a unified information space for the specification of building performance simulation results. In: Beausoleil-Morrison, I., Bernier, M. (Eds.), *Building Simulation 2005.* 9th International IBPSA Conference, Aug. 15-18, Montreal (Canada), pp. 671–676.
Mahdavi, A., 2011. People in building performance simulation. In: Hensen, J.L.M. (Ed.), Lamberts R. *Building Performance Simulation For Design and Operation.* Taylor & Francis Group, New York (USA).
Mahdavi, A., Glawischnig, S., Schuss, M., Tahmasebi, F., Heiderer, A., 2016. Structured building monitoring: ontologies and platform. In: Proceedings of ECPPM 2016: The 11th European Conference on Product and Process Modelling. Limassol (Cyprus).
Mahdavi, A., Taheri, M., 2017. An ontology for building monitoring. Journal of Building Performance Simulation 10 (5–6), 499–508.
Mahdavi, A., Taheri, M., 2018. A building performance indicator ontology. Proceedings of ECPPM 2018 385–390.
Mahdavi, A., Taheri, M., Schuss, M., Tahmasebi, F., Glawischnig, S., 2018. Structured building data management: ontologies, queries, and platforms. In: Wagner, A., O'Brien, W., Dong, B. (Eds.), Exploring Occupant Behavior in Buildings. Publisher: Springer.
Mahdavi, A., Wolosiuk, D., 2019a. Integration of Operational Data in Building Information Modelling: From Ontology to Application. *CLIMA 2019 Congress*, vol. 111. E3S Web Conf.
Mahdavi, A., Wolosiuk, D., 2019b. A Building Performance Indicator Ontology: Structure and Applications. Proceedings of the 16th IBPSA Conference, Rome, Italy, pp. 77–82, 2–4 September 2019.
McEvoy, A., Markvart, T., Castaner, L., 2011. Practical Handbook of Photovoltaics: Fundamentals and Applications, 2 ed. Elsevier, Amsterdam.
McNeel, R., Associates, 2020a. Grasshopper Visual Programming Language. Available from: https://www.grasshopper3d.com/ (accessed 10.09.2020).
McNeel, R., Associates, 2020b. Rhinoceros Version 6. Available from: https://www.rhino3d.com/ (accessed 10.09.2020).
Plotly Technologies Inc., 2015. Collaborative Data Science. Montréal, QC. https://plot.ly (accessed 10.09.2020).
Roudsari, M.S., Pak, M., 2013. Ladybug: A Parametric Environmental Plugin for Grasshopper to Help Designers Create an Environmentally-Conscious Design. Proc. of the 13th International IBPSA Conference.
Sandia National Laboratories, 2020. Sandia National Laboratories Photovoltaic Test and Evaluation Program. https://energy.sandia.gov/programs/renewable-energy/solar-energy/photovoltaics/photovoltaic-systems-evaluation-lab-psel/ (accessed 10.09.2020).
Schrack Technik GmbH, 2020. Photovoltaik Rechner - Berechnen von Rendite und Amortisation von PVAnlagen. https://www.schrack.at/tools/pv-rechner/ (accessed 28.08.2020).
Tukey, J.W., 1977. Exploratory Data Analysis. Addison-Wesley, Boston.
U.S. Department of Energy, 2020. Office of Energy Efficiency & Renewable Energy, Commercial and Residential Hourly Load Profiles for All TMY3 Locations in the United States. https://openei.org/doe-opendata/dataset/commercial-and-residential-hourly-load-profiles-for-all-tmy3-locations-in-the-united-states/ (accessed 28.08.2020).
Ward, G.J., 1994. The RADIANCE Lighting Simulation and Rendering System. Proc. of the 21st SIGGRAPH Conference.

Python Software Foundation, 2020. Python Language Reference version 2.7. Available from: http://www.python.org/ (accessed 10.09.2020).

The HDF Group, 2019. Hierarchical Data Format Version 5 (HDF5). https://www.hdfgroup.org/.

Wilcox, S., W. Marion., 2008. User's Manual for TMY3 Data Sets. National Renewable Energy Laboratory, NREL/TP-581-43156.

15

Digital City Science—a platform methodology for sustainable urban development

Jörg Rainer Noennig, Jan Barski, Katharina Borgmann and Jesús López Baeza
Digital City Science, HafenCity University (HCU), Hamburg, Germany

1. City science approaches in urban research

Hard science for the city In contrast to a broad range of disciplines that investigate the city with qualitative and "soft" methods—either based on descriptive and reflective approaches (sociology, anthropology, cultural studies) or on creative and artistic technique (urban design, landscape planning)—only few approaches claim to work with rigorous methods based on empirical evidence. One explicit attempt in the latter respect is the city science paradigm (Batty, 2013; Schwegmann et al., 2021). Evolved over the past half a century and now established as a field in research and study, it introduces instruments and methodologies of the "hard" sciences, namely mathematics and statistics, into discourses of urban development and planning (Batty, 1976). Targeting objective knowledge, it is a positivistic doctrine derived from rule-based, computational logic whose scientific rationality is grounded in systematic experimentation and replicability.

This chapter examines these "hard sciences of the city" in order to clarify their potential of integrating with recent debates on sustainable urban development. The task needs to acknowledge that city science, upon a closer look, is made of a diversity of scientifically not-too-closely related schools of thought. However, two traditions and anchor points of city science can be clearly identified: mathematical/computational intelligence and environmental systems ecology.

Computational intelligence A major ignition for computational city science, "A City is not a Tree" (Alexander, 1965), stands

Intelligent Environments. https://doi.org/10.1016/B978-0-12-820247-0.00013-8

out as an early application of mathematical description to urban systems. Written by an architect-turned-scientist, it triggered researchers from cartography, transportation, and geosciences, among others, to use formal models for the analysis and design of urban forms and infrastructures (Dantzig and Tatty, 1973; Batty, 1976). It coincided with somewhat premature applications of system dynamics for the computation of urban development (Forrester, 1969), an attempt to be revived in the 21st century when more refined models and stronger computational power became available. In the 1980s, the social structures of cities eventually became the subject of formal modeling. Prominently put forward by "*The Social Logic of Space*" (1983) and "*Space is the Machine*" (1990), Bill Hillier and colleagues extended mathematical urban theories to issues of community interaction and social life, venturing into cross-scale modeling of urban environments by way of topological models—an avenue expanded by the Space Syntax movement and subsequent studies into urban topologies (Huber, 2002). Continuing the thread of Forrester et al. systemic macroperspective examinations reignited when statistical models borrowed from natural and environmental sciences were applied to urban systems (Bettencourt et al., 2007). They created a theoretical framework that enabled cross-disciplinary investigations into urban complexity, especially the computation of dynamic "live" features of urban processes with social network models, multiagent systems, and cellular automata. The application of these models assumes that urban phenomena such as social exchange and innovation are determined by statistical rules similar to those in environmental and natural sciences.

Digitalization Empirical and positivist sciences aim to create objectivity and validity from the application of axiomatic principles, the conduct of replicable experiments, and methodical interpretation of data (Popper, 1959; Lakatos, 1977, 1978), and so does city science. Their scientific logic, in effect, drove city science discourses toward digital urban technologies and data production. Vice versa, the evolution of digital technologies had a catalytic effect too as it enabled the generation of large amounts of data—and thus of potential evidence—from the digital linkage of urban systems. Thus, a strong quantitative and evidence-based approach entered the realm of urban studies that had not been possible a few decades ago, when the collection and analysis of large urban data was an insurmountable task (Krizek et al., 2009). The short-circuiting of scientific data demands with new data-generating technologies has led to a new arsenal of techniques for urban analysis, modeling, and simulation. For understanding and generating urban structures, data science became a requisite.

While the technical opportunities of data-driven urbanism rapidly unfolded over the past years (commonly paraphrased as *smart city*), scientific interpretations of its implications are few. Prominently, William Mitchell in the *"City of Bits"* (1995) and Nicholas Negropontes in *"Being Digital"* (1995) reflected on the future effects of digital technologies on urban life and space. Subsequently, a number of dedicated research ventures at universities such as University College London, MIT, or HafenCity University (HCU) Hamburg (Ratti, 2004; Schwegmann et al., 2021) have created new digital instruments in support of data-based urban analysis and planning. For example, the cockpits for collaborative urban planning as developed by MIT and HCU combine analytic algorithms with tangible interfaces (lego tables or touchtables) in order to provide physical interaction with complex urban data (Noyman et al., 2017) (Fig. 15.1). Digital city science, however, has not yet become mainstream in urban studies and still counts as a young paradigm. Few studies have been made to assess the consistency and applicability of its theory, and to line out its scientific constraints and limitations. Notably, the discourse landscape is fragmented, mirroring a plethora of digital solutions which are pushing into the market of urban management and planning. Few attempts have been made to integrate data science, system dynamics, and urban complexity within a comprehensive scientific approach. Ambitious concepts which aimed to converge urban sociology, network theory, and data science into a "social physics" notion (Pentland, 2015) have been criticized for being overly deterministic and reductionist.

Convergence with urban sustainability On a parallel track, yet disconnected from the above-described evolution of Digital City Science, a second "hard science" discourse has moved to the center of urban studies. Growing from environmental ecology and systems research in the 1960s, sustainability has become a core topic in practically any institution dedicated to urban development and planning. Apart from its fundamental holistic perspective, sustainability research is based on the positivist methods and quantitative approaches of natural and environmental sciences, especially physics. Commonly, sustainability discourses assume a complex nexus of different spatial spheres and functional systems (social, environmental, economic). To grasp the complexities of environmental emissions, energy, and waste management, or material life cycles, urban sustainability discourses depend on data-based methods and high-performance computing. This

Figure 15.1 Tangible interaction with urban data: Cockpit for Collaborative Urban Planning at HafenCity University. HCU.

suggests a convergence with the approaches of Digital City Science that—as shown above—have grown from a different direction, but has reached a similar point in terms of scientific methodology and technological evolution.

While there exist other "hard science" approaches to urban issues that need to be considered, e.g., in the context of urban economics, the merger of the two highlighted streams into a scientific discourse on the digitally enabled sustainable city apparently becomes a key challenge and demands careful shaping. Reliable scientific approaches are required to comprehend and integrate the multiplicity of urban systems. Their interdependencies need to be balanced—in scientific modeling as well as in practical application. Concepts like the 1970s′system dynamics had already anticipated what the integration of urban complexity and sustainability may look like. At that time, the "limits to growth" in ecology had not been reached yet, but computer science and technology were still heavily constrained. Half a century later, the situation is different. Whereas sustainability has become a priority of humanity, eminent new approaches, methodologies, and tools have been developed especially in the realm of digital systems. They can be activated and aligned with scientific discipline in order to create reliable knowledge in support of sustainable urban development.

2. Principles, methods, and technologies

This chapter aims to outline the specific intelligence that Digital City Science could add in the context of other urban research disciplines. It puts aside the further discussion of sustainability matters at this place, in order to focus on the question: What turns Digital City Science into a scientific endeavor? The following paragraphs outline epistemological principles that form a framework for the systematic research and study of Digital City Science. It does so by giving a brief analysis and interpretation of the three key notions—"digital," "city," and "science"—in their relation to data, information, and knowledge theory.

"Digital" Nicholas Negroponte maintained in *"Being Digital"* (1995) that digitalization needs to be understood not only as a new linkage of highly diverse technological systems that were unrelated hitherto, but also their interconnection to humans. In human evolution, the index finger—lat. "digitus"—became the key instrument for indicating and counting. With similar meaning, but with massively expanded powers of indicating and counting, digitalization brings events and occasions to human attention and makes them measurable. It intimately connects human life with an expansive technological universe and makes all occurrences in this universe accountable. The Latin term "datum" means the "given," just as the input data that are given in a mathematical textbook equation. Any occasion produces such "given," even if unrecognized or unreported (Whitehead, 1929). Not all data are relevant, but by (digitally) indicating and indexing the datum of an event, relevance is created—and datum changes into information. Accounted for as relevant information, the human mind as well as technical apparatuses may generate sense or meaning from it on the basis of knowledge processing (Liew, 2007). However, the fact that unlimited data are being produced by the countless events in a digitally connected "world" makes a systematic selection, organization, and assessment a prerequisite for the generation of relevant information and knowledge. This process can be termed *data science.* It has evolved as a new discipline over the past years, not only as a connector between computer science and mathematics, but as a conditioner of knowledge production in an eventful, digitally connected world.

Against that background, digitally connected urban systems with their massive output of data about urban states and processes provide a particular case. They, too, require systematic data processing in order to generate knowledge that proves meaningful in the urban context (say: *urban data science*), mirroring the general principles of data science (data collection, management, and interpretation) in quantitative methods and mathematical models of the city.

"City" Digital city science, however, reaches beyond urban data science, i.e., the mere processing of urban data, as it takes a holistic perspective and acknowledges urban complexity. Cities are systems of systems: interwoven fabrics of technological, social, environmental, and cultural layers—dynamic organisms that escape deterministic description. Cities are multiple entities, consisting of individual districts and neighborhoods which possess their own multiple characteristics and identities (Fig. 15.2).

"Science" Scientific disciplines are "disciplined" by their axiomatic principles and their model evolution. Epistemology, the theory of science, holds that a rational and systematic

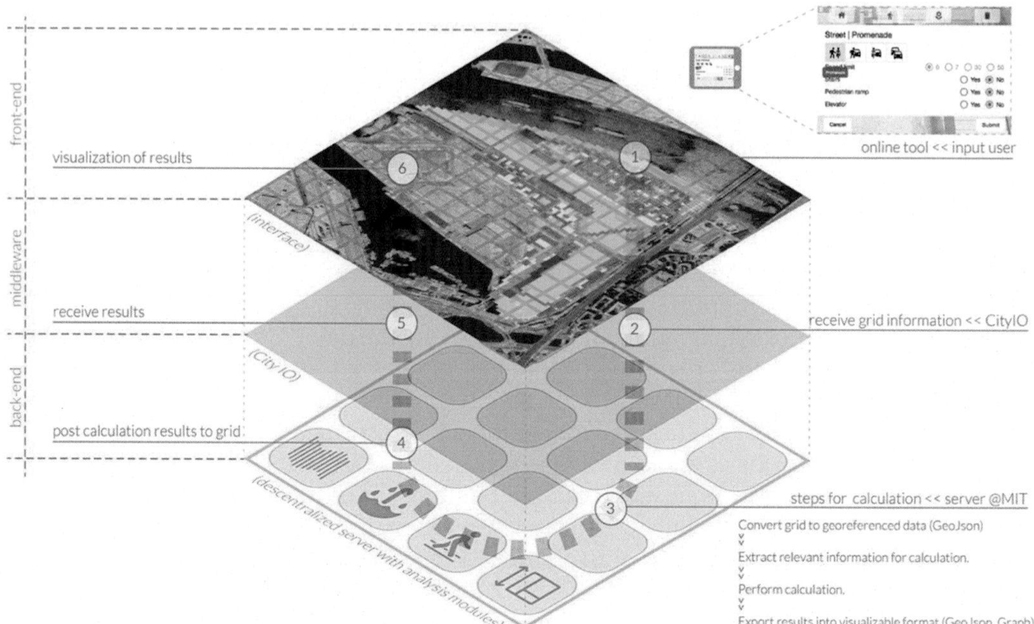

Figure 15.2 Multilayer analysis of urban systems: Concept diagram of a collaborative urban planning cockpit . HCU.

pursuit—*method*—is mandatory for the creation of valid and replicable knowledge (Whitehead, 1925; Popper, 1959, Lakatos, 1977, 1978). The difficulty in the case of Digital City Science lies in the fact that its method needs to connect two scientific cultures and practices: data and computer science on the one hand, and urban planning, development, and management on the other. Each side has unfolded its own rationalities and methodologies over the course of its disciplinary emancipation. Here, the scientific fundamentals of quantitative, data-driven approaches on the one hand encounter qualitative, value-driven, and normative practices on the other. Whereas data science works on computable abstract terms, urban sciences in contrast deal with aggregate socio-spatial complexes. A robust transdisciplinary methodology is needed to bridge these highly divergent spheres (Mittelstrass, 2003). It shall be termed here "Level 1 transdisciplinarity" (another level will be introduced in Section 3).

Organon A transdisciplinary methodology on Level 1 enables a scientific approach to cities that is qualitative and quantitative at the same time, complex *and* yet computable, and possibly predictable. It exploits the opportunities of digitalization (interconnecting, integrating, and cross-linking *all* urban systems) and of data science (processing large amounts of system data into knowledge). The list below outlines respective components that constitute the theoretical framework of Digital City Science. To form a bridging language between urbanism and data science, each component needs to be applicable to either side. Such multilateral connectivity not only gives proof of the validity of the proposed elements but also of the connective theory formed with them. It is noteworthy to mention that—in order to find transdisciplinary convergence points—it is often necessary to go back to earlier stages in the evolutionary path of the individual disciplines. Often, it is not the most advanced state of the disciplines that invites convergence, but some previous stage *before* they branched into the sophisticated discourses of the present.

Key Principles:

- Complexity: Open, large, and nondeterministic systems composed of interconnected layers. Complexity in data science: computational complexity (Hartmanis and Stearns, 1965). Complexity in urbanism: cities as socio-technical/socio-spatial systems (Healey, 2006).
- Computation: Rule-based algorithms for system analysis and synthesis. Computation in data science: mathematical theory of computation (McCarthy, 1963). Computation in urbanism: City operation systems and computation (Luque-Ayala and Marvin, 2020).

Key Methodologies:

- Visualization: Comprehension of complexity through images, diagrams, and maps. Visualization in data Science: knowledge representation, infographics (Tukey, 1977). Visualization in urbanism: Infrastructure topologies, geoinformation mapping (Kunze et al., 2012).
- Simulation: Anticipating future effects and impact on the basis of statistical models. Simulation in data Science: predictive analytics (Philipps-Wren, et al., 2021). Simulation in urbanism: Scenario planning (Waddell and Ulfarsson, 2004).

Key models:

- Dynamic Systems: Representing complexity with interconnected systems and agent populations. Dynamic Systems in Data Science: cellular automata, social network analysis (Forrester, 1987). Dynamic Systems in urbanism: movement flows, socio-spatial dynamics (Lopez-Baeza et al., 2020).
- Spatial Information: referencing objects and event data with topological coordinates. Spatial Information in data Science: vector spaces, data fields (Li et al., 2015). Spatial Information in urbanism: geo-information systems, building information models (Song et al., 2017).

These principles, methodologies, and models constitute the fundamentals for the development of Digital City Science tools and projects, as presented in Chapter 4. The epistemological framework is to give scientific validity to an otherwise highly application-driven production of digital solutions. Decision-makers in governments and authorities as well as professional city planners and developers are in need of effective, reliable instruments, which they can employ to support their decision-making. While global urban challenges create a clear demand for readily applicable tools—which need to be delivered urgently—it is the responsibility of science to provide them a valid theoretical base. The growing gravity of urban sustainability problems just adds criticality to this demand.

3. Convergence with urban sustainability

Framework condition Sustainability has become a central challenge in urbanism not only since the United Nations published the Brundtland report (UN, 1987) and listed the creation of sustainable cities and communities as one of the 17 priority goals (UN, 2015). Over the past decades, it became clear that climate change, resource scarcity, and environmental pollution dictate conditions that will strictly impact the development of cities—and vice versa. Whereas cities turn out to be the main catalyzers for changing environmental conditions, they are also epicenters where the effects of climate change are notable most directly, especially in the fast-growing urban agglomerations in Asia and Africa. Urban turnover of natural resources and energy is a main conditioner for the transformation of the planetary environment (Kousky and Schneider, 2003).

The declaration of an "urban age"—according to which the majority of the world population now lives in urban areas—has been criticized for methodological inconsistencies (Schmidt and Brenner, 2014). Still, the human exodus from rural to urban areas proliferates. In India, the majority of people is still living in the countryside; here the "urban age" is still to come— although agglomerations like Delhi, Kolkata, or Mumbai have grown to dimensions that are already beyond the urban scale.

To adjust such growth dynamics to the goals of sustainable development, coordinated measures have been taken, e.g., the declaration of the Paris Convention (UN, 2016) or the European Commission's 'Green Deal' (EU, 2020), which will impact urban policies too. Governments on all levels—international, regional, and local—are demanded to implement practices in urban planning and development that save resources, reduce emissions, and provide alternative infrastructures, especially for energy supply, mobility, and transportation. At the same time, however, it becomes clear that in contexts of rapid urbanization and informal city development, public governance is reaching limits of control and efficacy (Beermann, 2014).

Multidimensional sustainability Research has clarified that sustainability needs to be viewed from multiple, interconnected perspectives (Schreurs, 2008; Seghezzo, 2009). *Environmental sustainability* needs to ensure livable climate conditions, cyclical resource flows, and a minimization of ecological footprints. Here, decarbonization and the transition to renewable resources are key targets. *Social sustainability* aims to achieve just and healthy living conditions, and manage the issues of migration and demographic change. Overpopulation in the megacities accompanied by depopulating rural areas poses substantial threats not alone to social cohesion and stability. *Economic sustainability* as the basis of social welfare and development needs to balance production, consumption, and innovation, and secure jobs and income. New models of circular economy need to be established with feasible business models and value chains.

In view of the many more dimensions of sustainability, the call for comprehensive action comes with eminent challenges. Reductionist approaches that have addressed sustainability from few selected perspectives have been criticized as counterproductive (El-Haram and Horner, 2008). Sustainability measures need to encompass, inseparably, the multiple dimensions and metrics of sustainability. A methodological pluralism coupled with advanced forms of governance, stakeholder engagement, and participation becomes requisite (Baumgartner and Korhonen, 2010; Puppim de Oliveira et al., 2013). To enact comprehensive changes in societal mindset as well as in institutional behavior, and to pave the way for alternative forms of public governance and decision-making, effective means of research and foresight are needed that are able to anticipate the interwoven, circular networks of causes and effects. It further implies means of communication capable of conveying the necessary information to trigger transformation on a broad scale. Advanced computational modeling and network technologies for massive collaboration and communication may be key catalyzers for this end.

Multiobjectivity The conflict of targets poses a major challenge in the integrative and multidimensional pursuit of sustainability goals. Environmental protection, for example, may contradict economic growth targets, while rapid economic progress may lead to social destabilization. The synchronous targeting of multiple divergent yet interconnected goals appears to be a demanding theoretical task. It transcends well-established approaches of multicriteria analysis and optimization that consider a complex set of influencing factors in order to achieve a certain goal. In multidimensional sustainability contexts, complex combinations of factors need to be considered in order to achieve a complex set of goals that is not fixed but evolving over time. This implies a virtually infinite process of reassessment and reconsideration whose facilitation on scientific as well as on procedural level is demanding. In science, mathematical models of multiobjective optimization offer a suitable methodological approach. Enabling the efficient computation of meshes of interconnected influences and targets, they mirror a given environmental complexity with adequate algorithmic complexity (Zionts and Wallenius, 1976). Advances in machine learning and the growth of computational power over the past decades have made this theory applicable for complex problems of development, engineering, and planning (Tanaka et al., 1995). For a permanent reassessment of networked goals and influences on a procedural level, however, not only technical tools but also "societal and institutional algorithms" are necessary that would enable multistakeholder participation, collaborative decision-making, and deliberation on the broadest scale (Hemmati et al., 2002).

It is at this point where Digital City Science approaches—as described in the earlier chapters—connect to urban sustainability discourses. Based on algorithmic intelligence and complex data processing, they provide a scientific and technological platform that is able to exploit mathematical models for matching, learning, and optimization, and to complement them with interactive tools. On such a basis, advanced instruments become possible that support the analysis and understanding of urban complexity, especially the multiobjective modeling of dynamic environments. Collaborative and participatory digital tools that can be used online as web applications or on-site in the format of digital workshop facilitation, make such complexities understandable and interactable (Noyman et al., 2017; Landwehr et al., 2021).

Level 2 Transdisciplinarity The linkage to urban sustainability adds another layer to the transdisciplinary challenge of Digital City Science. Going beyond the above-described first-level convergence of urban research with data and computer science, this new dimension results in a "Level 2 Transdisciplinarity." To an already hybrid organon of Digital City Science, urban sustainability discourses provide another layer of external knowledge whose incorporation poses epistemological difficulties. Sustainability research is driven by descriptive methods of environmental and natural sciences. To a large extent, these are incompatible with "sciences of the artificial," e.g., computer engineering, software design, or urban planning whose approach is constructivist and generative (Simon, 1969). At this intersection, again, a transversal methodology is needed that can connect to discourses and models of either side. The creation of such transdisciplinary language is a central task for any science of the digital and sustainable city.

Environmental intelligence On a technological level, however, the opportunities are promising. Developments in the field of human–machine interaction such as tactile internet or gesture and language recognition have opened a vast panorama of new opportunities for learning, understanding, and shaping matters of complexity. The Internet of Things (IoT) and so-called Cyber-physical Systems (CPS) enable a fine-grained monitoring of environments on all spatial levels. Remote sensing, wireless communication, and data analytics present powerful means not only for registering climate states, resource flows, and human activity patterns but also for the purposeful management and organization of urban environments. Expanding network technologies and growing computation powers provide new capacities for data transfer and processing. The convergence and targeted exploitation of these technological achievements will be a key enabler for achieving urban sustainability. Still, they depend on scientific models and analyses in order to produce intelligence and insights that are useful in practice. Information comprehension and knowledge extraction from extensive data cannot be delegated to artificial intelligences alone: meaning emerges from clear notions and models, and from human experience gained in factual situations. In addition, current debates on lean data have emerged, having implications also for sustainability issues (Shcherbakov et al., 2014). The prevalent big data paradigm finds increasing opposition by calls for a new resourcefulness in the digital realm too. The history of science has shown that not masses of data but the coherence of theory is the key to understanding, discovery and innovation.

4. Sample studies and projects

A number of case studies and projects have been carried out at the HCU Hamburg to explore the potentials of the Digital City Science approach. The projects in the following paragraphs address sustainable urban development on different scales and levels: from supporting local urban design challenges in the spatial context of Hamburg, they span over urban and regional scale to solutions that explicitly target global development issues, and seek international application. Common to all presented ventures are:

- a modular system architecture and platform approach;
- a transdisciplinary setup with complex stakeholder compositions;
- a rapid project development from prototype to pilot application;
- an open-source character, targeting community building among users and developers.

The presented projects and systems aim for empowering city authorities, planners, and designers, as well as local communities to comprehend complex urban environments, and to make informed decisions about their future development. Despite being commonly conceived as generic (global) applications, they support specific user groups within specific application scenarios. This potential contradiction is resolved by a design which configures different levels of user interaction, the complexity of generated knowledge, and data consumption in response to the very context of usage. Such "responsiveness by design" and a built-in openness for future developments are key concepts of their design.

Global Scale: Toolkit for Open and Sustainable City Planning and Analysis In cooperation with the German Agency for International Cooperation (GIZ), a GIS-based digital toolbox was developed that enables authorities, communities, and researchers to implement geospatial applications without getting into a long-term vendor lock-in with commercial providers. The key idea of the Toolkit for Open and Sustainable City Planning and Analysis (TOSCA) is the provision of a robust and extendable GIS framework to local users who otherwise have little means to access and process spatial data for integrated urban planning and land use management. By design, the platform enables easy creation of custom-made analytic modules in support of specific challenges that can range from slum upgrading, through disaster management, to mobility planning. The usability of the system, in turn, is designed to facilitate multistakeholder participation as well as high-level decision-making. Created with an intention to allow global usage and replication, the system is applicable in any place in the world where basic georeferenced data are available (imported from Open Street Map, for example). The currently existing modules can analyze, among others, natural and topographical data, transportation networks, as well as social and demographic patterns. First pilot applications have been carried out in Asia and Southern America where the initial set of applications was used for the upgrading of informal settlements (India) as well as for anticipatory disaster management (Ecuador). For example, mapping the lahar flow from the volcano Cotopaxi onto the Ecuadorian city of Latacunga (Fig. 15.3) helps to anticipate the complex cascade of effects, leading from natural catastrophe (volcano eruption) through technical damage (defunct infrastructures) to social disaster (human casualties, abandonment of neighborhoods), thus enabling the preventive design of countermeasures.

To support comprehensive assessments of complex environmental issues, the Toolkit is applied and refined in close cooperation with local communities, research institutes, urban developers, and decision-makers. In the future, the system is supposed to grow into a comprehensive GIS platform carrying an array of digital instruments for integrated urban analysis and development. To amplify interest and contributions, the solution is promoted to potential users worldwide (state ministries, private enterprises, think tanks), as well as to the growing global community of software developers.

Regional Scale: Sustainable Development of Urban Regions Program Within the funding priority "Sustainable Development of Urban Regions" (SURE, 2020–25) of the German Ministry of Education and Research, HCU Digital City Science leads a

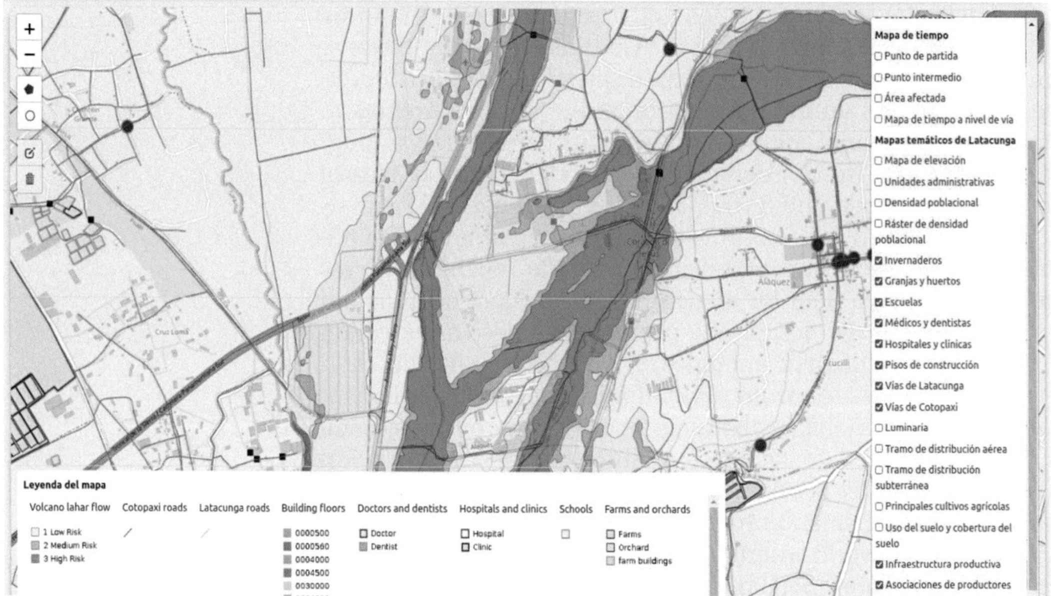

Figure 15.3 Toolkit for Open and Sustainable City Planning and Analysis: Scenarios of lahar flow from the Cotopaxi volcano in Latacunga, Ecuador. HCU.

consortium whose task is to synthesize and synergize scientific findings from 10 individual research projects. All projects directly relate to urban and regional development issues in South-East Asia, a region where some of the most critical urban development issues unfold. Targeting challenges in sustainable construction, urban waste management, or flood protection in highly populated areas, among others, the projects are supposed to discover novel scientific approaches, new technological solutions, as well as effective forms of governance and regulation. Some initiatives employ an explicit people-centered approach in order to test their strategies against the input and feedback of a broader societal audience. On that background, the main target of the synthesis research is (a) to converge the insights from the individual projects and to transfer them across the entire program and its stakeholders and (b) to analyze the long-term impacts of the projects within the scientific community as well as in their local contexts. To this end, a SURE knowledge platform provides algorithmic tools borrowed from business intelligence and digital linguistics to mine insights for the projects. Complementing these intelligent technologies for mining documents and data, also methodologies such as synergy workshops or communities of practice are applied to facilitate the research progress and to comprehend the intangible layers that relate to their socio-cultural context and specific localities. The synthesis project's other mandate is to enable an assessment of the impact of local sustainable urban development strategies (i.e., on authorities, specialists, and citizens but also on the built environment) as well as globally (i.e., on the international communities of scientists and practitioners). A key instrument for this is an interactive communication hub that allows collaboration between the 10 projects and the SURE synthesis researchers. On the institutional level, SURE is supposed to build a vital community of urban researchers and planners who will continue to share insights, approaches, and results from their work. Although the projects cover not only a large geographic area but also a broad panorama of topics, they are interconnected on a systemic level and therefore suggest knowledge transfer by way of tools such as interactive mapping or automated document analysis (Fig. 15.4). This may lead, in the long run, to connected regional communities of knowledge and to more unified and better-informed action toward sustainable urban development in the region itself.

Urban Scale: Migrant Integration Cockpits and Dashboards (MICADO): The project MICADO (2019–22) addressed one of the most pressing topics of social sustainability: the integration

Figure 15.4 Interactive map of selected projects locations in the funding priority Sustainable Development of Urban Regions. HCU.

of migrants into the local socio-economic systems of European cities. Funded by the Horizon 2020 program and coordinated by HCU Digital City Science, a consortium with stakeholders from Madrid, Antwerp, Bologna, Vienna, and Hamburg co-created a pan-European service platform in response to the European Commission's demand for broader implementation of Information and Communication Technologies (ICT) solutions into migrant integration processes. The MICADO platform provides digital assistant tools in order to support public authorities, civil society organizations, as well as migrants themselves in their efforts to make arrivals successful. With new means of visualization such as data stories or dashboards, new insights can be created for migration workers, and reliable pathways be outlined for migrants that guide them into local labor, housing, health, and education systems (Fig. 15.5). To this end, not only a transdisciplinary approach to cultural, societal, and technological aspects is needed, but also the linkage of data drawn from migrant individuals, local authorities, and international institutions. To this end, MICADO undertakes the task of connecting social sciences with software development, thus embodying the dual challenge that Digital City Science faces. Although the project delivered a generic *universal* solution, pilot applications of the platform prototype in each of the four partner cities have been carried out to ensure the appropriate uptake and customization in correspondence to specific local needs. For MICADO, too, the establishment of a committed community of users and developers was a key target, in order to secure the future development of the system beyond the funding period. As could be observed in the process of its design and development, MICADO has triggered the growth of novel structures across institutions, e.g., by the formation of the

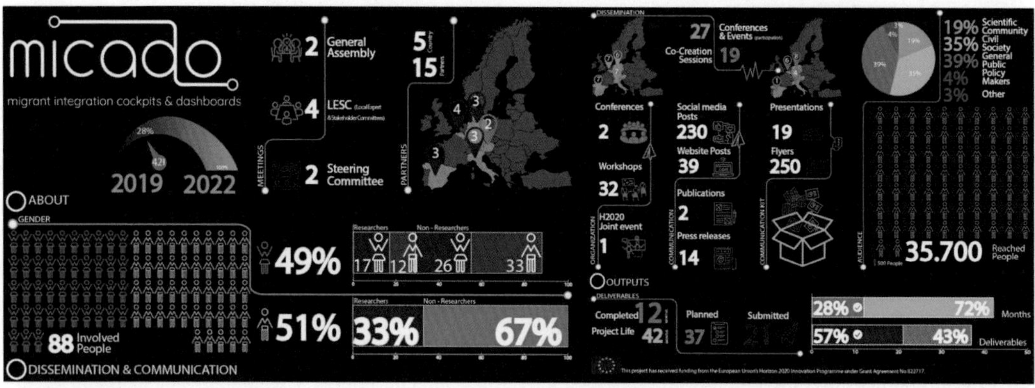

Figure 15.5 Data visualization—Dashboard with key performance indicators of the MICADO project. HCU.

so-called Local Experts and Stakeholders Committee (LESC). Originally, these communities were to function as sounding boards for the technical development process, yet they turned into informal exchange platforms for public authority actors, civil society organizations, and migrant communities. This suggests that—apart from the mere provision of a technology—the collaborative efforts toward its creation may already unfold substantial powers of cohesion and have a transformative effect on institutional processes.

Neighborhood Scale: Cockpit for Collaborative Urban Planning (COUP): To the urban design and landscape planning of the new innovation district "Kleiner Grasbrook" in Hamburg, a digital toolbox was developed, based on the idea of an interactive design and decision support system for architects and planners (Landwehr et al., 2021). The toolbox consists of a modular software infrastructure which links several analysis and simulation modules to user-friendly interfaces. The system is fed with a combination of existing geodata and design propositions for a new neighborhood. By using the web interface, designers and stakeholders are able to test the performance of the design scenarios in such fields as noise emissions, wind and thermal comfort, or pedestrian flow distribution. The COUP responds with two different formats to two different use cases: (1) A real-time feedback version intended to be deployed at the early phases (conceptual design) to test general design outlines and (2) a version delivering accurate performance reports for the later phase of functional planning when minor changes in the final design need to be tested. The tool is based on the CityScope concept developed by the MIT Media Lab, which partnered in the project along with HCU and HafenCity GmbH, a public urban development agency that is the commissioner of the architects and urban designers, who actually apply the software.

In practice, several intertwined simulations are intended to provide designers with detailed information about the impact of design changes on pedestrian accessibility (Fig. 15.6), noise pollution, social cohesion, or business feasibility.

Design and decision support systems like the COUP will give, in the medium run, urban projects a substantially broader basis of information and knowledge. They will introduce interactive, iterative, and agile work processes to the sphere of urban design and planning that (a) set up clients, planners, and consultants in new constellations and roles and (b) transcend linear stage-gate processes leading from conceptual design via design development to functional planning, etc. Different from the conventional procedures, they do not increase model complexity just in

Figure 15.6 COUP: Accessibility analysis of urban amenities—calculating the pedestrians flow within in relation to urban morphology using agent-based models. HCU.

correspondence to the progress of the design work. Instead they enable multilayer analysis with a variety of indicators and targets from the start, thus preventing what complexity science has termed dilemmas of concretization—the emergence of critical issues that become apparent only in the advanced phases of development.

5. Outlook: a new paradigm?

Converging megatrends The convergence of the two discourses, digital city and urban sustainability, not only creates a number of new research challenges (especially methodological ones, as the chapters above have shown) but generates impact beyond the scientific sphere. Two features make it a potential new paradigm in urbanism. On the one hand, it gives new meaning to the somewhat exhausted notion of the smart city, as it raises environmental and societal targets that reach further than the technology push that has been driving smart city ventures so far. On the other hand, by bringing into play the vast possibilities of computation and data science, it presents a "powertool" for a better understanding of complex environmental transformations, and for shaping the transition toward more sustainable environments.

The strength of such a paradigm lies in its comprehensiveness. While actions toward sustainability, inevitably, imply a holistic perspective that needs to encompass the diversity of systems and their linkages, digitalization provides the technical and methodological bases for integrating these systems and for creating connective models. Digitalization is a main vehicle for convergence, and by its epistemological constitution, Digital City Science is programmed for data and model integration. A fast-growing reservoir of environmental information, in combination with advanced theoretical models and computational power, forms a scientific apparatus that may tackle aforementioned challenges of multiobjectivity in the context of sustainability research.

Platform powers Tools and systems like the ones presented in the previous chapter pave the way for simulating environmental dynamics across spatial layers and social domains. They enable analysis and intelligent interpretations of multi-level systemic effects. To maximize their applicability, these solutions are designed as platforms that enable the plug-in of new features and modules. Their systems and components are open-sourced, replicable and shareable. Functional and compositional transparency is requisite to disseminate them broadly. In turn, the exposure to global data reservoirs will demand a further expansion of their analytic and synthetic capacities. By their technical DNA, these systems are designed to constantly evolve their functional range and specter of usage. Step-by-step, they can build up an internal complexity that is requisite to correspond to the complexities of the external world.

Managing complexity Through digital integration, parameters of the social, ecologic, economic, and political sphere become parts of one equation. Certainly, no complete representation is possible of either the social nor the physical world. Despite their infinite dimensions and qualities, approximations are possible still. The growing complexity built into models and tools enables explorative multilayer analyses. Being incomplete, insufficient, and reductionist though, they represent the best available means for framing the key issues of urban transformation. New forms of collective human reasoning in combination with artificial intelligence may complete their setup and equip them with higher level rationality in the future.

Future research and education The confluence of sustainable and digital city research creates new scientific demands.

Groundwork needs to be carried out, before all, in regards to methodology. As indicated in Chapter 3, a new level of transdisciplinary cooperation needs to be established that reaches beyond the fusion of data science and urbanism. Another widely incompatible scientific realm—sustainability research—needs to be interfaced too. Growing complexity, however, can lead to the disintegration of systems—on the technical as well as on the epistemological level. The creation of a valid methodology thus becomes a challenge of magnitude, comparable to the paradigm shift caused by the emergence of digital humanities. But there is a pressing demand for urban solutions placed at the intersection of digitalization and sustainability. To properly respond to the forces of a global sustainability market, this new transdisciplinary language needs to be established quickly. Schools and universities need to train experts in digital urban sustainability as a novel type of data scientists and as a new kind of urbanist.

Criticism A preliminary assessment of the Digital City Science approach in the context of urban sustainability should line out ex-ante limitations and risks in terms of sociotechnical impact. The digital city approach in its application to sustainability issues clearly has limitations and shortcomings. Insufficient data availability will incapacitate its mission. Moreover, there is the threat of negligence of locality: many digital solutions are generic and monorational. Adequate mechanisms need to be built into the systems and solutions that help to embed them into specific cultural and geographical contexts. Even without techno-colonial intentions, digital tools and platforms can exert strong manipulative powers. Data processing and visualization easily become subject to instrumentalization and technocracy. An accompanying and thorough analysis needs to reflect such risks from the start.

The appropriate integration of human dynamics will remain an issue on all levels. Formal and abstract system models can hardly comprehend the phenomenological wealth of urban life. Most models in the environmental or engineering sciences (CPS, IoT, BIM, CIM, GIS, etc.) are agnostic to social interaction, community sense, identity of place, collective memory, etc. While advancing fast on tracks of system and market rationality, they underrepresent human activity in the urban context—on the personal as well as on the collective level. Furthermore, a shortcoming of urban models and simulations has been their inability to represent the omnipresent influence of the intangible, nonrational, and erratic nature of anthropogenic systems. A subset of this are cultural differences, so commonly overlooked by the "one-model-fits-all" approach in urban design. These challenges form cornerstones of the discipline's future progress and maturing.

Next Steps The presented arguments provide a compass for the long-term evolution of Digital City Science. In the short and medium term, the work programme should focus on the creation of a transdisciplinary methodology—on the languages, models, and principles that can bridge between the scientific domains of urbanism, data science, and sustainability research. They are requisite for the paradigm shift toward digitally enabled sustainable cities.

References

Alexander, C., 1965. A city is not a tree. Architectural Forum 122 (No 1). April 1965.

Batty, M., 1976. Urban Modelling: Algorithms, Calibrations, Predictions. Cambridge University Press, 1976.

Batty, M., 2013. The New Science of Cities. MIT Press, 2013.

Baumgartner, R.J., Korhonen, J., 2010. Strategic thinking for sustainable development. Sustainable Development 18, 71–75.

Beermann, J., 2014. Urban partnerships in low-carbon development: opportunities and challenges of an emerging trend in global climate politics. URBE – Revista Brasileira de Gestão Urbana 6 (541), 170–183.

Bettencourt, L.M.A., Lobo, J., Helbing, D., Kühnert, C., West, G.B., 2007. Growth, innovation, scaling, and the pace of life in cities. PNAS 104 (17), 7301–7306. April 24, 2007.

Brenner, N., Schmid, C., 2014. The 'urban age' in question. International Journal of Urban and Regional Research 38.

Dantzig, G., Saaty, T., 1973. Compact City. Freeman, San Francisco, 1973.

El-Haram, M., Horner, M., 2008. A critical review of reductionist approaches for assessing the progress towards sustainability. Environmental Impact Assessment Review 28, 286–311. https://doi.org/10.1016/j.eiar.2007.09.002.

European Commission (EU), 2020. A European Green Deal. European Commission 2020.

Forrester, J.W., 1969. Urban Dynamics. MIT Press, 1969.

Forrester, J.W., 1987. Lessons from system dynamics modeling. In: System Dynamics Review 1987.

Hartmanis, J., Stearns, R.E., 1965. On the computational complexity of algorithms. Transactions of the AmericanMathematical Society 117, 285–306, 1965.

Healey, P., 2006. Urban Complexity and Spatial Strategies: Towards a Relational Planning for Our Times. Routledge 2006.

Hemmati, M., Dodds, F., Enayati, J., McHarry, J., 2002. Multi-stakeholder processes for governance and sustainability: beyond deadlock and conflict. Earthscan.

Huber, J., 2002. Urbane Topologie. Bauhaus University Press, 2002.

Kousky, C., Schneider, S.H., 2003. Global climate policy: will cities lead the way? Climate Policy 3 (4), 359–372.

Krizek, K., Forysth, A., Schively Slotterback, C., 2009. Is there a role for evidence-based practice in urban planning and policy? Planning Theory & Practice 10 (4), 459–478.

Kunze, A., Burkhard, R., Gebhardt, S., Tuncer, B., 2012. Visualization and Decision Support Tools in Urban Planning. https://doi.org/10.1007/978-3-642-29758-8-15.

Lakatos, I., 1977. The Methodology of Scientific Research Programmes. Cambridge University Press, 1977.

Lakatos, I., 1978. Mathematics, Science and Epistemology. Cambridge University Press, 1978.

Landwehr, A., Sievert, J., López Baeza, J., Luft, J., Bruns-Berentelg, J., Preuner, P., Noyman, A., Larson, K., Noennig, J., 2021. Reinventing the competition: CityScope platform for real-time analysis and decision-support in urban design competitions. International Journal of E-Planning Research (IJEPR) 10 (4). https://doi.org/10.4018/ijepr.20211001.oa8.

Li, D., Wang, S., Li, D., 2015. Spatial Data Mining. Theory and Application. Springer, 2015.

Liew, A., 2007. Understanding data, information, knowledge and their inter-relationships. Journal of Knowledge Management Practice 8 (2).

López Baeza, J., Noennig, J., Weber, V., Grignard, A., Noyman, A., Larson, K., Saxe, S., Baldauf, U., 2020. Mobility solutions for cruise passenger transfer: an exploration of scenarios using agent-based simulation models. In: Müller, B., Meyer, G. (Eds.), Towards User-Centric Transport in Europe 2. Lecture Notes in Mobility. Springer, Cham.

Luque-Ayala, A., Marvin, S., 2020. Urban Operating Systems: Producing the Computational City. MIT Press, 2020.

McCarthy, J., 1963. Towards a mathematical science of computation. In: Information Processing 1962. North-Holland Publishing Company, Amsterdam, pp. 21–28, 1963.

Mittelstrass, J., 2003. Transdisziplinarität – wissenschaftliche Zukunft und institutionelle Wirklichkeit, Universitätsverlag, Konstanz 2003.

Noyman, A., Holtz, T., Kröger, J., Noennig, J.R., Larson, K., 2017. FindingPlaces: HCI platform for public participation in refugees' accommodation process. In: 21st International Conference in Knowledge Based and Intelligent Information and Engineering Systems - KES2017. Elsevier: Procedia Computer Science.

Pentland, A., 2015. Social Physics. Penguin, 2015.

Phillips-Wren, G., Esposito, A., Jain, L.C., 2021. Advances in Data Science: Methodologies and Applications, Intelligent Systems. Springer International Publishing, 2021.

Popper, K., 1959. The Logic of Scientific Discovery. Routledge 1959.

Puppim de Oliveira, J.A., Doll, C.N., Suwa, A., 2013. Urban Development with Climate Co-benefits: Aligning Climate, Environmental and Other Development Goals in Cities. United Nations University: UNU-IAS Institute of Advanced Studies.

Ratti, C., 2004. Space Syntax: some inconsistencies. Environment and Planning B: Urban Analytics and City Science 31 (4), 487–499.

Schreurs, M.A., 2008. From the bottom up local and subnational climate change politics. Journal of Environment & Development 17 (4), 343–355.

Schwegmann, R., Ziemer, G., Noennig, J., 2021. Digital City Science. Researching New Technologies in Urban Environments (Perspectives in Metropolitan Research), Jovis 2021 *Forthcoming*.

Seghezzo, L., 2009. The five dimensions of sustainability. Environmental Politics 18 (No. 4), 539–556. July 2009.

Shcherbakov, M., Shcherbakova, N., Brebels, A., Janovsky, T., Kamaev, V., 2014. Lean data science research life cycle: a concept for data analysis software

development. Communications in Computer and Information Science 466, 708–716.
Simon, H., 1969. The Sciences of the Artificial. MIT Press, 1969.
Song, Y., Wang, X., Tan, Y., Wu, P., Sutrisna, M., Cheng, J.C.P., Hampson, K., 2017. Trends and opportunities of BIM-GIS integration in the architecture, engineering and construction industry: a review from a spatio-temporal statistical perspective. In: International Journal of Geo-Information, vol. 6, 2017.
Tanaka, M., Watanabe, H., Furukawa, Y., Tanino, T., 1995. GA-based decision support system for multicriteria optimization. Industrial & Management Engineering Fields 2 (2), 1556–1561. https://doi.org/10.1109/ICSMC.1995.537993.
Tukey, J., 1977. Exploratory Data Analysis. Addison-Wesley, 1977.
United Nations, 1987. World Commission on Environment and Development: Our Common Future (Brundtland Report). Oxford University Press, Oxford, 1987.
United Nations, 2015. Resolution Adopted by the General Assembly on 25 September 2015, Transforming Our World: The 2030 Agenda for Sustainable Development.
United Nations, 2016. Paris Agreement. United Nations Treaty Collection.
Waddell, P., Ulfarsson, G.F., 2004. Introduction to urban simulation: design and development of operational models. In: Handbook of Transport Geography and Spatial Systems.
Whitehead, A.N., 1925. Science and the Modern World. Cambridge University Press, 1925.
Whitehead, A.N., 1929. Process and Reality. The Free Press, New York, 1929.
Zionts, S., Wallenius, J., 1976. An interactive programming method for solving the multiple criteria problem. Management Science 22 (6), 652.

Further reading

Brenner, N., Schmid, C., 2011. Planetary urbanization. In: Gandy, M. (Ed.), Urban Constellations, Jovis (Berlin).
Helbing, D., 2008. Managing Complexity: Insights, Concepts, Applications. Springer, Heidelberg, 2008.
Hillier, B., 1999. Space Is the Machine: A Configurational Theory of Architecture. Cambridge University Press, Cambridge.
Hillier, B., Hanson, J., 1984. The Social Logic of Space. Cambridge University Press, Cambridge.
Kustra, M., Brodowicz, D., Noennig, J.R., 2017. Smart city sells – business models and corporate approaches on the smart city concept. In: Crabu, S., Giardullo, P., Miele, F., Turrini, M. (Eds.), Sociotechnical Environments. Proceedings of the 6ths STS Italia Conference, pp. 211–230.
Meadows, D., Meadows, D.H., Randers, J., Behrens, W.W., 1972. The Limits to Growth. A Report for the Club of Rome's Project on the Predicament of Mankind. Universe Books, 1972.
Mitchell, W., 1995. City of Bits: Space, Place, and the Infobahn. MIT Press, 1995.
Mitchell, W., 2003. Me++: The Cyborg Self and the Networked City. MIT Press, 2003.
Negroponte, N., 1995. Being Digital. Alfred A. Knopf 1995.

16

A software tool for net-positive urban design and architecture

Janis Birkeland
Faculty of Architecture, Building and Planning University of Melbourne, Parkville, VIC, Australia

1. Introduction

1.1 Overview

Given existential threats to society and nature, urban development must do more than restore ecosystems, regenerate communities, and revitalize local economies. Buildings must create "net-positive" public benefits, not just offset the negative impacts they add. "Net" is a whole-system concept and therefore includes the project's lifecycle, supply chain, and cumulative social and ecological impacts—everywhere. In this context, "net-positive energy" is a specious claim because, due to the laws of nature, energy cannot be increased without imaginary systems boundaries. Net-positive buildings would give back more than they take from both humanity and nature. Ecological regeneration is seldom "net" nature-positive because it only restores what remains of nature.

While urban design, planning, and architecture can improve community–society–nature relationships, they do not compensate for their past and ongoing damage. This would require increasing "ecological space" in real terms—as well as regenerating nature and improving human life quality. To be net-positive, therefore, buildings must contribute eco-positive public gains that overcompensate for their share of the adverse impacts of *all* urban development. This is possible. As one example, structural materials grown from mycelium in vertical spaces could return mining and cropland to wilderness while sequestering waste and carbon (Huynh and Jones, 2018). For other examples, see Birkeland (2020).

Intelligent Environments. https://doi.org/10.1016/B978-0-12-820247-0.00004-7

"Positive Development" is the theoretical scaffolding for transforming sustainable development from aiming for "no harm" to creating overall public gains (Birkeland, 2008, 2020). This paradigm produces new models, mindsets, methods, and metrics for urban planning and design. Positive Development aims to bridge the paradigm divide in sustainable development fields that has limited the interdisciplinary, cross-sectoral collaboration that whole-systems design change requires. The resulting new analyses, strategies, and tools unite linear-reductionist decision-making—choosing—with synergistic, multifunctional design: creating. One of these means to facilitate the necessary institutional and intellectual reframing is discussed here: "STARfish," a new computer app for net-positive design.

STARfish assists in designing multifunctional, adaptable, net-positive environments. It goes beyond the basic circular systems model. Closed-loop recycling systems can only aim for zero. They cannot, on their own, increase fundamental life-support systems, or "public estate" and "ecological base," as defined below. STARfish was devised for design re-education, and to help designers envisage the radically different environments needed to reverse social injustice and environmental devastation. STARfish sums cumulative—negative, restorative, and net-positive—impacts throughout all design stages. The app measures design impacts against stationary, not relative, biophysical baselines: namely, preurban ecological and regional social conditions. Thus, it facilitates genuine sustainability gains.

This paper distinguishes STARfish from rating tools and life-cycle analyses or "LCA." As explained later, green building rating schemes and LCA currently sanction "less-harmful" impacts and impede whole-systems sustainability gains. STARfish weds design with quantitative assessment. It visually displays and simultaneously calculates the interconnections among cumulative and remote upstream and downstream impacts to aid design synergies. Data from LCA or primary sources can be easily integrated into STARfish. The paper also highlights some unique features of STARfish diagrams and benchmarks, such as its fractal radar diagram and net-positive benchmarks. The open-source STARfish can be downloaded from the website (Birkeland, 2019).

1.2 Problems and prospects

Green design (Papanek, 1971; Vale and Vale, 1975) was slow to be adopted. Over time, it evolved into "conservation through eco-efficiency" and subsequently "nature-based design." Nonetheless, the potential of urban designers to contribute to equitable, eco-productive environments is immense. Cities could serve their myriad cultural and practical functions while being transformed into nature-health retreats that create the conditions for biophysical sustainability. They could function like reefs that seed their ocean bioregions. Instead, urban expansion and densification are eliminating the land and resources needed to sustain natural life-support systems and nature's intrinsic values. Meanwhile, most sustainable planning and urban design declarations only aim to leave human habitats "better than before construction" (e.g., Habitat III, 2016; SDGs, 2018).

Green building tools reflect this fatalism. Their influence is growing, as is cumulative, irreversibledamage. These tools include prescriptive certification schemes that reward best practice, design review processes, and principles against which experts judge design, data-driven lifecycle assessment methods, and tools that inspire creativity. They seek improvements over typical buildings, best practices, or current site conditions. Yet highly rated buildings often only perform slightly better than ordinary code-compliant buildings. Moreover, when green buildings claim to "use 50% less water," they still consume more water than "no building." Such relative standards encourage designers to use conventional building templates and then mitigate their impacts.

These assessment frameworks are really decision, not design, tools. Decision tools assist in simplifying complex choices and avoiding technical errors but generally exclude consideration of design strategies that can create multiple public gains. They retain the old illusion that the damage from the conventional industrial building model can be canceled out by reduction, recycling, value-adding, or regeneration. Hence, they inform efficiency or less waste, not the requisite socioecological gains that sustainability demands. Nevertheless, in large complex developments, building management and modeling tools are becoming a practical necessity and, due to competition, green building certification schemes are becoming a commercial imperative.

Green building certification and marketing schemes have certainly raised awareness. However, industry-led standards tend to reinforce current practices. They are beginning to prescribe and proscribe design processes and standards, especially in large commercial developments. To raise design quality, many local governments are replacing their own design review processes with these proprietary tools. Hence, commercial interests increasingly define "green buildings" and control the pace of reform. Despite the centrality of construction in global sustainability challenges, therefore, urban design standards are being abdicated to special interests. Meanwhile, worldwide, over 60% of biodiversity has been lost in under 50 years and disparities in wealth are escalating.

Design tools, policies, and regulations that only aim for "zero" cannot reverse biodiversity losses. They correspond with "weak sustainability," which frames the environmental crisis as a matter of better policies and decisions, rather than redesigning anachronistic institutional and physical structures. For example, weak sustainability purports to counter the industrial growth paradigm with "green growth." Yet it shares the same conceptual foundations that allow incremental trade-offs of nature (Kothari et al., 2019). A framework that optimizes choices among current options to "strike a balance" between economic growth, social upheaval, and ecological collapse, called the "triple bottom line," is a terminal process.

One reason that building tools emphasize impact reduction and efficiency over multiplying socioecological benefits is that design is still undervalued as a lesser subset of decision-making or "choosing" (Birkeland, 2012). Design has been marginalized as merely about aesthetics, or else just a means to communicate and express values. "Thinking" itself has been conflated with decision-making or linear-reductionist logic, as in computing. Fortunately, medical research now shows that designing and decision-making involve distinct cognitive functions and neural networks (Alexiou, 2009). Furthermore, many now recognize that sustainability is a design problem, not a matter of choosing among environmentally friendly products.

Although building rating tools reward responsible developers and designers for improving the built environment, they measure success against *unsustainable* norms. Therefore, as shown below, these tools conceal negative impacts, treat impact reductions as adequate or even label them "positive," disregard net-positive public gains, and ignore deteriorating contextual and global conditions. Thus, they fail to address the scale of the sustainability crisis, disrupt harmful industry conventions, or recalibrate urban design and decision-making. These schemes move the finish line nearer the starting block to achieve buy-in from status-seeking firms—when the challenge should be to save the planet and humanity.

Clearly, the standards and strategies of sustainable development and design need a fundamental *reset*. Sustainability dilemmas caused by traditional development processes can be traced to negative social constructs, mental headsets, and power structures. New ecologically sound systems of urban governance, planning, decision-making, and design are needed to convert cities from a problem into a sustainability solution. Positive Development reconceives these social constructs so that the urban environment can create net-positive sustainability gains. Before looking at how basic sustainability issues, such as environmental justice, biodiversity, and ethics, are neglected in rating tools, some maxims of Positive Development theory are briefly reviewed.

1.3 Positive development

Positive Development posits that, with a different design paradigm, cities can be retrofitted to increase nature, justice, and life quality, as summarized in *Net-Positive Design and Sustainable Urban Development* (Birkeland, 2020). The proposition that "development can save the planet" sounds paradoxical. This perhaps explains why it has only been hypothesized since after the turn of this century (Birkeland, 2003, 2005). Positive Development shows how urban environments can multiply public benefits, expand future social options, and increase nature and justice (Birkeland, 2007). To change the nature of the built environment, Positive Development *inverts* the dated conceptual frameworks that underlie the dominant paradigm:

- Closed-system models that "balance" resource inputs with outputs, waste produced with waste recycled, costs with benefits, and, in contemporary terms, "circular" systems that close resource loops.
- Dualistic, "either-or" mindsets that favor either side of the engrained divisions in western thought: qualitative-qualitative, technocratic-creative, competitive-cooperative, hard-soft, mechanistic-ecological, and so on.
- Transactional, versus transformative, processes that aim to "balance competing interests" by making trade-offs and offsets that do not account for, or compensate, the public costs of unsustainable development.

Positive Development deconstructs these and other deeply engrained precepts that have shaped weak sustainable development. It facilitates a paradigm shift from "do no harm" to "beyond zero" in all dimensions. Net-positive design means that structures externalize public gains, instead of just internalizing negative impacts. Quality design can cost less than conventional design that often features conspicuous consumption by using eco-positive design strategies, such as "design for eco-services," "eco-positive retrofitting," "green scaffolding," and "playgardens" (Birkeland, 2007, 2020). The Positive Development Test is a development that expands positive future options by increasing the "ecological base" and "public estate." These umbrella terms represent specific standards:

- The term *public estate* encompasses and expands the range of social sustainability issues affected by built environments. In most rating tools, social goals usually pertain to stakeholders' interests, such as "community building" and economic revitalization, not public needs. Access to unstable markets does not ensure environmental and resource security. Positive Development would provide direct, equitable access to the means of survival and well-being for everyone, especially in emergencies. This requires identifying and rectifying sustainability deficits in the bioregion, not merely within property lines. In STARfish, the social baseline is improvements in area-wide social conditions, opportunities, justice, and environmental security.

- The term *ecological base* encompasses ecosystem and biodiversity issues. Most rating tools are anthropocentric. They use adjectives like "ecological," but these usually refer to resources or benefits for stakeholders, such as healthy indoor air, water, and materials. At most, they encourage landscape regeneration. A sustainable construction should increase nature's positive ecological footprint, not merely reduce humanity's negative ecological footprint. This means that, unless rates of human consumption reduce radically, urban areas should increase space and support for ecosystems beyond what existed before urbanization, settlement, or industrialization. In STARfish, again, environmental impacts are assessed relative to predevelopment, not preconstruction, conditions.

The above concepts require preliminary analyses of socioecological conditions in the region. Usually, basic planning and design decisions are made "technocratically" before people with creative design thinking skills are included. Therefore, Positive Development provides general planning guidelines that are also relevant to less-developed regions, and a set of planning analyses for social and environmental issues to identify the regional social and ecological deficits that could be corrected by development. These frameworks can be used by planners, developers, designers, or community groups on any level from mind-mapping to data-intensive analysis. These 22 planning analyses will be transposed into the STARfish diagram below.

2. How STARfish differs from rating tools

2.1 Complex systems and total impacts

Rating tools do not treat buildings as complex systems, but rather as the sum of isolated variables. Lists of building components with scores for achieving certain percentages of reductions or additions conflict with the holistic way that creative people think. Some tools present lists of design principles in circles to

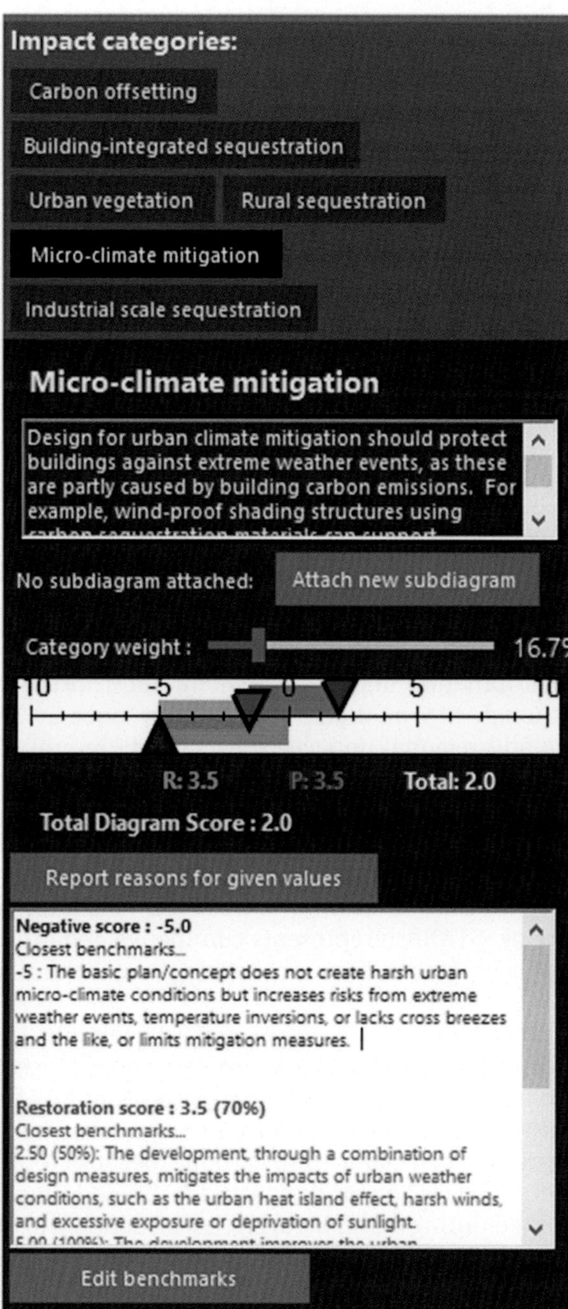
Impact categories:
Carbon offsetting
Building-integrated sequestration
Urban vegetation
Rural sequestration
Micro-climate mitigation
Industrial scale sequestration
Micro-climate mitigation
Design for urban climate mitigation should protect buildings against extreme weather events, as these are partly caused by building carbon emissions. For example, wind-proof shading structures using
No subdiagram attached:
Attach new subdiagram
Category weight :
-5
0
5
R: 3.5
P: 3.5
Total: 2.0
Total Diagram Score : 2.0
Report reasons for given values
Negative score : -5.0
Closest benchmarks...
-5 : The basic plan/concept does not create harsh urban micro-climate conditions but increases risks from extreme weather events, temperature inversions, or lacks cross breezes and the like, or limits mitigation measures.
Restoration score : 3.5 (70%)
Closest benchmarks...
2.50 (50%): The development, through a combination of design measures, mitigates the impacts of urban weather conditions, such as the urban heat island effect, harsh winds, and excessive exposure or deprivation of sunlight.
Edit benchmarks

Figure 16.1

convey holism, but they do not indicate actual interrelationships. STARfish can display the web of interconnections between actions and their cumulative outcomes throughout project supply chains or lifecycles. Conceivably, STARfish could even be converted into a three-dimensional "hologram" to assess complex multidimensional systems such as urban precincts, cities, or regions.

Rating tools do not encourage design synergies. They give points for known green techniques, so it is tempting to start with typical building forms and then add eco-technologies. Net-positive design would need to increase socioecological gains in most project elements, structures, and spaces. Tools that count design elements in one category cannot recognize or reward multifunctional outcomes. STARfish conveys visually how most actions have mutual gains, a combination of good and bad outcomes, or spill-over effects in several different impact categories. Showing how alternatives affect the whole system can help to uncover opportunities for multiplying positive functions on all scales.

Rating tools rarely consider actual site-specific environmental impacts. In fact, they were partly motivated to avoid the imposition of environmental impact assessment (EIA) in the building sector. Although EIA methods were initially poor at analyzing cumulative and regional impacts, they steadily improved. Certified green buildings often receive expedited approval processes without ecological assessments. Rating tools use surrogate targets to avoid counting embodied impacts, such as "percentage of water recycled." However, buildings that recycle 100% of their water may have caused excessive water or pollution during manufacturing. STARfish represents cumulative, remote negative impacts visually, rather than obscuring them behind rubbery numbers.

Rating tools often permit an unnecessary amount of carbon impacts by deeming certain emission levels "acceptable." Further, voluntary rating schemes cannot prevent buildings that emit excessive amounts of carbon emissions from being built. However, projects can claim "zero carbon," because tools usually exclude embodied carbon. As design and technology improve, the carbon emitted during manufacturing/construction will be higher than most new building's operating emissions. Undercounting embodied carbon means the potential for carbon sequestration is easily overlooked. Buildings can sequester their total lifecycle carbon emissions by permanent building-integrated vegetation alone (Renger et al., 2015). Therefore, STARfish incentivizes design that sequesters carbon.

Rating tools do not take into account the depletion of natural resource stocks. For example, as they reward negative impacts that are simply lower than average, standard water conservation targets seldom consider regional water scarcity. A water-efficient project in a drought-affected area could lower the water table or stream flow without this being exposed by the assessment. STARfish considers cumulative, incremental damage to whole-system sustainability, such as the depletion of local water resources. It is designed to assess impacts against optimal biophysical, regional conditions, to account for reductions in total resource stocks and flows as well as biodiversity and ecosystems.

2.2 Flexible tools and adaptable design

Rating tools generally use prescriptive rules based on past building conventions. Because each project's functions, site conditions, and socioecological context are unique, such rules often have suboptimal design outcomes. This helps to explain why some highly rated buildings have performed worse than ordinary ones (Newsham et al., 2009; Scofield, 2009). Because rating tools lack the flexibility to cover differing situations, most establish separate rules for different "building types," instead of requiring buildings to accommodate changing conditions or functions. STARfish can apply to any project because benchmarks are fixed, and impact categories can be added because alterations are transparent and subject to scrutiny.

Rating tools allow users to score enough points without addressing all the criteria. This equates to dispensations from the professed performance standards. Flexible performance standards are the opposite of flexible designs that can respond to changing climates and contexts. Although called "performance-based," these tools specify actions, not outcomes. For instance, some tools encourage "durable buildings." Durable buildings can be very wasteful if they must be demolished when conditions or needs change. In contrast, demountable, modular components and structural systems allow spatial expansion or contraction over time. STARfish rewards things that are not easily enumerated, such as adaptable or portable designs.

Rating tools rarely incentivize retrofitting, even though new buildings generally cause more sociocultural dislocation and environmental damage than renovations. If all old buildings were replaced with new green ones, the impacts would cause planetary devastation. Furthermore, new "green buildings" must soon be retrofitted if cities are to contribute to genuine sustainability. There are now rating tools for assessing retrofits, but it is usually easier to get a higher rating by constructing a new building on a greenfield site. STARfish, in contrast, can be used to identify deficits in existing buildings and compare their current performance to a proposed eco-positive retrofit.

Rating tools seldom encourage or accredit mixed or multiple building uses. Mixed-use developments generally have a more functional and social value per unit of resource. They tend to be more resilient and adaptable in their use of materials and spaces over time. Although designs for mixed and multiple building uses have long been considered best practices, they are seldom assessed because they are difficult to generalize and standardize. STARfish can add criteria and benchmarks for incentivizing multiple, mixed use, and adaptable design features. Generic rules for benchmarking to ensure additions are consistent with net-positive principles are set out below (Box 16.1).

Rating tools seldom consider the potential symbiotic uses of indoor/outdoor spaces. Space itself is intangible, but it can support multiple social and ecological functions. Spatial resources are rarely credited because rating tools only measure particular material elements. Often, an attached greenhouse or atrium designed to provide multiple benefits will only count in predetermined categories, such as insulation or air quality. Open spaces are also a means to accommodate change, such as enabling climate adaptation and mitigation through substantial urban greening and farming. STARfish can credit any negative, restorative, or positive impacts of spatial resources that affect human or environmental health.

2.3 Visualization, communication, and transparency

Rating tools are seldom transparent. Certification schemes are costly to use, but few users know why particular scores are awarded for certain actions or why some factors are given more weight. Uniform points and weightings are often recommended by expert working groups and/or endorsed by industry representatives, based on what is currently considered achievable. There can be legitimate reasons for modifying the weightings, such as priority local issues, unique project purposes, and unusual contextual situations. The rationales are published in an automated STARfish Design Report, so the community, clients, or councils can contest new benchmarks or dubious weightings and scores.

Rating tools that only record the "reduction" of impacts conceal the total negative impacts that have been caused. For decades, people have understood it is more rational to prevent

Box 16.1 General guidelines for creating new benchmarks

General guidelines for new benchmarks

Negative (black area)

−10 = This is the worst imaginable case. With respect to the specific impact factor, the product or design element is highly damaging, irreversible, and/or leaves a site completely degraded. Note that a green development is negative if it covers a greenfield site or occupies a site where harmful conditions already exist. This is because remedial, mitigative, or offset actions are not deducted in the black zone. In this tool, unlike most other tools, "less harmful" is negative, not positive. Therefore, doing nothing or constructing an ordinary (unsustainable) building can be negative because it is a lost opportunity.

−5 = Here the building or specific design concept being examined is harmful, even if it could be or is mitigated. For example, air pollution in the urban area is not excessive or the project adds more air pollution, but the resulting urban air quality is not bad. This discourages beginning with a polluting building technology and only reducing its impacts. In some instances, it may be appropriate to assess the "negative" impacts relative to typical buildings, code requirements, practices, or preconstruction site conditions. However, positive impacts (below) should be assessed relative to preurban ecological or regional social (whole-system) conditions.

Restorative or regenerative (green area)

50% = Restorative/regenerative actions reduce the negative impacts of the development or component, and/or improve the site and building with respect to the given impact factor. 50% means the design reduces, offsets, or regenerates a considerable portion of any existing damage and impacts of the development itself, but the overall impact is still negative compared to preurban or preindustrial conditions. For example, a development on a degraded site may restore the equivalent preurban vegetation and biodiversity on what remains of the land surrounding the new building, but it does not compensate for the land covered by the building footprint itself.

100% = This means the outcome in the impact category is zero, or the damage is completely offset, which is the current sustainable design target. What are called restorative or regenerative impacts seldom amount to eliminating 100% of the project's additional impacts or improving overall regional outcomes. Instead, zero usually means the equivalent of preconstruction conditions (vs. presettlement conditions). Here, 100% would mean the designs or actions eliminate all "added" negative impacts of the development itself. Although the negative impacts of the development may be offset by compensatory measures, they are not net positive in a global or whole-system sense.

Positive or net positive (blue area)

+5 = These are additional positive impacts and/or separate design elements or actions that, at least in combination, go beyond restoring the damage caused by the project in the given category. Whereas impacts are usually considered regenerative when they only benefit stakeholders, eco-positive design must create public benefits. For example, indoor air quality benefits stakeholders but not neighbors or nature. Public benefits usually require multifunctional design (a low-impact green roof provides many building services, but can also support endangered species, purify air and water, etc.). Positive impacts almost invariably require "design," not simply "decisions" (choosing among known products or designs).

+10 = Beyond +5 means major increases in the net ecological base and/or public estate. These designs or actions improve whole-system outcomes. They effectively expand future public options by preserving or increasing nature. For example, soil, air, or water quality does not have system boundaries, so their overall condition should be improved. This generally requires multifunctional, adaptable design and innovation, supplemented by net-positive offsetting. If a unique positive design feature is added that is unrelated to given impact categories, it can be placed on a new Leg, and/or a whole new impact category (a new Satellite diagram) can be added.

pollution than to try to decontaminate a complex environment later. Therefore, a project that treats its own toxic waste should *not* get a higher score than a project that avoids pollution in the first place. Nonetheless, buildings are only expected to offset their irreversible impacts. In STARfish, negative impacts and outcomes remain forever visible. This serves the added educational purpose of increasing awareness of the importance of preliminary designs and decisions.

Rating tools score projects relative to the norm, which indicates how "less bad" buildings are. Some tools even label waste reductions or resource savings as "positive." A project with no public value, such as a luxurious "playboy mansion," might be efficient and upcycle all its construction waste, yet be 100% wasteful. STARfish considers the community costs and benefits of projects, total resources used, and total waste generated, not merely the portion of waste reduced. By counting waste, including luxuries, separately from recycling, the incentive is to avoid waste by design, which reduces costly systems for processing and managing waste later.

Rating tools do not disseminate innovations very widely. Certification companies publish many case studies, but they are more promotional than educational. Again, they usually advertise how much "less" energy, water, carbon, or waste that a building causes, rather than explaining how the eco-technologies work. Like green building tours and magazines, they are inspirational yet provide little practical information for students and others. Further, new ideas and precedents are seldom attributed to their originators, which is inequitable. As the STARfish Design Report requires explanations for scores, future design teams can learn from and borrow innovations, while acknowledging the sources of ideas.

Rating tools usually set thresholds to simplify point scoring. That means, beyond a certain performance level, the scores do not change. In effect, therefore, thresholds treat a given percentage of reduction or gain as optimal, because additional positive or negative impacts will not count. Hence, designers have no incentive to design-in more efficient, multifunctional benefits beyond that threshold. For example, if the maximum points for using a certain percentage of recycled timber are exceeded, designers may feel free to use rainforest timbers surplus to need. Because STARfish has a sliding scale for estimating below or above zero impacts, it avoids thresholds.

2.4 Decision-making (reduction) versus design (multiplication)

Rating tools are often called "design tools" although they mainly help designers choose among building products or compare projects after basic designs are formed. Assessment is retrospective, whereas design creates something new. However, designers wanting a top rating may let the tool dictate the design. Rating tools also favor technological fixes because they focus on efficiencies or impact reductions. Mechanical equipment often has high embodied impacts. Tools seldom favor passive solar structures and spaces. While STARfish is primarily a design tool, it can compare preliminary and passive design alternatives before substantial time, effort, or money is invested in technical detail.

Rating tools seldom give adequate credit for nature-positive systems. They allow designers to meet standards by adding mechanical equipment instead of supporting eco-services that perform building functions in biophilic ways (Birkeland, 2007, 2016). Today, buildings are largely compilations of commercial materials and equipment. There are digital tools that calculate the thermal effects of building components, like wall and window assemblages, to ensure they meet energy standards. However, they tend to result in uniform metal and glass cupboards for caging people in towers. STARfish encourages natural systems and passive solar design to be maximized before mechanical products or systems are specified.

Rating tools do not support the cross-disciplinary, collaborative planning processes that sustainable design entails. Design is about synthesis, synergy, and symbiosis. In urban design, therefore, multiple perspectives, skills, and expertise are essential. Reductionist certification schemes do little to integrate the social, physical, and ecological sciences into urban design and decision-making. STARfish facilitates a mutual learning forum among scientists, designers, engineers, community groups, future building users, and others throughout the design stages. It incorporates scientific or engineering approaches, which generally emphasize "hard" technological solutions, along with "soft" social science analyses that help to identify local community deficits (Birkeland,2020, Chapters 7 and 8).

Rating tools appear to be scientific because they are numerical, yet most only assess things that are easy to assign numbers to. They exclude many issues that have not traditionally been measured, such as sustainability itself. They do little to motivate outcomes that have yet to be achieved. STARfish adds many new sustainability criteria that project teams must consider when generating public gains. As benchmarks are based on real-world outcomes, not improvements over current conditions, a building that does more harm than "no building" might get a negative score. Nevertheless, it should receive a higher score than a conventional building.

Rating tools are often operated by specialist assessors whose clients are developers. Many of them lack a substantial background in design or sustainability. Stories abound about how prescriptive rules were applied arbitrarily to exclude innovative design features that met the tool's intent. While some tools do not reward clever passive solutions that address site-specific problems, others reward "innovations" regardless of their actual socioecological outcomes. STARfish instead credits the on-ground results of innovations. Again, where an original solution with net-positive outcomes was not anticipated, users can add criteria according to the benchmarking principles in Box 16.1 if they state convincing reasons.

2.5 Ecosystems and biodiversity issues

Rating tools often confuse human and ecological impacts. Many count things as "ecological" that only concern human health and comfort, such as indoor air quality or biophilic amenities. Confused by the long list of factors under "environment" columns (that do not actually support nature), many have suggested that rating tools privilege ecology when they actually favor financial aspects: marketability and efficiency. More recently, there are tool upgrades that credit biodiversity "enhancement," without requiring compensation for the biodiversity lost during resource extraction (Birkeland, 2018). In contrast, STARfish encourages the provision of new ecological space for habitats and biodiversity incubators in urban environments.

Rating tools do not require real or net contributions to positive "offsite" ecological or microclimatic conditions. Although some tools now give credit for remediating offsite water or land or compensating for onsite biodiversity losses, that hardly ever constitutes nature-positive gains in the bioregion. Some rating tools consider "preserving" land elsewhere to be a net gain, but reservations do not increase the region's ecological carrying capacity or create biodiversity incubators. STARfish enables offsite actions that benefit the region's ecology to be credited. Conversely, negative offsite impacts are deducted, even if diverse, diffuse, or remote, by using a sliding scale between benchmarks.

Rating tools do not consider the "highest ecological use" of land. Within regulatory boundaries, developers (who are "the market") determine most land uses. Once a property is developed, more ecologically-appropriate land uses are effectively barred. This fundamental "opportunity cost" of development is seldom considered. Positive Development planning therefore begins with the highest ecological use. Once ecological land use parameters are ascertained by planners, compatible socioeconomic uses can be solicited. Where authorities permit a detrimental land use anyway, eco-positive functions can at least be included by design. STARfish also uses "net-positive offsetting" to increase total ecological gains (Birkeland and Knight-Lenihan, 2016).

Rating tools do not encourage designs that lower environmental risks on surrounding urban properties, even though these are often exacerbated by infill development. Sometimes, green building design mitigates hazards that may damage the project itself by, for example, constructing barriers against floods, fires, extreme winds, or the urban heat island effect. However, it seldom mitigates the environmental risks themselves, or the project's impacts on nearby properties caused by increasing urban density/expansion (e.g., overshadowing, urban flooding, subsidence, impermeable paving). STARfish counts actions that lessen environmental risks in the wider area, in addition to those that protect the project and site itself.

Rating tools do not compensate for ecological uncertainty and extinction rates. Some tools count biodiversity-friendly landscaping as an ecological gain, even when a new building covers most of a greenfield site. A green roof was labeled "positive" although the multistory building's floor area was many times that of the roof. Biodiversity credit schemes may give governments excuses for delaying legislation to increase urban biodiversity. Other tools count gains in landscaping relative to the degraded site conditions when ownership was transferred. As STARfish sets ecological benchmarks relative to preurban ecosystems, it does not give extra credit for selecting profitable degraded sites.

2.6 Social issues and community engagement

Rating tools mainly only count benefits to stakeholders. One reason is that, when they first appeared in the 1990s, many developers did not comprehend that sustainable design saves money. Hence, the emphasis was on promoting financial benefits for occupants and owners, such as energy savings and "worker health"—code for higher productivity and morale, less absenteeism, and fewer compensation claims. Efficiencies that saved money and risks for investors were therefore regarded as gains, although they generally only decreased the project's additional impacts. Benefits to stakeholders seldom address social issues in the region, whereas STARfish prioritizes contributions to the community.

Rating tools largely exclude community input in the development of their criteria and indicators, although these tools affect public welfare. While green building organizations seek their members' input and support, their tools are often developed by practitioners from the corporate sector. Input from the wider community is sometimes invited, but without a real opportunity to challenge underlying assumptions, processes or results. Government plans, policies, and rules, in contrast, can usually be challenged in open public hearings. The STARfish Report enables ordinary citizens to understand the design rationale and how projects may affect their environment, or to even make constructive suggestions.

Rating tools distract from wider social sustainability issues, such as exclusion, wealth disparities, destruction of the means of survival, and the exploitation of labor. Early on, the sustainability movement emphasized social issues (Commoner, 1971; Schumacher, 1973). However, with notable exceptions (e.g., Lyle, 1994; van der Ryn and Cowan, 1996; Wann, 1996), public costs and benefits were side-lined in the sustainable design literature, which focused on efficiency and energy—economics. Some "neighborhood scale" tools have been developed that count social benefits, but most do not deduct for negative social impacts. STARfish considers the project's negative social impacts in the region.

Rating tools do not really address environmental justice or equity issues. They seldom suggest ways that design might improve social conditions beyond the owner's legal liabilities, property lines, or project supply chains. Some tools give points that effectively reward developers for "not breaking laws," such as not condoning slavery or not creating unsafe working conditions for laborers. If not illegal, they should be. Government responsibility for protecting human rights, health, and safety should not be shifted to voluntary private-sector organizations. STARfish will incorporate Positive Development planning analyses that identify regional deficits and means to increase community-wide environmental justice and security.

Rating tools are not socially transformative. Although they have made sustainable design almost prestigious, they are slow to keep pace with growing public awareness about social sustainability issues. Green buildings reduce waste and expense while improving life quality for the well-heeled but do little for the underprivileged. Urban environments that perpetuate social problems cannot be rapidly reconfigured through voluntary "industry self-regulation" schemes. The rate that standards rise depends on the clients of certification companies: developers. Further, green building councils compete among themselves for financial sponsors: developers. In contrast, changes to STARfish can be made quickly in response to reasoned critique.

2.7 Transaction costs and omissions

Rating tools do little to encourage design that enhances traditional cultures or regional identity, let alone other local social needs, deficits or priorities. Net-positive design aims to contribute positively to the bioregion's unique cultural, economic, and bioregional characteristics. Some tools have been modified for application to developing countries, as they are expensive to produce from scratch. However, they usually have the same bureaucratic orientation and high transaction costs. As STARfish is benchmarked against regional social conditions, the criteria are transferrable to different countries, cultures, and socioeconomic conditions. Positive Development also provides design guidelines for disadvantaged regions (Birkeland, 2020, Chapters 13 and 14).

Rating tools involve administrative tasks that are not relevant to improving the schematic design. As most assessment tools require a fairly complete design to assess, the process comes too late to modify the basic plan. STARfish demands an investment in learning, but design education is a necessary precondition of sustainable design because a paradigm shift is required. It is free and could be used for community design "charrettes." While challenging, it creates a "game" in which a design team competes with itself. There is no advantage to cheating in this collaborative context but, if anyone did, it would be obvious.

Rating tools do not require an examination of alternative locations, site plans, or building forms that might have fewer impacts. Most sustainable designers understand that site selection and preliminary designs determine the majority of impacts. However, sites are usually selected on economic criteria alone, within regulatory constraints, before sustainability is considered. Average designers then begin with massing studies to maximize profitability, instead of conducting socioecological analyses. STARfish can enable quick comparisons of schematic site and building alternatives to help determine the best location and plan. The design can then be improved in an iterative process as quantitative information gradually materializes.

Rating tools do not influence the majority of "ordinary" buildings, and codes only enforce minimal standards. Hence, neither result in net sustainability improvements to the environment. A certification company can refuse to assess developments proposed near ecologically sensitive sites. However, a developer that is keen on certification will simply locate elsewhere. This means an even more harmful project will likely be built on that site instead. Further, rating tools are not used to ameliorate bad projects because they are expensive to use because of fees and compliance activity—and voluntary. Many developers are motivated more by profit than professional recognition.

Rating tools increasingly encourage the use of lifecycle assessment or give credit for using "BIM," or building management/modeling, tools, but as separate activities. While BIM facilitates efficiency on large, complex projects, it does not yet deal with most sustainability issues – hence it is not discussed here. Lifecycle assessment can include many social and ecological issues, but it generally only counts negative impacts or reductions in negative impacts. BIM and LCA should be integrated with STARfish to combine industry data with ethical considerations and design thinking. The following section explains how STARfish can avoid several of the conceptual problems with LCA.

3. How STARfish differs from lifecycle assessment

3.1 Problems with lifecycle assessment

LCA is a technical method for estimating the impacts of processes, products, or structures. It involves tracing the sources, transport and transformations of materials, energy, waste, and emissions at each stage of production, from cradle to grave. To the extent feasible, it quantifies their diverse impacts on human health, climate, ecosystems, resource consumption, and environmental "media" or air, water, and land. LCA is well suited for improving engineering systems because it can identify where wastes and impacts appear excessive in industrial or manufacturing processes. Once designs are sufficiently detailed to quantify materials, LCA data can be transferred into the STARfish app.

LCA aligns with the idea of "resource and energy balance:" a closed-systems, versus net-positive, framework. Circular systems cannot, in themselves, compensate for past socioecological damage. An LCA convention is to draw "system boundaries" to exclude remote, distant, or uncertain ecological impacts that are difficult to measure. "Recycling writ large," or closing loops at product, project, and urban boundaries, can conceal the gradual losses of ecosystem health and total resource stocks. Circular systems models are sometimes reminiscent of economic equilibrium theory, which ignored nature depletion. STARfish avoids this closed-system thinking and instead estimates changes in whole-system conditions as the design evolves.

LCA avoids some major omissions of rating tools by accounting for embodied resources and energy, although it has not considered net-positive outcomes. Like rating tools, LCA looks at single projects or processes, not spatial resources, or the urban context. Urban form can limit adaptability, exclude nature, or increase vulnerability to stochastic change like pandemics. Yet urban densification might score well on an LCA, because it values efficiency. That is, efficiency-based frameworks normally treat space as waste, not a valuable resource for multifunctional, adaptable design. STARfish recognizes contextual design issues and the need for public space to allow for unexpected challenges.

LCA purports to deal with complexity although it cannot calculate the myriad systemic impacts of pollution within different ecosystems, environmental media, and individual immune systems, because toxins often biomagnify over time. LCA can legitimize trading, offsetting, or credit schemes that effectively trade-off nature for development. As species extinctions and lost human lives are irreversible, compensation through restoration or offsetting cannot constitute reparation. Further, trade-offs cannot make segregated, fragile ecosystems resilient to global forces such as climate change. STARfish, therefore, creates "net-positive offsetting," which requires unavoidable damage to nature to be offset by increasing total ecological space and appropriate biodiversity.

LCA counts the supply chain impacts, such as the percentage of energy required to produce and operate the machinery and vehicles used for a construction project. However, it does not consider the contribution of construction projects to locking-in harmful industrial processes by, for example, prolonging the demand for fossilized energy. Generally, the sooner passive, renewable systems replace fossil fuels, the more resources, environmental-human health, and money will be saved. STARfish can compare basic systems, as if neither the current nor proposed energy systems yet existed. By discounting sunk costs, the whole-system costs and benefits of converting to sustainable systems become clearer.

LCA can give "more sustainable" products a commercial advantage by certifying product quality or checking the veracity of manufacturers' claims. For instance, a new biochar-based building material received an award for being "carbon positive" simply because biochar sequesters carbon. An LCA would have weighed in the pyrolysis used in producing the material. However, certified products tend to displace passive solar design, natural environmental systems, and organic materials, because the quality of organic materials is variable, and LCA favors materials whose performance is certified. STARfish can credit the multiple secondary benefits of organic materials, not just their resource or energy savings.

LCA has enabled much more accurate assessments. Comparing inputs to outputs at each stage of production to determine whether particular products or building components are more or less efficient than alternatives is important. However, choosing is not designing. Further, the "relative" resources saved are often less important than the public benefits relative to the resources consumed. Also, inert, easily enumerated substances, such as materials, pollution, and energy, are often separated from their effects on social sustainability. STARfish assists in visualizing how efficient usage may affect other issues, such as environmental justice, wealth disparities, local social needs and priorities, and so on.

LCA-based "design tools" are now emerging to fill the void created when rating tools marginalized EIAs to avoid dealing with the natural environment or complex socioecological systems in general. These nascent tools attempt to merge the gap between quantitative assessment and qualitative design. Although used in the early stages of design, most tend to be decision tools. That is, they use generic LCA data to simplify a designer's choices by providing information on the impacts of materials, based on quantities needed. Being based on standard products, these decision tools could undercut design. Some examples are discussed in the following section.

3.2 Problems with simplified LCA-based tools

LCA-based tools that use generic LCA data can often be misleading. For instance, one landscape rating tool provides the estimated carbon emissions of commercially available landscape products. However, it assumes that carbon emissions in transportation, construction, and end-of-life processes equal 30% of a project's operating emissions, which is hardly useful. Merely choosing the lowest-carbon "building blocks" currently on the market does not support design. Such a mechanical approach would not normally receive a passing grade in a landscape architecture studio class. STARfish discourages approaches that simply add up the carbon in "least bad" products and instead supports synergistic, adaptable, and multifunctional design.

LCA-based tools, being oversimplified, can have irregular outcomes. For instance, a so-called "climate-positive" tool gives credit for "megatons of CO_2 not released." This achievement is apparently gained by making improvements over a hypothetical development that the designer could have built instead. This is the "decoy effect." It is analogous to rating tools that award points for not breaking laws. In reality, the carbon emission and sequestration outcomes depend on design: a symphony of space, functions, and structures. There are many other socioecological factors to consider. STARfish aims to show how design can magnify and maximize benefits for nature and society.

LCA-based tools often conceal net impacts. For instance, a tool calls the conversion of "20% of existing concrete to crushed paving" climate positive. If an existing site has substantial concrete paving, it already increased the greenhouse effect, stormwater runoff, and land coverage. Crushing it increases permeability but generates new emissions, while 80% of the original harmful paving remains. Drilling drainage holes in the concrete and adding overhead shade or even "green scaffolding" would provide more positive functions relative to their impacts (Birkeland, 2020, Chapter 6). By exposing existing impacts, not just those caused during construction, STARfish reveals whole-system outcomes.

The above sections provided examples of how STARfish avoids the conceptual problems found in rating tools, LCA, and LCA-based tools. The following sections describe how STARfish does so, in part by making fundamental variations to the typical "radar" diagram (Fig. 16.2). First, it has a scale from −10 to +10, to enable the visualization and assessment of positive, not just less negative, impacts. Second, it adds Satellite diagrams to show cumulative and remote upstream-downstream impacts over the project lifecycle. After the advantages and disadvantages of radar diagrams are outlined, some of the unique aspects of STARfish diagrams are highlighted below.

3.3 Benefits of radar diagrams

Radar diagrams were used in "LCADesign," which was one of the first automated LCA software to read data from 3D computer-aided drafting "CAD" models. In most LCA tools, the impact factors are "normalized" or converted into the same numerical units so they can be easily summed. In radar diagrams, different elements, such as solids, liquids, or gases, keep their own conventional units. Only two conditions need to be known to create a scale. Such visual representations have an advantage over typical LCA processes because they indicate relationships

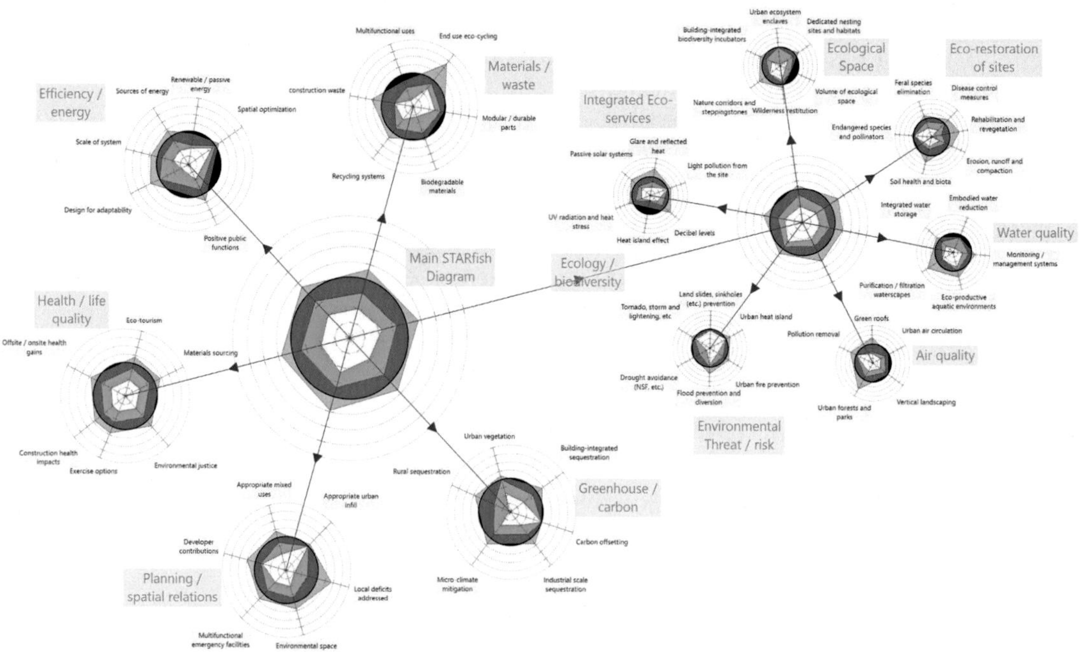

Figure 16.2 Typical radar diagram (scale from 0 to −1).

among impact factors. Thus, radar diagrams can highlight places needing design interventions.

Radar diagrams can avoid other problems caused by normalization. Converting everything to a common unit, such as energy, carbon, or money equivalents, facilitates arithmetic. However, sustainability involves incommensurable issues. Thus, for instance, as waste to landfill is commonly reported in units of weight or volume, local government recycling claims often fail to mention toxins. Similarly, as toxins are hard to measure because they have pervasive, unpredictable, or unknown systemic impacts, they have sometimes simply been left out of LCAs. Radar diagrams can provide a visual "gap analysis" without over-simplifying reality, omitting data, or reducing dissimilar phenomena to the same units.

Radar diagrams can help to avoid treating ecosystems or species as inert entities. Life is not a number, yet ecosystem services are still commonly converted to the costs of replacing natural services with mechanical systems (Heal, 2002). Monetary values can fluctuate wildly due to financial speculation and unforeseeable sociopolitical events. Further, unitization facilitates trade-offs between incongruent issues, such as biodiversity and energy. For instance, roads to accommodate more energy-efficient private cars will contaminate the land, air, and water, resulting in cascading biodiversity losses. Measuring everything in terms of energy can create tunnel vision, and reduce the value placed on nature.

3.4 Problems with radar diagrams

Radar diagrams reduce problems of normalization, unitization, and incommensurable values, but they also have limitations. The scales are usually from zero impact "0" to total damage "−1". This can only calculate the damage of component processes. Radar diagram do not count "beyond zero" or net benefits that can only be created by design. Drawing upon Positive Development, some have reversed the scale from "−1" to "0" but this still confuses reductions with gains. Some superimpose negative and positive impacts on the same radar diagram, including some alternative STARfish diagrams (Jones et al., 2020). This suffices for impact assessment but not design.

Radar diagrams, whether they show positive or negative impacts or both in an overlay, do not in themselves display cumulative or remote impacts over time or space. Therefore, they are not tailored for exploring basic planning alternatives, highlighting potential interventions in supply chains upstream, or suggesting opportunities to shape user behaviors and lifestyles downstream. A single diagram that does not distinguish regenerative from net-positive impacts, or does not go beyond zero, cannot envisage whole-system gains. STARfish satellite diagrams can expand in fractal patterns to expose opportunities for design synergies that create socioecological gains and positive spill-over effects over project lifecycles.

Radar diagrams, like STARfish, can include the social dimension, even if difficult to unitize and quantify, because scales with social and ethical benchmarks can be created. STARfish benchmarks incorporate whole-system concepts like "environmental space," or per capita share of resources, to capture social justice issues. In addition, losses of global life-support systems will continue to exacerbate poverty and wealth disparities unless we redesign cities. Escalating rates of population growth, consumption, urban development, and their systemic ramifications cannot be expressed in a single radar diagram. STARfish Satellites enable the interrelatedness of complex urban problems and solutions to be expressed and assessed.

4. Unique structure of STARfish

The above has shown that STARfish addresses basic problems with conventional radar diagrams as well as conceptual deficiencies common to most green building tools. If tools fail to inspire and incentivize whole-system benefits for nature and society, they cannot increase genuine sustainability. STARfish can provide a quantitative and qualitative picture of interrelated cumulative and remote impacts affecting or affected by a development proposal. This reveals opportunities for eco-positive design interventions that produce multiple, socioecological gains beyond project boundaries and throughout the lifecycle. That is, it is a "design tool" which approximates total impacts in real time while designers explore ideas.

Instructions and a video demonstration are provided on the website, and the app itself has pop-up explanations. Therefore, only some unique features of the STARfish app are discussed here. The core impact factors are represented as 'Legs' (radii). For a small project, a designer can begin with a Basic diagram (Fig. 16.3). More legs can be added later to accommodate more criteria. Satellite diagrams for clusters of related impacts can also be added. If transport, water, or air quality were critical issues, for example, Legs could be added to the Basic diagram, or some legs could grow satellite diagrams.

As each development has a unique context, a leg or satellite diagram pertaining to special geographic or cultural factors might be added, such as where a project affects an indigenous community. Any new benchmarks must follow basic principles that are discussed in Box 16.1. The rationale for new impact factors, weightings, and benchmarks is recorded, formatted, and printed

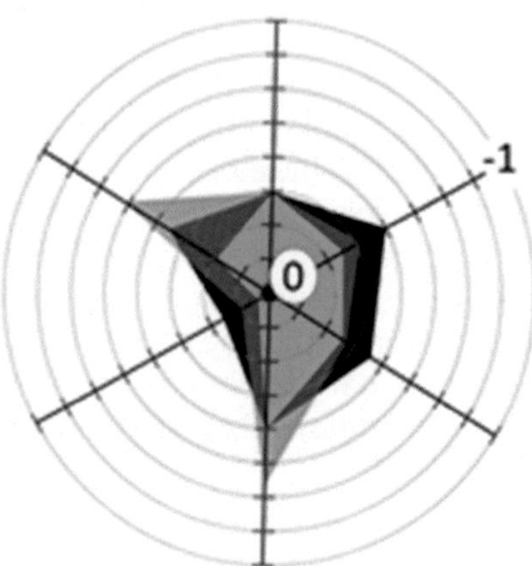

Figure 16.3 A Satellite STARfish (ZeroCircle version).

automatically in a STARfish Report. As mentioned earlier, this gives the users discretion, but it is totally transparent and can be challenged. Rating tools set universal rules regardless of the socioecological context and their obscure rationales rely on an appeal to authority.

The six Legs in the Basic diagram (Fig. 16.3) are impact categories commonly found in rating tools: Materials/waste, Ecology/biodiversity, Greenhouse/carbon, Planning/spatial relations, Health/life quality, and Efficiency/energy. This is to facilitate the exchange of information with other tools. The STARfish spreadsheet can be exported for any number of purposes. The diagram version in Fig. 16.3 is called a "ZeroCircle." A major difference between ordinary radar diagrams and STARfish is the bold circle in the middle of the diagram, which represents "net zero impact" as shown in Fig 16.3. The app provides a wide range of diagram types and aesthetic options to accommodate personal preferences or presentation purposes.

The black shape in the Basic diagram represents negative impacts, the green shape represents restorative/regenerative impacts, and the blue shape represents positive/net-positive impacts. If the outer point of a colored star/polygon shape meets the zero circle, that means the impact factor has no *net* impacts. Negative (black) impacts increase as the point moves from the zero circle along the Leg toward the center, which represents the worst possible case. Here, negative impacts never disappear so they cannot be hidden behind offsets. As restorative (green) actions only repair, revitalize, or regenerate, they start where the black point ends up and slide toward the zero circle.

Positive (blue) impacts begin from where restorative outcomes end up and move toward the outermost circle (+10): the best conceivable outcome. If a net-positive result in that impact factor is achieved, the blue shape extends outside the zero circle. Multifunctional and adaptable design improvements will reduce the black area and increase the white area inside and blue area outside the zero circle. An impossibly perfect design would be where ecological conditions compared to preindustrial times, and social conditions in the bioregion, are improved to the maximum extent possible. This hypothetical would appear as a blue polygon with a white center.

Fig. 16.4 shows a basic diagram with 'Satellites' attached to the Ecology/biodiversity Leg, shown to have six subcategories. This can be expanded into fractal satellites, virtually forever, so designers can explore and record ever more design improvements. For example, the water quality Leg in the Ecology/biodiversity satellite might have a satellite that examines means to improve the water quality and biota in nearby waterways. The tool defines negative, restorative/regenerative, and positive/net-positive benchmarks. These define real-world outcomes, rather than specifying well-known green design strategies. In this way, they can stimulate new design ideas for providing more socioecological benefits.

"Sliders" are used to estimate the various impacts (Fig. 16.5). As the red slider moves between "0" and "−10," benchmarks appear below it in red writing to help locate the slider along the scale. The green slider will go from that end point up to "0." Most rating tools stop at zero, or neutral. However, the blue positive/net-positive slider will go from that green point up to a theoretically possible "+10." To go beyond the zero circle, a combination of low-impact, multifunctional, adaptable design and net-positive offsetting would often be necessary. Examples are available (Birkeland, 2020, Chapters 5–6 and 13–14).

The summary or "Net Neg-Pos" diagram (Fig. 16.6) compares total good and bad outcomes. It happens to be shown here in a "pie diagram" format. However, a "bar diagram" may be preferrable to users or their clients. If the total impact in an impact category is negative, then a black pie slice appears. The larger the black pie slice, the worse the total impact. If the net impact is

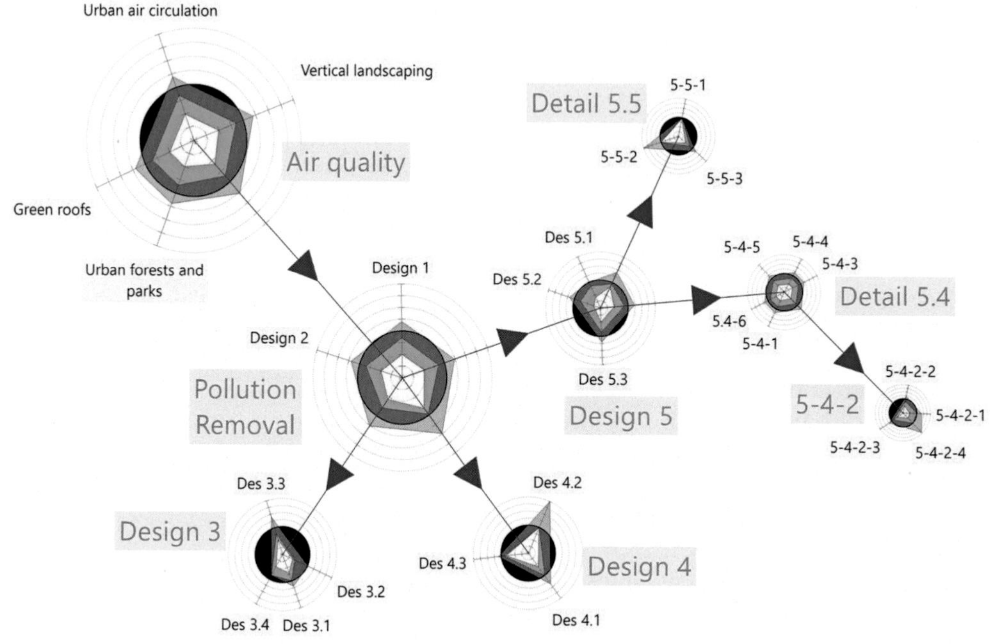

Figure 16.4 Satellite diagram.

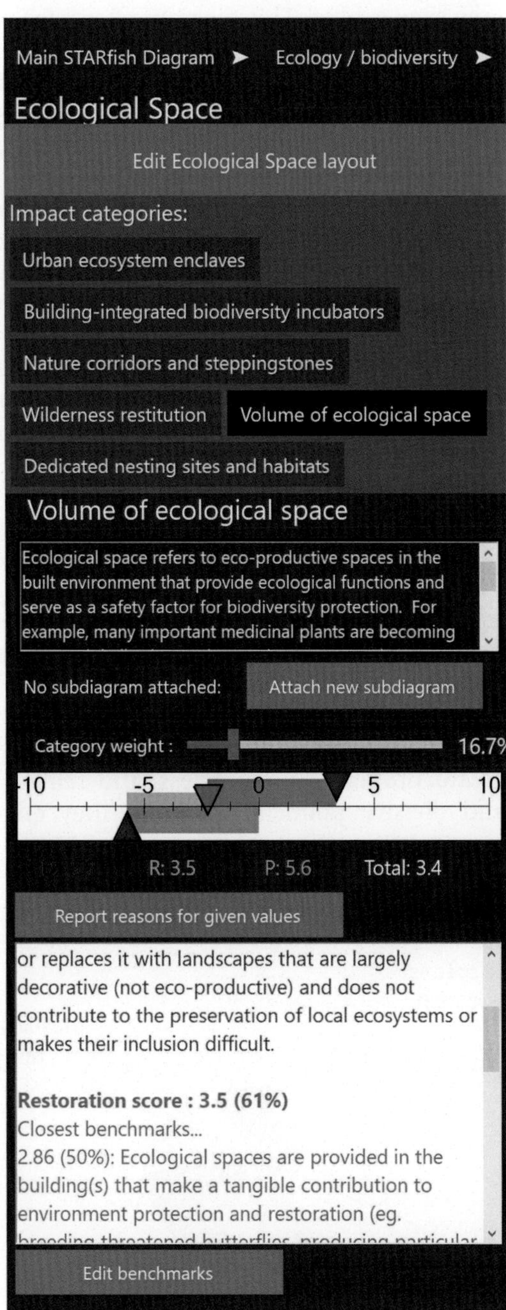

Figure 16.5 Sample slider.

positive, the pie slice is blue. This diagram allows for quick comparisons of design alternatives. Black areas indicate where to invest more attention to mitigation, efficiency measures, and positive design features.

The place for designers to insert new benchmark definitions appears under the sliders (Fig. 16.5). Box 16.1 is a "general" guide for adding benchmarks for new impact factors. This enables the flexibility to assess any site-specific problem or opportunity. Users can also eliminate criteria that are irrelevant to particular projects, as often found in prescriptive rating tools. Fundamental benchmarks cannot be changed by users. However, if a built-in benchmark is not relevant, the Slider can be left at zero. Exemplars of net-positive design concepts could be added as pop-ups. Designers would of course translate such examples into original site-specific applications.

5. Discussion and outlook

5.1 From choosing options to expanding options

There are many deeply rooted reasons for the belief that resource exploitation stimulates economic growth which, in turn, can solve the intractable systemic problems it causes, through the magical properties of competition, self-interest, markets, and private property. Nonetheless, the reified economic constructs and divisive political processes they engender are

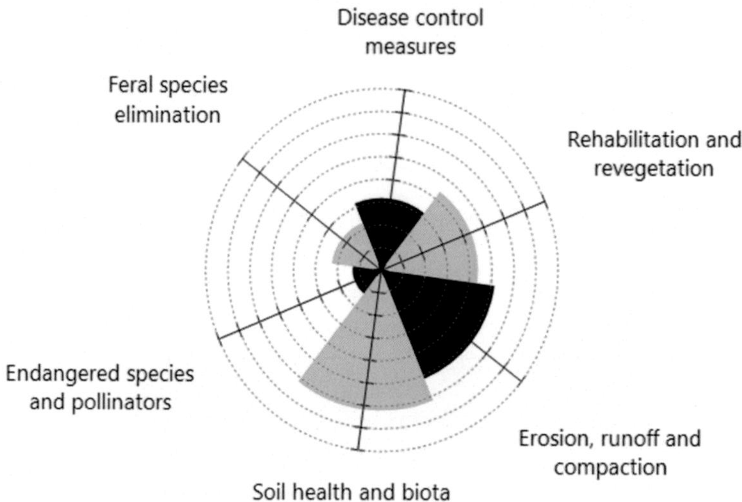

Figure 16.6 The summary (net Neg-pos) diagram.

destroying the life-support system. Although each land use allocation might leave remnants of land undeveloped, wilderness cannot survive endless partitioning. The fiasco of Australia's major river system illustrates this problem. The environment was treated as just another stakeholder among irrigators, industry, and farmers, for "balance," leading predictably to an ecological catastrophe (Kilvert, 2019).

Government decision frameworks have presumed that fair playing fields for using natural and human resources are created by "balancing conflicting demands." However, "interest balancing," via exchange and trade-off schemes, ignores the Earth's limits. This is reinforced by myopic decision theories, whose origins lay in military strategy. They are designed to optimize the relative position of particular groups, individuals or businesses, not everyone. As decision theories depict society as competitive and zero-sum, they are useful in "understanding" selfish behavior. They are less useful for imagining biophysical systems that reverse past design failures and increase overall public gains. This requires design thinking.

Even if these anachronistic decision systems could be altered to share dwindling resources equitably and maintain "sustainable yields" through regeneration and recycling practices, the ecological base would still decline. Nevertheless, many in the sustainability movement still hope that propagating enlightened values will somehow lead to fairer systems design. Sustainable design does not happen by itself, and policy choices do not change design paradigms and practices (Birkeland, 2014). Unlike markets, politics, and policy, design can avoid oppositional reactions. Moreover, it does not require changing consumer or voter demand first. However, design is, of course, also influenced by cultural constructs and institutions.

The cultural marginalization of design and subliminal association of planning with decision-making still impedes urban transformation. For instance, sustainable planning policies are seldom implemented because conventional infrastructure "decisions" precede design. Therefore, creating institutional and physical structures that foster eco-productive urban environments and symbiotic human—nature—society relationships requires the integration of quantitative, reductionist decision-making with qualitative, synergistic design. In Positive Development, design and decision-making are understood as complementary thinking skills. Both skills are combined in all tools: systems mapping analyses for regional planning issues, principles for eco-governance, design guidelines, and of course the STARfish for whole-system design and assessment.

5.2 Future prospects

STARfish and its parent philosophy, Positive Development, summarized earlier, were built upon a critique of the dominant physical and social construct in sustainable development. As they are disruptive, resistance is to be expected. With contemporary social media, however, congenital power-based obstacles can be surmounted. Some designers are already testing STARfish in their classes or own projects. A Brisbane project has committed to creating the first verifiably net-positive development; a researcher is investigating means to integrate economic accounting into the mix; another is applying net-positive concepts to eco-retrofitting. Satellites will be added to the STARfish diagram to increase its comprehensiveness.

STARfish could also be modified to assess global progress toward sustainability. For instance, the UN Sustainable Development Goals (SDGs) could be expressed as a STARfish diagram. However, this will require more sustainability-relevant and net-positive criteria and indicators. The current economics-based indicators that accompany the SDGs bear little relationship to sustainability. They were apparently compiled by statisticians. Most of the criteria and indicators implicitly call for economic growth without suggesting how the funding trade-offs could be decided. A table on the netpositivedesign.org website provides examples of alternative nature-based and ethics-based criteria that could replace or supplement these business-as-usual SDG indicators.

Time is of the essence. It took over 50 years for the now popular "circular" paradigm, or whole-system recycling, to take hold (Wolman, 1965). While essential, circular systems are no longer adequate. The cncept of net-positive design is only two decades old, and STARfish was only envisaged a decade ago. Several green building certification organizations have adopted some net-positive axioms, albeit not their substance, but they can adopt net-positive tools whenever they are ready. Meanwhile, younger generations are emerging. Educators, professionals, and students are welcome to request assistance in undertaking net-positive planning and design projects via the website or author.

References

Alexiou, K., Zamenopoulos, T., Johnson, J., Gilbert, S., 2009. Exploring the neurological basis of design cognition using brain imaging: some preliminary results. Design Studies 30 (6), 623–647. https://doi.org/10.1016/j.destud.2009.05.002.

Birkeland, J., 2003. Beyond zero waste. In: Societies for a Sustainable Future, Third UKM-UC International Conference. April 14–15. Canberra, UKM-UC conference Proceedings. In: https://researchprofiles.canberra.edu.au/en/publications/conference-proceedings-ukm-uc-third-international-conference-soci.

Birkeland, J., 2005. Design for Ecosystem Services: A New Paradigm for Eco-Design. SB05 Tokyo Action for Sustainability, The World Sustainable Building Conference, Tokyo, 27–29 Sept. http://www.sb05.com/.

Birkeland, J., 2007. Positive development: designing for net-positive impacts. In: BEDP Environmental Design Guide of the Australian Institute of Architects. ACT, Canberra. http://www.environmentdesignguide.com.au/.

Birkeland, J., 2008. Positive Development: From Vicious Circles to Virtuous Cycles through Built Environment Design. Earthscan, London, 978-1844075799.

Birkeland, J., 2009. Design for eco-services and design for environmental services. BEDP Environmental Design Guide of the Australian Institute of Architects. ACT, Canberra. http://www.environmentdesnguide.com.au/.

Birkeland, J., 2012. Design blindness in sustainable development: from closed to open systems design thinking. Journal of Urban Design 17 (2), 163–187. https://doi.org/10.1080/13574809.2012.666209.

Birkeland, J., 2014. Systems and social change for sustainable and resilient cities. In: Pearson, L., Newton, P., Roberts, P. (Eds.), Resilient Sustainable Cities. Routledge, London, pp. 66–82.

Birkeland, J., 2016. Net positive biophilic urbanism. Smart and Sustainable Built Environment 5 (1), 9–14. https://doi.org/10.1108/SASBE-10-2015-0034.

Birkeland, J., 2018. Challenging policy barriers in sustainable development. In: Dymitrow, M., Halfacree, K. (Eds.), Bulletin of Geography, Socio-Economic Series 40. Nicolaus Copernicus University, Toruń, pp. 41–56. https://doi.org/10.1080/01944366508978187.

Birkeland, J., 2019. Detailed Operating Instructions Are on the Website and App Itself. http://netpositivedesign.org.

Birkeland, J., 2020. Net-positive Design and Sustainable Urban Development. Routledge, London. https://doi.org/10.4324/9780429290213, 978-0429290213.

Birkeland, J., Knight-Lenihan, S., 2016. Biodiversity offsetting and net positive design. Journal of Urban Design 21 (1), 50–66. https://doi.org/10.1080/13574809.2015.1129891.

Commoner, B., 1971. The Closing Circle. Alfred A. Knopf, NY. -13: 978-0394423500 ISBN-10: 039442350X.

Habitat III, 2016. The New Urban Agenda. Adopted at the Habitat III Conference, Quito, Ecuador, United Nations, 20 October 2016. http://habitat3.org/the-new-urban-agenda/.

Heal, G.M., 2002. Nature and the Marketplace: Capturing the Value of Ecosystem Services. Island Press, Washington DC. -13: 978-1559637961, ISBN-10: 155963796X.

Huynh, T., Jones, M., 2018. Scientists Create New Building Material Out of Fungus, Rice and Glass. The Conversation. June 20. https://theconversation.com/scientists-createnew-building-material-out-of-fungus-rice-and-glass-98153.

Jones, D., Ashar, S., Vlieg, M., Baggs, D., 2020. Counting gains to beyond zero-impact futures. WIT Transactions on Ecology and the Environment 245, 97–108. Wessex, UK, WIT. https://www.witpress.com/elibrary/wit-transactions-on-ecology-and-the-environment/245/37596.

Kilvert, N., 2019. Drought, Climate Change and Mismanagement: What Experts Think Caused the Death of a Million Menindee Fish. ABC News. https://

www.abc.net.au/news/science/2019-01-16/what-caused-menindee-fish-kill-drought-water-mismanagement/10716080#.

Kothari, A., Salleh, A., Escobar, A., Demaria, F., Acosta, A. (Eds.), 2019. Pluriverse: A Post-development Dictionary. Tulika Books and Authorsupfront, Delhi and Chicago. -10: 8193732987 ISBN-13: 978-8193732984.

Lyle, J.T., 1994. Regenerative Design for Sustainable Development. John Wiley, NY. -10: 0471178438 ISBN-13: 978-0471178439.

Newsham, G.R., Mancini, S., Birt, B.J., 2009. Do LEED-certified buildings save energy? Yes, but .... Energy and Buildings 41 (8), 897–905. https://doi.org/10.1016/j.enbuild.2009.03.014.

Papanek, V., 1971. Design for the Real World: Human Ecology and Social Change. Pantheon Books, NY, 0394470362.

Renger, C., Birkeland, J., Midmore, D., 2015. Net positive building carbon sequestration. Building Research and Information 43 (1), 11–24. https://doi.org/10.1080/09613218.2015.96100.

Schumacher, E.F., 1973. Small is Beautiful: Economics as if People Mattered. Blond & Briggs, London. SBN 060803525.

Scofield, J.H., 2009. Do LEED-certified buildings save energy? Not really .... Energy and Buildings 41 (12), 1386–1390. https://doi.org/10.1016/j.enbuild.2009.08.006.

SDGs, 2018. Sustainable Development Goals. United Nations Department of Economic and Social Affairs. https://sdgs.un.org/.

Vale, B., Vale, R., 1975. The Autonomous House: Design and Planning for Self-Sufficiency. Thames and Hudson, London. ISBN0500930015 ISBN13: 978-0500930014.

Van der Ryn, S., Cowan, S., 1996. Ecological Design. Island Press, Washington, DC, 1559633891, 978-1559633895.

Wann, D., 1996. Deep Design: Pathways to a Livable Future. Island Press. ASIN: B0073NL32Q, Washington, DC.

Wolman, A., 1965. The metabolism of cities. Scientific American 213 (3), 178–193. https://www.scientificamerican.com/article/the-metabolism-of-cities/.

17

Strategies to improve energy efficiency in residential buildings in Ambon, Indonesia

Dieter D. Genske[1] and Abdelrahman M.H. Ammar[2]

[1] *Nordhausen University of Applied Sciences, Nordhausen, Germany;*
[2] *DSK GmbH Zentrale Wiesbaden, Wiesbaden, Germany*

1. Introduction

Carbon dioxide (CO_2) emissions from the world's 20 largest economies (so-called G20 countries), including Indonesia, are increasing. According to Climate Transparency (2019a), G20 emissions in the building sector grew faster than any other in 2018 (+4.1%), although average emissions have stabilized over the past decade. To meet the Paris Agreement climate targets (the so-called 1.5°C target), G20 countries must reduce their CO_2 emissions to at least 45% below 2010 levels by 2030 and achieve net-zero emissions by 2070.

The aim of this project is using urban planning tools to improve energy efficiency in residential buildings on Ambon and to demonstrate that Indonesia could achieve the respective climate targets of the Paris Agreement by 2030/2070. Therefore, this report is structured as follows: First, the conditions of Ambon Island such as climate, geography, and population are introduced. This is followed by a classification of the residential area and buildings on Ambon into prototypes and the estimation of energy flow within the different residential prototypes. In the second step, energy efficiency measures are proposed and their impact on energy demand and CO_2 emissions is studied. Then, two future scenarios for the residential energy situation on Ambon are developed and visualized as maps, one based on the freezing of the current energy situation (business-as-usual scenario) and the other based on the implementation of the energy efficiency measures (innovative scenario). The comparison of these scenarios is intended to illustrate the importance of taking effective measures to improve energy efficiency in the residential sector of Ambon.

Intelligent Environments. https://doi.org/10.1016/B978-0-12-820247-0.00019-9

The project is embedded in a larger project investigating energy self-sufficiency of the Maluku archipelago, which consists of thousands of islands. There are no power lines to these islands, and fuel delivery must also be minimized for cost reasons. So island solutions have to be found. These facts make the project area ideal to prove that island solutions to achieve energy autonomy are feasible, based on existing technologies and considering a limited budget. If energy self-sufficiency works in this environment, it should work in many places on the planet.

A key component in ensuring energy self-sufficiency is increasing the efficiency of energy use. In the project area, this primarily concerns the use of fuels, electricity, and biomass.

2. Methodology

In this report, the energy efficiency in the residential buildings on Ambon Island is studied. For this purpose, data from literature, statistical analysis, interviews, and surveys are used; also energy simulation software (DesignBuilder), geographic information system (QGIS), and planning tools (STAR model) are used. More details on the STAR model can be found in (Droege et al., 2018) and also online (www.starem.org).

On the one hand, this report is based on a quantitative approach, mainly on a review of literature dealing with STAR model. Such a literature review provides the method of employing the urban planning tool to improve energy efficiency. Also, the quantitative approach includes a review of literature dealing with energy consumption in a hot and humid climate such as Enteria et al. (2020) and Kubota et al. (2018), which provide a comprehensive overview of the factors that influence the energy situation in a region, such as a climate, history, architecture, and politics. In addition, the quantitative approach relies on the statistical analysis of climate, energy, and population data on Ambon from BPS-Statistics of Maluku Province (2020) and the Maluku government.

This report also follows a qualitative approach by conducting interviews and surveys about the energy situation on Ambon, which were conducted with Indonesian experts in Indonesian by Giovanni Pradipta and translated into English. In addition, the weekly meeting of experts and students at the University of Applied Sciences Nordhausen, who participate in the Project (Energy Atlas for Maluku archipelago), is a main pillar of the qualitative approach of this work. More details on Energy Atlas for Maluku archipelago can be found in Genske and Pradipta (2022).

3. Results

3.1 Geography, population, and climate of Ambon Island

The Maluku archipelago is composed of about 1000 islands. Ambon Island has the highest population and as well as the highest energy consumption in the archipelago. It covers a total area of 761 km^2, of which about 41% (or 310 km^2) is currently designated as Ambon City. In 2019, the population of Ambon City reached 478,616 (representing 77% of the total population of Ambon Island). The annual population growth rate is in the order of 4%. Considering the rural areas of Ambon Island, which are administratively part of Maluku-Tengah, the total population reached 621,085 in 2019. This accounts for about 34.4% of the population of Maluku Province (BPS-Statistics of Maluku Province, 2020; Miller, 1999). Fig. 17.1 shows a map of Ambon Island.

According to the Köppen climate classification, the island of Ambon is in a tropical climate zone. Since it is located close to the equator, the climate is hot and humid throughout the year. The tropical climate offers average air temperatures between 24 and 27°C, a low diurnal range and high relative humidity, and a lot of precipitation, especially during the monsoon season (Enteria et al., 2020).

3.2 Residential area prototypes and building types on Ambon

The residential area on Ambon Island was categorized into Spatial Urban Prototypes (SUPs) (Table 17.1 and Fig. 17.5). The basic idea of prototyping spatial units (urban as well as suburban and rural) goes back to the work of Everding (2007) and Everding et al. (2019). These prototypes have comparable spatial energy characteristics. They have a comparable energy demand per area, but also a comparable aptitude to produce renewable energy (for example, with photovoltaics, solar collectors, heat pumps, etc.). The concept has already been applied in some project areas, for example, in the Canton of Basel-Stadt (Switzerland) (Genske, 2013; Berger et al., 2011), in Hamburg (Germany) (Genske et al., 2010), or in the Lake Constance Region (Germany, Switzerland, Austria, and the Principality of Liechtenstein) (Droege et al., 2018). Based on this prototyping, planning maps for current and future energy demand can be developed, as well as planning maps for renewable energy production.

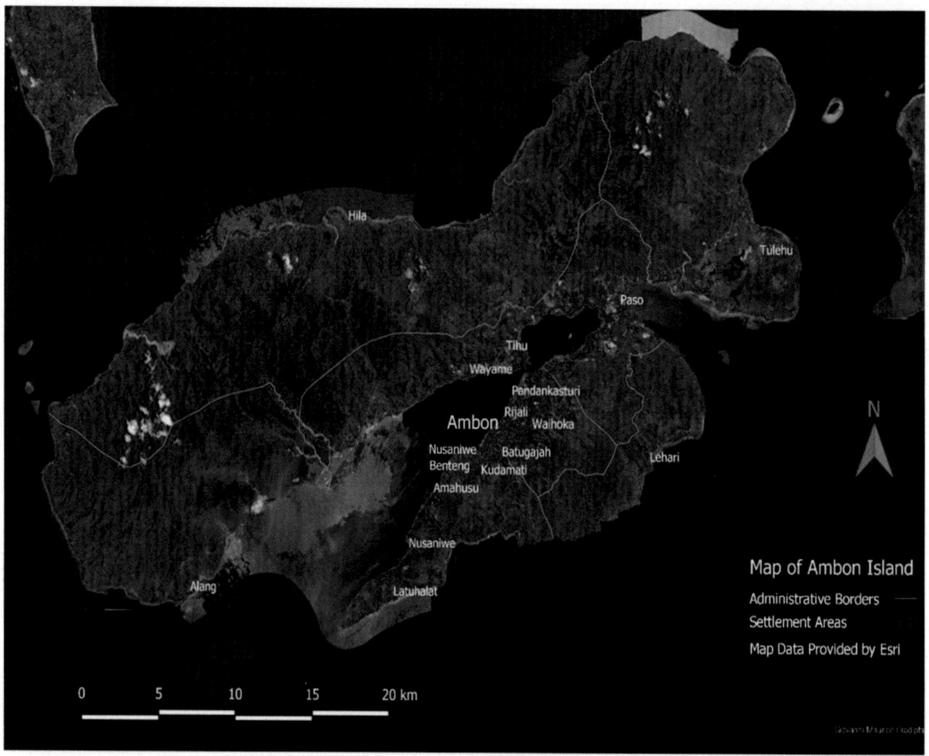

Figure 17.1 Map of Ambon Island showing the administrative division of the island and the places of residential settlements (map data provided by ESRI, www.esri.com).

Table 17.1 Residential prototypes on the island of Ambon and its main characteristics.

SUP	General definition	Location	Income level	Type of construction	Area proportions (from GIS data)
1	Rural, outside the city	Island borders, or in the woods	Low	Traditional	12%
2	Rural, connected to the city	City borders	Low to middle	A mixture between traditional the modern	28%
3	Urban, modern, and highly developed	Inside the city, far away from the city center	High	Modern	4%
4	Urban, middle	Inside the city, close to the city center	Middle to high	Modern	35%
5	Urban, mix-use (residential and commercial)	In the city center	Middle	Modern	9%
Shanty	Informal settlements	Inside the city	Low	Undefined, random build	12%

The categorization of urban prototypes on Ambon was based on an analysis of satellite imagery, data from maps and interviews, as well as observations on site. In addition, the historical development, the prediction of the income level, and the construction type of the buildings and their surroundings were taken into consideration.

In addition to the residential prototypes, the building styles on Ambon were also categorized, depending on their energy sources and construction details. This allows for greater accuracy in estimating energy demand and CO_2 emissions from the residential sector (Table 17.2).

3.3 Residential energy consumption and CO_2 emissions on Ambon, 2019

Residential electricity consumption on Ambon was estimated by projecting electrical systems and appliances in each building category, based on analysis of survey data and interview data conducted on Ambon for the Maluku Archipelago Energy Atlas. In contrast, household fuel consumption was estimated by identifying the main fuel type for each household category, based on data from BPS-Statistics of Maluku Province (2020).

Residential buildings in rural areas (RLC.1, RLC.2a, and RLC.2b), as well as informal settlements, record low electricity consumption because air conditioning is not used. The average electricity consumption of these houses was estimated to range from 83 to 215 kWh/month, distributed among lighting, entertainment, and ceiling fans. In contrast, the electricity consumption of the urban residential buildings (ULC.3, ULC.4a, ULC.4b, and ULC.5) is much higher, with a consumption rate between 168 and 568 kWh/month. More than 20% of this consumption comes from air conditioners, with the rest distributed between lighting and entertainment.

On Ambon, either kerosene or biomass is mostly used for cooking. In general, rural households still rely on the latter because they can collect it for free in the surrounding area. The situation in the city is changing; due to the lack of biomass and economic growth, households are increasingly relying on kerosene, with a small percentage (1%) consuming liquefied petroleum gas (LPG). In residential buildings that still rely on biomass fuels for cooking (RLC.1, RLC.2a, RLC.2b, and 30% of Shanty), the fuel is burned in a traditional way with low efficiency, resulting in a large consumption of biomass to obtain the actual energy needed for cooking. The biomass consumption

Table 17.2 Residential buildings on the Island of Ambon and its main characteristics.

Building	Spatial urban prototype (SUP)	Proportions %	Area (m^2)	Main building materials	Roof	Air conditioning	Cooking fuel
RLC.1[a]	1	12	100	Wood	Wood pitched roof with wood structure	No	Woodfuel
RLC.2a	2	20	100	Brick and concrete	Zinc pitched roof with wood structure	No	Woodfuel
RLC.2b	2	8	120	Brick and concrete	Brick pitched roof with wood structure	No	Woodfuel
ULC.3[b]	3	4	85	Concrete block	Brick pitched roof with aluminum structure	Yes	Kerosene and liquefied petroleum gas
ULC.4a	4	25	85	Brick and concrete	Brick pitched roof with wood structure	No	Kerosene
ULC.4b	4	10	100	Concrete block	Brick pitched roof with wood structure	Yes	Kerosene
ULC.5	5	9	200	Brick and concrete	Brick pitched roof with wood structure	Yes	Kerosene
Shanty	Shanty	12	50	Undefined, old used materials	Undefined	No	Woodfuel and kerosene

[a]Rural living construction.
[b]Urban living construction.

of these households is estimated according to Floor and van der Plas (1992) at 7.48 kg/day, which is equivalent to 997 kW/month. In contrast, the energy consumption of urban households using kerosene (ULC.4a and ULC.4b, 70% of ULC.3, and 70% of Shanty households) is estimated at 491 kWh/month. LPG fuel has the highest combustion efficiency, with LPG consumption per household estimated at 118 kWh/month.

The burning of fossil fuels to produce energy involves emissions of greenhouse gases such as CO_2, methane, and nitrous oxide. These emissions contribute to an imbalance of atmospheric gases, leading to global warming and climate change. In this work, direct CO_2 emissions are estimated, since they account for the largest share of emissions resulting from energy consumption. In addition, focusing on direct emissions allows for easy comparison of the model region with other regions in the world. CO_2 emissions from biomass combustion are also not considered, as they have no impact on the overall greenhouse gas balance in the atmosphere.

Electricity in Indonesia is generated from various energy sources, many of which are fossil. According to Climate Transparency (2019b), 61% of electricity in Indonesia in 2018 was generated from coal, 22% from gas, and 5% from oil. Therefore, direct CO_2 emissions can be estimated at 761 g CO_2/kWh of electricity. The CO_2 emission factor for LPG and kerosene is 227 g CO_2/kWh and 259 g CO_2/kWh, respectively (Darío and John, 2006).

To estimate the total energy consumption and CO_2 emissions of the residential sector on Ambon, the energy consumption per hectare for each SUP was calculated based on the estimates of energy consumption for each building category. The total electricity consumption of the residential sector for 2019 was thus estimated at about 222 GWh and fuel consumption at about 744 GWh, distributed among the residential prototypes. This consumption leads to about 255,000 tons of CO_2 emissions (Table 17.3).

Table 17.3 Total annual electricity and fuel consumption and CO_2 emissions on Ambon from the residential prototypes, 2019 (numbers are rounded for better reading).

		Electricity consumption		Fuel consumption		CO_2 emissions	
Spatial urban prototype (SUP)	**Area from GIS (ha)**	**MWh/ ha.a**	**Total (MWh/a)**	**MWh/ ha.a**	**Total (MWh/a)**	**t CO_2/ ha.a**	**Total (t CO_2/a)**
1	99	100	9861	1196	118,341	76	7506
2	223	182	40,658	1137	253,361	139	30,943
3	35	829	29,291	561	19,833	764	27,001
4	286	303	86,682	662	189,326	402	114,989
5	74	476	35,394	295	21,905	439	32,642
Shanty	92	227	20,952	1542	142,059	452	41,667

3.4 Energy efficiency measures in the residential buildings

Annual fuel consumption by the residential sector on Ambon accounted for about 23% of total fuel consumption in all sectors in 2019, while electricity consumption by the residential sector accounted for about 64% of total electricity consumption (Genske and Pradipta, 2022). Therefore, energy efficiency measures should be taken in the residential sector on Ambon to reduce consumption and rely on renewable energy sources. In this section, nine residential energy efficiency measures depending on energy consumption profile are proposed. Measures 1–3 are about energy efficiency of cooking fuels. They aim at switching to clean energy sources as well as reducing demand. Measures 4–7, on the other hand, are aimed at reducing electricity demand in residential buildings that use air conditioning, which is the case in urban areas. They focus on reducing cooling energy demand by improving the thermal performance of buildings. In addition, measures 8 and 9 provide renewable energy solutions (Tables 17.4 and 17.5).

Three urban residential prototypes (ULC.3, ULC.4b, and ULC.5) that use air conditioning for cooling are thermally simulated using DesignBuilder to investigate the impact of energy efficiency measures 4–7 on their thermal performance and thus on energy demand. DesignBuilder requires hourly data on the environmental conditions (i.e., temperature, humidity, wind speed, and solar radiation) at the building site. The site template (Ambon/Pattimura) was selected for all buildings. Next, DesignBuilder determined the climate template 'AUS_DARWIN_IWEC' of the city of Darwin in Australia for the Ambon/Pattimura site because weather data for Ambon was missing from the ASHRAE Weather data and the two cities have similar climatic conditions.

Table 17.4 Cooling energy required (kWh/month) in residential buildings (according to DesignBuilder simulation).

Building	Reference	With fourth measure	With fifth measure	With sixth measure	With seventh measure
ULC.3	481	400	307	372	476
ULC.4b	464	356	293	321	441
ULC.5	1274	1121	Not implementable	1003	1223

Table 17.5 Energy efficiency measures for the residential sector on Ambon.

Measure	Type of measure	Energy efficiency and environmental effectiveness	Impact determination method	Implementation in Spatial Urban Prototype (SUP)	Implementation	
					Start	Finish
1. Replacing traditional fuelwood with stove Save80	Temporary	• 80% reduction of fuelwood demand • Reduction of indoor air pollution • Protecting forests from unsustainable logging	After (Oliver Adria, 2014)	1 and 2	2020	2025
2. Conversion from kerosene to LPG	Temporary	• 18% reduction of CO_2 emissions factor of fuel • 76% reduction of energy needed for cooking	After (Thoday et al., 2018)	3, 4, and 5	2020	2030
3. Partial use of solar cookers	Temporary	30%–40% reduction of kerosene or LPG demand and their emissions	After (Oliver Adria, 2014)	3, 4 and 5	2020	2030
4. avoiding direct solar radiation inside building	Permanent	12%–23% reduction of cooling demand	Thermal simulation (see Table 17.4)	3, 4, and 5	2020	2040
5. Roof renovation of urban residential buildings	Permanent	37% reduction of cooling demand	Thermal simulation	3 and 4	2020	2040
6. Separate indoor spaces and cool specific zones	Permanent	21%–31% reduction of cooling demand	Thermal simulation	3, 4, and 5	2020	2025
7. LED lighting and efficient electrical appliances	Permanent	• 32%–53% reduction of lighting demand • 2%–5% reduction of cooling demand	Thermal simulation	All prototypes	2020	2025

Continued

Table 17.5 Energy efficiency measures for the residential sector on Ambon.—*continued*

Measure	Type of measure	Energy efficiency and environmental effectiveness	Impact determination method	Implementation in Spatial Urban Prototype (SUP)	Implementation	
					Start	Finish
8. Biogas for cooking	Permanent	Solid biomass waste recycling	After (Genske and Pradipta, 2022)	1 and 2	2030	2070
9. Photovoltaics on the roofs of residential buildings	permanent	100% reduction of CO_2 emissions from electricity	After (Patil, 2021)	All prototypes	2025	2050

Two-dimensional plans were drawn for the three residential building types. The building materials for the various building components that affect the thermal performance of the building have been defined, namely the glazing, ceiling, exterior and interior walls, and floor. Then, the buildings were simulated in the reference case (without measures) and in the case with measures for the month of March, as this is one of the warmest months on Ambon (Table 17.5).

3.5 Future energy situation scenarios of the residential sector on Ambon

According to the STAR model, it is possible to create scenarios for the energy situation by specifying certain factors and to visualize them with the GIS. In this way, the energy efficiency measures that are most suitable for achieving certain climate goals can be considered. The scenarios are not predictions, but projections into the future based on societal trends and guided by policy decisions (Droege et al., 2018).

In the following, two scenarios for future residential energy flows through 2100 are considered. The first scenario (business-as-usual scenario) is based on the principle of freezing the current state of energy policy but considering population and economic growth. Meanwhile, the second scenario (innovative scenario) assumes the introduction of energy efficiency measures into energy policy to achieve specific climate targets.

3.5.1 Population and residential area growth

Ambon Island population in 2019 was estimated to be around 621,085. Of these, 498,191 people live urban areas and about 122,894 in rural areas. The annual population growth rate in the latter was estimated at about 0.3% and in urban areas (Ambon City) at about 4% (BPS-Statistics of Maluku Province, 2020). Population growth in Ambon City has changed dramatically over the last 7 decades. According to United Nations, Department of Economic and Social Affairs, Population Division (2019), since 1950 until now, the population growth rate in Ambon City has been decreasing. It will decrease to 1.67% by the end of 2030 and to 1.40% by 2037. The development of rural areas on Ambon is also declining. According to BPS data, the population growth rate in rural areas was about 0.41% in 2010 and about 0.31% in 2019 (BPS-Statistics of Maluku Province, 2020). Therefore, and considering continued economic growth in the coming years, the population is growing while at the same time the growth rate is expected to decline steadily until the year 2100 (Table 17.6).

Population growth also means an increase in residential area, and since the relationship between residential area and population is a direct relationship, the growth rate of residential area was based on the expected population growth rate. In 2019, the ratio of residential area to population in rural areas was about 0.00262 ha/person, while the ratio in urban areas was

Table 17.6 Projections of population growth on Ambon every 10 years.

	Ambon city			Rural on Ambon island		
	Population projections	Annual population growth rate (%)	Population growth rate in 10 years (%)	Population projections	Annual population growth rate (%)	Population growth rate in 10 years (%)
2020–30	627,721	2.88	26	117,015	0.25	2.25
2030–40	715,602	1.54	14	118,595	0.15	1.35
2040–50	801,474	1.30	12	119,662	0.10	0.9
2050–60	881,622	1.15	10	120,739	0.10	0.9
2060–70	960,968	1.05	9	121,826	0.10	0.9
2070–80	1,037,845	0.90	8	122,922	0.10	0.9
2080–90	1,110,494	0.75	7	124,029	0.10	0.9
2090–2100	1,177,124	0.65	6	125,145	0.10	0.9

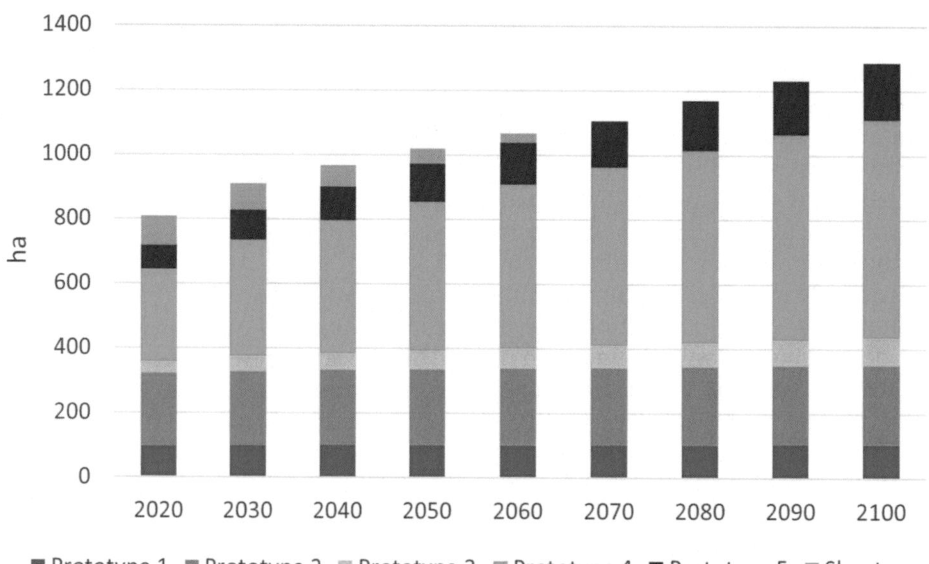

Figure 17.2 Projections of the growth of residential area on Ambon by urban prototypes.

0.00098 ha/person. Multiplying this ratio by population, the residential area can be estimated for the coming years. The only exception are informal settlements. This is a problem that many developing countries face and would like to solve. Economic and social growth in the coming years is expected to cause slum dwellers to move into domestic areas (in our case the fourth model housing prototype) and reduce the area of Ambon informal settlements until they disappear in 2070 (Fig. 17.2).

3.5.2 Business-as-usual scenario

The business-as-usual scenario assumes freezing the current energy situation and policies. However, one of the energy policies that have entered the implementation phase is expected to change the residential energy flows on Ambon by 2030. The Indonesian government's conversion program from kerosene to LPG in 2007 is considered one of the key energy policies for fuels in the country, and this program is expected to affect the energy situation on Ambon in the coming years, as its implementation phases in Maluku province only began after 2016 (Thoday et al., 2018). By analyzing the results of this program in the western regions of Indonesia such as Java and Jakarta between 2007 and 2015 and assuming that the phases of the program on Ambon will take place at the same tempo, it is estimated that 90% of households on Ambon that consume kerosene will switch to

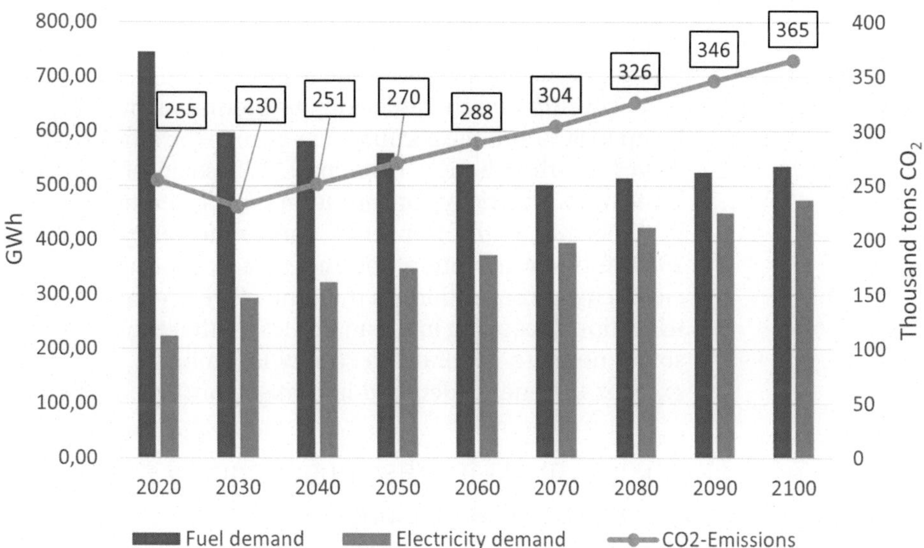

Figure 17.3 Projections of electricity consumption, fuel consumption, and CO_2 emissions from the residential sector on Ambon until 2100 according to the business-as-usual scenario.

LPG by the end of 2030. Therefore, it is assumed that in 2030, 45% of households will use biomass as their main fuel, 50% will use LPG, and 5% will use kerosene. Therefore, fuel consumption is expected to decrease significantly between 2020 and 2030 due to the impact of the kerosene-to-LPG program. Even after 2030, further decrease is predicted due to shrinking informal settlements that consume a lot of energy while burning wood. On the contrary, electricity consumption is expected to increase dramatically in the coming years due to population, economic, and social growth (Fig. 17.3, Figs. 17.6–17.8).

3.5.3 Innovative Scenario

In the innovative scenario is assumed that the energy efficiency measures and renewable energy technologies proposed in Chapter 4.4 will be implemented in residential prototypes on Ambon in the coming years to meet the climate targets for the years 2030 and 2070. To extend the innovative scenario up to 2100, the energy consumption as well as the CO_2 emissions in the residential sector was estimated for the coming decades. The energy efficiency measures reduce energy consumption and thus CO_2 emissions. Direct CO_2 emissions resulting from residential energy consumption were estimated within the innovative scenario. They are expected to decrease by approximately 40% by 2030 compared to 2020, and the residential sector on Ambon is expected to be emission free by 2070. The significant reduction in fuel consumption and emissions between 2020 and 2030 is mainly due to the first and second measures (Table 17.5). The first measure will improve the efficiency of biomass stoves in rural areas by up to 80% and the second will improve the efficiency of cooking stoves in urban houses by using LPG instead of kerosene. At the same time, electricity consumption is expected to increase slightly by 2050 due to the impact of energy efficiency measures. After 2050, fuel consumption continues to decline at the expense of electricity consumption, as the innovative scenario assumes electrification of cooking in urban homes. At that time, the potential of solar energy to generate electricity in Ambon's residential sector exceeds the energy demand in that sector (Figs. 17.4–17.8).

3.6 GIS maps for residential energy demand and their CO_2 emissions

The current energy situation on Ambon and future scenarios for it are visualized as maps using QGIS. Fig. 17.6 shows the current and future electricity consumption map. In the innovation scenario, electricity consumption per hectare is expected to increase by 2070, due to the electrification of cooking in urban households. In contrast, in the business-as-usual scenario, electricity consumption per hectare is expected to remain unchanged or increase slightly (Fig. 17.5).

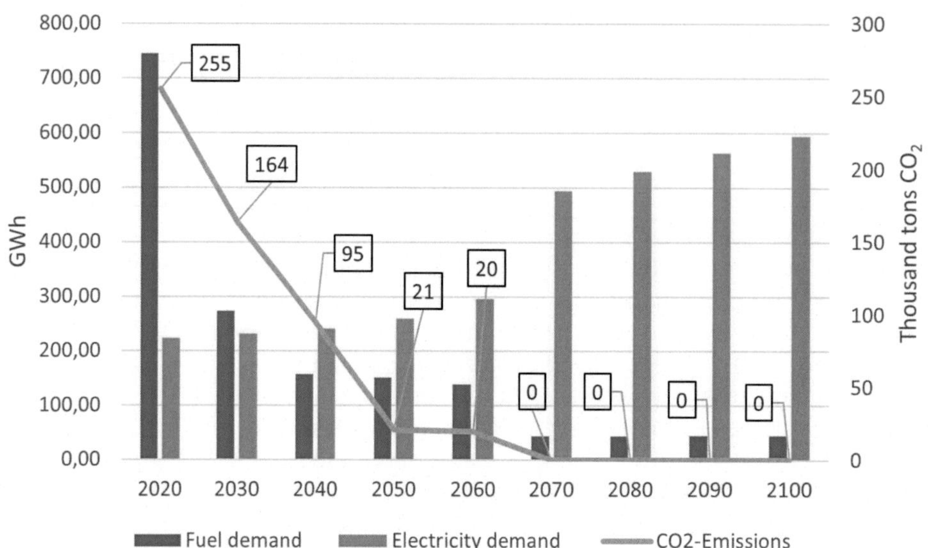

Figure 17.4 Projections of electricity consumption, fuel consumption, and CO_2 emissions from the residential sector on Ambon until 2100 according to the innovative scenario.

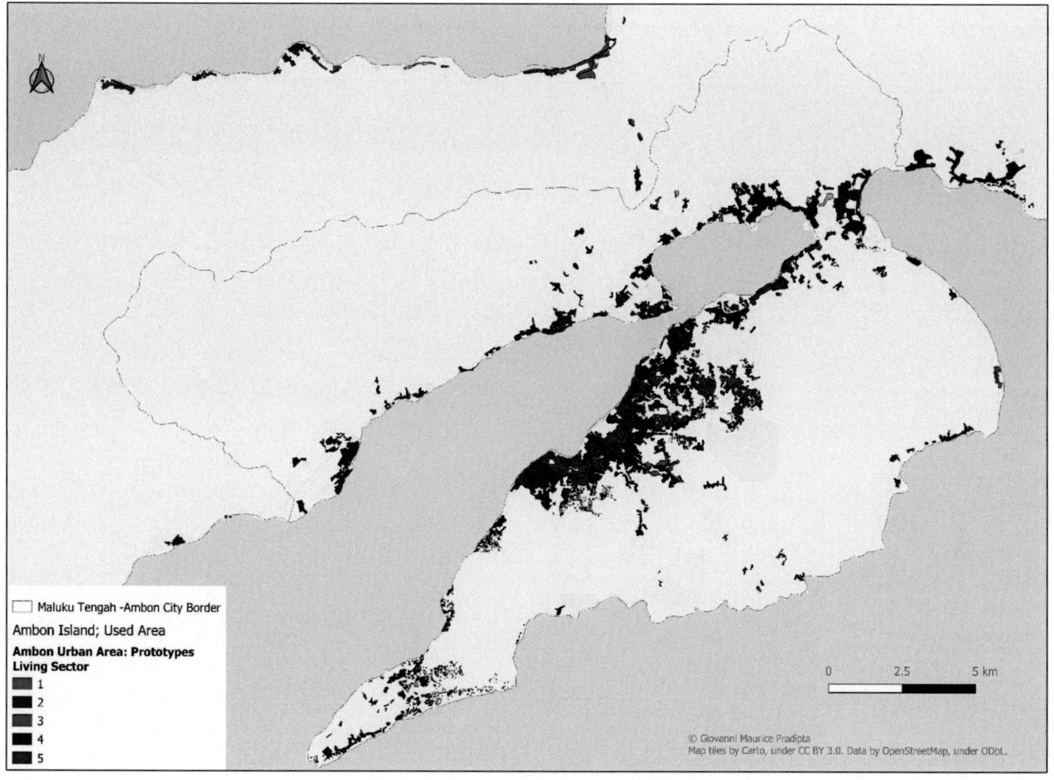

Figure 17.5 Map of residential prototyping.

Fig. 17.7 shows the current and future fuel consumption map. In contrast to electricity consumption, fuel consumption per hectare on Ambon is expected to decrease in both future scenarios, mainly due to electrification of cooking and the Indonesian government's program to switch from kerosene to LPG.

In the innovation scenario, energy efficiency measures lead to a reduction in CO_2 emissions from the residential sector until they are zero in 2070. In the business-as-usual scenario, emissions per hectare in urban areas are expected to decrease until 2030 due to kerosene to LPG program and then stop decreasing (Fig. 17.8).

4. Discussion

This chapter presented steps to improve energy efficiency in the residential sector on Ambon to reduce CO_2 emissions from this sector and achieve the goals of the Paris Climate Agreement using the STAR model. Therefore, the energy consumption profile

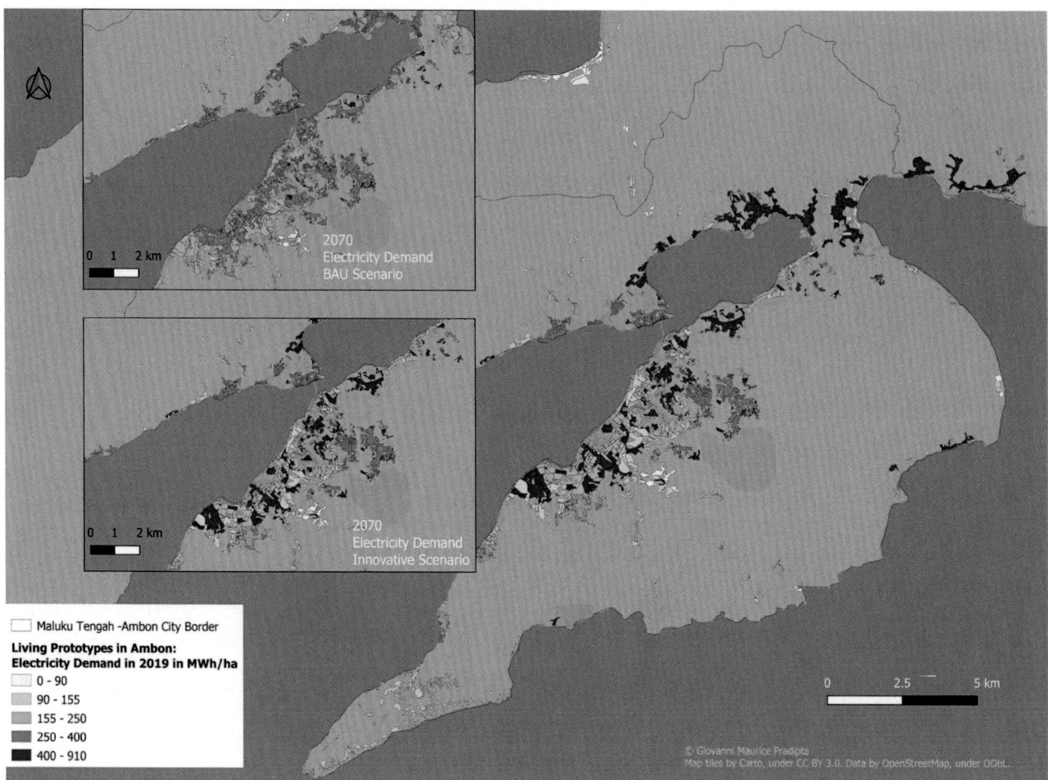

Figure 17.6 Map of electricity consumption in MWh/ha in 2019 and the future.

of the various residential buildings was first analyzed to determine the potential for energy efficiency in these buildings. The average annual energy consumption of residential buildings on Ambon in 2019 was estimated at 11 MWh/a. This consumption is not different from the average annual energy consumption of Indonesian households, which was estimated by Fukuyo (2018) to be around 12 MWh/a. In contrast, Surahman and Kubota (2018) estimated the average annual energy consumption of households in Jakarta and Bandung to be about 6 MWh/a. The difference in annual consumption between Ambon, Jakarta, and Bandung can be explained by the difference in the type of fuel used for cooking, as most households in Jakarta and Bandung use LPG, while kerosene and biomass are consumed mainly for cooking on Ambon.

In our research, nine measures to improve the energy efficiency of residential buildings are proposed. Although energy efficiency improvement is not limited to these measures, the nine

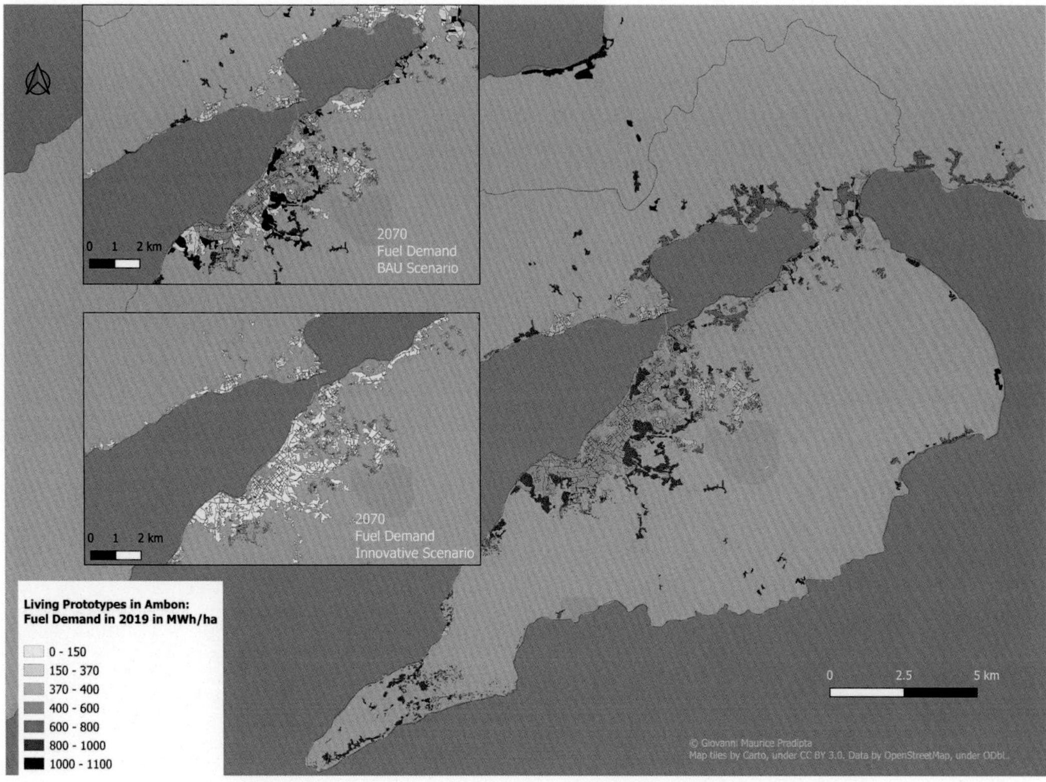

Figure 17.7 Map of fuel consumption in MWh/ha in 2019 and the future.

measures were based on the analysis of the energy consumption profile in residential buildings and the study of the greatest energy efficiency potential in these buildings. In addition, the potential of solar energy and biomass on Ambon was studied to demonstrate the feasibility to implement eighth of the nine measures proposed, which aim to apply photovoltaic and biogas technologies to the residential sector on Ambon See more about the potential of solar energy and biomass on Ambon in (Genske and Pradipta, 2022; Patil, 2021, In press)

The possibility of implementing energy efficiency measures and achieving the innovative scenario depends on several factors, the most important of which are energy policy and social acceptance. Except for some easy-to-implement and low-cost measures, most of the measures require government implementation or at least government support due to the cost, which means that the Ambon government needs to introduce a new energy policy that supports their implementation. In addition, the

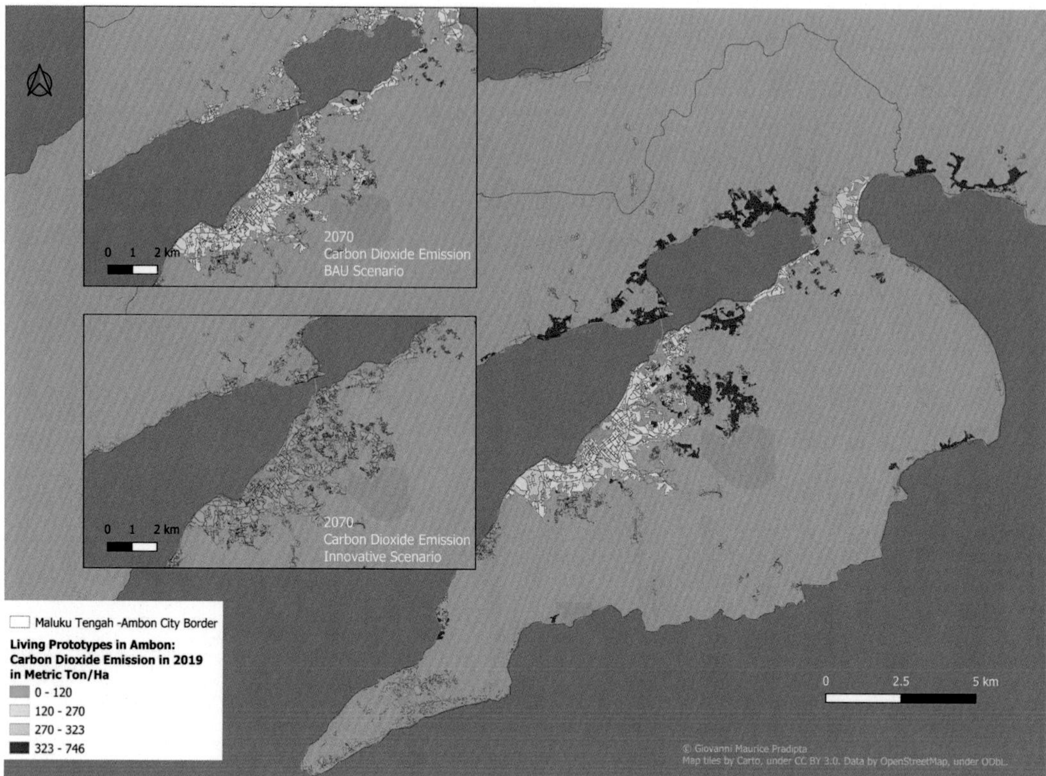

Figure 17.8 Map of CO_2 emissions in t/ha in 2019 and the future.

level of social acceptance of energy efficiency measures affects the possibility of their implementation. Therefore, it is recommended to first educate people through civil society institutions about the importance of implementing these measures in the future.

Using urban planning tools to improve the energy efficiency in the residential sector helps Ambon's planers and governments to put their energy goals and strategies for the future because this approach not only investigates the energy efficiency and its improvement strategies but also build future scenarios. In addition, this approach helps educate the community on the importance of taking energy efficiency measures in the future by showing future scenarios and comparing them in environmental, economic, and social terms. It should also be noted here that this approach is not limited to the residential sector or to the island model but is applicable to the business and transportation sector and to various urban prototypes.

5. Conclusion

Ambon is an island of the Maluku archipelago and forms one of its largest urban centers. The residential sector accounts for 20% of the total island area, which is divided between urban (Ambon city) and rural areas (Maluku-Tengah). The residential sector on Ambon, in addition to informal settlements, can be divided into five prototypes whose energy consumption profiles and energy sources differ. The total electricity consumption of the residential sector for 2019 was estimated to be about 223 GWh, and the total fuel consumption was about 744 GWh. This is associated with about 255,000 tons of direct CO_2 emissions.

Energy efficiency needs to be improved and renewable energy options need to be introduced in order to reduce energy consumption and CO_2 emissions from the residential sector. The first three energy efficiency measures presented in this chapter provided solutions to increase cooking fuel efficiency. In addition, measures 4–7 were presented to improve the building envelope and thermal performance to reduce cooling energy. The last two measures offered solutions related to renewable energy.

The future residential energy situation on Ambon and the achievement of Indonesia's climate goals are dependent on the change of energy policy and the implementation of such energy efficiency measures. If the energy policy on Ambon remains as it is, emissions and environmental impacts will increase with population growth, while the implementation of efficiency measures and the introduction of renewable energy options would allow for a 40% reduction in residential sector emissions by 2030 and zero CO_2 emissions by 2070.

The planning maps developed in this project serve on the one hand to record the current energy demand of the Ambon region. On the other hand, they also show possible future scenarios by visualizing possible development paths. They thus serve as a valuable aid for urban and regional planners on their way to shaping a sustainable, energy self-sufficient, fossil-free future.

References

Berger, T., Genske, D.D., Hüsler, L., Joedecke, T., Menn, A., Ruff, A., 2011. Basel auf dem Weg zur 2000-Watt-Gesellschaft (Broschüre zum Forschungsbericht). Basel Kanton Basel-Stadt, Amt für Umwelt und Energie (AUE) 30.

BPS-Statistics of Maluku Province, 2020. Provinsi Maluku Dalam Angka 2020. Maluku Province in Figures. https://maluku.bps.go.id/publication/2020/02/28/147f22b514ed12b9241f3f6f/provinsi-maluku-dalam-angka-2020–penyediaan-data-untuk-perencanaan-pembangunan-.html.

Climate Transparency, 2019a. Brown to green: the G20 transition towards a net-zero emissions economy. Climate Transparency 63. https://www.climate-transparency.org/wp-content/uploads/2019/11/Brown-to-Green-Report-2019.pdf.

Climate Transparency, 2019b. Indonesia country profile. In: Brown To Green: The G20 Transition towards a Net-Zero Emissions Economy: Climate Tranparency. https://www.climate-transparency.org/wp-content/uploads/2019/11/B2G_2019_Indonesia.pdf.

Darío, R.G., John, D.W., 2006. 2006 IPCC Guidelines for National Greenhouse Gas Inventories, vol. 2. Chapter 2: Stationary Combustion. Intergovernmental Panel on Climate Change—IPCC. https://www.ipcc-nggip.iges.or.jp/public/2006gl/pdf/2_Volume2/V2_2_Ch2_Stationary_Combustion.pdf.

Droege, P., Genske, D.D., Ruff, A., Schwarze, M., 2018. Building regenerative regions rapidly: the STAR energy model as regional planning tool. In: Droege, P. (Ed.), Urban Energy Transition: Renewable Strategies for Cities and Regions. Elsevier, pp. 579–634. https://doi.org/10.1016/B978-0-08-102074-6.00044-9.

Enteria, N., Awbi, H.B., Santamouris, M. (Eds.), 2020. Building in Hot and Humid Regions: Historical Perspective and Technological Advances. Springer.

Everding, D., Genske, D.D., Ruff, A., 2019. Bausteine des energetisch-ökologischen Stadtumbaus. In: Everding, D., Genske, D.D., Ruff, A. (Eds.), Energiestädte. Springer Berlin Heidelberg, pp. 1–66. https://doi.org/10.1007/978-3-662-44703-1_4-1.

Everding, D. (Ed.), 2007. Solarer Städtebau: Vom Pilotprojekt Zum Planerischen Leitbild. W. Kohlhammer, Stuttgart.

Floor, W., van der Plas, R., 1992. CO2 Emissions by the Residential Sector : Environmental Implications of Inter-Fuel Substitution (Industry and Energy Department Working Paper. Energy Series Paper; No. 51 Washington, D.C.). D.C. World Bank Group. http://documents.worldbank.org/curated/en/532881468741361244/CO2-emissions-by-the-residential-sector-environmental-implications-of-inter-fuel-substitution.

Fukuyo, K., 2018. Overview of energy consumption in hot-humid climates of Asia. In: Kubota, T., Rijal, H.B., Takaguchi, H. (Eds.), Sustainable Houses and Living in the Hot-Humid Climates of Asia. Springer, pp. 305–311. https://doi.org/10.1007/978-981-10-8465-2_30.

Genske, D.D., 2013. Basel on its Way to the 2000-Watt-Society. SITRA National Resource Wisdom Forum Helsinki, Finlandia Hall (key note).

Genske, D.D., Pradipta, G.M., 2022. Establishing Plus-Minus-Energy-Regions: The Maluku Archipelago in Indonesia. Springer Nature (in print).

Genske, D.D., Henning-Jacob, J., Jödecke, T., Ruff, A., 2010. Forcasts for the reference scenario/Forecasts for the excellence scenarios. In: Internationale Bauaustellung Hamburg. Energy Atlas: Future Concept Renewable Wilhelmsburg, pp. 79–120.

Kubota, T., Rijal, H.B., Takaguchi, H. (Eds.), 2018. Sustainable Houses and Living in the Hot-Humid Climates of Asia. Springer.

Miller, A., 1999. Resource Management in the Urban Sphere: Ambon's Urban Environment. In: CAKALELE. The Center for Southeast Asian Studies, pp. 7–37. https://core.ac.uk/download/pdf/5096205.pdf.

Oliver, A., 2014. Residential Cooking Stoves and Ovens: Good Practice Technology: Save 80 Stove. Wuppertal Institute for Climate, Environment and Energy. https://bigee.net/static/filer_public/2014/10/08/bigee_residential_cooking_stoves_good_practice_save80.pdf.

Patil, P., 2021. Design, Calculation, and Mapping of Electricity Generation Potential from Solar PV in Ambon, Indonesia [Master Thesis]. Hochschule Nordhausen, Nordhausen (in press).

Surahman, U., Kubota, T., 2018. Household energy consumption and CO_2 emissions for residential buildings in Jakarta and Bandung of Indonesia. In: Kubota, T., Rijal, H.B., Takaguchi, H. (Eds.), Sustainable Houses and Living in the Hot-Humid Climates of Asia. Springer, pp. 325–333. https://doi.org/10.1007/978-981-10-8465-2_32.

Thoday, K., Benjamin, P., Gan, M., Puzzolo, E., 2018. The mega conversion program from Kerosene to LPG in Indonesia: lessons learned and recommendations for future clean cooking energy expansion. Energy for Sustainable Development: The Journal of the International Energy Initiative 46, 71–81. https://doi.org/10.1016/j.esd.2018.05.011.

18

Transactive electricity markets: case study RENeW Nexus

Jemma Green, Peter Newman and Nick Forse
CUSP, Curtin University, Perth, Australia

1. Introduction

Western Australia's capital Perth has on average 300 clear-sky days a year and hence is an ideal place for roof-top solar to be demonstrated as part of the decarbonization transition. The rooftop solar revolution has been more successful than anyone ever anticipated in Perth with over 40% of households purchasing it and predictions of this moving to more than 70% this decade. On October 15th 2022 the grid hit a world record having 71% of its power supply provided by rooftop solar (Parkinson, 2022). But its addition to a centralized grid system (the SWIS or South West Integrated System) has caused many problems. These can be summed up as market and electrical instabilities highlighted by three key issues:

1. At an electrical level, the noontime oversupply of solar photovoltaics (PV) threatens the scheduling of electricity generation and creates reverse flows to distribution networks. This can burn out transformers and cause harmonics and voltage outages and demand even more equipment to stabilize the grid;
2. Wholesale prices for electricity vary significantly from extremely low or negative midday prices to regularly high evening peak prices and also cause issues to the scheduling of baseload generation as intermittent solar generation takes priority during daylight hours; and
3. Increased solar means ancillary services, which relate to frequency stability, get ever more expensive.

Up until now, the industry has employed a patch-and-fix approach to solving these problems in the hope that they will eventually go away. These are usually in the form of tariffs, but one tariff patch inevitably leads to another. Uncertainty pervades

Intelligent Environments. https://doi.org/10.1016/B978-0-12-820247-0.00009-6

the industry, consumers, and political realm as the transition to renewables is desired but it does not fit the present grid system. The need for a new model has been set out over many years and is likely to include a much more localized approach that makes the most of solar energy (Green and Newman, 2017a).

The premise for this study was that there could be a more systematic and scalable way to address the suite of related problems outlined earlier, using what has now been called transactive energy (Atamturk, 2014) and hence what we have called transactive electricity markets. The chapter examines how a case study—the RENeW Nexus project in Perth—was created to address this issue.

2. Research question

The case study asks the question: could a transactive electricity system, that is, a highly localized electricity market with clear and real-time price signals transacted between producers and consumers of solar energy, solve the suite of three problems described earlier?

The case study was set up using solar and batteries associated with smart systems to manage transactions through new software and blockchain-based accounting. The project aimed to assess the question about transactive electricity trading in two separate parts:

2.1 Can transactive electricity trading reduce stress on the grid?

A solar P2P trading trial, called Freo 48, involved households selling electricity to each other across the grid. There were 48 participants involved in the trial but the scheme was deliberately designed so it could easily be scaled up to a larger group without any significant investment, or special requirements other than a smart meter. The study looked at behavior to see if energy consumption patterns would change and arbitrage style activities would emerge and whether these would constitute demand response: the shifting of electrical use to reduce stress on the grid.

2.2 What are the effects of transactive electricity trading on payback times for a battery?

In a further part of the project, called Loco 1, a mathematical model was constructed to test typical payback times for a 10 and 15 kWh battery device in a normal household environment. The study went on to evaluate how the payback times could be shortened if the batteries are included in a virtual power plant (VPP) arrangement, evaluating the use of these distributed batteries when aggregated through a blockchain-enabled VPP platform for participation in grid balancing and network control services.

For this project, a transactive, localized energy market refers to a group of consumers (both households and businesses) within the same low-voltage distribution area downstream of the same feeder. Each market can be linked to other connected markets within that same part of a distribution network, such that any net energy export from one market, caused by a net excess of solar PV energy within it, could be used to supply another local energy market linked within that section of the distribution network.

3. Background

Electricity generation from rooftop solar presents a significant challenge to both electricity network operators and market operators as it requires the increased use of appropriate support services such as frequency control, voltage control, and peaking generation due to its intermittent nature. This is a universal issue but is particularly evident in Perth as the growth in roof-top solar as a proportion of the electricity system is very high, meaning that on some days this source is providing 80% of the input power.

The Australian Energy Market Operator (AEMO) is now considering how to manage the 1.1 GW of connected behind-the-meter PV (AEMO, 2018). Importantly, this solar PV generation is displacing synchronous generators (e.g., traditional thermal generators like coal) that provide a range of technical services to the grid (AEMO, 2019a, 2019b). As this kind of renewable generation becomes more common and displaces conventional generation sources, services will need to be procured from alternative sources or new services may be required to appropriately manage a more variable energy mix (AEMO, 2019a, 2019b). AEMO highlights this future thus: "The SWIS could become inoperable under its present operating parameters."

Electricity generation and distribution systems are changing significantly. Electricity supply is becoming a hybrid of centralized and distributed systems as a result of increased rooftop solar generation and more recently, battery storage in the network. These systems are collectively called distributed energy resources (DERs) and are not controllable in the sense that traditional generation assets are, causing new challenges to grid stability. Changes are needed to ensure a stable and low-cost energy system, and a wide variety of solutions are being investigated such as changes to market rules, tariffs, increased technical standards, and two-sided markets. Energy trading is one such solution that has been proposed to solve these issues and complement other solutions (Energy Transformation Taskforce, 2019). Energy trading can occur via solar systems or from coordinating battery sources to form a VPP.

The SWIS requires a minimum amount of net demand at any one time, stated by AEMO as 700 MW, below which it risks a cascading failure of the entire network (AEMO, 2019a, 2019b). Due to the large proportion of DERs in the SWIS causing a sharp reduction in demand during the day, there is an expected increase of hours per year below this limit from 10 h/year in 2022 (potentially requiring the disconnection of up to 60,000 households through the shutoff of distribution feeders in areas with particularly high DER export) to 150 h/y in 2026 (up to 300,000 households) (AEMO, 2019a, 2019b).

Related issues including ramping, load-shedding, restart services, dispatch of out-of-merit generation, and increased frequency of negative trading intervals are stated as issues by AEMO (AEMO, 2019a, 2019b; Energy Transformation Taskforce, 2019b). To avoid these problems, changes must be made to Western Australia's energy market, regulations, and systems (Energy Transformation Taskforce, 2019c).

To address the issues outlined earlier, various industry bodies, regulators, market operators, and network operators propose a number of potential solutions. The WA State Government has established an Energy Transformation Strategy and Energy Transformation Taskforce to develop a Whole of System Plan and DER Roadmap (Energy Transformation Taskforce, 2019a). The Government is examining possible changes to market rules and regulations to ensure system security and reliability, while also deriving as many benefits as possible from the increase of DERs in the SWIS (Energy Transformation Taskforce, 2019b). Some of the proposed areas for reform include:

- changes to retail tariffs and network tariffs to implement time-of-use pricing and locational network pricing (Energy Transformation Taskforce, 2019c; Legislative Assembly, 2020);
- updates to inverter technical standards to mandate all inverters have their advanced capabilities and two-way communications enabled by default (AEMO, 2019a, 2019b; Energy Transformation Taskforce, 2019a);
- changes to the Western Australia's wholesale energy market (WEM) market rules to allow large-scale batteries to participate in the wholesale market (Energy Transformation Taskforce, 2019b; Economic Regulation Authority, 2018);

- the increased use of standalone power systems, microgrids, and community batteries in areas where it is economic to do so (Energy Transformation Taskforce, 2019c; Legislative Assembly, 2020; Creating The Rural Network Of The Future: Stand-Alone Power Systems, 2019); and
- further investigation into the ways that DER can support the network (e.g., through aggregation into a VPP that provides localized network support) (Energy Transformation Taskforce, 2019a).

Consumer energy trading has been cited by the Australian Energy Market Commission (AEMC) as having the potential to help resolve some of the issues cited above (Integrating Distributed Energy Resources For The Grid Of The Future, 2019; Annual Report 2018–2019, 2019). There can be no single silver bullet to solve the problems facing the SWIS and other Australian energy markets such as the National Electricity Market (NEM). Transactive electricity markets through P2P and VPP energy trading are potential solutions that could help alleviate some of the problems while complementing other solutions, potentially making them more effective (Wu et al., 2019).

Transactive energy trading, including P2P and VPP trading, is being examined by industry bodies to deliver system and market benefits. The rule-maker for the NEM, the AEMC, is looking to reward consumers for sustainable behavior and views such energy trading as part of how consumers will interact with the electricity system. This is summarized by "*The Commission's vision for the future electricity system is one of two-way trade of electricity and services in a wholly connected energy market*," adding that the energy services will be provided with dynamism, and the "... *electricity network is becoming a trading platform* ..." (Integrating Distributed Energy Resources For The Grid Of The Future, 2019).

AEMO, which operates WEM, has echoed the AEMC's vision of a two-sided market, calling for "*changes to the WEM Rules to allow 'multiple trading relationships', whereby an end consumer can benefit by offering services to the market* via *a third-party aggregator while retaining a relationship with their retailer*" and changes to regulations and metering provisions to reach a point where "*residential customers can trade their energy between themselves (peer-to-peer), either as part of an embedded network or outside of an embedded network.*" (AEMO, 2019a, 2019b). As is happening in other countries, such as Japan, aggregators could act as P2P buyers of energy from consumers for both solar and battery sourced electricity (Movellan, 2019; Colthorpe, 2020).

Future energy trading platforms would need to be capable of integrating with the market operators' market dispatch platforms and would also require AEMO's cooperation to do so. The AEMC highlights in its 2018–19 annual report that Australian energy markets will continue to become more consumer-centric: "*The technology revolution offers opportunities and benefits for customers to take control of how they buy, sell and use energy. Over time, this should allow for greater utilisation of the existing stock of generation and network capacity, lowering average costs for all consumers*" (Annual Report 2018–2019, 2019). Activities, such as customer energy trading can be considered consistent with the WA State Government's view, outlined in their DER Roadmap report, of an energy system whereby consumers can use their DER systems to provide network services to the Distribution Service Operator and participate directly in the Wholesale Market (Energy Transformation Taskforce, 2019a). Without a market mechanism such as a localized energy market enabled by P2P trading, the focus of consumers will be on load defection. But with a market mechanism, they are incentivized to have a new relationship with the grid where they provide network services and energy to their neighbors.

Due to a lack of research into the topic, there is a need to investigate the potential of transactive electricity trading systems to address and resolve some of the challenges facing Australian energy markets and networks. Specifically, transactive electricity trading has the potential to create a localized energy market of consumers (both households and businesses) within the same low-voltage distribution area that gives residential customers a more cost-reflective rate for the electricity they use and produce during the day. These lower electricity costs could act to shift usage behaviors to the daytime when energy is cheapest, alleviating network problems associated with lack of daytime demand and the reverse flow of energy. Additionally, it could produce a number of noneconomic benefits such as empowering consumers with a greater sense of agency and control by allowing them to participate in the market directly (Annual Report 2018–2019, 2019).

In summary, Western Australia's energy system is facing significant challenges in accommodating the rapid increase in DERs. In the mix of potential changes required to address these challenges, regulators are beginning to investigate the possibility of a decentralized, transactive electricity market that allows greater direct customer participation, incentivizing the optimal physical generation and network outcomes for the energy system - a marked change from the current highly-centralized model, which built the physical system first and designed the market later.

4. The project: RENeW Nexus—a study of localized transactive, electricity markets

The RENeW Nexus project was conceived to understand the potential of localized, transactive electricity markets and how technology platforms can facilitate more efficient outcomes to the energy system ("Smart Cities And Suburbs" 2020). The project was supported by the Australian Government through the Smart Cities andand Suburbs Program.

The RENeW Nexus project arose from a project called white gum valley where 100 units of medium and low density housing were set up to share rooftop solar provided on their site through a shared battery system (Green and Newman, 2017b). As a part of the project, in Fremantle, Western Australia (Fig. 18.1), a solar P2P trial called Freo 48 was run that consisted of two Phases: Phase 1 included 18 participants and ran for 7 months—November 2018 to June 2019. Phase 2 initially had 30 participants (a single participant withdrew after 2 months due to the increase in costs) and ran from October 2019 to January 2020. A subsequent trial called Loco 1, consisting of the modeling of a VPP, was undertaken to better understand the financial benefits prosumers could realize from having a battery installed and participating in a VPP as

Figure 18.1 The white gum valley (WGV) project at the eastern outskirts of fremantle combined apartments, single residential buildings, and development types of other typical use patterns, to trial peer-to-peer trading with integrated storage and a shared EV-charging station. The Fulcrum Agency (2020).

well as the benefits to the energy system. Another aspect of the RENeW Nexus project is the Loco 2 trial being run at the East Village at Knutsford project. This project is being developed by DevelopmentWA in Fremantle, Western Australia and involves a microgrid with a 670 kWh shared battery system that will facilitate 36 households trading excess energy with each other via the battery (Byrne et al., 2020).

As was outlined in the DER Stocktake (Energy Transformation Taskforce, 2019b), the purpose of these trials was:

- To demonstrate proof of concept test for P2P electricity trading;
- To understand the value of P2P for customers and project partners; and
- To trial the technological interoperability between the Power Ledger platform, Synergy (energy retailer), Western Power (network operator), and supporting technologies, and test the Power Ledger platform capability as a client P2P solution.

A secondary objective of the trials was to investigate whether P2P energy trading had the potential to incentivize customers to stay connected to the grid and change energy consumption patterns throughout the day to better support the grid and deal with reverse flows of energy due to excess solar electricity during the day. Similarly, this water supply network mirrors this which can be modeled alongside the energy infrastructure in place. Fig. 18.2 alludes to a similar process to energy trading with collecting, storing, and consuming water, while using blockchain technology to facilitate when the best time to utilize mains water and when it is advantageous to utilize collected or filtered water that is stored on site.

The Freo 48 trial provided the opportunity to assess participants' perception of and experience using energy trading technology. It also provided an opportunity to assess any behavior change and/or changes in energy consumption habits by consumers, though these insights were limited by a lack of historical consumption data with which to quantify any changes.

This chapter summarizes the localized energy project, looking at the integration of the Freo 48 trading results, modeling of additional VPP benefits, customer insights provided through multiple surveys, as well as information collected in workshops and discussions undertaken between project partners. The chapter also provides an analysis of barriers and best-case scenarios for localized energy trading and the benefits to the system and the next steps that could be taken by the relevant stakeholders.

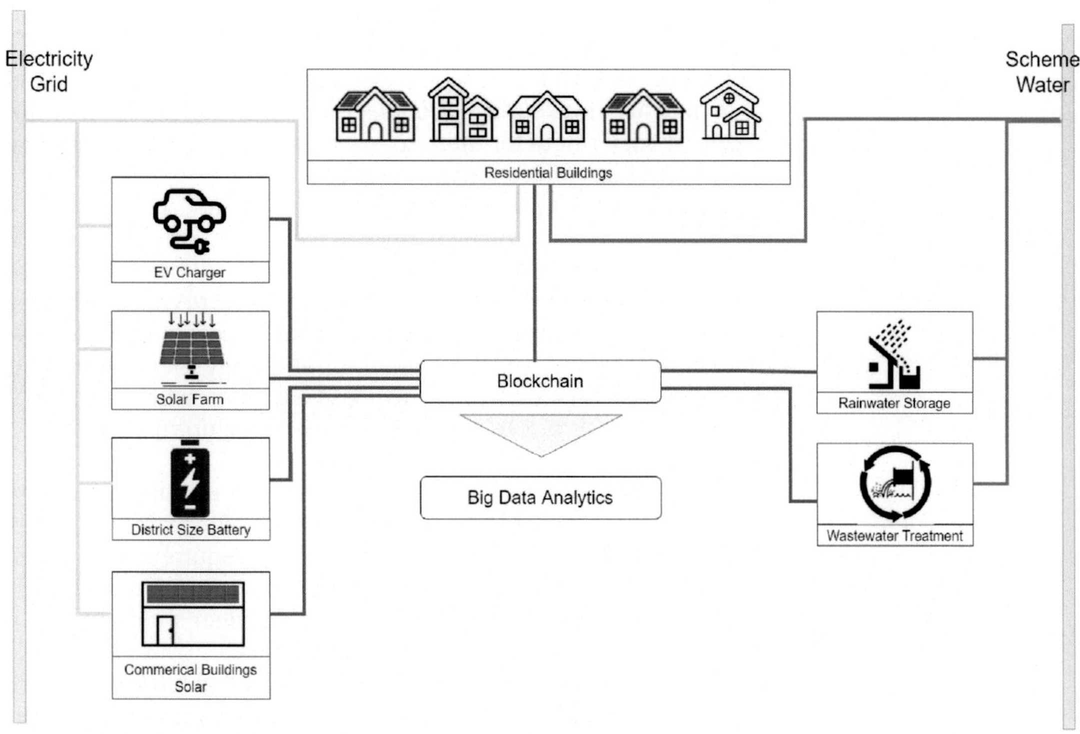

Figure 18.2 Technical data flow diagram in the power/water cooperative using blockchain analytics.

5. Methodology

5.1 Freo 48

A solar P2P trading trial, called Freo 48, was undertaken and involved households selling electricity to each other across the grid. Freo 48 had two parts: Phase 1 and 2.

Participants set their own rates for the energy they bought and sold from each other as part of a world-first in dynamic P2P pricing that was introduced in Phase 1. Prosumers with the lowest sell prices and consumers with the highest buy price had first priority for trading, with the transaction settling at the buyer's price.

Allowing participants to set their rates dynamically had the practical effect of creating a localized energy marketplace that uses pricing incentives to balance out the supply of exported energy and consumer demand. If there was an excess of energy available for purchase, prosumers were incentivized to reduce the price to make sure their energy was sold, and consumers could afford to set their prices higher. The reverse is also true—when there was a deficit of exported energy, prosumers could afford to raise the price and consumers would have to lower their preferred price to ensure their demand would be satisfied. The pricing worked as a normal marketplace would—that is, if the prosumers are receiving high prices for their exported energy then the consumers are paying high prices and vice versa.

If P2P energy supply was greater than demand in any given interval, the most expensive energy was sold back to the retailer at a fixed price of 4.0c/kWh (Phase 1) and 3.5c/kWh (Phase 2). If there was more energy demand than supply, the buyers with the lowest offers bought energy from the retailer at a preset rate. Participants had visibility over the quantity of energy they traded and over energy consumed from the grid at times when solar P2P trading does not occur (when the sun is not shining).

To facilitate the solar P2P trading:

1. Granular interval data from real-time electricity meters installed at the participant's house was first communicated to energyOS's platform. NB: this is not a requirement for P2P trading, it can also be done with a revenue-grade smart meter.
2. Data was then transferred to Power Ledger's system via a secure Application Programming Interface.
3. Trading was then carried out on a per-interval basis (i.e., every 30 min) by matching prosumers and consumers based on their preferred buy and sell prices. This real-time data was not compliant with state regulations for use in billing customers, so the retailer passed through a data file at the end of each month, which contained the readings taken from the network operator's advanced meters installed at each property to reconcile any differences. No major differences were found, with the only discrepancies occurring when the real-time meters went offline.
4. All transactions for the month were rerun using the network operator's data file and aggregated into a summary file which was then passed through to the retailer via secure file transfer.
5. This data was input into the retailer's customer billing system, used to invoice the customers for the energy they bought and sold, both from the grid and each other.

Each participant's real-time bidirectional energy flow data was measured by a Saturn South three-phase mini-meter. These DIN-rail-mounted electricity meters were installed in participants' switchboards, or in a standalone IP-rated enclosure where the switchboard proved unsuitable. Readings from the mini meter were wirelessly communicated to an SS9002 ESBox LT gateway device that was connected to each participant's router, which in turn fed the readings to energyOS's platform.

The tariffs used in each Phase of the trial were designed to reflect the relative proportions of the various underlying costs of providing energy to the consumer, that is, a combination of network costs, which cover the cost of building, maintaining, and administering the transmission and distribution networks, capacity costs and retailer's energy costs. The network and capacity costs are fixed and distributed evenly across the residential consumer base in line with Western Australia's *Uniform Tariff Policy* (Energy Policy WA, 2021).

The tariffs used were "unbundled" (i.e., the fixed and variable costs were separated out) to ensure that a solar P2P energy market could be created. Participants paid fixed charges of $3.30 per day, consisting of a $1.10 capacity charge paid to the retailer and a $2.20 network charge for the network operator, plus a variable trading fee charged by Power Ledger (0.5c per kWh traded P2P). These fixed charges were determined by the retailer and network operator calculating the average per-connection charges required to recover their respective fixed capacity and network costs for supplying the entire residential customer base.

Households in the SWIS usually pay these costs through a combination of the fixed charge component and variable energy charge component of the residential tariff. The network operator elected to provide a discount to the network charge component of 9%, bringing it down to $2.20 (from $2.40).

The rates for energy not purchased via solar P2P trading were charged on a time-of-use basis and differed between the two trial phases. These rates were based on the average of WEM balancing market prices for the preceding 12 months of each trial period, adjusted for marginal loss factors. Table 18.1 documents the

Table 18.1 Phase 1 and 2 tariffs.

Rate	Time	Phase 1 tariff	Phase 2 tariff
Retailer everyday peak rate	3:00p.m.–9:00p.m.	9.90 c/kWh	7.80 c/kWh
Retailer everyday off-peak rate	All other times	5.72 c/kWh	4.90 c/kWh
Retailer buy back rate	Daily	4.00 c/kWh	3.50 c/kWh
RENeW Nexus P2P energy rate	Any time	Set by participants	Set by participants
Power ledger transaction fee	Any time	0.50 c/kWh	0.50 c/kWh
Retailer capacity charge	Daily	$1.10/day	$1.10/day
Network operator network charge	Daily	$2.20/day	$2.20/day

Note: Prices include GST.

tariffs used in each trial (Standard Electricity Prices and Charges: South West Interconnected System, 2020). All energy purchased from the retailer is hereby referred to as being "bought from grid", as opposed to energy purchased from peers.

Any energy that was exported by a prosumer and not traded P2P was sold back to the retailer at a predetermined rate. This was set at 4.0c/kWh for Phase 1 and 3.5c/kWh for Phase 2. Both these rates are significantly lower than the Renewable Energy Buyback Scheme (REBS) rate (currently set at 7.135c/kWh), a government-funded feed in tariff subsidy in Western Australia aimed at incentivizing the installation of rooftop solar PV systems (Electricity Industry (Licence Conditions) Regulations, 2005).

Learnings from Phase 1 were integrated into Phase 2. Many participants in Phase 1 had a below-average daily energy consumption and therefore saw an increase in costs due to high fixed charges, calculated based on an average customer consumption profile. Recruitment for Phase 2 was initially targeted at households that consume between 11 and 16 kWh/day, but this band was expanded above 16 kWh/day late in the recruitment period due to difficulties attracting participants that threatened the trial's viability.

The ratio of prosumers to consumers was also modified from Phase 1 to 2. The Phase 1 cohort consisted of ~70% prosumers, which led to an overabundance of exported solar energy during the day. The ratio was reversed for Phase 2, initially consisting of 67% consumers to 33% prosumers. This new ratio not only balanced the amount of exported energy but was more representative of the overall mix of households with DERs in the SWIS today—estimated by the Australian PV Institute as 28.8% of households in the SWIS ("Australian PV Institute Solar Map", 2021). As one consumer installed a solar PV system during the middle of the trial, the ratio changed to 62% consumers to 38% prosumers. This highlights the need to achieve the requisite market composition, that is, matching buyers and sellers throughout the day as well as grid stability. This is also discussed in the DER Roadmap's vision for a Distribution Market that is balanced by the coordinated dispatch of DER systems. This demonstrates that the introduction of distributed batteries could provide a more efficient way of dealing with this issue by storing some of this surplus solar electricity which can then be dispatched at times of day for which there is demand (Energy Transformation Taskforce, 2019c).

5.2 Loco 1

In a further part of the project, called Loco 1, a mathematical model was constructed to test typical payback times for a 10 and 15 kWh battery device in a normal household environment. The study went on to evaluate how the payback times might be shortened if the batteries were included in a VPP arrangement.

In this analysis, prosumers can use their energy in any one interval for either P2P or VPP trading, but not both during the same interval. Using a battery coupled with VPP would mean that consumers could purchase locally sourced energy from prosumers with batteries throughout the day, not just when the sun was shining. It also means that batteries could help the grid in dealing with reverse energy flows and provide system services to stabilize the grid, and in doing so pay back the investment a prosumer made in the battery faster.

To investigate these potential system benefits and the ability to deliver localized energy markets, an analysis was undertaken taking account of market conditions, average user profiles, and using the Power Ledger VPP energy trading platform. This system provides an interface to VPP operators to inform the DER dispatch decisions and uses a blockchain to create a market mechanism that provides secure trading and fast settlement between customers and energy retailers. Batteries connected to VPP software need to be capable of receiving dispatch instructions from a software control layer, so customers with eligible systems could bring their own DER systems into the VPP. The only other hardware requirements are a smart electricity meter and an internet connection.

Western Australia's energy market, the WEM, has two distinct markets—a capacity market that pays generators for the available capacity they could provide to the market if required (regardless of whether they actually generate electricity or not), and an energy market for the electricity that has actually been generated. The energy market comprises three parts: Bilateral Contracts between market participants (settled off-market), the Short Term Energy Market (STEM) (a day-ahead market to adjust positions), and the Balancing Market (a market for generators to meet actual instantaneous system demand). Market customers need to purchase from the Balancing market to account for any differences between their net contracted position (STEM + Bilateral purchases) and their actual energy requirements. Historical half-hourly STEM price data was used to determine when the VPP discharged to bid into the STEM rather than offsetting the consumers' energy use. The STEM was chosen as the market that the VPP would dispatch into since a price forecast is required to determine an opportunity for arbitrage—the Balancing Market has ex post (after the fact) price determination so no price forecast is available.

To determine the benefits that a residential VPP could offer in the SWIS, which could also contribute toward localized energy markets, two models were constructed. The first model used the residential A1 tariff, LFAS, and STEM pricing information for 2019 and an average Perth household's energy consumption and demand profile to determine the financial benefits for an individual consumer from participating in a VPP. A second model was created to determine the degree to which this VPP could contribute toward localized energy autonomy.

The first model assumed that:

- User consumption of 20 kWh/day. This is above the SWIS average of 13.426 kWh/day as it was assumed that smaller customers had less financial incentive to install battery systems.
- Two options were analyzed where a prosumer household had a 5 kW solar system and a 3.3kW/10 kWh battery or an 8 kW solar system and a 5kW/15 kWh battery. These were chosen as they are the typical sizes that are currently being sold in the market. Modeling on a larger system was done to examine the benefit of having a higher discharge capacity and longer discharge duration.
- The P2P trading rate was set at the REBS FiT rate of 7.135 c/kWh +10%.
- The VPP was 10 MW in size and could bid into the WEM as a scheduled generator.
- The batteries received a capacity credit for providing LFAS services. The 10 kWh battery was able to provide 2.5 kW of power postapplication of derating factors; the 15 kWh battery was able to provide 3 kW.
- All consumers were within the same low-voltage distribution network.
- If there was an STEM high-price event or LFAS dispatch opportunity, the battery would dispatch for the highest value event, otherwise, all energy exported to the grid was traded P2P. VPP participants can participate in both P2P trading and a VPP providing grid services, but not both during the same interval.

6. Results

6.1 Freo 48

6.1.1 Phase 1

Phase 1 of the Freo 48 trial led to a financial loss for a majority of the participants—17 of the 18 households (94%) experienced higher costs than they would have received under the regulated A1 tariff. Contributing factors are outlined below:

- Because energy generation costs are a relatively small component of delivering electricity to households in the SWIS (approximately 15%–20%), reduced daytime energy costs were not sufficient to offset high daily fixed charges for the majority of participants. All participants that were worse off had an average consumption below 11.5 kWh/day. Unbundled tariffs that reflect system costs via a high fixed-supply charge favor higher energy consumption because higher energy use brings down the per-unit cost.
- The suboptimal ratio of prosumers and consumers (70% prosumers to 30% consumers) led to limited demand of P2P energy (more supply than demand) resulting in more rooftop solar electricity being sold to the retailer than traded P2P (18.0% of exported energy sold P2P vs. 82.0% sold back to the retailer) attracting a lower rate (4.0 c/kWh and a trading cost of 0.05 c/kWh traded) than otherwise received from the REBS (7.135c/kWh). In addition, the P2P trades that cleared were on average below the REBS rate, which also relates to the relative cost of the off-peak time-of-use tariff (5.72c/kWh) used in the trial.

Any participants that were financially worse off compared to the A1 tariff were credited the difference after the trial ended.

Participants in Phase 1 consumed 35,796 kWh of total electricity. Of that total, 6901 kWh (19.3%) was purchased from peers, with the remaining 28,894 kWh (80.7%) purchased from the retailer. Note that these totals include consumption at night when there is no possibility of purchasing solar energy P2P. When narrowed to daylight hours (5:00a.m.–7:30p.m. in Phase 1), the percentage of energy sourced from peers changes to 34.1% (6901.36 kWh), reducing the local markets' need for grid-supplied energy to 65.9% of their daylight consumption. This highlights the ability of localized energy markets to source a significant portion of consumption from themselves and in doing so deal with system challenges from reverse energy flows from excess solar. Fig. 18.3 shows these amounts as a percentage of their respective import/export type.

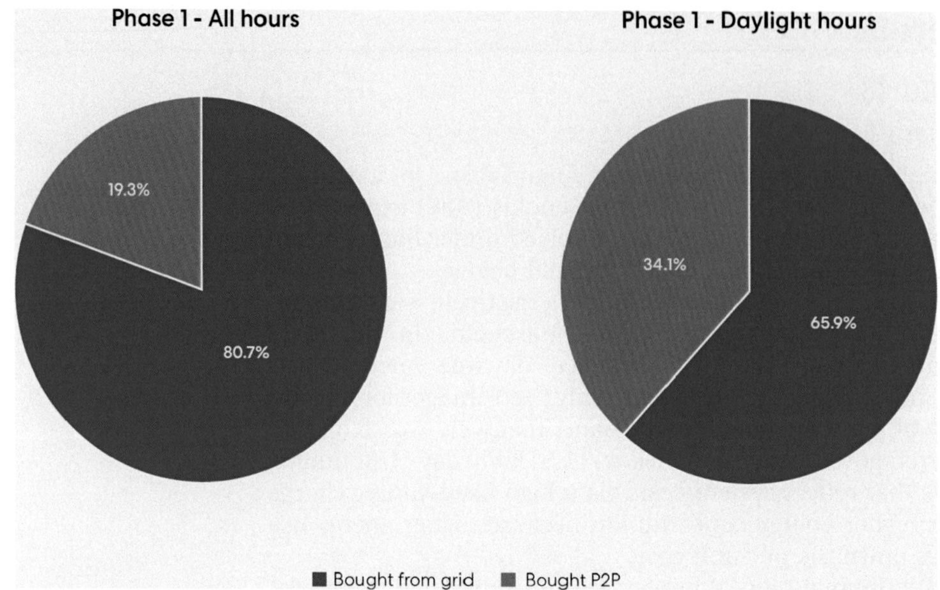

Figure 18.3 Relative consumption volumes for trial Phase 1, all hours versus daylight hours.

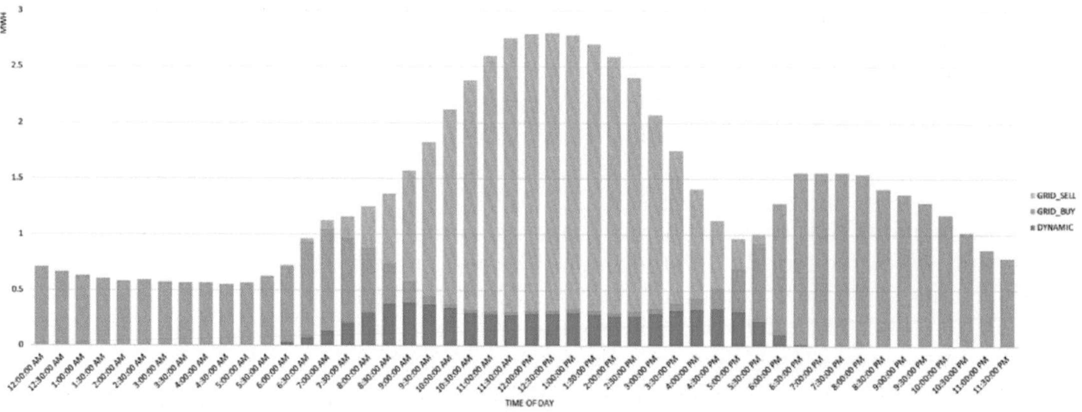

Figure 18.4 Summary of Phase 1 transactions, averaged per half-hourly interval.

The prosumers in Phase 1 exported a total of 38,264.92 kWh into the grid over the course of the trial. Of that generation, 6901.36 kWh (18.0%) was traded P2P and 31,363.56 kWh (82.0%) was sold back to the retailer at the default buyback rate. Fig. 18.4 shows the total consumption and generation for Phase 1 figures averaged over 30-minute intervals. The large amount of "spilt" exported solar energy in Phase 1 clearly demonstrates the need for more consumers with daytime consumption to absorb the daytime solar generation.

6.1.2 Phase 2

Phase 2 aimed to address some of the learnings from Phase 1. The prosumer-to-consumer ratio was reversed to reduce the amount of exported energy sold to the grid, with the new cohort initially consisting of 20 consumers and 10 prosumers. Customers with a historical average of 11–16 kWh were recruited to take part in the trial, which aimed to cover the $3.30 total daily fixed costs when compared against using the A1 tariff.

These measures were moderately effective, with the percentage of "spilt" energy (i.e., exported solar PV energy that was sold to the grid instead of P2P) reduced to 61.2% in Phase 2 compared to 82.0% for Phase 1. This was still above the expected level however and can be explained by:

- Below-average targeted consumption by numerous participants. Despite recruitment based on the historic energy use of 11 kWh/day, many customers during the trial period had an average daily consumption below this level.
- Seven consumers never logged into the platform and were therefore not able to set up their system and trade. In Phase 1 all participants logged in, thereby reducing the amount of participating consumers. Additional recruitment was not undertaken to address this deficit in consumers.
- Not enough local energy demand during daylight hours. Even though more consumers were added to the Phase 2 trial, their total consumption during daylight hours (5:30 a.m.–7 p.m.) was not enough to consume all the excess exported energy from the prosumers. This suggests that while the trial participants consumed a relatively large amount of energy, the majority of this consumption was not during daylight hours when the prosumer solar PV systems are generating. Despite the excess of generation in the middle of the day, highlighted in Fig. 18.6, ~65% of participants' demand during daylight hours was still sourced from non-P2P generation sources. These figures highlight the mismatch between consumer demand and the availability of solar PV-generated energy.

Fig. 18.6 shows these totals of relative generation and consumption plotted over the relevant 30-minute interval. Participants in Phase 2 consumed a total of 41,164.24 kWh, of which 8224.78 kWh (20.0%) was sourced P2P and the remaining 32,939.46 kWh was sourced from the retailer (80.0%).

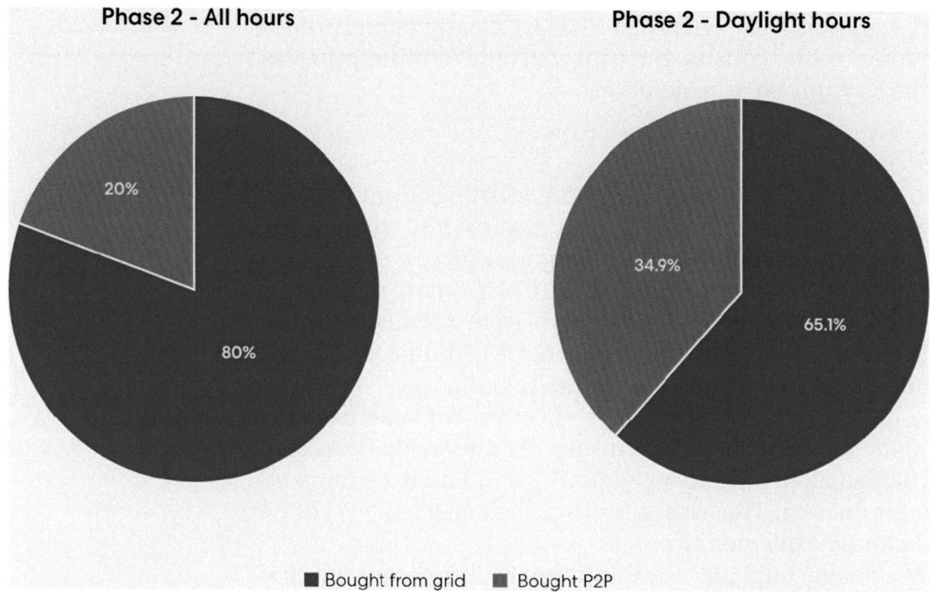

Figure 18.5 Relative consumption volumes for trial Phase 2, all hours versus daylight hours.

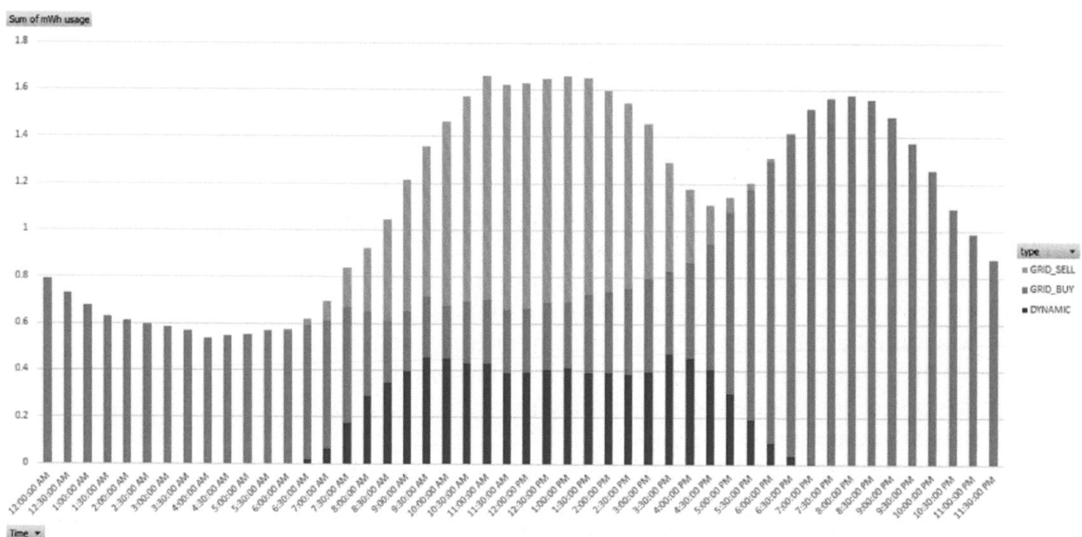

Figure 18.6 Summary of Phase 2 transactions, averaged per half-hourly interval.

When only daylight consumption is factored in these totals (i.e., between 5:30 a.m. and 7:30 p.m. in Phase 2), the percentage of consumed energy sourced from peers increased to 34.9%

(8224.78 kWh) and the remaining 65.1% was sourced from the grid (15,319.77 kWh). Fig. 18.5 shows the average percentage of energy bought in Phase 2, between all hours and daylight hours.

Prosumers exported a total of 21,176 kWh, of which 38.8% was traded P2P and the remaining 12,951 kWh (61.2%) was sold back to the retailer for the default buyback rate.

Phase 2 resulted in a financial benefit for a majority of participants: 18 of the 29 participant households (62%) experienced lower costs than if they had been charged the A1 tariff whereas 11 participants (38%) experienced higher costs.

These results can be explained due to two major factors:

- P2P trades constituted a very small percentage of the participants' overall costs. Of the registered participants subsequently traded P2P, percentages of P2P trades as part of their overall cost across the trial ranged from 0.1% to 10.2%, with an average of 2.8% and a standard deviation of 2.6%. Any savings derived from purchasing P2P energy instead of grid energy was minor due to the volumes and small price difference involved.
- Average consumption volume (measured in kWh/day) was a much better predictor of a participant's end financial position. A total of 77% (14/18) participants that saw a financial benefit had a consumption level above 11 kWh/day, whereas 80% (10/12) of the participants were worse off compared to the A1 tariff which had a consumption below 11 kWh/day.

6.1.3 Technical outcomes

To facilitate real-time solar P2P trading, additional metering hardware was installed in customers' homes. Real-time metering was intended to provide participants instantaneous feedback on their energy consumption, which in turn was hypothesized to influence their energy consumption behavior. Real-time metering, however, is not essential for P2P energy trading and the cost and disruption of installing these additional meters to enable this functionality was not seen to be justified by the benefit of having live data. Remotely read interval meters (usually called "smart meters" or "advanced meters") are currently being installed in the SWIS which would instead suffice for solar P2P trading. Future planned upgrades to the network operator's metering infrastructure (both hardware and software) could reduce the time delay between trade and confirmation of the trade. It should be noted that the brand of meter is not relevant, the only requirement for participation in P2P trading is a smart meter with remote communication capabilities and the ability to provide this data regularly and reliably.

The Power Ledger platform and the retailer's billing system were integrated smoothly, with minor modifications to the retailer's systems required to accept trading results and ensure consumption and trading data matched 100%. The data provision from the network operator to the retailer proved adequate for the trial's needs.

6.1.4 Recruitment

The recruitment of consumer participants proved to be more difficult than was originally anticipated.

In Phase 2, all participants fitting the criteria were targeted with an email. Within the City of Fremantle and the suburbs of North Coogee, Palmyra, and Hamilton Hill, there are some 20,000 households. Due to the high daily fixed charges in the trial, only 200 prosumers were identified as fitting the daily consumption criteria of 11–16 kWh/day, whereas approximately 3000 consumer households were identified as fitting this daily consumption criterion.

Although there was a small pool of 200 eligible prosumers, recruitment of the 10 prosumers to the trial was relatively straightforward. By contrast, it was significantly more difficult to attract 30 consumers from the 3000 candidates.

It is hypothesized that prosumers have a greater awareness of electricity markets, having already made a significant investment in their solar PV system and are thus more motivated to participate in schemes or projects that maximize the return on that investment. Consumers, by contrast, have not made such an investment and therefore lack a deeper understanding of reasons to participate. This highlights the need for proactive engagement and communication in offering new products and tariffs into the market.

6.1.5 Survey results

Seven trial surveys and workshops were undertaken from Phase 1 and Phase 2 participants to gain insights into the participants' experiences during each phase:

- Phase 1
  - A pretrial survey (48 respondents);
  - Two post-trial participant surveys (10 respondents and 12 respondents, respectively);
  - Two workshops, one pretrial and one posttrial; and

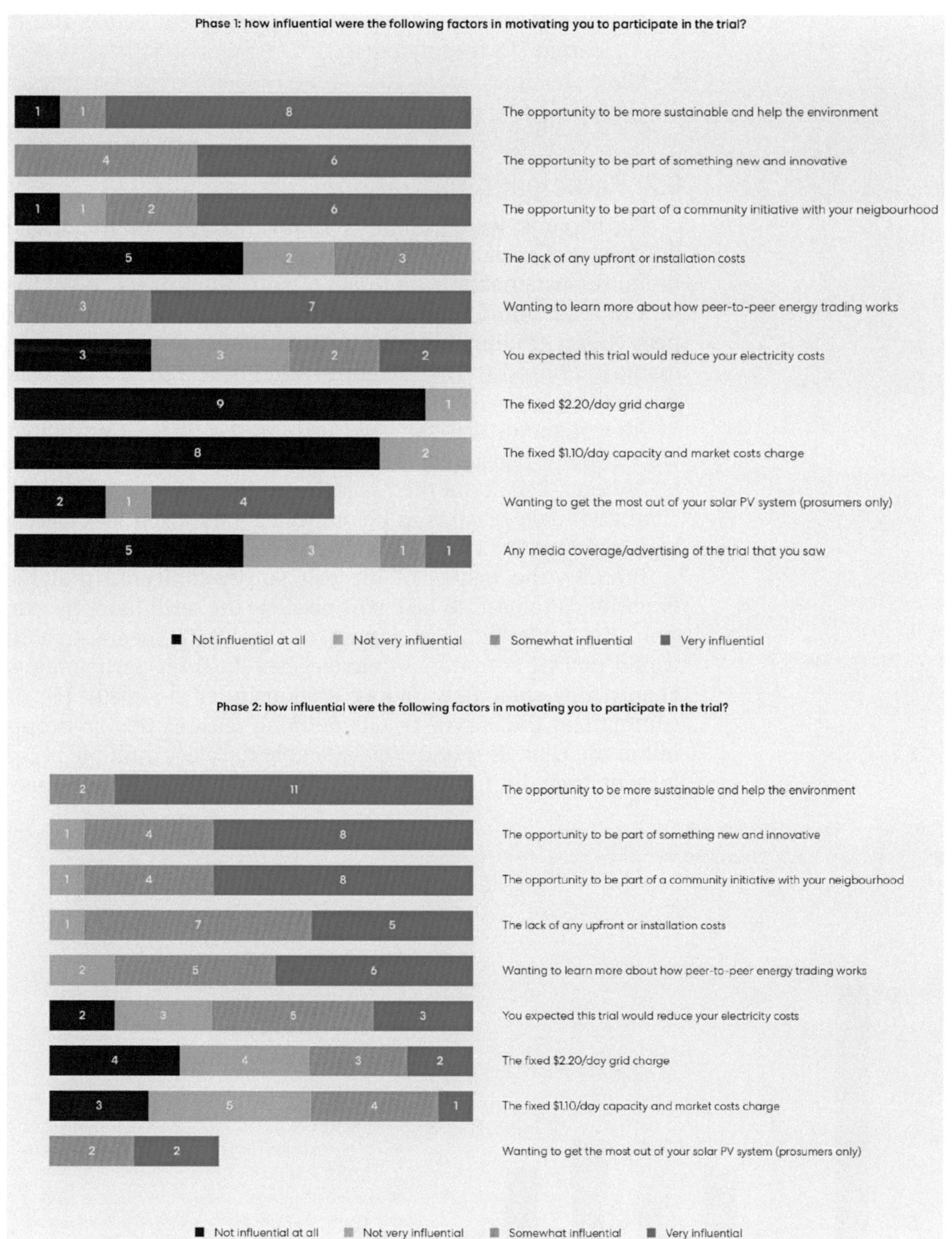

Figure 18.7 Phase 1 (*above*) and Phase 2 (*below*) participant motivations for participation.

 - An exit survey of recruits that withdrew before the trial started (13 respondents).
- Phase 2
 - A post-trial participant survey (13 respondents).

6.2 Participant motivations

Participants were primarily motivated to join the trial for nonfinancial reasons. The key reasons given were; wanting to be more sustainable, to be part of something innovative, to be part of a community initiative and to learn more about peer-to-peer energy trading. Fig. 18.7 outlines the responses from participants in Phase 1 ($n = 10$) above and Phase 2 ($n = 13$), below, respectively.

An exit survey was sent by Curtin to the Phase 1 participants who initially registered their interest but did not actually sign up. When asked about their reasons for withdrawing, participants cited two main reasons as being because the fixed fees were too high and that the trial tariff rewards big energy users.

Broadly, the results of the exit survey indicated that these households refused to take part because the tariff (and, by extension, the underlying economics of the SWIS) meant that they would not see a material financial benefit from participating in energy-only solar P2P trading (Wilkinson et al., 2020). Fig. 18.8 summarizes the survey results defining reasons people dropped out of the trial. Respondents were able to select multiple reasons for why they did not want to participate in the trial and then to

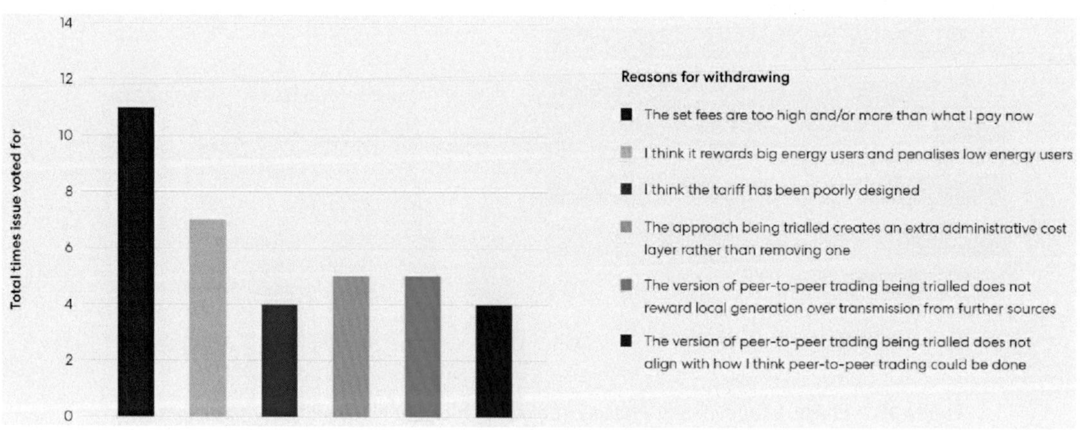

Figure 18.8 Participant motivations for withdrawing from the trial.

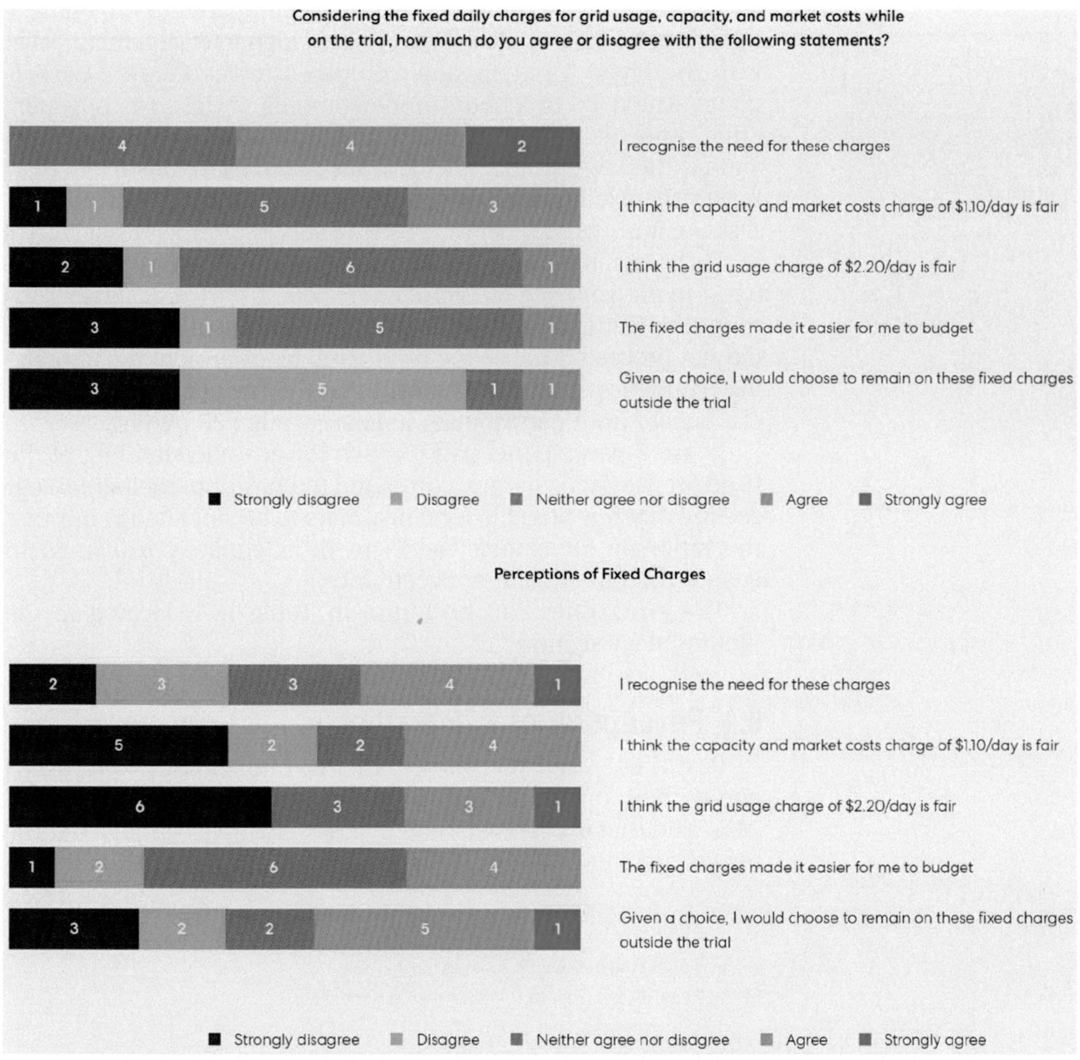

Figure 18.9 Phase 1 (*above*) and phase 2 (*below*) participant perceptions of the trial's fixed charges.

rate these in order or priority. The height of the bars indicates the number of times the reason was voted for.

6.3 Perception of pricing

Generally, there were mixed perceptions of the charges used in the trial tariffs in both Phase 1 and 2. Participants in Phase 2 perceived the fixed charges more negatively and were less likely to recognize the need for these charges compared to the Phase 1 participants. This is likely due to the higher engagement level with the Phase 1 participants compared to the Phase 2 participants, which led to a better understanding of the costs of generating and delivering electricity. Unsurprisingly, participants viewed the low variable energy rates much more positively relative to the fixed charges. Fig. 18.9 displays the results from Phase 1 above and Phase 2 below, posttrial surveys, respectively.

These sentiments were also shared by those who registered interest in participating but withdrew before it started. A survey conducted by Curtin University from Phase 1 indicated that households did not proceed because the tariff (and, by extension, the underlying economics of the SWIS) meant that they would not see a financial benefit from participating in energy-only P2P trading.

Phase 2 participants had a much lower understanding of the need for the fixed charges, compared to Phase 1 participants, suggesting that it is possible for consumers to accept change but that the rationale for change needs to be adequately explained to ensure there is consumer acceptance.

The exact rates can be found in Table 18.1, located in the Methodology section.

6.4 Perception of P2P trading

Posttrials, when the participants of both phases were asked about their understanding of P2P trading, a majority (17/23, 74%) said that they understood it very well or well enough—these results are shown in Fig. 18.10.

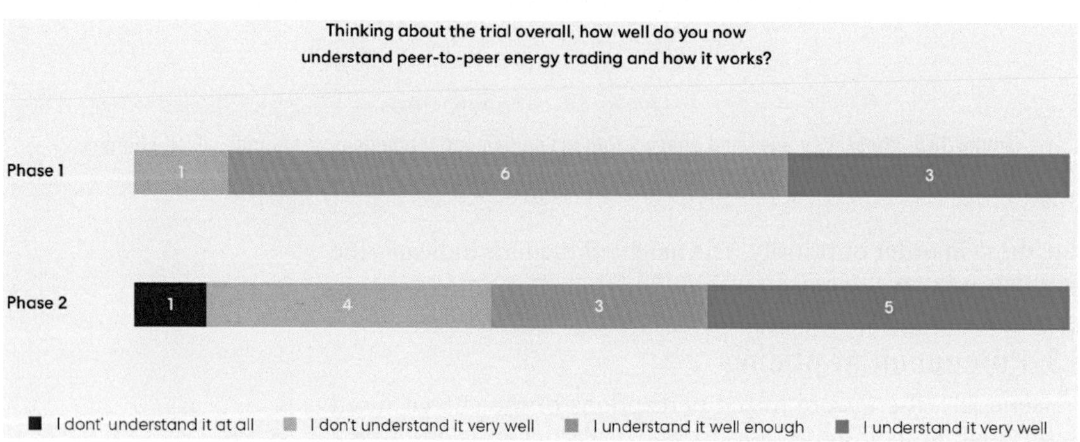

Figure 18.10 Participant motivations for withdrawing from the trial.

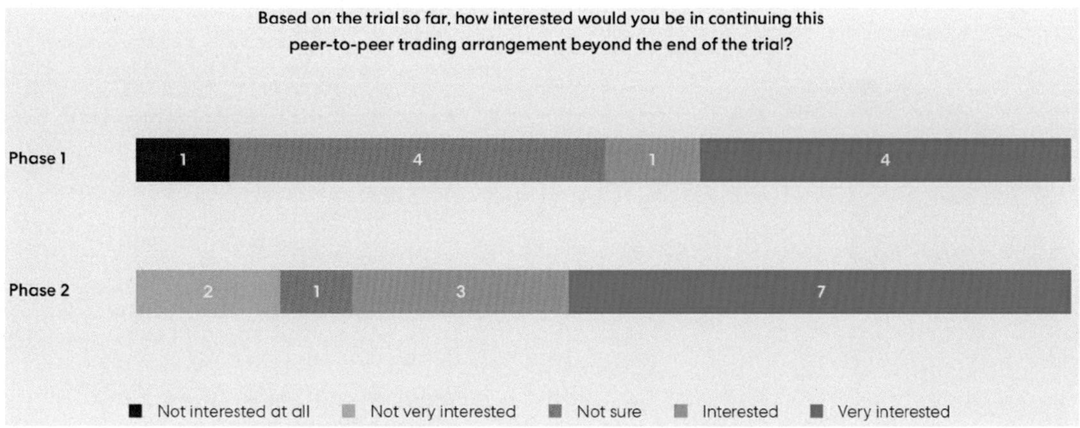

Figure 18.11 Participants' desire to continue with P2P trading.

When asked if they would continue with P2P trading outside of trial, most Phase 1 participants were interested or undecided whereas a clear majority of Phase 2 participants were interested. Fig. 18.11 outlines these findings and some of the reasons given for why they were interested.

When asked about whether participants would actually continue with P2P trading, 78% (18/23) said they would continue if it saved them money or did not cost them any extra, while 22% (5/23) of the participants said they would regardless of whether it cost them money. Fig. 18.12 breaks down the participants' savings expectations from each trial phase, Phase 1 above and Phase 2 below.

When the Phase 2 participants were asked about their experience with using the Power Ledger platform, 42% (5/12) had a positive or very positive experience using it. 50% (6/12) had a neutral experience, with the single participant (8%, 1/12) citing a negative experience.

6.5 Perceptions of energy use

A secondary aim of the trials was to investigate whether solar P2P could encourage participants to shift their consumption to the middle of the day (when solar generation is at its maximum) and away from the morning and evening peaks.

The results of the posttrial surveys indicated that participants were significantly more aware of their energy usage habits. A majority of participants (69%) in both phases stated they considered shifting their energy usage to daylight hours when tradable

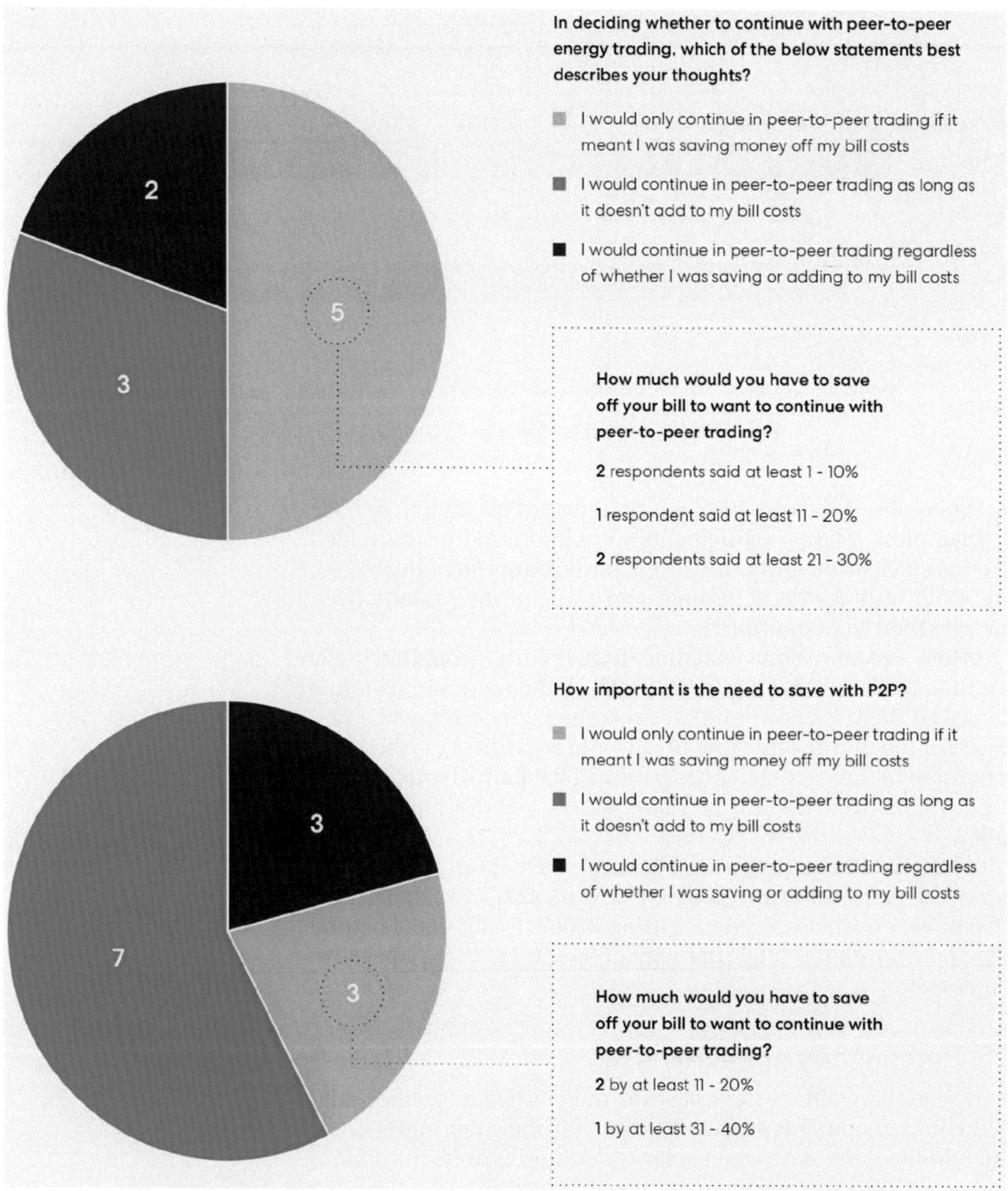

Figure 18.12 Participant expectations of savings required to continue with P2P trading.

energy was available (P1: 7/10, P2: 9/13) and most of this subset (75%) stating they made an effort to alter their usage habits (P1:

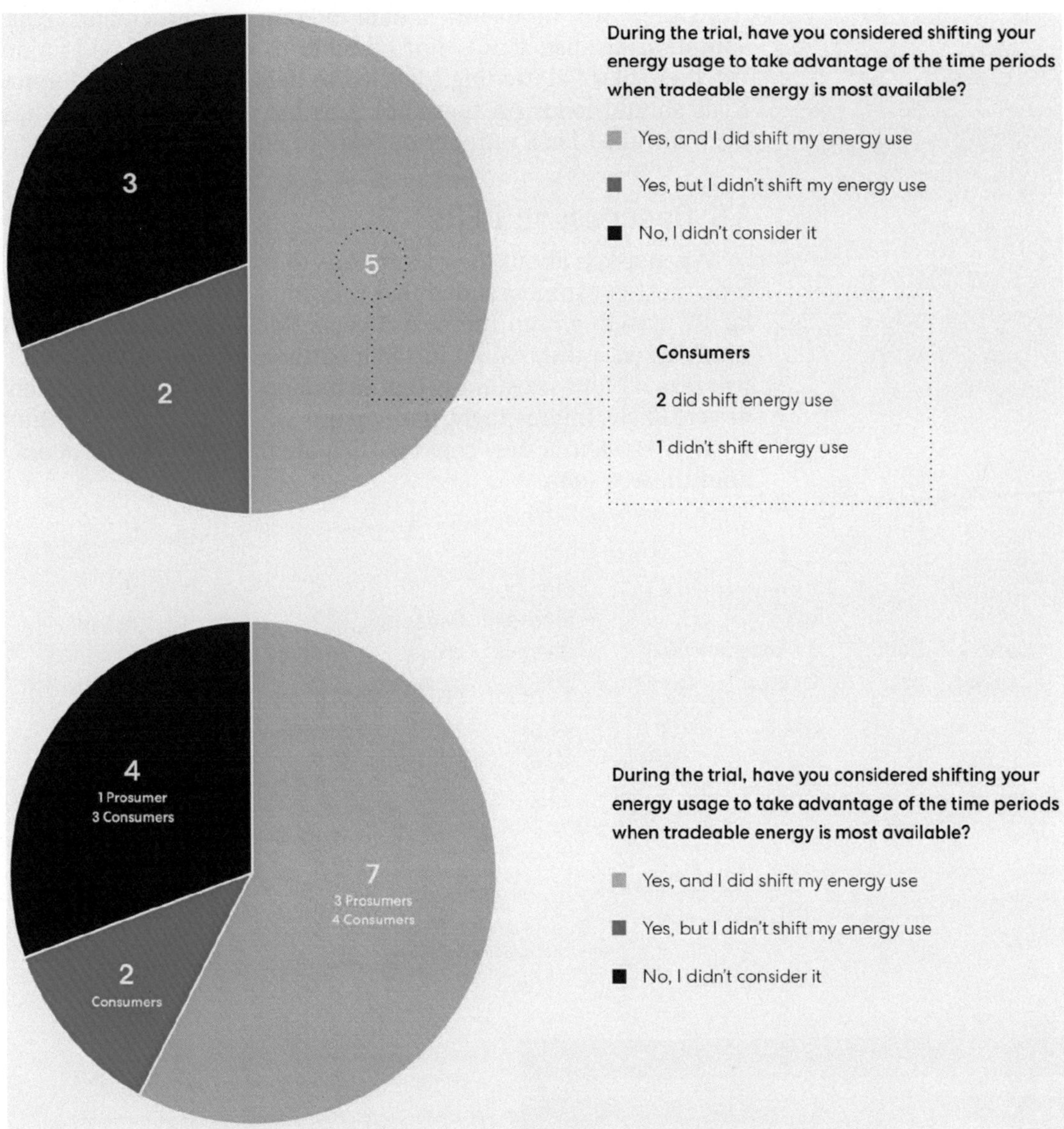

Figure 18.13 Participants' subjective evaluations of their energy usage behavior.

5/7, P2: 7/9). This indicates that participation in P2P energy trading did make users more conscious of their energy use and were inclined to change their behavior depending on the price of electricity. Fig. 18.13 outlines the participants' subjective evaluations of whether their behavior changed during the trial, separated by trial phase. Phase 1 above and Phase 2 below.

As there was no historical data to compare participants' consumption against, it was not possible to objectively determine whether solar P2P trading trials led to behavioral change. Future trials should focus on households with a smart meter that has been installed for a number of years to enable a comparison.

6.6 Openness to DERs

When asked about their intentions to purchase a solar PV system, most consumers stated that they intended to purchase a solar PV system within the next 5 years. Most consumers said no when asked if they would install a battery system within 5 years, whereas all four prosumers that responded said they were likely or very likely. Interestingly, participants were more likely to install a battery system if they could participate in a VPP. Fig. 18.14 outlines these results.

Battery capacity	Battery cost	Self-consumption savings	P2P revenue	Energy arbitrage revenue (VPP)	Capacity credit payment	LFAS revenue (VPP)	Total income	Payback period self consumption	Payback period (self consumption + VPP)
10 kWh	$11,775	$913.86	$110.11	$35.54	$98.22	$313.00	$1470.73	12.88 years	8.00 years
15 kWh	$15,175	$937.86	$297.84	$42.65	$117.86	$376.00	$1772.18	16.18 years	8.56 years

Note: all fields are annualized.

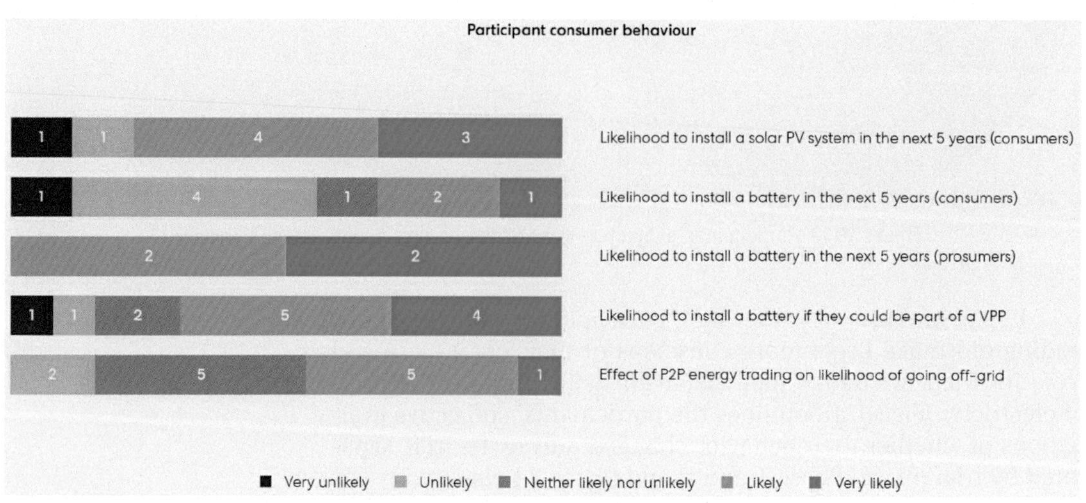

Figure 18.14 Participant consumer behavior.

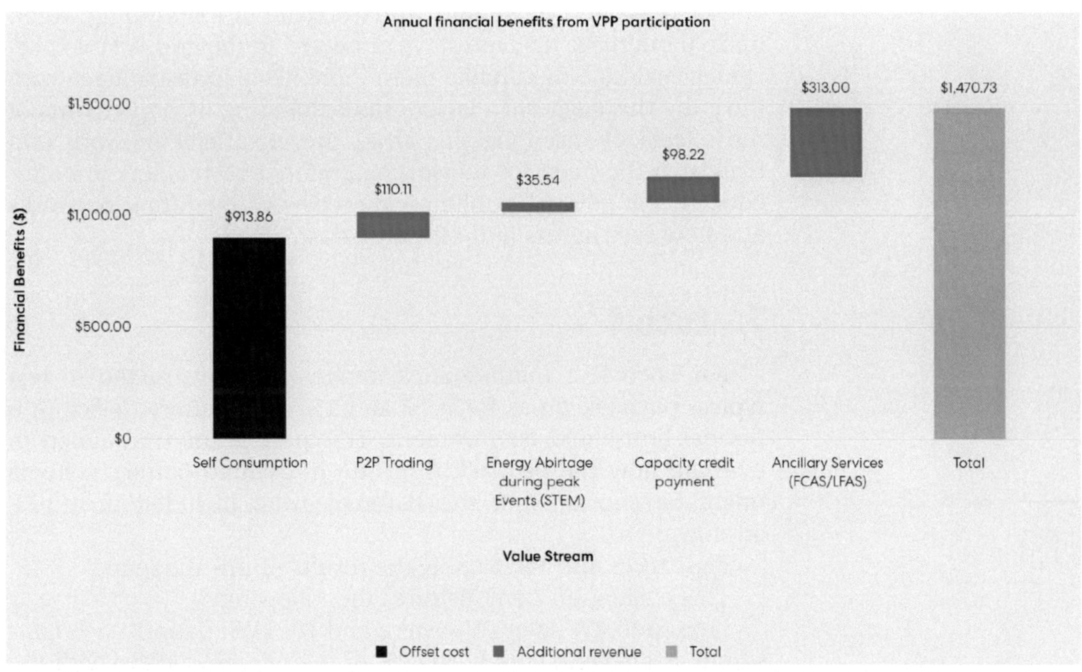

Figure 18.15 VPP benefits for an average SWIS consumer with a 5 kW solar PV system +10 kWh battery.

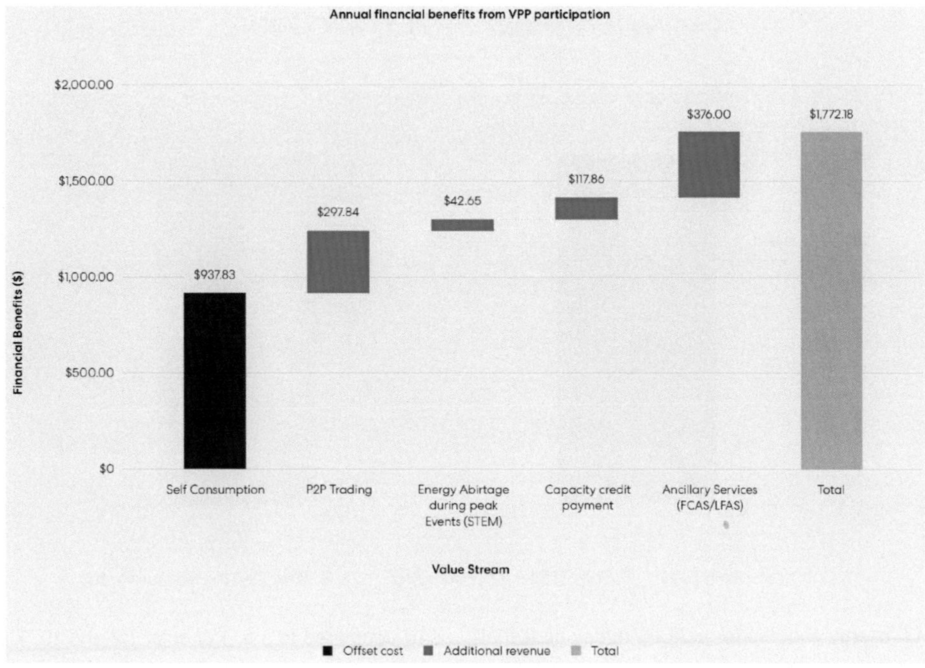

Figure 18.16 VPP benefits for an average SWIS consumer with an 8 kW solar PV system +15 kWh battery.

When asked if being able to participate in P2P trading would make them more likely to stay connected to the grid, a large percentage said it would make them more likely to disconnect from the grid. This suggests a lack of understanding by participants of the effects of disconnecting from the electricity network and highlights the need for network operators and retailers to better educate the general public on the costs of operating networks and how their tariffs and bills are constructed.

7. Loco 1

For Loco 1, a mathematical model was constructed to test typical payback times for a 10 and 15 kWh battery device in a normal household environment. This part of the trial aimed to evaluate how the payback times on household battery systems might be shortened if the batteries were included in a VPP arrangement.

Figs. 18.15 and 18.16 show the results of this modeling.

This evaluation demonstrates the following:

From a 5 kW solar PV system and 10 kWh battery each consumer was able to supply 86.87% of their energy needs, with the remaining 13.13% being supplied from the grid. The results of

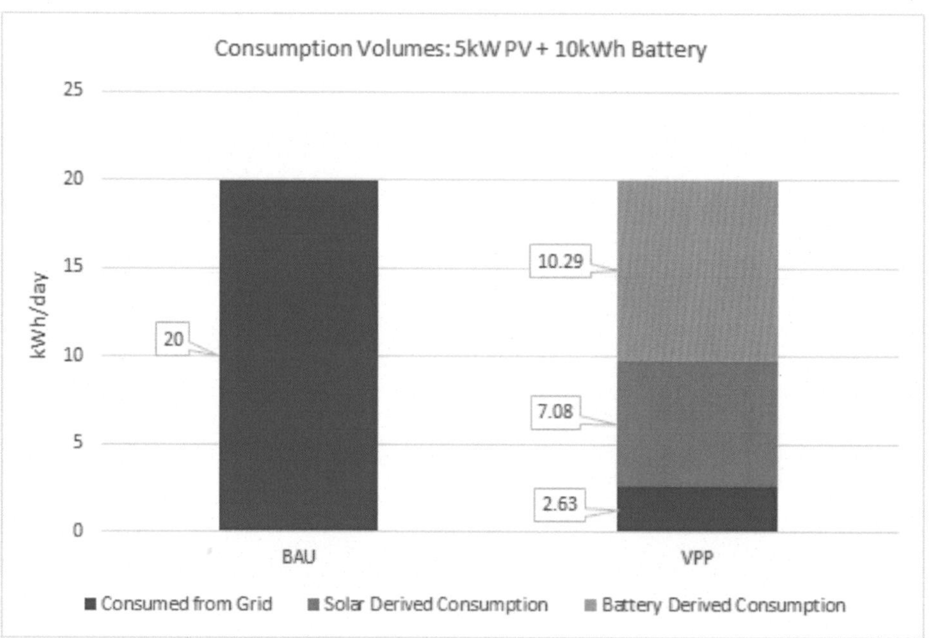

Figure 18.17 Energy sources for a 20 kWh/day household—BAU compared to a 5 kW solar PV and 10 kWh battery.

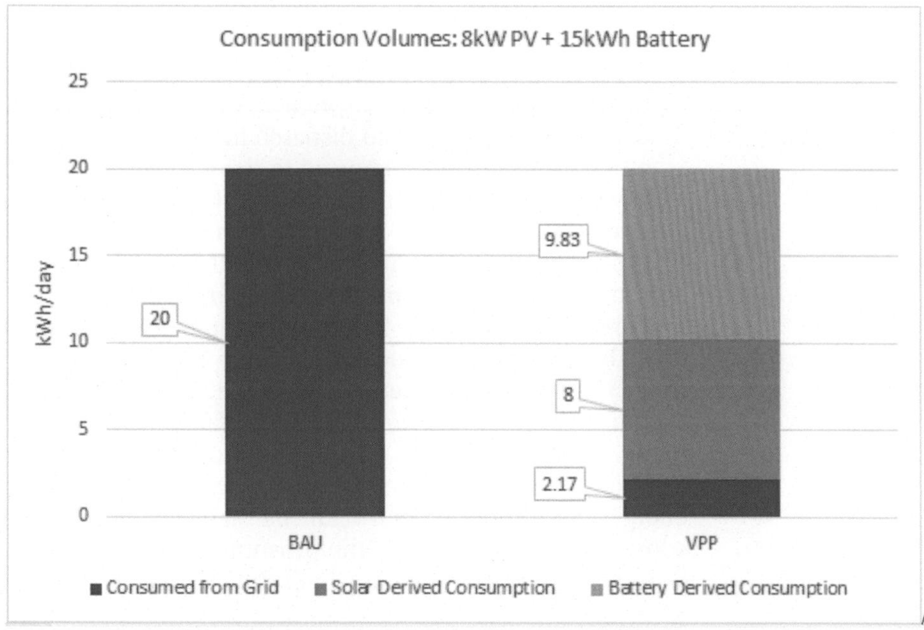

Figure 18.18 Energy sources for a 20 kWh/day household—BAU compared to an 8 kW solar PV and 10 kWh battery.

this can be seen in Fig. 18.17. From an 8 kW solar PV system and 15 kWh battery the household was able to supply 89.14% of their energy needs. The results of this can be seen in Fig. 18.18.

A primary purpose of the RENeW Nexus project was to examine the potential for localized, transactive electricity markets in the SWIS and how they can contribute to the required system outcomes. For this purpose, a second set of modeling was conducted to determine the degree to which a VPP can increase localized energy markets. Specifically, to what degree can a community meet its own energy needs, measured inside a localized distribution area, on a half-hourly basis and reduce its reliance on external energy sources, and in doing so, contribute toward providing grid services in a more cost-effective way. The second model used the following assumptions:

- The market consisted of 29% of prosumers with a combined solar and storage system who were participating in a VPP and 71% being consumers with no solar PV or storage system. This is consistent with the overall percentage of prosumers and consumers in the SWIS of 28.8% ("Australian PV Institute Solar Map", 2021).
- The results of the first model were used as electricity import and export kWh values for the prosumers.

- Consumers had a daily consumption of 13.436 kWh, which is the average consumption of a household in the SWIS (Residential Electricity Price Trends, 2019).
- If there was an STEM high-price event or FCAS dispatch opportunity, the battery would dispatch for the highest value event, otherwise, all energy exported to the grid was traded P2P.
- It was assumed that there were dispatch instructions being given by the market operator using a Distributed Energy Resource Management System (DERMS) layer to match prosumer export with consumer demand.

Three scenarios were incorporated into the analysis to evaluate the potential for localized energy markets, which in this project is defined as a market within the same low-voltage distribution area downstream of the same feeder, to meet local demand. The degree to which the community can provide localized energy autonomy is defined as the percentage of local energy consumption that can be satisfied from both self-consumption (provided by the prosumer's batteries) and energy exported from the prosumer households, that is, energy traded across the grid.

The results are summarized here (Fig. 18.19):

Scenario	Percentage of prosumers	Solar PV system size (kW)	Battery system size (kWh)	Degree of localized energy autonomy
1	29%	5	10	11%
2	29%	8	15	30%
3	50%	8	15	68%

Overall discussion of the findings

- Under scenario 2, renewable energy autonomy would sit at 30.22% due to the self-consumption provided by prosumers having a battery installed, as well as the VPP dispatching

Scenario	Percentage of prosumers	Solar PV system size (kW)	Battery system size (kWh)	Degree of localised energy autonomy
1	29%	5	10	11%
2	29%	8	15	30%
3	50%	8	15	68%

Figure 18.19 Results for each modeled VPP scenario.

energy from their batteries to meet their neighbor's energy needs. Increasing the percentage of VPP participants in the local area to 50% (i.e., scenario 3) increased local energy autonomy to 67.9%.

- The usual consumer benefit from installing a home battery system is that the prosumer consumer needs to procure less energy from the market as well as the system benefit of dealing with reverse flows of energy. By also participating in a VPP, households could sell battery-sourced energy to the STEM and LFAS markets, as well as electricity from the battery to their neighbors. Providing these services could yield a 36% increase in annual financial benefit for the household with a 5 kW solar PV and 10 kWh battery system, decreasing the payback period from 13 to 8 years and incentivizing households to install more solar PV and battery systems. This could also reduce or avoid the need for network augmentation, reducing the need for adding further costs to the network and grid tariffs.

Overall, this suggests the possibility of offering a low-cost market mechanism for trading electricity that would encourage solar and storage to be sized to contribute services to the grid, rather than just self-supply. This would need to be investigated, whether it be inclusion in the existing dual-market structure (i.e., the capacity market) or within a two-sided market structure, each could seek to resolve physical issues in the network by creating the right economic incentives for prosumers to strategically install and operate DER assets.

While the VPP modeled for this chapter focused on household battery systems, it should be noted that businesses with commercial-scale battery systems could also participate in a VPP if they meet the requirements outlined previously.

8. Conclusions

The RENeW Nexus project was intended to look at the potential for and benefits of localized, transactive electricity markets. This is defined as a market that exists within the same low-voltage distribution area downstream of the same feeder. Each market could be linked to other markets such that any net energy export from one market, caused by a net excess of solar PV energy within it, could be used to supply another local energy market linked within a section of the distribution network. This involved looking at the potential for communities to sustain more of their own consumption from local solar PV energy and battery energy via P2P trading, and the benefits that can be derived from a VPP from a grid and consumer perspective.

The trial results showed transactive electricity trading was a success from a technical standpoint. Participant demand for energy trading was highly dependent on the price structure. Due to the trial tariff structure and the high daily fixed costs involved, participants' financial outcomes relative to the comparison rate (the default residential tariff) were largely dependent on their daily energy consumption rather than their trading volume. Participants that had a high energy consumption (>11 kWh/day) were almost always better off compared to the residential A1 tariff, because the low per-kWh rate used in the trial meant that they were penalized less for consuming more. Low consumers (<11 kWh/day) were almost always worse off since the high fixed fees meant they had a large monthly cost regardless of their consumption, whereas under the A1 tariff they paid less due to the relatively higher volumetric component.

The survey results showed participants were generally enthusiastic about the trials and energy trading, with participants from both phases wanting to be part of an innovative sustainable community project. However, the survey also showed some participants may not have fully understood the rationale for paying for the grid and how energy was priced. This highlights the need for utilities to clearly and effectively educate the general public on any new concepts or changes that are made to the electricity system.

The most significant result was that the coupling of prosumers with batteries either through their own or a community battery enables them to monetize their excess solar at all times of the day, without any subsidy, and also provide services to the grid. This will need some rule changes but government subsidies can be reduced and system benefits can be delivered to the network in a more efficient way.

Ultimately, the value for allowing customers to trade electricity is that retailers can procure electricity and network services from their customers, providing new income streams to battery owners, while decarbonizing the grid more rapidly and effectively.

Glossary

ACCC Australian Competition and Consumer Commission

AEMC Australian Energy Market Commission

AEMO Australian Energy Market Operator

API Application Programming Interface

BAU Business as Usual

C&I Commercial and Industrial

COAG	Council of Australia Governments
CSIRO	Commonwealth Scientific and Industrial Research Organisation
DER	Distributed Energy Resources
DNSP	Distribution Network Service Provider
ERA	Economic Regulatory Authority
FCAS	Frequency Control Ancillary Service
GW	Gigawatt
kW	Kilowatt
kWh	Kilowatt-hour
LFAS	Load Following Ancillary Service
MW	Megawatt
MWh	Megawatt-hour
NEM	National Electricity Market
P2P	Peer-to-peer
PV	Photovoltaic
REBS	Renewable Energy Buyback Scheme
SPS	Standalone Power System
STEM	Short-Term Energy Market
SWIS	South West Interconnected System
TNSP	Transmission Network Service Provider
ToU	Time of Use
UK	United Kingdom
VPP	Virtual Power Plant
WA	Western Australia
WEM	Wholesale Energy Market
WOSP	Whole of System Plan

References

AEMO, 2018. Microgrids and Associated Technologies. Ebook, Nineteenth ed. Australian Energy Market Operator Limited https://www.parliament.wa.gov.au/Parliament/commit.nsf/luInquiryPublicSubmissions/DE299CB91F2A0B8448258279002434BB/$file/20180413%20-%20MAT%20-%20Sub%20No.19%20-%20AEMO.pdf.

AEMO, 2019a. 2019 Electricity Statement of Opportunities. Ebook. Australian Energy Market Operator Limited. https://www.aemo.com.au/-/media/Files/Electricity/NEM/Planning_and_Forecasting/NEM_ESOO/2019/2019-Electricity-Statement-of-Opportunities.pdf.

AEMO, 2019b. Integrating Utility-Scale Renewables and Distributed Energy Resources in the SWIS. Ebook. Australian Energy Market Operator LimitedAEMO. https://www.aemo.com.au/-/media/Files/Electricity/WEM/Security_and_Reliability/2019/Integrating-Utility-scale-Renewables-and-DER-in-the-SWIS.pdf.

Atamturk, N., 2014. Transactive Energy: A Surreal Vision or a Necessary and Feasible Solution to Grid Problems? California Public Utilities Commission, Tech. Rep.

Annual Report 2018-2019, 2019. Ebook. Australian Energy Market Commission, Sydney. https://www.aemc.gov.au/sites/default/files/2019-11/AEMC%20Annual%20Report%202018-2019.PDF.

Australian PV Institute Solar Map, 2021. Pv-Map.Apvi.Org.Au. https://pv-map.apvi.org.au/historical.

Byrne, J., Mouritz, M., Taylor, M., Jessica, K., Breadsell, 2020. East Village at Knutsford: a case study in sustainable urbanism. Sustainability 12 (16), 6296. https://doi.org/10.3390/su12166296.

Colthorpe, A., 2020. 'Repowering' Japan: Reporting from PV Expo in Tokyo, Part 2—PV Tech. PV Tech. https://www.pv-tech.org/repowering-japan-reporting-from-pv-expo-in-tokyo-part-2/.

Creating The Rural Network Of The Future: Stand-Alone Power Systems, 2019. Ebook. Perth: Western Power. https://www.westernpower.com.au/media/3177/stand-alone-power-systems-round1-brochure-20190222.pdf.

Economic Regulation Authority, 2018. Report to the Minister for Energy on the Effectiveness of the Wholesale Electricity Market 2018. Ebook. Perth: Economic Regulation Authority. https://www.parliament.wa.gov.au/publications/tabledpapers.nsf/displaypaper/4012365ae79dcabf169e53fd482583d90005d956/$file/2365.pdf.

Electricity Industry (Licence Conditions) Regulations, 2005 (WA): https://www.legislation.wa.gov.au/legislation/prod/filestore.nsf/FileURL/mrdoc_32111.pdf/$FILE/Electricity%20Industry%20(Licence%20Conditions)%20Regulations%202005%20-%20%5B01-b0-01%5D.pdf?OpenElement.

Energy Policy, W.A., 2021. Household Electricity Pricing. Wa.Gov.Au. Accessed May 27. https://www.wa.gov.au/organisation/energy-policy-wa/household-electricity-pricing.

Energy Transformation Taskforce, 2019. DER Roadmap: Appendix B—DER Project Stocktake. Energy Transformation Taskforce, Perth.

Energy Transformation Taskforce, 2019. Distributed Energy Resources Roadmap. Ebook. Energy Transformation Taskforce, Perth. https://www.wa.gov.au/sites/default/files/2020-04/DER_Roadmap.pdf.

Energy Transformation Taskforce, 2019. Energy Transformation Strategy: A Brighter Energy Future. Department of Treasury, Perth.

Green, J., Newman, P., 2017a. Citizen utilities: the emerging power paradigm. Energy Policy 105, 283–293. http://www.sciencedirect.com/science/article/pii/S0301421517300800.

Green, J., Newman, P., 2017b. Planning and Governance for Decentralised Energy Assets in Medium-Density Housing: The WGV Gen Y Case Study. Urban Policy and Research. https://doi.org/10.1080/08111146.2017.1295935.

Integrating Distributed Energy Resources For The Grid Of The Future, 2019. Ebook. Sydney. https://www.aemc.gov.au/sites/default/files/2019-09/Final%20report%20-%20ENERFR%202019%20-%20EPR0068.PDF.

Legislative Assembly, 2020. Taking Charge: Western Australia's Transition to a Distributed Energy Future. Parliament of Western Australia, Perth.

Movellan, J., 2019. End of the Residential FIT in Japan. Post FIT Recs Go to RE100 Companies. Renewable Energy World. https://www.renewableenergyworld.com/solar/end-of-the-residential-fit-in-japan-post-fit-recs-go-to-re100-companies/#gref.

Parkinson, G., 2022. Rooftop solar smashes demand and supply records in world's biggest isolated grid. Renew Economy. October. https://reneweconomy.com.au/rooftop-solar-smashes-demand-andsupply-records-in-worlds-biggest-isolated-grid/.

Residential Electricity Price Trends 2019, 2019. Ebook. Australian Energy Markey Commission, Sydney. https://www.aemc.gov.au/sites/default/files/2019-12/2019%20Residential%20Electricity%20Price%20Trends%20final%20report%20FINAL.pdf.
Smart Cities And Suburbs, 2020. Department of Infrastructure, Regional Development and Cities. https://infrastructure.gov.au/cities/smart-cities/index.aspx.
Standard Electricity Prices And Charges: South West Interconnected System, 2020. Ebook. Synergy. https://www.synergy.net.au/-/media/Files/PDF-Library/Standard_Electricity_Prices_Charges_brochure.pdf.
The Fulcrum Agency, 2020. The White Gum Valley (WGV) Project at the Eastern Outskirts of Fremantle Combined Apartments, Single Residential Buildings and Development Types of Other Typical Use Patterns, to Trial Peer-To-Peer Trading with Integrated Storage and a Shared EV-Charging Station [image] Available at: https://www.thefulcrum.agency/case/wgv.
Wilkinson, S., Hojckova, K., Eon, C., Morrison, G.M., Sandén, B., 2020. Is peer-to-peer electricity trading empowering users? Evidence on motivations and roles in A prosumer business model trial in Australia. Energy Research & Social Science 66, 101500. https://doi.org/10.1016/j.erss.2020.101500.
Wu, W., George, Q., Schleiger, E., Bratanova, A., Graham, P., Spak, B., 2019. The Future of Peer-To-Peer Trading of Distributed Renewable Energy. CSIRO. Ebook. Brisbane. https://data61.csiro.au/~/media/D61/Files/19-00178_DATA61_REPORT_RenewNexus_WEB_1905301.pdf.

Further reading

Advanced Meters Puts the Power in Your Hands, 2020. Western Power. https://www.westernpower.com.au/our-energy-evolution/projects-and-trials/advanced-meters-puts-the-power-in-your-hands/.
AEMO, 2020. AEMO Virtual Power Plant Demonstration. Ebook. Australian Energy Market Operator Limited. https://arena.gov.au/assets/2020/03/aemo-virtual-power-plant-demonstration-knowledge-sharing-report-1.pdf.
Australian Competition, Consumer Commission, 2017. Retail Electricity Inquiry: Preliminary Report. Commonwealth of Australia, Canberra.
CSIRO, 2013. The Future Grid Forum's Analysis of Australia's Potential Electricity Pathways to 2050. Ebook. CSIRO, Newcastle. https://www.csiro.au/~/media/EF/Files/Future-grid-forum-change-choice.
Department of Treasury, 2018. Improving Access to the Western Power Network. State of Western Australia.
Lavine, M., 2017. Bloomberg—Are You A Robot? Bloomberg.Com. https://www.bloomberg.com/opinion/articles/2017-02-17/dole-food-had-too-many-shares.
Minister for Mines and Petroleum; Energy; Corrective Services, 2020. State Government Rolls Out First Community Battery in Perth. https://www.mediastatements.wa.gov.au/Pages/McGowan/2020/02/State-Government-rolls-out-first-community-battery-in-Perth.aspx.
Power Ledger White Paper, 2019. Ebook. Power Ledger, Perth. https://www.powerledger.io/company/power-ledger-whitepaper.
Vorrath, S., 2018. WA govt considers home battery incentives. In: Solar Tariff Review. Reneweconomy. https://reneweconomy.com.au/wa-govt-considers-home-battery-incentives-solar-tariff-review-36744/.

19

The Insight Engine 2.0: the body and biomimetic systems as intelligent environments

Bill Seaman, Quran Karriem, Dev Seth, Hojung Ashley Kwon and John Herr
Duke University, Durham, North Carolina

1. The body as intelligent environment

Although researchers have made great strides in exploring new forms of artificial intelligence and extended intelligence (EI), the human body/brain/mind/environment is perhaps still the highest-level intelligent system known to be in existence. The inclusion of evidence from other intelligent living species, choosing alternate definitions of intelligence or systems of communication than those employing human natural language for communication, interpretive purposes, and social exchanges of information, falls outside of the scope of this research. For this text, we will focus on human sentience production. A statement from the Allen Institute exemplifies part of the kinds of research we are interested in:

> *The human brain is what makes us who we are. It's also arguably the most complex structure in all of biology. We believe that to truly understand the brain, we must study it on multiple scales, from the genes that make individual neurons unique to the circuits that drive behavior. We map the brain through comprehensive atlases that we share with the global neuroscience community to accelerate their work … Our neuroscience research falls into three broad categories: We describe the fundamental parts of the brain, its cells, synapses and circuits. We study the brain's computation, how those parts come together to represent information about our environment. Ultimately, we aim to understand cognition itself, or how the millions of different*

Intelligent Environments. https://doi.org/10.1016/B978-0-12-820247-0.00014-X

> *molecules and electrical synapses that crisscross the brain translate into thoughts, memories, behavior.*
>
> **(Allen Institute for Brain Science, undated)**

The body is an ultracomplex biomachine, with a complexity greater than all "human-made" systems. Robert Rosen early on saw the limitations of the machine metaphor in relation to biological research. In a book published in 1999, *Essays on Life Itself,* Rosen points to a particular form of limit:

> *I have attempted to introduce, and to motivate, a concept of complexity. A system is called complex if it has a nonsimulable model. The science of such complex systems is very different from the science we have become used to over the past three centuries. Above all, complex systems cannot be completely characterized in terms of any reductionistic scheme based on simple systems. Since the science is different, so too are technologies based on it, as well as any craft pertaining to the systems with which that science deals.*
>
> **(Rosen, 1999, p. 307)**

Perhaps we can devise an ultracomplex simulable model given the potentials of new computational systems—or we can work toward building a system to explore complex mathematics and logic that enable new forms of modeling ultracomplex systems? Perhaps this is one of the highest goals of our project. Rosen, in the 1999 text suggests:

> *It is too early to tell how such ideas will develop in the future. My purpose here has been to introduce some of the flavors of the concept of complexity, how it pertains to basic biological issues, and how it may force a complete reevaluation, not only of our science, but of our concepts of art and of craft as well. Indeed, it may turn out, as it has before, that the pursuit of craft may provide the best kind of probe to guide our science itself.*
>
> **(Rosen, 1999, p. 307)**

Our project seeks to provide a technological platform to aid in the research of such future ideas related to complexity.

In their paper entitled *Es are Good: Cognition as enacted, embodied, embedded, affective and extended,* Dave Ward and Mog Stapleton from the School of Philosophy, Psychology and Language Sciences, University of Edinburgh, present the following perspective:

> *We present a specific elaboration and partial defense of the claims that cognition is enactive, embodied, embedded, affective and (potentially) extended. According to the view we will defend, the enactivist claim that perception and cognition essentially depend upon the cognizer's interactions with their environment is fundamental. If a particular instance of this kind of dependence*

> *pertains, we will argue, then it follows that cognition is essentially embodied and embedded, that the underpinnings of cognition are inextricable from those of affect, that the phenomenon of cognition itself is essentially bound up with affect, and that the possibility of cognitive extension depends upon the instantiation of a specific mode of skillful interrelation between cognizer and environment. Thus, if cognition is enactive then it is also embodied, embedded, affective and potentially extended.*
>
> **(Ward and Stapleton, 2012a,b)**

Humans learn from embodied actions in the natural environment and via human interaction with the extended environment of our technological man-made information systems. Language as being primarily logocentric potentially needs to be reunderstood related to our internet use, pervaded with images and sound as well as text … not to mention visualization and sonification modalities. Fields of meaning of image, sound, and text act upon each other with an ongoing meaning summing as the associations of the media interactant are enfolded in the production of meaning. Thus, as individuals, we each weave our own understanding of meanings based on the history of our embodied interactions, learning, our self-reflection, and creative thought. Interacting with various natural and electronic environments is central to this building up of our intelligence and knowledge production over a lifetime. A paper by Joichi Ito from the MIT Media Lab discusses a related form of EI:

> *But beyond distinguishing between creating an artificial intelligence (AI), or augmenting human intelligence (IA), perhaps the first and fundamental question is* where does intelligence lie? *Hasn't it always [in relation to computation and sociality, emphasis Seaman], resided beyond any single mind extended by machines into a network of many minds and machines, all of them interacting as a kind of networked intelligence (Hidalgo, 2016) that transcends and merges humans and machines? (Ito, 2016)*

We humans attribute intelligence to other beings, and/or to systems which display intelligent behavior that we interact with linguistically. Thus, intelligence can be described as linguistic and social by nature and arises in sentient beings through learning—through a myriad of forms of knowledge production. This also becomes a meta-system, as the system systematically pays attention to its own self-organization.

This means that the human body is embedded in the larger natural and manmade environment that we are living within, existing in a delicate balance. We exist in a time where that balance is being tipped in a very dangerous direction. Réne Thom (1989) talks about a tipping point in his book *Structural Stability and Morphogenesis: An Outline of a General Theory of Models* where he discusses his Catastrophe Theory. Bob Rosen (1985) discusses related ideas in relation to biological systems in his book *Anticipatory Systems*. As we make predictive models about our future environment, the one where we as human intelligent environments are nested, we must begin to make careful choices about how we move forward environmentally. A. H. Louie in a text called *Robert Rosen's Anticipatory Systems*, provides Rosen's definition:

> *Now what is an anticipatory system? Here is Robert Rosen's definition:*
>
> *An anticipatory system is a natural system that contains an internal predictive model of itself and of its environment, which allows it to change state at an instant in accord with the model's predictions pertaining to a later instant.*
>
> *Note, in contrast, that a reactive system can only react, in the present, to changes that have already occurred in the causal chain, while an anticipatory system's present behavior involves aspects of past, present, and future. The presence of a predictive model serves precisely to pull the future into the present; a system with a "good" model thus behaves in many ways as if it can anticipate the future. Model-based behavior requires an entirely new paradigm, an "anticipatory paradigm", to accommodate it. This paradigm extends – but does not replace – the "reactive paradigm" which has hitherto dominated the study of natural systems. The "anticipatory paradigm" allows us a glimpse of new and important aspects of system behavior.*
>
> **(Louie, 2010)**

How can we humans become intelligent environments that better anticipate? Here I imagine new forms of AI that can function as supportive Anticipatory Systems. In part, this is discussed later as one of the pragmatic benchmarks of the Neosentient—thinking in imagined space before acting. Humans live in relation to their environment. Our species depends on a series of conditions to survive—relative temperature, oxygen for breathing, food for sustenance, clothing and shelter protecting us from adverse conditions, etc. We also live in a delicate balance with other organisms, animals, insects, bacteria, and viruses. Where a dominant culture has sought to conquer nature historically, many of us now seek ways to live in harmony with it. Yet, our behaviors and habits have changed our relation to the environment over time, and also the potential relations surrounding our own bodies and their machinic malleability, including both internal and external prosthetics. Our relation to the pervasiveness of machines has been both positive and negative.

The Anthropocene is discussed by Jos Lelieveld from Nature Magazine:

> *Paul J. Crutzen discovered how atmospheric pollutants can destroy stratospheric ozone, which protects Earth from harmful ultraviolet radiation. He shared the 1995 Nobel Prize in Chemistry for this work with F. Sherwood Rowland and Mario J. Molina, who had shown that such pollutants included chlorofluorocarbons. Combining rigorous research with a gift for communicating, Crutzen championed the term 'Anthropocene' to describe what he regarded as a new epoch, characterized by human dominance of biological, chemical and geological processes on Earth. He has died, aged 87 [in 2021].*
>
> **(Lelieveld, 2021)**

How can society, its individuals and groups, begin to tackle such global problems as a matter of urgency? Could new kinds of intelligent systems help answer such difficult global questions? What role does human sentience play in our coming to know the world, and developing new approaches to taking care of it? Can we develop new forms of AI and EI to help us in our tasks to anticipate future environmental problems? How could a new kind of intelligence be defined, one that might function as a collaborator to help us solve environmental problems, and push back against the effects of the Anthropocene and human destructive forces?

2. The Neosentient model environment

Seaman and Otto E. Rössler wrote a book called *Neosentience, The Benevolence Engine* (Rössler and Seaman, 2011). It provides hundreds of microchapters and background on the potentials and uniqueness of Neosentient research. Since then, Seaman has been working on a system to enable transdisciplinary research to develop this model of Neosentience. Central is developing an extended intelligence system, which seeks to help author a higher-order intelligent system. Initially, a transdisciplinary search engine and intelligent database was set up for testing as a closed system—The Insight Engine 1.0, where participants were invited to contribute papers and textually annotated media objects. We are now working toward a new open system, with additional AI aspects enfolded to assist with the processes it enables. The goal is to arrive at a model for an intelligent autonomous learning robotic system via transdisciplinary information processes and information exchanges. The long-term focus of this research is to develop an ultracomplex system, one that seeks to abstract human sentience via biomimetics. The ultimate goal of this model is to potentially enable Neosentience to arise via a robotic system's functionality. We call the transdisciplinary database and intelligent system designed to access it in a relevant manner for differing researchers, The Insight Engine 2.0. Thus, we develop the intelligent database and visualization system, such that the Insight Engine 2.0 can help work toward the creation of a higher-order intelligent system—The Neosentient entity, exploring the abstraction of human sentience in a machinic system. It must be noted that the first generation of the Insight Engine was already under production in 2012 as a closed system, with documentation presented publicly on the internet in 2014. Others have subsequently taken up our system's title. Why do we do this you ask—because this system may in its own way help unlock new approaches to human knowledge production that are unique, potentially helping us to solve the kinds of problems mentioned earlier through positive human/machine interaction.

Research related to this goal is accomplished through the use of an intelligent transdisciplinary database, search engine, a natural language Application Programming Interface (API), a dynamic set of visualization modes, and a series of independent collaborators, as well as computational collaborators—what we have entitled Micropeers—*The Insight Engine 2.0* (I_E). Rössler and I in the Neosentience book developed pragmatic benchmarks to define our Neosentient robotic entities, as opposed to the Turing Test (1950): the system could exhibit well-defined functionalities: It learns—through the enactive approach [and we may explore other approaches like conversation theory from Gordon Pask (1976)]; it intelligently navigates; it interacts via natural language; it generates simulations of behavior; it metaphorically "thinks" about potential behaviors before acting in physical space; it is creative in some manner; it comes to have a deep situated knowledge of context through multimodal sensing by abstracting and adopting the embodied, embedded approach; and it displays mirror competence. Seaman and Rössler have entitled this robotic entity *The Benevolence Engine*. They state that the interfunctionality of such a system is complex enough to operationally mimic human sentience. Benevolence can in principle arise in the interaction of two such systems. Synthetic emotions would also become operative within the system. The System would seek to be benevolent in nature.

I am working initially with a team of researchers at Duke University to define and articulate this new system to, in the long run, help a group of transdisciplinary researchers build a model for a higher-order intelligent system. The System development team for the Insight Engine 2.0 consists of Professor Bill Seaman, Ph.D., Computational Media, Arts and Cultures, Duke University; John Herr, Duke's Office of Information Technology; Dev Seth, Computer Science student, Duke University; Hojung (Ashley) Kwon, Computer Science student, Duke University, Quran Karriem, Duke Computational Media, Arts and Cultures Ph.D. researcher, with Seaman being the primary investigator. Many of the ideas for this text have been discussed together with this team and more formally in a series of abstracts that have been developed for a special session of a 2021 conference entitled—Theoretical and Foundational Problems (TFP) in Information Studies (TFP, 2021). These abstracts will later form the basis for a series of elaborated individual papers to be published in the conference proceedings (Burgin, forthcoming).

3. The enacted, embodied, embedded, extended approach, abstracted via biomimetics

The goal is to enfold the embodied, embedded, enactive, and extended approaches to understanding cognition in the human and then seek to articulate the entailment structures that enable this set of dynamic interrelations to function – I have earlier called this intra-relations. Ward and Stapleton, mentioned earlier, lay out a rich history of texts related to cognition as enacted, embodied, embedded, affective, and extended:

> *Over the past twenty years several claims about human cognition and its underpinnings have gained currency. Human cognition (henceforth 'cognition') can sometimes be* extended *– the material vehicles underpinning cognitive states and processes can extend beyond the boundaries of the cognizing organism (Clark and Chalmers, 1998; Hurley, 1998; Clark, 2008). Cognition is* enactive *– that is, dependent on aspects of the activity of the cognizing organism (Varela et al., 1991; Hurley, 1998; Noë, 2004; Thompson, 2007). Cognition is* embodied *– our cognitive properties and performances can crucially depend on facts about our embodiment (Haugeland, 1998; Clark, 1997). Cognition is* embedded *– our cognitive properties and performances can crucially depend on facts about our relationship to the*

> *surrounding environment (Haugeland, 1998; Clark, 1997; Hurley, 1998). Finally, cognition is* affective *(Colombetti, 2007; Ratcliffe, 2009) – that is, intimately dependent upon the value of the object of cognition to the cognizer. (Ward and Stapleton, 2012a,b).*

Because there are many different biological as well as machinic information systems involved in mapping and articulating such biological processes, as well as functioning as an extension of cognition, this necessitates a new transdisciplinary holistic approach to the study of the body and how the body as intelligent environment relates to the environment external to the body. What is at operation in the body that enables sentience to arise? The answer to this question requires a transdisciplinary approach to the problem. It would involve the body's bioabstraction (the machinic reframing of the body's functional biological structures) via biomimetics, to enable entailment structures to be reunderstood and reapplied in defining a model for a Neosentient system, in part articulating a new branch of AI. The idea is to define a transdisciplinary holistic approach which seeks to examine dynamic, time-based Mind/Brain/Body/Sensing/Environment relationalities.

The full entailment – the study of the structures at operation in the body – and the later potential emulation of the body's functionality especially related to what I have called the creation of an ultracomplex network of simulable models, after Rosen's ideas presented earlier, has to my knowledge not been achieved. This is due in part to the distributed nature of the mind/brain – as it falls in relation to the operation of the body – where a small event in one part of the brain might not be able to be picked up in terms of the resolution of a technological scan, yet it might shift elements of thought. One researcher discusses this in relation to emotions:

> *Even with expensive technologies and tools, it turns out that understanding the brain isn't as clear cut as researchers might have hoped. In the early days of brain scanning, researchers often focused on locating regions for different emotions in the brain. Over time, it became evident that emotions don't map neatly onto specific brain regions, but rather stem from a complicated network of interconnected brain regions.*
>
> **(American Psychological Association, 2014)**

This inability to define entailment structures in the brain is also potentially due to data processing strategies. A more recent paper from 2020 states: "studies have shown that measurement of laminar functional magnetic resonance imaging (fMRI) responses can be biased by the image acquisition and data processing strategies." (Bause, 2020) What new technologies will have to be developed to undertake such scanning tasks that successfully encompass the biological functionality of the entire body?

Interestingly, the paradox central to our problem set—researchers must come to know the human body better to elucidate its functional abstraction, explored in the articulation of a new form of combinatoric n-dimensional bioalgorithm, or other computational approach arising out of the research. Ward and Stapleton state: "... when we say that cognition depends on 'our activity', or upon 'bearing relations to an environment', the phrases within the quotation marks can be cashed out in many different ways" (Ward and Stapleton, 2012a,b). In terms of the enactive paradigm, Ward and Stapleton suggest that: "To be a cognizer, in the sense which interests the enactivist, is to manifest an appropriate degree of attunement to the objects, features, threats and opportunities present in the immediate environment" (Ward and Stapleton, 2012a,b). We must acknowledge that the Anthropocene poses many potential threats to future existence. Additionally, the idea of creating intelligent systems to help us anticipate and articulate approaches to solving our most difficult environmental problems becomes a future goal for an alternate version of the Insight Engine, informed by a different database and set of researchers. I will return to this concept later in this text. Ward and Stapleton continue: "The features of the environment to which the system is attuned are not inert and independent of the system, but dependent upon, and specified at least partly in terms of, the system's activity and capacities." (Ward and Stapleton, 2012a,b).

4. Embodied computation

There are a number of labs undertaking Embodied Computational research. One sits in the MIT Department of Architecture (Kilian, 2018). Another example is the *Embodied Computation Lab* at Princeton University, also in its architecture department. The lab building itself also represents an Intelligent Environment. It is described as follows:

> *This is a facility for interdisciplinary research on robotics, sensors, and everywhere that computers meet the physical world and become 'embodied computation'. The building is both an experiment and a research instrument. Just as biologists use a*

> *microscope to study organisms, architects will use this structure to study buildings.*
>
> **(Embodied Computation Lab, 2017)**

There are other sites undertaking theoretical research into *Embodied Computation*, including the Emergence Lab at Duke that Bill Seaman codirects with John Supko as part of the Computational Media, Arts and Cultures program at Duke University. The Insight Engine and the goal of defining a model for a Neosentient system is just such a research area. Seaman has been working on notions surrounding re-embodied intelligence and theoretical aspects of Embodied Computation for over 20 years (Seaman, 2021). Seaman's early paper *(Re) thinking—The body, generative tools and computational articulation* is one good example also (Seaman, 2009). Seaman has been actively recouping aspects of research from this earlier period, in terms of the initial study of Bionics, related to the work of Heinz von Foerster. The Biological Computer Lab run by Heinz von Foerster is described in the book: *An Unfinished Revolution? Heinz von Foerster and the Biological Computer Laboratory | BCL 1958–76* (Müller and Müller, 1976).

5. The Insight Engine 2.0—focusing on the production of a model for neosentience

The pragmatic goal is to make the Insight Engine function in such a way as to "point" to potential new research data across disciplinary boundaries by using advanced information processing, computational linguistics, a natural language API, and additional forms of AI acting as Micropeers—AI collaborators—to enable intelligent bridging of research questions, and the development of new informational paradigms through bisociation, after Koestler (1964) and poly-association (Seaman). These Insight Engine information systems are being designed to support researchers, to empower them to access relevant transdisciplinary information from the database, to contribute to the higher order goal over time of articulating a functional Neosentient model, as an "extended" approach to knowledge production, accessible via the internet. Such a model is informed from many intellectual perspectives and transdisciplinary conversations to be facilitated by the I_E system, a list-serve, and future information-oriented gatherings. I often call this a multi-perspective approach to knowledge production, and in this case to sentience production.

The Insight Engine 2.0 seeks to embody a series of intelligent processing structures, visualization systems, and the mapping of relationalities related to the corpus of papers, books, media objects, keywords, abstracts, diagrams, etc. initially driven by texts and textual annotations. We are also in the process of researching new forms of visual pattern recognition, and sonic recognition systems that will later potentially be integrated. They will potentially extend the search engine capability and help outline the articulation of a very new variety of Bioalgorithm—informed by the biofunctionality of the human body. The system is being made operational via a game engine and thus adds new forms of interaction and computational functionality—like giving "gravity" to ideas that might attract each other in a self-organizing manner, exploring new functionalities for a physics engine.

Biological structures are to be abstracted and then rearticulated in a biomimetic manner in the Neosentient model. This model for the operative approach to the arising of Neosentience is sought through this dynamic system of systems and seeks to be interactive with the environment, building new knowledge up somewhat like humans do, through pattern-flows of multimodal sense pertubations (embodied computation), as well as incorporating a layering of other potential learning systems. Meta-levels of self-observation and the development of language (both natural and code languages) to articulate such contextual learning are central for embodiment in the system, as well as the set of pragmatic benchmarks that define the Neosentient entity as described earlier.

6. Bisociation and poly-association

Central to the Insight Engine is the exploration of processes related to bisociation as discussed in Arthur Koestler's book, *The Act of Creation* (Koestler, 1964):

> *I have coined the term 'bisociation' in order to make a distinction between the routine skills of thinking on a single 'plane', as it were, and the creative act, which, as I shall try to show, always operates on more than one plane ... We learn by assimilating experiences and grouping them into ordered schemata, into stable patterns of unity in variety. They enable us to come to grips with events and situations by applying the rules of the game appropriate to them. The matrices which pattern our perceptions, thoughts, and activities are condensations of learning into habit.*

> *The bisociative act connects previously unconnected matrices of experience ...*
>
> **(Koestler, 1964)**

In the Insight Engine, the interactant can choose two different papers, and/or textually annotated media objects, and the system will facilitate a transdisciplinary search relevant to both choices. The system can make available links to a series of relevant works in a hierarchy of relationality. One can also define how many of these works can be called up at a time. Additionally, there are "categories of research" and one can operate under a given category or based on the overarching set of categories. I have also coined the term poly-association. This is when an interactant chooses multiple works and the system defines a relationality between them and then undertakes a search for relevant items from the database. These two methodologies, bisociation and poly-association, enable interesting new forms of transdisciplinary bridging. Using this system, one will be able to articulate new forms of relationality that might not otherwise surface, especially because often scientists and researchers from different disciplines publish in different journals and intellectual domains.

7. Some visualization strategies in the Insight Engine 2.0

The interactant can choose from a series of visualization systems with different functional qualities to explore relevant data. This also enables participants to explore particular categories of interest as well as different visualization systems that they might be leaning toward. The basic visualization interfaces are the following:

- The Micropeer system will potentially be active under the surface in all of the visualization systems. This will include a set of sliders where interactants can set levels for different kinds of AI activities as an active collaborator functioning in all of the differing visualization environments.
- An unnamed system originated by Dev Seth and his research team [personal discussion between Seth with Seaman and I_E Research Team]) is to be used in concert with the database, the natural language API, and micropeers. This is a potential second space in which researchers can share their ideas, do intelligent searches, read abstracts, make annotations, and potentially generate bisociations (Koestler) and poly-associations. This will be a next-generation intelligent canvas

that will allow users to create, curate, and collaborate around traditional files and web-native content. Here intelligent agents work with human users to generate meaningful insights from networks of data.

- A mathematical system is used, based on point-cloud data of a high-dimensional search space. The visualization makes a set of superimpositions, where overlapping points represent differing forms of relationality between the papers (or annotated media objects) that have been called up based on an intelligent search mechanism.

The central search avenue in the point cloud system is research papers. In terms of bisociation, the three axes in the space represent alignment among papers (x-axis), author relationalities (y-axis), and publication date (z-axis). Each point in the 3D space is a research paper; meanwhile, in a system where many point clouds are overlaid, each set of intersecting points represents associations among papers, authors, or concepts discussed in the papers. On each point, along with the general information about it represented with the three axes, other information that the paper represents such as its keywords are potentially overlaid as multidimensional vectors. Depending on how much information about the paper we want to represent with the point, the number of dimensions of the vectors can vary. Users will be able to search for specific papers using these numerical intersection points related to a high-dimensional numerical intersection of the content such as cosine distance. This introduces a different way of visualizing intersections among research papers from the other methods discussed in this text.

- Along with the 3D point cloud, a knowledge tree can be a way to represent associations among authors. Each author can be represented as a tree-like visualization with their individual papers and/or research papers that the author searched for and collected. There are different ways of using this part of the system, perhaps relevant to researchers from differing research domains. Potentially, earlier papers are located near the bottom of the tree, composing its roots, and more recent papers are located near the top of the tree, composing its leaves. The information about each author will be updated over a set time period so that the trees can "grow" by receiving and adding new publications about authors they represent, and/or annotated media-object publications like diagrams and even 3D environments (in the future links to such 3d environments on-line). Users will be able to see this information by hovering the cursor over the tree (or selecting it with an aura-like visualization tool). This visualization interface of Insight Engine 2.0 will look like a forest composed of multiple trees. Users will be able to zoom in and out and make choices from a number of vantage points. The distances among trees will be determined based on information gathered about authors that are represented in the Insight Engine and their interactions with the system; the trees of authors whose works are closely related to each other's papers in terms of research topics or authors who collaborated on the same paper will be located closer to each other, given one interactive choice. Users will be able to change categories based on where the trees are distributed in the forest and explore the reorganization of the trees into different formations, as an operative relational database. Also, there will be bridges between trees that represent collaborations among authors, bisociations, and poly-associations. At the end of each bridge will be an element that composes a tree, namely a research paper. This connection can represent different "categorical" relations between authors, and also collaborations among authors; it may represent the research topic of one paper being inspired by that of others or two papers discussing the same issue. Overall, the visualization will look like a forest with varying distances between trees and bridges connecting trees. A terrain will also be generated with chosen information. Users will be able to search for specific authors and papers or multiple authors and papers to visualize associations among them, zoom in and out and move through the trees, and make new bisociations and poly-associations.

8. The World Generator 2.0—programming by Quran Karriem

Another method of visualization involves a 3D space is through a rolodex/shelving-like wheel structure, which borrows its inspiration in part from Giulio Camillo's Memory Theater (Fabrizi, 2019). The wheel is divided into different sections, each representing an academic discipline and/or one of the research topic areas discussed in the following section, as well as potential 3D models, still images, videos, media objects, and sound. Each section will be composed in part of research papers that are relevant to the topic they represent. Users will be able to change the selection of papers loaded into each section based on their interests or have the visualization world-space auto-loaded based on particular menu choices.

Data will be loaded into the world in a series of concentric rings visible from the center of the environment via one choice of the interactant, also forming a Camillo-like memory theater structure. Papers that are more strongly related to topics represented by sections of the wheel will be closer toward the center if the interactant chooses this menu choice related to auto-loading. As mentioned earlier, we are using a game engine to facilitate this 3D world generating systems exploring informatics.

The section will vertically extend toward the circumference of the wheel and include information about authors and research papers relevant to the discipline. As in the two other models described earlier, users can either search for an individual author or a paper or associations among multiple authors and papers. Associations among those elements composing each section of the wheel world will be represented as lines connecting the sections. By hovering over a part of an association (or specific menu selection), users will also potentially be able to see an automatically generated summary of it, such as how the papers that are linked in the association are related to each other. These functionalities can be empowered by Natural Language Processing (NLP) and knowledge graph-building APIs like Diffbot, which already have the functionality of extracting associations among entities in a graph using NLP. In the end, the visualization will look like a spider web with lines going out from the center of the wheel with horizontal lines connecting different parts of the vertical lines as related to the different topic areas, discussed next.

9. Initial research areas for the Insight Engine 2.0

We will have a set of overarching research areas that have been developed over time, which the system will pay attention to. Each research area will have a Micropeer. There will also be a micropeer that is observing the entire system and corpus populating the database. These different research areas include the following (although new research areas will be added as needed):

- Neosentience
- n-Dimensional combinatoric bioalgorithm development
- Bodily entailment structures
- Mindful awareness—self-observation
- Second-order cybernetics
- Neuroscience

- Neuroscience and the arts
- AI and the arts—computational creativity
- Biomimetics
- The connectome
- AI
- AI and ethics
- EI—extended intelligence
- Embodied computation
- Robotics and situated knowledge production
- The biological computer lab (cybernetics and second-order cybernetics)
- Science fiction
- The history of AI
- Bridge building between disciplines
- Transdisciplinarity—a multiperspective approach to knowledge production
- Information—new approaches
- Approaches to learning—conversation theory, etc.
- Robotics and situated knowledge production
- Computational intuition
- Android linguistics (Evan Donahue);
- Related new forms of mathematics.

10. Two different approaches to Neosentience—one top down (Rössler), one bottom up (Seaman)

Seaman and Rössler's book—*Neosentience, The Benevolence Engine* discusses in part two different approaches to the arising of Neosentience [Synthetic Sentience] in an autonomous robotic system. The book has a unique structure of many microchapters. In the Neosentience book, Rössler discusses his "Brain Equation" as a top-down approach to Neosentience production and is skeptical of arriving at a bottom-up approach without taking a vast amount of time. *The Insight Engine* is discussed in the book as potentially functioning as a midwife to the ideas that might make up a new bottom-up approach. The Insight Engine 2.0 is by no means going to provide answers to the vast set of questions that are enfolded in our ultracomplex information-oriented problem set of problem sets. Yet, by chipping away at the problem, new partial solutions and exciting ideas about AI will be encountered. Additionally, many different research areas, which to some extent may have very different worlds for their historical research publication, will potentially get bridged and perhaps open up areas that are formed out of the bridging of discussion across disciplinary domains. This presents an exciting set of areas related to new knowledge production.

11. A new combinatorial *n*-dimensional bioalgorithm

Cognitive behavior is approached through a series of information-oriented processes. Central is to define all of the entailment structures that inform the emergent arising of sentience in the human. Our scanning technologies currently have limitations related to scale and time-based data acquisition. This suggests one area of new technological development. Researchers would seek to abstract many different mappings of subsystems abstracted from operations in the body and form them into a continuously self-organizing, switching and shunting network of ultracomplex biomechanisms. The many different mappings would inform the construction of a bottom-up model related to achieving the functionality of an autonomous Neosentient robotic system. This would happen over time, by first chipping away each subsystem's functionality and relationality to other systems in the human. Here, clues are taken from the embodied, embedded, enactive, and extended paradigm discussed earlier. These approaches are interrelated. Unlike historical approaches exploring the brain and its functionality as the center of AI research, this holistic approach becomes an active methodology for understanding how the body, focusing on multimodal sensing systems working in conjunction with the brain/mind, and different kinds of memory, form an ultracomplex dynamic system informing sentience production in an embodied, enactive manner.

What are some of the areas of study that are necessitated by this shift in attention to the entire body? Can we abstract aspects of the nervous system into our new n-dimensional combinatoric bioalgorithm? What is the best way to accomplish this? The difficulty is that sentience may only arise out of this deep complexity. We ask, at what level of complexity will our self-aware Neosentient techno-species begin to have a deep self-knowledge, always learning and applying new knowledge into the functioning of the intelligent system (read new form of intelligent environment)? Pragmatic benchmarks are used to define Neosentient robotic entities (as opposed to the Turing Test) discussed earlier.

12. Why *n*-dimensional?

If we think of the brain as a distributed system that brings partial systems into a distributed group network where the brain enables numerous different kinds of neurons each with specific specialties to function together to support thought, language, action, introspection, feeling, emotion, etc. then, when shifting attention, be it environmental or built out of the memories of experiences that call for it—new self-organizing shunting systems will function in a mind/brain-like manner. I think of this as an n-dimensional system functioning as an operational network being brought to life by a distributed, neuroplastic, electro-chemical-like code over time which is abstracted biomimetically through a mixed system including neuromorphic chips, neural nets, and code (or new forms of computation arising out of this research).

How can we reunderstand what is at operation in this ultra-complex environment, and translate this into a new bio-algorithmic form? Do we need to invent a new form of n-dimensional shunting mathematical system? Because this code is built in a biomimetic manner emulating a system of 100 billion neurons being configured and reconfigured over time, then along with the huge nature of the combinatorics at play, comes the notion of dynamic recombination *over time*—this is also why I call it n-dimensional—it of course will have the living dimension of the interoperationality of the brain/mind, but it also will have time, sensual experience, and this includes the internal experience of thinking about experience—self-reflection. It also will have a similar but different repetition of experiences, thoughts, and the ongoing deepening of networks of associations between patterns (Hebb). Pattern flows of sense perturbations will potentially contribute in an enactive manner and in real time define the dynamic shunts of neuronal passages, playing out a living dimensional code structure that is forever being further articulated. How can we biomimetically attempt to model and reembody such a code in a synthetic environment? Is this a singular substrate or a hybrid of many different computational substrates? Might this also be defined as a mixed analog and discrete system given neurons and neural transmitters and the efficacy of synapses in touch with both varieties of signal?

13. Ethics and redefining notions of bias

A large area of our research process in constructing both the Insight Engine 2.0 and the World Generator 2.0 is concerned with selection biases and the limits of intelligent systems to instantiate ethical solutions while operating within the constraints of an imperfect world. Our position is that a system that meaningfully "avoids biases" while using tools that come out of a biased society is a paradox and impossibility, and yet nevertheless one we must continually strive toward circumnavigating inappropriate bias. We have to work in the world as it exists, with an ideal in mind for the one we want to build. Humans and human societies are unavoidably biased, and our machines inevitably produce recursions of those biases. Our position is that the best we can do is to instantiate shifts in our biases: to direct them toward explicitly and universally prohuman ends. Some part of that is being overt about inclusion and consent, and also openness to the notion of a potential counter-history as curators of the system. Much of AI, artificial life, etc. falls prey to a "great (white) man" theory of history. It is increasingly common knowledge that intelligent systems are subject to imperfections in data collection rely on analysis of human artifacts that contain racist and misogynist assumptions, to name just a few of the issues.

But we maintain that the limits to the notion of an "objective" artificial intelligence run deeper than "bad data": we cannot fix it just by fixing the data, or by including more data. *How* researchers collect and create the data is important, as is the data subject's consent to inclusion within our project (invited researchers?). The computer's very mode of operation is constrained by the course of cryptography and military science in Western epistemology. As data-based and computational thinking predates the computer and therefore the very idea of computation as we know it, it is a product of a specific time and belief structure in the history of cybernetic and precybernetic thought, with all its promise, all its limitations, and all of its problematics. The system's intelligence can really only work with what we give it; we are in a relationship of cobecoming with our machines and cannot meaningfully separate the origins of today's sociotechnical effects.

For us, the notion of an "autonomous system" is an oxymoron that has roots in outmoded ideas about (human) individuality. Any cursory inquiry into the actual functioning and maintenance of any technical assemblage will show that they all require human investment and bureaucracy to persist. We view the Insight Engine and World Generator as systems that will help us glean new insights about our corpus but will always need to be steered and observe that it is no coincidence that the most sophisticated intelligent systems today belong to Google, Facebook, Apple, Amazon, and Microsoft; corporations that command massive amounts of internal and external, direct and indirect human labor and capital. The engineers that have invented and implemented the contemporary forms of machine learning and deep learning are largely sponsored by or work for these firms. At present, the outputs of the real instantiations of these algorithms are closely monitored and controlled by human will and toward ends consistent with what we have come to know as data capitalism. That is its bias, though we tend to naturalize the operativity of such systems and view it as objective. We view as fallacious the widespread idea that a technical system might be unbiased. We need to explicitly bias them toward universalist prohuman rather than antihuman or posthuman ends. In the most widely known accounts, posthuman agency is understood as *distributed* agency. The notion of distributed agency has long been associated with egalitarian or communitarian ideals, but we want to draw attention to the fact that the mere existence of technical systems does not inaugurate any such increase in freedom and in fact has been instrumental to emergent forms of surveillance and protocological control. And, finally, we want to reject ideas of transcendence through technology. Too often we simply forget that generative techniques, machine learning and intelligent systems in general, are contextualized and trained on corpuses. Systems cannot include "everything" and are therefore always already selections, which at some level of operational abstraction, require a human decision. In our research into the World Generator, it is our goal to define a new set of questions that help us unveil new approaches to issues in the ethics of technosociality.

14. The scope of the research

The system will bring together a series of technologies from the research of diverse scientists and second-order cyberneticists, as well as complex-system theorists, and artists articulating aspects of the creative process, to help map this time-based set of relationalities that bridge mind/brain/body—multimodal sensing systems, and environment. It is apparent that we will need new scanning technologies to accomplish this mapping. Additionally, we will need new forms of intelligent databases [like the Insight Engine 2.0] to help keep information about our various systems organized in a meaningful, relational manner. We will need transdisciplinary teams to tackle such a problem set of problem sets. We will seek to collaborate with disparate researchers to help us understand what is at operation in the humans contributing to sentience production, and how many different systems must become interoperative to achieve the eventual arising of Neosentience. It must be noted that at every stage human intelligence is at operation steering the system based on the individual wishes of interactants and/or teams of researchers.

No single discipline of science, the humanities and/or the arts can tackle such a difficult information-related problem set. A special transdisciplinary team of teams would need to arise out of the use of the Insight Engine 2.0.

We are discussing here a holistic, embodied approach, where researchers will need to define bridging languages between research domains that may not have talked to each other in the past. Micropeers [collaborative AIs] and a natural language API within the Insight Engine will help accomplish intelligent searches and suggestions about potential relevant approaches across domains of study. An international listserv would be created to facilitate intercommunication between researchers from around the world.

With the development of a new variety of computer code, researchers will need to discuss new approaches to combinatorial shunting that will facilitate mind/brain functionality as it is in communication with the entire body. One interesting area is in the employment of Neuromorphic chips. These chips may function in tandem with multiple systems emulating different aspects of conscious and unconscious thought.

To create synthetic sentience modules (viz. the dimensional components relating to speech, cognition, emotion, etc.), we will need inspiration from existing biological complex systems that incorporate these modules. The three fundamental questions here for philosophers of mind and consciousness, neuroscientists, and psychologists, are as follows: (a) What is the correct ontology that bridges psychological concepts with real-world neurological entities? (b) What are the neural correlates that map onto this ontology? (c) How, in the distributed mind, do disparate sensing systems integrate information? (sensor fusion). Knowing at least approximate answers to these three questions is crucial to building sentience modules, because synthetic modules will simply be uniquely implemented but functionally equivalent versions of the biological modules (based on the concept of multiple realizability, due to Hilary Putnam in "Minds and Machines" (1960)) or the principle of the psycho-physical parallelism discussed by von Neumann (1955) in the Mathematical foundations of quantum mechanics.

Sustainable AI and EI

In the Insight Engine 2.0, although initially designed to study sentience and create a model for a Neosentient robotic system, there is good reason for an Intelligent Environmental system to be developed to explore *Advanced Systems for a Healthy Planet.* One would need to create a database related to the Anthropocene, renewable forms of energy, core foci on sustainability, etc. This would call for the appropriate funding and set of people to upkeep the system and steer the insight engine in a new direction.

Could AIs or micropeers be set to work on a problem on their own and/or in conjunction with human collaborators? Could new solutions be found that humans alone have not found given the abilities of computational systems to make research from vast bodies of papers and textually annotated media objects. Such research combining intelligent human and computational potentials may help define new approaches to this vast problem set as it relates to the Anthropocene, as well as anticipating new kinds of solutions, and/or changing paths of behavior in an environmentally sustaining, proactive manner. Like the Insight Engine 2.0, an overarching set of categories to be searched would be defined by a series of researchers interested in the Anthroposcene and the difficult problems that have arisen due to human mindlessness. These papers would be transdisciplinary in nature and this new version of the insight engine would become a repository for differing approaches to such problem-solving. The intelligent natural language API would assist in making connections between texts that have never before been articulated, especially across disciplinary domains. This would be achieved via bisociation and poly-association, as discussed earlier. The space would also function as a social meeting site, promoting discussion on a series of relevant topics.

One other technological goal is to make AI and EI computing sustainable. Can we develop new computational technologies to help computers function that use only minute amounts of energy, and do not create waste heat during use? If the Neosentient is an autonomous robot, what new form of battery might they run on that is sustainable in relation to minimal material use and renewable power consumption? How can we educate people to the possibility of making changes in their lifestyles, habits, and lives that historically may have been lived without a thought for the environment – thereby dramatically reducing the environmental footprint? This may represent a huge paradox at the heart of our project, related to the technological and resource dependency of solutions.

15. Conclusion

We have given ourselves a very difficult and interesting task. We have discussed the body as an intelligent environment that depends on natural language – and code-based language working in conjunction with it, to help us research and solve a set of deep and complex transdisciplinary problems. This also includes meta-levels of self-understanding. We are treating the body as a whole, ultracomplex system. We are devising an elaborate set of human/computational systems to work together with a diverse body of researchers to bring new forms of emergent insight to light related to the topic of human sentience production and in particular the biological functionality at operation in the body that enables sentience to arise as an emergent property of that biofunctionality. In particular, we seek to employ the holistic, nonreductive concepts of *enacted, embodied, embedded, affective and extended* approaches to cognition research. Ross Ashby, a cyberneticist, early on worked on related problems in his text *Design For A Brain* (Ashby, 1960) explored an early approach to the complex biomechanisms leading to thought production and in particular to adaptive behavior. Cybernetics provided an approach to create complex models that cross disciplinary domains. Along with second-order cybernetics, this research has also now been taken up by complex systems theory. Ashby in his later book *An Introduction to Cybernetics* states:

> *Cybernetics offers one set of concepts that, by having exact correspondences with each branch of science, can thereby bring them into exact relation with one another ... It has been found repeatedly in science that the discovery that when two branches are related, this leads to each branch helping in the development of the other branch. The result is a markedly accelerated growth in both (Ashby, 1957:1).*

This becomes a central driving problem in the development of an intelligent database and a series of ways to promote transdisciplinary knowledge discovery and knowledge production across a series of linked domains. Others have written about the creation of autonomous learning systems, that is, Ray Kurzweil in *The Singularity is Near: When Humans Transcend Biology* (Kurzweil, 2005), and How To Create a Mind (2012). Another set of very early related works was by John Haugeland called Mind Design (Haugeland, 1981) and Mind Design II (Haugeland, 1997), but this was more related to making something work, accomplishing some intelligent task, as compared to looking at how the body works and reembodying that through biomimetics. *Principles of*

Synthetic Intelligence: PSI an architecture of Motivated Cognition is also fascinating by Bach (2009). The upshot here is that we are now in a position to work in a much more holistic manner exploring mind/brain/body/environment/and sensing systems through biomimetics. Yet this is a highly daunting task and requires researchers from multiple fields to work together to find a set of relevant solutions.

Our current focus for the system has initially been centered on defining a model for Neosentience production based on the study of entailment structures and human biofunctionality via biomimetics. Research related to this goal is accomplished through the use of an intelligent transdisciplinary database, search engine, a natural language API, a dynamic set of visualization modes, and a series of independent AI collaborators (Micropeers)—*The Insight Engine 2.0* (I_E), as well as informed input from a transdisciplinary set of researchers, their papers, models, data sets, etc. The Insight Engine 2.0 is an intelligent information exchange environment designed to empower new forms of research across disciplinary domains in the service of creating a model for a synthetic variety of autonomous intelligent environment, A Neosentient entity. The potential of defining a new form of ultracomplex *n*-dimensional combinatoric bioalgorithm inspired by human biofunctionality is also a long-term goal.

We discussed the potential repurposing of Insight Engine 2.0, an open-source project, to tackle problems related to the Anthropocene. We look forward to working on this in the future.

There are numerous researchers in the field that individually have developed articulate ideas about elements of the research cited earlier, from multiple perspectives—too many to mention in this context, although many of both my historical papers and the papers of others that have been cited point to important precursors that we would suggest following up on. The unique element here is the empowering of transdisciplinary communication across historical disciplinary lines as well as the ability to explore many new connections that would not be easily facilitated in a nonhuman/machine-driven intelligent environment. Here we believe many disciplines could perhaps build bridges to multiple other disciplinary domains. We believe the set of tasks is difficult but, even if a model for Neosentience is not immediately achieved, we believe new knowledge will be unleashed via the above set of research methodologies. Our perspective is positively long-term: while current scientific research is often expected to achieve new knowledge in a relatively short time, the transdisciplinary research in our problems is expected to be operating for many years to come. I believe many positive research artifacts and papers that will be supportive in an ongoing transdisciplinary manner to this research set of processes will arise out of the employment of this system of systems.

References

Allen Institute for Brain Science, (undated Unlocking the Mysteries of the Brain, https://alleninstitute.org/what-we-do/brain-science/research/(accessed 19 May, 2021).

American Psychological Association, 2014. Scanning the Brain, New Technologies Shed Light on the Brain's Form and Function. https://www.apa.org/action/resources/research-in-action/scan. (Accessed 19 May 2021).

Burgin, M., Proceedings of Papers Forthcoming, Theoretical and Foundational Problems (TFP) in Information Studies. https://tfpis.com (accessed 16 May, 2021).

Clark, A., 1997a. The dynamical challenge. Cognitive Science 21 (4), 461–481.

Clark, A., 1997b. Being There: Putting Brain, Body and World Together Again. MIT Press, Cambridge, MA.

Clark, A., 2008. Supersizing the Mind: Embodiment, Action, and Cognitive Extension. Oxford University Press, Oxford.

Clark, A., Chalmers, D., 1998. The extended mind. Analysis 58 (1), 7–19.

Colombetti, G., 2007. Enactive appraisal. Phenomenology and the Cognitive Sciences 6, 527–546.

Embodied Computation Lab, 2017. https://architizer.com/projects/embodied-computation-lab/. (Accessed 16 May 2021).

Fabrizi, M., 2019. Spatializing Knowledge in Giulio Camillos Theatre of Memory. http://socks-studio.com/2019/03/03/spatializing-knowledge-giulio-camillos-theatre-of-memory-1519-1544/. (Accessed 15 May 2021).

Haugeland, J., 1981. Mind Design: Philosophy, Psychology, and Artificial Intelligence. MIT Press, Cambridge Mass.

Haugeland, J. (ed.), 1997. Mind Design II: Philosophy, Psychology, Artificial Intelligence. MIT Press, Cambridge, Mass.

Haugeland, J., 1998. Having Thought: Essays in the Metaphysics of Mind. Harvard University Press, Cambridge MA.

Hidalgo, C.A., 2016. Networked Intelligence. PubPub. Retrieved from. https://v3.pubpub.org/pub/networked-intelligence. (Accessed 14 May 2021).

Hurley, S., 1998. Consciousness in Action. Harvard University Press, Cambridge, MA.

Ito, J., 2016. Extended Intelligence. https://www.academia.edu/24233625/Extended_Intelligence. (Accessed 14 May 2021).

Ashby, R., 1957. An Introduction to Cybernetics. Chapman and Hall LTD, London, pp. 1–1.

Ashby, R., 1960. Design For A Brain. Chapman & Hall, London.

Bach, J., 2009. Principles of Synthetic Intelligence: PSI an architecture of Motivated Cognition. Oxford University Press, Oxford.

Bause, J., Jonathan, R.P., Stelzer, J., In, M.-H., Philipp, E., Pablo, K.-F., Aghaeifar, A., Lacosse, E., Pohmann, R., Scheffler, K., 2020. Impact of Prospective Motion Correction, Distortion Correction Methods and Large Vein Bias on the Spatial Accuracy of Cortical Laminar fMRI at 9.4 Tesla. https://www.sciencedirect.com/science/article/pii/S1053811919310250. (Accessed 19 May 2021).

Kilian, A., 2018. Architectural Robotics – Embodied Computation. https://architecture.mit.edu/building-technology/lecture/architectural-robotics-embodied-computation. (Accessed 20 May 2021).

Koestler, A., 1964. The Act of Creation. Macmillan Company, New York.

Kurzweil, R., 2005. *The Singularity is Near: When Humans Transcend Biology.* Viking, New York.

Lelieveld, J., 2021. Paul J. Crutzen (1933–2021), Obituary, 24 February 2021, Nature. https://www.nature.com/articles/d41586-021-00479-0. (Accessed 29 May 2021).

Louie, A.H., 2010. Robert Rosen's Anticipatory Systems. https://www.researchgate.net/publication/228091658_Robert_Rosen%27s_anticipatory_systems. (Accessed 15 May 2021).

Müller, A., Müller, K.H., 2008. An Unfinished Revolution? Heinz von Foerster and the Biological Computer Laboratory | BCL 1958-1976. Echoraum Press, Vienna.

Noë, A., 2004. Action in Perception. MIT Press, Cambridge, MA.

Pask, G., 1976. Conversation Theory, Applications in Education and Epistemology. Elsevier.

Ratcliffe, M., 2009. Existential feeling and psychopathology (and response to commentaries 'Belonging to the world through the feeling body'). Philosophy, Psychiatry & Psychology 16 (2), 179–211.

Rosen, R., 1985. Anticipatory Systems, Philosophical, Mathematical, and Methodological Foundations. Dalhouse University, Nova Scotia, Canada. Pergamon Press, Oxford, New York, Toronto, Sydney, Paris, Frankfurt.

Rosen, R., 1999. Essays on Life Itself. Columbia University Press.

Rössler, O., Seaman, W., 2011. Neosentience/the Benevolence Engine. Intellect Press, London.

Seaman, B., 2009. (Re) Thinking – the Body , Generative Tools and Computational Articulation. https://billseaman.com/Papers/TA%207.3%20(Re)Thinking%20copy.pdf. (Accessed 16 May 2021).

Seaman, B., 2021. (billseaman.com).

Thom, R., 1989. Structural Stability and Morphogenesis: An Outline of a General Theory of Models. Addison-Wesley, Reading, MA. ISBN 0-201-09419-3.

Thompson, E., 2007. Mind in Life: Biology, Phenomenology, and the Sciences of Mind. The Belknap Press of Harvard University Press, Cambridge, MA.

Turing, A.M., 1950. Computing machinery and intelligence. Mind 59, 433–460.

Varela, F.J., Rosch, E., Thompson, E., 1991. The Embodied Mind: Cognitive Science and Human Experience. MIT Press, Cambridge, MA.

von Neumann, J., 1955. Mathematical Foundations of Quantum Mechanics (Trans. R.T. Beyer). University Press, Princeton, NJ.

Ward, D., Stapleton, M., 2012a. Es are Good, Cognition as Enacted, Embodied, Embedded, Affective and Extended. https://www.researchgate.net/publication/258832836_Es_are_good_Cognition_as_enacted_embodied_embedded_affective_and_extended. (Accessed 14 May 2021).

Ward, D., Stapleton, M., 2012b. Cognition as enacted, embodied, embedded, affective and extended, Dave Ward & Mog Stapleton. In: Paglieri, F. (Ed.), ProQuest Ebook Central. John Benjamins Publishing Company. Created from duke on 2021-05-15 07:07:14. https://www.researchgate.net/publication/258832836_Es_are_good_Cognition_as_enacted_embodied_embedded_affective_and_extended. http://ebookcentral.proquest.com/lib/duke/detail.action?docID=979716 (accessed May 14, 2021) found in Consciousness in Interaction : The role of the natural and social context in shaping consciousness.

Further reading

IS4SI, 2021. https://summit-2021.is4si.org/. See also https://tfpis.com/the-book-of-abstracts/.

Pask, G., Conversation theory, https://web.cortland.edu/andersmd/learning/pask.htm (Accessed 15 May, 2021).

Pavid, K. (Date not set) What is the Anthropocene and Why Does it Matter, https://www.nhm.ac.uk/discover/what-is-the-anthropocene.html (accessed 14 May, 2021).

Index

Note: 'Page numbers followed by "*f*" indicate figures and "*t*" indicate tables and "*b*" indicate boxes'.

Printed in the United States
by Baker & Taylor Publisher Services